D1104519

HISTORICAL DICTIONARY
OF
TUDOR ENGLAND,
1485–1603

HISTORICAL DICTIONARY
——————OF——————
TUDOR ENGLAND,
1485–1603

Ronald H. Fritze, *Editor-in-Chief*
Sir Geoffrey Elton, *Advisory Editor*
Walter Sutton, *Assistant Editor*

GREENWOOD PRESS
New York • Westport, Connecticut • London

Library of Congress Cataloging-in-Publication Data

Historical dictionary of Tudor England, 1485-1603 / Ronald H. Fritze,
  editor-in-chief ; Sir Geoffrey Elton, advisory editor ; Walter
  Sutton, assistant editor.
     p. cm.
  Includes bibliographical references and index.
  ISBN 0-313-26598-4 (alk. paper)
   1. Great Britain—History—Tudors, 1485-1603—Dictionaries.
  2. England—Civilization—16th century—Dictionaries. 3. Tudor,
  House of—Dictionaries.   I. Fritze, Ronald H., 1951- .
  DA315.H5 1991
  942.05—dc20   91-9153

British Library Cataloguing in Publication Data is available.

Library of Congress Catalog Card Number: 91-9153
ISBN: 0-313-26598-4

First published in 1991

Greenwood Press, 88 Post Road West, Westport, CT 06881
An imprint of Greenwood Publishing Group, Inc.

Printed in the United States of America

The paper used in this book complies with the
Permanent Paper Standard issued by the National
Information Standards Organization (Z39.48-1984).

10 9 8 7 6 5 4 3 2 1

For My Parents

Harold† and Eleanor Fritze

Contents

Preface

British history has been blessed by many fine reference works including the classic *Dictionary of National Biography* (1885-1901). In the field of historical dictionaries, two excellent works cover the entire span of British history: Sigfrid H. Steinberg and I. H. Evans, *Steinberg's Dictionary of British History*, 2nd ed., 1970, and J. P. Kenyon, *A Dictionary of British History*, 1983. They provide brief entries on many topics, but only the Kenyon volume contains biographical entries. Neither work supplies bibliographies to guide further reading. Until quite recently, what has been lacking are specialized historical dictionaries or encyclopedias covering shorter periods of English and British history and providing more detailed entries with suggestions for further reading.

The purpose of this work is fill that gap for the age of the Tudors from 1485 to 1603. The primary geographical focus is England, but a number of articles on Scottish and Irish history are included, particularly where it had an impact on England. Political, diplomatic, military, and religious topics predominate among the entries, but representative entries on social, economic, and intellectual topics have been included. As such, this work is fairly traditional in its chronological and topical emphases.

The dictionary consists of 295 entries written by 66 contributors. Sixty-six entries are biographical while the remainder concern events (the battle of Bosworth Field), laws (Act of Six Articles), institutions (Parliament), and special topics (exploration). Individual entries range from 250 to 2,000 words in length and include selected bibliographies for additional reading. Cross-references are indicated by the related terms appearing in capital letters when it is mentioned in another entry.

Editing a contributed volume has reminded the editor, once again, of the high quality of the people engaged in British studies in higher education throughout the world. I have no horror stories to share with other, less fortunate editors of contributed projects. Instead, I would like to thank all the contributors for their help and excellent work. I also want to thank the Faculty Senate and administration of Lamar University for providing me with development leaves that I used to work on this book and other projects. One can only hope that they will continue and expand this excellent program. My colleagues in the history department at Lamar University have been generous in their encouragement of this project—in particular, my assistant editor, Professor Walter Sutton, who helped with the preparation of camera-ready copy and never seems to be at a loss when it comes to unraveling a problem of word processing. The past and present secretaries of the history department, Dee Sherrill and Randy Landry, gave their assistance whenever they could. I would especially like to thank Professor Kevin Smith and Denise Parsons of the sociology department for allowing this project to be printed on their laser printer. Their generous instincts for cooperation fall into the best traditions of the university as a community of scholars. Sir Geoffrey Elton, the advisory editor, contributed much essential guidance from the start through the finish of this project. Once again, I stand amazed at his ability to read a manuscript closely in a brief period of time. All who know him, especially his students, understand the value of both his advice and his friendship for any scholar of Tudor England. Finally, I would like to thank Karen Campbell for making the world a better place.

Contributors

Dr. Michael V. C. Alexander, Department of History, Virginia Polytechnic Institute and State University, Blacksburg, Virginia, U.S.A.

Dr. Don S. Armentrout, School of Theology, University of the South, Sewanee, Tennessee, U.S.A.

Dr. Christopher Baker, Department of English, Lamar University, Beaumont, Texas, U.S.A.

Dr. Barrett L. Beer, Department of History, Kent State University, Kent, Ohio, U.S.A.

Dr. Gary Bell, Department of History, Sam Houston State University, Huntsville, Texas, U.S.A.

Dr. Michael Bennett, Department of History, University of Tasmania, Hobart, Australia.

Dr. Douglas Bisson, Department of History, Belmont College, Nashville, Tennessee, U.S.A.

Dr. Eugene Bourgeois, Department of History, Southwest Texas State University, San Marcos, Texas, U.S.A.

Dr. Gerald Bowler, Canadian Nazarene College and Department of History, University of Manitoba, Winnepeg, Manitoba, Canada.

Dr. Robert C. Braddock, Department of History, Saginaw State University, University Center, Michigan, U.S.A.

Dr. C. W. Brooks, Department of History, University of Durham, England.

Dr. Eric Josef Carlson, Department of History, Gustavus Adolphus College, St. Peter, Minnesota, U.S.A.

Mr. Brian Christian, Department of History, Louisiana State University, Baton Rouge, Louisiana, U.S.A.

Dr. Lesley Cormack, Department of History, Queen's University, Kingston, Ontario, Canada.

Professor Ian B. Cowan, Department of Scottish History, University of Glasgow, Scotland.

Dr. John Crangle, Department of History, Benedict College, Columbia, South Carolina, U.S.A.

Sir Geoffrey Elton, Regius Professor of Modern History (retired), Clare College, Cambridge University, Cambridge, England

Ms. Connie Evans, Department of History, Louisiana State University, Baton Rouge, Louisiana, U.S.A.

Dr. Ann E. Faulkner, Department of History, Loyola University, Chicago, Illinois, U.S.A.

Dr. Ronald H. Fritze, Department of History, Lamar University, Beaumont, Texas, U.S.A.

Dr. M. A. R. Graves, Department of History, University of Auckland, New Zealand.

Dr. Richard Greaves, Department of History, Florida State University, Tallahassee, Florida, U.S.A.

Dr. Steven Gunn, Merton College, Oxford, England.

Dr. Sheldon Hanft, Department of History, Appalachian State University, Boone, North Carolina, U.S.A.

Dr. Richard Harrison, Dean, Disciples Divinity House, Vanderbilt University, Nashville, Tennessee, U.S.A.

Dr. Rudolph W. Heinze, Department of History, Oak Hill College, London, England.

Dr. Mark Heumann, Department of English, Western New England College, Springfield, Massachusetts, U.S.A.

Dr. Dale Hoak, Department of History, College of William and Mary, Williamsburg, Virginia, U.S.A.

Dr. Daniel W. Hollis, Department of History, Jacksonville State University, Jacksonville, Alabama, U.S.A.

Dr. Janis Butler Holm, Department of English Language and Literature, Ohio University, Athens, Ohio, U.S.A.

Dr. Peter Holmes, Hills Road Sixth Form College, Cambridge, England.

Dr. Ralph Houlbrooke, Department of History, University of Reading, England.

Dr. Sybil Jack, Dean, Department of History, University of Sydney, Australia.

Dr. David Lamburn, University of York, England.

Dr. Carole Levin, Department of History, State University of New York at New Paltz, New York, U.S.A.

Professor David M. Loades, Department of History, University College of North Wales, Bangor, Wales.

Dr. James E. McGoldrick, Department of History, Cedarville College, Cedarville, Ohio, U.S.A.

Dr. Roger B. Manning, Department of History, Cleveland State University, Cleveland, Ohio, U.S.A.

Dr. David B. Mock, Department of History, Tallahassee Community College, Tallahassee, Florida, U.S.A.

Dr. Michael Moody, Huntington Library, San Marino, California, U.S.A.

Dr. Gerald Morton, Department of English, Auburn University, Montgomery, Alabama, U.S.A.

Dr. John S. Nolan, Department of History, Marymount University, Arlington, Virginia, U.S.A.

Dr. Mary O'Dowd, Department of Modern History, Queen's University of Belfast, Northern Ireland.

Dr. Andrew Penny, The King's College, Edmondton, Alberta, Canada.

Dr. Ronald Pollitt, Department of History, University of Cincinnati, Cincinnati, Ohio, U.S.A.

Dr. D. L. Potter, Department of History, University of Kent at Canterbury, England.

Dr. Steven Rappaport, Department of History, New York University, New York, New York, U.S.A.

Professor W. Stanford Reid, Department of History, University of Guelph, Ontario, Canada.

Dr. Richard Rex, St. John's College, Cambridge, England.

Dr. Peter Roberts, Department of History, University of Kent at Canterbury, England.

Dr. Mary Robertson, Henry E. Huntington Library, San Marino, California, U.S.A.

Dr. William B. Robison, Department of History, Southeast Louisiana University, Hammond, Louisiana, U.S.A.

Dr. Vivienne Sanders, Head of History, Dame Alice Harpur School, Bedford, England.

Dr. Beverley Schneller, Department of England, Millersville University, Millersville, Pennsylvania, U.S.A.

Dr. Anthony Sheehan, Department of German, Queen's University of Belfast, Northern Ireland.

Dr. Martha C. Skeeters, Department of History, University of Oklahoma, Norman, Oklahoma, U.S.A.

Professor Arthur J. Slavin, College of Arts and Sciences, University of Louisville, Louisville, Kentucky, U.S.A.

Dr. J. P. Sommerville, Department of History, University of Wisconsin, Madison, Wisconsin, U.S.A.

Dr. Walter A. Sutton, Department of History, Lamar University, Beaumont, Texas, U.S.A.

Dr. Ronald J. VanderMolen, Department of History, California State University, Turlock, California, U.S.A.

Dr. Dewey D. Wallace, Jr., Department of Religion, George Washington University, Washington, D.C., U.S.A.

Dr. Retha Warnicke, Department of History, Arizona State University, Tempe, Arizona, U.S.A.

Dr. Ann Weikel, Department of History, Portland State University, Portland, Oregon, U.S.A.

Dr. Mary Winkler, Institute for the Medical Humanities, University of Texas Medical Branch, Galveston, Texas, U.S.A.

Dr. D. R. Woolf, Department of History, Dalhousie University, Halifax, Nova Scotia, Canada.

Dr. Jenny Wormald, St. Hilda's College, Oxford, England.

Professor Joyce Youings, Department of History, University of Exeter, England.

Introduction

The last forty years have witnessed a remarkable expansion of our knowledge of the Tudor century of British history, an era once thought of as well and completely worked over. In effect, hardly any of the writings produced before about 1950 any longer offer either synoptic or detailed information useful to current scholarship. Yet the age of the Reformation, of Henry VIII and Elizabeth I, of William Shakespeare and William Camden, retains its hold on a wide range of people, general readers as well as students, a fact which makes it desirable to provide a reasonably up-to-date guide to our present knowledge and understanding. This Dictionary aims to serve that manifest need. It is hoped that the right topics have been covered; certainly the coverage is various enough and includes all the approaches to learning that are being employed. There has been no attempt to impose some general interpretation or point of view, and contributors have been left to their own devices. What the editors looked for, and what indeed they got, were proven standards of learning–knowledge based on real work in the sources and ability to present that knowledge in concise but comprehensible form. How far they have succeeded in their efforts is something that users will judge for themselves. Meanwhile, the editors express their gratitude to all those who so readily contributed to the enterprise.

Geoffrey Elton

HISTORICAL DICTIONARY
OF
TUDOR ENGLAND

A

Admonition Controversy. The first major polemical dispute among Elizabethan Protestants, the *Admonition* controversy erupted in the spring of 1572 shortly after Queen ELIZABETH quashed a bill in the House of Commons that would have empowered bishops to exempt godly ministers from using disputed sections of the BOOK OF COMMON PRAYER. The authors of the *Admonition to the Parliament* were two young London preachers, John Field and Thomas Wilcox. Ostensibly framed as an address to Parliament, the *Admonition* in fact was primarily intended for popular consumption and enjoyed a wide readership by August 1572, when the third edition appeared. The authors presumably had no real expectation of persuading Parliament to embrace the PRESBYTERIAN polity they espoused but sought to expand their base of support by denouncing and satirizing perceived weaknesses in the Church of England. The first part of the *Admonition*, written by Wilcox, used measured tones to indict the state establishment for its failure to manifest the external signs of a true church. Casting aside restraint, Field appended a searing denunciation of the Church of England for its "popish" practices, its liturgical "mass book," and its self-serving prelates. Instead of rallying the godly to enlist in a united crusade, the *Admonition* fractured PURITAN ranks, as men such as JOHN FOXE, Anthony Gilby, and Thomas Lever expressed disapproval. London magistrates imprisoned Field and Wilcox for a year, although the two men remained unrepentant.

The controversy intensified in November with the publication of an anonymous *Second Admonition* and an *Answere to a Certen Libell*. Commissioned by MATTHEW PARKER, archbishop of Canterbury, the latter work came from the pen of JOHN WHITGIFT, master of Trinity College, Cambridge, and vice-chancellor of the university. Whitgift's defense of the state church brought Thomas Cartwright into the fray. A native of Royston, Hertfordshire, Cartwright had been educated at Clare Hall and St. John's College, Cambridge, and had subsequently been a chaplain to the archbishop of Armagh. Appointed Lady Margaret professor of divinity at Cambridge in 1569, Cartwright so angered Whitgift by his unfavorable comparison of the Church of England to the primitive church described in the Book of Acts that the vice-chancellor deprived him of his chair in late 1570. Cartwright thereupon sought refuge on the Continent but returned in April 1572, approximately two months before Field and Wilcox issued the first *Admonition*. Twelve months later, in April 1573, Cartwright's *Replye to an Answere Made of M Doctor Whitegifte Againste the Admonition* appeared. Whitgift's *Defense of the Answere to the Admonition* (1574) elicited further rebuttals from Cartwright in a *Second Replie* (1575) and *The Rest of the Second Replie* (1577).

At root the *Admonition* controversy was less a dispute over formal theology than it was practical implications for the life and structure of the church. To describe the debate as a struggle between rival clerical interest groups is to miss the fundamental point that the underlying issue involved the very nature of worship and piety—the core of the Christian life. Cartwright placed much emphasis on the role of bishops and college masters as impediments to further reformation, a criticism undoubtedly sharpened by his own deprivation at Whitgift's hands. The most crucial issue in the debate focused on the relationship of the invisible and visible churches, and in this sense the controversy was certainly theological. Whereas Whitgift insisted on sharply distinguishing the invisible church and its spiritual government from the visible church with its external rule and ceremonies, Cartwright blurred the distinction by arguing that the church's government must be wholly spiritual and that its divinely bestowed discipline must be used to establish and maintain a godly community. Unlike Whitgift, who embraced a vision of the visible church as the gathering place of both the wheat and the tares, the godly and the profane, Cartwright advocated the use of excommunication to purge the church of manifestly evil persons and thereby to create a congregation of visible saints. Cartwright also favored the exclusion of Catholics and known sinners from the Sacraments. Such differences led the two men to advocate different views of the relationship between church and state. Whitgift made no significant division between a Christian commonwealth, many of whose officers were concerned with supporting true religion and punishing sin, and the church. Cartwright, however, distinguished sharply between the church, whose polity must be presbyterian, and the state, whose officers were subordinate to ecclesiastical discipline only in spiritual matters.

After a warrant for Cartwright's arrest on charges of "dangerous dealings and demeanors in matters touching religion and the state" was issued on 11 December 1573, he returned to the Continent, where he spent time at Heidelberg, Basel, Geneva, Antwerp, and other places. Suffering from poor health, he returned in 1585 to England, where the bishop of London committed him to prison. Released the same year, Cartwright was appointed master of the hospital at Leicester in 1586; he retained his affiliation with the hospital until his death on 27 December 1603.

Bibliography: P. Collinson, *The Elizabethan Puritan Movement*, 1967; P. Lake, *Anglicans and Puritans? Presbyterianism and English Conformist Thought from Whitgift to Hooker*, 1988; D. J. McGinn, *The Admonition Controversy*, 1949.

Richard L. Greaves

Advancement of True Religion, Act for the (1543, 34 and 35 Hen. VIII, c. 1). Also known as the Act Concerning Bible Reading, this Conservative statute attempted to limit the reading of the ENGLISH BIBLE to the upper ranks of society and so prevent unauthorized religious discussions and innovations.

The early 1540s were a time of many religious tumults as Conservatives and Reformers struggled for control and jostled for HENRY VIII's support. Furthermore, by that time, the struggle had spread to the countryside as Protestant ideas began to reach more and more people. Conservatives felt that the true doctrines of the church were being threatened by the increasing circulation of books, sermons, songs, and plays containing false beliefs, especially WILLIAM TYNDALE's translation of the Bible and its Protestant annotations.

In 1543, the religious Conservatives led by STEPHEN GARDINER, the bishop of Winchester, were in the ascendent. On 4 April, they secured the acceptance of the KING'S BOOK, a very traditional and orthodox doctrinal statement by CONVOCATION. This victory was followed by the introduction of a bill into the House of Lords on 8 May for regulating printed books. That bill received a second reading on 10 May and ultimately evolved into the Act for the Advancement of True Religion. It appears to have been composed hastily and to have received many alterations before it attained its final form.

The preamble of the Act for the Advancement of True Religions justified itself by citing the king's duty to suppress the many erroneous religious opinions that were springing up throughout England. Immediately following the preamble, the statute began by forbidding the keeping and use of Tyndale's Bible or any books or writings contrary to the official doctrines of the Church of England as they had been established by Henry VIII since 1540. Printers and booksellers were then forbidden to deal in such books or suffer fines of £10, confiscation, and even perpetual imprisonment. Those people owning such forbidden books were also to get rid of them or face a fine of £5. At the same time, possession of an English Bible was allowed so long as it was not Tyndale's translation and if it did not contain any annotations or if they were blotted out. Also excepted from the law were royal proclamations, statutes, and official liturgical books; any books possessing a royal license; and those religious songs and plays that did not discuss doctrine. The law then went on to forbid preaching on, or the public reading of, the Bible by unauthorized persons on penalty of one month's imprisonment. Those nobles, gentry, and merchants who were heads of households were specifically allowed to read the Bible to their families. But the statute went on to forbid men of the lower orders and all women to read the Bible even in private unless given permission by the king. Then, somewhat contradictorily, the statute allowed the women of the nobility and gentry privately to read the Bible. Reading of any officially approved statements of doctrine was allowed for all persons, although no unauthorized person was to engage in any open discussion of the Scripture. Severe penalties were also provided for those clergy and laymen who preached or taught contrary to official doctrine while the provisions of the ACT OF SIX ARTICLES (1539) were confirmed. Finally, the statute gave Henry VIII the power to alter its provisions any time as he saw fit. Enforcement of the act was given to the ordinaries of each diocese supported by two justices of the peace.

The Act for the Advancement of True Religion represented another attempt by Conservative forces to roll back Protestantism in England. To accomplish their purpose, they gave Henry VIII a significant expansion of his prerogative powers over the Church of England. Basically, the new law made the king the ultimate judge of what constituted correct doctrine and true books on religion. At the same time, the statute also contained sufficient exceptions to make it a weak tool for combatting Protestant Bible reading. Therefore, the effect of the statute turned out ultimately to be disappointing to the Conservative cause.

Bibliography: S. E. Lehmberg, *The Later Parliaments of Henry VIII, 1536-1547*, 1977.

Ronald Fritze

Agriculture. Agriculture was at the very center of the Tudor economy. Except for fish, wine, and a very few luxuries such as spices and dried fruits from the Levant, English farmers grew all of the food supplies and almost all of the basic raw materials for English industry. The latter included hides for leather, tallow for soap and candles, wool and vegetable dyes for the clothing industry, horses for traction and transport, and hemp and linen for canvas and cordage. The POPULATION of England grew from 2.3 million in the 1520s to 4.1 million in 1601 and made heavy demands on English agriculture. This demographic pressure was sustained through the middle of the seventeenth century and produced an inflationary spiral of prices for foodstuffs and land that is called the Price Revolution. Ultimately this demand stimulated the Agricultural Revolution, but in the shorter run agricultural production could not be expanded rapidly enough to avoid dearth and even crises of subsistence in years of deficient harvests. Although the LONDON market required imports of grain, cereal production in England did, on average, increase, and England remained a net exporter of grain until the crisis of the 1590s reversed that trend. The growing of grain became a more profitable enterprise than it had been in the fifteenth and early sixteenth centuries. However, mercantilistic regulation was applied to the grain trade because the government needed to insure adequate supplies for the populace, since even local shortages could cause dearth and precipitate food riots. The export of raw and semifinished wool, once the keystone of medieval England's foreign trade, fell off in the second half of the sixteenth century because the expansion of the domestic clothing industry consumed more raw wool. Falling prices of raw wool suggest that domestic consumption also declined; England actually began to import this commodity when trends in fashion dictated a preference for finer Spanish wools. Yet, in sum, England remained more nearly self-sufficient in agricultural commodities than did other comparable European countries.

The most important European development in Tudor agriculture was the transition from subsistence farming, within the context of peasant society, to a more commercially oriented kind of agriculture. This change was promoted by an expanding market, which resulted from demographic expansion; the deployment of a larger proportion of the labor supply into rural industries, which made craftsmen dependent upon others for food supplies; and the rapid growth of the London market. The commercialization of agriculture hastened the disintegration of peasant society, which consisted of small copyhold tenants operating their farms mostly with family labor, and increasingly concentrated land resources in the hands of yeoman farmers and gentry, who were aware of the new commercial opportunities and willing to supply the demands of distant markets. The latter increasingly employed landless laborers working for wages to cultivate their fields while smallholders found themselves squeezed by rising rents and declining standards of living. The diminished consumption of agricultural produce by those who tilled the land diverted greater amounts of food into the marketplace. Marginal lands were brought into cultivation and undoubtedly added to the total produce but did nothing to increase the yield per unit of land, which generally remained low throughout the sixteenth century. The cultivation of grain seldom returned more than four or five bushels for every bushel sowed. Convertible husbandry, which abolished the distinction between arable and pastoral land and eliminated the wasteful fallowing of arable fields, provided a technological breakthrough that significantly increased yields. When the planting of nitrogen-fixing, artificial grasses or leys, such as clover, sainfoin, and lucerne, replaced bare fallows in the new system of crop rotation, yields of both grain and fodder crops generally doubled per unit of land. However, the impact of the Agricultural Revolution remained highly selective before the middle of the seventeenth century.

Agrarian historians discern something like forty distinct farming regions in England and Wales, which were determined by the type and quality of soil, elevation, temperature ranges, and precipitation. To these environmental constraints English farmers added their own peculiar adaptations and specializations. One basic adaption was the mixed farming of the more fortunate lowland region of southern and eastern England, where farmers grew both cereals and grass but kept animals primarily to plough and manure their arable fields. In regions with thin or sandy soils such as the southern downlands, the Lincolnshire wolds, or the brecklands of East Anglia, heavy manuring by great flocks of sheep was necessary to maintain the fertility of the arable fields. This adaptation was called sheep-corn husbandry. In the highland zone, which included Wales, the west, and the north of England, poor soils predominated on the moors and mountains, and the cooler and wetter climate precluded cultivation of cereals except in a few favored vales. These conditions neccesitated the practice of pastoral farming with regional specializations in wool or cheese and butter production. In addition there were other local adaptations in the woodland pasture of forests where the mass of beech and oak trees and browsewood fed cattle and pigs. The fenlands of eastern England and other wetlands along the eastern and southern coasts and the Thames estuary were flooded too frequently to permit grain production prior to the great drainage schemes of the seventeenth century, but with their lush grasses and proximity to the London market they were well situated to fatten cattle brought from the highland zone. Economic demand stimulated by sustained demographic expansion tended to increase specialization in the various farming regions as they became integrated into larger markets.

Environmental differences and regional specializations in agriculture also contributed to variations in patterns of settlement and social structure. Nucleated villages, where the influence of parson and squire was much in evidence, constituted the usual pattern of settlement in lowland England, where mixed farming predominated. The extension of cultivation in the early modern period created severe shortages of pasture and common grazing and made life more precarious for smallhold tenants. Such communities were less able to absorb surplus population and were obliged to tax householders to pay the costs of poor relief. Pastoral and sylvan regions displayed a more dispersed pattern of settlement characterized by small hamlets and isolated farm houses, and consequently the influence of the manor house and the parsonage was weaker. Their lower population densities and more abundant commons and wastes attracted the surplus populations of arable villages and elicited fears that unenclosed commons would become "nurseries of beggars." If endowed with resources of water power and wood or mineral fuel, pastoral and sylvan regions were likely to spawn protoindustrial economies with populations of cottagers and artisans who were thought to be ungovernable. Consequently, agricultural reformers called for ENCLOSURE of commons not only to bring more land under cultivation but also to impose a greater degree of social regulation upon populations of artisans and cottagers, who were perceived to be masterless, "idle," and potentially seditious.

Bibliography: Joan Thirsk, ed., *The Agrarian History of England and Wales*, Vol. 4: *1500-1640*, 1967; C. G. A. Clay, *Economic Expansion and Social Change: England, 1500-1700*, Vol. 1: *People, Land and Towns*, 1984.

Roger B. Manning

Amicable Grant (1525). Although it has been denounced as "attempted extortion" and "the most violent financial exaction in English history," the Amicable Grant of 1525 is remarkable chiefly as a tax that provoked such extensive opposition that it was never collected. HENRY VIII and Cardinal THOMAS WOLSEY, the lord chancellor, demanded a non-refundable grant or forced loan to finance a war against France. The tax was to be administered in two stages. First, commissioners in each county were to persuade persons liable to the tax to agree to an assessment based on valuations made for a forced loan in 1522. The clergy were to pay one-third of their yearly revenues or of the value of their moveable goods if these were above £10. Clergy with goods valued below £10 were to pay only 25%. Although there is no official record of the assessment proposed for the laity, Edward Hall, the chronicler, wrote that assessments varied according to a sliding scale from 17% on incomes about £50 per year to 5% on incomes between £20 and £1. As the government encountered opposition, the demands were reduced. The second stage—the actual payment of the assessments—never occurred.

Wolsey has been traditionally viewed as the author of the Amicable Grant, but recent research suggests that the tax was the product of a consensus among the king and his principal councillors. Once the tax was agreed upon, Wolsey; THOMAS HOWARD, the 3rd duke of Norfolk; CHARLES BRANDON, the duke of Suffolk; and WILLIAM WARHAM, archbishop of Canterbury, worked loyally and energetically to secure compliance. The proposed grant, while unpopular and impolitic, was neither new nor unconstitutional. It was based on the Crown's historic PREROGATIVE right to ask subjects for financial aid when an emergency created necessity. In the past kings had borrowed money and collected benevolences, which were unauthorized taxes. Parliament declared a Yorkist benevolence illegal by a statute of 1484, but HENRY VII, pleading military need, successfully levied one in 1491. In 1522 the government imposed a substantial forced loan. Non-parliamentary taxation based on the doctrine of necessity opened the door to potential abuse by the government because the king and his advisers alone determined whether an emergency actually existed.

In 1525 Henry VIII needed tax revenue for an invasion of France. His foreign policy, inspired by memories of the Hundred Years' War and the conquests of Edward III and Henry V, sought to recover former English posssession on the Continent. Wars were still the sport of kings and noblemen in the early sixteenth century and were begun with little thought of human costs. Since England lacked sufficient military power to attack France unilaterally, Henry VIII's policy required an alliance with Charles V. After an imperial army captured the French king at Pavia, England had an opportunity to attack its historic enemy under extremely favorable circumstances. Two years earlier, in 1523, Henry had allied with Charles V against the French, ostensibly to defend the king's honor and to punish France for its failure to uphold previous diplomatic commitments. Although the army commanded by the duke of Suffolk achieved far less than the king had hoped, the invasion whetted his appetite for another campaign. The humiliating defeat of the French at Pavia encouraged Henry to look beyond military conquests and lay claim to "the whole crown of France." Achieving this grand design required tax revenue because it was impossible for the government to finance foreign invasions exclusively from Crown lands and customs duties. While Parliament provided revenue for the campaign of 1525, Henry and Wolsey decided to finance the proposed attack on France with the Amicable Grant.

Resistance to the Amicable Grant developed not because of opposition to the king's foreign policy but because of the taxpayers' claim that they were too poor to pay. While subjects traditionally avoided a direct refusal of financial assistance on the grounds of poverty, the government eventually accepted this argument. The tax burden had increased in recent years, and actual collections were slow. Previous taxes had provoked opposition, but the Amicable Grant led to vigorous protests over a wide area of the country. In the textile towns of southwest Suffolk riotous assemblies estimated to number in the thousands threatened the use of force. When rioters at Lavenham were asked who their captain was, John Grene, a Melford weaver, retorted that his men knew no other captain but poverty. The bulk of the persons indicted in Suffolk were poor men who protested spontaneously against the tax. No evidence survives to suggest that clothiers conspired with their workers to oppose the Amicable Grant. As popular discontent mounted, the government retreated. Henry VIII stated that he never knew of the tax while Wolsey denied giving his assent. Yet Wolsey's reputation suffered as public indignation was directed at him not the king. The Amicable Grant revealed the inability of Henry VIII's government to implement an ambitious financial program. Lacking the revenue required for an attack on the French, the king shifted his foreign policy away from Charles V and formed an entente with France.

Bibliography: G. W. Bernard, *War, Taxation and Rebellion in Early Tudor England: Henry VIII, Wolsey and the Amicable Grant of 1525*, 1986.

Barrett L. Beer

Angers, Treaty of (1551). This treaty was the result of the rapprochement between England and France that took place after the treaty of Boulogne in 1550. Unable to rely on the benevolence of the emperor, the government of JOHN DUDLEY, the duke of Northumberland, saw closer ties with France as a source of security, while remaining suspicious of French policies in general. For its part, the French court needed to remove uncertainties about English intentions as it faced a renewal of war with the emperor in 1551.

On 12 May 1551, William Parr, marquess of Northampton, was commissioned to go to France primarily to conclude a marriage treaty between Edward and Henry II's daughter, Elisabeth. His instructions required him to ask the French king for the handing over of MARY, QUEEN OF SCOTS first, but this was a matter of form. The embassy was a splendid one; Northampton was accompanied by 31 dignitaries and over 200 servants and was greeted ceremonially in all the towns he passed through, including Paris and Orleans, on the way to Nantes. Negotiations on the treaty began on 20 June, and the request for Mary was turned down. The substantial talks concerned the size of the "dote" or financial payment that was to accompany the marriage and compensate England for the termination of the old pension. Northampton had been instructed to demand 1.5 million ecus and come down no lower than 800,000. This demand was greeted by the French negotiators with amused incredulity. Further instructions from England told Northampton to reduce his demand to 600,000 ecus, in which case EDWARD VI would not abandon any of his titles and pension claims. Finally, on 2 July he was authorized to ask for 400,000 ecus and accept 200,000, with the costs of transporting the princess to England in a seemly way. This latter sum was agreed at Nantes on 17 July, and the treaty was signed at Angers, to which the king had removed, on 19 July.

The treaty was in the form of an agreement to conclude a marriage contract "per verba de praesenti," not binding until carried out. Elisabeth de Valois was only six at this time, and the marriage was envisaged within one month of her twelfth birthday (in 1557). Half the money was to be paid on the day of solemnization and the second half a year after that, and arrangements were made for the princess's dower in traditional fashion, with land and rents of 10,000 marcs.

On balance it seems unlikely that either side regarded this marriage as a serious proposition, not only because of the ten year age difference but also because of religious difficulties. The English envoy assured Simon Renard, the imperial ambassador in France, that whatever the French might claim, the treaty was not directed against the emperor. Indeed, the instructions of Northampton had specifically ruled out the conclusion of an offensive or defensive alliance. It seems, therefore, that the main purpose of the alliance, from the point of view of Northumberland and his advisers, was to acquire a degree of freedom of action in negotiating between the major powers. A trend, however, was created in which England for the next two years enjoyed closer relations with France than for the previous twenty years.

Bibliography: *Calendar of State Papers, Foreign, Edward VI*; *Spanish Calendar*; W. K. Jordan, *Edward VI: The Threshold of Power*, 1970.

David Potter

Anglicanism. In the sixteenth-century Church of England the predominant faction advocated a Protestantism expressed by Reformed theologians and by English forms of church order and liturgy; or, as put by advocates of this position in 1556, "we would have the face of an English church." The doctrinal basis for this position was adiaphora, "indifferent things;" church matters not legislated by Scripture were to be left to churches themselves. Though this Pauline and Reformed doctrine was initially intended to promote unity by allowing cultural differences among believers, it became the critical source of contention between those who claimed that Scripture did indeed prescribe most religious practices (the PURITANS and precisians) and those who defined religious practices according to national cultural traditions (Anglicans, formalists).

Those traditions had been promulgated as a "reformed" and "English" way in the 1530s and 1540s, when Tudor churchmen and political advisers created a national religious establishment to suit King HENRY VIII and to promote their own notions of proper religious reform. The new Anglican religious establishment had various features: an ambiguous theology; a hierarchical polity that in part had its own economic foundations but also fell prey to the king and his advisers; a liturgy defined in a Royal Primer; and controlled access to Scripture. Under King EDWARD VI, this Anglican establishment was pushed toward a theology that would please Continental Reformed theologians such as Heinrich Bullinger, Martin Bucer, and John Calvin. This Reformed theology was evidenced in the Forty-two Articles; however, liturgy followed a more formalized, ritualistic tradition, as evidenced in the BOOK OF COMMON PRAYER. Reformed churchmen like JOHN KNOX resisted some of the liturgical formalities, to the effect that the BLACK RUBRIC was added to the Prayer Book, a rubric designed to allay fears that Roman Catholicism remained in English worship. Within the Church of England, then, there were two broad Reformed factions, in addition to those who wanted to return to the Roman Catholic fold.

The two Reformed factions initially squabbled over the Prayer Book, but controversies also developed over many other issues: church polity, church discipline, vestments, preaching, and Sabbath observance. In these and other issues, the predominant party maintained that English practices had to prevail, practices that were incorporated into the law, promoted by the monarchy, and enforced by the English ecclesiastical hierarchy, while their puritan opponents demanded full loyalty to Scripture, that is, as interpreted by the prophet-like puritan preacher.

The Prayer Book disagreements that had originated under King Edward became full-blown during the MARIAN EXILE. Opponents of the book, led by John Knox, claimed that to many Roman Catholics "superstitions" were retained in the Prayer Book. By contrast, proponents of the "English way" contained in the Prayer Book aggressively maintained that worship must conform fully to the book's directions. Led by Richard Cox (later bishop of Ely), this group used nationalistic as well as theological arguments to support their position. Each group appealed to John Calvin for support, and each in turn received it; however, the Prayer Book party received its most critical aid from the source upon which it would continue to rely during Queen Elizabeth's rule—the state. The Frankfurt town council expelled Knox and his followers, many of whom fled to Geneva, while proponents of the Prayer Book group reestablished English liturgy. When the exile ended, many Prayer Book proponents also gained high positions in the Elizabethan Church of England and soon conformed to Queen Elizabeth's version of Protestantism.

Queen ELIZABETH and her leading bishops proceeded to develop a national church in which they primarily emphasized conformity to episcopal polity and to traditional rituals. This national church was accomplished by clerical appointments, an ACT OF UNIFORMITY, a revised prayer book, a broadly Calvinist doctrinal position in the THIRTY-NINE ARTICLES, and church discipline based on outward conformity in worship rather than on an ideological inquisition. The CONVOCATION of 1563, for example, resisted the puritan faction's desire to employ Continental examples of liturgy, church government, and discipline. The convocation left discipline in the hands of bishops and ecclesiastical commissions. For the remainder of Elizabeth's rule, puritan leaders pressed for change, only to be resisted by the queen and most of her episcopal appointees. At the same time, there was not complete harmony between the ruler and her bishops; for, while the bishops envisioned a church with some independence, she treated it more as an institution that must conform to national needs—as interpreted by the queen herself. Also, since she was usually bent on personal popularity, she often let puritans blame her bishops for policies she herself had privately urged.

Though Queen Elizabeth personally preferred an elaborate liturgy, she left it to her prelates and other clerics to define what comprised Anglicanism, rightly understood. Proponents of an Anglican way produced various works more fully to define their church and to react to criticisms. Archbishop MATTHEW PARKER's BOOK OF HOMILIES provided concise homilies suitable for reading in worship services. The homilies contained much Reformed theology and strongly emphasized social and political conformity, as did Parker's Advertisements, the archbishop's response to puritans in the VESTIARIAN CONTROVERSY. In *Apologia Ecclesiae Anglicanae* [Apology for the Church of England] (1562), Bishop John Jewel defended the national church, and Archbishop JOHN WHITGIFT's Lambeth Articles (1595) expanded on the Calvinist doctrines of predestination as already contained in the Thirty-nine Articles. Further, a biblical antidote to the Geneva Bible was the Bishop's Bible, by means of which Archbiship Parker hoped to avoid a puritan interpretation of controversial texts, for the Geneva version contained side notes and footnotes that Parker considered too prejudicial and "sharp." RICHARD HOOKER's *Of the Laws of Ecclesiastical Polity* (books 1-4, 1593; book 5, 1597) became the standard rebuttal of puritan charges against Anglican liturgy and polity (books 6-8 were published in the Stuart era).

The theological issues that divided Anglican churchmen from their puritan critics are well told in the old accounts by John Strype and Bishop Gilbert Burnet, and most of the controversies were rehashed during the nineteenth century. Modern scholarship by M. M. Knappen, Perry Miller, and William Haller emphasized the use of puritanism and thus left the impression than puritanism was opposed by an equally well-defined Anglicanism. The antidote to that approach has been to emphasize a broadly reformed and antipopish consensus in the Tudor church. This view is epitomised in Patrick Collinson's *The Religion of Protestants* (1982), while the older theological distinctions are maintained in William P. Haugaard's *Elizabeth and the English Reformation* (1968). Though not an "ism" in the modern philosophical sense, the Anglican "formalist" approach to English Protestantism was a strong one, especially in the eyes of contemporary critics, the puritans. This Anglicanism was Calvinist, though not of the scholastic variety; it was episcopal and thus rejected presbyterian principles of discipline, and its proponents insisted on Prayer Book conformity—"the face of an English Church."

Bibliography: Patrick Collinson, *The Religion of Protestants*, 1982; William Haugaard, *Elizabeth and the English Reformation*, 1968.

Ronald J. VanderMolen

Anglo-French War of 1512-1514. From the moment of his accession in 1509, HENRY VIII was eager to establish his reputation in Europe as a warrior prince and to emulate his famous predecessors on the English throne in making war on the traditional enemy, France. Until 1511, however, the caution of his councillors and the difficulty of finding reliable Continental allies restrained his ambition. In that year the dispatch of a force to the Netherlands under the veteran Sir Edward Poynings to assist the Habsburgs against France's ally the duke of Guelders was followed in November by English adherence to the anti-French Holy League of Spain, Venice, and the papacy. An English fleet put to sea to fight the French in the next spring but met with no great success, while an army of some 12,000 men sent to Spain for a joint invasion of Gascony failed dismally. King Ferdinand of Aragon wished to use the English troops merely to distract the French while he conquered Navarre. Without his promised help, the inexperienced commander Thomas Grey, marques of Dorset, would not advance, and the army dissolved into a diseased, drunken, and mutinous rabble whose quarreling captains returned home in November to humble themselves before the king's anger.

In 1513 Henry turned to the more practical course of attacking northern France from CALAIS and securing the support of the emperor Maximilian—at some cost in English subsidies—as well as that of Ferdinand and the pope, by the treaty of Mechlin in April. The spring's naval campaign was again unfruitful, and it resulted in the death of the rash lord admiral, Sir Edward Howard. In May Ferdinand devalued the treaty of Mechlin by making a truce with France. Yet Henry pressed on, sending two divisions of his huge army—19,000 men under George Talbot, earl of Shrewsbury, and Charles Somerset, Lord Herbert—across the Channel and through Calais to begin the siege of Therouanne in June. In July the king left Calais to join them with the remaining 16,000 or so troops, skirmished with French forces on the march across Artois, and met up at Therouanne with Maximilian, who brought plenty of flattery and advice but not the promised army. Henry's arrival enabled the establishment of an effective blockade around the town, one consolidated by English victory at the Battle of the Spurs on 16 August, when French cavalry trying to revictual Therouanne collided with the bulk of Henry's force and fled ignominiously, leaving a number of distinguished prisoners in the king's hands. This discouraged the garrison, which agreed on 22 August to surrender under terms. The town and its defenses were destroyed, and Henry moved on to tackle the greater prize of Tournai, a French enclave in the Netherlands, probably at Maximilian's instigation. Tournai's defenses were weak, and after six days' intensive bombardment and the storming of one of the gates by CHARLES BRANDON, Viscount Lisle, the citizens surrendered on 21 September. Henry determined to keep the city and did so until 1518, spending some £230,000 on its garrison and fortifications only to sell his conquest back to France under the TREATY OF LONDON for a mere £120,000.

Henry planned another major campaign for 1514, under the treaty of Lille, which again promised Spanish and imperial intervention, but one by one his allies deserted him. The death of the bellicose Pope Julius in 1513 and the accession of the more pacific Leo X were followed by the conclusion of truces with the French by Ferdinand and Maximilian. Henry sought help from the Swiss, who had recently defeated the French in Italy, and in June his fleet raided the area around Cherbourg. But in August he upstaged his inconstant allies by making peace with Louis XII of France and giving his sister Mary as Louis's bride.

The war was more significant for its effects on internal politics and the development of government than for any alteration of England's international position. THOMAS WOLSEY owed his rise to power to his very able administration of the war effort, while the campaign of 1513 brought Brandon a dukedom and Somerset an earldom to match the rewards given to the Howards for their victory against the Scots at FLODDEN FIELD. The great cost of the war, over £900,000—perhaps eight or ten times the king's ordinary annual revenue—destroyed the solvency established by HENRY VII, led to the introduction of the lay subsidy as an effective instrument of parliamentary taxation, and necessitated measures of retrenchment and financial reform that consolidated Wolsey's power. Meanwhile the search for popular support for the conflict brought new initiatives in the use of printed propaganda by the Crown. Henry had made his mark on European affairs, but his expensive victories seem only to have tempted him to further intervention.

Bibliography: C. G. Cruikshank, *Army Royal: Henry VIII's Invasion of France 1513*, 1969.

S. J. Gunn

Anglo-French War of 1522-1525. The unification of the Netherlands, the Spanish monarchies, and the Holy Roman Empire under the control of Charles of Habsburg (Charles V) in 1519 made conflict inevitable between Charles and Francis I of France, his rival for the inheritance of the dukes of Burgundy, for dominance in Italy and for European hegemony. Henry VIII, bent on the maintenance of an honorably important role in Continental affairs, saw the chance to commit England's weight to the struggle, either to impose peace on the rivals or to support one against the other in the hope of tangible gain. In 1520-1521 HENRY VIII and his chief minister, Cardinal THOMAS WOLSEY, tried hard to arbitrate between Charles and Francis under the terms of the TREATY OF

LONDON of 1518 but simultaneously prepared to take advantage of alliance with Charles to attack France should English mediation fail, as it had done by the autumn of 1521. The TREATY OF BRUGES in November 1521 committed Henry to declare war on France almost immediately and to lead an invasion in person in spring 1523 in coordination with a similar enterprise by Charles; it also promised a desirable marriage between Henry's daughter and prospective heir, Mary, and the emperor.

English involvement in the war in 1522 was limited to a naval raid on Brittany and a destructive but desultory campaign in northern France, both led by THOMAS HOWARD, earl of Surrey (later 3rd duke of Norfolk). Meanwhile Wolsey occupied the year with preliminary preparations for the Great Enterprise, as Henry's promised personal invasion was known. A thorough and innovative survey of the nation's military resources was carried out, and its registration of landholding and wealth was then used as the basis of assessment for very productive forced loans. Nevertheless, by the treaty of Windsor in June 1522, the Great Enterprise was further delayed until 1524, probably as a result of English concern about the threat from a Scotland dramatically stirred up by the French.

In 1523 a new opportunity opened for Charles and Henry with the treason of Charles, duke of Bourbon, constable of France. He agreed to recognize provisionally Henry's claim to the French throne and to raise a large rebellion against Francis; Charles's forces were to attack from Spain, and Henry's were to combine with an army from the Netherlands to meet Bourbon near Paris. Henry's army under CHARLES BRANDON, duke of Suffolk, marched over the Somme in October 1523 to threaten the capital, but the Spanish forces barely crossed the border, Bourbon's revolt misfired, and the German mercenaries hired for the constable with Henry's money were defeated in eastern France. Suffolk retreated and was then forced to abandon his campaign entirely by cripplingly harsh weather, mutinies among his troops, and the dispersal of his auxiliaries by the insolvent government of the Netherlands, which placed more value on the concurrent conquest of Friesland than on ventures into France. Henry was disillusioned with his allies but emboldened by Suffolk's initial success. As a result, his policy in 1524 was more than usually fluid, and attempts to stir up Charles and Bourbon and to urge on the Great Enterprise and preparations for another campaign by Suffolk alternated with recriminations about his confederates fecklessness and even with tentative negotiations with the French.

The battle of Pavia in February 1525 revived the flagging Great Enterprise, as Francis was captured by Charles's commanders in Italy, leaving his kingdom apparently at Henry's mercy. Plans for an invasion under Henry's own command were pushed ahead, and Charles was urged to partition France with him. But such a campaign necessitated drastic fiscal expedients, as the reluctance of Parliament to grant the large subsidy demanded by Wolsey for the invasion of 1523 had shown. An ambitious plan to raise an Amicable Grant was set in motion but foundered on widespread refusal to pay. Charles's evident reluctance to indulge Henry's ambitions and the snub of his jilting of Princess Mary combined with the failure of the AMICABLE GRANT to encourage further talks with France. On 30 August a peace treaty was signed at The Moor (or Moor House), Wolsey's residence in Hertfordshire. By this Henry won what he could from the French—enlarged annual pensions, but no territorial concessions—before the anticipated settlement between the emperor and the captive French king threatened to make England irrelevant in European affairs.

The war exposed the frail foundations of Tudor intervention in Continental conflict, for despite Wolsey's efforts neither the financial nor the military resources at Henry's disposal sufficed to compete with the greater powers or make any lasting impact on the old enemy France. Charles V proved too unreliable an ally to be willingly of much help in furthering Henry's dreams of conquest and too powerful to be coerced into doing so. At the same time those dreams were shown to be unrealistic only in their breadth, and when Henry returned to war with France two decades later he determined successfully on small but concrete territorial gains.

Bibliography: G. W. Bernard, *War, Taxation and Rebellion in Early Tudor England: Henry VIII, Wolsey and the Amicable Grant of 1525*, 1986; S. J. Gunn, "The Duke of Suffolk's March on Paris in 1523," *English Historical Review* 101 (1986): 596-634; P. J. Gwyn, "Wolsey's Foreign Policy: The Conferences at Calais and Bruges Reconsidered," *Historical Journal* 23 (1980): 755-72.

                                                                    S. J. Gunn

Anglo-French War of 1543-1546. The last war waged by HENRY VIII against Francis I, it is conventionally regarded as his most capricious and wasteful campaign. It must, however, be seen in the context of Henry's designs upon Scotland and the increasingly complex diplomatic and religious struggles in Europe during the 1540s.

The signal for a move toward war was the deteriorating relationship between Emperor Charles V and Francis I from 1540 onward. The French were busy refortifying their northern frontier in 1541 in the expectation of war, and this activity gave rise to conflicts on the borders of the CALAIS Pale. Henry VIII was putting pressure on Scotland, the old ally of France, and the French were prepared to back up Scottish resistance. Toward the end of 1541 Scottish participation was mooted in a French-led, anti-imperial alliance in which England was to have no part. Henry also had a useful *casus belli* to hand. Francis I had not paid his pension to England since 1536 on the grounds that Henry had failed to come to his aid against the emperor in that year.

While substantial talks between England and France were going on as late as April 1542, parallel talks with the imperial ambassador, Eustace Chapuys (which he thought might be used to get better terms out of the French), were being held. It seems possible that Henry VIII had provisionally opted for the imperial alliance by May 1542 and in June and July was negotiating for German mercenaries with a view to starting hostilities in the spring of 1543. Though war between France and the emperor was declared on 30 July 1542, England remained neutral for the obvious reason that the problem of Scotland had to be dealt with before the launching of a full-scale campaign in France. This was done by an unanswerable ultimatum and the fortuitous victory of Solway Moss (22 November 1542). On 11 February 1543, a secret Anglo-Imperial Treaty of Mutual Aid, drafted by Chapuys, was signed in London. It provided for mutual defense to cover attacks against England or the Low Countries. Within two years there was to be a joint campaign against France. War was to be signalled by a joint embassy to demand the restoration of Henry VIII's pension, restoration of fortresses to the emperor, and an end to French dealings with the Turks.

War was delayed until late June 1543 since the French were anxious to prolong the peace with England and Henry VIII had still to settle the affairs of Scotland to his advantage. By that time it was impossible to arrange for a substantial campaign, though Henry acquitted his obligations under the treaty by commissioning Sir John Wallop on 7 July with a force of 5,000 men (mainly foot) to operate against the French for 112 days. Setting out from Calais on 22 July, they burnt French territory as far as the area of Doullens. In August, Henry agreed that Wallop should join the emperor's siege of Landrecies, where the English gained useful experience in attacking modern fortifications.

The real strategic plans for the Anglo-French war were negotiated in England by Fernando de Gonzago as a declaration of intentions dated 31 December 1543. This provided for the campaign to start by 20 June 1544, with two armies of invasion led by the sovereigns in person and each consisting of 35,000 foot and 7,000 horse (the English force was to include the German troops provided for in February 1543). The aim would be a concerted thrust towards Paris.

The date set for the start of the campaign was too late in the season to accomplish its aims. Moreover, Henry VIII showed a distinct reluctance to appear himself in the field as the date approached and did so only when the emperor's determination to go ahead threatened him with the loss of face. Crossing the Channel at the end of June, the king joined the main army under CHARLES BRANDON, the duke of Suffolk's command (3 July), while THOMAS HOWARD, the 3rd duke of Norfolk, was directed to besiege Montreuil with a smaller force. The total English army was about 30,000 men, the full 42,000 being impossible to raise in time.

Almost as soon as Henry landed in France (13 July), he was in receipt of secret messages for peace from the French court and, though he dallied with them, was not yet prepared to agree to terms. Boulogne had become his main goal, which was a weaker place than Montreuil, so there was a chance of success. Negotiations with the French court were going on constantly through Cardinal du Bellay during the siege, but it was with the emperor that the French concluded a treaty at Crêpy-en-Laonnois (18 September 1544). This came too late to release French forces to relieve Boulogne, which had surrendered on 14 September while a relieving army was on the way. Meanwhile, Montreuil held out, and Norfolk raised the siege on 28 September on the approach of the French army under the Dauphin. Henry returned to England as soon as he decently could, leaving only a garrison of 3,300 men in Boulogne.

That Boulogne did not immediately fall to the French counterattack is surprising, since it was faced by a French army of 50,000 men. Scarce supplies, bad weather, and a failed assault on the night of 12-13 October persuaded the Dauphin to withdraw his army, and Boulogne was safe for the time being.

The ability of the English to cling on at Boulogne against all the odds dominated English policy for the rest of the 1540s. It made a rapprochement with France difficult and generated ruinous expediture by the need to build modern fortifications and employ German mercenaries. The war itself became one of large-scale skirmishes around Boulogne until the summer of 1545, when Francis I and the French admiral d'Abnebault mounted a celebrated naval campaign in the Channel. It achieved little more than burnings on the Isle of Wight and the humiliation of Henry VIII when the *Mary Rose* accidentally sank in face of the enemy.

Diplomacy began to shift with the death of Francis I's son Orléans in September 1545, since his marriage into the Habsburg family had been a crucial element of the peace of Crêpy. France began to move toward a more active role in Germany in support of the Protestants, who took the view that their security depended on peace between England and France. A Protestant deputation led by Jakob Sturm actually set up an arbitration conference between England and France on the border of the Calais Pale in November 1545, but this failed as neither side was prepared to make the necessary compromises, either on Boulogne or on French interference in Scotland. English diplomacy, largely conducted in this period by WILLIAM PAGET, had to reckon with the determination of his aged king not to relinquish his last conquest.

Neutral mediation continued in the person of a Venetian gentleman with contacts in England, Francesco Bernardo, who approached the French diplomat Jean de Monluc. As a result, direct Anglo-French talks started early in May at Campe halfway between Guînes and Ardres. The negotiations were unusually protracted because of the difficulty of agreeing on the sum that was to be paid for Boulogne (both arrears of the pension and compensation forfortifications erected) and the English demand for the handing over of Mary Stuart (see MARY, QUEEN OF SCOTS) before they would include Scotland in the treaty. There was, however, now agreement that England would keep Boulogne for a term of eight years until the indemnity should be paid. It was finally agreed that this should be 2 million French crowns (roughly £400,000) and that the "perpetual" pension should be renewed. The Boulonnais was to be kept by England, and Scotland was at least "comprehended" in the treaty on the French side.

The treaty of Campe or Ardres was signed on 7 June 1546, settling the immediate problems but leaving plenty of scope for further discord. The status of Scotland, the erection of fortifications after the treaty, and the exact delimitation of the frontier were all to contribute to growing hostility between England and France after 1547, but, for the moment, the field was open for Anglo-French cooperation on the issue of the emperor's increasingly alarming plans in Germany.

Bibliography: J. D. Pariset, *Les relations entre la France et l'Allemagne au milieu du XVI e siecle*, 1981; D. L. Potter, "England and France 1536-50," Cambridge Ph.D. thesis, 1973; G. Salles, "La guerre et les négotiations entre Francois Ier ex Henry VIII.....Sept 1544–June 1546," *Positions de théses...à l'Ecole des Chartes*, 1983.

David Potter

Anglo-French War of 1549-1550. A renewal of the conflict temporarily settled by the treaty of Campe, 1546. After the deaths of HENRY VIII and Francis I, attempts to reach a closer understanding represented by the two treaties negotiated by Baron de La Garde in England (11 March 1547) were abandoned. The new French king, Henri II, refused to ratify them (April 1547), and EDWARD SEYMOUR, the protector Somerset, was in no position to press the matter. Henri II was determined to recover Boulogne, having been humiliated in failing to recover it in 1544, but, in view of the triumph of Charles V in Germany, was not immediately able to put his plans in effect. However, the failure to ratify La Garde's treaty led to increasing border hostilities with the English, who were themselves busy digging in at Boulogne. They also refused to accept full Scottish comprehension in the 1546 treaty, despite French demands. Somerset's invasion of Scotland and victory at Pinkie accelerated French aid to the Scots, which had already been decided on in September 1547. In April 1548 French troops arrived, with more landing in the summer. French and English forces were thus clearly engaged against each other, notably in the protracted siege of Haddington (from September 1548), but an even larger French force under Paul de Termes had to be sent in the spring of 1549. Meanwhile, at Boulogne Gaspard de Coligny was sent to start work on the fort Chatillon at the mouth of the harbor (May 1548).

Why was open war delayed until 1549? A prerequisite for France's declaring war on England was a clear understanding that the emperor would not fulfill his treaty obligations to the English (and would refuse to see these as including Boulogne). This condition was not established until late June 1549, when the failure of WILLIAM PAGET's mission to the emperor was known.

In early July news arrived in France of the seriousness of the WESTERN REBELLION. The moment seemed opportune to act, and a plan was probably formulated by 19 July. It was a relatively modest one for the French army to take the outlying fortifications of Boulogne and then see what happened. The army assembled at Abbeville on 10 August while already on the 8th, the French ambassador Odet de Selve went to the Privy Council to deliver the declaration of war.

In view of his preoccupations at home, Somerset could do little to reinforce Boulogne, and reverses there were used against him in the struggle for power in September. Henri II was leading an army in the field for the first time since his accession. Leaving Abbeville on 14 August, he had set up camp at Boulogneberg on the 22nd. By the beginning of September he had captured the outlying fortresses and cut Boulogne off, except by sea, but the king failed to press his advantage and departed. His army remained and dug in for a long siege over the gruelling winter months. The English garrison of Boulogne was still strong, and the Dunette still capable of dominating the harbor. All that the French could do during the winter months was to bombard the English positions from the other side of the estuary.

Edward Fiennes, Lord Clinton, the English commander, had made overtures to Gaspard Coligny, the French commander, as early as 25 September but had been rebuffed. By the New Year, negotiations seemed a more attractive prospect. After the fall of Somerset, Paget pressed constantly for a more realistic attitude toward Boulogne in the new regime. In France, the prospect of assembling a new army to besiege Boulogne was daunting. The cost of 12,500 foot in Picardy in January was 224,323 livres. As in 1546, it was an Italian intermediary, a Florentine merchant named Antonio Guidotti with contacts in England and France, who got the talks started.

Commissioners for peace were appointed by both sides in January, and the first meeting took place on 18 February. Negotiations were not easy, but Paget had already argued the case for abandonment forcefully at home and won. The question was, On what terms? The treaty of Boulogne signed at the Oultreau fort on 24 March was the result of some hard bargaining. Boulogne was to be handed back to France before the time stipulated in 1546 for £400,000 (133,000 ecus), a sum lower than envisaged in 1546 but higher than the French had originally offered and just enough to cover the cost of the English building of new works at Boulogne since 1545. The French wished to abolish the pension (not paid since November 1546), but the English maintained their claim while failing to have it restored. In effect it ceased to be an issue after 1550, though English face had been preserved on the matter. In Scotland, Henri II had taken on the role of protector with possession of Mary Stuart (later MARY, QUEEN OF SCOTS) and expected a full English evacuation. The English policy of dominating Scotland was abandoned, though not by the treaty. The French had wanted to conclude a marriage treaty between Edward VI and Henri II's daughter Elisabeth and showed in this desire that they were already thinking in terms of a closer alliance with the new regime in England. The English negotiators, though, had no power in the matter of a marriage treaty, and it had to wait for the following year. Boulogne was handed over in April, and a new phase in Anglo-French relations began.

Bibliography: D. L. Potter, "The Treaty of Boulogne and European Diplomacy" *Bulletin of the Institute of Historical Research* 131 (1982); D. L. Potter, "Docu-

ments concerning the Negotiation of the Anglo-French Treaty of March 1550,"
Camden Miscellany 28, 1984: 58-180.

David Potter

Anglo-French War of 1557-1559. This conflict was not particularly England's
war, but rather England's involvement in the last stage of the Valois-Habsburg
struggle, which had been going on intermittently since at least 1519. A series of
confrontations between Pope Paul IV and Philip II of Spain during 1556 led to an
outbreak of fighting. Henry II of France entered the war against Spain in January
1557 and provoked a flurry of activity in England. By terms of the marriage
treaty that had united Philip and MARY I in 1554, the former was not permitted
to call upon English support for the war he was then fighting. Philip put pressure
on the PRIVY COUNCIL for England to enter the war. It was due to French
provocation that the council eventually declared war on 7 June. This decision was
popular with the military aristocracy, who hoped for employment and profit in
Philip's service, but unpopular in the country at large, particularly in the merchant
community of London. In July 1557 the imperial army of Philip II was poised in
Cambrai for an invasion of northeastern France. By the end of the month it was
besieging the town of St. Quentin. On 10 August the constable of France, Anne
de Montmorency, advancing incautiously to the relief of the town, fell into an
ambush. He was routed and captured along with 7,000 troops in one of the most
decisive battles of the entire war. St. Quentin held out until 27 August, when it
succumbed to a direct assault in which some 2,000 English troops took part. The
English acquitted themselves well, suffering some 200 casualties, although not as
well as they subsequently claimed and pretended. Philip II lacked the resources
to follow up this double victory, and the expected advance on Paris never
materialized. By early November the English troops had returned home, and the
main army went into winter quarters.

The disaster of St. Quentin left the French in urgent need of some striking
success to bolster their flagging morale. In November 1557 the duke of Guise was
recalled from Italy to provide leadership, and eventually it was decided to make
the target the poorly maintained English fortress at CALAIS. Although the
English government received some warnings of the French preparations, it
ignored them. Guise attacked on 1 January 1558 and captured the crucial harbor
fortress of Rysbanck the next day. This capture prevented the reinforcing of the
rest of the fortress, and by 21 January the last of the English forces surrendered.
Although the English government initially considered a counterattack, it was
abandoned by the end of February. The loss of Calais left a long legacy of
bitterness and recrimination.

Philip's forces continued to experience problems during the first half of 1558.
In May negotiations for peace began, which made it even more important for
Philip to score a victory. Fortunately for him, the French general de Termes made
a serious tactical mistake. Advancing toward Gravelines, he allowed his

forces to be caught between the army of the Count of Egmont and an imperial fleet commanded by Galindez de Carvajal on 13 July. Philip's victory at Gravelines was less dramatic than at St. Quentin but was nevertheless significant. English forces supposedly assisted at this action, but there is no conclusive evidence that they did.

Peace negotiations continued throughout the autumn of 1558 with much hard bargaining. Both sides needed peace, but neither trusted the other. The main issue, apart from the restoration of Calais to England, was the duchy of Savoy. Philip II wanted to regain independence for his ally, Emmanuel Philibert. The French eventually agreed to his wishes. The Treaty of Cateau-Cambresis, which eventually resulted on 3 and 4 April 1559, was generally regarded as a success for Philip II. It was a success won by making concessions at the expense of others. As long as Mary was alive, Philip felt some obligation to recover Calais for England. When she died and Elizabeth succeeded to the throne on 17 November 1558, Philip was freed from an aging and childless wife and any obligation to England. Efforts to recover Calais for England ceased, and Philip agreed in February 1559 to marry Elizabeth of Valois, the daughter of Henry II. The continuing threat of French aggression compelled England to remain on good terms with Spain in spite of its disappointment over Calais.

The importance of the Treaty of Cateau-Cambresis has been exaggerated by subsequent events. Henry II was killed a few weeks later in a tournament, with disastrous consequences for France. There were no further major hostilities in Europe for the next fifty years. With hindsight, Cateau-Cambresis can be seen as a turning point in the history of the sixteenth century and as the final end of forty years of endemic warfare. But it did not look that way at the time—least of all to those who signed it.

Bibliography: C. S. L. Davies, "England and the French War, 1557-59," in *The Mid-Tudor Polity, c. 1540-1560*, eds. J. Loach and R. Tittler, 1980; D. M. Loades, *The Reign of Mary Tudor*, 1979; D. Potter, "The duc de Guise and the Fall of Calais, 1557-8," *English Historical Review* 98 (1983): 481-512.

David M. Loades

Annates, Acts Concerning (1532 and 1534). (23 Hen. VIII, c. 20; 25 Hen. VIII, c. 20). By 1532, HENRY VIII was becoming increasingly insistent that his demand for a divorce from CATHERINE OF ARAGON be approved. Continued resistance by the papacy led to a series of acts in Parliament that were designed to put pressure on the church to accede to Henry's demands. The end result would be a separation from Rome by way of legislative action.

The first Act Concerning Restraint of Payment of Annates to the See of Rome, sometimes called the "Conditional Restraint of Annates," forbade the payment of a special fee, called annates or first fruits, to the papacy. Annates were the equivalent of a year's income from the lands that were owned by the highest offices in the church—bishops, archbishops, and abbots. The nominee to one of these positions could not receive full approval for the office from the pope until after such fees had been paid. Annates thus served as a significant source of income for the Holy See, and Henry assumed that a threat to their continuance might force the pope to consider seriously his request for a divorce.

The 1532 act was not to become law until final approval came from the king, with the clear understanding that if the pope would grant the king's divorce, the law withholding annates from Rome would not be put into action. There was significant resistance to the bill in the House of Lords, where the legislation originated, and there was some reluctance also in Commons. Some, even among the bishops and abbots who had been forced to pay these fees, were loathe to be disloyal to the pope. Others, particularly in the House of Commons, may have been fearful of economic reprisals from some of their Roman Catholic trading partners on the Continent, especially those under the rule of Emperor Charles V. The king personally visited Parliament several times in order to win approval of the law. The vote in the House of Commons took place in the presence of the king.

In 1533, since the pope had not given in, Henry VIII completed the procedures to end the payment of annates. The law further provided that if the pope tried to interfere by delaying or denying approval of nominees, they could be consecrated without the pope's blessing. In addition, the act anticipated the possibility of excommunication or interdict and stated that if the pope should take such action, the king and the people of England could lawfully "continue to enjoy the sacraments, ceremonies and services of Holy Church, any papal censures notwithstanding."

The next year Parliament passed a second law forbidding the payment of annates, with severe penalties awaiting any who would defy king and Parliament. This law went further and put into formal law the traditional practice of the king's choosing his own bishops and abbots. Cathedral chapters and monasteries were ordered to elect the person nominated by the king within twelve days or stand in danger of being charged with PRAEMUNIRE (serving as an agent of a foreign government against the interests of England). Further, the king would then be permitted to appoint the bishop (or abbot) directly.

The result of these pieces of legislation was to sever the authority of Rome over the English church by removing the pope's role in approving those to serve in the positions of greatest power and influence in the church and by claiming authority of the king and English church to proceed regardless of any action by the papacy. The use of annates, money, as an instrument of persuasion failed. But Henry was nevertheless able to insure that his own people were appointed to lead the sometimes wealthy and generally influential cathedrals and monasteries.

Bibliography: S. E. Lehmberg, *The Reformation Parliament*, 1970.

Richard L. Harrison, Jr.

Anne Askew Affair (1546). Anne Askew is one of the most famous martyrs of the English Reformation. Her story is significant not only as the drama of a young woman standing steadfast in the face of combined ecclesiastical and political forces but for its social and historical implications.

She was born in 1520, the daughter of a Lincolnshire knight, Sir William Askew. Her father was a man with connections at court and enlightened-enough views to educate his daughter to a degree somewhat uncommon for their time and station. This fact would have bearing on the young woman's future, for she began early in life to study WILLIAM TYNDALE's Bible. By her adolescence she had begun to be recognized in her family circle for the combination of enthusiasm, stubborn assurance, and argumentativeness that would characterize her short life.

Seeking to provide for his daughter before his death, Sir William made arrangements in 1540 for her to marry a wealthy landowner, Thomas Kyme. This marriage proved to be unhappy largely because Kyme was a strong adherent to the old faith while Anne had become a convinced and ardent Protestant. In time, Anne came to believe that her husband had joined with the papist clergy to prevent her from practicing her beliefs. In 1543 the couple separated, and Anne returned to her childhood home. In the flurry of gossip surrounding the event, Thomas Kyme's spiritual advisers counseled that he bring his wife home and force her to abjure her heretical and disobedient activities. Anne, however, claimed that her marriage was not valid in the eyes of God and sought a divorce. After losing her suit at the Bishop's Court at Lincoln, she determined to take her case to the Court of CHANCERY in London. This move to London in 1544 brought her into the wider political context against which her personal religious drama was played out.

Anne Askew arrived in London at a crucial period in the English Reformation. The path of reform in England had not been direct, and this lack of directness had led in the last years of HENRY VIII's life to power struggles between Reform and Conservative factions. Thus, questions of theology and ecclesiastical reform had become inextricably intertwined with the ambitions of powerful individuals or families. In 1546 the line between the factions had become very clearly drawn, with the Protestant cause in the ascendency. Henry's queen, CATHERINE PARR, was an intelligent and learned woman devoted to the Protestant cause, which had strong and able leaders, including the Earl of Hertford, EDWARD SEYMOUR, uncle to Prince EDWARD. Moreover, after 1545, Parliament contained a sizeable group friendly to Protestantism. Each faction understood that it was necessary to win Henry's support before his death left a minor as king because his favor would determine the future of the Reformation for the next generation.

The Conservative faction, led by STEPHEN GARDINER, bishop of Winchester, and THOMAS WRIOTHESLEY, lord chancellor, intended to use Henry's deep horror of heresy to further their political and religious ends. If Henry could be made to connect highly placed Protestants (including his queen) with the cancer of heresy and sedition, then, the Conservatives reasoned, their ascendency would be assured. Into this cauldron of personal ambition and animosity, high politics, and religious controversy walked Anne Askew. As her case unfolded, it became clear that she would become a mere pawn in a ruthless game that, finally, had little to do with true religious conviction.

Anne had come to London to procure a divorce from her husband on religious grounds, and she soon became the center of a circle of gospel readers. It is clear that she enjoyed her role of Protestant heroine and sufferer for the true faith. She was steeped in Scripture and not reluctant to speak of what she espoused. Moreover, she was pert and witty to the point of recklessness. In other words, she made enemies, and by June she had come to the attention of the authorities. On 13 June 1545 she was arrested and presented for trial at Guildhall "for certain words spoken . . . against the Sacrament." No witnesses appeared, and although her replies to her inquisitors were so witty as to be rude, she was released.

Unfortunately, she came to the notice of Thomas Wriothesley, who sent one of his clerks to spy on her. On his evidence she was again arrested on suspicion of heresy and was taken to the house of the lord mayor of London. There she was questioned by the mayor and the bishop's chancellor. Again, her answers were considered disrespectful, and she was sent to prison there to be interrogated by a priest in the service of Bishop EDMUND BONNER. On 25 March the bishop himself questioned her and hoped to force her to sign a confession of orthodox belief. Upon being given the paper, she wrote her own equivocal statement. The authorities returned her to prison, but her friends bargained for her release. Finally, she heeded their advice and left London. She did not, however, return to her husband but went to her brother's home.

While she remained in South Kelsey, the situation in London worsened. The Conservative faction began a veritable witch-hunt for heretics in high places. Gardiner determined to consolidate his forces and overthrow his enemies, and, with the eager assistance of Thomas Wriothesley and Richard Rich, a campaign began to extirpate heretics and enemies at one blow. Anne Askew was again arrested and on 19 June was brought before the PRIVY COUNCIL at Greenwich and then sent to Newgate Prison because she refused to live with her husband and because "she was very obstinate and heady in reasoning in matters of religion." Now, she faced heresy charges in earnest. Rich and Wriothesley were determined to use her to implicate members of the court; others were cautious about trying and executing a gentlewoman. Therefore, all proceeded with caution. Canon lawyers and theologians visited her, and Gardiner himself interrogated her on the subject of the Sacrament. Finally, she came to trial with three others. All were found guilty. Two of her codefendants recanted and were pardoned. She, however, was returned to prison to await execution at the stake.

This trial should have ended the matter, but Rich and Wriothesley were fixed on forcing the implication of others, especially the queen. Therefore, they undertook a desperate and highly illegal course of action. Although already tried and condemned, Anne was taken to the Tower, where the two tried to force her to reveal the names of her coreligionists. When she refused, they placed her on the rack, and they themselves removed their gowns and applied the torture. She must by now have completely given herself over to suffering martyrdom and remained steadfastly silent. They returned her to the Tower and, finally, to Newgate to await her death. Word of her torments and of her courage quickly spread, and rather than regarding her as an odious heretic, people began to regard her as a heroine. From prison she wrote to friends and to fellow prisoners in the hope of making the truth of her story known. She also demonstrated the force of her faith in prayers for her enemies.

On 16 July 1546, she, John Lascelles, and two others were taken from prison to Smithfield, where they were burnt at the stake in the presence not only of Rich and Wriothesley but of a large crowd of spectators and supporters.

Thus ended the brief life of Anne Askew. The Anne Askew Affair did not, however, end here. In using her to pursue its end of destroying Reformed influence at court, the Conservative faction failed. Even before Anne's execution, Henry had angrily defended his queen before Wriothesley, and the despicable story of Anne's torture, along with the appalling spectacle of the execution of a woman of her rank, led to a wide anti-Conservative reaction. In effect, her death helped to sway the country on the side of Reformation again; the end of 1546 saw the downfall of the Conservative faction and Gardiner's disgrace. Anne's friends smuggled her accounts out of prison and to the Continent. They were printed in Marburg in 1547 and soon were being read throughout Protestant Europe.

Bibliography: John F. Davis, *Heresy and Reformation in the Southeast of England, 1520-1559*, 1983; Derek Wilson, *A Tudor Tapestry*, 1972.

Mary G. Winkler

Anne of Cleves (1515-1557). Anne of Cleves was the fourth wife of HENRY VIII and the daughter of John, duke of Cleves, who had renounced papal authority while avoiding heretical extremes. She was Henry's choice among several candidates after the death of JANE SEYMOUR. The two-year search for a new wife began almost immediately after the former queen's death. Where Henry's earlier marital decisions had been based on dynastic considerations, this marriage arose out of political and religious necessity. Although there had been tentative negotiations for marriage with Christina, duchess of Milan, and with a French princess, the necessity of a Protestant alliance was pressed by THOMAS CROMWELL. In 1539 the emperor Charles V and the king of France signed the Treaty of Toledo, agreeing not to negotiate with England separately, and Pope Paul III promulgated a bull absolving Henry's subjects from allegiance to their sovereign. Under these circumstances, England, needing a Protestant alliance, looked to Germany. Anne appeared a suitable candidate. Cromwell negotiated the alliance, and England and Cleves signed the marriage treaty on 6 October 1539.

Unfortunately, instead of the serene beauty attributed to her in the Hans Holbein portrait, Henry saw a "Flanders mare." He seems to have found her physically repugnant, and upon her arrival in England in January 1540, he said, "If I had known as much before as I know now, she would never have come into this realm." The marriage was never consummated, and by Easter Henry had displayed an interest in one of her ladies-in-waiting, CATHERINE HOWARD.

The Habsburg-Valois alliance had begun to break down, leaving Henry free from his former need for a Protestant alliance. Because Cromwell had orchestrated the German marriage in order to secure England as a Protestant state, Henry turned to him to facilitate an annulment. Cromwell, not wanting to advance the Conservative cause through the king's marriage to Catherine Howard, hesitated. His hesitation helped bring on his downfall, while Henry achieved his annulment in July 1540. Anne of Cleves remained in England, the king's "dear sister," until her death seventeen years later.

Bibliography: Paul Rival, *The Six Wives of Henry VIII*, 1936.

Mary G. Winkler

Apprentices, Statute of (1563), (5 Eliz. I, c. 4). Also known as the Statute of Artificers, this law consolidated 150 years of economic legislation, regulated the service of all hired employees, and required youths to serve apprenticeships in trade, industry, or husbandry. Parliament enacted this bill in an effort to strengthen the English economy by improving the quality of manufactured goods and to enhance the stability of society by addressing the issue of growing numbers of vagrants and persons dispossessed by enclosure.

This act served three purposes. First, it established a procedure whereby JUSTICES OF THE PEACE would annually fix wages of all occupations at certain rates. Ths statute thus limited inflation of wages and prices of goods. Once established, wage rates would be certified by the chancellor, approved by the PRIVY COUNCIL, and announced by the sheriffs. The rates were for maximum, rather than minimum, wages and established national control of wage rates. Those employers who ignored the statute and paid higher wages were imprisoned and fined. Workers who received higher rates were jailed.

Second, the statute established minimum working conditions. It stipulated the length of the workday and varied hours between winter and summer. Employers were required to engage their workers for periods of at least one year. Workers were prohibited from leaving before the term of their contracts had expired. Unmarried women aged twelve to forty were also required to enter service.

Third, the act created a national system of apprenticeship. Apprenticeships were now required to be served for seven years, during which the master was completely responsible for the apprentice's care, conduct, and occupational training. The 1563 act required youths to serve apprenticeships in industries and trades as well as farming. Apprentices in the trades served until age twenty-one (age twenty-four in corporate towns in an effort to restrict the growth of poor households). Apprentices engaged in husbandry were required to serve until age twenty-one, or twenty-four if they so agreed. Masters were, however, permitted to discharge apprentices for misbehavior. The number of apprentices was limited to three for each journeyman in textiles, shoemaking, and tailoring. Apprentices also had to satisfy occupational and property qualifications, which varied among trades. Employers could hire only those who had completed the seven-year apprenticeship. Artisans could not establish shops until they had first served an apprenticeship. Apprentices were bonded until age twenty-one to make sure they fulfilled their contracts. In addition, justices of the peace received the authority to apprehend those who fled.

The Statute of Apprentices was a significant piece of legislation and was in force for over 200 years. It established a uniform, national system of apprenticeship in place of the many local variations. By formalizing the apprenticeship process and by standardizing the period of service, it encouraged economic stability. The statute also established standards for industrial regulation that lasted until the mid-eighteenth century, when they were undermined by rapid industrial change.

Bibliography: M. Davies, *The Enforcement of English Apprenticeship, 1563-1642*, 1956.

David B. Mock

Archpriest Controversy. Disputes among Roman Catholics during the reign of ELIZABETH I arose from time to time. The hardships and frustrations of exile and persecution contributed to divisions caused by clashes of personality and policy and by rivalries and differences between regular and secular clergy.

The death of Cardinal William Allen in 1594 removed a valuable unifying force in Rome and also raised the question of how the English should run their mission and their church, now that the man who had in some senses been the leader was gone. Two disputes erupted, one in Rome and the other in England and they prepared the ground for the later Archpriest Controversy. In Rome in 1595, for the third time in its recent history, the English seminary was disturbed by student troubles, directed in this case against the Jesuit governors of the college. Robert Persons returned from Spain to Rome to solve this problem with great skill and speed. The second dispute occurred in 1594-1595 among the thirty or so priests interned in Wisbech Castle in Cambridgeshire by the government of Elizabeth. Personalities, trivialities, and persecution played their part here as at Rome and again the leadership of Jesuits raised a question of corporate loyalty and rivalry. Briefly, the rules of collegiate life proposed by the Jesuit William Weston were rejected at Wisbech by a group of secular priests led by Dr. Christopher Bagshaw and Thomas Bluet, both later prominent Appellants. The

"Stirs at Wisbech ran their course in the years 1594-1595, manuscript documents passing from one side to another, until in the end a reconciliation of sorts was achieved.

The Wisbech problems revealed the need for a greater degree of organization in the English mission, which had been discussed since the beginning of the missionary effort. An obvious solution was to consecrate one or two English bishops, but it was also obvious that such men would be in grave danger in England. Persons in 1598 solved the problem to his satisfaction by securing from the cardinal-protector of the English nation the creation of a new officer, an archpriest, who was, with twelve assistants, to become head of the English mission. Persons was influenced in making this proposal by the serviceable system of organization developed in England by Henry Garnet, the head of the small English Jesuit mission there, and Persons expected the new archpriest to work closely with his Jesuit counterpart, an expectation that made very sound sense. The scheme, however, was flawed in two vital respects. First, there seem to have been no consultation of the English secular clergy and even some suspicion that Persons, by using the cardinal-protector to make the appointment, was attempting to steamroller his plan. Second, the choice of George Blackwell as archpriest was poor, since he soon showed himself a weak leader and since his closeness to the Jesuits made him suspected as a mere puppet of Persons.

The secular clergy, or at least a portion of them, objected to the appointment of Blackwell and appealed to Rome on two occasions, hence their name—the Appellants. The first appeal was taken to Rome in 1597 by William Bishop and Robert Charnock, whom Persons was able to rebuff easily and firmly. They were denied access to the pope, imprisoned, and then banished to France. This action had the effect of intensifying the quarrel. A second appeal was taken to Rome in 1602 by Bagshaw and Bluet from Wisbech and by two others, Anthony Champney and Francis Barneby. After lengthy discussions at Rome, the matter was settled in a compromise. Blackwell remained, and there was a succession of archpriests in England until 1625, but the archpriest's powers were substantially reduced by the pope, and his links with the Jesuits were cut. Blackwell was ordered to appoint three of the Appellants as his assistants. The controversy had been accompanied by the publication of over twenty printed books, largely on the Appellant side; now the pope commanded that this unseemly public debate should cease.

The controversy has been variously interpreted. Clearly there were different ideas about how to run the mission, although in fact Persons and the Appellants differed more over details than in substance. The jealousy felt by the secular clergy for the Jesuits was probably the most significant element in the whole story. The Appellants were important because they raised the question of toleration for Catholics in a very practical way. This matter had been discussed, by Persons, among others, on and off for years but the Appellants tried to do something about it by negotiating with the government through Richard Bancroft, bishop of London. The plan was for Catholics to renounce political involvement

and to condemn the Jesuits as the cause of all previous plots and hence persecution. Clearly the Appellants could not go far with such a plan in Rome, and in the
end it seems that the English government was not sincere. Elizabeth denounced
both seculars and Jesuits in a proclamation of November 1602 and ignored the
Proclamation of Allegiance given to her by thirteen Appellants early the next year.

Bibliography: T. G. Law, *The Archpriest Controversy* 2 vols., 1896-1898; A. O.
Meyer, *England and the Catholic Church Under Queen Elizabeth*, 1916.

P. J. Holmes

Armada, Spanish (1588). In 1588 England faced the threat of invasion from
Philip II of Spain, who sent an armada of 130 ships commanded by the duke of
Medina Sidonia to escort Spanish troops across from the Netherlands under the
duke of Parma. Neither England nor Spain officially declared war, but they were
involved in the religious wars in France and the Netherlands and from 1585 to
1604 fought each other directly. Tradition regards the "Enterprise of England" as
the result of religious and commercial rivalry and its defeat as a victory for a
superior English navy. The modern view is more complex. ELIZABETH I and
Philip II wanted to avoid war, but conflict was inevitable not only because of
religious antagonism and the struggle for wealth but also because of domestic
politics and the complicated international situation in the 1580s. While the English
had expected a Spanish invasion for some time, they were surprised when the
armada appeared. Finally, the English victory affected the outcome of the war less
than other circumstances.

Philip used his marriage to MARY I from 1554 to 1558 to claim the English
throne. He was also the most powerful ruler in Europe and the hope of Catholics
everywhere for winning the English back to Rome. But prior to the 1580s, he
showed little interest in a crusade against England. Though he ordered the duke
of Alba to prepare an invasion in conjunction with the RIDOLFI PLOT in 1571,
he was unenthusiastic, and he ignored papal attempts against Ireland in 1579 and
1580. New developments in the 1580s forced him to change his mind. After
Philip inherited the Portuguese throne in 1580, Elizabeth gave sanctuary to the
pretender, Don Antonio, and aided his unsuccessful attack on the Azores in
1581-1582. She also supported Calvinist insurgents against Philip in the
Netherlands, and after the assassination of their leader, William of Orange, in
1584, she officially extended English protection to the Dutch in 1585. Sir
FRANCIS DRAKE's voyage around the world in 1577-1580 increased Philip's
concern for his empire's safety. His fears were proved realistic by Drake's raids
on Baiona and Vigo and Caribbean shipping, as well as by English attacks on
Spain's Newfoundland fishing fleet. Also worrisome were English offers of
friendship to Fez-Morroco and the Ottoman Empire in 1584-1585, especially
given the internal threat in Spain from the Moriscos. When the French duke of
Anjou died in 1584, the new heir to Henri III was the Huguenot Henri Bourbon

of Navarre. This development and Dutch overtures to the French in 1585 created the possibility of an Anglo-Dutch-French alliance against Spain, though even without this alliance Philip refused to allow a Protestant on the French throne without a fight. That same year the Spanish king was reconciled with the powerful Catholic Guise family in France, and so was left more open to plots to place MARY, QUEEN OF SCOTS—whose mother was a Guise—on the English throne.

England's concern about a Spanish invasion was not unrealistic. When the marquess of Santa Cruz suggested it to Philip in 1583, the king rejected the idea as impractical, but in 1585 he reconsidered and began negotiating with Pope Sixtus V for financial aid and the right to name Mary's successor if she replaced Elizabeth. Philip considered two plans in 1586—Santa Cruz suggested sending an invasion force from Spain, and Parma recommended transporting men from the Netherlands. The king combined the two proposals and determined to send an armada from Spain and soldiers from the Netherlands. He was preparing for it in 1587, even before Elizabeth's execution of Mary, Queen of Scots in February (for her role in the BABINGTON PLOT of 1586) and Drake's April raid on Cadiz. But Philip met repeated delays in procuring men, ships, and provisions, and Santa Cruz died on 30 January 1588. Though his replacement, the duke of Medina Sidonia, was more competent than contemporaries realized, the further postponement of the enterprise was damaging, for Sir FRANCIS WALSINGHAM's English intelligence network had learned of the plan.

In England, though, defense was not the only concern. An interventionist party—led by Walsingham and ROBERT DUDLEY, the earl of Leicester, encouraged by Drake's exploits, and incensed by Philip's seizure of foreign ships in 1585—wanted an offensive war to open up the Portuguese Empire and use the riches thus obtained to carry on the fight in the Netherlands. But they were opposed by the more cautious WILLIAM CECIL, Lord Burghley, and Elizabeth herself, whose reluctance to make war is well known. In fact Drake's expeditions merely broke even, and Leicester's campaign in the Netherlands became one of attrition, so that even after Cadiz, the queen preferred a peaceful settlement. Still, by fall 1587, she could not ignore the Spanish mobilization, and by spring the peace talks had stalled.

Elizabeth agreed in May 1588 to allow Drake to attempt a preemptive srike against the armada off Lisbon. Lord Admiral Charles Howard, earl of Nottingham sailed from the Thames to Plymouth with almost 100 ships and left 40 under Lord Henry Seymour to guard the English Channel. Thrice between 30 May and 10 July, the English attempted to reach the Spanish coast, but each time the wind blew them back. Meanwhile the armada sailed from Lisbon on 30 May, but bad weather forced it to put in at La Coruna on 19 June for supplies and repairs, and it was unable to put to sea again until 22 July. Howard and Drake had learned of this event and concluded that the invasion was off, so the appearance of the Spanish fleet off the Lizard on 29 July was a surprise.

Fortunately, most of the English fleet was still at Plymouth and hastily put to sea and gaining the weather gauge (wind advantage) on 31 July. Thanks to Sir

JOHN HAWKINS the English had a centralized naval administration, which the Spanish lacked. This, superior tactics, greater maneuverability, and the longer range and more rapid fire of their guns gave the English the advantage in skirmishes off Portsmouth, Plymouth, and the Isle of Wight on 31 July and 2 August, and 4 August. The turning point was Medina Sidonia's halt off CALAIS on 6 August, necessitated by poor communications with Parma—the fault of Philip. The English sent fireships among the Spanish on 7 August and did considerable damage to the armada before a "Protestant wind" blew it into the North Sea. Howard broke off pursuit on 12 August; the armada sailed home around Scotland and Ireland and lost many more men and ships than in the actual fighting.

The English victory was indecisive, however. The war continued, Drake's PORTUGUESE EXPEDITION in 1589 failed, and Philip attempted invasions again in 1596 and 1597. But the victory of 1588 convinced English Protestants that God was on their side and made loyalists of many English Catholics unwilling to countenance foreign invasion. It also shattered the image of Spanish invincibility and over the long run made peace with the English a compelling alternative in Spanish foreign policy and made empire more attractive and attainable for the English.

Bibliography: Simon Adams, *The Armada Campaign of 1588*, 1988; Geoffrey Parker and Colin Martin, *The Spanish Armada*, 1988; M. J. Rodriguez-Salgada, et al., *Armada*, 1988.

William B. Robison

Army. It is somewhat anachronistic to speak of a Tudor "army" for England did not possess a permanent, standing army of any significant size during the sixteenth century. There were only a tiny number of people who could be considered professional soldiers in Tudor England. These were the some 200 Yeomen of the Guard, also known as the Beefeaters, primarily a ceremonial palace guard; the small permanent garrisons at Berwick, Dover, and CALAIS; a small group of gentlemen pensioners who served in part as the royal cavalry; the 850 mounted "gendarmes" organized by JOHN DUDLEY, duke of Northumberland; and the royal officials employed in the ordnance office at the Tower of London. To obtain a viable field army for temporary offensive or defensive purposes, Tudor monarchs relied on a variety of recruitment methods. The feudal levy was one such means. It was based on the obligation of the landed magnates to supply men and arms for their monarch. HENRY VII and HENRY VIII regularly used the feudal levy to fill their armies. By ELIZABETH's reign, however, this expedient had become too unwieldy and too costly. The Crown occasionally hired foreign mercenaries to augment its armies. Until 1560, mercenaries were always found in English armies, usually to correct shortages of pikemen, heavy cavalry, or troops with firearms. Sometimes the government contracted with private citizens by indentures to supply a company of troops for a sum of money. Other people were given special commissions to raise troops for the government. The most significant source of men and arms came from the county militia, and by the reign of Elizabeth it had become the main component of the Tudor army.

Dating from Anglo-Saxon times, the county militia embodied the obligation of all able-bodied men aged 16 to 60 in each county to own arms and defend the country from invasion. In spite of some efforts to change things late in Elizabeth's reign, the county and its sub-units, the division and the hundred, remained the chief administrative unit for militia affairs throughout the Tudor era. Prior to 1558, various medieval statutes regulated the militia. They limited the way the central government could use the militia. Each county's militia could serve only within that county, otherwise the Crown must pay for the full cost of the troops serving outside of their own county. In practice, the central government often ignored these geographical restrictions and used militia in other parts of the country or even overseas.

The true reorganization of the militia began under Queen MARY with two statutes passed in 1558. The Act for the Having of Horse, Armour and Weapon (4 & 5 Philip and Mary, c. 2) required lay citizens to supply military equipment on the basis of their wealth and in so doing effectively established the counties' obligation to finance their own militia. An Act for the Taking of Musters (4 & 5 Philip and Mary, c. 3) regulated the periodic taking of musters, during which local authorities were to call out and to inspect men, horses, and equipment. It also required some rudimentary training and drill. Both statutes also contained provisions for the enforcement of these regulations. As in many aspects of local government, the LORDS LIEUTENANT and their deputies (especially after 1585), the sheriffs, the JUSTICES OF THE PEACE, and certain other commissioners supervised these musters.

Most other major improvements and innovations in the Tudor army occurred after the statutory reorganization of 1558. The only significant earlier reform was the use of the lieutenancy during Edward VI's reign. Prior to 1558, the English army was deficient in firearms when compared to the Continental armies. As a result, many of the foreign mercenaries hired by the Tudors were skilled in firearms. It was only after 1570 that the English government began to supply native troops with the latest muskets and other firearms in significant numbers. Previously they had relied upon the antiquated longbow and the ineffectual bill, which consisted of a wooden shaft seven feet long capped with a metal point and blade. The creation of the trained bands was a development closely related to the increasing use of firearms. By 1573 the PRIVY COUNCIL had begun a program to train about 10% of the militia intensively in the use of firearms and horses. Members of the trained bands were intended to serve as the backbone of the national defense and were often used in foreign expeditions. The counties had to pay for this new training, and that requirement aroused much local opposition.

A further attempt to improve the militia involved the introduction of two new military officers at the county level: the muster-master and the provost-martial

The muster-master, a professional soldier, became a permanent addition to the militia during the 1580s and served as the agent of the central government. His responsibilities included (1) the training of the militia in the use of firearms, (2) the oversight of the care and preservation of local supplies of arms and armor, (3) the selection of the proper men for various duties, and (4) the inspection of the troops. Originally the Crown chose and paid for the muster-master. By 1588 the lords lieutenant were appointing muster-masters, and the counties were paying for their service. This additional expense again provoked local resistance. Provost-martials were also Crown appointees and enforced martial law in the localities, particularly the policing of ex-soldiers returning from overseas duty.

Tudor armies generally suffered from problems of poor organization and administration. These maladies stemmed largely from the localized nature of recruitment, financing, and equipping of the troops. Armies were usually divided into large and unwieldy units called wards. The massive force of 42,000 men that Henry VIII used to invade France in 1544 consisted of three such wards numbering 13,000, 16,000, and 13,000 men, respectively. Wards were further divided into companies. These companies were the basic unit of military organization. They included 100-150 infantry, of which 60% carried firearms, 30% were pikemen, and 10% were billmen and another 60-100 cavalry. A captain commanded each company and was responsible for the arming, clothing, and feeding of his men as well as the disbursement of their pay. Country gentlemen, usually amateurs, generally filled the position and often engaged in corruption. During the 1580s the intermediate-sized unit of the regiment was introduced. It consisted of a number of companies under the command of a colonel. This addition improved the chain of command by allowing better communication between the colonels and their individual companies and the generals commanding the entire army.

England was not a great land power during the sixteenth century and lacked generals of the caliber of the duke of Parma. Tactics on the battlefield consisted of little more than raids and skirmishes between small bodies of troops. Warfare in the sixteenth century was conducted with great slowness. Improvements in fortifications tended to emphasize the defensive side of warfare. As a result, strategic thinking focused on the conducting of lengthy sieges of fortified areas and the garrisoning of towns to withstand attackers.

Warfare has always been an expensive enterprise, and during the sixteenth century the cost of the latest fortifications or firearms and warfare's slowness only made it more so. Ordinary Crown revenues were not sufficient to pay for either a standing army or even an occasional one. Additional help from Parliament was needed and given, although not always adequately. The central government also increasingly called on the localities to pay for the costs of the militia. Corruption by contractors and officers further added to the costs of war. Captains of companies routinely pocketed "dead pays," that is, ten extra payments for every 100 men under their command. The foreign ventures in the Netherlands from 1585 cost nearly £100,000 annually while the war in Ireland from 1595 to 1603 drained the EXCHEQUER of an astronomical £1,800,000. Opposition to these continued expenditures from the hard-pressed taxpayers grew in the last two decades of Elizabeth's reign. The Crown tried to ease popular discontent by making the financial burden more equitable, but it had little success. Tudor England, like every other early modern state, was bound by the fiscal reality that warfare was expensive and prolonged warfare was ruinous to the domestic economy.

Bibliography: Lindsay Boynton, *The Elizabethan Militia, 1558-1638*, 1967; C. G. Cruickshank, *Elizabeth's Army*, 2nd ed., 1966.

Eugene J. Bourgeois II

Art. One cannot write about art in England during the reign of the Tudors without discussing three important cultural influences. One is the influence of HUMAN-ISM on the visual arts, and another is the influence of Evangelical Protestantism. The third is the use of art to support the increasing authority of the monarchy.

The Renaissance style, the result of decades of development in theory and practice, came relatively late to England. It came late because humanism was a relatively late import and because art was commissioned mainly in the service of late medieval religious practices. Renaissance art developed chiefly in the heady atmosphere of the Italian republics—most notably Florence—and reached its culmination under the patronage of the church. It grew out of an attitude toward existence that stressed the centrality of humanity and that sought order and harmony in theories of proportion and mathematical perspective. In England this style never took root enough to grow and bear its own distinctive native fruit.

If we look to the reign of HENRY VII, we find few of the conditions necessary for the growth of the artistic style of humanism. The English aristocracy were essentially indifferent to the arts, and when they commissioned works of art, they tended to desire works expressive of the almost feverish concern with death and afterlife. Thus the very real expression of artistic concern is to be found in tomb sculpture, grave monuments, funerary chapels, and so forth. Although the duke of Urbino presented Henry VII with the gift of Raphael's *St. George and the Dragon*, there is little suggestion that the style of this gift impinged on the consciousness of its recipient or of his court.

It is in the reign of his son HENRY VIII that the Italian style first finds a truly welcome reception. Under Henry VIII, a new spirit animated artistic patronage. The young king was eager to bring the New Learning to his court, and with the New Learning came the new art. It is only in Henry's reign, when Italian artists and sculptors were employed at court, that the Renaissance style had its first real influence on English cultural life.

The most famous proponent of the new art in England, however, was a German, Hans Holbein (1497-1543). It is, in fact, through Holbein's eyes that we see Henry, his court, and the humanist circle associated with the names of

Erasmus and Sir THOMAS MORE. Hans Holbein, the Younger, the son of the Augsburg painter, Hans Holbein, the Elder, made his first visit to England in 1526. He had attracted the notice of Erasmus when both were residing in Basel, and the scholar in turn introduced the painter to Thomas More. Although More praised his work in glowing terms, he perceived that Holbein might have difficulty establishing himself among an aristocracy that still favored Gothic art and architecture. Nevertheless, he introduced the artist to court. Although he has become justly acclaimed for his portraits, his first work at court was as a decorator for the Master of Revels (1527). At the time of his visit he executed a number of portraits for private donors (*e.g.*, Thomas More, Archbishop WILLIAM WARHAM, Nicolas Kratzer). He went home to Basel in 1528 but was back in England in 1532, a casualty of Reformation iconoclasm. During the second visit he entered regular, royal employment. Although Henry thought of art as primarily a service to enhance the pomp and ceremony accompanying royal power, he gave the servant-artist Holbein the politically important commission of painting portraits of his prospective brides. Unfortunately, Holbein lost favor with Henry after the appearance of ANNE OF CLEVES did not measure up to her portrait.

Holbein's work represents a Renaissance style that synthesizes the idealizing and theoretical aims of Italian masters with interest in particularity and detail found in northern art. Combining the pragmatism of a very keen observer with the flattering results that attend the universalizing tendencies of geometric construction, he achieved portraits that looked modern to his contemporaries and that continue to exert a strong fascination and appeal.

How art in Tudor England would have developed had the Protestant Reformation not occurred cannot be known. What is known is that this religious movement had crucial consequences for artistic style and patronage in both Protestant and Catholic countries. Where the use of religious art was equated with idolatry, artists were forced to emigrate or find new forms of employment. Division between Catholic and Protestant lands also affected sources of artistic influence. From the time of the Reformation in England, Italian art—bent increasingly on proclaiming the doctrines of Catholicism—lost influence. Instead, England looked to the Lowlands for sources of artistic nourishment. Many artists on the Continent, losing their livelihood by reason of Reformed teaching on art, emigrated to England and hoped to secure royal patronage. None of these was of the rank of Holbein, and it would not be until the reign of Elizabeth that England produced native painters who even approached his skill.

Moreover, it was not until the reign of ELIZABETH that the arts played a major role, for neither EDWARD VI nor MARY patronized the arts. From the beginning of Henry's reign to the end of Elizabeth's, England experienced great religious upheaval and social change. These were reflected in the art of the period. In 1509 Henry had been a pious Catholic, and the church was a potent force in the political and cultural life of the nation. By the king's death in 1546, he had become the head not only of the state but of the church as well. Instead of journeying to shrines and praying at altars, the people turned to their Bibles and prayer books. Instead of statues of the Virgin and pictures of the saints, the nobility cultivated the portrait and the decorative arts. In general, Elizabethan art took a new role—that of celebrating the monarchy through symbolic and allegorical representations of the queen. The Renaissance fascination with personality and character was subsumed in glorifying the individual as servant of the state. The need to harmonize both interests was satisfied by the development of miniature painting—what the Elizabethans called the art of limning. The two major exponents of this genre were Nicholas Hillyard (1547-1619) and Isaac Oliver, a French emigre (1551 or 1556-1617). These miniatures, essentially works of art worn as personal adornment, were romantic, theatrical, melancholy, poetic, and heavily laden with allegorical symbolism. They were visual poetry. As such, they exemplified the central qualities of Elizabethan art. During the sixteenth century, religious themes lost their grip on English artistic imagination, as did the ideals that sustained Renaissance humanism. Instead, under the hands of native craftsmen and northern European religious exiles, England developed an art that, in reflecting religious ferment and the rise of the centralized state and absolute monarchy, was essentially decorative and theatrical without participating in torments and ecstasies of Mannerist art on the Continent.

Thus, the art of the Tudor period managed to reflect intellectual trends and social stresses without ever becoming a dominant factor in cultural expression. The Renaissance humanist style imported from Italy and southern Germany never fully took root, and the to-and-fro of religious controversy left little opportunity for art to play its traditional role as a vehicle for religious transcendence. Instead, by the end of Elizabeth's reign it had become a vehicle for proclaiming the authority of a monarch and her servants and of attesting to a new cultural vision.

Bibliography: Margaret Aston, *England's Iconoclasts*, 1988; Maria Dowling, *Humanism in the Reign of Henry VIII*, 1986; Eric Mercer, *English Art 1553-1625*, 1962; Graham Reynolds, *English Portrait Miniatures*, 1988; John Rowlands, *Holbein*, 1985.

Mary G. Winkler

Attainder, Act of. An act of attainder is a legislative action that imposes penalties upon a person for a crime, usually TREASON. In England such acts were passed as statutes by PARLIAMENT, acting as the highest and final court of the realm, and often affirmed previous convictions in lower courts and commonly imposed forfeiture on the person attainted.

Attainder had its origins in the early fourteenth century, became more punitive and useful to kings, and reached its greatest potency in the Tudor era. Initially attainder denoted the finding of guilt by final legal judgment, normally by a common law court; however, attainder might also denote guilt established by battle, outlawry, or ancient royal prerogative. By 1350 the word *attaint* denoted the legal consequences of conviction (particularly the extinction of civil rights) to the person found guilty and his property. Prior to 1458 there were several types of parliamentary attainder, but afterward one type evolved providing for the punishment of rebels. Acts of attainder were passed declaring peasants killed during the Peasant's Revolt of 1381 without due process of the law to be convicted felons. Acts of attainder were used by the Crown to confiscate the property of rebels and still withstand the challenges of the heirs that such confiscations were illegal. Kings used acts of attainder to secure final appellate affirmation of punishments and confiscations. Frequently, attainder was used in an in absentia proceeding against persons who had committed treason and could not be apprehended and tried in the common law courts.

Fifteenth-century attainder acts usually provided for forfeiture of the victim's property including lands held in fee simple and fee tail and lands in uses. Jack Cade's attainder in 1450 contained the novel provision that his heirs should be declared corrupt of blood and be denied the right to inherit. By 1450 attainder was used not only to affirm criminal convictions but also to supplement the common law process of outlawry.

During the Wars of the Roses, attainder was used not only against fugitives accused of treason but also against persons in custody. A further abuse of attainder occurred when Henry VIII used it as a way of condemning someone by legislative act and so avoiding a hearing under common law. Such acts were final and could not be appealed or questioned since parliamentary acts were final, being the acts of the highest court in England. The use of attainder continued into the seventeenth century, when it was last used in 1697 against Lord Edward Fitzgerald, and it was not formally abolished until 1870. Even then attainders could still be used in cases of outlawry until 1938.

Bibliography: J. R. Lander, "Attainder and Forfeiture, 1453-1509," *Historical Journal* 4 (1961): 120-51; S. E. Lehmberg, "Parliamentary Attainder in the Reign of Henry VIII," *Historical Journal* 18 (1975): 703-24.

J. V. Crangle

Augmentations, First and Second Courts of. The court of the Augmentations of the King's Revenues was established as a court of record by act of Parliament in 1536. It was given responsibility for the administration of the lands and property of the monasteries as they were dissolved (see DISSOLUTION OF THE MONASTERIES). It was accommodated on the site of the offices formerly belonging to the Auditors of Foreign Accounts, which stood between the EXCHEQUER and the inner gateway at Westminster. It had four principal officers, headed by a chancellor (Richard Rich, Edward North): with a treasurer (Thomas Pope, Edward North, John Williams); an attorney (John Onley, Robert Southwell, Walter Henley) and a solicitor (Robert Southwell, Walter Henley,

Nicholas Bacon). There were also in the first court ten auditors and seventeen ushers and messengers.

In the first court, the administrative structure in the counties made the general receivers, each with one or two counties in his care, responsible for receiving the revenues from the property of houses situated within their counties, regardless of where that property lay. Daily management of the property remained with local bailiffs or receivers and of the local courts with the stewards. The auditors had fixed circuits, usually of four to six counties, which they traveled once a year after Michaelmas to hear the accounts of bailiffs, receivers, and general receivers. The general receivers were required to send the revenues to Westminster twice a year but to keep on hand what might be required locally. In practice, the receivers in the more distant counties received particular or general warrants to pay money locally. The captain of Berwick on the borders with Scotland, for example, received regular payments in this way. The final audit took place in the central court after Easter before the principal officers, who allowed the receiver "supers" for money that had not been paid. These misunderstood arrears which comprised a variety of dues, some, in fact, not due the monarch at all, have given rise to the belief that the court was inefficient. While certain receivers became indebted, however, the revenues were generally collected and expended promptly and competently. Calling in the receivers to finalize their accounts in 1546 did not yield an enormous backlog of recoverable revenue.

The central court was responsible for renewing leases and appointments to all lesser local offices. It also pursued defaulters on payments of all sorts. It dealt with all the legal problems that arose and heard by English bill such things as cases around the issue of the leases, offices, and other concessions granted by the monasteries and the problems of levying the debts owed to the monasteries. Moveable monastic goods were variously dealt with. Ordinary household items were usually sold by commission by the local receiver and auditor; valuable books and plate-ware were sent to the monarch, and important resources such as lead were handled by the council. Whether continuing monastic pensions should be paid centrally or locally was a contentious matter that varied over time and place.

Land was sold by a commission established for the purpose from time to time and was not the responsibility of the court except insofar as its officers had to supply the commissioners with the necessary documentation involved in the certification required for the sales. Usually, however, the chancellor, at least, was on the commission, and the court was the repository responsible for custody of records accompanying the purchases and for insuring that installments were paid on time. Payments for the purchases often, but not invariably, came to the treasurer of augmentations, who also paid money as required by warrant from the monarch.

By 1546, so much land had been alienated that the necessity for not one but two courts responsible for royal estates was questionable. Moreover, the division of responsibility among all the courts was partly to blame for some of the more glaring errors in administrative practice. Amalgamation of the first Court of Augmentations with the Court of General Surveyors promised long-run economies, even if the pensions that had to be awarded to those compulsorily retired were initially costly.

The second court had additional central officers, including two general surveyors to handle the additional accounts now in its care. Additional local surveyors, making a third royal officer in the counties, were appointed to control false statements of values and costs. All property was grouped by county, regardless of the location of the original owner, and the auditors' circuits were reorganized and the internal rules were tightened up to eliminate identified loopholes. Despite these changes, the second court seems to have been slightly less efficient than the first. Two or three receivers were so heavily in debt by 1553 that their estates were eventually extended, and auditing the accounts of the last treasurer, Sir John Williams, was a complicated and protracted exercise. Part of the blame doubtless lay with the general financial crisis in the last years of EDWARD VI's reign.

After lengthy hesitations, therefore, the government decided in January 1554 to amalgamate the court with the Exchequer. The effect of this change on the local administration once the immediate period of confusion had passed was minimal; the records continued in the same form, and the roles of the officers were virtually identical.

Bibliography: W. C. Richardson, *History of the Court of Augmentations*, 1961; J. Youings, *The Dissolution of the Monasteries*, 1971.

Sybil Jack

Ayton, Treaty of (1497). This treaty ended the hostilities between JAMES IV and HENRY VII that resulted from the Scottish king's support of the pretender PERKIN WARBECK.

James IV had withdrawn his active support of Warbeck after the abortive invasion of England in 1496. But, in spite of peace feelers from Henry VII, serious negotiations did not begin until September 1497. At that point, however, results came quickly. A seven-year truce was concluded on 30 September, and later on 5 December the peace was extended to the lifetime of either monarch.

Initially the Treaty of Ayton appeared to be a simple truce that showed little potential for long-term success. Relations between England and Scotland remained tense. Both kings, in fact, genuinely desired better relations after more than a decade of hostility. In the case of James IV, this policy came to dominate in spite of opposition from his nobles. A further treaty in 1502 betrothed Henry VII's daughter Margaret to James IV, and they were married in 1503. This marriage alliance indicates the increasing acceptance of the fledgling Tudor dynasty by the other rulers of Europe. It also established the critical dynastic link between the Tudors and the Stuarts that ultimately brought JAMES VI and I to the throne of England upon the death of ELIZABETH and the failure of the Tudor line in 1603.

Bibliography: Agnes Conway, *Henry VII's Relations with Scotland and Ireland 1485-1498*, 1932, reprint 1972.

Ronald Fritze

Azores Expedition (1591). This project was initially planned by JOHN HAWKINS after FRANCIS DRAKE's unsuccessful PORTUGUESE EXPEDITION. In July 1589 he presented a plan for a continuous blockade of the Azores by two squadrons of six principal and six smaller ships in four-month rotations, a blockade that could profitably intercept Spanish treasure fleets from the Americas, prevent Philip II from rebuilding his navy, and pressure Spain to make peace. This project left half of the queen's navy to protect England.

Reluctantly the queen approved the project, and the first contingent was to set sail in February 1590. The detection of a Spanish fleet at Corunna delayed this departure and allowed the *Galeones*—the Peruvian treasure fleet—to reach Spain with five million ducats for Philip II's naval activities. While Hawkins went to Corunna in June, Sir Martin Frobisher took the first blockade convoy to station off the Azores, where he saw little activity.

Hawkins, supplied for six months, relieved Frobisher, but events off Brittany prompted an insecure queen to recall Hawkins's squadron in October. Fear of the Azores blockade forced Philip to suspend the *Flota*—the main Caribbean treasure fleet—and caused a slowing of Philip's rearmament program and an accumulation of trade and treasure in Spanish colonies. The queen, disappointed by the lack of profit, appointed new commanders. In mid-April 1591 the squadron, refitted for blockade duty under Lord Thomas Howard and Sir Richard Grenville, set sail. Howard's fleet included six ships of the line, three of which were *pinnaces*.

Because England's blockade was intermittent, many small convoys reached Spain and enabled Philip to gather a substantial fleet to protect the *Flota* during the most dangerous part of its voyage. In late August 1591 Admiral Alonso de Bazan arrived in the Azores with 55 ships, including 20 heavily armed *apostles*. Unaware of Bazan's armada, Howard anchored off Flores Island to resupply, to exchange ballast, and to treat sick sailors.

Bazan began the Battle of Flores by attacking the English from the east with his whole fleet. Howard boldly sailed toward them and escaped with most of his squadron before the wind died. Grenville in the *Revenge*, protecting the fleet's rear, chose to follow Howard rather than run. Becalmed, the *Revenge* was quickly grappled and surrounded. For nearly 15 hours, from the afternoon of 9 September until the following morning, Grenville's crew valiantly defended their ship, sank two Spanish vessels and inflicted serious damage on 15 others. His men ignored their mortally wounded captain's order to destroy the ship and surrenndered.

These brave seamen were immortalized in Raleigh's *True Defense* and by Tennyson's moving poem, "The Revenge."

Shortly after Grenville died on the Spanish flagship and Bazan had gathered most of the *Flota*, a cyclone hit the Azores, sinking the *Revenge*, and causing the destruction or capture of 70 of the 120 vessels in Bazan's flotilla.

Despite Grenville's heroics, the Queen was disturbed by the knowledge that the *Revenge* was the sole ship of her fleet ever to surrender, and the blockade was abandoned. While Grenville's bravery boosted British spirits, the Azores expedition had little effect on the war with Spain.

Bibliography: A. L. Rowse, *Sir Richard Grenville of the* Revenge, 1937.

Shelton Hanft

B

Babington Plot (1586). In 1586 came the last of a series of conspiracies to murder ELIZABETH and restore MARY, QUEEN OF SCOTS. A group of young men planned to murder Elizabeth as the inaugeration of the enterprise of England. The original conspirators were Thomas Morgan, Mary Stuart's agent in Paris, and a Jesuit priest named John Ballard. He recruited a young Catholic Derbyshire gentleman, Anthony Babington, who had been a page in the household of George Talbot, the earl of Shrewsbury, and thus had probably been acquainted with Mary and cherished a romantic devotion to her. In 1580 Babington had traveled to France for six months, where he had met a number of Catholic English exiles and also met Morgan. On his return he settled in London as a student at Lincoln's Inn and was one of a clandestine group protecting JESUIT MISSIONARIES in England. Thus he was a natural for any conspiracy centered around Mary Stuart. What the conspirators did not know was that, with the aid of the renegade Catholic spy Gilbert Gifford, in 1585 Sir FRANCIS WALSING-HAM had tapped into Mary Stuart's secret means of correspondence, so that all letters to and from Mary Stuart went through his hands.

After a great deal of initial planning, Babington wrote to Mary on 12 July 1586 and outlined plans in almost final form for the invasion of England, the murder of Elizabeth, the rescue of Mary, and Mary's assumption of power as queen of a restored Catholic nation. Babington assured Mary there were six noble gentlemen, all with positions around the court, who were ready to undertake the "tragical execution" of Elizabeth. Babington was so enthralled with the project and the immortality that would come to him as a result that he actually had his portrait painted with the six potential assassins. This was almost all that Walsingham needed, but he waited for a reply in Mary's own hand before he arrested the conspirators. On 17 July Mary responded, strongly encouraging Elizabeth's murder and her own rescue. Walsingham forged a postscript asking for the names of all those committed to the murder. He wanted irrefutable evidence to convict the assassins. Babington, however, delayed sending the names, and it was too dangerous to wait longer. Walsingham on 4 August began the roundup of those involved. Babington escaped but was captured 14 August and taken to the Tower. Soon after, Mary was invited to go out to hunt, and while she was away from Chartley, she was met by a guard and escorted to a neighboring house. Meanwhile her two secretaries were imprisoned and all her papers seized.

When the conspirators were apprehended, the citizens of London celebrated. Under interrogation Babington confessed every detail of the conspiracy, fully implicating Mary Stuart. At his trial on 13 and 14 September he tried to place all the blame on Ballard. Babington and his co-conspirators were quickly tried and condemned. On 20 September Babington and six of the principal conspirators were taken from Tower Hill to St. Giles's field and hung, drawn, and quartered. Though Elizabeth had wanted an example made of the traitors, she quickly sickened of the barbarity, and on the next day when seven more were executed, at the queen's command they were allowed to die before their bodies were mutilated.

Though called the Babington plot, the conspiracy did not originate with Anthony Babington. The plot is significant because it was Mary Stuart's approval of the plans—especially of Elizabeth's murder—that led to her trial and eventual execution. The Babington Conspiracy was the final conspiracy of Mary Stuart's life and directly caused her death on 8 February 1587.

Bibliography: A. G. Smith, *The Babington Plot*, 1936.

Carole Levin

Bail Act (1487). The Bail Act (3 Hen. VII, c. 4) was enacted by HENRY VII with the advice of the PARLIAMENT of 1487 and was explicitly designed to remedy abuses resulting from a previous act dating from 1483, the first year of the reign of Richard III, which included the release, on the taking of bail money, of murderers and felons against the due form of the law "to the great displeasure of the King and the annoyance of his people." As the 1483 act granted to every JUSTICE OF THE PEACE, acting alone, full and absolute discretion to incarcerate or free on bail prisoners and persons arrested for light suspicion of felony. This discretion was abused with the result that too many suspects who should have been denied bail because they constituted an intolerable threat to society were, in fact, freed on bail.

The Bail Act empowered justices of the peace in every shire, town, and city to release prisoners bailable by the law within their jurisdiction until the next meeting of the courts of general sessions of the peace or Gaol Delivery. However, the act required that a minimum of two justices approve each release on bail and that at least one such justice be of the Quorum. Furthermore, the act required that the justices of the peace, or one of them, certify bail to the next general sessions of the peace or general Gaol Delivery, on pain of forfeit to £10 for every default.

The Bail Act did not originate the practice of taking of bail and was applicable only to certain cases, but it furthered the evolution of the right to bail under English law.

J. V. Crangle

Barnes, Robert (1495-1540). Perhaps the most significant agent for the transmission of Martin Luther's influence to England, Barnes was born at Lynn in Norfolk, near Cambridge. He joined the Austin friars while still an adolescent and eventually became prior of the Augustinians at Cambridge. In 1517 he went to the University of Louvain during the time when Erasmus was there, and when Barnes returned to his friary in 1521, he introduced the academic methods of humanism to his brethren there. He was by then a doctor of divinity and a respected scholar and preacher. The martyrologist JOHN FOXE concluded that Prior Barnes "made a great part of the house learned (which before was drowned in barbarous rudeness)."

Soon after introducing the study of classical literature at his friary, Barnes began intense study of the New Testament, on the basis of which he became a critic of ecclesiastical abuses and corruptions. The influence of Thomas Bilney, another Cambridge scholar, seems to have led Barnes to adopt Protestant doctrinal views and to join a circle of reform-minded clerics who met clandestinely at the WHITE HORSE INN to study the Bible and Luther's writings smuggled from Germany. Barnes became the most prominent figure among these "Cambridge Germans."

Barnes became a biting critic of ecclesiastical wealth and clerical negligence, which he denounced in a tactless manner. At Christmas 1525 he preached at St. Edward's Church, Cambridge, and thereby incurred the charge of heresy for denying that Christians have a right to sue one another in civil court and for insulting remarks about Cardinal THOMAS WOLSEY, chancellor of England. Although Wolsey was generous toward his critic, church authorities ordered Barnes to recant or die as a heretic. He recanted in a public ceremony at Paul's Cross in London but still had to spent six months in Fleet Prison, after which he endured confinement at the Austin houses in London and Northampton.

While under house arrest Barnes used his considerable liberty to distribute the New Testament in the forbidden version of WILLIAM TYNDALE. This action brought the sentence of death by burning, but the accused escaped to Antwerp after a ruse that made it appear he had committed suicide. He soon went to Germany, where he became a close friend to Luther. At Wittenberg he became a learned Lutheran theologian. While there he began writing his *Vitae Romanorum Pontificum*, the first history of the papacy by a Protestant author, which he completed in 1535. As a reformer-in-exile Barnes tried to influence his homeland through his writings, especially his *Supplication unto King Henry the Eighth* (1530), by which he affirmed loyalty to his monarch HENRY VIII, while he assailed England's prelates as opponents of royal authority.

Barnes's *Supplication* impressed THOMAS CROMWELL, the king's chief minister, who obtained for its author a royal promise of safe-conduct to return to England in 1531. Although Henry made Barnes a royal chaplain, the king still suspected him of heresy, and Sir THOMAS MORE sought to destroy the Reformer. Barnes left for Germany, where he served Henry as occasional ambassador to the Lutheran princes during a period when his king negotiated half-heartedly for an alliance with the German Protestant states. Barnes represented Henry intermittently in this endeavor until his death in 1540.

While serving as a diplomat, Barnes contined to hope that Henry would embrace the Evangelical faith and lead England to adopt the Reformation. It became evident by about 1536, however, that the king's interest in Lutheran Germany was entirely political. Luther and Barnes lost hope for the conversion of the English monarch, although Barnes continued to seek an Anglo-German alliance.

Henry VIII used Barnes also in the effort to gain Lutheran support for his divorce from CATHERINE OF ARAGON. The Reformer failed in this undertaking, as in his attempt to secure an alliance with the German states, and by 1536, when he returned to England, Barnes was falling from the king's favor. Cromwell's efforts to obtain some financial reward for Barnes produced very little. Henry, nevertheless, regarded him as potentially useful, should he wish to make further overtures to the German princes. The Reformer, always loyal to his king, allowed Henry to use him without regard to reward.

While Barnes was on his final diplomatic mission for the king of England, Parliament passed the ACT OF SIX ARTICLES (1539), which reaffirmed the basic theology of medieval Catholicism as the doctrinal position of Henry's Church of England. This act made it impossible for Barnes to achieve an Anglo-German agreement.

Although the situation in England had become dangerous for Protestants, Barnes went home in August 1539. By that time Cromwell was in disfavor, and his attempts to aid Barnes only increased the peril to both of them. Rather than seek obscurity, Barnes boldly preached Lutheran doctrines that caused conflict with Bishop STEPHEN GARDINER, a former friend and protector, who then accused the Reformer of heresy. When Gardiner denounced justification by faith alone, Barnes defended Luther's teaching vigorously. Henry demanded that Barnes recant and apologize for attacking Gardiner. The recantation was actually an evasion that insulted Gardiner further and led to a sentence of death. A bill of attainder condemned Barnes to die in flames on 30 July 1540. He expired in the company of two other Protestants. Before he died, Barnes affirmed allegiance to the Apostles' Creed and expressed full confidence in the merits of Christ's sacrifice to save him. He reiterated his loyalty to Henry VIII, although by his refusal to recant, he denied that the king was lord of his conscience.

Bibliography: James E. McGoldrick, *Luther's English Connection*, 1979; Neelak S. Tjernagel, *Lutheran Martyr*, 1982.

James Edward McGoldrick

Bastard Feudalism. The term *bastard feudalism* describes a system of affinities among noblemen and their retainers that developed in the later Middle Ages and persisted throughout the Tudor period. Titled noblemen—and sometimes lesser gentry—kept bands of followers sworn to loyalty and frequently armed, gave them livery or badges to wear as signs of their allegiance, rewarded their service with land, money, or office, and maintained them in legal proceedings, sometimes through embracery, that is, illicit interference with the judicial system. Noble retinues were not quite private armies, for they were seldom kept in arms in large numbers for very long. Also a nobleman typically had three kinds of retainers—household servants, men bound in his service by indenture, and those recruited for emergencies, and it was only the latter whose primary purpose was always military. However, in that capacity noble retinues were both valued and feared by the Crown, which never in the fifteenth and sixteenth centuries sought to abolish but only to control them. Prior to the existence of standing armies these bands were essential to the monarch during both foreign wars and internal rebellions, yet when sufficiently large they could make overmighty subjects of their masters and seriously threaten law and order within the realm.

In the late medieval period the Crown made several attempts to restrict noble retinues and prevent their unlawful or disorderly behavior. A statute of 1390 prohibited retaining by anyone other than a nobleman, and Edward IV's act of 1468 was intended to limit retainers to menial servants, officers, and men learned in the law; however, neither attempt was entirely successful. When HENRY VII came to the throne at the end of the Wars of the Roses, he sought to eliminate hostile peers through acts of attainder, while insuring the loyalty of the remaining nobility through an unprecedentedly extensive (and unpopular) use of bonds and recognizances. Also in 1504 Parliament passed the act *De Retentionibus Illicitis*, the last and best-known statute of liveries, which outlawed retaining without a royal license. This lapsed at Henry VII's death, however, and HENRY VIII and his children operated on the basis of the 1468 act and used royal PROCLAMATIONS to remind their subjects of the law but issued large numbers of licenses to keep retainers.

It is an irony of the Tudor age that noble retinues were both a threat to good order and necessary to preserve it. Henry VII had to entrust considerable responsibility for keeping the peace to the Howards, who had opposed him at BOSWORTH, though this paid off in his reign and later for Henry VIII during the PILGRIMAGE OF GRACE, MARY at the time of WYATT'S REBELLION, and ELIZABETH throughout her reign. The nobility and the greater gentry were routinely placed on commissions of the peace, of oyer and terminer, for musters and array and other local government bodies. Fortunately for the Crown, most lacked the provincial, landed power base that would have enabled them to offer the sort of opposition faced by monarchs on the Continent. Still Cardinal THOMAS WOLSEY, during his ascendency, found it necessary to proceed against a number of magnates in STAR CHAMBER for illegal maintenance, embracery, and retaining, and it was, in part, allegations of the latter that led to BUCKINGHAM's downfall in 1521. THOMAS CROMWELL, also reluctant to depend upon the loyalty of the nobility, attempted to turn over their function to special councils in the north and in the Marches of Wales in the 1530s. Elizabeth faced serious opposition from noble retinues during the NORTHERN REBEL-LION of 1569 and as late as 1600 from the ESSEX REBELLION.

At the beginning of the Tudor era the Crown had to rely, aside from occasional use of mercenaries, on two sources for its ARMY: private retinues of the nobility and the local militia raised by commissions of muster or array. Although various reforms were made throughout the period, the armed retinues arising out of Bastard Feudalism remained an integral part of the Crown's military forces and essential to effective local government.

Bibliography: G. R. Elton, ed., *The Tudor Constitution*, 1982; J. R. Lander, *Crown and Nobility, 1450-1509*, 1976; Penry Williams, *The Tudor Regime*, 1979.

William B. Robison

Benefit of Clergy, Act Concerning (1512). Promulgated in response to excessive abuse of clerical privilege, this statute (4 Hen. VIII, c. 2) denied immunity from civil penalty to those members of the clergy below the rank of priest, deacon, or sub-deacon who were found guilty of murder in a civil court.

Long overburdened by the "legitimate" financial demands of the church, English laymen in the early years of the sixteenth century were outraged at the number of crimes committed by the clergy, who invariably pleaded immunity to escape civil penalties for their actions. Clerical penalties were notoriously lax, and large numbers of criminals, in their quest to elude secular punishment, seized upon the privilege.

Passed with the proviso that it be subject to renewal by the next Parliament, the act was debated by the PARLIAMENT of 1515 in light of the case of RICHARD HUNNE, whose supporters alleged that he had been killed in the bishop of London's prison in December 1514 by his clerical jailers. Parliament divided on the issue of laymen's exercising authority over the clergy. This inherent challenge to royal authority led HENRY VIII to call a conference at Blackfriars to debate the implications of clerical privilege. Rejecting a plea to adjourn the matter to Rome, Henry expounded his belief that questions on clerical and temporal authority were to be referred to the Crown alone. The king dissolved Parliament, effectively killing the renewal of the act.

Bibliography: A. F. Pollard, *Wolsey*, 1929, reprint, 1978.

J. V. Crangle

Berwick, Articles of (1560). The newly crowned ELIZABETH I was a most insecure sovereign, beset by a variety of foreign threats. Nowhere were the dangers more present than along the northern border with Scotland where the long-standing French involvement was underscored by MARY, QUEEN OF SCOTS also becoming the queen of France in 1559. It was also rumored that the 3,000 French troops in Scotland supporting Mary's regent were to be joined by more troops in late 1559 or early 1560 to suppress the brewing Protestant revolt.

Elizabeth decided to intervene before French influence became too great and directly threatened England. Her admiral William Winter, instructed to act without implicating his sovereign, successfully turned back the majority of the French reinforcements that sailed into the Firth of Forth area during December 1559. Next the queen dispatched Thomas Howard, 4th duke of Norfolk, to Scotland in January 1560 to aid the Lords of the Congregation, the Protestant faction opposed to the French-dominated regency. After arriving at Berwick, Norfolk reached an agreement with the Lords of the Congregation on 27 February 1560 known as the Articles (or treaty) of Berwick.

The articles bound the rebellious Scottish lords and the English to each other both offensively and defensively. Elizabeth became the implicit protector of Scottish civil and religious liberties by agreeing to send an army to their aid. The Scottish lords, in turn, promised to send troops to England in the event of a French invasion. While the agreement left Mary Stuart's royal prerogatives intact, it clearly asserted the English perception of Scotland as a vassal state. In particular the English voiced their opposition to any union of the Scottish and French Crowns. An English army of 6,500 men marched into Scotland on 28 March and besieged the French at Leith. This action began a struggle that ended successfully for Elizabeth with the TREATY OF EDINBURGH in that same year.

Bibliography: J. B. Black, *The Reign of Elizabeth, 1558-1603*, 2nd ed., 1959; Conyers Read, *Mr. Secretary Cecil and Queen Elizabeth*, 1955.

Gary Bell

Berwick, Treaty of (1586). The Treaty of Berwick of 1586, the second of that name from the Elizabethan period, is one of the most important treaties signed by England's last Tudor. It not only secured the realm's so-called postern gate, Scotland, but also laid the foundation for the Stuart sucession and the eventual union of the two kingdoms.

The formal treaty was signed at Berwick on 5 July 1586. It pledged England to a formal alliance, providing for armed assistance by each if the other was invaded by a third force. It also guaranteed that neither country would enter into a treaty with a foreign power prejudicial to the other. Finally, it undertook to bind the two monarchs to maintain the religion professed currently in their respective realms. This agreement also implicitly recognized JAMES VI's right of succession to the English throne since an explicit recognition by ELIZABETH I was out of the question. The English had already begun providing James VI with a subsidy in May 1586 that allowed him to increase his independence from his refractory nobles.

The French had tried to sabotage the negotiations but failed to outmaneuver the skillful English diplomats. Orchestrated by Sir FRANCIS WALSINGHAM in London, the treaty was a masterstroke for the English. It bore immediate fruit when the English and the Scots began to cooperate in pacification of their border in an attempt to settle the centuries-old tension found along their common frontier.

The treaty did run into some serious obstacles. James VI was aggrieved by the niggardliness of his pension and fumed that he had signed too quickly. The most serious challenge came a little later in February 1587 with the execution of MARY, QUEEN OF SCOTS by the English. His dignity stung, James VI came under enormous pressure to respond militarily to that act and to contravene the treaty. But as James put it to ROBERT DUDLEY, earl of Leicester, "how fond and inconstant I were, if I should prefer my mother to my title." His mother's troubles were less important than the prize of England. An argument can even be made that the Treaty of Berwick signed Mary's death warrant. By assuring the Scottish king's dependence on the English, it freed them to remove the constant threat that Mary had posed to the English royal succession since 1568. Similarly the fear of foreign, more specifically French, intervention through Scotland was rendered even less likely than had been the case with the TREATY OF BLOIS in 1572. The Treaty of Berwick strengthened England's position in European international relations and also served as the first substantial step toward the uniting of the English and Scottish Crowns.

Bibliography: Susan Doran, *England and Europe 1485-1603*, 1986; Wallace T. MacCaffrey, *Queen Elizabeth and the Making of Policy, 1572-1588*, 1981.

                                                                                    Gary Bell

Bible, English. The rise of English as a respectable vernacular in the late Middle Ages combined with the appearance of PRINTING, the revived linguistic studies of HUMANISM in the fifteenth century, and the onset of the Reformation to produce conditions favorable to the appearance of an English Bible. WILLIAM TYNDALE became the first Englishman to translate the Bible using the revived studies of Greek and Hebrew. Initially, in 1523 he tried to interest the humanist bishop Cuthbert Tunstall in sponsoring a translation. When his proposal was rejected, a merchant of London named Humphrey Monmouth became his patron instead. Travelling to Germany in 1524, Tyndale tried to publish a New Testament at Cologne but was driven off by hostile ecclesiastical authorities. He moved to Worms, where in 1525 he managed to bring out 6,000 copies of a quarto New Testament. By April 1526, it was selling in England, where it immediately superseded the hand-copied Bibles of the LOLLARDS. Tyndale's New Testament generated so much demand that it was reprinted in 1526, 1530, and 1534. George Joye brought out his own revision and correction of Tyndale's translation in August 1534, which competed with the publication of the new, corrected edition of Tyndale's New Testament, which was published in November 1534 and again in 1535 in a further corrected edition.

Tyndale did not live to translate the entire Bible. On 17 January 1530, he brought out a translation of the Pentateuch. During the next year he published Jonah, and in 1534 he produced a revision of Genesis. He also translated Joshua-II Chronicles, which did not appear in print while he was alive. Meanwhile, his sometime associate and sometime competitor George Joye also translated a substantial portion of the Old Testament.

Scholarship on the biblical languages was in a formative stage in Tyndale's day. Still, he managed to use the scholarly tools that were available to the best advantage, although he made some mistakes with the Hebrew. Stylistically, Tyndale used everyday colloquial English, presented in a happy voice and organized as a dramatic narrative. Latinisms were avoided. To aid his style, he liked to vary his choice of words so that the same Hebrew and Greek words were given several different English equivalents.

Needless to say, clerical and secular authorities in England did not like Tyndale's translating enterprise. His word usage implicitly supported the cause of the Reformers, for example, the use of congregation in place of church. His prefaces were explicit in their promotion of Lutheran doctrines. Even when these were left out, however, the existence of an English Bible invited the literate laity to read, to study, and ultimately to form their own religious opinions. Therefore Bishop Tunstall prohibited the Worms New Testament in 1526 while HENRY VIII banned it in 1530.

Miles Coverdale, another former associate of Tyndale's, first managed to publish a complete English translation of the Bible. He included the Apocrypha in his translation, although he began the practice of setting it off from the rest of the Old Testament. Not possessing a knowledge of the biblical languages, Coverdale was forced to use the best available Latin and German translations along with Tyndale's translation. Beginning his work of translation in 1534, he soon published it on 4 October 1535. The first Coverdale translation was Protestant in its language and so not authorized, although Queen ANNE BOLEYN showed a strong interest in it. When it was reprinted in folio and quarto editions in 1537, however, it claimed to have royal license. Other reprints appeared in 1550 and 1551.

Meanwhile the advance of Protestantism through the upper reaches of English society and government softened official opposition to English translations of the Bible. At the urging of Archbishop THOMAS CRANMER, the CONVO-CATION of Canterbury in December 1534 petitioned Henry VIII for an English Bible. Cranmer started a project to have the bishops revise Tyndale's New Testament, but it failed. Anne Boleyn and Cranmer both encouraged Henry VIII to have an English Bible placed in every church. Apparently he adopted their suggestion since that requirement appears in THOMAS CROMWELL's unissued injunctions of 1536.

In 1537, the Mathew Bible appeared in folio. Although it was claimed that a "Thomas Mathew" produced it, that was merely a pseudonym for John Rogers, another friend of Tyndale's. It was not a new translation. Instead, it was a combination of earlier translations. The New Testament, the Pentateuch, and Joshua-II Chronicles were from Tyndale while the rest of the Old Testament was Coverdale's, with some revision and a new translation by Rogers. Furthermore, it included some 2,000 notes derived from humanist and Protestant writers.

The Royal Injunctions issued on 5 September 1538 commanded the parishioners of every church to pay half the cost of purchasing the largest available English Bible. There were two English Bibles available to satisfy the order. One was the definitely Protestant and more scholarly Mathew Bible, and the other was Coverdale's less scholarly edition of 1537, which claimed to be officially licensed. Since neither Bible was particularly satisfactory to many people, it was decided to publish an acceptable official revision of the Bible.

Thomas Cromwell began the planning of the Great Bible with the approval of Cranmer. Coverdale was made editor, and the work was to be printed in Paris. During June, August, and December 1538, Cromwell received advance sheets from the new edition. Just as the project neared completion, the inquisitor-general of France swooped down and seized everything. English diplomatic pressure caused King Francis I to obtain the release of all of the materials except the printed sheets. After this delay, work on the project recommenced in London, and the Great Bible went on sale in November 1539. This new edition was largely based on the more scholarly Mathew Bible. It eliminated the Protestant prologues and marginal notes but retained Tyndale's Protestant word usage. Supported by episcopal and royal injunctions, the Great Bible was in considerable demand. Further revisions were made, and a second edition was published in April 1540 with a preface by Cranmer. It managed to survive the Conservative resurgence that followed Cromwell's fall, and the order authorizing its placement in churches was renewed in 1541. Soon after a conservative effort to produce a Catholic translation foundered on the unacceptability of the overly Latinate version proposed by Bishop STEPHEN GARDINER and on institutional inertia. The Act for the Preservation of True Religion in 1543 (34 and 35 Hen. VIII, c. 1) did forbid unlicensed people from the lower ranks to read any Bible at all. Under EDWARD VI, however, the order for churches to purchase the Great Bible was renewed while in MARY I's reign there was no official banning of English Bibles, although many were burnt through private initiative.

The reign of Mary I (1553-1558) stimulated a new chapter in the history of the English Bible through the appearance of the Geneva Bible. The MARIAN EXILES at Geneva produced their own translation of the Bible for use in missionary work. In 1557, William Whittingham translated the New Testament and Psalms and used Tyndale's translation as his guide. He was joined in this enterprise by Anthony Gilby and Thomas Sampson, and in 1560 they brought out a complete Bible based on the best available sources and scholarship. It was definitely intended to be a Bible for the people. The text was supplemented by helpful and scholarly headnotes, marginal notes, and alternative translations that were strongly CALVINISTIC. Furthermore, the Geneva Bible was printed in the more readable Roman type rather than Black Letter and was produced in the cheaper and handier quarto size. For ease of reference, it was the first English Bible to divide chapters into verses. As a result of these many congenial features, the Geneva Bible quickly became the household Bible of England. There were ultimately 140 editions printed as it immediately superseded the Great Bible, staved off its first competition from the Bishops' Bible, and remained popular into the 1640s in spite of the appearance of the Authorized Version in 1611.

The radicalism of the Geneva Bible did not endear it to the Church of England's leadership, which organized the production of the Bishops' Bible as an acceptable alternative. In 1561, Archbishop MATTHEW PARKER proposed the revision of the Great Bible. The work was divided up among various bishops and scholars (all of whom ultimately became bishops) and began in 1566 under Parker's supervision. Using the Great Bible as their starting place, the translators were instructed to revise only those sections that distorted the meaning of the original languages. They finished their work quickly, and it was published in 1568. Oddly enough, the Bishops' Bible never became the official translation of the Church of England, nor did it ever become popular with the English people. It did, however, provide the official basis for the work on the famous Authorized Version.

Faced by the challenge of the numerous Protestant versions of the Bible, Elizabethan Catholics responded by preparing and publishing their own version at Rheims College. Gregory Martin began translating the Vulgate in 1578 and worked at the rate of two chapters a day. Eventually the Rheims New Testament appeared in a quarto edition in 1582. Martin's translation employed many Latinisms, which later had much influence on the Authorized Version. Its notes took a very combative stance toward Protestant doctrine. As a result, the Rheims New Testament attracted the ire of Protestant controversialists. Because of Martin's death in 1584, succeeding English Catholic exiles were unable to finish the translation of the Old Testament until 1610, when it was published at Douai. This translation came too late to have any influence on the form of the imminent Authorized Version (sometimes known as the King James Version) of 1611, the most famous of English Bibles.

Bibliography: F. F. Bruce, *History of the Bible in English: From the Earliest Versions*, 1978; Gerald Hammond, *The Making of the English Bible*, 1983.

Ronald Fritze

Bible, Welsh. Various narrative sections of the Bible were translated from Latin into Welsh during the Middle Ages. In addition, there are stories of a Welsh Pentateuch and a Welsh translation of WILLIAM TYNDALE's New Testament circulating in the early sixteenth century. A complete and undisputed translation of the Bible into Welsh did not occur, however, until ELIZABETH I's reign in 1588. William Salesbury, a Protestant and the most learned Welshman of the Tudor era, laid the foundation for a translation by publishing the first English-Welsh dictionary in 1547. His translation of the liturgical Gospels and Epistles from the Vulgate into Welsh soon followed in 1551. Later, in 1563, at the instigation of Richard Davies, a Welsh Marian exile and the bishop of St. David's, Parliament passed a law (5 Eliz. I, c. 28) ordering the Welsh bishops to secure a translation of the Bible and the BOOK OF COMMON PRAYER into Welsh by 1566. Davies received little assistance from the other bishops, although he and Salesbury began a fruitful collaboration. Their Welsh translations of the New Testament and the Book of Common Prayer appeared in 1567. Salesbury did most of the work of translation along with providing marginal notes and introductory materials based on the Geneva Bible. Davies translated only I Timothy, Hebrews, I and II Peter, and James while Thomas Huet, the Protestant precentor of St. David's Cathedral, was brought in to translate Revelation. The translation was based on the best available Greek texts, although Salesbury's renderings of Welsh were considered by many to be somewhat idiosyncratic.

When the partnership of Davies and Salesbury dissolved in 1576 over the etymology of a single Welsh word, the work of completing the translation of the Bible into Welsh was taken up by William Morgan. He began by translating the Pentateuch, and when his activities were brought to the attention of Archbishop JOHN WHITGIFT, he found a ready patron. As a result, Whitgift placed Morgan in charge of a project to produce a completely new Welsh translation of the Bible, along with the Apocrypha, which included a revision of the Salesbury-Davies New Testament. Beginning in 1578, Morgan and his assistants completed their work in late 1587. The new Welsh Bible became available from the printer in 1588 shortly after the defeat of the Spanish Armada. Its first printing consisted of 1,000 bulky, folio volumes selling for what Morgan considered was the exorbitant price of £2. This translation was based on the best available Hebrew and Greek texts and was judged as excellent by contemporaries. The daunting task of Protestantizing Wales was greatly aided by its appearance. Furthermore, posterity has credited Morgan's Bible with the salvation of Welsh as a living language.

Bibliography: S. L. Greenslade, ed., *The West from the Reformation to the Present Day* Vol. 3: *The Cambridge History of the Bible*, 1963.

Ronald Fritze

"Bill and Book" (1584-1587). PURITANS dissatisfied with the polity of the Church of England as well as purportedly unscriptural and "popish" elements in the BOOK OF COMMON PRAYER made bold attempts in the Parliaments of 1584-1585 and 1586-1587 to introduce Genevan-inspired reforms. Apparently at the behest of PRESBYTERIAN ministers, a London physician and member of the House of Commons, Dr. Peter Turner, submitted a bill early in the 1584 session that proposed to place the government of the state church in the hands of ministers and elders meeting at the congregational and shire levels. According to this system the clergy of each county would have complete authority to deal with ecclesiastical matters and power to eject ungodly or heretical ministers. Turner's bill also proposed to replace the Book of Common Prayer with the Form of Prayers and Administration of the Sacraments, the liturgy formerly used by JOHN KNOX's congregation of MARIAN EXILES at Geneva. The bill's authors wanted even family prayers to conform to the confession of faith embodied in the Form of Prayers. Following the lead of Sir CHRISTOPHER HATTON, the House, most of whose puritan members were chary of the clerical-oriented Presbyterian polity, refused to consider the bill.

Undaunted by their failure and fortified by surveys of the clergy in London and eleven shires underscoring the need for reform, the Presbyterians renewed their efforts in the ensuing Parliament. Presented to the Commons by Anthony Cope, member for Banbury, Oxfordshire, the new bill was more revolutionary than its predecessor in calling for the abolition of all existing laws and customs pertaining to the liturgy and polity of the Church of England. These would be replaced with a revised edition of the Genevan liturgy, the Form of Common Prayers, printed by the Dutchman Richard Schilders, which increased the role of the ministers in ecclesiastical polity. Unlike 1584, when Turner lacked overt support among his fellow members, Cope had the backing of Presbyterian allies, including Job Throckmorton, who later wrote the anonymous MARPRELATE TRACTS. Queen ELIZABETH, who had previously ordered the Commons not to involve itself in religious issues, prevented the House from having the Form of Common Prayers read by ordering the speaker to submit both the bill and the book to her. An irritated Peter Wentworth, member for Northampton, thereupon made an impassioned statement on behalf of freedom of speech in Parliament. For their efforts, Cope, Wentworth, and three colleagues were imprisoned in the Tower of London. Not until 4 March, nearly a week after Cope's speech of 27 February, did most members of the House discover the full import of the bill from government spokesmen, who underscored the ramifications of repealing all extant religious legislation. The "bill and book" episode exacerbated divisions within the state church, as reflected especially in CONVOCATION's denunciation of the Presbyterian effort for its "absurd" divinity, in the polemic of Richard Bancroft against the puritans, and in the vitriolic attack on bishops in the Marprelate tracts.

Bibliography: P. Collinson, *The Elizabethan Puritan Movement*, 1967; J. E. Neale, *Elizabeth I and Her Parliaments, 1584-1601*, 1957.

Richard L. Greaves

Bishops' Book (1537). The TEN ARTICLES of July 1536 which were intended "to stablyshe Christen quietnes and unitie amonge us," failed to achieve their purpose. Their ambiguity, especially on the Sacraments, was unsatisfactory to many, and so a new formulary, the *Institution of a Christian Man*, usually known as the *Bishops' Book*, was completed in July 1537. The *Bishops' Book* was drawn up by a large assembly of bishops and divines who were convoked by the king "to compile certain rudiments of Christianity and a Catechism." Probably before the assembly began to meet in February 1537 a debate took place among the bishops in Parliament on the subject of the four Sacraments that had been omitted from consideration in the Ten Articles. Statements on these Sacraments were drawn up, probably before the assembly met, and the original plan may have been to reissue the Ten Articles including these statements. However, since a different type of formulary including material of a catechistical nature was needed, the assembly, under the presidency of THOMAS CROMWELL as vicegerent, drew up a considerably more detailed statement of faith.

Agreement on all major points was reached by the beginning of May 1537, and two months were spent completing the final draft of the book, which was finished by the middle of July. On 24 July Edward Foxe, who played the leading role in compiling the book, wrote Cromwell to inquire if the book was to go out in the king's name or that of the bishops. However, despite repeated requests for HENRY VIII to correct the work, the king did not read it before publication, and it was eventually printed with a preface asking the king to grant his approval and stating that without it the bishops acknowledged that they had no right either to assemble or to publish anything that resulted from their assembly. Attached to the preface was the king's reply that he had merely "taken as it were a taste" of the book since he had not had sufficient time to give it a thorough reading. As a result the book was published without royal approval. When, at the end of the year, months after it was published, Henry read the book, he found much that he did not like, and he sent a series of some 250 proposed alterations to Archbishop THOMAS CRANMER in January 1538. Cranmer responded with a frank and sometimes sharp criticism of Henry's revisions. Along with comments on many minor matters such as Henry's bad grammar, Cranmer was especially critical of Henry's tendency to dilute any statement tending toward Lutheran doctrine of justification by faith alone. As a result the king never accepted the *Bishops' Book*. It was eventually revised by a committee, which presented the more conservative and anti-Lutheran statement of faith known as the *KING'S BOOK* to CONVOCA-TION in 1543.

Since the *Bishops' Book* was the product of an assembly representing a variety of different views, it is not surprising that it was a compromise document. The book incorporated much that was in Ten Articles and sometimes used the exact wording, but it was considerably longer. It also included much that was ignored in the Ten Articles. It was organized in the catechistical form, providing a detailed exposition of the Creed, the Sacraments, the Ten Commandments, the Lord's Prayer, and the *Ave Maria*. Although portions of the book reflected the influence of Luther, it was a somewhat more conservative document than the Ten Articles in that all seven medieval Sacraments were accepted and defined.

The book began with an exposition of the Apostle's Creed in which the statement on the church set forth the English doctrine of a universal church made up of free and equal national churches in which no one church "is head or sovereign over the other." It specifically rejected the authority and superiority of the Roman church over any of the national churches and stated that the unity of the Catholic church was not destroyed by differences in "outward rites, ceremonies, traditions and ordinances." Although all seven medieval Sacraments were included in the section on Sacraments, a distinction was made between the three chief Sacraments (Baptism, the Eucharist, and Penance) and the lesser four since, according to the book, only the first three conveyed grace for the forgiveness of sins and were necessary for salvation. The description of the three chief Sacraments was taken from the Ten Articles. The exposition of the Commandments and the Lord's Prayer reflected the influence of *Marshall's Primer*, published 1533/34 which contained a good deal of Lutheran material. Consequently, part of Luther's exposition of the Commandments was included in the book. The *Bishops' Book* concluded with somewhat ambiguous articles on "Purgatory" and "Justification" taken from the Ten Articles.

Bibliography: E. G. Rupp, *Studies in the Making of the English Protestant Tradition*, 1947; J. J. Scarisbrick, *Henry VIII*, 1968; text is included in C. Lloyd, ed., *Formularies of Faith Set Forth by Authority During the Reign of Henry VIII*, 1825.

Rudolph Heinze

Black Rubric. A footnote printed in black and inserted in the second BOOK OF COMMON PRAYER (1552). It was added at the last moment before distribution to correct the notion that the practice of kneeling at communion might involve veneration of the elements.

The Prayer Book revisions carried out during the latter half of EDWARD VI's reign and finally approved for publication failed to satisfy fully the radical Protestant faction then gaining currency in governmental circles. John Hooper, bishop of Gloucester, has been portrayed as the leader of this group, though in the end the continuing fulminations of JOHN KNOX, one of Edward's royal chaplains, appears to have had the deepest impact in swaying the PRIVY COUNCIL's mind about the need to alter the book on the very eve of its scheduled diffusion.

The practice of kneeling at communion during the reception of the host was one that the more aggressive among the anti-Romanist party in England wished to see abolished or drastically modified so as to avoid the popular connotation of adoration. Knox had evidently already begun to substitute sitting for the practice of kneeling in his own services in the north. When invited to preach in London in connection with his royal obligations, he held forth against kneeling in such a manner that considerable alarm was generated within the council circle.

Accordingly, the printer was ordered to place a hold on the supply until some problems could be rectified, while THOMAS CRANMER, archbishop of Canterbury, was given what was obviously for him the distasteful task of taking a second look at the matter. Undoubtedly tiring of pressures for further changes, Cranmer defended the book as it then stood. He expressed opposition on procedural grounds, knowing that Parliament would not be consulted in this instance due to time constraints. Knox continued his spirited attack and achieved at least partial success, so that on 27 October 1552, the council instructed the lord chancellor to see to the inclusion of the explanation that had by now been endorsed by the king. Cranmer was thus overruled, although the order to insert the footnote appears to have been carried out rather haphazardly—once again owing to the advanced stage of the proceedings. Cranmer's opposition can best be seen in terms of his desire for outer concord and not so much on personal or theological grounds, since he was acutely aware of the proceedings of the Council of Trent where the traditional veneration of the host was being upheld. He even expressed the need to guard against the practice in a letter to John Calvin dated a mere three weeks before the ACT OF UNIFORMITY was approved. For his part, Knox instructed the members of his parish community to observe the stipulation on kneeling in the interest of concord, though he seems to have continued to hold that the subject of kneeling was not an indifferent matter.

The black rubric was dropped in the 1559 Elizabethan Prayer Book, though its essence was likely transmitted by sympathetic clergy for years following. The so-called ornaments rubric was added at that time, however, together with an alteration in the words of administration associated with the communion service. Both changes appear to have been made according to the personal desires of the queen and her circle.

The new rubric ordered that church ornaments and priestly garb should conform to the standards current in the second year of Edward's reign. Though intended to clarify a controversial issue and establish an acceptable mean, the rather obscure historical reference to Edward's second year generated turmoil for centuries and was interpreted by some as a reference to the first Prayer Book and by others as a throwback to the traditions in use prior to the establishment of the Reformation. Much of the confusion stemmed from the fact that the first Prayer

Book, though passed in 1549, was not to be used officially until the third year of Edward's reign. Difficulty in interpretation was also introduced later on by the Advertisements of 1566 and their intended relationship to the Elizabethan ACT OF UNIFORMITY. What is clear, however, is that ornaments fell into the category of things indifferent to ELIZABETH and her circle, though they were useful if controlled by the Crown and not the ecclesiastical hierarchy. In seeking to understand the official attitude on the subject, one must also remember that Elizabeth's own chapel employed both candles and the crucifix. As if to make the situation bearable for the hard-line Protestant faction, however, the standards prescribed do not seem to have been strictly enjoined, though the bishops accepted the wearing of the cope during communion and the surplice at other times. The rubric underwent modification in 1662.

Bibliography: Norman L. Jones, *Faith by Statute: Parliament and the Settlement of Religion 1559*, 1982; Francis Proctor, *A New History of the Book of Common Prayer: With a Rationale of Its Offices*, revised by W. H. Frere, 1958; Paul Rust, *The First of the Puritans and the Book of Common Prayer*, 1949.

Andrew Penny

Blois, Treaty of (1572). One of the most famous Elizabethan treaties, this agreement created a defensive alliance between England and France and set the stage for the Anglo-Scottish TREATY OF BERWICK in 1586.

Sir Thomas Smith and Sir FRANCIS WALSINGHAM negotiated the agreement, which was signed on 19 April 1572. It was ratified in a magnificent and costly ceremony during May that served to indicate the importance that both France and England attached to improving their foreign relations. Relations between England and France had been strained during the early 1560s as a result of France's capture of CALAIS in 1558. War had broken out between the two nations in Scotland in 1560 and in France during 1562-1564 while a general distrust dominated the times of peace. Sir Thomas Smith's mission to France during 1567 made it clear that the loss of Calais was permanent in spite of promises made by France in the treaties of Cateau-Cambresis and TROYES. Meanwhile the growing power of Habsburg Spain was forcing England and France to drop their hostilities and unite against the common danger. England also had its own special problems with Spain because of religious antagonisms, English incursions into the Spanish monopoly in the New World, and Spain's involvement in the RIDOLFI PLOT against Queen ELIZABETH.

The Treaty of Blois was no diplomatic revolution, but it did accomplish what five years earlier would have been considered impossible—it formed a defensive alliance between France and England. Each side pledged 6,000 soldiers and eight ships to the other in case of invasion. This understanding even promised mutual aid if either party was attacked for religious reasons, something that Catholic France had no particular reason to expect but that was a real fear for Elizabeth due to her recent excommunication by the papal bull REGNANS IN EXCELSIS of 1570. Charles IX of France declined to include such inflammatory stipulations in the formal treaty, although he expressed the same sentiments clearly in a private letter of understanding that preceded the signing. Finally, the French promised a staple port for the marketing of English cloth, whose trade had been badly disrupted by the closure of the Low Countries to English merchants.

Blois was a modest treaty, easily abrogated, but it did bring England some measurable benefits. England could now temper its wariness of France. Indeed, there followed a period of Anglo-French accord that even saw highly publicized, if insincere, attempts to marry, at various times, the Virgin Queen Elizabeth to either of the younger brothers of Charles IX. The rapprochement with France also provided a useful counterbalance to the growing threat that Spain posed. Finally, the treaty was another element in the continuing attempt to neutralize the northern frontier, where the traditional French client state of Scotland was slowly being subjected to English supervision. The French abandonment of the cause of MARY, QUEEN OF SCOTS and of intervention in Scotland were just two implicit aspects of the Treaty of Blois. It set in motion the events that gave England first ascendency over, and then integration with, Scotland.

Bibliography: M. Dewar, *Sir Thomas Smith: A Tudor Intellectual in Office*, 1964; N. M. Sutherland, *The Massacre of St. Bartholomew and the European Conflict, 1559-1572*, 1973; R. B. Wernham, *Before the Armada: The Emergence of the English Nation, 1485-1588*, 1966.

Gary Bell

Boleyn, Anne (1507-1536). Second wife of HENRY VIII, Anne was born in 1507 to Elizabeth Howard, a daughter of THOMAS HOWARD, 2nd duke of Norfolk, and Thomas Boleyn, a descendant of Edward I through his maternal grandfather, the 7th earl of Ormond. The paternal grandfather of Thomas was Geoffrey, who served as lord mayor of London. While on a mission to the Netherlands in 1513, Thomas won an invitation from the regent Margaret for Anne to be educated in the Habsburg nursery at Malines. In 1514, when Mary, sister of Henry VIII, was wed to Louis XII, Anne left Malines to join her in Paris. After Louis's death in 1515, his widow returned home as the wife of CHARLES BRANDON, duke of Suffolk, leaving Anne with Claude, the consort of Francis I.

Educated with Claude's young sister Renee, Anne learned to speak French fluently and acquired musical and social skills. About 1521 she entered the household of Margaret, duchess of Alencon, the king's sister, and was introduced to French humanism. She was recalled home in late 1521 by her father, who, with the support of THOMAS HOWARD, earl of Surrey (later 3rd duke of Norfolk), planned to marry her to the heir of Piers Butler, earl of Ormond.

She is next heard of on Shrove Tuesday 1522 at the home of Cardinal THOMAS WOLSEY, where she participated in a pageant with her sister Mary and Henry VIII, among others. About a year later, the Butler marital scheme having been dropped, Anne exchanged *de futuro* vows with Henry Percy, heir to the earl of Northumberland, a betrothal broken up by Wolsey for political reasons. While she was rusticated, her sister, now wife to William Carey, became the king's mistress.

Sometime in the winter of 1526-1527, having arrived at the conclusion that his marriage with CATHERINE OF ARAGON, his brother's widow, violated biblical law, Henry ordered Wolsey to hold hearings on the validity of the union. Shortly afterward he fell in love with Anne, the queen's new maid of honor. About that time, Anne also attracted the attention of Thomas Wyatt, who wrote poetry in her honor. In late December 1527, Pope Clement VII issued a bull permitting Henry to wed Anne in the event that his first marriage was invalidated.

During the next year, beginning with her departure from court in June because of the sweating sickness, which she contracted, Henry addressed seventeen love letters to her, but their wedding plans were further delayed when Catherine appealed the case to Rome in 1529. It has been argued that Anne had remained so embittered by the Percy episode that in cooperation with Norfolk and Suffolk she took advantage of Wolsey's inability to obtain the divorce to bring about his fall. The evidence for this doubtful theory is the gossip of men friendly to Catherine, such as Eustace Chapuys, the imperial ambassador. While Wolsey's failure was costing him royal favor, Anne's father was gaining higher noble status, becoming earl of Wiltshire and Ormond in 1529; subsequently, she was addressed as Lady Anne Rochford. In 1531 when THOMAS CROMWELL, Henry's new minister, obtained from the CONVOCATIONS qualified acceptance of the king as their supreme lord, Catherine was banished from court.

On 1 September 1532, in preparation for taking Anne to CALAIS for a meeting with Francis I, Henry ennobled her as the lady marquess of Pembroke. The death a few days earlier of WILLIAM WARHAM, archbishop of Canterbury, made possible the appointment of THOMAS CRANMER as his successor and the preparation by Cromwell of a statute to forbid appeals of marital cases to Rome. By December Anne was with child, and on 25 January 1533 she was secretly wed to Henry. On 1 June, after Cranmer had invalidated the king's first marriage and declared the second fully valid, Anne was crowned queen and on 7 September she gave birth to Elizabeth.

The modern historian E. W. Ives has argued without much evidence that Anne and Cromwell formed a faction to foster reform in the church. Anne may have alerted the king to the works of Simon Fish and WILLIAM TYNDALE, but Henry had long been reading heretical books, and most of the clerics she patronized, some independently of Cromwell, had from at least 1530 actively worked for the divorce. Although she favored men like Cranmer who were to be Marian martyrs, she also supported a few like Nicholas Heath who later persecuted the reformers. A study of her extant statements indicates that her beliefs were compatible with Catholic doctrine.

The speculation that Anne's fall occurred because, following Catherine's death on 7 January 1536, she attempted, as a French ally, to thwart an Anglo-Imperial rapprochement, thereby angering Cromwell enough to lead a conspiracy against her, cannot be substantiated; indeed, she had only recently been offended by the refusal of Francis to approve the betrothal of his son to her daughter. Anne lost the king's favor because the male fetus she miscarried in January 1536 (she had previously had a miscarriage in 1534) seems to have been deformed, an ill omen for her since it was believed that God visited children with deformities as a punishment for their parents' sexual sins. In late April and early May, five gentlemen of the privy chamber, all reputed to be libertines—her brother George, Lord Rochford (born c. 1503), Sir Francis Weston, Henry Norris, William Brereton, and Mark Smeaton (who alone confessed to the charges)—were convicted of having had adulterous and incestuous relations with her.

Just before her arrest on 2 May, Anne confronted her husband, holding the perfectly formed Elizabeth in her arms as an attempt to prove her honor, and she sent Norris to her almoner to swear her innocence. On 17 May Cranmer invalidated the royal marriage, two days after a commission had found her guilty of sexual crimes then associated with witchcraft. Anne was beheaded on Tower Green on 19 May with a sword wielded by a Calais executioner and was buried at St. Peter ad Vincula.

Almost fifty years later, Nicholas Sander, a Catholic-Reformation priest, described her as a witch, she had been very tall, he said, with sallow skin, a sixth finger, a tumor on her throat, and a gobber tooth. The few extant contemporary accounts of her appearance are silent about deformities but do assert that she was of medium height with a small neck and somewhat dark complexion. Modified versions of Sander's fables gained credibility largely because she was executed for acts associated with witchcraft.

Bibliography: E. W. Ives, *Anne Boleyn*, 1986; R. M. Warnicke, *The Rise and Fall of Anne Boleyn: Family Politics at the Court of Henry VIII*, 1989.

Retha Warnicke

Bond of Association (1584). By October 1584 the various plots against ELIZABETH in favor of MARY, QUEEN OF SCOTS had come to alarm her PRIVY COUNCIL greatly. Should Elizabeth be assassinated, no one could even legally avenge her murder, since all royal officials would lose their commissions at the death of the monarch. As a result, Mary Stuart could easily succeed to the throne. To deal with this situation, Sir FRANCIS WALSINGHAM, with WILLIAM CECIL, Lord Burghley helping with revisions, drafted the Bond of Association. With each subsequent draft the bond became more violent, so that in its final version it had an element of lynch law to it. The first clause of the bond bound its members to obey the queen and withstand, pursue, and exterminate all people who attempted to harm her. It was the next clause, however, that made the bond so crucial. In its final wording, the bond pledged those who signed that in the event of an attempt on Elizabeth's life, no only would this disallow the succession of the person for whom the attempt was made, but the signatories would also kill that person by whatever means they could. Though Mary Stuart was not mentioned by name in the bond, it was aimed at her. If an attempt was made on Elizabeth's life, Mary Stuart was to be killed, whether or not she was a party to this action. Not only Mary would be killed; though wording was ambiguous, people accepted that it included not only the claimant but heirs of the claimant. JAMES VI, particularly if he were to claim the throne, would also be hunted down. Since the pope had sanctioned Elizabeth's assassination, the Protestants would also meet violence with violence.

Copies of the bond were sent all over England so loyal Englishmen could join the association if they wished. The response was enthusiastic, as thousands of people added their names and seals, though some loyal Protestants were distressed by the lawlessness of the bond and refused to sign it. When Parliament passed the QUEEN'S SAFETY ACT (1585) the bond was amended to agree with it, and James was removed from punishment unless he himself was shown to be involved with any plot. While Elizabeth claimed in 1586 that she knew nothing of the bond until she was shown the document with the signatures of thousands of her subjects appended, she was probably aware of the scheme, though it is doubtful she either saw or approved of its final form.

Bibliography: John Neale, *Elizabeth I and Her Parliaments, 1584-1601*, 1957.

Carole Levin

Bonner, Edmund (1500?-1569). Bishop of London, Bonner is famous chiefly for his part in the persecution of Protestants during the MARIAN REACTION.

Educated in canon and civil law at Oxford, Bonner entered the service of THOMAS WOLSEY, whose chaplain he remained until the cardinal's fall. His talents attracted the attention of HENRY VIII and THOMAS CROMWELL, and he was sent on a number of foreign missions. Bonner appeared in Rome in 1532 to protest the papal position on the royal divorce and informed the pope that Henry wished to appeal to a general council of the church. During the next ten years he was appointed to embassies to the empire, Denmark, and France and won a reputation for diplomatic clumsiness and a bullying manner.

Bonner was supported in his career by being given a number of ecclesiastical preferments, including that of archdeacon of Leicester. He was named bishop of Hereford in 1538 and was translated in the next year to London. As bishop of London he was always in the forefront of the prosecution of goverment religious policy. In his first years in the post he was responsible for the enforcement of the unpopular SIX ARTICLES and took part in the examination of the Protestant martyr ANNE ASKEW.

Under Henry VIII Bonner accommodated himself to the king's wishes in matters of religion—he accepted the ROYAL SUPREMACY and wrote a glowing preface to STEPHEN GARDINER's *De Vera Obedientia* (1536) in which he supported the ROYAL DIVORCE and attacked papal pretensions. He was, however, less willing to go along with religious innovations during the reign of EDWARD VI. Instructed by the PRIVY COUNCIL in 1549 to preach against Catholic rebels and defend the proposition that the royal power was as great during the rule of a minor as during that of an adult, Bonner instead spent his sermon upholding transubstantiation. Despite a spirited defense in which he attacked his Protestant accusers, such as HUGH LATIMER and John Hooper, he was imprisoned in the Marshalsea and replaced as bishop of London by NICHOLAS RIDLEY.

When MARY I gained the throne in 1553, Bonner was released and returned to his bishopric and the turmoil surrounding the queen's attempt to reintroduce Catholicism. He was vigorous in his efforts to educate his flock in what was now required of them religiously. His visitations enquired into forbidden practices and beliefs, and he wrote a series of instructional works: a book of *Homilies* and *Profitable and Necessary Doctrine* in 1555 as well as a child's catechism, *An Honest Godlye Instruction* in 1556. It was, however, the 1555 reintroduction of burning for heresy that contributed most to making Bonner a central figure in the history of the Marian Reaction.

One of every three burnings during the reign of Mary I took place in his diocese, and Protestants soon came to blame him for the atrocities and called him "Bloody Bonner" or "The Butcher of London." His coarse and abusive manner (made worse, some said, by his own mistreatment in prison under Edward VI) only served to add to his reputation for cruelty. Some of this notoriety may be misplaced. Bonner seems to have preferred arguing and frightening his prisoners into submission rather than putting them to death. But his diocese was directly under the eye of the government, a position that made it difficult to escape exercising the severity that Mary and her advisers demanded. Certainly he was chastised on more than one occasion for his foot-dragging and the leniency of his proceedings.

For a short time after the accession of ELIZABETH I, Bonner remained in possession of his see. He attended Parliament and the convocation of 1559 but refused to take the Oath of Supremacy and was placed under arrest and once again jailed in the Marshalsea. Even in prison he continued to be a thorn in the side of the Protestants, as he avoided the death penalty for twice refusing the Oath by challenging the legitimacy of the ordination of his accuser. Bonner died in 1569, still so unpopular that he was buried in secrecy to avoid a riot.

Bibliography: Gina Alexander, "Bonner and the Marian Persecutions," *History* 60 (1975): 374-91; John Foxe, *Acts and Monuments*, 8 vols., 1837-1841.

Gerald Bowler

Book of Common Prayer (1549 and 1552). A response to the mid-sixteenth century need to provide a uniform pattern of worship for the reforming English church and thus a vehicle for further reform in the direction that seemed desirable to the dominant governmental and ecclesiastical authorities. The Prayer Books of 1549 and 1552 (each of which was established by an ACT OF UNIFORMITY) should be seen as part of a long-standing process to streamline and revise official worship in England. The first involved a significant revision of traditional orders, particularly the Sarum Use, and was considerably influenced by the Breviary of Francisco de Quinones, while the second demanded a more Protestantized format than the first.

The Prayer Books did not appear suddenly from out of nowhere during the Edwardian years but were part of a continuum of reform that began during the overturning days of HENRY VIII's reign. They reflected an instinct for beauty, the art of compromise in English dress, and careful attention to the social and political realities of the times. The assumption that undergirded the book's revisions was that the practice of common prayer should have a vital spiritual role in the community as a whole and that each and every individual had a part to play in erecting Christ's earthly kingdom in its English manifestation. In all of this, the mind of THOMAS CRANMER, archbishop of Canterbury, figured prominently.

Cranmer's religious ideal not only embraced regular attendance at worship but, even more vitally, emphasized the need for active participation and appreciation on the part of all the godly. Communion was therefore not an odious obstacle or even a necessary inconvenience prescribed by the national church but rather, an opportunity for spiritual assessment and reckoning that should lead to fundamental changes in life-style and behavior for all recipients—in fact, it contained the essence of being converted when properly comprehended and observed.

Early Reformational attempts to come up with an acceptable pattern for the English church had dealt with both doctrinal and ceremonial matters at the same time. These included the *BISHOPS' BOOK* (1537), the ACT OF SIX ARTICLES (1539), and the *KING'S BOOK* (1543). In 1541, the *RATIONAL OF CEREMONI-AL* was produced by an episcopal commission set up by THOMAS CROMWELL, the King's vicegerent in spiritual matters. It gave specific attention to the Mass and baptism. Two years later, CONVOCATION established its own reforming commission as a result of pressure from Henry to see the service books more fully revised. The notion of royal approval (and even insistence) for reform was thus embedded in the process carried on under Cranmer's supervision years before its culmination in the Edwardian and Elizabethan periods.

The first year of Edward's reign brought the appearance of Injunctions, a *BOOK OF HOMILIES*, and a bill concerning the nature of Holy Communion and the necessity of receiving in both kinds. An *Order of Communion* followed around Easter 1548 and was later incorporated into the Prayer Book itself.

The push for a comprehensive, definitive service book began in September of that year with a royal proclamation that looked forward to the speedy production of a regularized form of worship. The task was entrusted to a group known as the Windsor Committee (possibly the same men who had come up with the *Order of Communion*), which may have had a form in hand by the opening of the second parliamentary session and the sitting of convocation in late November. Debate on the Prayer Book, which predictably centered on the nature of the presence in the Sacrament, occurred in the House of Lords before the adjournment for Christmas but did not receive a first reading until 7 January 1549. When matters came to a vote on 15 January, two lay peers were joined by a minority of eight bishops in opposing the proceedings.

The first Prayer Book, like most Reformational movements in England, represented a compromise. Despite some clear Protestant overtones (such as that regarding the sole mediatorial authority of Jesus Christ), it did not sit well with hard-line Reformers such as John Hooper, bishop of Gloucester, as of 1551. Criticism was also expressed by Martin Bucer, whose influence in Edwardian proceedings was considerable. Pockets of organized resistance to the issuance of the book were evident in 1549 during the WESTERN REBELLION in Cornwall and Devon. Here, opposition to alterations in the Mass and the use of the vernacular demonstrated considerable (though undoubtedly misinformed) opposition to the reform tide then gaining the upper hand at official levels. Not all Englishmen appreciated the downplaying of the mysterious elements in the Sacrament nor the opportunity to be more fully engaged with the meaning of the rite itself. Presumably, changes in ritual were harder to accept than alterations in theology, owing to their obvious visualization. Concern was also expressed by the rebels regarding the appropriation of religious foundations and the setting forth of the Scriptures in English, indicating a wellspring of Conservative sentiment presumably, though not necessarily exclusively, driven by clergy favouring certain aspects of the old order. No opposition was expressed toward the ROYAL SUPREMACY, however, nor was accommodation with the papacy required in the list of demands. The majority of the realm's parishioners obviously went along with the book with its royal and parliamentary backing through the first ACT OF UNIFORMITY (1549, 2 and 3 Edw. VI, c. 1). No penalties were enjoined for laymen who failed to attend the official services or who enjoyed other forms.

Ultimately, however, it was not conservative dissatisfaction but the demand for further reform that led to the imposition of the second Prayer Book in April 1552. The procedural details surrounding its approval are somewhat obscure, though one can assume a prominent role for Cranmer, who was often in touch with the new bishop of London, NICHOLAS RIDLEY, during these days. Input was also forthcoming from Peter Martyr and Bucer, not to mention John Calvin, who expressed his fear openly to Cranmer that the archbishop might come to the end of his life without having accomplished the necessary work of clarification and improvement. The episcopacy was engaged in relevant activity as well.

In the end, Cranmer was probably left the responsibility of tying the submissions together. He was well prepared for the task, since he had likely seen the first effort as a kind of temporary measure and had been increasingly withdrawing himself from state matters throughout the last half of Edward's reign. Unfortunately, the process incurred his displeasure at the very end when the council caved in to a pressure group led by Hooper and insisted upon the printing of the BLACK RUBRIC to avoid the notion of veneration of the Sacrament while in the posture of kneeling. In this form, then, the book was enforced by the second Uniformity bill (1552, 5 and 6 Edw. VI, c. 1) of the reign, along with the Ordinal of 1550. As the original statute was never repealed, the new measure was packaged as a refinement rather than a radical innovation. It is also noteworthy that the type of dissent evident following the imposition of the first Prayer Book was absent after the publication of the second and that these measures, together with the settling upon the FORTY-TWO ARTICLES of religion in the next year, helped to make England more formally Protestant than at any other point in its history. A delay in implementing the bill (and thus the Prayer Book) for some seven months was written into the proceedings, partly to allow for the production of the anticipated articles and partly to give Cranmer time to use the propaganda value contained in the new order as grounds for convening a European-wide Protestant assembly.

The second Prayer Book may be seen as a predictable extension of the Reformational principles that underlay the first effort. The goal of both was to define not only the individual's role in divine worship but also that of the nation as a holy community. It was thus viewed as the means whereby the godly kingdom of Christ might be instituted at that crucial stage in England's history, with the church of Christ leading the way into the future.

In terms of doctrinal development, one notes a much closer approximation to the Continental Reformed mainstream by 1552. Justificatory theology is inseparably linked to faith, with no room for good works in the salvation schema, while the death of Christ is represented in a stricly Protestant light. The mass has given way entirely to the notion of communion, and the 1549 reference to the intercessory status of the saints and the Virgin Mary is omitted. For all of its intent, however, the book enjoyed the briefest of exposure before being summarily abolished by the first Parliament of Mary's reign in the fall of 1553. Worship was thence to be conducted after the form that prevailed during the final year of her father's rule.

The second Prayer Book remained popular with Protestant sympathizers, however, including those who fled the purge and took up residence in various Continental cities of refuge. Thus it was not surprising that Elizabeth should be pressured to see to its restoration. The tone of the 1559 book, though in many ways similar to that of 1552, was intended to remove the most virulent anti-Romanist sentiments, and the communion theology was broadened to permit a variety of persuasions. In some ways, the language of the Elizabethan Prayer Book with regard to the Sacrament can be seen as a combination of the best aspects of the worlds of 1549 and 1552, even permitting Anglo-Catholics as well as Swiss Reformed to feel generally satisfied with its terminology—an act of political genius if not courageous ethics. Some could assume an openness to real presence doctrine therein (including the corporeal sense), while others would prefer to stress the reality minus the corporality of Christ's presence. In addition, the black rubric disappeared, but one dealing with priestly vestments during communion (the so-called ornaments rubric) was inserted. These changes were all part of the moderate settlement in religion determined by Elizabeth and her advisors.

Bibliography: John E. Booty, "Communion and Commonweal: The Book of Common Prayer," in Booty, ed., *The Godly Kingdom of Tudor England: Great Books of the English Reformation*, 1981: 139-216; W. K. Jordan, *Edward VI*, 2 vols., 1968, 1970.

Andrew Penny

Book of Homilies (1547). One of the obstacles retarding the growth of a Reformed church in England was the lack of an adequately trained, preaching clergy. THOMAS CRANMER first proposed the writing and authorization of model sermons or homilies to deal with this problem in the reign of HENRY VIII and in 1542 CONVOCATION agreed to the plan. Within a year a book of homilies consisting of 12 sermons was compiled and edited by Cranmer who probably wrote at least five of them. However, Henry VIII refused to authorize a book that might conflict with the *KING'S BOOK* which was being prepared at the same time; consequently, the *Book of Homilies* was not officially issued until EDWARD VI's reign.

In January 1547 Cranmer revived the plan to issue a *Book of Homilies*. Although he asked STEPHEN GARDINER to contribute, Gardiner refused replying that he was satisfied with the *King's Book* which made the homilies unnecessary. When the homilies were authorized by royal PROCLAMATION in July 1547, Gardiner protested that the proclamation was unconstitutional because the content of the homilies conflicted with the theology of the *King's Book*. It was, therefore, in violation of an act of PARLIAMENT, 34 & 35 Hen. VIII c. 1, which forbad teaching contrary to the *King's Book*. Although Gardiner's protest was largely ignored, his argument was not without substance. Three of the homilies written by Cranmer, (3) "Of the Salvation of all Mankind," (4) "Of the True and Lively Faith," and (5) "Of Good Works," dealt with the theology of justification. Although Cranmer did not teach the full Protestant doctrine of justification, and emphasized the need for a "true and lively faith" which was manifested in good works and Christian living, his contention that human beings were justified by faith without works seemed to contradict the doctrine of the

King's Book that both faith and "other gifts of the grace of God, with a desire to do good works" were necessary for salvation.

The homilies were used throughout the reign of Edward VI, although recent research suggests that at the end of the reign a large number of rural parishes had still not purchased the *Book of Homilies*. In MARY's reign they were suppressed by royal proclamation; but the new archbishop, REGINALD POLE, who also appreciated the value of the homilies for instruction, commissioned a book of Catholic homilies to expose the errors of Protestantism. However the plan was never carried out, and in 1559 ELIZABETH reinstated the first *Book of Homilies*. A second book with 21 additional sermons was issued in 1563, although it was not published in final form until 1571 when the final homily, "Against Rebellion," was added in response to the NORTHERN REBELLION of 1569. The author of most of the new homilies was John Jewel, but both MATHEW PARKER and EDMUND GRINDAL also contributed sermons.

The homilies contained both instruction in Christian doctrine and Christian living. They were biblically based and denounced what the homily "Of Good Works" called "false doctrine, superstition, idolatry, hypocrisy, and other enormities and abuses" that had grown up in the Middle Ages as a result of tradition rather than biblical teaching. Although the homilies played a role in the demise of Roman Catholicism and the triumph of Protestantism at a time when there were relatively few able Protestant preachers, the regular repetition of the same sermons over a long period of time must have also led to boredom and uninspired preaching. It is not suprising that as more university trained clergy, who were both Protestant in their convictions and able preachers, became available some of those most committed to biblical preaching began to question the usefulness of the *Book of Homilies*.

Bibliography: Ronald B. Bond, "Cranmer and the Controversy Surround the Publication of Certayne Sermons on Homilies, 1547," *Renaissance and Reformation* 12 (1976): 28-35; Horton Davies, *Worship and Theology in England from Cranmer to Hooker 1534-1603*, 1970; and *Sermons or Homilies Appointed to be Read in Churches*, reprint, 1986.

Rudolph W. Heinze

Bosworth Field, Battle of (1485). The battle of Bosworth Field was the culmination of a brief campaign by Henry Tudor, earl of Richmond, and his adherents to overthrow Richard III, king of England and Wales. Since October 1483 Henry Tudor, who had lived as a penniless exile in Brittany for over a decade, had hoped to seize the throne from Richard III, whom the English blamed for the disappearance and probable murder of his nephews, Edward V and Prince Richard.

That Henry was able to embark for his homeland in the summer of 1845 was largely owing to the attitude and policy of the French government. Charles VIII feared that Richard III would reopen the Hundred Years' War. Accordingly, the French authorities hoped to keep Richard tied down and agreed to subsidize a conspiracy against him. In November 1484 they sent 3,000 *livres tournois* to help Henry equip his troops, and in June of the following year they dispatched at least 1,500 men to fight alongside his band of 400-500 Englishmen.

Had Henry been able to count on a force of only 2,000 men, he would never have risked a pitched battle against Richard III, who could rally at least five times as many troops. But the Tudor claimant was relatively certain of some assistance from Scotland, since James III was still smarting from Richard's seizure of Berwick Castle in 1482. Obviously, Richard III would never willingly hand it back, but Henry Tudor might do so for a consideration; to that end James sent 1,000 men to assist the pretender once the latter had set foot on English soil.

Finally, Henry could rely on military support from WALES. As the acknowledged head of the House of Tudor, he was the leader of an old Welsh family, and for many years there had been a prophecy that a great Welshman would appear one day and conquer England. Attempting to exploit that prophecy, Henry wrote letters to the main Welsh chieftains during the early months of 1485 and requested their aid against Richard II. The greatest Welsh landowner, Rhys ap Thomas, promised that he and his fellow magnates would supply as many as 4,000 troops, provided Henry launched his campaign against the English ruler from Wales. With that pledge of support in hand, the pretender felt ready to embark on his hazardous expedition by 1 August.

Henry and his troops landed at the Welsh port of Milford Haven on 7 August. Early the next morning they set out for Haverfordwest, and within a week Rhys ap Thomas and other Welsh magnates appeared with over 2,500 retainers. Thereupon Henry felt he could safely arrive at Shrewsbury and crossed the border into western England on 16 August.

Meanwhile, at Nottingham Castle, the waiting Richard had learned that the long-dreaded invasion was at last underway. On 11 August he alerted his principal supporters to be ready to meet him with their retainers at Leicester within a week. For some reason he himself did not set out until 19 August. Within two days he had passed through Leicester and arrived at the base of Ambien Hill, two miles south of the little town of Market Bosworth. Because Henry and his men were now only a short distance away, a pitched battle was almost bound to occur the next day.

About 8:00 a.m. on Monday, 22 August, the battle of Bosworth Field began when Henry's vanguard under John de Vere, earl of Oxford, the ablest commander on either side, charged the king's position on the slopes of Ambien Hill. Richard III had about 10,000 men in his army, whereas his opponent had only 5,800. Yet morale was considerably higher among the rebels, since Henry's troops believed in their cause. As for Richard's chief lieutenants, Henry Percy, earl of Northumberland, was a lukewarm adherent at best and remained safely at the rear with his men. Thomas, Lord Stanley and his brother Sir William were even more notorious trimmers, having always managed in past years to be on the winning side, whether Lancastrian or Yorkist. At this juncture the Stanleys' sympathies were with the pretender, who was Lord Stanley's stepson, owing to that peer's marriage to Henry's widowed mother, Lady Margaret Beaufort. But, contrariwise, the Stanleys had enjoyed great benefits from Richard III's largesse, and the king had also taken the precaution of making Lord Stanley's eldest son a hostage for their support. Because of the Stanleys' mixed feelings, they remained on the sidelines until the climax of the battle when, calculating the side that was likely to win, they threw themselves into the fray and assured the victor's success. Of Richard III's main adherents, only Sir John Howard, duke of Norfolk, and his son THOMAS, earl of Surrey, fought wholeheartedly for their sovereign. Norfolk, a man in his sixties, was killed within the first thirty minutes, while Surrey was wounded so badly that he begged for someone to put an end to his suffering.

As for Richard himself, he fought demonically, believing this battle to be his best chance to save himself and his throne. Therefore, Richard took a major part in the combat and made a furious effort to reach and kill his rival. He unhorsed the experienced warrior Sir John Cheyney, and he ended the days of Sir William Brandon, the rebel standard-bearer. Before he could engage Henry in direct combat, the latter's guardsmen closed about him, and he was slain, fighting manfully, albeit wildly, to the last.

Once the conflict ended about 10:00 a.m., the crown Richard had worn on his helmet into battle was found in the dust and taken to Lord Stanley. Stanley, in turn, rode to his stepson's side and bade him dismount and kneel. Then he crowned him HENRY VII, king of England and Wales, and declared that a new reign had begun.

Bibliography: Michael J. Bennett, *The Battle of Bosworth*, 1985.

Michael V. C. Alexander

Brandon, Charles, 1st Duke of Suffolk (c. 1484-1545). Courtier, councillor, and military commander, Charles Brandon owed his place at court to his father's heroic death at BOSWORTH FIELD and his uncle's position as master of the horse to HENRY VII. In the first five years of HENRY VIII's reign he gradually emerged from the circle of courtiers who jousted and revelled with the king to a unique position in Henry's friendship, which brought him rewards in office, wardships and land, the post of marshal and second-in-command of the king's army in France in 1513, and the titles of Viscount Lisle (1513) and of duke of Suffolk (1514). His role seems to have complemented that of the rising administrator THOMAS WOLSEY, and they cooperated closely in the forging and maintenance of peace with France in the period 1514-1515.

Early in 1515 Brandon temporarily incurred Henry's anger by marrying the king's sister Mary without royal permission in France following the death of her husband King Louis XII in 1515. Though Henry forgave the couple, they were forced to surrender to him a portion of Mary's dower income, and Wolsey's concurrent rise to clear supremacy in the government lessened Brandon's political role, as did the duke's inflexibly Francophile views on foreign policy. In the following years he faced the difficult challenge of establishing himself as a local magnate in East Anglia. The king had granted him the forfeited estates of Edmund de la Pole, earl of Suffolk, but these provided insufficient resources to enable Brandon to compete effectively with the Howards and the De Veres, and he had to rely heavily on his numerous but rarely distinguished cousins for local support. Meanwhile his East Anglian commitments drew his attention away from the offices he held in North Wales, where he involved himself only to use the Crown's revenues as a source of personal credit and otherwise left his deputies and the local gentry to exploit his authority to their own ends; in 1525 he lost these posts in Wolsey's reorganization of Welsh government.

The 1520s brought Brandon back to the forefront of affairs. In 1523 he led an Anglo-Dutch army across the Somme to threaten Paris but was forced to withdraw by adverse weather, widespread mutinies, and the failure of England's allies to press the French on other fronts. In the AMICABLE GRANT risings of 1525 and the public order problems generated by grain shortages and interruptions to the cloth trade in the period 1527-1528, he worked with THOMAS HOWARD, 3rd duke of Norfolk, to keep Suffolk and Norfolk under control. In 1529 Wolsey's decline and fall renewed Brandon's political importance, as he joined Norfolk and others at the head of the new regime as lord president of the council.

This was a false dawn, and in the early 1530s Brandon's uneasy relations with ANNE BOLEYN and THOMAS CROMWELL made his life uncomfortable at a time when Henry's affection for him seemed to have waned. In East Anglia his affinity came increasingly into conflict with that of the Howards, and in 1533 he grudgingly surrendered the office of earl marshal, which he had held since 1524, to Norfolk at the king's command. In 1535 he submitted to a disadvantageous exchange of lands with the Crown in return for the cancellation of the debts of his late wife, Mary (d. 1533).

The Lincolnshire rising of October 1536 gave Brandon the chance to regain the king's favor. He led an army to confront the rebels and after their dispersal pacified the county. In the wake of the rebellion Henry ordered him to reside in Lincolnshire, where his new wife, Catherine, Lady Willoughby, had her inheritance. Within three years he had exchanged almost all his East Anglian estates for the lands of dissolved monasteries and other Crown property in Lincolnshire and make himself the county's greatest landowner. In the 1540s he continued to expand his estates and influence there and built up a more powerful and cohesive local following than he had ever led in East Anglia.

During his last years he was active at court (as great master of the household from 1539), in the House of Lords, and in the privy council, taking a more responsible part in the government than at any other time. He commanded the army on the border with Scotland almost continuously from October 1542 to

March 1544. In summer 1544 he accompanied Henry to France and won the king's gratitude for his important role in the capture of Boulogne. In summer 1545 he led the army that defended the southern coast against threatened French invasion, but on 22 August he succumbed to an apparently sudden illness and died.

Brandon's religion was Conservative but not rigid. He patronized some Reformist clergy, apparently at the request of followers whose views were more radical than his own or perhaps of his last wife, who was moving in evangelical circles by the end of his life and was to choose exile under Queen MARY. Though his two sons by Mary Tudor predeceased him, the two sons by Catherine Willoughby survived him to become the 2nd and 3rd dukes of Suffolk, both dying in 1551.

Bibliography: S. J. Gunn, *Charles Brandon, Duke of Suffolk c. 1485-1545*, 1988.

S. J. Gunn

Bristol, Treaty of (1574). This treaty was an attempt to end the deterioration of Anglo-Spanish relations that had been taking place since the late 1560s. Both countries had seized the other's shipping in early 1569, and trade was seriously disrupted. By 1572 ELIZABETH I and Philip II were ready to settle their problems. A preliminary agreement reached at NYMEGEN during 1573 restored trade for two years. The next year diplomats met at Bristol in August 1574 to reach a permanent agreement on mutual compensation for losses to shipping. The Treaty of Bristol was signed on 21 August 1574 and received full English ratification on 28 August. As a result of this agreement the steady decline of Anglo-Spanish relations was arrested for six years. The English conceded to being the net debtor in the financial reconciliation and claimed only slightly less than £70,000 while allowing Spain to take almost £90,000. The problem of illegal trading and raiding in the Spanish New World by JOHN HAWKINS and FRANCIS DRAKE was ignored by the treaty. In fact, sporadic seizures of the other's shipping by both nations continued after the ratification of the treaty. In spite of these problems, the treaty did contribute to a full restoration of commercial and political ties almost to the level of 1568. Both sides made sincere efforts to exhibit good faith. The next year Philip II expelled English Catholic dissidents from Louvain, and so met a long-standing English request. Elizabeth reciprocated by agreeing not to harbor rebels against the king of Spain. All of these efforts ultimately proved futile as England and Spain were too far apart in their religious, political, and economic goals to arrest for very long the slide into open warfare that the crisis of the period 1569-1570 had presaged.

Bibliography: G. D. Ramsay, *The Queen's Merchants and the Revolt of the Netherlands*, 1988.

Gary Bell

Brittany Expeditions (1591-1595) were sent during the final phase of France's long civil war, in which Henry IV, a Protestant, sought to regain Crown lands from a rebellious Catholic League assisted by Spain. They were launched as much to allay ELIZABETH's fear that Philip II might capture and use France's Channel provinces to attack England as to appease the new generation of courtiers, led by her favorite, the impetuous ROBERT DEVEREUX, earl of Essex, who sought fame and foreign adventures.

In October 1590 Spanish troops landed at Blavet in upper Brittany and, supported by the Catholic League, captured the towns of Blavet and Hennebon. They put great pressure on Brest, on the royalist government, and along the northeastern Channel coast. The duke of Parma increased the pressure on this Protestant region by marching from the Low Countries to relieve the siege of Paris. Shortly thereafter Elizabeth agreed to aid Henry after receiving only vague promises of repayment of her earlier loans and possible English occupation of recaptured towns. The French diplomats shrewdly exploited Essex's desire for glory to assist their cause.

An expedition of 600 men was sent in March 1591 under the command of the veteran Sir Roger Williams, who helped break the siege of Dieppe. In May, a second force of 3,000 troops, under the command of Sir John Norris, followed. They initially helped the royalist governor, de Dombes, defend Paimpol and then were ordered to protect Brest. Despite much pleading, the queen's favorite was kept from these enterprises because Essex's secret marriage had angered the queen. After a reconciliation, Essex was finally allowed the adventure he craved and given command of a third English army of nearly 4,000 men, an army that he helped to raise. They were sent to Dieppe in August to join Henry's mercenaries in an expedition to besiege Rouen.

After a foolhardy dash across 130 miles of enemy territory to meet with Henry IV at Compiegne, Essex returned to his forces while the French king occupied himself elsewhere. During this long summer hiatus Essex's forces were depleted by desertions, malaria, dysentery, and disillusionment. On the route to Rouen Essex joined the siege that captured Gournay on 27 September and lavishly rewarded his subordinates and provoked Elizabeth's displeasure. She recalled him in early October and harshly criticized him. When he returned, he found his forces numbering one-quarter of their initial total and bearing the whole burden of the siege of Rouen until Henry's forces arrived in mid-November. While Essex and his troops behaved bravely in a series of skirmishes, the siege proved futile, and he returned to London. News of Parma's advance brought Essex's rapid return, but winter weather delayed Parma. Essex surrendered his command in

January 1592 after the governor of Rouen declined his challenge to settle the siege by personal combat.

Parma finally relieved Rouen in April 1592, after Elizabeth had refused French requests for additional aid. She provided occasional assistance, as she did in the spring of 1592 to harass Parma, whose return to the Netherlands bogged down in the Somme, but this had little significance. Meanwile the Spanish challenged Norris's forces at Craon in May 1592 and inflicted a crushing defeat.

English distrust of Henry IV limited further assistance. Believing the English could not save him and suspicious of their continued demands for a major seaport, Henry proclaimed his conversion to Catholicism in July 1593 but gained little immediate assistance and was forced to renew his English alliance.

During the winter of 1593-1594, Spanish troops moved from Blavet to Crozon, where they constructed a fort designed to close Brest's access to the sea. In response an expedition of eight warships and 4,000 men under the joint command of Norris and Sir Martin Frobisher was organized and dispatched in July after Henry IV agreed to accept the total cost of the expedition. It landed in early September and began besieging Crozon. On 7 November the fortress fell to a combined onslaught of Frobisher's guns and Norris's soldiers. Norris was severely wounded, as was Frobisher, who died shortly after.

England had sent nearly 20,000 men to France over five years with fewer than half returning home. While these expeditions taxed English resources, they also frustrated Spanish ambitions without weakening English forces in Ireland and the Netherlands. The victory at Crozon assumed added importance after Parma's successor seized Calais in April 1596 and England launched the 1596 CADIZ EXPEDITION.

Bibliography: R. B. Wernham, *After the Armada: Elizabethan England and the Struggle for Western Europe, 1588-1595*, 1988.

Shelton Hanft

Bruges, Treaty of (1521). Anglo-Imperial alliance concluded at Bruges on 25 August 1521. By the time of this treaty, Emperor Charles V was at war with France and wanted England as an ally. The English under THOMAS WOLSEY tried to maintain an appearance of impartially arbitrating the Franco-Habsburg conflict. According to the treaty negotiated at Bruges, Charles V and HENRY VIII agreed to declare war on France in March 1523 and, respectively, to field armies of 80,000 and 40,000 soldiers for an invasion. In addition, the English promised to declare war on France by November 1521 if a state of war existed at that time between Charles V and the king of France. The pope was also to be a member of this alliance, although his contribution was to be spiritual rather than military. France was to be placed under papal interdict, and, furthermore, the pope was to grant dispensation for a marriage between Charles V and Princess MARY. Both parties agreed for obvious reasons to keep the provisions of this treaty very secret, although the French soon began to suspect that the English and the Imperialists were plotting against them. This treaty marked a further increase in cooperation between Charles V and Henry VIII against France. Although Cardinal Wolsey continued his efforts to negotiate a peace between Charles V and Francis I, he failed. As a result Henry VIII went to war as a junior partner of the emperor in the fruitless ANGLO-FRENCH WAR OF 1522-1525.

Bibliography: Peter Gwyn, "Wolsey's Foreign Policy: The Conferences at Calais and Bruges Reconsidered," *Historical Journal* 23 (1980): 755-72.

Ronald Fritze

Buckingham, Treason Trial of the Duke of (1521). Edward Stafford, 3rd duke of Buckingham, born at Brecknock Castle in Wales on 3 February 1478, was the son of Henry, the 2nd duke, and Catherine Woodville. His father was attainted for rebellion against Richard III in 1483, but HENRY VII restored the younger Stafford to his dukedom in 1485. He married Eleanor Percy, daughter of the 4th earl of Northumberland in 1489 and had a son and three daughters. Buckingham was a soldier, a knight of the Bath (1485) and the Garter (1495), Lord High Steward at HENRY VIII's coronation (1509), a privy councillor (1509), and a justice of the peace in several counties and was at the FIELD OF CLOTH OF GOLD and Henry's meetings with Charles V in 1520. However, as the highest-ranking member of the old nobility, Buckingham resented his lack of influence at court. He despised and often criticized the lowborn THOMAS WOLSEY, notably when the latter's foreign policy clashed with his own pro-imperial sentiments, and he was angry over his expenses in France in 1520. More importantly, he was a threat to the king because he had vast lands and ties to many peers and as a descendant of Edward III and nephew of Edward IV was a potential successor to Henry if he had no male heir. Failing to keep order in his Welsh lands and high-handed with his tenants, he alarmed the king in 1520 by asking to arm his retainers to quiet the troubles there. Already in 1519 the king had reprimanded Sir William Bulmer for wearing Buckingham's livery at court. Then late in 1520 Wolsey received an anonymous letter accusing the duke of treason.

Henry summoned Buckingham on 21 April 1521 and had him followed. After seeing Wolsey, Buckingham was arrested by Sir Henry Marney and 100 yeomen, who took him to the Tower of London. On 8 May he was indicted for high treason for compassing the deposition and death of the king by words and deeds between 10 March 1511 and 4 November 1520. He pled not guilty. The trial was held on 13 May at Westminster, before Chief Justice John Fyneux, in the Court of the High Steward, the duke of Norfolk. This procedure was correct for cases involving peers when Parliament was not in session. The jury, not packed, included ten greater nobles (all but the aged earl of Arundel), nine barons, and the prior of St. John's of Jerusalem. The only witnesses were Charles Knevet, a former official on the duke's estates; Robert Gilbert, his chancellor;

John Dellacourt, his chaplain; and Nicholas Hopkins, his confessor. Knevet probably wrote the letter, though it could have been any of the others or Margaret Geddynge, a former servant. As was normal, Buckingham had no lawyer, did not know the charges beforehand, and was unable to cross-examine the witnesses, though he was allowed to speak in his own defense, and careful attention was given to correct procedure. After long deliberation, the jury unanimously found him guilty. He was convicted of treason by words, for which there was precedent in the fifteenth century, even though the statute of 1352 required an overt act. Despite the queen's plea for a pardon, he was beheaded on Tower Hill on 17 May, after admonishing observers to avoid his errors (Henry exempted him from being hung, drawn, and quartered). He was posthumously expelled from the Order of the Garter, and in 1523 Parliament passed an act of ATTAINDER declaring his property forfeit to the king.

Bibliography: Barbara J. Harris, *Edward Stafford, Third Duke of Buckingham, 1478-1521*, 1986; Carole Rawcliffe, *The Staffords, Earls of Stafford and Dukes of Buckingham, 1394-1521*, 1978.

William B. Robison

C

Cadiz Expedition (1596). A massive land and naval attack on the main port of Spain, Cadiz, under the joint command of ROBERT DEVEREUX, earl of Essex and Charles, Lord Howard of Effingham.

By the middle of the 1590s, Philip II of Spain, in an effort to revenge the loss of his 1588 armada, had once again readied himself to launch an offensive attack against England. Apprised of this new attempt, the English PRIVY COUNCIL authorized a preemptive assault upon the chief Spanish port of Cadiz, to take place in the spring of 1596. A Spanish attack upon the French port of Calais delayed the fleet's launch, and ELIZABETH I dispatched an expeditionary force under Essex to aid in the French defense. Calais fell to Spain anyway, and now no choice was left but to proceed with the plan to attack Cadiz.

Despite reluctance on Elizabeth's part, the expedition sailed from Plymouth during the first week of June. At the end of June, nearing Cadiz, the English were cheered to learn that the port was virtually unprotected and unaware of the attack to come; further, a rich merchant fleet bound for the Indies rested at anchor outside Cadiz. The first attack, by sea, proved successful, and Essex, with a small contingent, was able to penetrate to the center of the town. Ignoring the merchant fleet, Howard brought the remainder of the English troops to reinforce Essex, a move that assured the complete domination of Cadiz. The port was sacked, although Essex gave orders that the churches were to be left alone, and women, children, and the religious were to be evacuated. The systematic plundering of Cadiz yielded great treasure, but the Spanish kept the merchant fleet that Howard had ignored out of English hands, the duke of Medina Sidonia ordered its destruction two days after the fall of Cadiz.

Essex seized the glory of the moment, named himself governor of Cadiz, and promptly knighted sixty-eight of his comrades-in-arms. However, the lure of an expected treasure fleet from the Azores outweighed the earl's plans for a permanent Spanish base, and on 1 July, the town was fired and the English fleet set out to claim further spoils. Unable to find the treasure fleet and disappointed by the lack of suitable adventures, Essex returned the slowly deteriorating flotilla to Plymouth.

Expecting a hero's welcome, Essex was taken aback at Elizabeth's attitude. Cheated of expected treasure—for the troops had absconded with much of the wealth found at Cadiz—and stung at the earl's presumption in knighting his compatriots, the queen turned on Essex and held him responsible for the mistakes of the expedition. Though London celebrated the victory—and Essex's role in it—Elizabeth refused to vindicate the earl, who turned to the people for validation of his military prowess. Shaken by the appointment of ROBERT CECIL to the office of PRINCIPAL SECRETARY during his absence, Essex became ever more convinced that the road to success meant the coupling of military exploits with the popular support of the masses. Reckoning without Elizabeth's jealousy of her people's love, the earl, intoxicated by his victory at Cadiz, began to lay the foundations for his eventual fall and execution.

Bibliography: Robert Lacey, *Robert, Earl of Essex*, 1971.

                                                                                  Connie S. Evans

Calais. The last English outpost on the Continent after the close of the Hundred Years' War in 1453 came into English hands shortly after Edward III's victory at Crecy in 1346 (though it was not formally ceded to England until the treaty of Bretigny in 1360). Considered a part of the realm of England rather than a possession surrounded by hostile territory, Calais constituted a rich commercial center for trade with Europe. The leading regulated company of the later Middle Ages, the Mayor and Company of the STAPLE, established the wool mart there in 1363. During the reigns of HENRY VII and HENRY VIII the company became responsible for the payment of the Calais garrison by entering into engagements known as Acts of Retainer; ultimate authority over the town and its environs (the Pale of Calais), however, rested with a royal official, the lord deputy, and with his council. The corruption, disorder and incompetence that characterized the administration of Arthur Plantagenet, Lord Lisle, induced THOMAS CROMWELL in 1535 to create a royal commission to investigate affairs and recommend reforms. These were embodied in the Calais Act (27 Hen. VIII, c. 3), which aimed at integrating Calais into the realm along with the other "outliers," IRELAND and WALES. This statute reorganized the civil and military establishment at Calais, legislated against the sale of offices, separated the garrison from civilian interference, and attempted to place finances on a firmer footing. (After 1536 Calais was represented by two burgesses in Parliament). Despite this ambitious program, Calais remained a financial and military liability for the Tudors.

As both the country's first line of defense and a potential infiltration point for subversive elements, the town of Calais was heavily fortified, and its garrison remained the most costly military expenditure sustained by the Tudor monarchy. The boundaries of the Pale, concerning which there were constant disputes with France, embraced an area of approximately 120 square miles. The town of Calais was surrounded by rectangular walls, roughly 1,200 yards in length and 400 yards in width. The fortifications were circumscribed by a moat, and its inner defenses included the Calais Castle (which was in ruins in the year of Calais's fall) and the tower of Rysbank, which dominated the spit of land north of the harbor. Lightly held strongpoints protected the approaches to Calais, but the backbone of the Pale's defenses remained the powerful outforts of Newnham Bridge, Guisnes, and Hammes. All three had been rebuilt during the years 1539-1542; Newnham Bridge had its own commander, an artillery complement of fifty-five guns, and the protection of marshes and watercourses. Hammes was a pentagonal castle built on a large mound; in 1547 it possessed thirteen brass culverins and seventy-one iron cannons, dominating much of the marshy area of the Pale. By far the strongest of the defenses, however, was Guisnes Castle, nearly square in shape and surrounded by earthen walls and a moat. Guisnes was heavily garrisoned and armed with 56 brass pieces and over 200 iron pieces. Despite these elaborate fortifications Calais proved vulnerable to assault by an enemy both familiar with the terrain and cognizant of the difficulties of maintaining the elaborate network of defenses even with a large, experienced garrison force.

England's entry into the Habsburg-Valois war in 1557 posed an immediate danger to Calais, but one that went unheeded by MARY I, her husband, Philip II of Spain, and her privy council. During January 1558, the duke of Guise with 27,000 French troops attacked and captured Calais. No reinforcements arrived from England or from Philip II's domains in the Low Countries (see ANGLO-FRENCH WAR OF 1557-1559).

Though Calais represented England's past greatness and remained a key strategic outpost, the PRIVY COUNCIL, doubting both the cost and feasibility of such an enterprise, made no effort to recover it. When peace negotiations between Henry II of France and Philip began at Cateau-Cambresis, the latter regarded Calais as expendable. The privy council was persuaded to yield it just before the queen's death in November 1558. To obtain peace with Scotland and secure England's northern border, in 1559 ELIZABETH I reluctantly ceded Calais to France. The clause of the treaty of Cateau-Cambresis that provided that Calais would be returned to England in eight years went unfulfilled, largely because of the unsuccessful assistance that Elizabeth extended to the Protestant party in France. Under the terms of the TREATY OF TROYES (11 April 1564) England lost Calais and forfeited the indemnity promised by the treaty of Cateau-Cambresis.

Bibliography: G. A. C. Sandeman, *Calais Under English Rule*, 1908.

Douglas Bisson

Calais [Gravelines], Treaty of (1520). Anglo-Imperial alliance concluded near CALAIS on 10 July 1520. It occurred in the immediate aftermath of the more glamorous meeting of the FIELD OF CLOTH OF GOLD between HENRY VIII and Francis I of France during June. Henry VIII and Emperor Charles V had previously agreed to the meeting at Calais at an earlier negotiation on 11 April. Basically, both parties renewed their existing treaties with each other at the meeting of 10 July and promised to give each other military assistance. They also agreed not to make any separate treaties with France during the next two years, and there was some discussion of a future marriage between Charles V and the young princess MARY. Such a marriage alliance would have involved breaking an existing agreement from 1518 for the princess Mary to marry the French Dauphin. Furthermore, both rulers agreed to have a joint meeting with France at Calais in August 1521. But, in spite of the English efforts to appear as an impartial arbiter between France and the Habsburg lands, these negotiations with Charles V aroused French suspicions and did represent a movement away from the principles of the TREATY OF LONDON. Meanwhile, the revolt of the Communeros in Spain (June 1520-April 1521) distracted Charles V's attention from negotiations with France. By the time of the meeting at Calais in early August, neither the Imperialists nor the English were negotiating in good faith with the French. Instead, a few days later on 27 August, Charles V and Henry VIII concluded a definite military alliance against France in the TREATY OF BRUGES.

Bibliography: Susan Doran, *England and Europe 1485-1603*, 1986.

Ronald Fritze

Calvinism, English. John Calvin's *Institutes of Christian Religion* remains the basic work for understanding Calvin's own theological system as well as his approach to doing theology; however, both of these parts of Calvin's thought were modified by his admirers to meet social realities and theological controversies. English Calvinism was no exception. Calvin himself was deeply indebted to Renaissance humanist scholarship, and, as a result, he left many theological problems unresolved and viewed many ecclesiastical practices as "things indifferent" (adiaphora); that is, he left their formulation to local or national traditions as long as the formulations did not violate Scriptural demands. Essential in Calvin's theology were the universal Christian beliefs found in the orthodox creeds, but those beliefs were seen through the eyes of Pauline theology and an ongoing scholarly interpretation of the Scriptures. For this approach Calvin was indebted to Lutherans such as Martin Luther and to Philip Melanchthon as well; he also learned much from Reformed theologians such as Ulrich Zwingli and Martin Bucer. Calvin's theology, then, reflected a broad Protestant worldview, but one that was shaped by St. Paul's theological system, which Calvin applied in his biblical studies and in his efforts to systematize theology. Similarly, admirers of Calvin's theology reflected Calvin's older theological attachments as well as new scholarship and new practical realities. Calvin's Dutch, French, and English followers, for example, developed their own brand of Calvinism, both in theology and in practical affairs.

John Calvin's English admirers demonstrated their loyalty to him during the reign of Queen MARY, when English exiles in Frankfurt-am-Main appealed to Calvin to resolve their ecclesiastical disputes. While there appears to have been a theological censensus among the rivals, they could not agree on matters of liturgy and church government. JOHN KNOX and his followers held out for the liturgy and polity then being used by Reformed churches on the Continent, while Richard Cox's associates wanted to rely exclusively on the BOOK OF COMMON PRAYER and demanded loyalty to exile leaders who formerly had been the more prominent leaders in England. During the disputes each faction, in turn, appealed to Calvin—and each received his support. Apparently, what Calvin thought were essential matters did not correspond to his admirers' choices; while he urged both factions to forget their squabbles, the Frankfurt disagreements over liturgy and polity carried over into the reign of ELIZABETH.

English Calvinists, though they revered Calvin, differed from him on how they should approach matters of liturgy and church government as well as on what practices should be established. During Elizabeth's reign they disagreed over many practical issues: clerical vestments, liturgical order, church offices, clerical authority, and sermon content and style. English ecclesiastical leaders who advocated Calvin's theology of "indifferent things" modified his views to require conformity to "English ways." They adhered to traditional English worship and to the governmentally appointed church hierarchy that had come down from HENRY VIII, and they approached the English traditions as though God had ordained them specifically for English society and thus significantly modified the theology of adiaphora. Consequently, they castigated violators and critics of the ANGLICAN system as "precisians" or "PURITANS" who had unacceptable loyalties. Practically, that system became embodied in Elizabethan ecclesiastical laws and was promoted by Archbishops MATTHEW PARKER and JOHN WHITGIFT and by bishops such as Richard Cox and John Jewel, author of *Apologia Ecclesiae Anglicanae*. Various ideas were incorporated into this Anglican view, including the notion that it was closest to what the early church fathers had created, plus the coherent theology of John Calvin. Thus, proponents of this version of English Protestantism are correctly labelled "English Calvinists," though ecclesiastical practices were to follow traditional English usage as enacted by English law and administered by bishops and ecclesiastical commissions.

The more famous admirers of Calvin, the "precisians" or "puritans," modified the Genevan Reformer's ideas in two ways: they claimed to have discovered the most biblical way to worship and to organize the church, and they adhered to scholastic methods when doing theology. For the most part these puritans remained within the Church of England and hoped for better times, that is, a time when their version of Scripture, not national customs, would fully prescribe English theology and ecclesiastical practices. Proponents of this view saw in Geneva the best example of contemporary biblical Christianity and tried to change Anglican ways to reflect Genevan Calvinism. First, they criticized liturgical practices, such as how the communion table was to be positioned (they opposed any resemblance to an altar), and prescribed holy days, baptismal practices (especially baptism by women), and clerical vestments. This last matter became especially famous in the VESTIARIAN CONTROVERSY of the 1560s. Thomas Sampson and Lawrence Humphrey, along with other clerics, were deprived of their ecclesiastical offices for refusing to wear the clerical surplice. They preferred the Genevan scholar's gown instead. Puritan Calvinists saw the clerical surplice and the other practices cited above as evidence that England was not as fully Reformed as Calvinist Geneva had become.

Second, puritans criticized how the Church of England was organized and governed, for they saw among Dutch and Genevan Calvinists a more biblical system of discipline and church polity, Presbyterianism. Presbyterianism involved clerical-lay cooperation in that clerical and lay leaders were approved by congregations and employed a system of mutual discipline by means of consistories, classes, and synods rather than by means of a governmentally appointed hierarchy and ecclesiastical commissions. Some Presbyterians, such as Thomas Cartwright, became exile spokesmen for radical puritanism, while others, such as Edward Dering and Laurence Chaderton, conformed to the Anglican polity. The conformists, however, did continue to press for change. They promoted it in Parliament, in Cambridge University, and in a "classical" movement within the Church of England. Clerics in Cambridge and in the broader classical movement, for example, employed a system of mutual censorship by means of prophetic exercises. This involved meeting with colleagues to exegete texts and to criticize each other's views, the desired result being a Scriptural sermon that fulfilled the preacher's true calling—biblical prophet.

Orthodox doctrine and proper theological methods also became issues among English Calvinists, largely because most Calvinists found it necessary to refine the doctrine of election. Anglican doctrine held to predestination as it had been briefly stated by John Calvin, and this orthodoxy was sufficient for most leaders in the Elizabethan church. Genevan, French, and Dutch Calvinists, however, refined the doctrine by employing scholastic techniques as well as biblical scholarship, and the puritan Calvinists followed this newer path to Calvinist orthodoxy. Broadly termed "Protestant scholasticism," among English puritans such as William Perkins and William Ames this meant using the Ciceronian scholastic technique developed by Petrus Ramus. Other puritans, such as Laurence Chaderton, used the scholastic methods that Peter Martyr Vermigli and Theodore Beza had derived from Aristotle and the medieval scholastics.

The most famous product of Calvinist scholasticism was federal, or covenant theology, which emphasized double predestination as the means of CALVINISM, salvation and reprobation and sanctification as the means of assurance; however, this highly systematized version of Calvin's theology was not accepted by all theologians. In the 1590s at Cambridge University, William Barrett and Peter Baro raised the issues of assurance of salvation and the efficacy of Christ's death and opposed the "Calvinist" majority, who emphasized reprobation and federal theology. Archbishop Whitgift, though he opposed the puritan Calvinists' Presbyterian and iconoclastic views, supported their version of predestination and incorporated it in his Lambeth Articles. Whitgift's successor, Richard Bancroft, refused to support this type of Calvinism and opted instead to allow continued discussion of the theological issues that divided Calvinists and Lutherans alike—predestination, reprobation, assurance of salvation. While the THIRTY-NINE ARTICLES contained a statement of election that would satisfy John Calvin, Calvinists continued to disagree on the full meaning of the doctrine.

As seen above, English Calvinism in Tudor England was a widespread movement composed of various, often hostile factions that disagreed over liturgy, theology, and church polity. Historians such as M. M. Knappen (*Tudor Puritanism*, 1939), William Haller (*The Rise of Puritanism*, 1938), and John T. McNeill (*The History and Character of Calvinism*, 1954) juxtapose Puritan Calvinism against a broader Anglicanism. That view has been challenged by a wide range of scholars who come to the subject from various angles. Basil Hall, in "Calvin Against the Calvinists" (in G. E. Duffield, ed., *John Calvin*, 1966), emphasizes the differences between John Calvin and the scholastic Calvinists who followed Beza, while Perry Miller (*The New England Mind*, 1939) traces the course of Ramus's scholasticism in radical puritan thought. Others emphasize a broad, evangelical consensus in Tudor England. Patrick Collinson (*The Religion of Protestants*, 1982), Nicholas Tyacke (*Anti-Calvinists: The Rise of English Arminianism*, 1987), and Peter Lake (*Moderate Puritans and the Elizabethan Church*, 1982) pursue this consensus view with abundant research. Though with great merit, this latter approach may too successfully play down what were critical disagreements within English Calvinism. The various factions within English Calvinism could all lay claim to Calvinist orthodoxy, depending on the point at which they chose to stop reforming the Church of England and to stop refining John Calvin's theology. The vestments dispute of the 1560s, the ADMONITION CONTROVERSY of the 1570s and 1580s, and the doctrinal conflicts within Cambridge University were all struggles among English Calvinists. While they can be seen, in part, as stemming from an anti-popish, Protestant consensus, they also illustrate diverse understandings of what it meant to have a properly reformed Christianity. Disagreements among Tudor English Calvinists produced bitter results in the seventeenth century.

Bibliography: G. E. Duffield, ed., *John Calvin*, 1966; Peter Lake, *Moderate Puritans and the Elizabethan Church*, 1982.

Ronald J. VanderMolen

Campbell, Archibald, 5th Earl of Argyll (c. 1535-1573). Archibald Campbell was born in the mid-1530s, son of the 4th earl, whom he succeeded in 1558. Thus in his mid-twenties he became one of the most important nobles in SCOTLAND. This importance was shown by the fact that in the same year that he became earl he was commissioned, along with JAMES STEWART, prior of St. Andrews, the half brother of MARY, QUEEN OF SCOTS and later the earl of Moray, to take the maternal Crown to the Dauphin of France, whom Mary married. He refused the commission, perhaps because he favored the Protestant Reform movement, as he had in 1557 when he signed the band of the "Lords of the Congregation of Jesus Christ," the alliance of the Protestant nobility.

In spite of his professed Protestantism, he was one of those nobles who gave their allegiance to Mary of Guise, the Queen Mother and regent. Although known to be a Protestant, he was a member of Mary's council, and when troubles developed in Perth, he was one of the commissioners who arranged a treaty with the Lords of the Congregation. When this peace was broken by the regent's forces, he joined the Congregation. At this time Argyll was actively negotiating with the English and was, to a considerable extent, responsible for obtaining their help in expelling the French forces sent to support Mary of Guise. However, when Mary, Queen of Scots returned from France in August 1561, after her husband's death, he gave her his support, which she appreciated, even calling herself his sister, and made him a privy councillor. This all changed when she married HENRY STEWART, Lord Darnley. Argyll opposed the marriage and as a result was forced into exile.

On his return to Scotland a short time later, it is suspected that he may have been involved in Darnley's murder. It is certain that he was opposed to Mary's next marriage to JAMES HEPBURN, earl of Bothwell. Argyll apparently favored her imprisonment in Lochleven Castle and carried the sword of state at the coronation of her young son, JAMES VI. All this changed again when Mary escaped, for he then became a commander of her forces and led the army supporting her at the battle of LANGSIDE in May 1568. His swooning at the beginning of the battle may have been one of the causes for the defeat of the royalist forces and resulted in Mary's flight to England. In 1570 he finally submitted to James VI and was restored to his position as a privy councillor.

With the appointment of JAMES DOUGLAS, earl of Morton, as governor, in 1572 Argyll again came into prominence, being appointed lord high chancellor of the realm for life. He did not enjoy this office for very long as he died on 12 September 1573 and was succeeded by his brother Colin. Argyll was married twice, first to Jane, the natural daughter of JAMES V, in 1561, but he divorced her in 1571. He then married Jane, daughter of Alexander Cunningham, the 5th earl of Glencairn, in June 1573. He had no legitimate offspring but fathered three illegitimate sons and two illegitimate daughters.

Bibliography: Jane Dawson, "The fifth Earl of Argyle, Gaelic Lordship and Political Power in Sixteenth-Century Scottland," *Scottish Historical Review* 67 (1988): 1-27.

W. Stanford Reid

Canon Law. Throughout medieval Christendom obedience was owed to the church's rules or canons imposed by authority in matters of faith, morals, and discipline. While England was not known for its canonists, William Lyndwood codified the English provincial canon law, understood as subject to Roman canon law, in the fifteenth century. His *Provinciale*, first published in 1432 and accepted by both Canterbury and York CONVOCATIONS, thus became the law enforced by the CHURCH COURTS in England. It was printed in English in 1534, the same year Parliament acted to pursue recodification of the canon law.

The REFORMATION PARLIAMENT, which met from 1529 through 1536, convened under the shadow of HENRY VIII's attempt to have his marriage to CATHERINE OF ARAGON invalidated by the papacy. Attempting to intimidate the pope and weaken resistance from the English clergy, the king used Parliament's anti-clericalism to end the clergy's independent ecclesiastical jurisdiction, including the enactment and enforcement of canon law. The assault on the Church began when PRAEMUNIRE charges were brought against THOMAS WOLSEY, later leading clerics, and finally in 1531 the whole clergy. The latter were charged for their exercise of independent jurisdiction in ecclesiastical courts. By buying a pardon, however, the clergy for the moment maintained the church's independent exercise of ecclesiastical jurisdiction and thus, the integrity of canon law.

In 1532, following the COMMONS SUPPLICATION AGAINST THE ORDINARIES, the king presented three articles to convocation demanding that the clergy give up their independent power to legislate. The first required the king's license for any new law; the second, that a committee of thirty-two (including sixteen clergy and sixteen lay members of the upper or lower houses of Parliament) study canon law and decide what should remain and what should be excluded; and finally, that the remaining laws have the king's approval. Existing canons would remain in force as long as they did not conflict with laws, statutes, and customs of the realm or damage the ROYAL PREROGATIVE. Threatened with parliamentary action on these matters and implicitly with charges of praemunire, convocation, after much discussion and protest and in a diminished form (which has been characterized as a "rump"), submitted to the king's demands. In 1534 Parliament passed a bill confirming the SUBMISSION OF THE CLERGY (25 Hen. VIII, c. 19). Since no committee to examine canon law had been appointed in the interim, the act called for a committee of thirty-two to do so. While it appears that an informal working group of four had completed a draft for recodification in the autumn of 1535, no committee as authorized by the statute was appointed, and Parliament reenacted this bill in 1536 and added a three-year deadline for completion of the committee's work from the end of Parliament's meeting (27 Hen. VIII, c. 15). THOMAS CROMWELL may have hoped the deadline would speed completion of the project. Still, no committee was appointed, and in 1544 another statute extended the king's authority to appoint the commission over his lifetime (35 Hen. VIII, c. 16). This statute differed from previous measures in that a collection of new laws rather than one of old, unobjectionable laws was required. In January 1546 Archbishop THOMAS CRANMER, at the king's request, made arrangements for the draft completed some ten years earlier to be forwarded to the king. This survives in the British Library and is prefaced by a letter from the king, written to give it legal force. However, no committee was appointed, and a recodified canon law was not effected during Henry's lifetime. (Henry's letter, however, prefaced JOHN FOXE's 1571 edition of the Edwardian manuscript of reformed canon law, published with some Elizabethan modifications, even though the contents of this manuscript differed considerably from the Henrician.)

In 1535 Henry VIII prohibited the study of canon law (which he thought popish) at Oxford and Cambridge, with the result that the civil law and lawyers grew dominant in the English church courts. In 1545 a statute (37 Hen. VIII, c. 17) authorized doctors of civil law to practice in the courts Christian even if they were lay and married. The civilians educated themselves in canon law both by working in the church courts and by studying in the great library at Doctors' Commons, established in London in 1511 for advocates practicing in ecclesiastical courts. It survived until 1857.

The project for reforming the canon law resumed during the reign of EDWARD VI. In 1547 the lower house of convocation presented Archbishop Cranmer with a petition asking that the long deferred commission of thirty-two be appointed. In 1550 a bill revived the scheme for revision of canon law by a commission of thirty-two, authorizing a working period of three years, dating from the first day of the session, 4 November 1549 (3 and 4 Edw. VI, c. 11). For reasons not clear, Cranmer and several bishops, including both Conservatives and Reformists, did not support the bill. On 6 October 1551, the privy council directed the lord chancellor to commission 32 named persons, including eight each of bishops, theologians, civilians, and common lawyers, for the work on canon law, but it is uncertain that they were actually commissioned. A subcommittee of eight of these, including Cranmer and the theologian Peter Martyr, received 4 November 1551 a commission to work on the project and draft a code for subsequent revision and ratification by the whole committee of 32. The membership of this subcommittee was changed in a subsequent commission on 11 November 1551. An extant commission shows that on 12 February 1552 the commission of 32 was constituted, with several changes from the list of 6 October 1551. The work proceeded, with Cranmer and Peter Martyr contributing substantially, but apparently it was foreseen some months ahead of time that it might not be completed by the deadline. A bill was brought into Parliament to extend the time, but it was not passed, and at the king's death 6 July 1553 the project, though substantially complete, had received no further official attention. While it is known that the king was eager for the reform of the canon law, JOHN DUDLEY, duke of Northumberland, may have opposed authorization of the collection, to which in 1571 John Foxe, with no apparent authorization from the manuscript, gave the title *Reformatio legum ecclesiasticarum.*

Perhaps obstacles to its ratification were created by the document's passage on the eucharist, which made clear that bread and wine remained after consecration. While the document also made substantial revision of the laws on matrimony, it left traditional control of such matters as marriage, tithes, testaments, perjury, slander, and benefices in the ecclesiastical courts. Heresy would still have been tried in church courts, which would have handed recalcitrant offenders, "all other remedies having been exhausted", to the secular arm for burning.

The document disappeared from view during the reign of MARY and appeared again in the first Parliament of ELIZABETH's reign. A bill to appoint a committee for reforming the canon law was passed by the Commons in 1559, but it met with no success in the Lords, probably because of opposition from the court. The reform of canon law was part of the radical program presented to the lower house of convocation in 1563, and in 1571 it again came before the House of Commons. Foxe's edition of the *Reformatio* was brought into Parliament and discussed before the project was buried in committee. It undoubtedly was opposed by the queen both because of its content and because of her view that Parliament should not meddle in canon law. Cranmer's reformed code was never enacted, and no action was taken modifying canon law until 1604. Though from the time of the Submission of the Clergy there was some confusion in church courts about just what their law was, a body of law combining the old canons and statute was used.

Bibliography: R. H. Helmholz, *Roman Canon Law in Reformation England*, 1990; D. Logan, "The Henrician Canons," *Bulletin of the Institute of Historical Research* 47 (1974): 99-103.

Martha C. Skeeters

Carberry Hill, Battle of (1567). On 15 June 1567, the army of MARY, QUEEN OF SCOTS and her husband, JAMES HEPBURN, earl of Bothwell, faced that of the Confederate Lords, eight miles west of Edinburgh. To call what happened a battle, however, is a misnomer. Throughout a blazingly hot day, the armies faced each other; Bothwell was prepared for single combat, but those whom he challenged, Morton and Lord Lindsay, were not. The queen's soldiers gradually drifted away. At the end of the day, agreement was reached: Bothwell would depart, and the queen would give herself up to the Lords, who would preserve her safety and honor. It was the end for Mary Stuart. She was brought back to Edinburgh in a state of nervous collapse, and was greeted to howls from her subjects of "Burn the whore. . . kill her. . . drown her." She was taken to Lochleven Castle, where in July she miscarried of twins, and on 24 July was forced to sign her abdication. Five days later her son JAMES VI was crowned at Stirling. In August, her brother JAMES STEWART, earl of Moray, prudently absent until it was all over, as he had been in 1566, returned to threaten her with execution and to become regent. It was a terrible and a heart-rending story. Inevitably it creates sympathy for the queen and considerable reservations about the men who treated her thus.

   Yet these Confederate Lords were not simply hardheaded—and hearted—politicians, intent on her destruction. Many had been previously loyal nobles and Mary's officers of state, headed by her secretary William Maitland of Lethington. Desertion on this scale, therefore, suggests a state of desperation with Mary that could not simply be set aside, however horrible the personal consequences. Mary's actions since the murder of Darnley, beginning with her tactless breaking of the rules of royal mourning and going on to her frantic creation of faction with the Bothwell marriage, and the increasingly visible evidence that a monarch who had never given strong direction to affairs was now wholly incapable of rule, had forced even those who had supported her into the recognition that she was impossible to serve. It might have been said of her, as Archbishop William Laud said of her grandson Charles I, that she "knew not how to be or be made great." Some like the earls of Huntley and Erroll, solved their problem by staying away; others threw in their lots with men like Glencairn and Morton, opponents of the queen since the years 1565-1566. By doing so, they ensured a brutal but perhaps inevitable end to four years of lack of rule and two of ever-increasing misrule.

Bibliography: Gordon Donaldson, *All the Queen's Men*, 1983; Jenny Wormald, *Mary Queen of Scots: A Study in Failure*, 1988.

Jenny Wormald

Carthusian Martyrs (1535). The Carthusians, who had only nine English houses, were the strictest and most respected of the religious orders in early Tudor England. The order, especially its London house, proved the most willing to resist the ecclesiastical revolution of the 1530s. The London prior, John Houghton, and proctor, Humphrey Middlemore, initially refused the oath to the succession in 1534, but Edward Lee, archbishop of York, persuaded them to swear it. However, the explicit repudiation of papal supremacy required of them in 1535 was too much. Houghton, together with the priors of Axholme and Beauvale (Augustine Webster and Robert Lawrence), was summoned before THOMAS CROMWELL. Having refused the oath of supremacy, they were committed to the Tower and were tried for high treason on 28 April, together with Richard Reynolds (of the Bridgettine house at Syon) and John Hale (vicar of Isleworth). Their defense, that they had not "maliciously" denied the supremacy, initially impressed the jury, but, after a judicial ruling that any denial was ipso facto malicious, the jury, threatened by Cromwell, found them guilty. On 4 May they were hung, drawn, and quartered. The resistance of the London house did not end here. Three more members (Middlemore, William Exmew, and Sebastian Newdigate) were arrested, condemned, and executed on 19 June. In 1536 four remaining ringleaders, Maurice Chauncy, John Foxe, John Rochester, and James Walworth, were sent away, the first two to Beauvale Charterhouse, the others to Hull. After the PILGRIMAGE OF GRACE, Rochester and Walworth were executed for denying the supremacy (11 May 1537). Meanwhile, the remaining thirty London Carthusians were subjected for two years to the rule of William Trafford, whose own initial rejection of the supremacy had been overcome by a personal interview with Cromwell in 1535. On 18 May 1537 all but ten of them swore to the supremacy. Soon afterward they surrendered their house. The other ten were left to starve in Newgate jail. Only one, William Horne, survived the summer—to be executed on 4 August 1540. The other charterhouses gave way without overt resistance, although Mount Grace was reluctant. The prior, John Wilson, was won round by Cuthbert Tunstall, bishop of Durham. Even so, he had to imprison four of his brethren for several months before they would conform; and it was from Mount Grace that George Lazenby, a Cistercian of Jervaulx, had received the advice that led him to martyrdom in 1535. Many Carthusians were clearly malcontents. In the 1540s, after the dissolution, Maurice Chauncy and several others fled abroad to resume their Carthusian profession at Bruges. Under MARY I, Chauncy led some of them back to refound the house at Sheen, where they were joined by fifteen other former Carthusians, including Wilson and the last prior of Witham, John Mitchell. In the first year of Elizabeth's reign, Chauncy accepted the government's offer of exile and led his small community for the last time from England's shores.

Bibliography: M. Chauncy, *The Passion and Martyrdom of the Holy English Carthusian Fathers*, translated and edited by G. W. S. Curtis, 1935; L. E. Whatmore, *The Carthusians under King Henry VIII*, Analecta Cartusiana 109, 1983.

Richard Rex

Catherine of Aragon (1485-1536). Queen and first wife of HENRY VIII, born on 16 December 1485, at Alcala de Henares, Catherine was the youngest child of Isabella of Castile and Ferdinand of Aragon. At the age of three she was betrothed to Arthur, Prince of Wales, and during childhood at the itinerant and tumultuous Spanish court, she was educated to be a queen. The lessons of Catherine and her sisters ranged from sewing and baking to hunting and falconry. They also read devotional works and received instruction in the classics from the leading humanists who were their tutors.

Catherine was only fifteen years old when she arrived in England in October 1501. She and the fourteen-year-old Arthur were married on 14 November in St. Paul's Cathedral. In spite of their youth it was decided that they should live together, and before Christmas they moved their court to Ludlow in Wales. The evidence, however, supports Catherine's later testimony that the marriage had not been consummated when Arthur died on 2 April 1502.

The young widow settled her household in London, with debts piling up as negotiations began for her marriage to the new Prince of Wales, the future king Henry VIII. Although the parties agreed that her marriage to Arthur had not been consummated, the Spanish nevertheless insisted on a dispensation from Rome removing the potential canonical impediment to the marriage. The ensuing treaty, concluded on 23 June 1503, called for a two-year waiting period until Henry reached the age of fourteen. In the meantime Catherine and her suite would live as guests of HENRY VII. In 1504, however, when Isabella died and Ferdinand's position was altered and weakened, Henry VII delayed the marriage and cut off Catherine's allowance. Her father also refused to contribute to her expenses. There followed extremely difficult years when those close to Catherine advised her to give up hopes for the marriage and leave England. She refused, and her endurance was rewarded. Upon the death of Henry VII in April 1509, English policy changed, and her marriage to the heir went forward. Henry and Catherine were married at Greenwich on 11 June, and on Midsummer's Day, Catherine, wearing white, was borne through the streets on a glittering litter to be crowned with her husband at Westminster.

The young couple began their marriage amidst continuous festivities; the new king took great pleasure in performing for his wife, perhaps his first love, in tournaments and masks, and basked in her approval. Their early years together were happy. They shared their mutual interests in the New Learning, in hunting, music, and dancing. They also shared an interest in foreign affairs, and the young king received with respect Catherine's experienced and intelligent judgment. Early in the reign her influence brought a renewal of the alliance with Spain, and when the king fought in France during the summer and autumn of 1513, he had her proclaimed governor of the realm. During his absence she was largely responsible for the success of English troops against the Scots at FLODDEN in September. In the following year, after her father proved a treacherous ally, Catherine withdrew from advising her husband in diplomatic matters and rarely intervened thereafter.

Catherine began the first duty of a queen, bearing children, within a few months of her marriage, but between 1509 and 1518, pregnancy after pregnancy (at least six) left only one surviving child, MARY, born on 18 February 1516. As her mother had done before her, Catherine took pains with the education of her daughter, turning to the prominent Spanish humanist, Juan Luis Vives, to develop a program of education for her. He, in turn, dedicated to Catherine his treatise, *The Instruction of a Christian Woman*.

Henry's disappointment at the lack of a male heir was assuaged by the betrothal of Mary to Catherine's nephew, the emperor Charles V, in 1522. Their son would inherit the Habsburg and Tudor lands. When in 1525 Charles changed his mind in favor of marrying a Portuguese princess, Henry was angry and disappointed. While the queen's personal and political significance diminished along with her youth and declining reproductive capacity, she still did not fear for her position as wife. If she noticed the king's dalliance with ANNE BOLEYN, she undoubtedly thought little of it. It was not his first infidelity. When she got wind of the king's secret plans for divorce in May 1527, she was outraged, but she blamed THOMAS WOLSEY, her longtime enemy, completely; she remained to the end a loyal apologist for Henry. However, when faced with Henry's assertion that theirs was no marriage because she was, in fact, his brother's wife, Catherine took an unwavering position. She knew she was a virgin when she had married Henry, and he knew it, too. Thus, she was the king's lawful wife. Between 1527 and 1533 she rejected assertions to the contrary from deputations of dignitaries and refused suggestions that she enter a nunnery. Although she denied the authority of the court that convened at Blackfriars to consider the case in June 1529, she confronted the king there publicly for the only time; she dropped to her knees before him to speak and put it to his conscience whether or not she was "a true maid" when "ye had me at the first." Henry was silent; he never testified on the point.

With her many pleas to the emperor and the pope unheeded, Catherine faced lonely, desolate years with few stalwart friends. She saw Henry for the last time in 1531 when, without saying goodbye, he rode off from Windsor in a hunting party that included Anne Boleyn. Her humiliation was complete when he married the pregnant Anne in 1533. By the time the pope spoke out, on 23 March 1534, it was far too late. Parliament had secured the succession for Anne's baby daughter, ELIZABETH, born in September 1533, and pronounced the Princess Mary a bastard. Moreover, the separation of the English church from Rome was underway.

Throughout, Catherine refused to relinquish the title of queen or compromise her conscience in spite of ill treatment and fear of poisoning. Moved from house to house, denied the company of her daughter, bereft of her jewels, her household impoverished, she still refused to be other than a loyal wife and queen. She made no attempt to escape and refused to countenance the imperial ambassador Eustace Chapuys's plans for a rebellion, even though the imperial ambassador had proven himself her faithful friend and tireless advocate.

Under these stressful circumstances, Catherine died at Kimbolton, Huntingdonshire, on 7 January 1536. While at the time her poisoning was rumored, it is likely that she died of cancer of the heart. She held to the end that she was Henry's lawful and loving wife, writing him on the morning of her death that above all things she desired to see him again and assuring him of her forgiveness. She was buried with the ceremony accorded a dowager princess, a title she had always refused, in Peterborough Abbey.

Much loved by the English people, Catherine of Aragon had, under the most difficult of circumstances, shown herself a woman of principle and endurance. Moreover, she never retreated from the purpose for which she was born, for which she set sail from Spain in 1501—to marry a king and set the descendants of Isabella and Ferdinand on his throne. When her daughter Mary ascended the throne in 1553, history proved her successful.

Bibliography: G. Mattingly, *Catherine of Aragon*, 1950.

Martha Skeeters

Cecil, Robert (1563-1612). Robert Cecil was Queen ELIZABETH's leading advisor in the final years of her reign. He was born, slightly deformed by a hunchback, on 1 June 1563. Robert was the second son of WILLIAM CECIL, Lord Burghley, and of Mildred, the daughter of Sir Anthony Cooke. His early education was by private tutor, but in about 1579 he began to attend St. John's College, Cambridge, and in 1584 he travelled in France, where he briefly studied at the Sorbonne. Cecil sat for Westminster in the Parliaments of 1584 and 1586 and for Hertfordshire from 1589. In 1588 he was a member of Henry Stanley, earl of Derby's unsuccessful mission to the Spanish Netherlands to negotiate peace with Spain. Cecil married Elizabeth, daughter of Lord Cobham, in the following year. He was knighted by the queen at Theobalds in May 1591 and sworn a member of the PRIVY COUNCIL in August. It was in the 1590s that his real service to the Crown began.

Sir Robert was groomed for power by his father, and he was already ably carrying out the work of secretary of the state long before he was officially appointed to that post in 1596. The pressures of intermittent naval warfare with Spain, war in IRELAND, and a series of bad harvests placed considerable strain on the Elizabethan system of government (see LATE ELIZABETHAN CRISES). Moreover, the 1590s saw a crisis of political leadership. Between 1588 and 1591 ROBERT DUDLEY, earl of Leicester; Sir Walter Mildmay; Sir FRANCIS WALSINGHAM; and Sir CHRISTOPHER HATTON—leading royal advisors—all died. ROBERT DEVEREUX, earl of Essex, took their place as a rival focus of power to the Cecils and brought a new bitterness to factional struggles. He was a rival determined to monopolize all patronage at court, and he and Cecil soon clashed over the expenses of the CADIZ EXPEDITION (1596). Further conflict arose over which of them should obtain the profitable and powerful post of master of the Court of Wards, which fell vacant on the death of Lord Burghley in 1598; Sir Robert secured the appointment. Cecil maneuvered Essex into accepting the virtually impossible task of subduing Ireland, and the latter's unauthorized return on September 1599 after only six months—and after making an ill-judged truce with the earl of Tyrone—gave Cecil the upper hand. Essex fell from royal favor, and his disastrous attempted coup of February 1601 completed his destruction and left the way open for Cecil to "rule both court and crown."

Factional problems were not the only ones faced by Cecil. The enormous cost of the Irish wars added greatly to royal financial difficulties. The Crown responded by requests for additional parliamentary subsidies, but Cecil also began to explore extra-parliamentary means of obtaining income. His exploitation of MONOPOLIES resulted in the vigorous expression of discontent by members of the House of Commons in 1601, despite Cecil's somewhat tactless attempts to silence complaints. Though Sir Robert was an outstanding administrator, he rarely displayed much skill in managing the House of Commons. Under pressure, Elizabeth and Cecil revised their policy on monopolies and withdrew those patents that caused most complaint, while attempting to retain the theoretical ROYAL PREROGATIVE to impose others should circumstances allow.

Later, under JAMES VI and I, Cecil went on to try to obtain firm legal support for extra-parliamentary levies by engineering Bate's Case (1606) as a test case for impositions. The Great Contract of 1610 was Cecil's final attempt to establish a more rational, efficient basis for the royal finances by exchanging feudal fiscal rights of wardship and purveyance for a regular land tax income; however, it met with no success.

The fall of Essex also enabled Cecil to establish good relations with James VI and to insure the king's peaceful succession to the Crown of England on Elizabeth's death. Essex had done his best to convince James that Cecil was firmly opposed to the Stuarts and plotting for the accession of the Spanish Infanta; indeed, he accused Cecil of this at his trial, and Catholics abroad—such as Robert Parsons—promoted the rumor. Furthermore, Elizabeth—as Cecil well knew—was implacably opposed to any action to guarantee her successor's claim. These factors conspired to ensure the secrecy and caution of Cecil's dealing with James VI; he even dismissed his private secretary, Simon Willis, to prevent him from discovering these negotiations.

When James gained the English throne, he displayed his gratitude for Sir Robert's assistance by elevating him to the peerage as Baron Cecil of Essindene in 1603, and he was later given the title of Viscount Cranborne (1604) and then earl of Salisbury (1605). From 1608 he held the office of lord treasurer. Cecil acted as James's leading adviser until ill health cut short his career. In 1612 he died of cancer.

Cecil did not succeed in solving all the problems of the late Elizabethan era. As a politician he was skillful in his manipulation of Essex's weaknesses, of Catholic divisions, and of royal fiscal prerogatives. Like his father, he was a conscientious administrator who chose his servants well and enriched his family, while still serving the monarch faithfully. Cecil did help to ensure the smooth transition from the Tudor to the Stuart dynasty, but many of the difficulties that faced the former lived on to plague the latter.

Bibliography: A. Cecil, *A Life of Robert Cecil, First Earl of Salisbury*, 1915; P. M. Handover, *The Second Cecil: The Rise to Power 1563-1604 of Sir Robert Cecil, Later First Earl of Salisbury*, 1959.

J. P. Sommerville

Cecil, Sir William, Lord Burghley (1520-1598). PRINCIPAL SECRETARY and lord treasurer in the reign of ELIZABETH I, Cecil was born and baptized at Bourne, Lincolnshire, but spent most of his youth at Stamford. In 1535 he was admitted to St. John's College, Cambridge University. He left the university without taking a degree and continued his education in the law at Gray's Inn. This educational step may have been dictated by his father, who tried to prevent his marriage to Mary, the sister of the Protestant scholar, Sir John Cheke. The marriage took place however, and a son, Thomas, was born in 1542. Cecil's election to Parliament in the same year launched his long and distinguished political career. His first wife died in 1544, and he then married Mildred, the well-educated daughter of Sir Anthony Cooke, an increasingly important courtier. This marriage connection probably led to his introduction to EDWARD SEYMOUR, Lord Protector Somerset.

Cecil served his apprenticeship for high government office in the reign of EDWARD VI. He entered Somerset's service in 1547 and helped organize the army for the invasion of Scotland, where he fought at the battle of Pinkie. On his return, he was elected to Edward VI's first Parliament. In 1548, when his friend from Cambridge days, Sir Thomas Smith, became a secretary of state and was sent abroad, he replaced him as one of Somerset's personal secretaries and as master of requests in the protector's household. There he gained valuable experience. Cecil survived the first political crisis of his career in October 1549, when Somerset was removed from power. He was with the protector when he was arrested; he was put in the Tower, but by 25 January 1550 he had secured his release and soon found favor with JOHN DUDLEY, earl of Warwick, who made him a secretary of state and a privy councillor in September 1550. His position as secretary placed him at the center of power, yet in 1553 he was not one of the councillors fatally implicated in the attempt to substitute the Protestant LADY JANE GREY for the Catholic MARY Tudor after Edward VI's death. He signed the documents to alter the succession, and with his fellow councillors proclaimed Lady Jane queen, but when the tide turned, he was one of the first to seek Mary's pardon after she had been proclaimed queen on 19 July 1553. Mary I did not retain Cecil as a secretary or as a member of the privy council primarily for religious reasons, but he continued to sit in Parliament during the reign and performed other tasks for the Marian government.

Elizabeth I fully recognized and utilized Cecil's particular political and administrative talents. She had employed Cecil as her surveyor since 1550, and she probably interpreted his conformity during Mary's reign as admirable obedience to his ruler. His appointment as her principal secretary at the very beginning of her reign was one of Elizabeth's most astute decisions. A practical, pragmatic politician, he became her most trusted advisor. Cecil's willingness to do the long hours of administrative work for his queen and his prodigious written record attest to his central role in the development of many successful Elizabethan programs. For the first meeting of the new council on 20 November 1558, Cecil prepared a long, sensible list of military, diplomatic, legal, economic, religious, and even routine measures designed to secure Elizabeth's smooth succession to the throne and to help the new ruler begin to extricate England from its precarious situation. The reaction of Philip II and the pope to a Protestant queen was uncertain. England was at war with France; peace needed to be negotiated quickly to alleviate the financial strain of war and to provide some external stability until urgent internal problems, such as the religious settlement, could be resolved. The first steps toward the religious settlement were taken in the 1559 Parliament with Cecil's aid. As a member of Parliament and the queen's secretary, Cecil was in a position to play a central role in the House of Commons as it fashioned a compromise between Catholic and Protestant theology and ecclesiastical governance. While Cecil served his queen effectively in helping her obtain the famous *via media*, which characterized ANGLICANISM in later years, he personally wanted a more thoroughly Protestant England. He worked steadily toward that end as Elizabeth's trusted advisor and as master of the Court of Wards, where he was able to influence the education of minor Catholic heirs. By the end of Elizabeth's critical first year as queen, Cecil had proved his worth; peace had been concluded with France, and a religious settlement had been enacted without serious disruption at home or abroad. Cecil then turned his attention to the fiscal reforms begun in Mary's reign. The recoinage of 1560, achieved with the advice of Sir Thomas Smith and the aid of the experienced Sir Walter Mildmay, put royal finance on firmer ground. Simultaneously, the question of the insistence of Scotland's MARY, QUEEN OF SCOTS on her claim to the English throne, and Elizabeth's marriage and the succession became pressing issues. Like all other councillors, Cecil believed the queen should marry as soon as possible to secure a peaceful succession, but the councillors did not always agree on the candidates, and Cecil found himself at odds with the royal favorite, ROBERT DUDLEY, later earl of Leicester. Elizabeth's resistance to marriage proved a difficult political challenge. When persistent conciliar pressure did not move the queen, Cecil and others first devised a plan to provide for the succession if the queen died without a designated heir and continued the pressure on her through Parliament. Although Cecil sympathized with the Protestants and opposed Catholic powers in foreign relations, he was not ideological and consistently worked to preserve England's safety in an increasingly hostile European world. Still, when the threats to his queen or country became serious enough, he advised firm action. He supported the defense of the Netherlands against Spain, opposition to the Holy League, and the execution of Mary, Queen of Scots.

Over the years as PRINCIPAL SECRETARY and then as lord treasurer after 1572, Cecil's advice to his queen was not always popular with his fellow councillors or courtiers, but to say there were factions in Elizabeth's government is to exaggerate the disagreements. In general, Cecil tended to identify with or lead the Protestants and the noninterventionists on the council. He often disagreed with the favorite Robert Dudley over the candidates for the queen's hand in marriage and over the conduct of foreign policy, but religious preference and loyalty to Elizabeth united them. The Conservative, Catholic northerners singled him out for criticism at the time of the NORTHERN REBELLION in 1569; at times critics temporarily tried to neutralize his influence with Elizabeth, but she knew how valuable he was to her successful governance. As he aged, he groomed his son ROBERT as his replacement, but he continued to serve his queen personally until his death in 1598. He lived long enough to advise and support Elizabeth through most of her reign, and he deserves much of the credit for her success.

Bibliography: S. Adams, "Eliza Enthroned? The Court and Its Politics," in *The Reign of Elizabeth I*, ed. Christopher Haigh, 1984; C. Read, *Mr Secretary Cecil and Queen Elizabeth*, 1955; C. Read, *Lord Burghley and Queen Elizabeth*, 1960.

Ann Weikel

Challenge Sermon. In April 1559 the Acts of SUPREMACY and UNIFORMITY were passed by PARLIAMENT against the resistance of the Marian bishops, and the main supports of the ELIZABETHAN SETTLEMENT OF RELIGION were in place. The settlement aimed at keeping the peace by avoiding divisive precision in its doctrine and worship. It was in defense of this settlement that John Jewel preached the Challenge Sermon of 26 November 1559 at St. Paul's Cross in London.

Preaching on Cor. 11: 23, Jewel lamented that even holy things can be abused, and pointed to communion in one kind, the adoration of the Sacrament, and private Masses, as egregious examples of deviations from God's prescriptions for worship. To these points Jewel added others, including the bishop of Rome's headship of the universal church, and he challenged the Roman Catholics to provide evidence from Scripture, the Fathers, general councils, or the primitive church that any of these practices had existed during the first 600 years after Christ. If his adversaries could provide such evidence, Jewel "would give over and subscribe unto him." He repeated the sermon on two occasions in March 1560, once at court and once again at St. Paul's Cross and extended the challenge until it included twenty-seven points centering on the nature of the Mass and of the eucharist. Jewel avoided the main questions in the doctrinal debates between Protestants and Romanists and selected what he saw as the weakest aspects of the Roman Catholic position. He nevertheless viewed the issues as of major importance, since he believed that much wider conclusions about Roman Catholic teachings as a whole would follow if they could be shown to have erred on these points.

In the Challenge Sermon, Jewel took the initiative and attempted to force the Catholics on the defensive and so to counter the assumption, too often successfully instilled by the Roman church, that it was the Protestant innovators who were bound to defend every item of their platform. Furthermore, Jewel prudently aimed in the sermon "to hold only the negative" and to oblige his opponents to provide authority and support for their established ways. His negative stance provoked no hidden disagreements among the defenders of the Church of England about the precise doctrines to which it was committed.

The Catholics could not afford to ignore so public and persistent a challenge, particularly as Jewel was consecrated bishop of Salisbury in January 1560. Henry Cole, the Marian dean of St. Paul's, responded almost immediately and attempted to contest the terms of the challenge. Confined to Fleet Prison from 1560, Cole could organize no proper reply, but others took up the cause. From Louvain, Thomas Harding, John Martiall, and John Rastell all published replies to Jewel in 1564. Jewel's *A Reply unto M. Hardings Answer*, in turn, provoked responses by Nicholas Sander and Thomas Stapleton. However, the debate over the Challenge Sermon rapidly became absorbed in the wider debate between the Church of England's defenders and the Catholic exiles. The publication by Jewel of his *Apologia Ecclesiae Anglicanae* in 1562 was itself a major reason why the debate assumed broader proportions.

The significance of Jewel's Challenge Sermon lay partly in its propaganda value at a formative time in the Church of England's development. Jewel seized the initiative and placed the Protestants on the offensive. Its more lasting significance lay in the breadth of the terms in which Jewel posed his challenge. He did not base his case narrowly on the Scriptures but showed a willingness to accept the authority of the Fathers and the early church—and this was to become a significant characteristic of much that was written in defense of the Church of England in ensuing centuries.

Bibliography: J. E. Booty, *John Jewel as Apologist of the Church of England*, 1963.

J. P. Sommerville

Chancery. As the second largest department of state, the Tudors made Chancery less an administrative-political agency of royal jurisdiction and more a legal apparatus of the judicial system. Thus, the Court of Chancery soon occupied a prominent place beside other central courts.

In its medieval origins, Chancery emerged as a writing office of the Crown under the supervision of the chancellor who retained the Great Seal. By the Tudor era, the Great Seal's importance was reduced because many state documents and correspondence originated either through the Signet Seal of the king's secretary or the Privy Seal of the council. By the sixteenth century, the Court of Chancery's legal activities definitely superseded its administrative functions. The Tudors utilized Chancery as well as the Court of REQUESTS and the Court of STAR CHAMBER to provide remedies at law that both assured their own political authority and guaranteed full justice to their subjects.

As a result of various social and political changes over the years, the medieval system of COMMON LAW justice was sometimes inadequate to provide individuals with appropriate relief. The need for prerogative courts such as Chancery, Requests, and Star Chamber was not due to a Tudor scheme to rise above the restraints of the law, but rather was due to the increased litigation, which required additional courts. Controversies sometimes arose because of the courts' use of new enforcement instruments: the subpoena and the injunction, the former requiring parties to appear and the latter enjoining parties from continued actions prior to adjudication. Moreover, these courts relied on equity when no acceptable remedy was available at common law. Despite the opportunity and perhaps the temptation to abuse its prerogatives in Chancery, the Crown almost always allowed the court to secure justice for the parties without interference. In short, the Crown provided new means for remedies but did not use its influence to prejudice the outcome.

At the beginning of the Tudor period, the chancellor was regarded not only as the chief administrative officer of the council but also as the most important political official of state. That situation continued until the chancellorship of THOMAS WOLSEY. Because of his wealth, prestige, and connections, Wolsey often acted independently in his administration of Chancery. Despite his weaknesses, Wolsey possessed certain administrative skills, and he felt an obligation to provide justice to litigants in Chancery. However, his fall from political power in the late 1520s coincided with a political transformation in royal government. Because THOMAS CROMWELL was the new political force in the 1530s, the office that he held, PRINCIPAL SECRETARY, gained political ascendency over the chancellor. From that point forward, the chancellor assumed primarily a legal function in central government, and the office was most often held by lawyers instead of ecclesiastics, as in the past.

By the reign of ELIZABETH I, the narrow role of the Chancery and the chancellor was entrenched. Chancery was a court of law, and the chancellor was the chief legal officer. True, the secretarial responsibilities involving the Great Seal remained, but gone was the expectation that the chancellor would lead political affairs and that royal policy originated in Chancery. Also, while earlier equity procedure had been haphazard and vague, it became clear and public in regard to matters ranging from evidence to the quality of ink and paper. A complainant requested the issuance of a subpoena from Chancery. If it was issued, both sides prepared their pleadings by deposing witnesses and gathering evidence as well as presenting various motions. The judges' decisions might be based on either common law jurisdiction (i.e., certain writs, the Crown's business, or affairs of royal officers) or the more frequent equitable jurisdiction (i.e., when no general law applied, including matters relating to the protection of uses and trusts or enforcement of contracts, or if by the enforcement of an existing law an injustice would be done, for example, due to forgery or fraud).

The Tudors adjusted their administrations to the needs of the times. The dramatic social, economic, and religious changes wrought during the century caused them to innovate with new instruments or powers less than to modify and augment existing structures in response to needs. The increased reliance on equity in Chancery manifested the Crown's quest to solve practical dilemmas to the benefit of both the state and individuals. Tudor interest in equitable solutions furthered the growth of the concept of due process of law, which became a hallmark of later English legal principles.

Bibliography: W. J. Jones, *The Elizabethan Court of Chancery*, 1967.

Daniel W. Hollis III

Chantries, Act Dissolving the (1547). This statute (1 Edw. VI, c. 14) was a second attempt to deal with what was seen to be an undesirable remnant of medieval Catholicism, chantries consisting of foundations that provided for the saying of Masses for the dead according to the wishes of the patron.

A Henrician measure against chantries (1545, 37 Hen. VIII, c. 4) had lapsed with the death of the sovereign in 1547. Giving the Crown new revenue opportunities to exploit during strained circumstances, the bill had been aimed at endowed establishments deemed to be badly run at the time and also at the practice of dissolution by some of the patrons themselves. In addition to chantries, other matters such as guilds, colleges, hospitals, free chapels, and stipendiary priests fell within the purview of the royal intention. Where no evidence of mismanagement was involved, commissioners were nonetheless required to conduct appropriate investigations, after which some dissolutions occurred.

The question of chantries resurfaced in Parliament toward the end of 1547. By this time, the Protestant direction of state affairs had become more pro- nounced, and a hard-line approach toward practices that were deemed to rest on superstitions was being manifested. Parliamentarians expressed concern about the non-spiritual aspects of the intended process, however, as they did not wish to endanger any worthwhile social function associated with the endowments, such as schooling, relief for the underprivileged, and ultimately, hospitals. Once again, provisions were made for commissioners of inquiry, who were appointed on 14 February 1548 and who had finished their assessments by the summer of that year.

The changes associated with the act were not at all sudden but could be foreseen in the BOOK OF HOMILIES set forth by the administration in July 1547 and in the Injunctions that were applied in the fall of the same year. The principle of intercession for the dead could not be expected to survive long in any form as the focus shifted increasingly to the matter of being prepared for the final judgment.

The chantries legislation was first introduced in the House of Lords on 6 December 1547 and passed nine days later after considerable turmoil, which included the opposition of THOMAS CRANMER, archbishop of Canterbury, and other ecclesiastics. Nevertheless, lay opinion was unanimously in favor of the bill and carried the day. The bill's route in the House of Commons was more complex; after the Lords' bill was read a second time on 17 December, a new, Commons-sponsored one was evidently introduced and given all three readings on the same day (21 December). The final bill proved more acceptable since it was less embracing, removed corporations and secular guilds from the force of the measure as required in the original, and thus permitted a smoother passage through the Commons. These institutions were simply relieved of those funds that had been designated for questionable religious functions. Subsequently, the Lords accepted the Commons new bill on 24 December, and royal assent was added on the same day.

The actions aimed against chantries in 1547 were partially motivated by the usual thirst for property and shortage of funds at the ruling levels. Doubtless, the spiritual aspect carried weight with some policymakers, as the chantries' association with medieval belief systems would seem to guarantee an eventual termination.

The extent of the damage to the social fabric resulting from the stipulations of the act is open to question. On the one hand, some rural facilities appear to have perished at the time, while the government reneged on its commitment to supply new ones with the pertinent monies. On the other, the lack of governmental largesse appears to have stimulated private interests to step into the breach in some cases. Overall then, the majority of the old hospitals and schools came through the tribulations in recognizable form, and were reendowed by ROYAL PREROGATIVE by the time of Edward VI's demise. Predictably, endowments associated with lamps and obits did not fare as well. In addition, there were instances in which the government permitted towns to buy back properties formerly used as hospitals and schools and use them for new purposes (including new schools). The deleterious effects would thus appear to be not as severe nor as lasting as once surmised. Most of the incomes pertaining to the chantries were meager, and the surveys revealed that many of the assets and funds connected with the foundations had been withdrawn by the founders prior to the Dissolution.

Bibliography: Alan Kreider, *English Chantries: The Road to Dissolution*, 1979; J. J. Scarisbrick, *The Reformation and the English People*, 1984.

Andrew Penny

Chaseabout Raid (1565). There are events in the history of Scotland in which drama, dignity, and crisis give way to an element of farce. The Chaseabout Raid is one. In August 1565, the mainstay of MARY, QUEEN OF SCOTS's government, JAMES STEWART, earl of Moray, rebelled. The queen and her new husband, HENRY STEWART, Lord Darnley, naturally took action, and set off to meet the rebel army. They never did so. Mary revelled in the activity and talked of her desire to live the life of a soldier. Darnley strutted in splendid armor. Both sides "chased" round southern Scotland for some weeks, without ever making contact, until in early October Moray gave up and fled to England to suffer a public dressing down from Elizabeth, the queen who would not tolerate traitors—but who still proceeded to give him asylum.

There was, however, nothing farcical about the underlying cause. It is easy to assume that Moray rebelled out of pique, because Mary's marriage threatened his preeminent position; and certainly his claim to defend the Protestant cause did not bring him widespread Protestant support. It has also been correctly pointed out that men in the summer of 1565 did not have our advantage of hindsight about the Darnley marriage. Nevertheless, there were warning signs enough. In May 1565, the English ambassador Thomas Randolph had noted the change in Mary, now much less concerned with her realm than obsessed with Darnley. Even more alarming were other signs of change. Foreign doubts about her commitment to the Catholic cause, evident by 1564, now gave way to papal enthusiasm for the Darnley marriage; her refusal to ratify the acts of the Reformation Parliament, and abolish the Mass was now accompanied by the ominous declaration to the General Assembly of the Kirk in June that she would not jeopardize "the friendship of the king of France, the ancient ally of this realm." By September her enthusiasm for papists at home and abroad was being reported to the English court. Although Protestant fears of a Catholic League, in which the Scottish queen had a part, were unfounded, rumor had its own potency. There was, therefore, an already significant shift in Mary's attitudes and actions in the summer of the marriage to Darnley.

This shift does not make lack of support for Moray surprising. Personal animosity and rivalry played their part. Far more importantly, men at no time in Scotland readily rebelled against the monarchy; a long tradition of loyalty to the Stewart (Stuart) dynasty and the recognition of the security and stability that the Crown alone could offer meant that rulers had to go much further than Mary had as yet done to provoke open and widespread reaction. Perhaps, therefore, the notable thing about the Chaseabout Raid was not that so few supported Moray, particularly among the ranks of the Protestant lairds, but that several magnates actually did, such as ARCHIBALD CAMPBELL, earl of Argyll. It was a messy affair, in which the queen triumphed. Even so, in this event her threat to the Protestant cause was so half-hearted as to make fears on that score turn out to be groundless. But Moray was right to fear. Lack of will and ability rather than opportunity ensured Mary's failure to do anything for the Catholics, and many came to share his awareness that the Darnley marriage marked the end of political stability and the beginning of the slide to disaster.

Bibliography: Antonia Fraser, *Mary Queen of Scots*, 1969; Gordon Donaldson, *All the Queen's Men*, 1983; Maurice Lee, Jr., *James Stewart, Earl of Moray*, 1953.

Jenny Wormald

Christian Brethren. The Christian Brethren or the Brethren in Christ are difficult to describe and define because there is little evidence about them. The primary document that survives is the "Communication of Sebastian Newdigate to Mr. Denny of a Society of Christian Brethren formed for the distribution of Lutheran books," which is in JOHN FOXE's *Acts and Monuments*. Sometimes they were known as the "evangellycall brethrene," and there is the possibility that the term *Christian Brethern* was a synonym for the *known men*, a name Foxe claimed was given to the Lollards because of their claim to "know" Scripture.

Most likely the Christian Brethren were a society for the publication and distribution of proscribed books and for the subsidizing of scholars, such as WILLIAM TYNDALE, who continued their work in the comparative safety of exile on the Continent. They supported the publication of John Frith's *Burial of the Mass*, in which he denied transubstantiation. Forming an underground network of "godly lerned men which labour in the vyneyarde of the Lorde to bryng the people of this realme to the knowledge of Christes gospell," they could be found in the UNIVERSITIES, the inns of court, and the merchant community of London and among English merchants abroad.

While there was a connection between the "known men" and the Christian Brethren, not all the first Episcopal Reformers during the reign of HENRY VIII who were connected with the Christian Brethren were LOLLARDS. The Christian Brethren simply joined those who shared the cause of reform, especially the publication of books. It is difficult to determine who was a member because very early the term became a general reference to any and all Reformers. THOMAS MORE was aware of the Christian Brethren and referred to "this blessed new bitched brotherhood" and "this new broached brotherhood." THOMAS CROMWELL seems to have protected them at times. This organization linked those committed to reform in England with Reformers on the Continent, especially those at Antwerp. The existence of the Christian Brethren clearly demonstrated that the Reformation in England was under way before the rupture between Henry VIII and the papacy.

Bibliography: S. Brigden, "Thomas Cromwell and the 'brethren'," in *Law and Government Under the Tudors*, ed. C. Cross et al., 1988: 31-49; E. G. Rupp, *Studies in the Making of the English Protestant Tradition*, 1949.

Don S. Armentrout

Church Courts. Ecclesiastical courts separate from the temporal courts had existed in England since the eleventh century. They administered the CANON LAW of the Roman church (much of it publicized in England by means of local legislation), supplemented in certain respects by local customs. Their most important task was to see that clergy and laity fulfilled their religious duties. It thus fell to them to insure proper administration of the Sacraments, adequate standards of clerical conduct and competence, lay attendance at church services, sufficient repair of church buildings, and the purchase or replacement of necessary liturgical equipment. It was the courts' responsibility, too, to enforce the payment of tithes, originally designed to support the clergy, and various other dues, including oblations and mortuaries. Determination of the validity of marriages and wills (strictly speaking, testaments) also belonged to them. Matrimony was a Sacrament, and the church had successfully claimed the authority to decide in particular cases whether it had been, or could be, lawfully celebrated. The church did its utmost to discourage sexual relationships outside of marriage, and its courts punished fornication and adultery. The development of the last will, closely associated with the last rites, had been strongly encouraged by the church so as to facilitate bequests to pious uses for the health of testators' souls, and when disputes arose, the courts sought to ascertain and implement their wishes. Another major task for the courts was the punishment of defamatory words, regarded as serious breaches of Christian charity.

The church courts performed much non-contentious work, such as the probate of wills and the issue of licenses and dispensations, besides being responsible for the correction of offenders and the settlement of disputes. In correctional cases the charge was "objected" against the putative offender, who had to clear himself, especially by means of purgation—swearing his innocence and producing a specified number of compurgators who swore that they believed him. Failure in purgation normally led to the imposition of penance or, in less serious cases, to a warning to perform a neglected duty or desist from irregular behavior. In cases between parties the plaintiff or "pars actrix" had to substantiate a written statement of his or her case, usually by the production of two or more witnesses. Most cases were peacefully settled or abandoned before coming to sentence, but in those that ran the full course, judges usually dismissed successful defendants or ordered unsuccessful ones to take appropriate action, for example, to pay tithe or a legacy, solemnize a marriage, or seek the forgiveness of a defamed plaintiff. To enforce compliance with their commands, ecclesiastical judges had two main sanctions: suspension from church entry and excommunication (exclusion from dealings with other Christian people).

Within England, there were three main levels in the court hierarchy, in ascending order: the archdeaconry (two or more in most dioceses), the diocese (twenty-one before the Reformation, including four in Wales, and twenty-six afterward), and the province (two—Canterbury, by far the larger, and York). Many parishes were exempt from archdiaconal control and came under direct episcopal supervision; others were exempt from episcopal control. The scope of archdiaconal jurisdiction varied greatly from one diocese to another. At every level, the visitation, a judicial tour of the jurisdiction, was the main vehicle of supervision and correction; bishops were normally entitled to conduct one every three years. In many archdeaconries, all dioceses, and both provinces, there were also less mobile tribunals, the busiest being the consistory courts, which carried out the bulk of the non-contentious work and heard cases between parties. In practice there was usually no rigid demarcation between the types of business transacted in and out of visitations. Appeals lay from one level to the next; the episcopal and archiepiscopal consistory courts heard both appeals and cases of first instance. (The provincial consistory court of the archbishop of Canterbury, sitting in London, was called the Court of Arches, its York counterpart the Court of Chancery.) Before the Reformation the papal court acted as the jurisdictional keystone of the system above the provincial level; appeals to it were often referred to judges delegate appointed by special commissions. The resulting High Court of Delegates was henceforth the final court of appeal in ecclesiastical causes.

The relationship between the church courts and the temporal power had always been important. The precise extent of the church's jurisdiction varied from one country to another, and within medieval England it changed in the course of time as the result of a complex process of give-and-take. Writs of prohibition enabled the king's judges to remove from the church courts cases over which they claimed jurisdiction, for example, ones concerned with real property or debts and chattels not connected with marriages and testaments. (In practice the fifteenth-century church courts heard large numbers of "breach of faith" cases concerned with debt; this activity was seriously challenged only from the 1490s onward.) A number of medieval acts of Parliament were intended to regulate or limit various aspects of ecclesiastical jurisdiction; the third statute of PRAEMUNIRE (1393), one of three designed to prevent cases determinable in the king's courts from being drawn out of England, was later invoked against the English church courts, especially under HENRY VIII. The church courts also depended fairly heavily on the cooperation of the "secular arm," for example, for the arrest of obdurate excommunicates and for the execution of heretics; they had a very restricted right to imprison and could not impose fines or capital punishment.

The Reformation radically altered the position of the church courts. The existing law of the church survived, insofar as it was compatible with the laws of the realm (Act for the SUBMISSION OF THE CLERGY, 1534): new draft codes of ecclesiastical law were never implemented. But the doctrine and liturgy enforced by the church courts were fundamentally changed. The ultimate responsibility for the maintenance of religious orthodoxy was attributed to the Crown by the 1534 ACT OF SUPREMACY, including a relatively narrow definition of heresy. CONVOCATIONS continued to legislate, but only within boundaries set by the decisions of the Crown in and out of Parliament. From 1529 onwards a stream of new acts of parliament affected almost every area of the church courts' activity. The royal supremacy had tangible administrative and institutional results in the shape of royal visitations to implement major new policies (1535, 1547, 1559), the short-lived innovation of a vicegerency in spirituals (1535-1540) and the more lasting establishment of the Court of HIGH COMMISSION in 1559. With a mixed lay and clerical membership, authority to fine and imprison, and powers that extended over the whole country, this court was a uniquely effective weapon for dealing with offenders against the ecclesiastical laws.

Historians' assessments of the church courts used to be all too heavily dependent upon satirical literature and the bitter invective of their opponents—especially Protestants on the eve of the Reformation and PURITANS after it. The courts were thus widely believed to have been oppressive and corrupt and, after the years 1533-1534, increasingly archaic and ineffectual. Thorough study of their own records has helped to demonstrate their abiding usefulness to society, the extent to which their corrective jurisdiction depended upon lay support and cooperation, and the considerable demand for the remedies they offered. The latter influenced the development of the COMMON LAW in respect of matters as various as defamation, debt, uses, and usury.

Bibliography: R. H. Helmholz, *Canon Law and the Law of England*, 1987; R. A. Houlbrooke, *Church Courts and the People During the English Reformation, 1520-1570*, 1979; M. Ingram, *Church Courts, Sex and Marriage in England, 1570-1640*, 1987; R. A. Marchant, *The Church under the Law: Justice, Administration and Discipline in the Diocese of York, 1560-1640*, 1969.

Ralph Houlbrooke

Cloth. Cloth was the most important manufactured item for export and domestic consumption in Tudor England. In the high Middle Ages there had been an urban woolen cloth industry of considerable size. These cloths, however, proved inferior to those manufactured by the carefully regulated industry of Flanders. The latter depended upon the superlative wools of England, especially the fine, short staple wool produced in the Welsh Marches and Lincolnshire. By the sixteenth century, however, virtually all English wools were being draped in England; by 1550 the industry had come to employ more persons than any other occupation in the realm save farming.

All of the processes leading to the production of woolen cloth could be performed in a peasant household; thus England escaped the scrupulous regulation that characterized the town-based cloth industry of the Continent. A statute of 1552 described some three dozen kinds of English woolen cloth but this varied production fell into three broad categories: woolens, traditional worsteds, and the so-called New Draperies, which consisted of new fabrics of mixed wool and worsteds. The woolens included the traditional broadcloths, as well as kerseys, friezes, dozens, and the "cottons" of Lancashire and Wales; the woolens and worsteds came to be known as the "Old Draperies." The highest-quality broadcloths were woven in the west country—Gloucester, Wiltshire, and Somerset;

East Anglia tended to specialize in worsteds and the New Draperies; the northern counties manufactured the cheaper, coarser cloths that were worked on a narrow loom by a single weaver. The kersey was first woven in the village of Kersey in Suffolk, but the technique of manufacturing these cloths came to be disseminated to Yorkshire, Berkshire, and Hampshire. Similarly, the tiny hamlets of Castle Combe in Wiltshire and Coggeshall in Essex manufactured cloths whose fame was known in Antwerp and Frankfurt. Regardless of geography, the processes involved in production remained dependent upon what kind of cloth was made. Woolens generally used wool of medium length, though the much prized broadcloths employed the best short-staple wool available; worsteds generally used long staple wool. Woolen cloth was felted together to achieve strength, while the warp (long threads) and weft (the cross threads that run across the warp) gave strength to worsteds. Wool for the Old Draperies had to be carded, spun, and fulled; after fulling it was dried on hooks, then dressed or shorn. The last process was the dyeing, though the clothiers who carried cloth to London for export preferred cloths to go undyed and undressed, so that they might be finished by the cunning hands of the Flemish clothmakers. The worsteds underwent a similar process, though the wool was combed, not carded, and the New Draperies employed a mixture of carded and combed wool.

Though independent spinners and weavers survived in much of the north and in corporate towns where the guilds gave them protection, the clothiers or "broggers in wool" began to place themselves between the artisan and the buyers (despite the statutes of 1545 and 1552 that prohibited middlemen dealing in wool). By the end of the Tudor age there is considerable evidence that such middlemen dominated the cloth trade in the west country. While the domestic system was clearly developing, no factories had appeared, despite the enduring popular fiction associated with "Jack of Newbury," the entrepreneur behind the Winchcombe kersies that proved so popular in Antwerp. Large workshops did appear, but a single master and a handful of apprentices might easily perform all the requisite processes from carding to shearing to dyeing.

The volume of Tudor England's cloth output remains a subject of some controversy. While the Venetian ambassador in 1610 could justly observe that cloth constituted the "chief wealth of this nation," exports may be tentatively estimated, but the domestic consumption can only be guessed. P. J. Bowden's estimate that the domestic market was one-half that of exports would appear to be low; while export was the desideratum of the country clothiers, enough cloth had to be retained to meet the needs of Englishmen, and much English cloth proved too coarse for the demanding standards of the Antwerp buyers. The evidence suggests that the number of cloths exported quintupled from 1450 to 1550, with the annual cloth shipments of the MERCHANT ADVENTURERS Company exceeding three-quarters of a million pounds in value about 1560. (This figure does not include the New Draperies, which were an increasing part of the total number of cloths exported.) The Great Debasement stimulated the export of cloth to a new high by lowering the price that the buyers in Antwerp had to pay for

English wares; the attempt to revalue the COINAGE in 1551 thus led to a precipitous decline in the number of cloths shipped to Antwerp. Yet clothshipments recovered quickly to a level only slightly below that of the artificial peak of the 1540s (i.e., 100,000-110,000 shortcloths a year), and the number of cloths exported remained fairly steady between 1559 and 1603. Despite the fears of Tudor statesmen that a downturn in the cloth trade would engender widespread disorder in the clothing counties, no disturbances comparable to the agrarian rebellions of the years 1548-1549 ever developed.

The export trade remained firmly in the hands of the Merchant Adventurers of England, the chartered company that during the first half of the sixteenth century displaced the Merchants of the STAPLE as the greatest TRADING COMPANY of the realm. The country clothiers reached them through the great cloth market maintained in London at Blackwell Hall on Basinghall Street. There the clothiers came each week with their packs of cloth (standard broadcloths were 26-28 yards in length and 1.75 yards in width, though broadcloths were actually "cloths of account," which only tenuously corresponded to actual goods sold) from Thursday to Saturday to sell their wares to individual Adventurers or privileged foreigners such as the merchants of the STEELYARD (the Hanseatic League). The cloths were transported and sold in packs of ten, each weighing seventy pounds; their care involved considerable labor, for they had to be regularly unfolded and brushed to prevent damage by moths.

Most of the cloth brought to London was destined for sale in the four annual marts held in Antwerp and its dependency, Bergen-op-Zoom. The broadcloths purchased in these Brabant towns usually ended up in Germany, while the kersies and dozens were sold chiefly in Italy and the Mediterranean countries. Dyed cloths constituted a small proportion of goods sold abroad and were sent mainly to Spain, Russia, and the Baltic; the greatest number of broadcloths and kersies went undyed to Antwerp, where they were finished according to the demanding standards of Europe's leading cloth mart. The proximity of Antwerp to the trade routes of northern, central, and southern Europe thus freed the Adventurers from toilsome journeys with their cloth packs and made the trade even more lucrative and inviting.

Despite the prosperity enjoyed by the Adventurers during ELIZABETH's reign, WILLIAM CECIL and other councillors remained worried about the concentration of the cloth trade in Antwerp. Sir Thomas Smith worried about the influx of imported luxuries that attended the Adventurers' traffic and the unfavorable balance of trade that followed from it. Cecil feared for the security of the trade itself and noted the power of Philip II to interrupt the flow of exports between the Low Countries and England (which occurred 1563-1564 and 1568-1573). The solution to the latter problem appeared to rest with the project of removing the Antwerp staple to England and placing the cloth mart at London, Ipswich, Hull, or York. An English staple, however, would require that the Continental buyers make a sea journey, and the more plausible alternative was the placement of the staple at more congenial towns. Philip's enmity and the dangers posed by the Dutch revolt drove the Adventurers to take up residence in Emden, Hamburg, Stade, and Middelburg during Elizabeth's reign. More important-ly,English commerce began to diversify both in the "vents" sought and, later, in the goods carried. Attempts were made to recover the Baltic trade routes lost during the fifteenth century to the Hansa, while the founding of the Levant Company marked the attempt to penetrate the Mediterranean market. The celebrated EXPLORATIONS for a northeast passage had the practical goal of selling woolen cloth and acquiring valuable naval stores in return (rather than the "trifles" that Smith deplored). Indeed, Richard Hakluyt's *Principal Navigations* (1589, dedicated to ROBERT CECIL) urged such projects not from curiosity but for the purpose of finding a vent for woolen cloth. While the number of cloths vented by the Muscovy and Levant Companies never matched the number sold by the Adventurers, the continuing search for such markets reveals the overwhelming importance of the cloth trade and the industry that created it.

Bibliography: D. C. Coleman, *Industry in Tudor and Stuart England*, 1976; Eric Kerridge, *Textile Manufactures in Early Modern England*, 1986.

Douglas Bisson

Coinage and Monetary Policy. Following the economic trends of the sixteenth century, Tudor coinage and monetary policy fluctuated at wide extremes. Crown attempts to exploit the coinage for fiscal gain combined with occasional inefficiency, corruption, and inflation to complicate valuations and the quality of coin production.

During the reign of HENRY VII and the first seventeen years of HENRY VIII's reign, English coins retained their late medieval reputation for quality. Henry VII introduced an important new coin, the gold sovereign, in 1489, with a face value of twenty shillings. The first Tudor devaluation came in 1526 under Chancellor THOMAS WOLSEY when the sovereign's face value was increased to 22s.6d., although the weight (240 grs.) and fineness (23 carats, 3 1/2 grs.) were not altered. Wolsey also introduced other changes, all of which produced a less than satisfactory profit for the Crown. What concerned Wolsey and, later, THOMAS CROMWELL was the public's tendency to hoard English coins, which were superior to Continental coins, and thus reduce the circulation.

Debts from wars with Scotland and France in the 1540s led the government to manipulate the coinage to raise revenue again. The result was a debasement that involved reducing the weight and fineness of the precious metals in the coins while retaining the face value. An initial experiment in 1542 with the Irish coinage led two years later to an application to English coins. The period of the "Great Debasement" lasted from 1544 to 1551, during which time the weight of gold sovereigns declined forty-eight grams and the fineness decreased more than three carats. Silver coins were debased also. Soon, the new bad coins drove the old good coins out of circulation. The shortage of currency in the economy also affected inflation of prices. During the Great Debasement years, the principal mint at the Tower of London was enlarged and other regional mints increased their output of the cheapened coins.

The effects of debasement were somewhat different for English consumers and merchants engaged in foreign trade. Domestically, consumers faced price hikes on many crucial items while merchants such as the Company of MERCHANT ADVENTURERS found the debasement increased demand for English goods, especially cloths, on the Continent. Crown profits from the debased coins resulted from the differences between the costs of purchasing and minting the coins and the face value of the coins. The profits were not inconsiderable, perhaps £1.3 million, yet the damage to the reputation of the government and the inflation for royal subjects suggest that on balance the policy was unwise. Although inflation was constant throughout the sixteenth century, it increased most dramatically in the 1540s during debasement. Foodstuffs doubled in price over the decade while manufactured goods rose in price by 70%. Wages rose only slightly in the period so that the real purchasing power of consumers declined by about 59%.

The reform of the coinage, begun in 1552, owed much of its impetus to the advice of Sir Thomas Gresham (1519-1579). He was the son of a successful merchant with connections in the Low Countries, especially the financial entrepot of Antwerp. Gresham became a royal agent in 1551 to help restore the loan credibility of England with Antwerp's financial houses. Within two years, Gresham helped to eliminate the Crown's debt by restoring the debt service in Antwerp at improved, that is, lower rates. Gresham also served as a royal agent in Antwerp under MARY and ELIZABETH. He supported Sir Thomas Smith and WILLIAM CECIL's efforts to end the debasement of the coinage in 1552. A decade later, Gresham championed the plan to recall debased coins from the reigns of Henry VIII and EDWARD VI along with a new issue of coins minted with an increased fineness and weight. In 1570, Gresham opened a Bourse or financial exchange in Bishopsgate Street, London, modeled after the Antwerp exchange. At his death in 1579, Gresham left an endowment for a college bearing his name in London (GRESHAM COLLEGE).

The relationship of economic activity, such as trade and inflation, to the coinage is not easy to demonstrate, yet even the most skeptical economic historian recognizes the connection. For example, although cloth exports rose in the late 1540s, there were factors other than the debased coinage that may have affected the trade, including economic conditions on the Continent. The Antwerp-London exchange rate in sterling reached a high of 27s.2d. in February 1544 but declined to a low of 12s.9d. in July 1551. It then recovered gradually as the debasement ended to reach a recovery high of 23s.5d. in February 1562. The debasement also seriously affected the supply of gold and silver coins. The number of gold coins fell between 1542 and 1551 by almost 50% whereas the number of silver coins increased almost fourfold in the same years. Clearly, silver rapidly displaced gold as the metal of choice in English coins thereafter.

Fiscal exploitation of the coinage for profit was a sign of government desperation and not a careful financial plan. Even with the stabilization and issue of a new coinage under Elizabeth, debasement had taken its toll. For example, the weight of silver in the penny declined by 35% from Henry VII's reign to the end of Elizabeth's. Gold coins under Elizabeth accounted for only 14% of the total produced. Still, English coinage and monetary policy were on a much sounder base at the end of the sixteenth century than during the mid-century debasement years. Government policy changes after 1551 created renewed confidence in English coins, even though they were not as intrinsically valuable as under Henry VII. For a time at least, government officials and monarchs were chastened to avoid the desperate resort to devaluation and debasement as a means of instant profit.

Bibliography: C. E. Challis, *The Tudor Coinage*, 1978; J. D. Gould, *The Great Debasement*, 1970.

Daniel W. Hollis III

College of Physicians (1518). Henry VIII chartered the Royal College of Physicians in 1518 to eliminate quackery and malpractice, insure public health, and give physicians control over their profession. The college also protected physicians from competition, like a medieval guild. Its principal founder was Thomas Linacre (c. 1460-1524), the king's physician, who studied at Oxford and Padua, though Cardinal THOMAS WOLSEY was also influential. An important preliminary was the parliamentary act of 1511 that confirmed the long-standing right of the UNIVERSITIES to license physicians, while giving the church responsibility for licensing surgeons, barber-surgeons, and barber-tonsors. This act recognized physicians as a separate group and restricted the activities of all other practitioners. The creation of the college followed a serious epidemic in London in 1517.

Subsequent parliamentary acts confirmed the college's charter and gave it the right to charge membership fees and license physicians (1523), reduced surgeons to craft status (1530), allowed physicians to practice surgery and amalgamated surgeons and barber-surgeons into a single company (1540), allowed unlicensed practitioners to treat illness and injury and further distinguished the respectable medicine of physicians from that of others (the "Quack Act," 1542), and enhanced the college's ability to proceed against those who evaded its authority (1553). Around 1563 Dr. John Caius completed a detailed set of statutes providing for officers, procedures for admission, discipline, examinations, meetings, corporate ritual, feasts, and symbols. Further revisions culminated with the *Statuta Vetera* in 1601. The college was involved in London politics and enjoyed various privileges, though it was not always on good terms with the city. Traditionally, the foundation of the college has been seen as the beginning of modern medicine in England; in fact, it set back medical science there by as much as two centuries. The study of physic at Oxford and Cambridge continued to follow an essentially scholastic curriculum based upon the inaccurate humoral theory of Hippocrates and Galen and emphasizing abstract principles and rhetorical disputation. Tudor physicians failed to benefit from medical advances on the Continent. Also, there was little attention to actual clinical practice—most physicians seldom laid hands upon their patients. The exclusion of surgeons from the college (unlike the short-lived College of Medicine established in 1423) kept out those with the most practical experience—the Hundred Year's War had given surgeons the chance to experiment with new techniques on the wounded and to dissect cadavers without ecclesiastical interference. The decline of warfare under the Yorkists and the Tudors eliminated the opportunity for clinical practice, and from 1511 on the status of surgeons was progressively reduced. The quality of medicine practiced by physicians changed little during the sixteenth century, for while Galenic medicine declined, it was not until William Harvey's work in the 1620s that English medicine even began to improve.

Bibliography: George Clark, *A History of the Royal College of Physicians of London*, vol. 1, 1964; Robert S. Gottfried, *Doctors and Medicine in Medieval England, 1340-1530*, 1986.

William B. Robison

Common Law. Despite the fact that it is one of the most characteristic of English institutions, the common law is more difficult to define than might at first be expected. At the end of the sixteenth century, it was frequently taken to be synonymous with the law of England in the most general sense, and this usage is often followed, correctly enough, by modern historians. However, influenced as they were by scholastic Aristotelian legal theory, Tudor lawyers were usually more precise. Writing early in the reign of HENRY VIII, Christopher St. German explained that the law of England in fact rested on "six different grounds": the law of reason, the law of God, diverse general customs of the realm, diverse principles called maxims of the law, various particular customs, and statutes made in PARLIAMENT. Of these six, only the third, the "general customs," were correctly called the common law.

At the same time, the common law could also be distinguished from other kinds of positive law that were used within the realm. Thus in *The First Part of the Institutes of the Laws of England*, the most famous of Tudor and Stuart lawyers, Sir Edward Coke, defined the common law as the common customs of the realm, but he then went on to list fourteen other varieties of law. These included the particular customs of local manorial and borough courts, the CANON LAW, the civil (Roman) law that was used in CHURCH COURTS and the Court of Admiralty, the law merchant, and the law relating to Crown and Parliament. In addition, although it was sometimes a subject of controversy, the common law was usually contrasted with the law of equity, a branch of the law of reason, which was administered by the Court of CHANCERY.

As these distinctions suggest, the varieties of English law could be divided largely along lines created by the jurisdictions of the various courts, and this fact provides a key to the most practical working definition of the common law. It was simply the law administered in the principal royal courts that sat in Westminster Hall in London, King's Bench, Common Pleas, and the EXCHEQUER. The claim of the common law to be the law of England rested on the general importance of these courts and the lawyers who worked within them.

At the beginning of the Tudor period, the Common Pleas was by far the busiest court in the realm. Its jurisdiction covered real actions concerning property, actions of debt, actions of trespass, and trespass on the case. The kinds of disputes involved could range from quarrels about the payment of rent for the possession of land to the collection of debts, allegations of assaults and defamation, or, for example, suits against medical practitioners for failing to carry out cures effectively. Unlike the Common Pleas, the King's Bench had a criminal as well as a civil jurisdiction. But up until the 1530s there were restrictions on the power of the King's Bench to hear "common pleas", especially actions of debt, from beyond London and Middlesex. These restrictions were overcome by the development of a notorious series of legal fictions associated with the Bill of Middlesex and writ of *latitat*, which enabled the court to encroach on the jurisdiction of the Common Pleas and to offer the procedural advantage of enabling plaintiffs to arrest and hold to bail the defendants from the very early stages of a lawsuit. This brought forth complaints both from some of the defendants and from the Common Pleas, but by the end of the Tudor century the jurisdiction of the King's Bench was roughly similar to that of the Common Pleas, although Common Pleas still heard about three times as many suits as its rival.

By comparison with the King's Bench and Common Pleas, the Exchequer was a poor third in terms of the amount of litigation it handled in the sixteenth century. The Exchequer was primarily a department of state responsible for the king's revenues, but over the years it had developed both a common law jurisdiction, or "plea side," which was presided over by the barons of the Exchequer, and an "equity side" with procedures that followed closely those of the Court of Chancery. In either case, the Exchequer courts were available only to those litigants who claimed (often fictitiously) that they owed the king some obligation or who could show that the king's interests were in some other way connected with their own affairs. Finally, these judicial branches of the Exchequer should not be confused with the court of Exchequer Chamber, which, in fact, took its name from the place where all the judges and serjeants-at-law assembled to decide on particularly difficult cases that were referred to them from the other courts.

The most important single fact about the common law courts during the Tudor period was that there was a remarkable growth in the amount of litigation that was brought before them. The increase was feeble and sporadic during the reign of

HENRY VII and was very seriously set back during much of the 1510s, 1520s, and 1530s by a sequence of outbreaks of epidemic disease in London, bad harvests, and civil unrest. But, from the 1550s and throughout the reign of Elizabeth, the amount of legal business increased steeply. Although exact measurements are difficult to make, by the end of the reign of Elizabeth a combined total of about 50,000 new suits were commenced in King's Bench and Common Pleas each year, at least ten times more than in the late fifteenth century. Procedural changes, markedly greater activity in the land market, the more extensive use of credit, and other social and economic changes account for much of the increase, but the emphasis that the Tudor state placed on the ideology of the rule of law and a decline of local jurisdictions also played a part.

By 1600, the amount of litigation entertained by the common law courts per head of population in England was greater than at any time before or since. Furthermore, the litigants, both plaintiffs and defendants, came from a wide cross-section of the population. About 30 % can be classified as belonging to the landed gentry, but the rest were smaller yeoman, husbandman farmers, urban merchants, and artisans. There was also a broad geographical range. London, East Anglia, and the western counties of Somerset, Devon, and Wiltshire were notably litigious, but most geographical regions generated hundreds of cases. The one major exception was the north of England, where the COUNCIL OF THE NORTH, which was firmly established in the reign of Henry VIII, exercised a regional jurisdiction that mirrored those in London. In addition, there were the traditional feudal enclaves, the duchy of Lancaster, and the palatinates of Chester and Durham, each of which had its own chanceries and courts of pleas and put restrictions on the flow of legal business from its area to London.

Common law procedure, which was based on writs issued out of the courts, was notoriously complex, but it facilitated this juridically unusual situation in which people from distant parts of the country did their legal business through a set of central courts in London. If, for example, a provincial farmer thought he needed to go to law, he usually engaged a local attorney, who travelled to London and purchased the writs that would be necessary to initiate the action. These were designed to force the defendant to acknowledge the summons and answer the plea that was being entered against him. Most lawsuits never went much further than this step, but if the case did develop and was found to hinge on points of law, these were argued out by counsel before the judges sitting in Westminster Hall. The resulting give-and-take, plus the rulings of the judges on controversial issues, formed the substance of the law reports that were compilations of the notes lawyers took while observing the arguments in court. If there were no difficult questions of law, or once those that existed had been resolved, writs were issued to summon a jury to try the general issue of whether the defendant was guilty or not.

At this point the case returned to the provinces, where it was tried before a jury when the court of assize met in the locality from which the disputants came. The assizes were judicial tribunals composed of common law judges and serjeants-at-law who were empowered by royal commissions to hear civil and criminal cases throughout provincial England. Twice every year these senior lawyers divided themselves into six so-called circuits, which consisted of a group of adjacent counties: the Home, the Midland, the Norfolk, the Oxford, the Northern, and the Western. Two assize judges and an accompanying retinue of lawyers then rode into the major county town of each shire on their circuit and stayed there a day or two to hear cases.

The powers of the assize judges were based on three separate royal commissions in addition to the commission of assize itself. First, they were authorized to hear the civil lawsuits that had arisen in the three common law courts in London and been sent for trial by jury in the country by means of the writ *nisi prius*, which ordered the jurors to appear before the judges when they came into the county. Next, two further commissions enabled them to exercise the most important criminal jurisdictions within the realm. The commission of *oyer and terminer* (to hear and determine) allowed them to handle major felonies such as treason and murder. The commission of gaol delivery ordered them to deal with prisoners in the local gaols (jails) and with suspects who had been bound over by the JUSTICES OF THE PEACE to appear at assizes. Although there were local variations, by the mid-sixteenth century there was a general demarcation between the jurisdiction of the assize judges, who tried criminals charged with felonies and therefore subject to the death penalty if found guilty, and the justices of the peace, who dealt at quarter sessions with less serious offenses, which were classed in law as misdemeanors.

The meetings of assizes were major events in the administrative and social calendars of the localities. Justices of the peace, leading members of the gentry, and constables, who were usually yeomen farmers, were expected to appear. Members of the lesser gentry served as grand jurors, and yeomen, or sometimes husbandmen, acted as trial jurors for both criminal and civil cases. The proceedings were normally opened with a sermon, followed by a charge to the grand jury in which one of the assize judges held forth about the benefits of the rule of law or even made a statement explaining some aspect of royal policy, before listing the large number of statutory offenses on which the grand jury should make presentments if any malefactors were known to it. Sometimes the grand jury also presented local grievances of an administrative or political nature. In addition, it was responsible for sifting through criminal indictments to see whether there was a "true bill," or case for the defendant to answer. If there was, he was then sent to be tried before the petty jury.

Frustratingly little is known about civil (*nisi prius*) trials at assizes, but historians have begun to piece together a picture of the criminal trial by compiling and comparing statistical data about the nature of criminals, jurors, indictments, convictions, and sentences. Those accused of criminal offenses were not permitted to call on the help of lawyers to prepare or present their defense (the judges were supposed to look out for their interests), and trials usually lasted no longer than a matter of minutes. The number of indictments increased in the later sixteenth century, and Elizabethans certainly thought themselves in the midst of a crime wave. At the same time, however, many more people were indicted than were convicted, and of those convicted, considerably fewer faced death by hanging than would have been the case if the full rigor of the law had been enforced against them. Some historians conclude that the assize judges must have dominated the trials and the disposition of felons. Others argue that the way in which prosecutions were brought and the role of the grand and petty juries in determining the fate of the accused meant that the local community had a much greater influence on the process than did the professional lawyers or formal legal ideas.

A problem with the second of these interpretations is that it tends to imply an opposition between "popular" attitudes held by the majority of ordinary people and ideas that were shaped by the common law and espoused by an elite of gentry and legal professionals. Although more research needs to be done on the subject, there are several reasons for thinking that such a dichotomy is excessively simple, especially for the latter part of the Tudor century. First, there is the fact that so much of the litigation that was brought into the central common law courts had to do with the interests of people from outside the political and social elite. They were admittedly not often representatives of the poorest sections of Tudor society, but they were certainly not from the richest. Second, the increase in litigation in the common law courts was accompanied by a great growth in the size of the legal profession. By 1600, the ratio of lawyers per head of population was rapidly approaching that of early twentieth-century England.

The Tudor period was one of considerable change in the legal profession, which, in general, can be divided into three groups. The attorneys were the practitioners usually consulted first by someone with a legal problem. With social origins in the lesser gentry and yeomanry, they learned their profession by serving as clerks to older practitioners, and they gained the formal qualifications to practice by being sworn as officers in one or another of the courts. By contrast with the attorneys, who were experts in the procedural law, another group of lawyers, who in many respects were the ancestors of the modern barristers, specialized in pleading before the courts and in the more theoretical aspects of legal learning. The most senior of these practitioners, the serjeants-at-law, enjoyed a monopoly right of audience before the court of Common Pleas, and judges were normally appointed from among their ranks. In the other courts, however, the serjeants shared the work with lawyers known variously as counselors-at-law or apprentices of the common law, men whose social origins were slightly more elevated than those of the attorneys and who hoped themselves one day to become serjeants.

All of these lawyers were associated with the inns of Chancery and inns of court, unincorporated societies that occupied sites in Holborn, midway between the city of London and the courts at Westminster Hall. In the later fifteenth century the eight inns of Chancery—Clifford's Inn, Clement's Inn, Barnard's Inn, Lyons Inn, New Inn, Thavies Inn, Furnival's Inn, and Staple Inn—were primarily places that provided young students with preliminary training in the elements of the common law before they moved on to the inns of court, but by the end of the sixteenth century they were dominated instead by attorneys who lived and worked in them when they came up to London from the country for the four legal terms of the year. Similarly, the four inns of court—Gray's Inn, Lincoln's Inn, the Inner Temple, and the Middle Temple—served as the term-time residences for the couselors-at-law. However, the inns of court were also the places where young students came to undertake the long and difficult task of learning the law. The inns provided some educational exercises such as moots and lectures by senior lawyers on statutes, and the "call to the bar" at one of the inns was the crucial qualification for gaining the right to plead in any of the major royal courts, including Chancery and Star Chamber. The degree of instruction offered by the inns of court should not be exaggerated, and the legal inns served nearly as much as residences for country gents who came up to London for the social life as they did as law schools. Nevertheless, the vitality of their intellectual life in this period warranted their claim to be "the third university of England," and there is no better illustration of the growing importance of the common law and the common lawyers in the sixteenth century than the fact that admissions to the inns of court increased from around 50 each year in the early sixteenth century to well over 200 a year in the years around 1600.

Bibliography: J. H. Baker, *The Reports of Sir John Spelman. Volume 2*, Selden Society, 1978; C. W. Brooks, *Pettyfoggers and Vipers of the Commonwealth: The "Lower Branch" of the Legal Profession in Early Modern England*, 1986; J. S. Cockburn, *A History of English Assizes 1558-1714*, 1972; W. R. Prest, *The Inns of Court Under Elizabeth and the Early Stuarts 1590-1640*, 1972.

C. W. Brooks

Commons' Supplication Against the Ordinaries (1532). This document was drafted by THOMAS CROMWELL, possibly as early as 1529. Certainly, in that year a similar ecclesiastical reform measure was introduced, then quietly shelved. Several interim drafts suggest a continuing interest in the subject, perhaps both to test and manipulate civic opinion. By March 1532 the body politic was ready to embrace censure of the clergy, and the supplication was presented on 18 March to HENRY VIII on behalf of the Commons by House of Commons Speaker Thomas Audley.

The Common's Supplication Against the Ordinaries contained a long list of specific grievances against the ecclesiastical establishment. These included, ecclesiastical legislation not being subject to lay concurrence, a prevalent and pervasive unfairness in the CHURCH COURTS, ungodly prelates, fees demanded for administration of the Sacraments, capricious persecution of heresy, and a church calendar containing too many holy days to be compatible with the labor needs of England's developing economy. The primary complaint lay with the higher clergy; in fact, it made much of their abuse of the lower clergy. A particularly widespread, albeit illegal, practice was what amounted to the extortion of large payments for such routine episcopal duties as institution of a parish priest into his situation. Collectively, the complaints exemplified a more basic issue—the fundamental jurisdictional war between church and state. Although the Commons requested permission to produce corrective legislation that amounted to a revolution in church-state relations, it carefully sweetened the supplication with protestations of orthodoxy and condemnations of heresy, both sincere to some degree. The supplication further claimed to seek to return ancient rights to the state rather than to impress new ones.

The CONVOCATION of the clergy had begun its own reform program the previous January and seemed zealous about continuing in that vein. However, these moderate reforms stopped short of any decrease in convocation's power. Besides, any real self-reform by convocation would obviate the Commons's rationale for increased lay control of the institutional church.

Thus, on 12 April 1532, Henry referred the Supplication to his bishops via Archbishop WILLIAM WARHAM along with a request for a formal reply. Bishop STEPHEN GARDINER probably crafted this answer, a defiant apologetic for an unfettered church whose sins Gardiner considered venial and individual rather than major and corporate. Its contents gave rise to the king's famous remark, "Well-beloved subjects! We thought that the clergy of our realm had been our subjects wholly, but now, we have well perceived that they be but half our subjects." All of this was a thoughtful prelude to the Act for Submission of the Clergy (1534).

Bibliography: G. R. Elton, *Reform and Reformation: England 1509-1558*, 1977; H. Gee and W. J. Hardy, *Documents Illustrative of English Church History*, 1896.

Ann E. Faulkner

Commonwealth Men or Party. These are terms used by some twentieth-century historians to describe a group at the court of EDWARD VI who were supposed to have supported EDWARD SEYMOUR, duke of Somerset's, attempts at reform. His fall from office and the accession of MARY I are said to have ended their influence.

The mid-Tudor period was one of considerable discontent. POPULATION growth, inflation, debasement of the COINAGE, religious uncertainty, the DISSOLUTION OF THE MONASTERIES, and new, aggresive landholding practices created dangerous feelings of dislocation and crisis among the English. This turmoil also produced a body of reform-minded thought aimed at restoring England's social wholeness. The term Commonwealth Men has been applied to the authors of these reforming sermons, tracts, and pieces of legislation.

HUGH LATIMER has been called the leader of this group, partly because of his sermons for the Edwardian court in 1549 and 1550 and partly because of his misidentification with an agitator labeled "that Commonwealth [man] called Latimer" in a contemporary letter. According to Latimer, the principal cause of the crisis was a moral collapse. The rich, he claimed, had been infected by a spirit of covetousness and irresponsibility. Their ENCLOSURES and rent increases improved their position at the expense of the poor, who reacted with violence. This moral diagnosis was echoed by many of the writers identified with the Commonwealth Party, such as the pamphleteer Robert Crowley, who called the rich "cormorants" and "greedy gulls" who swallowed other men's homes and farms without regard to law. The preacher Thomas Becon claimed that in no age had the devil been more active or covetousness more evident while John Hooper, the bishop of Gloucester, saw the poor man's position eroded by the rich, who wanted to monopolize the very earth. None of the Commonwealth Men, however, advocated violence as a solution to social oppression, and in 1549 they condemned both the religiously motivated rebels of the west and those peasants of Norfolk who sought economic reform.

Despite their nonviolence, the Commonwealth Men were blamed for inciting rebellion, as was John Hales, who, as a member of the commission on enclosures and author of parliamentary legislation, was critical of the expansion of sheep farming for its displacement of peasants and reduction of the supply of grains and dairy produce. Landowners, however, obstructed his work and the reforming legislation. Magnates also used the excuse of the uprising to bring down Somerset, who was identified with soft-hearted social policies, and to discredit Hales.

Recent historical work has demolished the idea of a Commonwealth Party, and has shown that these men mentioned were not formally linked to each other or to Somerset. There is no doubt, though, that they were part of a powerful contemporary ideal of the "commonwealth," a belief that government and social relations should be guided by the needs of the whole community and not the wealthy few. This ideal was not confined to the Edwardian period but sprang from medieval antecedents. Moreover, such thinking continued in the writings of the MARIAN EXILES and in much of the economic and social outlook of the Elizabeth PURITANS.

Bibliography: G. R. Elton, "Reform and the ' Commonwealth-Men' of Edward VI's Reign," in *The English Commonwealth, 1547-1640*, ed. P. Clark, A. G. R. Smith, and N. Tyacke, 1979; W. R. D. Jones, *The Mid-Tudor Crisis, 1539-1563*, 1973.

                                                                          Gerald Bowler

Convocations. The name for the two ancient assemblies of the clergy in the provinces of Canterbury and York, the singular term convocation sometimes refers to both convocations together and sometimes to the convocation of Canterbury alone. The province of Canterbury was much larger than York, and its assembly met virtually simultaneously with PARLIAMENT. Thus, usually Canterbury first considered and acted upon important ecclesiastical matters, and York followed suit. Convocations met to vote the clergy's subsidies to the Crown, to receive and promulgate canon law, and occasionally to deal with heretics or heretical writings. The convocation of Canterbury usually convened in London at St. Paul's Cathedral and infrequently at Westminster, while the convocation of York customarily gathered in York at St. Peter's Cathedral (York Minster). Each convocation had two houses. The upper house included the presiding archbishop, bishops, and before the Reformation, mitred abbots. The lower house included lesser officials (such as priors of religious orders, other conventual and cathedral dignitaries, and archdeacons and deans), proctors or representatives of cathedral chapters, and proctors or representatives of the lower clergy. The two convocations occasionally met together as a legatine assembly under the auspices of a papal legate. In the two centuries before the Reformation the archbishops of both Canterbury and York customarily received legatine powers, although a special legate could supersede them. By the sixteenth century both had equal rights of jurisdiction, directly dependent upon the pope, and only honorary precedence had been left to the archbishop of Canterbury, including the right to crown the monarch. Early in the reign of HENRY VIII, THOMAS WOLSEY, archbishop of York as well as papal legate, cardinal and chancellor, gained exceptional precedence over Archbishop WILLIAM WARHAM of Canterbury, who did not hold legatine powers. In 1534, with the destruction of papal power, the archbishop of Canterbury received authorization to issue all ecclesiastical licenses and faculties (25 Hen. VIII, c. 21).

During the meeting of the REFORMATION PARLIAMENT (1529-1536), convocation was assailed by king and Parliament alike. Threatened with PRAEMUNIRE charges in 1531, the convocations admitted Henry VIII head of the English church "as far as the law of Christ allows" and after paying over £118,000, received the king's PARDON OF THE CLERGY. In 1532 following the COMMONS SUPPLICATION AGAINST THE ORDINARIES, the monarch extracted from the convocation of Canterbury a SUBMISSION OF THE CLERGY, which represented a turning point in the constitutional history of the church. Ratified by Parliament in 1534 (25 Hen. VIII, c. 19), it curtailed the power of convocation to assemble, deliberate, or legislate. Thereafter, convocation could be summoned only under the monarch's writ and, in time, needed the royal license to legislate and royal assent to the legislation. The earliest known royal assent to canons after their enactment was issued in 1598; the earliest license, in 1604. After the supremacy act of 1536 (29 Hen. VIII, c. 10), first William Petre, Thomas Cromwell's deputy, and then Cromwell himself appeared at the convocation of Canterbury as representatives of the king who were empowered to exercise the rights involved in the ROYAL SUPREMACY. Though laymen, they were allowed to preside, and thus convocation acknowledged the king's right to the presidency. But this right is not known to have been exercised again by the sovereign either in person or by deputy.

It is noteworthy that the Submission of the Clergy and other legislation by convocation were put into statute by Parliament. That Parliament for the first time confirmed grants of taxes voted by convocation in the years 1540, 1542, and 1545 suggests a significant incursion into the most important function of convocations, taxing the clergy. While another traditional function of convocations, the prosecution of heretics, was left unchanged by the Reformation, there are no known cases in which sentence was passed on a heretic after 1534.

The continued existence of the convocations of Canterbury and York after the end of the Reformation Parliament in 1536 left an appearance of continuity that disguised only slightly the weakened condition of the remaining institutions, now thoroughly dominated by the Crown and, to a lesser extent, by Parliament.

Bibliography: F. Makower, *The Constitutional History and Constitution of the Church of England*, 1895; G. Trevor, *The Convocations of the Two Provinces*, 1852.

Martha Skeeters

Cornish Rebellion (1497). During the spring of 1497 a massive revolt occurred in southern England because of HENRY VII's persistent demand for war taxation. Although a crisis situation had arisen with Scotland, the king was primarily interested in adding to the cash surplus on hand at the EXCHEQUER. He therefore found it convenient to exaggerate the danger posed by JAMES IV.

Since November 1495 the king of Scots had provided to a Yorkist impostor, PERKIN WARBECK, who claimed to be the younger son of Edward IV. In mid-September 1496 James IV led an invasion of northern England on Warbeck's behalf but retreated within a week because no local support for the impostor materialized. The English monarch quickly saw how he could use this incident as a pretext to require additional sums from his wealthier subjects. On 24 October a Great Council opened at Westminster and authorized Henry to raise whatever money he could by means of a benevolence. In spite of public discontent, royal agents raised nearly £57,390, or more than 50% of the Crown's total yearly income at that juncture.

Henry was not satisfied with the result, however, and summoned Parliament to meet in January 1497. After an opening speech from Cardinal JOHN MORTON, who stressed the perilous nature of the diplomatic situation, the Lords and Commons agreed to a grant of £120,000 for the maintenance of two armies. An additional £120,000 was authorized if the war with Scotland became protracted. CONVOCATION agreed to contribute a further £40,000 to the king's war chest. Once assured of generous financial aid, Henry mobilized the armies, but after a brief raid across the border, the king renewed his earlier offers to James IV for an eventual dynastic alliance between the two Crowns.

Meanwhile in southern England, especially in Cornwall, where the mining industry had long been depressed, there were bitter protests against the demand for war taxation. Since the northern counties were exempt from most forms of taxation owing to their special obligation for border defense, irate Cornish landowners felt it was incumbent on northerners to pay for the campaign, which, in any event, was "a small commotion" that would soon be over. The Cornish protestors, who numbered over 15,000, were led by Thomas Flamank and Michael Joseph, a lawyer and a blacksmith, respectively. At Flamank's urging, the protestors resorted to the constitutional fiction that, because the monarch was clearly well intentioned, his councillors alone were to blame. The obvious strategy was to march on London and inform Henry of their views. He would then select new advisers and cancel the demand for war taxation.

Early in May the rebel band set out from Bodmin for the capital. At Taunton they encountered and summarily executed a royal tax collector. When they reached Wells, they were joined by Lord Audley, a nobleman in serious financial straits. After passing through Wiltshire and Hampshire, they took the Great Road north toward London. Meanwhile Henry had posted sentries throughout the capital and mobilized an army at Henley-on-Thames. On 14 June he merged his troops with the larger force of approximately 10,000 men under Lord Daubeney, who was encamped on Hounslow Heath and poised to defend London from assault.

After a brief skirmish in Surrey, Flamank and Joseph led the rebel bands toward the border of Kent, the center of several previous peasant uprisings. During the past generation, the people of Kent had enjoyed prosperity and felt little sympathy for the Cornish insurgents. Furthermore, the armed tenants of Lord Cobham and the earl of Kent were strong enough to block the rebels' advance and caused many of them to become dejected. When Henry refused to negotiate while they still had arms, the weak-in-heart stole away under the cover of darkness.

Early on 17 June Lord Daubeney launched a fierce attack on the rebels' camp at Blackheath. Because the insurgents had inadequate weapons and no cavalry, it briefly appeared that they would be routed within the hour. But they rallied and captured large numbers of the royalist vanguard, including Lord Daubeney himself. However, the rebels were no match for John de Vere, earl of Oxford, England's finest general, who commanded the royalist center. When Oxford charged their exposed flank, they were overwhelmed. More than 1,000 Cornishmen perished during the battle, while the king's losses did not exceed 300. Hundreds of fleeing peasants were captured and forced to pay small fines totaling approximately £9,000 in order to recover their freedom. As for the main rebel leaders, Flamank and Joseph were both taken alive and sent to London to stand trial. Speedily convicted of high treason, they were hung, drawn, and quartered at Tyburn. Lord Audley was also sentenced to die, but as befitted his noble rank, he was beheaded at Tower Hill.

Meanwhile in July 1497 James ordered Warbeck to leave his realm, and the crisis between England and Scotland was resolved. With the end of the war, Henry had no real justification for collecting the second installment of £120,000 authorized by Parliament seven months earlier, so the complaints about war taxation died away.

Bibliography: M. V. C. Alexander, *The First of the Tudors*, 1980; R. B. Wernham, *Before the Armada*, 1966.

Michael V. C. Alexander

Council of the North. The Council of the North under the Tudors was a modification of a Lancastrian and Yorkist institution, aimed at establishing the power of the Crown north of the River Trent with a supreme executive authority in the hands of royal officials. It was part of the Tudor policy to bring about a unitary state and was directed at reducing the power and influence of great northern magnates such as the Percys and at the same time providing a cheap and readily accessible royal court of justice in the north.

The history of the council under the Tudors falls into two distinct phases. The period up to 1537 was largely experimental, during which the council's existence was not continuous. Under HENRY VII it is probable that his mother, the Lady Margaret Beaufort, countess of Richmond, and her council were responsible for the government of the north, but under HENRY VIII it was the council of HENRY FITZROY, duke of Richmond, that provided a model for the later council.

After the PILGRIMAGE OF GRACE the council ceased to be used as a temporary expedient and became a permanent feature of the Tudor system of government, along with the councils in WALES and the West Country. From the appointment of Cuthbert Tunstall, bishop of Durham, as lord president in 1537 there was an unbroken sequence of holders of such office (except for a brief period from 1596-1599 under Archbishop Matthew Hutton), the most energetic of whom was Henry Hastings, 3rd earl of Huntingdon. From this point onward the council performed purely administrative and judicial functions, having no responsibility for the management of royal or baronial estates. The council's jurisdiction covered the whole of England north of the Trent, except for the palatinate of Lancaster and for a time after 1541, the Borders. The council exercised in the north the administrative and judicial functions of the PRIVY COUNCIL. Under the terms of its instructions the council was to hold four sessions each year, in York, Newcastle, Hull, and Durham. However, after 1556 the council rarely sat at Hull; it sat occasionally at Carlisle instead of Durham, and from 1582 onward sessions were always held only at York. Based at the King's Manor in York, the abbot's lodgings of the suppressed abbey of St. Mary's, the council consisted of a president, vice-president, and councillors. The councillors consisted of three or four lords and invariably included the archbishop of York, the bishop of Durham, the deans of both cathedrals, and about half a dozen knights, including the leading landowners, royal officials, and lawyers. From about 1568 onward the common lawyers sitting on the council were bound to attend sittings. Supporting the councillors were officers including secretaries, an attorney, examiners of witnesses, clerks, a sheriff, and collectors of fines.

The authority of the council was derived from instructions given to the successive lords president, and commissions of the peace and oyer and terminer. Its work covered two broad areas: administrative and judicial. In its administrative capacity royal proclamations were made and orders were transmitted to local justices of the peace and sheriffs. This task was not always easy, and in spite of being responsible for the nomination of JUSTICES OF THE PEACE, the council found it difficult to insure the cooperation of Yorkshire gentry. The council was responsible for reducing the north to order after the collapse of the Pilgrimage of Grace, enforcing Henry's religious settlement, and restraining recusancy and enforcing the break with Rome under ELIZABETH. Its administrative functions also included responsibility for defense, organizing musters, watches, and beacons along the coast, and taking steps to suppress piracy. In its supervision of local authorities the council intervened in disputes between towns, as in that between Hull and York over the lead trade, and in internal disputes in towns such as York, Newcastle, and Beverley. It sought to insure the election to Parliament of those well disposed to the government. The enforcement of statutory enactments dealing with the regulation of trade and vagrancy also fell within its jurisdiction. The busiest and most effective period of the council's work was under the presidency of Huntingdon.

The council's judicial activity included criminal and civil matters. Its criminal jurisdiction enabled it to deal with cases of TREASON, murder, and felony. Toward the end of the century it is clear that its civil jurisdiction had come to be of the utmost importance. Combining the functions of the Court of STAR CHAMBER and the Court of REQUESTS, it was said in 1607 to be dealing with 2,000 cases a year. It provided to inhabitants of the north a court more accessible than those at London to deal with private suits, land tenure cases, and debt.

Intrigues at court affected the relative importance the council gave to these administrative and judicial functions. In periods of court faction under EDWARD VI, during the period 1566-1570 and at the end of Elizabeth's reign, administrative responsibilities declined. By the early seventeenth century the council was becoming increasingly unpopular; it was abolished by the Long Parliament, and its records were lost during the Civil War.

Bibliography: Claire Cross, *The Puritan Earl*, 1966; R. R. Reid, *The King's Council in the North*, 1921.

D. J. Lamburn

Council of the West. This was one of the three, and by far the shortest-lived, of the regional councils newly erected or re-established by THOMAS CROMWELL. In 1539 the southwest of England was regarded as a potentially troublesome area, HENRY VIII being only too well aware of the CORNISH REBELLION in 1497 to protest against royal taxation and of lingering support for the cause of his own cousin, Henry Courtenay, marquess of Exeter, who had been executed in 1538 as a known religious Conservative and a potential claimant to the throne.

As Courtenay's replacement in the southwest as the leading landowner, the king and Cromwell had chosen Sir John Russell, a native of Dorset and already well tested in royal service. Early in 1539 he was given a substantial estate, largely in Devon and all of it former monastic property, and the title of baron Russell. His task was to pacify the region and to employ local energies in surveying the coastal defenses against a possible invasion by the Catholic powers of Europe. To this end there were associated with him a dozen or so of the leading knights and gentlemen of the area, each of them already of proven loyalty.

The idea of constituting Russell and his helpers as a council possessing not only administrative but also certain judicial powers was no doubt Cromwell's. Indeed the Council of the West was an almost exact copy of the COUNCIL OF THE NORTH and equally costly. Its members were also provided with generous expense allowances. Russell was an active president, and in its short life the council was usefully occupied. But the immediate crisis that had led to its establishment quickly passed, and with the fall of Cromwell in 1540 the Council of the West was quietly allowed to disappear. However, John Lord Russell, later 1st earl of Bedford, continued to serve as the Crown's "man" in the southwest and to be the first of a long line of LORDS LIEUTENANT.

Bibliography: P. Williams, *The Tudor Regime*, 1979; Joyce Youings, 'The Council of the West', *Transactions of the Royal Historical Society*, 1960.

Joyce Youings

Court. *Court* is an ill-defined term that in its widest sense encompassed the whole entourage within a ten to twelve mile radius of the king's person known as the "verge," where, for reasons of convenience and safety, COMMON LAW was suspended. In its narrowest, but equally misleading sense, *court* means simply the royal HOUSEHOLD. The former sense is misleading because many of those who followed the king and thus came under the jurisdiction of Household officials were specifically prohibited from entering the king's palace. The latter sense is misleading because it excludes not only such officials as the king's secretary and members of the PRIVY COUNCIL, who certainly had access to the king, but also such domestic departments as the Stable and Wardrobe, which were separate administrative units by the sixteenth century but which still catered to the king's personal needs. The master of the horse, for example, was certainly one of the most powerful "courtiers," and his authority rivaled that of the lord chamberlain when the king was out-of-doors. Although not a member of the Household, he was certainly a member of the court. The number of regulations issued between the mid-fifteenth century and the beginning of the seventeenth testifies to the difficulty of imposing definition and order upon the court.

The actual terms *court* and *courtier* evolved in the fifteenth century when the king's entourage became less a fighting unit and more the ceremonial unit through which the king demonstrated his dignity and power. As the king became a better lord than even his richest subjects, his court became the arena for all those with political ambitions. Access to the monarch was the key to personal monarchy, and any post that brought its holders to the king's attention was worth pursuing. For this reason the common usage of *court* equated it with the Royal Household. It was this meaning that Sir James Croft had in mind when he wrote: "The Court is divided into two governments, the Chamber and the Household."

The Household, or more often the Household Below Stairs, consisted of about twenty departments charged with providing the enormous meals served the king and his followers. They did everything from acquiring the provisions and preparing meals to washing up and disposing of the scraps to the poor. These departments were staffed by men from modest backgrounds who worked their way through the ranks to sergeant, usually the chief officer in each department. Departments were supervised by "particular clerks" who, in turn, came under the supervision of the Counting House, or Board of Greencloth, whose cofferer and subordinate clerks paid the bills and enforced the rules. Over these career servants were the lord steward and controller, prominent courtiers who tended to be more concerned with their own perquisites and prerogatives than the efficient service of the king.

The Chamber, or Household Above Stairs, consisted of a host of servants in less well-defined departments. Their titles depended on their physical proximity to the king as determined by the structure of the palace where the court happened to be lodged. As the older, undifferentiated great hall of medieval castles gave way to specialized apartments, the structure of the Household had to be adjusted. No matter where they served, servants above stairs combined catering to physical needs, protecting the king's person and, most importantly, creating the image of majesty. Status was determined by rank and nearness to the king. All were subject to the rule of the lord chamberlain and vice-chamberlain, except for the king's most intimate servants in the Privy Chamber, which enjoyed the status of a third department of the court. The Privy Chamber was under the eye of the king and his most personal servant, the groom of the stool.

The composition and shape of the Household was surprisingly constant under the Tudors. True, HENRY VII created the Privy Chamber as a separate department to which he could retreat to carry out the detailed work for which he is famous, but his son changed it from a bureaucratic unit to an office concerned with jousting and other court entertainments in which the king took part. Thus HENRY VIII's Privy Chamber differed in degree, but not in kind, from the chamber from which it had emerged. The advent of two reigning queens changed the public side of the Privy Chamber, and it disappeared by the end of ELIZA-BETH's reign.

THOMAS CROMWELL's attempt to impose his bureaucratic mind on the structure of the court was more short-lived. Shortly before his fall, Cromwell reorganized the court and brought it under one paymaster and one administrator, called the lord great master of the household in imitation of the French. This attempt to subordinate the Household above and below stairs to the Counting House was never completely successful. The lord steward's position was abolished, but the lord chamberlain survived a temporary eclipse and managed to reassert himself in the reign of EDWARD VI. MARY officially abolished the post and its four subordinate masters of the Household, who assumed their former duties in the Counting House. As the incumbents died off, their replacements were given their old titles, and Cromwell's experiment of imposing order was ended. Courtiers never did get used to being supervised by bureaucrats.

The one enduring aspect of the reforms of 1539 and 1540 was the creation of an elite new bodyguard, the Band of Gentlemen Pensioners. Cromwell had opposed the move because of the expense and because an extra guard was not necessary since the Yeomen of the Guard set up by Henry VII could be expanded if needed. Although an earlier attempt to set up an honorific guard called the "Spears" proved premature, it showed the king's thinking. The fifty pensioners and their three officers were socially superior to the guard. Their purpose was to fight for the king when he went to war and ornament the court during peacetime. Following the natural tendency for posts at court to multiply, the fifty pensioners were soon supplemented by a group of reversionaries, the gentlemen-at-arms. JOHN DUDLEY, duke of Northumberland, also attempted to create a much larger Household force, the *gens d'armes*, but chronic shortage of money soon ended this effort.

The advent of a minor and two women changed the pensioners' service from martial to ornamental, although they could still be called upon to fight, as they were in Northumberland's attempted coup and WYATT'S REBELLION. Although few pensioners made it to the top, with the Privy Chamber closed to males, a place in the Band of Gentlemen Pensioners was still desirable, because it served as a substitute for the more intimate service in the Privy Chamber denied to the ambitious.

The court experienced conflicting pressures throughout the Tudor period. On the one hand, there was pressure from the accountants to keep costs down by restricting the numbers permitted to enter the court and by eliminating waste in the royal kitchens. On the other hand, since the court was the stage upon which monarchy presented itself, there was pressure to increase the numbers and conspicuous consumption to make it as magnificent as possible. The struggle between grandeur and economy could not be resolved until the court ceased to play any political role.

Bibliography: D. Loades, *The Tudor Court*, 1987; D. Starkey et al., *The English Court*, 1987.

Robert C. Braddock

Cranmer, Thomas (1489-1556). As archbishop of Canterbury in the reigns of three Tudor monarchs he played a leading role in the initial establishment of a Protestant church in England. His contributions were especially significant in the formulation of doctrine and liturgy as well as in the official adoption and dissemination of an ENGLISH BIBLE. His doctrine of the "godly prince" provided a justification for the ROYAL SUPREMACY, but it also resulted in tensions with his other religious beliefs that proved especially difficult to resolve when at the end of his life he owed allegiance to a Roman Catholic ruler.

Cranmer was born at Aslocton, near Nottingham. He was the second son of a small landholder. Although often described as a "gentle scholar," he retained throughout his life his skill at riding and his love of hunting, which he learned in his youth. After his father's death in 1501, his mother sent him to Cambridge. He received his arts degree in 1511 and became a fellow of Jesus College. He resigned after marrying in 1515, but, when his wife died in childbirth, he was restored to his position as fellow. He took his master's degree, was ordained, and began to lecture in divinity before receiving his doctorate in 1523. By this time he seems already to have developed a deep commitment to biblical studies as well as an anti-papal position. Although there is no evidence that he attended Erasmus's classes while he was at Cambridge, the influence of HUMANISM is especially evident in Cranmer's approach to the Bible.

In the summer of 1529 Cranmer's suggestion that the European universities be consulted on the legality of Henry's second marriage, mentioned during a chance meeting with Edward Foxe and STEPHEN GARDINER at Waltham, resulted in his being asked to write on the subject. Shortly afterward he was invited to join the king's service, first as part of an embassy to Rome headed by ANNE BOLEYN's father and then as ambassador to the emperor in 1532. He also received preferment in the church. In 1531 he was appointed a royal chaplain and in the following year archdeacon of Taunton. While in Germany he met the Nuremberg Reformer Andrew Osiander and secretly married his niece, Margaret.

When WILLIAM WARHAM died in August 1532, Cranmer was appointed archbishop of Canterbury. His appointment is somewhat surprising since he was relatively unknown and certainly not as experienced as a number of other potential candidates. Although the influence of the Boleyn faction probably played a major role in the decision to select Cranmer, his knowledge of the faith and practice of the early church and his antipathy to papal interference in provincial affairs, combined with his unquestioning loyalty to his prince, were qualifications that must have especially commended him to HENRY VIII.

Although Cranmer was consecrated archbishop with papal approval and he took the traditional oath of obedience to the papacy, he stated in writing that he did not thereby bind himself to do anything contrary to king or country or to refrain from the reformation of the church. Within a month of his consecration Cranmer declared the king's marriage to CATHERINE OF ARAGON null and void, and in June he presided at the coronation of Anne Boleyn.

During Henry VIII's reign Cranmer balanced loyalty to a "godly prince" with efforts to bring about reform in the church. He played a major role in the first Henrician formularies of faith, the TEN ARTICLES (1536) and the BISHOPS' BOOK (1537), which reflect the influence of Continental Lutheranism, and he courageously corrected the king's theology (as well as his grammar) when Henry wrote a critical appraisal of the Bishops' Book. Cranmer supported THOMAS CROMWELL in acquiring the king's approval for an official English translation of the Bible, which the 1538 Injunctions ordered placed in every parish church. He also worked for moral and educational reform. Despite his subservience to the king he courageously interceded for many who fell from Henry's favor, including JOHN FISHER, THOMAS MORE, Anne Boleyn, and Thomas Cromwell. Cranmer retained his office even after the Catholic party came into ascendency in the 1540s, and he continued his work for reform. He defended the English Bible, wrote a series of homilies that were officially adopted in Edward VI's reign, and prepared an English litany, which received the king's approval in June 1544. Despite theological differences the king continued to support his archbishop when his enemies plotted against him, and before Henry died in January 1547, he called Cranmer to his bedside.

During EDWARD VI's reign Cranmer had the opportunity to introduce the type of far-reaching reform that was denied him earlier. Although his theology was a good deal more radical than it had been in Henry's reign, his approach to reform continued to be moderate. This was reflected in the gradual introduction of Protestantism in the early years of the reign, which is especially evident in the 1549 BOOK OF COMMON PRAYER, which even Gardiner found acceptable. Criticism of its moderation led to a second, more clearly "Protestant" prayer book in 1552, which broke entirely from the Latin Mass. Cranmer's major theological work, *The True and Catholic Doctrine of the Lord's Supper*, is a well-written defense of his new eucharist theology. He was also largely responsible for the FORTY-TWO ARTICLES, which, while clearly presenting a Protestant definition of essential doctrines, avoided the extremes of some Continental formularies.

When Edward died, Cranmer became a traitor to Queen MARY in response to the dying wish of his king as he supported LADY JANE GREY's claim to the throne. However, in Mary's eyes heretical doctrines were a more serious crime than treason. Although initially imprisoned for treason, he was eventually convicted of heresy and burnt at the stake on 21 March 1556. During the final months of his life he signed a number of recantations in response to persistent and clever appeals to his ERASTIAN beliefs. However, before going to the stake, he retracted his recantations and died courageously.

Bibliography: P. N. Brooks, *Cranmer in Context*, 1989; Jasper Ridley, *Thomas Cranmer*, 1962.

Rudolph W. Heinze

Cromwell, Thomas (1485?-1540). Statesman and administrator, Thomas Cromwell was the son of Walter, a Putney cloth worker and alehouse keeper who was frequently in trouble with the law until his death in 1514. Our knowledge of his son's early years once depended on tradition only. This put him in Italy from 1503 to 1511 and then in the Netherlands, where he was apparently a factor in the cloth trade until he returned to London in 1514.

We now know from documentary sources the facts behind the traditions. We cannot verify that he was at the battle of Garigliano in 1503. But he did soldier in Italy before he entered the service of the Frescobaldis, the Florentine merchant-bankers with whom he remained on intimate terms into the 1530s. We cannot confirm the tale that he studied accounting at Venice. But it is beyond doubt that Cromwell was trading at Syngsson's Mart at Middelburgh in 1512, within a year of the time JOHN FOXE placed him in Rome on business for the Marian guild of Boston in Lincolnshire.

What is most important is that Cromwell was at the papal court in 1514 and perhaps earlier, as a member of the household of Cardinal Christopher Bainbridge (1464?-1514). Curia records show him as a deponent in lawsuits involving English clergy until Bainbridge's death in June 1514. Then, Cromwell returned to England with others of the cardinal's household and entered THOMAS WOLSEY's service, probably by late August 1514, when Cromwell's hand first appears in Wolsey's papers. This early connection with Wolsey explains Cromwell's work in 1517 and 1518 for the Boston guild, when he twice went to Rome to seek enlargements of their indulgences. Wolsey had been their patron, and Cromwell seems to have taken over that work as he rose in Wolsey's service.

Cromwell's familiarity with the Curia explains that rise, for Wolsey, unlike Bainbridge, had never been resident in Rome and depended heavily for his relations with successive popes on returnees who had lived there. Cromwell's earliest work for the cardinal concerned ecclesiastical affairs, and before being sworn to Wolsey's domestic council in 1519, this expertise counted for more than the strong common law business Cromwell built or his useful marriage to Elizabeth Wykes, a widow and the daughter of a cloth merchant trading in the Low Countries. By her he had a son, Gregory and a daughter whose name is lost.

The years 1523-1524 marked a turning point in Cromwell's career. He sat in the Commons in 1523 and must have attracted notice, if the vigorous speech preserved among his papers was in fact delivered. It condemned the war in France and the failure of measures to edify the Commonwealth. In 1524 he joined Gray's Inn and in the same year took charge of Wolsey's dissolution of thirty religious houses to provide the foundation of a school at Ipswich and Cardinal's College at Oxford. It was also in 1524 that Cromwell for the first served as a Crown commissioner. He had extensive business dealings with Richard Pynson, the king's printer, and had acquired a knowledge of publishing that was to distinguish his mastery of the press in the 1530s.

He remained Wolsey's factotum until 1530, serving him well and with loyalty—a thing Henry VIII noticed and prized in all servants. But the fall of

Wolsey was a near thing for Cromwell. He made his own will at the time of Wolsey's arrest and, after other bids to enter the 1529 Parliament failed, secured Taunton, a seat managed for Wolsey by Sir William Paulet. Once in the Commons Cromwell shone. By 1531 he was sworn to the king's council. Memoranda show that in the 1531 session Cromwell was the council's parliamentary man of all work. At the session's end he removed the unresolved bills to his own study (as he was to do again in 1532), perhaps under royal command, for Henry had ordered Cromwell to prepare legislation for 1532, and in that session Cromwell managed the campaign against the clergy and their formal submission.

Sometime in 1533 he began to serve as Henry VIII's PRINCIPAL SECRETARY. He also had begun that accumulation of seemingly small offices connected with royal finance—the Jewel House, Hanaper, and others—by which he gained control over the management of Crown revenues. Combining the secretarial office which he held until April 1540, and parliamentary management, even after he entered the Lords on being named Privy Seal, Cromwell put his stamp on royal business. He directed the propaganda war for the ROYAL SUPREMACY and policed dissent from it. As the king's vicegerent and vicar-general in spirituals he managed all phases of the DISSOLUTION OF THE MONASTERIES. He also played a crucial role in arranging Anne Boleyn's fall and death on treason charges in May 1536.

Cromwell, in fact, managed, if he did not originate, the major steps following from the DIVORCE and shaping the constitutional revolution by which papal power in England was overthrown. In foreign policy he became the champion of an alliance with the Lutheran states in northern Europe. Indeed, his zealousness for reform may have overridden his good judgment by the autumn of 1536. During the PILGRIMAGE OF GRACE he was singled out for condemnation by the northern rebels. His 1536 Injunctions leaned toward evangelical reform. So, too, did the BISHOPS' BOOK of 1537, which was in advance of the king on points in Sacramental theology. From the late 1520s he had been deeply involved with a circle of religious radicals.

By 1538 the council had hard evidence that Cromwell had protected SACRAMENTARIANS at a time when Henry VIII was marking limits to reform by a vigorous assault on any deviance in eucharistic matters. Cromwell's set of 1538 Injunctions had set in motion an iconoclast campaign and also ordered the setting up in every parish church of a Bible in English, the printing and publishing of which he had managed at every stage, first in Paris and then in London.

When the Great Bible appeared in 1539, the ground had already been cut out from under Cromwell by the combination of evangelical commitment, significant failures in foreign policy, in particular, the abortive Lutheran alliance and the thwarted union with Scotland, and his failure to establish an exclusive control in court, council, and Privy Chamber.

Historians have relied too much on the 1539 Act to Abolish Diversity of Opinion (31 Hen. VIII, c. 14) and the fiasco of the marriage to ANNE OF CLEVES in explaining Cromwell's arrest on 10 June 1540, just two months after his creation as earl of Essex, and his subsequent execution on 28 July. His enemies, led by Gardiner and THOMAS HOWARD, 3rd duke of Norfolk, succeeded because Cromwell had failed in the most important thing of all: maintenance of the confidence of the king. He had led in religion where the king would not go. The 1540 articles of attainder were cooked on treason but not on aiding and abetting heresy and heretics. Supreme as a manager and executive, he was never so in the more intimate arenas of Henrician politics. This fact is more important in grasping his achievement than the still current and unanswerable questions about Cromwell's exact role in the creation of the Royal Supremacy, the ideas behind the Reformation, or the alleged TUDOR REVOLUTION IN GOVERNMENT. The fact is that Henry VIII never surrendered control in things that mattered to him: marital life, religion, and foreign affairs—however much power he lodged in his chief minister for a time.

Bibliography: G. R. Elton, *Policy and Police*, 1972; G. R. Elton, *The Tudor Revolution in Government*, 1953; A. J. Slavin, *Thomas Cromwell on Church and Commonwealth*, 1969.

A. J. Slavin

D

Dee, John (1527-1608). Among the leading intellectual figures of Tudor England, few can have been as closely involved with so many cultural currents as John Dee, the Elizabethan "magus." Dee's father was a minor official in the household of Henry VIII. The younger Dee was educated at St. John's College, Cambridge, where he boasted he had studied eighteen hours a day. His studies included mathematics, rhetoric, Greek, and Hebrew. After becoming a fellow of the college for a brief period in 1547, he proceeded M.A. in 1548. In 1547 and again in 1548 Dee traveled abroad, on the second occasion becoming a student at Louvain, where for two years he studied the civil law. Though Dee was offered a chair in mathematics at the University of Paris, he declined it, lest teaching duties reduce his free time. From 1570, for most of the rest of his life, he resided at Mortlake, near Kew.

Although Dee remained a valued adviser to councillors such as WILLIAM CECIL, Lord Burghley, ROBERT DUDLEY, earl of Leicester, and Sir FRANCIS WALSINGHAM, his official connections never brought him wealth or high office, and he was not always in great favor. In 1555 he was briefly imprisoned for having cast a horoscope of the Princess Elizabeth. Though he was released, the incident was one of several that left him with a lifelong reputation as a wizard and conjuror. This made him suspect to ecclesiastical authorities and to the populace; many years later, in 1583, a mob looted Dee's library on his departure abroad. Despite his evil public image, he was held in high esteem by Queen Elizabeth, who consulted him for medical and astrological advice.

Dee was the author of nearly eighty works, most of which remain unprinted. Many were published abroad, where he was more favorably regarded, including his most famous work, the *Monas Hieroglyphica* (Antwerp, 1564). This enigmatic tract is perhaps the most important English example of the Hermetic movement. Hermes Trismegistus was a mythical ancient sage whose writings inspired Renaissance scholars such as Dee to seek the perfection and unification of human knowledge. Dee's Hermeticism was heavily influenced by occult writers such as Henry Cornelius Agrippa (1486?-1535), and by the neoplatonic tradition of Giovanni Pico della Mirandola (1463-1494) and Marsilio Ficino (1433-1499); it involved the manipulation of numbers and symbols as a way of disclosing truths hidden to ordinary men.

Dee's geographical interests led him to act as adviser to explorers such as Martin Frobisher, Humphrey Gilbert, and FRANCIS DRAKE. He was fascinated by British history and antiquities and proposed as early as 1556 the establishment of a national library to house the nation's books, manuscripts, and treasures; in the 1580s, he proposed a scheme for the reform of the calendar to bring it in line with the Gregorian reform being enacted abroad. Like most of his contemporaries, he subscribed to the belief that Britain had once been united under ancient warrior kings such as Arthur; he envisioned England as a great imperial power, and in 1577 he published a tract on navigation largely devoted to advocating the creation of a powerful "Pety-Navy-Royall" to defend England's waters against pirates, foreign powers, and persons practicing unlawful fishing.

In the 1580s, Dee's ambition to master all knowledge led him to attempt to communicate with angels through a series of assistants or "scryers," who would gaze into a crystal or "shew-stone" and relay the instructions of angels to Dee. Among these scryers was Edward Kelley (1555-1595), an unsavory charlatan. Kelley, who was obsessed with the desire to change base metals to gold through alchemy, interested Dee in that art. He accompanied Dee on his trip to the Continent between 1583 and 1589. During that time, Dee visited Poland and was the guest of the emperor Rudolf II in Prague until he was expelled in 1586. Dee and Kelley parted in 1589, and the former returned to Mortlake. Dee's last two decades were spent in relative seclusion. He was rewarded with the mastership of Christ's College in Manchester, where he lived from 1595 to 1604, when he returned to Mortlake. He died in near penury in 1608.

Having provided a model for Prospero in *The Tempest*, Dee has since his death been considered everything from an eccentric wizard to a founder of modern science. In reality, he was neither; he was merely the most accomplished English representative of intellectual traditions such as Hermeticism, which had greater influence on the Continent. Because of his wide interests, he was also the prototype of a new species of scholar-gentleman, the virtuoso, whose greatest day was to come in the seventeenth century.

Bibliography: Nicholas Clulee, *John Dee's Natural Philosophy*, 1988; Peter French, *John Dee: The World of an Elizabethan Magus*, 1972; W. Shumaker, *Renaissance Curiosa*, 1982.

D. R. Woolf

De Facto Act (1495). (11 Hen. VII, c. 20). The De Facto Act was passed by Parliament in 1495 to protect persons from suffering the loss of their property as a result of serving the king in the suppression of rebellions. The law was passed in 1491 during a Yorkist rebellion in support of PERKIN WARBECK, the pretender.

The De Facto Act declared that it would be unreasonable, unconscionable, and against the law to deprive a loyal subject of the king of his property for doing his duty to the king. Therefore, the act provided that no person serving the king in his wars, whether foreign or domestic, should be convicted or attainted of high treason or for other violations of the statute relating to treason. Included were the prohibition of the penalties of forfeiture of life, lands, tenements, rents, possessions, chattels, or any other things. Loyal military servants were discharged from any vexation, trouble, or loss. The act also prospectively voided any future acts and processes that might penalize persons for military service to the king.

Parliament passed this act in a session that commenced on 14 October 1495, and it was captioned: "'AN ACTE' that noe p[er]son going with the Kinge to the Warres shalbe attaynt of treason." The statute was clearly designed to reassure those fighting on the side of HENRY VII against rival claimants that they would suffer no material loss on the grounds of TREASON for their military service and loyalty to the king.

Bibliography: A. F. Pollard, "The De Facto Act of Henry VII." *Bulletin of the Institute of Historical Research* 7 (1929): 1-12.

J. V. Crangle

Defender of the Faith (1521). The title "Defender of the Faith" (*Fidei Defensor*) was bestowed on HENRY VIII by Pope Leo X in 1521 in recognition of the king's services to the church in writing the *Assertio Septem Sacramentorum* against Martin Luther. The *Assertio* was a refutation of Luther's *De Babylonica Captivitate Ecclesiae* (1520), a radical reappraisal of the church's Sacraments first brought to Henry's attention in January 1521. Although Henry began work by himself in April, contemporary rumor had it that he received considerable help. THOMAS MORE was asked to examine the final draft, and he testified to the involvement of other contributors. The most likely helpers were the ten theologians from Oxford and Cambridge called to London by THOMAS WOLSEY in May 1521 for conference about Luther. The book, though still unfinished on 12 May, was printed by Pynson in June. It was not immediately published. Wolsey dispatched John Clerk to Rome with a presentation copy for the pope and a batch of further copies for subsequent distribution to selected European princes and universities. But first, Clerk was to obtain the coveted title that should put Henry on an equal footing with the kings of France and Spain (*Christianissimus* and *Catholicus*). Clerk presented the *Assertio* to Leo in September, and on 2 October the pope and cardinals agreed to grant the title *Fidei Defensor* to Henry (among other titles considered but rejected were *Apostolicus* and *Orthodoxus*). The title was conferred by a papal bull dated 11 October and accompanied by a brief of 26 October. However, the expediting of these instruments was delayed by Leo's death, and they did not reach England until 1522. Once the title was secured, the *Assertio* was released to the public. Though best known now for the brief but firm avowal of papal primacy that later so embarrassed Henry, the *Assertio* was an effective exposition of the seven Sacraments, of which the eucharist received the fullest treatment. It became one of the best-selling attacks on Luther of the decade. Luther himself dashed off a caustic reply, the *Contra Henricum Regem* (1522), which in turn elicited counterblasts from Thomas More, JOHN FISHER, John Eck, and others. As for the title itself, Leo conferred it on Henry alone and not on his heirs—although Henry clearly thought otherwise, as the title *Fidei Defensatrix* was applied to his wife, CATHERINE OF ARAGON. Clement VII confirmed the title in a bull of 1523 that left the question of heritability at best ambiguous. But Henry was inseparably attached to his new title. After the "Break with Rome" he annexed it forever to the Crown by a statute of 1543 that was repealed by MARY, who nevertheless continued to use the title, but reenacted by ELIZABETH.

Bibliography: J. Mainwaring, "Henry VIII's Book *Assertio Septum Sacramentorum* and the Royal Title of 'Defender of the Faith,'" *Transaction of the Royal Historical Society* 8 (1880): 242-61; R. A. W. Rex, "The English campaign against Luther of the 1520s," *Transactions of the Royal Historical Society* 39 (1989): 85-106.

Richard Rex

De Heretico Comburendo **(1401).** (2 Hen. IV, c. 15). Law providing statutory authority for secular authorities to assist in the punishment of heretics. LOLLARD criticisms of the papacy and the English church aroused the anger of the clerical hierarchy, and at the request of William Courtney, archbishop of Canterbury (1381-1396) letters patent were issued against them in 1382 and 1384. The church's ability to resist heresy was further strengthened when Parliament in 1401 passed the statute *De Heretico Comburendo* (On the burning of a heretic) with the support of the new king, Henry IV (1399-1413). Later it would be used against Protestants in general. The statute accused the "new sect" of usurping the office of preaching and prohibited them from circulating their "new doctrines and wicked, heretical, and erroneous opinions." It acknowledged that diocesan bishops could not correct the Lollards because they went from diocese to diocese. Therefore, they needed the aid of the king. All persons possessing heretical writings were ordered to hand them over to the bishops within forty days. Those convicted by ecclesiastical courts of refusing to abjure their heresy, or of relapsing into it, were to be handed over to the officers of the secular courts to be burned. The law was later expanded (2 Hen. V, stat. 1, c. 7).

   De Heretico Comburendo was repealed under HENRY VIII in 1534 (25 Hen. VIII, c. 14) and also under EDWARD VI in 1547 (1 Edw. VI, c. 1 2). It was revived in the autumn of 1553 when MARY I's first act of repeal was passed by Parliament and abolished nine acts concerning the church that had been passed in the reign of Edward VI. In January 1559 ELIZABETH's Supremacy Act (1 Eliz. I, c. 1), restoring the ancient jurisdiction, was passed. It repealed the heresy act of Philip and Mary. The act was employed for the last time by a Tudor in 1575. On Easter, 3 April 1575, some Flemish Anabaptists were gathered for worship at a house near Aldersgate, London. They were arrested and brought before Bishop Edwin Sandys of London for questioning. Some recanted, but five refused and were condemned to death. Of these five, two, Henry Terwoot and John Pieters, were burnt at the stake at Smithfield.

The last time the statute *De Heretico Comburendo* was brought into force was under JAMES VI and I. Two men were burnt for heresy at London and Lichfield in 1612. Later, near the end of the reign of Charles II (1660-1685), *De Heretico Comburendo* was totally abolished (29 Char. II, c. 9), and heresy was again subjected only to ecclesiastical correction.

Bibliography: H. Gee and W. J. Hardy, eds., *Documents Illustrative of English Church History*, 1910; J. Guy, "The Legal Context of the Controversy: The Law of Heresy," in *The Complete Works of St. Thomas More*, Vol. 10: *The Debellation of Salem and Bizance*, 1987.

                                                                    Don S. Armentrout

Desmond Rebellion (1579-1583). This rebellion was an uprising in Munster led by Gerald Fitzgerald, the 14th earl of Desmond. Desmond's motivation in this revolt appears to been the defense of Catholicism in Ireland, though his delay in joining the Catholic Crusade at its onset casts some doubt on this assertion.

It was in fact Desmond's rival, James Fitzmaurice, who precipitated the Munster War. Having toured the Continent from 1575 seeking support for his idea of spreading the Counter-Reformation to Ireland, Fitzmaurice eventually persuaded Pope Gregory XIII to finance an expedition to Munster and declare this action to be a crusade. On 17 July 1579, Fitzmaurice arrived in Dingle Bay with between 300 and 700 Italian and Spanish troops. Carrying the papal banner and in the pay of the pope, this force was accompanied by Dr. Nicholas Sanders, an English Catholic acting as the papal envoy. They established a camp at Smerwick and appealed to Irishmen "to join in the defense of the catholic faith."

Despite the death of Fitzmaurice in a skirmish on 18 August the crusade quickly found supporters among the Irish. Leadership was assumed by John and James Fitzgerald, the younger brothers of Desmond, indicating the reluctant earl's support for the crusade. This was certainly assumed to be the case by the chief English official in Dublin, Sir William Pelham, who drove Desmond irrevocably into the camp of the rebels by declaring him a traitor on 2 November 1579.

This precipitous action angered Queen ELIZABETH, who had hoped to limit the scope of the Munster rebellion by negotiating with Desmond. Now forced into an expensive war, in 1580 she dispatched a new lord deputy, Arthur, Lord Grey De Wilton, to Dublin with reinforcements commanded by prominent gentlemen such as Sir Walter Raleigh and EDMUND SPENSER.

Upon his arrival in Ireland in August 1580, Grey was confronted with two immediate challenges. The first was a revolt in the Pale led by James Eustace, Viscount Baltinglas, who mustered his troops within 25 miles of Dublin. Overconfident of his army's ability, Grey rashly attacked Baltinglas in the valley of Glenmalure and was repulsed with heavy losses. This rebuff encouraged the rebellion, and support for Desmond grew.

In September, the rebels were encouraged further by the landing of a second papal force of 700 men at the Smerwick fort. This time, Grey acted more effectively, joining forces with the loyal Thomas Butler, earl of Ormonde, and laying siege to the invader's camp on 7 November. Within four days the papal troops marched out in surrender, only to be massacred by the fiercely Protestant Grey.

This merciless action broke the back of the Catholic Crusade. Convinced that no help would reach them from the Continent, Desmond's followers gradually slipped away and made their submissions. Dr. Sanders died of dysentery in 1581, James Fitzgerald was captured, Baltinglas fled to Spain, and in January 1582, John of Desmond was killed, leaving the earl with no supporters. Ormonde laid waste to Munster in fierce campaigning from 1580-1583, inspiring Spenser to write of the devastation in *A View of the State of Ireland*. The rebellion finally ended on 9 November 1583, with the capture of Desmond, who was killed when his followers attempted to rescue him.

The rebellion set the stage for the Munster Plantation, by denuding the province of over 30,000 of its inhabitants. Further, the Irish bards, historians, and gallowglasses were likewise dispossessed because of their support for the rebellion. Thus a long step was taken toward the Elizabethan colonization of Ireland.

Bibliography: R. Dudley Edwards, *Ireland in the Age of the Tudors,* 1977.

John Nolan

Devereux, Robert, 2nd Earl of Essex (1567-1601). Becoming a court favorite of the elderly ELIZABETH I at the age of seventeen, Devereux enjoyed a spectacular, if short-lived, career as a courtier and military leader during the waning years of the last Tudor queen's reign.

The eldest son of Walter Devereux and his wife, Lettice (nee Knollys), Robert inherited the title at the age of nine following his father's death. Walter, lacking the time to consolidate the Devereux fortunes, bequeathed little more than his titles to the young earl and left behind substantial debts. Virtually penniless, his mother, Elizabeth's first cousin, secretly married ROBERT DUDLEY, earl of Leicester, within two years of her husband's death. Essex, under the guardianship of WILLIAM CECIL, Lord Burghley, was sent to Cambridge in 1577 and attained his master's degree by 1581. Realizing that his fortunes lay at COURT, the earl became the protege of Leicester, who saw an opportunity to bolster his own standing with Elizabeth by bringing his articulate, handsome, and charming stepson to the notice of the queen.

Essex attracted Elizabeth's immediate attention and began to jockey with the other established courtiers for her favor and the prizes that accompanied that favor. Essex soon began to benefit from Elizabeth's indulgence but was unable, through his own profligacy, to stabilize his debts. The earl also sought to distinguish himself through military exploits; serving with Leicester in the Netherlands and during the Armada crisis, Essex began to earn a reputation for bravery and leadership.

Following Leicester's death in 1588, Essex emerged as Elizabeth's chief favorite but tarnished her regard by participating in a series of rash adventures designed to achieve wealth and glory. By 1592, the earl turned his aspirations to the construction of a power base that would counterbalance the influence of Burghley and his talented son, ROBERT CECIL. Essex sought ways to increase his domination at court, precariously balanced between success and failure in his attempts to consolidate his faction. Elizabeth, amused at times and exasperated at others, managed to check Essex through stern warnings and the threat of dismissal from court.

In 1596, the earl scored an unqualified military success with the capture of the Spanish port of Cadiz. However, the venture did not replenish the coffers of the queen, who had subsidized the fleet, and she turned on Essex as the author of this oversight. Stung by the queen's attitude and apprehensive of the appointment of Robert Cecil as PRINCIPAL SECRETARY, Essex appealed to the people of London to validate his success, whose approbation fed his vanity. The IS-LAANDS VOYAGE, in 1597, designed to reinforce his ascendency, ended in ignominious failure and marked the beginning of the Earl's downward spiral.

Sent by the queen to IRELAND in 1599 to quell the rebels in that intransigent country, Essex realized that the commission represented his last best chance to redeem himself in Elizabeth's eyes. A massive investment of time, money, and troops notwithstanding, he constructed a private truce with the earl of Tyrone, the Irish rebel leader; it was rejected out of hand by Elizabeth, who viewed the agreement as treasonable. Essex set off for London to plead his case personally but was rebuffed by the queen, who ordered him into a brief confinement.

Stripped of his patent on sweet wines, Essex became convinced that he was the victim of a conspiracy. Amassing the remnants of his court faction, Essex engineered a rebellion in January 1601, its aim to rescue the queen from her evil councillors, chief of whom was Cecil. Entering London by early February, Essex was initially successful, but a tactical mistake, combined with a lack of public support, led to his defeat and eventual surrender. Tried and condemned quickly,

Essex was executed on 25 February 1601, a victim of rash desire and self-delusion.

Bibliography: Robert Lacey, *Robert, Earl of Essex*, 1971.

Connie S. Evans

Dispensations Act (1534). (25 Hen. VIII, c. 21). Officially entitled "An Act for the exoneration of exactions paid to the see of Rome," this statute followed hard on the heels of the confirmatory ACT IN RESTRAINT OF ANNATES and dealt with all other papal revenues besides annates. It was drafted by THOMAS CROMWELL and introduced into the House of Commons early in 1534. Fears about some of its provisions were expressed in the House of Lords, and it was then amended by the lord chancellor, Thomas Audley. A memorandum drawn up by Cromwell before the session suggests that he had originally thought of the withdrawal of further revenues as a means of bringing pressure to bear upon the pope. At the last moment a proviso was added empowering the king to abrogate the act at any time before 24 June, but this was never invoked.

The preamble takes the form of a petition from the Commons complaining that the king's dominions have been greatly impoverished by a range of papal exactions, including pensions, taxes, PETER'S PENCE, procurations, bulls of provision, and the costs of judicial proceedings as well as dispensations "and other infinite sorts of bulls, briefs and instruments." The "bishop of Rome" is accused of usurpation and of falsely persuading the king's subjects that he has the full power to dispense with "all human laws, uses and customs of all realms which be called spiritual." But the realm of England, recognizing no superior under God but the king, is subject to no human laws save those freely accepted by Crown and people. It is therefore reasonable that the king and the Lords and Commons "representing the whole state of your realm in this your most High Court of Parliament" should have full power and authority not only to dispense with those and all other human laws of the realm but also to change or rescind them.

The act then provides that no impositions whatsoever shall henceforth be paid to the pope. Nobody shall seek from him any sort of instrument or writing. Dispensations and licenses of the sorts hitherto obtained from Rome "for causes not being contrary or repugnant to the Holy Scriptures and laws of God" shall be granted by the archbishop of Canterbury. Those costing four pounds or more at Rome are also to be confirmed under the Great Seal. One major proviso firmly denies that the king or his subjects intend this act to stray from the path of true Catholic orthodoxy. Another safeguards from any interference by the archbishop of Canterbury all monasteries and other institutions that enjoy exemption from his authority, giving the king the supervisory powers hitherto vested in the pope and other foreign churchmen. It also forbids members of religious orders to attend any congregation or assembly (e.g., general chapter) held abroad.

The most important administrative consequence of the act was the establishment of the archbishop's Court of Faculties, issuing dispensations for such diverse activities as non-residence, holding benefices in plurality, eating meat in Lent, and marrying without banns or within the prohibited degrees (soon to be curtailed by 32 Hen. VIII, c. 38). Its chief constitutional significance lay in the fact that it deprived the pope of such powers as he still possessed in England.

Bibliography: D. S. Chambers, *Faculty Office Registers 1534-1549*, 1966; S. E. Lehmberg, *The Reformation Parliament 1529-1536*, 1970.

Ralph Houlbrooke

Dissolution of the Monasteries. In 1500 in the whole of England and Wales there were very nearly 900 communities of monks, regular canons, mendicant friars, nuns and canonesses, the houses for women consisting of about 6% of the total. The individual religious numbered nearly 12,000, the proportion of men and women being about the same as in the number of separate communities. Also resident within the monastic precincts were numbers of lay servants, both outdoor and indoor, and a sprinkling of men and women who, as lay corrodians, mostly quite elderly or invalid, had in some way compounded for their board and lodging for life. Also dependent to some extent for their livelihood on monastic resources were a few non-resident farm laborers and a host of lay officers in receipt of fees, the latter ranging from receivers and chief stewards to manorial bailiffs. Most houses also acknowledged a tenuous link with the lineal representatives of their founders.

All the monasteries and other religious houses depended almost entirely for their material support on their endowments, which consisted of mostly landed property producing regular rents and other seignorial dues. Most had long given up large-scale active farming of their land, retaining only a home farm for domestic needs, but some still worked considerable demesne, especially the more profitable sheep pastures, right up to the time of the Dissolution. Much of the remaining demesne in hand was leased in the early 1530s, mostly to local gentlemen. Also valuable in producing income, some of it still in kind or on short lease, were the parish tithes that many monasteries had been allowed by their diocesan bishops to impropriate to augment their resources. Rectorial or great tithes were usually accompanied by the right of presentation to vicarages, and there were also some advowsons to rectories.

By the mid-1530s the number of religious persons had declined somewhat, so much so that in some cases the communities were no longer viable. These included the 29 houses dissolved by Cardinal THOMAS WOLSEY between 1524 and 1529, apparently with the pope's approval. Such piecemeal dissolution might have continued but with THOMAS CROMWELL's appointment as HENRY VIII's deputy as supreme governor of the church in England early in 1535, steps were taken to close down a substantial number of religious houses as a measure of reform and to augment royal income. Following a nationwide survey of the location and resources of all monastic houses, the findings of which were set down in the VALOR ECCLESIASTICUS, Parliament was persuaded in 1536 to provide for the dissolution of all in receipt of incomes of less than £200 (27 Hen. VIII, c. 28). About a quarter of the 300 or so houses caught by the act were subsequently exempted, albeit temporarily. The simultaneous erection of the COURT OF AUGMENTATIONS (27 Hen. VIII, c. 27) allowed for the immediate appointment of regional officers to take charge of the Crown's new estate and arrange for those men and women religious who were still in residence and wished to continue in the religious life to be accommodated in larger houses of their orders. At this stage only existing heads or governors of houses, that is, abbots, abbesses, and so forth, were awarded pensions payable by the Crown.

Subsequent events, including the PILGRIMAGE OF GRACE, in which a handful of monastic communities was implicated, soon caught up with the larger houses. Individual monasteries, each for its own reasons, started the ball rolling, and gentle inducement, accompanied by considerable lay pressure, added to the trickle of surrenders to the Crown's officers. Finally, specially appointed bodies of commissioners were sent on regional circuits to mop up the remainder. Beginning with Furness Abbey, Lancashire, in April 1537, the whole operation was complete with the surrender of Waltham Abbey in Essex in March 1540. The houses of Friars were dealt with separately in 1538. There was one further act of Parliament providing for surrender, each community now simply handing over its possessions by a simple deed of gift signed by all, or almost all, of the religious persons still in residence. An act of 1539 (31 Hen. VIII, c. 13) merely assured the legality of the king's title to the former monastic property for the benefit of grantees.

With no longer any alternative accommodation to offer to the religious, the government of Henry VIII, intent on avoiding the making of martyrs around whom opposition might gather, now provided all those who departed without fuss with pensions for their lives. These were reasonably adequate except for the younger men and women, who received very little, but there was also no provision for inflation. In the case of heads of houses, except for the few who were recalcitrant and paid with their lives, the pensions were generous. There was also the provision for the men to be given "capacities," that is, licenses, to accept secular benefices. Corrodians and all those with indentures of appointment to lay offices received annuities. The fears of nearly all monastic tenants were put at rest by the statute of 1536, which set up the Court of Augmentations, and the royal commissioners charged with the task of taking the surrenders made at least some provision for the immediate need of lay servants. It cannot then be argued that the Dissolution added substantially to the number of paupers, although much suffering must have been caused to those already in need by the cutting off of casual monastic charity. Although closely linked chronologically with Henry VIII's breach with Rome, the Dissolution was not one of its direct or inevitable consequences. No attempt was made to convict the religious of harboring Roman loyalties, which few of them did, and even without his new statutory powers Henry VIII would no doubt have effected at least a degree of diversion of monastic resources into his own coffers. Nor, on the other hand, was there any reason that monasticism should not have remained a feature of the Protestant church in England.

With the dissolution of the larger houses the regional and central officers of the Court of Augmentations found themselves administering an estate scattered throughout every county in the Crown to the tune of nearly £200,000 a year, but even before the surrender of the larger houses had begun, the sites of the smaller monasteries, with all or part of the property appertaining to them, were disposed of by the Crown to especially favored laymen. At this stage a great many of the royal grants took the form of outright gifts or were made in exchange for other property acceptable to the Crown. But beginning late in 1539, by which time most of the larger houses had surrendered, there was a spate of sales of former monastic property to all who could raise the Crown's price. Most of the direct purchasers were knights, gentlemen, and men of affairs, including many lawyers, but many small traders and yeomen farmers and a few husbandmen bought at second hand from the many dealers who operated in this greatly expanded land market. Much of the property, largely manorial, which went, usually on favorable terms, to the nobility eventually returned to the Crown through political misfortune, including the large grants obtained before his fall by Thomas Cromwell. Much of this was resold, and indeed in the long run the greater part of the former monastic estate came to rest in possession of medium landowners, mostly knights, esquires, and mere gentlemen. The standard purchase price laid down in 1539 was twenty times the net annual value of the property, but in the course of time the Crown was able to increase the multiplier to take account of the length of existing leases in a time of rising land values. By the end of the reign of Henry VIII (1547) well over half the former monastic property had passed out of Crown hands and had been sold largely to pay for the king's foreign wars. By 1558 the total disposed of was probably over three-quarters, the remainder being sold by Queen Elizabeth and her early Stuart successors.

Some of the men and women religious who had been young at the time of the Dissolution were in receipt of their pensions until toward the end of the century, a handful for even longer. But the original intention, the permanent augmentation of royal income, was defeated by a combination of pressure on the Crown to share its good fortune with those of its subjects able to bend its arm and of the escalating cost of war.

Bibliography: David Knowles, *The Religious Orders in England*, Vol. 3, 1959, reprinted as *Bare Ruined Choirs*, 1976 and 1985; Joyce Youings, *The Dissolution of the Monasteries*, 1971.

Joyce Youings

Divorce, Royal. Early in 1527, HENRY VIII expressed doubts that his marriage with CATHERINE OF ARAGON was valid. Henry was Catherine's second husband; she had previously been married for five months to his brother, Arthur, who died in 1502. CANON LAW forbade marriage between two people closely related by marriage, an impediment called "affinity," but legal precedents allowed the pope to grant special permission to marry when the marriage would serve a good end, such as peace. Since a marriage between Henry and Catherine would maintain peace between Spain and England, Pope Julius II dispensed them to marry in spite of the impediment of affinity in the first degree.

During the nine years after their marriage in 1509, Catherine was often pregnant, but only one daughter lived to adulthood. By the early 1520s, the queen had become physically unattractive and morbidly pious. She also represented a failed diplomatic policy, since Henry had broken with her Habsburg relatives. Worst of all from Henry's perspective, she was unlikely to have another child, and he worried about the future without a legitimate male heir.

The king had discovered passages in the Bible that he believed applied to him. A passage in Deut. (25:5) ordered the brother of a man who died childless—as Arthur had done—to marry the widow to produce an heir for him, but Henry dismissed this passage as a Jewish law that was no longer binding. The crucial texts for him were those from Lev. (18:16, 20:21) that declared it was an unclean thing for a man to marry his brother's wife; the punishment was childlessness. Not having a legitimate male heir was (to Henry) the same thing. He concluded that the pope had not had the power to dispense him to violate God's law (as recorded in Lev.); the pope could dispense only from human laws. Henry soon sincerely believed that God was punishing him (and England) for his sin by denying him a son.

In May 1527, at Henry's instigation, Cardinal THOMAS WOLSEY and Archbishop WILLIAM WARHAM secretly convened a court to charge the king with incest, find him guilty, and annul his marriage. Henry personally chose the legal argument used from the start of the proceedings: his marriage violated divine law and the pope could not dispense for that. It was a difficult case but one he chose carefully. According to legal consensus, coitus created affinity. Catherine had always maintained that she and Arthur never had sexual relations; if she was a virgin when Arthur died, no impediment of affinity existed between Henry and Catherine. What existed was the impediment of "public honesty" (or "affinity by contract"), a modern (not biblical) proscription from which the pope certainly had the power to dispense. Since Julius had not done so, the marriage was technically illegal, but there was ample precedent for a retroactive dispensation, which Catherine could request. Henry did not deny Catherine's virginity at their marriage. Instead he argued that affinity was not created by coitus but by the marriage contract, a legally untenable position with centuries of precedent against it. He was forced to do so because of his determination to marry ANNE BOLEYN, the sister of Mary Boleyn, Henry's former mistress. Henry clearly saw his legal difficulty: if affinity was created by sexual relations, he was related to

Anne Boleyn in the same degree of affinity as he was to Catherine, and so he argued that the indispensable affinity was created by Catherine's contract with Arthur. It was the only possible case against the Aragon marriage that did not block his plan to marry Anne.

Wolsey, kept in the dark about Henry and Anne, had never accepted this argument. Anxious to protect papal authority, Wolsey preferred to argue that the dispensation had been only technically defective, thus rendering the marriage invalid. This argument did not preclude the pope's issuing a proper, retroactive dispensation that would bind Henry more tightly to Catherine than ever, so Henry rejected that approach.

Since Catherine could appeal the judgment of an English court to the pope, Henry decided to have Wolsey empowered by the pope to convene a legatine court in England. (There was no appeal from legatine courts because a legate acted as the pope's substitute.) For centuries popes had stretched legal points to accommodate well-intentioned kings. England needed a legitimate male heir; Catherine could not produce one. Since Henry made a consistent case, with biblical support, to give some color of legality to his request, he had reason to expect that the pope would assist. Clement, however, was unwilling either to aggravate Catherine's nephew Charles V (whose armies controlled Italy) or to acknowledge the limitations on papal dispensing power upon which Henry insisted.

Beginning in the summer of 1527, Henry dispatched several envoys to the pope seeking a commission for Wolsey to decide the case in England. After many failed attempts at compromise, Clement VII issued the commission jointly to Wolsey and Cardinal Lorenzo Campeggio and gave secret instructions to Campeggio to stall as long as possible. Campeggio arrived in London (ill with gout) in October 1528. While recuperating, he pressed Catherine to provide a solution by entering a nunnery and conveyed a desperate papal suggestion that Henry request a dispensation to commit bigamy, which the king refused.

The legatine court did not meet until 31 May 1529. Catherine appeared but rejected the court's authority and smuggled a letter to the pope requesting that he recall the case to Rome, and he did on 16 July. The order took weeks to arrive, and the court continued hearing witnesses until 23 July, when Campeggio announced a summer recess. Once Clement's advocation arrived, Campeggio returned to Rome, while Wolsey, increasingly unpopular, without influence, and hated by Anne Boleyn, was dismissed as chancellor for his failure to obtain a divorce for Henry.

Henry seemed ready to accept the Roman trial scheduled to begin in June 1530, and he turned to the universities of England and Europe for help. Some foreign universities did issue favorable judgments, but Cambridge and Oxford were deeply divided, and bitter debate preceded their responses to the king, neither of which helped Henry, since they stated that marriage to the widow of one's brother was against God's law only if she had had sexual relations with the first man.

Suddenly in August, Henry instructed his ambassadors to tell the pope that the case ought to be returned to England because Englishmen could not be cited abroad to answer to a foreign jurisdiction, though the envoys could offer the surprised pope no proof of this novel claim. In September, Henry added that he, as king of England, recognized no superior on earth. He learned this idea from the *Collectanea satis copiosa*, a manuscript of excerpts from ancient sources compiled by Edward Foxe, which he read with exceptional care. The sources in the *Collectanea* aimed to show that the king had imperium, final authority in all temporal and spiritual matters in his kingdom, and that kings rightly exercised authority over the church. After reading the *Collectanea*, Henry pursued an entirely new policy, for he saw his conflict with the pope differently; it was a crusade to regain lost rights that he had a duty to restore, and Henry entangled the honor of England with his conscience's private business.

In October, Henry raised the possibility of Parliament's enacting that the archbishop of Canterbury hear the case, in spite of any papal prohibition, but this possibilty was received with horror, and he set aside plans for a parliamentary solution. By January 1531 rumors about the divorce, still officially a secret, were spreading, and Henry agreed that Parliament should be informed and convinced of the justice of his actions. Soon after, the government launched a propaganda campaign to secure the support of the country. The favorable judgments of the foreign universities together with a long, tedious treatise on the indispensability of Levitical marriage restrictions were published in Latin, with an English translation, *The Determinations of the Universities*, soon after. *The Glasse of Truthe*, a livelier work with more popular appeal, argued that the pope had ignored God's law, unjustly delayed the king's divorce and harmed not only the king, who was forced to remain in a sinful marriage, but also England, which was denied a male heir to the throne. The *Glasse* also publicly raised doubts about Catherine's virginity and printed wedding-night boasts by Arthur about his sexual exploits with Catherine. The *Glasse* went farther than earlier works by suggesting that Parliament should provide a solution for the king. While practically all books supporting Catherine were effectively suppressed or destroyed, she continued to have supporters on the council and in parliament, and pro-Catherine sermons were ubiquitous; Henry himself endured one on Easter Sunday 1532.

That same year, some of Henry's councillors returned with more success than before to the quest for a parliamentary solution. The greatest obstacle to the divorce was Catherine's right of appeal to Rome, and it was increasingly clear to THOMAS CROMWELL and Thomas Audley that the divorce and papal authority were irreconcilable. The Act in Conditional Restraint of ANNATES (23 Hen. VIII, c. 20) was a turning point. Although Henry saw the bill only as a way to bully the pope by threatening to cut off revenue, Cromwell and Audley saw it as a precedent for the limitation of papal authority by statute. Parliament was not yet ready for radical measures, but Cromwell's careful exploitation of anti-clerical-ism, resulting in the COMMONS SUPPLICATION AGAINST THE ORDINAR-IES, paid dividends. Once the clergy submitted to the sovereignty of the king,

Parliament was willing to act. By January 1533, Anne was pregnant, and she and Henry secretly married. In the same month, Henry nominated THOMAS CRANMER, one of his most trusted agents over the past few years, to replace WILLIAM WARHAM, who had died in August 1532, as archbishop of Canterbury. In April 1533, Parliament, using arguments derived from the *Collectanea satis copiosa*, passed the Act in Restraint of Appeals (24 Hen. VIII, c. 12), which enacted that all ecclesiastical cases, including appeals, were to be heard in English church courts. While Parliament debated, the prelates ruled Henry's marriage invalid, and once the act passed, Cranmer issued the official annulment and declared Henry's marriage to Anne valid.

Rome continued to support Catherine. In July, the pope excommunicated the king and declared the Boleyn marriage invalid. In March 1534, a Roman court upheld Henry's first marriage. Clement VII died in September and was replaced by Paul III, who continued to support Catherine until her death in January 1536 ended the story of the King's Great Matter.

Bibliography: Henry Ansgar Kelly, *The Matrimonial Trials of Henry VIII*, 1976; J. J. Scarisbrick, *Henry VIII*, 1968; Edward Surtz, S.J., and Virginia Murphy, eds., *The Divorce Tracts of Henry VIII*, 1988.

Eric Josef Carlson

Douglas, Archibald, 6th Earl of Angus (1489?-1557). Born in on about 1489, he succeeded his grandfather, the 5th earl, about December 1513, shortly after the death of his wife, Margaret Hepburn, daughter of Patrick, 1st earl of Bothwell. In early 1514 he married Margaret Tudor, widow of JAMES IV, thereby invalidating her legal rights as tutrix to her infant son, JAMES V. Having quarrelled with his wife over her pro-English policies, he was initially on good terms with the governor John Stewart, the duke of Albany, who arrived from France on 18 May 1515. However, on his return to France in 1517, rivalry between Angus and James Hamilton, 1st earl of Arran, both members of a council of regency, led to an incident on 30 April 1520 known as "Cleanse the Causeway" when Arran and his associates, in attempting to seize Edinburgh, were repulsed by the Angus Douglases. The latter's triumph was, however, short-lived, and with Albany's return in 1521, Angus withdrew to France, where he remained until about June 1524. A month earlier Arran (next in succession after Albany to the throne) had engineered a coup d'ètat by his erection in May 1524 of the twelve-year-old king; he thus ended Albany's governorship but also facilitated Angus's reinstatement. Returning via London, where he promised to uphold English interests north of the border, he regained his former influence by an ostensible reconciliation with his wife. In fact political stability was seriously threatened by the personal relationship between them. In a bid for sole power Angus, breaking an arrangement of 1526 whereby the king was safeguarded by four magnates in turn, retained permanent custody and procured on 14 June 1526 another erection of the king, then fourteen years old. Real authority, however, lay with Angus, who became chancellor in 1527 while James remained a virtual prisoner. Despite his alienation from the queen mother and the magnates, Angus held sway for two years while Margaret plotted against him and in 1528 not only obtained her long sought for divorce but also succeeded in effecting her son's escape to Stirling Castle, where the assembled magnates declared Angus and his associates banished and their estates forfeited. When attempts at reconciliation failed, Angus retired to England and left James to vent his spite against his kinfolk. The king's death in 1542 facilitated his return and restoration, and he thereafter continued to promote Anglo-Scottish relations; he unsuccessfully took to arms in 1543 when the governor, the earl of Arran, abrogated the TREATIES OF GREENWICH. He did not, however, condone English invasions and on 27 February 1545 led his countrymen to victory at Ancrum Moor, but success eluded him at Pinkie in 1547 when his command of the van contributed to the Scottish defeat. With peace temporarily achieved in 1550, the earl, once described as a "young witless fool," died of an attack of erysipelas at Tantallon Castle before 22 January 1557 and was survived by his third wife Margaret, daughter of Robert, Lord Maxwell.

Bibliography: P. Buchanan, *Margaret Tudor: Queen of Scots*, 1985; J. B. Paul ed., *The Scots Peerage*, Vol. 1, 1904, 190-93.

Ian B. Cowan

Douglas, James, 4th earl of Morton (c. 1516-1581). James Douglas was the second son of Sir George Douglas, master of Angus, and Elizabeth Douglas, heiress of Pittendreich. In 1548 he was captured by the English at Dalkeith and remained in England until 1550. This experience seems to have made him pro- rather than anti-English, as later became clear.

In 1552 he was made a member of the privy council. He also became one of the nobles who favored the rising Protestant movement and signed the "band" of the Lords of the Congregation in 1557, although he was not active in his support. Instead he seemed to be more interested in maintaining his political alliance with Mary of Guise, the regent. It was not until 1560 that he really came into the open as a member of the Protestant party, by supporting the Parliament's decision to establish the Scottish Reformed Church. His Protestantism did not seem to have caused him trouble after the return of MARY, QUEEN OF SCOTS from France in 1561. The next year he was made chancellor of the realm, and the same year he was created earl of Morton. Yet despite his apparent support of Mary, Morton was actually in the opposition, being one of those who planned and carried out the murder of David Rizzio (1566), for which he was exiled to England for nine months. He may also have been involved in the murder of HENRY STEWART, Lord Darnley, Queen Mary's husband, in the following year. While at first he seemed to support Mary, he eventually became one of the leaders of the party that forced her to abdicate and find refuge in England. During the subsequent regencies of the earls of Moray, Lennox, and Mar, Morton wielded considerable power. In fact after the assassination of JAMES STEWART, the earl of Moray, in 1570, he seems to have become the real ruler of the country. Thus it was logical that on the earl of Mar's death in 1572 he became regent.

During the preceding regencies, there had been constant political conflict, even civil war, with those nobles, such as the Hamiltons, who sought the return of Mary from England. In July 1570, however, a truce was arranged between the two groups. During the negotiations Morton had played a part, and when he took over as regent a few months later, he did his utmost to keep the peace. Yet while he enforced the law rather rigorously against the rebels and criminals, he himself acquired much wealth by various means and became seen as an avaricious ruler. At the same time he sought to maintain a close relationship with England and was particularly desirous that the Church of Scotland should conform to the English pattern, which brought him into conflict with the extreme Reformed element, led by Andrew Melville. To add to this problem, he alienated some of the most powerful nobles by his dictatorial policies. Consequently in 1578 he was forced to resign the regency but soon returned, without the title of regent, to rule the country.

With the arrival from France in 1579 of Esme Stewart, seigneur d'Aubigny, who became an immediate favorite of the young JAMES VI, Morton lost much of his influence. Moreover, many of the Scottish nobles opposed to him found in Esme Stewart, now duke of Lennox, a leader who could break Morton's control. The result was that in December 1580 Morton was accused of participating in Darnley's murder, found guilty, and executed the following June. He was survived by his wife, Elizabeth, daughter of the 2nd earl of Morton, one legitimate daughter, four illegitimate sons, and probably three illegitimate daughters.

Bibliography: G. R. Hewitt, *Scotland Under Morton, 1572-80*, 1982.

W. Stanford Reid

Drake's Circumnavigation. This famous voyage originated as a reconnaissance mission for possible future colonization of South America by England. The plan, drawn up in mid-1577, called for a voyage down the Atlantic coast of the continent through the Strait of Magellan and up the western coast to around 30° latitude. When Queen Elizabeth granted permission for the voyage that summer, preparations began in earnest. A fleet of five ships was assembled (the *Pelican, Elizabeth, Marigold, Swan,* and *Christopher*) totaling some 325 tons with a total complement of 160 men.

The expedition left Plymouth on 13 December 1577, reaching Africa near Cape Cantin twelve days later on Christmas Day. Drake proceeded to sail south down the African coast, where he seized several Portuguese and Spanish fishing boats and used their catch to increase his larder before the trip across the Atlantic. On 21 January 1578 Drake left the coast of Africa and set sail for the Cape Verde Islands and South America. In the Cape Verdes Drake had the good fortune of capturing the *Santa Maria*, whose pilot, Nuño da Silva, was familiar with the Guinea-Brazil route. Soon after leaving the Cape Verde Islands, around 1 February, a rift developed between the sailors and the gentlemen on board. Drake accused Thomas Dougherty, one of the gentlemen, of treason and later had him tried and executed.

On 5 April, some two months after leaving the Cape Verdes, the expedition came within sight of the Brazilian coast. After surviving a thick fog soon followed by a sudden storm, the ships slowly made their way south until they reached the Plate estuary on 14 April. They sailed up the estuary to the Bay of Montevideo, where the men killed a number of seals for fresh meat. After several weeks, Drake continued the journey south and reached Cape Tres Puntas on 12 May and St. Julians' Bay around 20 June. It was at St. Julians' that Dougherty was tried and executed. Drake remained at St. Julians' for close to two months before setting sail for the Strait on 17 August with only three ships—the *Pelican*, the *Elizabeth*, and the *Marigold*.

They reached the strait three days later, whereupon Drake had his flagship, the *Pelican*, rechristened the *Golden Hind*. The passage through the strait took 14 days, and they came into the Pacific on 6 September 1578. The three vessels made their way northwest for three days when they encountered a heavy storm that drove the ships back to the Strait. It was during this storm that the only vessel of the voyage was lost; the *Marigold* disappeared from view of the other two ships and was never heard from again. By 7 October the two remaining ships rejoined near the strait but were soon separated by a storm once again. The *Elizabeth* sought shelter within the strait, where her crew waited three weeks for the *Golden Hind* before weighing anchor and returning to England.

Drake, meanwhile, had been blown south by the storm to Cape Horn. After replenishing his stores in the Elizabethides, he set sail northwest for the western coast of South America. He continued on this course until 16 November, when, realizing his charts were wrong, he set a new route to the northeast heading for the previously agreed upon rendezvous at 30°. Making his way up the coast of South America, he reached the Valdivia River on 23 November. In early December Drake looted a ship in the harbor of Valparaiso and then sacked the town. From there he continued north until he reached the rendezvous point and waited a week before continuing on to Salada Bay, where he remained from 22 December 1578 to 19 January 1579, making repairs.

Upon leaving the bay, Drake continued north examining the coast and looking for prize ships. On 5 February he seized one ship of silver and coin and destroyed another. At Callao, the port of Lima, Drake learned that the *Cacafuego*, loaded with a rich cargo of silver, had just left for Panama. He managed to overtake and capture the ship in early March. Soon after, Drake had another great stroke of luck when, on nearing Panama, he captured a bark carrying two pilots familiar with the Philippines route.

Avoiding the Gulf of Panama, the *Golden Hind* sailed north, sacking several villages on the Mexican coast. They remained on a northerly route until early June, when they finally turned back south. On 17 June, the expedition put in at Drake's Bay on the California coast, where they remained until 23 July. Then, making use of the knowledge of the two captured pilots, Drake set sail southwest in search of the trade winds that would carry him across the Pacific. After arriving on the eastern edge of the Caroline Islands in September, he sailed west to Mindanao and then south to the Moluccas. At Ternate, Drake managed to obtain six tons of cloves from the local sultan. Drake then spent four weeks making repairs on a small island near Celebes before again fixing a course for the Moluccas. Soon after setting sail, however, a storm blew him along the eastern coast of Celebes, where the *Golden Hind* ran aground on a submerged rock. To float her off, Drake had three tons of cloves and two guns thrown overboard. More bad weather drove Drake west along the north coast of Timor, then east along the south coast of Java, where he remained until 26 March 1580 before heading across the Indian Ocean for the Cape of Good Hope. The remainder of the voyage was uneventful, and the *Golden Hind* arrived back in Plymouth harbor on 26 September 1580, almost three years after the expedition had begun. Of the 160 men who had began the expedition approximately 100 made it back to England.

Bibliography: Derek A. Wilson, *The World Encompassed: Francis Drake and His Great Voyage*, 1977.

Brian Christian

Drake, Sir Francis (c. 1540-1596). Francis Drake was born, probably in 1543, into a Devonshire family of yeoman status. His grandfather, John, held land at Crowndale on the estate of John Russell, the earl of Bedford, and his father, Edmund, appears to have been a seaman and self-taught preacher of the Protestant persuasion. Bedford's heir, Lord Francis Russell, himself a strong Protestant in later years, was Francis's godfather, a fact that indicates that his father already enjoyed a certain reputation. Edumnd Drake shortly after became a preacher at Chatham and, after ELIZABETH's accession, vicar of nearby Upchurch. So he brought up his numerous brood of twelve sons within easy reach of the sea, and Francis seems to have learned the rudiments of his trade in the Thames estuary and along the north Kent coast. He was related to the well-established Plymouth merchant family of Hawkins and sailed on two of JOHN HAWKINS's voyages—to Guinea in 1563 and to the Caribbean in 1566—before being given his first command in 1567. This was the 50-ton *Judith*, and the expedition was the ill-fated slaving venture that was ambushed by the Spaniards at SAN JUAN D'ULLOA in 1568. This experience, together with the strong Protestantism that he had learned from his father, gave him a lifelong hatred of Spain and a violent contempt for Spaniards that caused them to nickname him El Draque (the dragon). In 1569 he married Mary Newman of Plymouth and returned to the Caribbean in command of the *Swan*. By that time he seems to have become a full-time privateer, whose exploits were hard to distinguish from piracy since there was no state of war between England and Spain. He soon began to acquire (in England) the reputation of a romantic adventurer, particularly for his attack on Nombre de Dios in 1572 and his attempt to ambush a mule train of silver on the Isthmus of Panama. In 1577 he was chosen, as a captain of proven skill and enterprise, to command a secret expedition of obscure purpose mounted by a syndicate inspired by JOHN DEE and FRANCIS WALSINGHAM. The queen herself was heavily involved, and that involvement appears to have been the main reason for the secrecy, because whatever the voyage was originally intended to achieve, it certainly involved trespassing into waters over which Spain claimed exclusive control. The choice of Drake as commander was in itself a provocation, given his reputation.

The expedition sailed from Plymouth in December 1577, with Drake in command of the 100-ton *Pelican* and four smaller vessels. Proceeding through the south Atlantic, the ships made their way through the Strait of Magellan. By the time he reached the Pacific, Drake had lost his small consorts, but the Spaniards were taken completely unaware, and for months he was able to sail at will, capturing both settlements and ships. He returned to Plymouth in September 1580, having incidentally circumnavigated the globe, and carryied plunder to the value of about £500,000 sterling. This immense sum (about three years' normal revenue for the English Crown) touched the queen's heart in a way nothing else could do. Drake was knighted on board his ship and allowed to keep a sufficient share to purchase Buckland Abbey and establish a gentry family. In 1585 he commanded the first naval operation of the war against Spain, sacked San Domingo, Cartagena and St. Augustine in Florida, and administered to those vulnerable colonies a lesson that they were quick to learn. Two years later, in an almost equally successful raid on Spain itself, he destroyed a great quantity of supplies being prepared at Cadiz for Philip's cherished armada against England and also captured the *San Felipe*, valued at £114,000. As vice admiral of the fleet that eventually opposed the SPANISH ARMADA in July 1588, his role was more controversial and less heroic. Although he played a leading part in the decisive engagement at Gravelines, he is more than suspected of having ignored fleet discipline and explicit orders in order to make a prize of *Rosario*, an exploit that could have damaged the whole English operation.

No action was taken against him, but his favor was somewhat diminished, and when a similar indiscipline ruined the effectiveness of the English counterstroke against the Biscay ports in 1589, he returned in virtual disgrace. For five years he was not employed in the queen's service and became instead mayor of Plymouth and the city's member of Parliament. In 1595, however, he was allowed, with Hawkins, to return to the Caribbean in an attempt to repeat his exploit of ten years before. This time the aging adventurers found the whole area heavily fortified and defended, and after a number of abortive landings, both died at sea, Drake succumbing to yellow fever in January 1596.

Bibliography: J. Corbett, *Drake and the Tudor Navy*, 1898; R. B. Wernham (ed.), *The Expedition of Sir John Norris and Sir Francis Drake to Spain and Portugal, 1589*, 1988; N. Williams, *Francis Drake*, 1973.

David M. Loades

Drama. When, on 22 August 1485, Henry Tudor defeated Richard III at BOSWORTH FIELD, English drama consisted of little more than a handful of morality plays and several cycles of mystery plays that had been performed at various times during the fifteenth century by amateur players on improvised stages or pageants, decorated carts, pulled through city streets. By 1592, when the plague broke out in London and the playhouses were closed, England had several professional theatres and acting companies, the government had begun regulating the activities of both, the university wits—CHRISTOPHER MARLOWE, Thomas Kyd, John Lyly, and others—had written their major plays, and a little-known playwright named WILLIAM SHAKESPEARE was beginning the most significant literary career in the history of Western drama. In short, at the end of the Tudor period—and 1592 is a somewhat arbitrary designation given that ELIZABETH I was to reign for eleven more years, but for the study of the drama it is an appropriate one—the foundation was well in place for the development of the finest drama and most distinctive theatrical enterprise produced by a Western culture, that of seventeenth-century England.

The Tudor drama is fascinating historically, if not always invigorating aesthetically. At the beginning of the period, the only plays that existed in England were religious dramas—the mystery plays, which developed from the church liturgy to present a biblical plot; the miracle plays, which dramatized the story of a church saint; and the morality plays, which presented the conflict of the vices and virtues and were thus drawn more from the church homily. English playwrights had not yet rediscovered the classical plays of Greece and Rome, nor had they developed a native tradition. What took place, then, during the Tudor period was the secularization of the drama as the basic themes and devices from the religious plays were reshaped by the influence of the classical plays, particularly those of Seneca, and by the emergence of a native element.

The first form of English drama that developed during the Tudor period was the secular morality play. Many of these plays were in fact not secular plays as such. In John Rastell's *The Nature of the Four Elements* (c. 1519), for example, the theme is that through the study of nature man can come to a better understanding of God. While not containing the emphasis on man's salvation of the religious moralities, this play is allegorical, and its focus remains didactic. A similar play written in the late fifteenth century is *Mankind*, which presents the conflict of its peasant hero as he attempts to ward off the influence of the comic vice characters Titivillus, Newgyse, Nowadays, and Nought. Again, the theme is religious and the purpose didactic; however, the buffoonery and foul language of the characters point up the movement toward secular drama.

Directly related to these plays are the political moralities and moral interludes popular during the reigns of HENRY VII and HENRY VIII. The best of the early political moralities is John Skelton's *Magnyfycence* (c. 1515), which dramatizes the conflict of the monarch character Magnyfycence as he is led astray by such court flatterers as Counterfeit and Folly, only to be left destitute until returning to the path of Good Hope and Redress. Clearly, the best writer of moral interlude was John Heywood. What most distinguishes his moral interlude from the other forms of morality play is its diminished didacticism and its greater emphasis on entertainment. The characters are drawn from ordinary life, and the comic element is increased. In Heywood's best drama, *The Play of the Weather*, for example, a group of characters appeal to Jupiter for weather that would suit their purposes. The action centers on the debate that breaks out until Jupiter announces that the weather will remain as it is.

Of the Tudor playwrights, the first to make use of the classics were the writers of school plays who knew primarily the Roman dramatists Seneca, Plautus, and Terence. The Roman plays provided both style and content to dramatists who were interested in writing plays completely free from religious didacticism. Two notable comedies appeared during this period of transition, *Ralph Roister Doister* (c. 1534-1541) written by Nicholas Udall, headmaster of Eaton, and *Gammer Gurton's Needle* (c. 1563), which is generally ascribed to John Still. Although both plays present English characters and are somewhat akin to the medieval farce, they are heavily indebted to the influence of Plautus, particularly Udall's work, which is a rework of the Roman playwright's *Miles Gloriosus*. The action follows the efforts of the braggart Ralph and his agent, the parasite Merigreek, as he attempts to woo the widow Christian Custance, who is already betrothed to the absent merchant Gawin Goodluck. Although ponderous in both action and language, the play is superior to *Gammar Gurton's Needle*, which is a coarse treatment of its buffoonish country characters in search of Gammer's mislaid, needle which shows up painfully in the breeches of her servant Hodge. Both plays particularly establish the influence of classical writers and the fusion of this influence with a strong native element, both of which were important in the move toward a professional drama.

Also a school drama, the first English tragedy was the play *Ferrex and Porrex, or Gorboduc* (1561), written by two students at Inner Temple, Thomas Sackville and Thomas Norton. The play takes its subject from English legend, but it is handled in the vein of the Roman playwright Seneca, whose revenge tragedies were profoundly to affect later English writers of tragedy, including Shakespeare. *Gorboduc* presents the political turmoil that results when King Gorboduc divides his kingdom between his sons Ferrex and Porrex. The play suggests the growing use of the drama to make a political statement.

Early Tudor playwrights had seen the possibilities in the drama to promote political and/or theological positions. When Henry VIII broke with Rome, the tendency to use the literary form for this purpose increased. Throughout his reign, as well as the reigns of EDWARD VI and MARY, dramas had been written and performed to support partisan positions regarding the religious and concomitant political struggles in Tudor England. Elizabeth recognized the power of the drama in this context and in 1559 banned the performance of unlicensed plays and attempted to discourage works dealing with religious and political subjects.

For several years, these measures were sufficient, if not always entirely effective, in controlling the emerging professional theatre. However, as the drama expanded and the number of plays written and performed increased, the government enhanced its control. In 1572, the government stipulated that no nobleman below the rank of baron could sponsor a troupe of professional players. Also in the 1570s the religious cycles were suppressed, thus giving greater momentum to the secular dramas performed by professional troupes. Finally, in 1574, the government extended its control of the drama further when the master of revels, an official royal position, was given complete control of the theater as the licenser of all plays and acting companies. While not completely successful, this measure generally gave the government control of the growth of the drama and anticipated the 1604 measure that extended the right to maintain licensed companies only to members of the royal family.

In 1574, the master of revels licensed under the sponsorship of ROBERT DUDLEY, earl of Leicester, and the direction of James Burbage the first major professional troupe. Nine years later, the master of revels hired from existing companies twelve actors to establish the Queen's Men, which remained the leading company until the closing of the theatres in 1592. These and the other professional troupes were organized according to a sharing plan, whereby the financial backing and resulting profits were distributed among the primary members of the company. These shareholders generally included some of a troupe's actors, particularly those who were deemed crucial to the company's success. More often actors were householders or part-owners of the theatre in which the company performed and shared profits through that financial arrangement. Of the twenty to twenty-five members of a company, half would have been hired men who worked on limited contracts and were essentially the jack-of-all-trade participants in a company's activities. They would have served as actors, stage managers, musicians, prompters, and so on.

The first permanent professional theatres were built in England during 1576. The Theatre was an open-air design somewhat akin to the bear-baiting arena, which some scholars speculated was the model for the Elizabethan public theatres in general. Such theatres have been classified "public" because they played to diverse audiences. The Theatre, built by James Burbage, was located in Shoreditch, on the south bank of the Thames River. This, the first permanent theatre in England, was soon followed by several other public playhouses, most of which were also located on the Bankside: The Curtain (1577), Newington Butts

(1579), The Rose (1587), The Swan (1595), Shakespeare's theatre, The Globe (1599), The Fortune (1600), The Red Bull (1605), and The Hope (1613). The second theatre built in 1576 was The Blackfriars, an indoor structure of remodeled rooms in a monastery. It was designed for performance of plays presented to an aristocratic audience and is thus classified a private theatre. From these two first theatres grew the two Tudor traditions of indoor and outdoor staging, although the term outdoor is somewhat misleading.

Most of the outdoor theatres were built on the same basic design. The stage was located within a circular structure resembling a bear-baiting arena or inn yard. It was covered by a roof that not only afforded protection from the weather but also contained whatever simple stage machinery a company employed. A two-level facade spanned the rear of the stage with entrance and exit passages on the first level and a balcony set on the second. Behind the facade, often a curtain, the actors had room to change into costumes—as many played dual roles—and otherwise prepare for their entrances. The floor of the stage contained a trapdoor for the entrance of supernatural characters such as Mephistopheles in Marlowe's *Doctor Faustus*. The second-level balcony was often used to signal changes in location that accompanied act and scene changes.

Surrounding the stage in an outdoor Tudor theatre was a three-story circular structure that provided covered sections and railings along which the ranking members of the audience could stand to observe the performance. In the pit in front of the stage stood the common folk, or groundlings, who paid a penny to watch a play. These often unruly spectators were notorious for calling down poor performances and weak plays before their hoped-for two-week run was completed. They often were, in this sense, much more rigorous critics than those whom a twentieth-century playwright faces, and their power to determine the success of a playwright or play was pronounced.

In one very important respect the development of a professional theatre changed the literary profession in England. Previously, only those writers who were able to secure the patronage of a member of the nobility were able to devote themselves to their literary pursuits. Their numbers were few, and often their efforts restricted by the need to develop themes and to master forms that would ensure that they kept the favor of their patron. By writing scripts for the theatre, however, a dramatist could generate a respectable income and, within the still fairly broad government guidelines, probe ideas both intellectually and artistically challenging. And although the theatres in general and the public theatres in particular provided a popular form of entertainment, the Tudor drama had developed from a foundation largely built on the influence of classical literature, thus giving it respectability. Not surprisingly, therefore, the first major play-wrights to produce scripts for the professional theatre were university-educated members of the literati, the so-called university wits: John Lyly (1554-1606), George Peele (1557-1596), Robert Greene (1558-1592), and Christopher Marlowe (1564-1593). Lyly and Peele had been educated at Oxford, Greene and Marlowe at Cambridge, and Kyd at neither, although he had a sound classical training from his days at the Merchant Taylors' school.

When John Lyly turned to writing for the stage, he had already achieved literary success through the publication of his novel *Euphues* (1578). His plays, though structurally weak and encumbered by sluggish plots, were extremely popular, largely because Lyly was able to write effective dialogue. Probably the most interesting of his plays is *Galathea* (1585), which is set in the English countryside, where the people are beset by the curse of Neptune, which can be appeased only by the sacrifice of a virgin to the sea monster Agar. To save their children, two fear-stricken fathers disguised their daughters as boys, only to have them pursued by the nymphs of Diana acting under Cupid's spell and to fall in love with each other.

George Peele, in many ways a superior writer to Lyly, further developed the use of the native element in English comedy. Peele's most successful play was *The Old Wives Tale*, a romantic comedy in which the characters in a story told by the wife of the simple smith Clunch come to life on the stage. Her story deals with a wizard who has stolen the daughter of a king and her brothers' efforts to rescue her. Peele's ultimate success was, however, with language, as he was able to employ a variety of verse forms and to use them to enhance his characterizations.

Although Robert Greene is perhaps best remembered for referring to Shakespeare as an "upstart crow," he was in fact the best writer of comedy among the university wits. His *Friar Bacon and Friar Bungay* (1591) was a major success and stands as the first major romantic comedy in English literature. The main plot pivots on a love triangle involving Prince Edward, Lady Margaret, and Lacy, sent by the prince to woo on his behalf the lovely maid, but the comic subplot involving Friar Bacon is the better part of the play.

Thomas Kyd's reputation rests on the lasting popularity and significance of *The Spanish Tragedy* (1586). This play employs all of the devices ascribed to the influence of Seneca: a mad hero, a plot of murder and revenge, a vengeful ghost, and a dumb show. In the play, Balthazar, son to the viceroy of Portugal, is captured by Horatio and Lorenzo. The tables turn and Lorenzo and Balthazar murder Horatio and suffer the revenge of his father.

Decidedly the most gifted dramatist of the university wits was Christopher Marlowe. By the time he was killed at age twenty-nine, Marlowe had written a body of dramatic literature that is far better than what Shakespeare wrote by the time he was the same age. In his very first play, *Tamburlaine* (1587), Marlowe established himself as the poet of the Tudor stage through his mastery of blank verse in the speeches of his dynamic central character. What this play and the *Second Part of Tamburlaine* both lacked, however, was structure and characterization. His next effort, *Doctor Faustus* (c. 1590), also has problems with its structure; however, Marlowe did solve many of his problems with characterization. Unlike the flat Tamburlaine, Faustus is a multidimensional character whose soul is tormented not just by his bargain with Mephistopheles but by his growing realization that he never receives those things that he requests. It was with *Edward II* (1592) that Marlowe's command of language, structure, and character came together. In this play, he probes with delicacy and astuteness the motivations of the stubborn but vulnerable Edward as well as those of Edward's adversaries, most notably the Machivellian Mortimer. He shows himself also capable of writing a play with more than one major character. Ultimately, however, in this and all of Marlowe's plays, it is the richness of language which defines the genius of the Tudor period's most impressive playwright.

What explains the advances in the theatre and dramatic literature of the Tudor period is the richness of the period itself. The Reformation came to England early in the period and with it, political crisis, which explains why the secular plays evolve so quickly out of the medieval religious dramas. The period was marked by English nationalism, which created the interest in the native element. And it was the period during which Englishmen rediscovered the classics, perhaps the most important influence on the growing dramatic tradition. All three influences put together prepared the stage for Shakespeare and BEN JONSON, England's two greatest playwrights.

Bibliography: Thomas Marc Parrott and Robert Hamilton Ball, *A Short View of Elizabethan Drama*, 1943; A. P. Rossiter, *English Drama from Early Times to the Elizabethans*, 1967.

Gerald W. Morton

Dudley, John, Duke of Northumberland (c. 1504-1553), de facto ruler of England during Edward VI's last years (October 1549-July 1553); a great soldier and unscrupulous politician popularly remembered for his treasonous attempt to bar Mary Tudor from the succession.

Dudley was the eldest son of Edmund Dudley, HENRY VII's attainted councillor. Upon Edmund's execution in 1510 (see EMPSON AND DUDLEY, AFFAIR OF), Dudley became the ward of Sir Edward Guildford, a seasoned captain and master of the armory whose daughter, Jane, he married in 1526. (There were eight sons, including ROBERT DUDLEY, the Elizabethan earl of Leicester.) Frequent duty overseas prompted Guildford to assign his young half-brother, Sir Henry, with Dudley's upbringing at court. A gentleman of the Privy Chamber and one of HENRY VIII's most intimate companions, Sir Henry organized the king's jousts; this experience and Dudley's natural prowess explain the young man's training for the tournament and war and his subsequent service as soldier and courtier. At nineteen he was in France, where (as Guildford's lieutenant) he was knighted in battle (November 1523). His appearances at COURT (at coronations, christenings, and jousts) and honorable attendance—he accompanied THOMAS WOLSEY to France (1527) and the king and ANNE

BOLEYN to CALAIS for their meeting (1532) with Francis I—bear witness to his royal preferment.

In November 1534 Dudley was returned to the House of Commons at a knight of the shire for Kent. He sat in the Parliament of 1536 (the one that condemned Anne Boleyn) and perhaps that of 1539. In the meantime he was acquiring by purchase and gift an extensive landed base in Staffordshire, where he was named sheriff in 1536 for his assistance in raising 200 men against the PILGRIMAGE OF GRACE. Following an embassy to Spain (1537) he was sent to Calais (1538) as deputy to Arthur Plantagenet, Viscount Lisle (who had married his mother in 1510). Lisle's disgrace (1540) and death (1542) paved the way for Dudley's own creation (12 March 1542) as Viscount Lisle and a summons to the House of Lords.

The third ANGLO-FRENCH WAR OF 1543-1546 brought Dudley to the fore as one of the king's chief commanders. Vice admiral since 1537, he was appointed lord admiral (26 January 1543) at about the same time he was admitted to the king's Privy Chamber (1542 or 1543) and the PRIVY COUNCIL (23 April 1543) and installed a knight of the Garter (5 May 1543). Military engagements on land and sea stamped him as a hardened, successful warrior—storming Leith, burning Edinburgh, and taking Boulogne in 1544; sweeping the Channel of enemy craft and attacking Normandy in 1545 and 1546; and—as "Lieutenant General of the Army and Armada upon the sea in outward parts against the French" (March 1546)—leading English envoys to Paris to obtain Francis I's signature to the Treaty of Camp (July 1546), which he had helped to negotiate.

In the 1540s Dudley's comrade-in-arms was EDWARD SEYMOUR, the earl of Hertford, with whom at court he forged an alliance against factious "Conservatives." Dudley reckoned, correctly, that on King Edward's accession (28 January 1547) real power would pass to Seymour, the boy-king's uncle (and later the duke of Somerset) and the religious Reformists in Seymour's camp. An executor of Henry VIII's will—and thus a member of the council that Henry had appointed to govern during King Edward's minority—Dudley supported Somerset's creation as lord protector; for his support he was made earl of Warwick (16 February 1547) and (on surrendering the admiralty to Somerset's brother) chamberlain to the king's household (until 1 February 1550).

Ambition eventually made enemies of the two men, though during the Protectorate (1547-1549) they were one in matters of policy. Somerset's chief policy was war, a war in Scotland that also engaged France. Dudley helped secure a quick victory at Pinkie (September 1547), but Somerset's strategy of garrisoning Scotland, adopted against his advice, bankrupted England, and when the rebellions of 1549 brought war on a third, domestic front, he and the Conservatives on the council overthrew the protector (October 1549).

Myth, not fact, gives Dudley a butcher's part in supressing KETT'S REBELLION. Martial honor and government policy dictated that he offer pardons to the rebels, an act that he bravely undertook in person in their camp. At

Dussindale, a rearguard action (27 August 1549), he tried to prevent a massacre; the responsibility for slaughter that day lay with uncontrollable subordinates.

A master of intrigue, Dudley more than once countered the treachery of dangerous court rivals with cunning and duplicity. His sham Catholicism at the time of the coup (1549) disoriented the Conservatives, who, it developed, were really bent on destroying him. In the struggle for control of the council (October 1549-February 1550), he called on THOMAS CRANMER to move the king to appoint new members, all of them Reformists who could be expected to support him. His own appointment as great master of the Household (20 February 1550) carried with it the presidency of the council, an office empowering him to govern effectively as king in council; he outlawed the Conservatives, reinstated Somerset, brought in his own clients, seized the levers of royal patronage, and became the duke of Northumberland (11 October 1551). Discovering that Somerset, meanwhile, meant to undo him, he reluctantly rigged his execution (January 1552), an act (so he said) that burdened his conscience thereafter.

As governor, Dudley sought to restore order, a precondition of financial stability. He abandoned war, stabilized the currency, liquidated the king's foreign debts, and (through WILLIAM CECIL) reorganized government by council, the basis of Cecil's later, Elizabethan "system." Obsessed by security, he mustered a short-lived gendarmery, the nucleus of England's first standing ARMY. Neglecting the NAVY, he nonetheless patronized overseas EXPLORATIONS—tentative steps toward maritime expansion.

Under his rule Reformist divines also effected a religious revolution, establishing for the first time officially the doctrines and liturgy of the Protestant Church of England: a new Ordinal (1550), a catechism (1553), and the FORTY-TWO ARTICLES of Faith (1553). In religion Dudley was certainly no idealist; he backed this stage of the Reformation because it enriched him with confiscated church property. The Reformers denounced him for this, as they knew how much the king admired him (contemporaries spoke of Dudley's great charm and bearing). At any rate, Dudley was careful to encourage a boy for whom Protestantism had become a sacred dynastic cause.

By tying his fortunes officially to Protestant reform—a policy furthered by those he had planted in Edward's Privy Chamber—Dudley had bound himself politically to the Catholic Mary's exclusion. In June 1553, when it became clear that Edward VI was dying, he adopted the desperate (and, in the absence of parliamentary approval, illegal) scheme by which the king, in an amended "Devise," willed the Crown to LADY JANE GREY (whose marriage to Dudley's son, Guildford, had been arranged in May). But the swiftness of Edward's demise (6 July 1553) caught Dudley by surprise. He had failed to secure Mary's person beforehand, and his last-minute "conversion" to Catholicism did not win her pardon. He was beheaded on Tower Hill on 22 August 1553.

Bibliography: Barrett L. Beer, *Northumberland: The Political Career of John Dudley, Earl of Warwick and Duke of Northumberland*, 1973; Dale Hoak, "Rehabilitating the Duke of Northumberland: Politics and Political Control, 1549-53," in *The Mid-Tudor Polity c. 1540-1560*, ed. J. Loach and R. Tittler, 1980.

Dale Hoak

Dudley, Robert, Earl of Leicester (1532?-1588). Robert was the fifth son of JOHN DUDLEY, duke of Northumberland, the queenmaker *manqué* of 1553. In 1550 he had contracted a love match with Amy Robsart, the daughter of a Norfolk squire, when both bride and groom were eighteen years old. At that stage in the family fortunes it is highly unlikely that any more ambitious marriage alliance was envisaged for this younger son, for all his manifest gifts and charm. In his prime his enemies were to make much of the fact that both his father and his grandfather, Edmund Dudley, had been executed for treason against the Tudors, and he was to be vulnerable to the charge of being an *arriviste*.

He first met ELIZABETH at the COURT of her brother EDWARD VI, and she is reported to have been impressed from the outset. But on her accession in 1558 his name was not immediately linked with hers as a possible suitor. After he was sworn of the PRIVY COUNCIL in April 1559, Elizabeth seemed incapable of concealing her affection for him and did nothing to dispel the rumors that she might marry him. In 1560, while Dudley was in attendance on the queen at court, Amy Robsart fell downstairs at Cumnor Place and broke her neck, and the ensuing scandal threatened to touch the sceptre itself. Certain circumstances point to suicide brought on by despair, and the coroner's verdict of death by misadventure did little to quell the suspicions of Dudley's complicity in murder. He is unlikely to have been guilty of any greater offense than neglect of his wife. Although her death released him from one restraint upon his grandiose ambitions, the suspicious circumstances attending it introduced a new, and ultimately insuperable, obstacle.

His intimacy with the queen was probably not as scandalous as the gossips would have us believe. For all her early infatuation with him in 1560 and 1561, Elizabeth does not appear to have abandoned herself to passion. She soon recovered her dignity and independence when Dudley overplayed his hand, and he seemed never to have had as much influence with her again. In 1564 she proposed him as a suitor to MARY, QUEEN OF SCOTS, and to make him a more eligible consort for her he was created earl of Leicester and endowed with gifts of land and privileges to support his state. Mary was secretly insulted to be offered Elizabeth's cast-off lover and "horse-keeper" as prospective husband. Leicester later made out that he was not a willing collaborator in the proposals, which Elizabeth may not have expected to succeed except as a diplomatic ploy to prevent Mary's seeking a foreign prince as consort.

During her summer progress in 1575 Elizabeth was entertained by Leicester at Kenilworth Castle with elaborate festivities, which included a pageant designed in cryptic terms as a formal proposal of marriage. The queen did not respond to this public gesture, and three years later, after extricating himself from a liaison with Lady Douglass Sheffield, Leicester married Lettice Knollys at a secret ceremony. When Elizabeth learned of this, the earl was banished from the court, and his influence was at a low ebb during the French courtships of the queen. When the prospect of a foreign marriage faded in 1581 and 1582, he recovered favor at court and rounded on those Catholic courtiers who had promoted Anjou's suit.

In his periods of disgrace, Leicester was dependent on WILLIAM CECIL's good offices as an intermediary with the source of all favor. Cecil seems never to have exploited these situations for his own advantage, a service that was not reciprocated when Dudley himself was in the ascendent, for in 1560, 1564, and 1569 he intrigued for the secretary's dismissal. Once he abandoned his ambition to marry the queen, he and Cecil seemed to have reached a modus vivendi. Faction—rivalry, not merely over the distributions of patronage but over the sharing of power—remained a latent danger in the court politics of the reign. The danger posed by Catholic plots to the queen's life and the regime caused the privy councillors to close ranks in 1584 as subscribers to the oath or BOND OF ASSOCIATION.

Leicester had more to lose than any other subject from the queen's premature demise. Yet none of the allegations that he made subversive contingency plans to assure his position should Elizabeth predecease him can be substantiated. Even so, his historical reputation has suffered from the long-lasting effect of the libel published against him in 1584 and known subsequently as "Leicester's Commonwealth."

As premier courtier and favorite, Leicester seems to have been content to hold the Household offices of master of the horse (from 1559) and lord steward (from 1584), rather than any of the great offices of state. His activities as a patron of parliamentary candidates in shire and borough elections met with indifferent successes and do not suggest that he was seriously concerned to build up a major following in the House of Commons. He was the first nobleman to sponsor a company of actors, and his protection of "Leicester's Men" sat uneasily with his patronage of PURITANS. He told another puritan, Thomas Wood, in 1576, defending himself against criticism for inconstancy in the cause, "I never altered my mind or thought from my youth touching my religion." It would be difficult to document such consistency or commitment on his part, and he cannot so easily be exculpated from the charge of cynical opportunism in matters of church and state. His protection of the puritan campaign for a preaching ministry and the religious education of the laity was necessarily constrained by the queen's aversion to the "precisians." From early on in the reign he had taken a keen interest in ecclesiastical preferments and in securalizing bishops' lands, though he may have acted from mixed motives.

Leicester cast himself in the role of champion of embattled CALVINISM on the Continent, and from as early as 1572 he had schemed to be appointed commander of an English expeditionary force to aid the Dutch rebels against their Spanish overlord. When he finally achieved this ambition in the years 1585-1586, the campaign he conducted was a miserable failure. He was rash enough to accept without Elizabeth's permission the title of governor general of the Netherlands conferred by the estates and was forced to relinquish it when she repudiated his action. He was not a successful general, but neither was he the political lightweight he is made out to be in so many historical accounts. His loyalty to the queen cannot be seriously questioned; he had recovered favor again by the time of the SPANISH ARMADA, and he was at her side when she delivered her famous speech at Tilbury. As commander of these land forces he was denied his moment of glory when the armada was repulsed at sea. He died of a fever on 4 September 1588 at Rycote on his way back to Kenilworth, much lamented by Elizabeth, who preserved "his last letter" to her (as she marked it) as a special keepsake.

Bibliography: Wallace T. MacCaffrey, *Queen Elizabeth and the Making of Policy, 1572-1588*, 1981; Eleanor Rosenberg, *Leicester, Patron of Letters*, 1955.

Peter Roberts

E

Edinburgh, Treaty of (1560). The English intervened militarily in Scotland on 28 March 1560 in compliance with the ARTICLES OF BERWICK, their agreement with the Scottish Lords of the Congregation. Unfortunately, while the English besieged the French forces at Leith, they had failed to defeat them decisively. Expenses were mounting, and the Spanish made their displeasure with the English actions known. As a result, Queen ELIZABETH ordered WILLIAM CECIL, the leading advocate of intervention in Scotland, to negotiate a peace.

Cecil and the English commissioners proceeded north on 27 May 1560. Negotiations among the English, French, and Scottish commissioners began at Newcastle on 8 June but shifted to Edinburgh on 18 June. There they agreed that while the military situation of the English besiegers of Leith was poor, it was worse for the besieged French. With supplies declining and with no hope for succor from France (the English controlled the seas), the French cause was further crippled by the death of the regent Mary of Guise. As a result, Cecil managed, for the worried Queen Elizabeth, to turn a potential setback into an advantageous treaty, which he concluded on 6 July.

In the treaty, it was agreed at the beginning that MARY, QUEEN OF SCOTS would abandon displaying the English royal arms with her own. Of more substance, the French agreed to evacuate Scotland and dismantle their strongholds at Leith and Dunbar. Furthermore, they promised that they would stop interfering in Scottish affairs and that no French official would hold a position in the Scottish government. A twelve-member governing council consisting of five chosen by the Protestant-dominated Scottish Parliament and seven chosen by the queen of Scots would rule the country. No mention was made, however, of the much sought English-Scottish alliance that the Protestant rebels had hoped to include.

The Treaty of Edinburgh was a striking success and laid the foundations for English domination over, and eventual incorporation of, Scotland. Queen Elizabeth, however, was not at all satisfied. The French had refused to return

CALAIS or pay an indemnity of 500,000 crowns, as she had desired. Cecil narrowly managed to conclude the treaty just before a royal ultimatum to break off negotiations arrived. Mary, Queen of Scots was even more unhappy with the treaty. She refused to ratify it, but the death of her husband, Francis II, left her without significant French support; besides, the French troops in Scotland were forced to withdraw anyway, leaving her with little authority there. From that point onward English influence in Scotland remained strong.

Bibliography: C. Read, *Mr. Secretary Cecil and Queen Elizabeth*, 1955; R. B. Wernham, *Before the Armada: The Emergence of the English Nation, 1485-1588*, 1966.

                                                                                                Gary Bell

Edward VI (1537-1553). Succeeded his father, HENRY VIII, as king of England and Ireland at the age of nine (28 January 1547); he died of pulmonary tuberculosis at fifteen (6 July 1553) after a brief and troubled reign.

Edward's birth (12 October 1537) at Hampton Court provided Henry VIII with a legitimate male heir, the object of the dynastic policy that had triggered the Reformation of the 1530s. Edward's mother, JANE SEYMOUR, was Henry's third queen; her sudden demise (24 October 1537) left the infant Edward—painted by Holbein at fourteen months—in the care of Lady Margaret Bryan, two nurses, four "rockers," and three physicians. His later portraits (ninety-nine in all) show an intelligent, grey-eyed lad of fair complexion and slight build. "He had a somewhat projecting shoulder-blade" and was nearsighted and perhaps slightly deaf, said the Italian doctor, Cardano; though "decorous" and "handsome," a noticeably "grave aspect" made him seem an "old man" at times. He was of a reportedly pleasant disposition, and his frequent illnesses indicated no inherent frailty; he was an active boy of some stamina who ran at the ring and enjoyed the martial games of the court.

Edward's rigorous formal education, which commenced in 1544, rivalled the best that Renaissance HUMANISM could offer; his tutors included England's foremost scholars and educational theorists—Richard Cox (chancellor of Oxford), Roger Ascham (author of *The Schoolmaster*), Sir Anthony Cooke (a learned courtier), and John Cheke (Regius Professor of Greek at Cambridge and Edward's principal teacher). His schooling completed by June 1552, he was (at fourteen) a prodigy of the classroom whose facility in ancient and modern languages—he could read, write, and speak Greek, Latin, and French—rhetoric, dialectic, history, geography, political theory, ethics, music, cosmography, and mathematics (including the science of navigation; he owned and knew the use of the astrolabe, quadrant, and dial-ring) clearly surpassed that of even well-rounded masters of arts.

For Reformist court preachers (Thomas Becon, Martin Bucer, HUGH LATIMER, John Ponet et al.), Edward was England's Josias, and in their weekly sermons before him they pounded home the obligations of the godly prince, especially his sacred duty to promote "true religion"; here was the anti-papal Protestant program, and Edward absorbed it all, writing down in now lost ledgers "every notable sentence" (said WILLIAM CECIL), "especially if it touched a king." Edward's tutors were also zealous Protestants, and there can be no doubt that the lessons they devised reinforced the message of the sermons.

After his scripturally based religious studies, Cheke reckoned Aristotle's *Politics* to have been Edward's most important reading, important, that is, for the precepts that were supposed to inform a prince's understanding of politics and history. In his self-styled "Chronicle," the unique, political diary of sorts that Cheke bade him compose, Edward laconically recorded news of Turkish maneuvers with as much emphasis as that given to festivities at court or the executions of his uncles. Contrary to views that place Edward on "the threshold of power" in the years 1551-1553, his much discussed "state papers" (memoranda for business in council, etc.) provide no evidence of a direction of affairs or management of men; he composed them after the fact from lists and notes supplied him by his secretaries and clerks. He was certainly cognizant of contemporary evils; how, as an adult, he would have responded to them remains conjectural.

There is no evidence that Edward devised his government's policies. Full power and authority during his minority technically lay with the executors of Henry VIII's will. In fact Edward's uncle, EDWARD SEYMOUR, duke of Somerset, governed both the king and England until October 1549, when he was overthrown by the council, in which leadership subsequently fell to JOHN DUDLEY, duke of Northumberland (then earl of Warwick). Like Somerset, Northumberland sought to control Edward by planting his own friends in the king's Privy Chamber. (Somerset's brother, Thomas, had challenged this type of control in 1549 and was therefor executed.) Edward's speeches in council (1551-1552), said a French eyewitness, were themselves evidence of the success of Northumberland's efforts; the duke and his men had so drawn the king to them that after careful priming, Edward willingly decreed their designs as his own.

This appreciation was essentially corroborated by Sir John Gosnold, solicitor general and one of those charged with framing Edward's "Devise" for the succession, and it explains how the scheme to make LADY JANE GREY queen appeared to be of Edward's invention. Already seriously ill in January 1553, Edward believed himself divinely appointed to preserve the church reformed in his name. Since this belief required the exclusion of his sister, Mary—on the grounds, as he said on his deathbed, that her Catholicism endangered true religion and presaged civil war—he was persuaded to revise the holograph draft of his "Devise" in such a way as to leave the Crown not to the (then) unborn heirs male of his cousin, Jane, as first decided, but to Jane herself, who on 21 May 1553 had been forced to marry Northumberland's son, Guildford Dudley.

Edward died at Greenwich, and he reportedly prayed to "defend this realm from papistry." He was buried on 8 August 1553 in an unmarked grave in Westminster

Abbey; an Elizabethan plan for a monumental tomb commemorating him as a Protestant "imperial" king was never realized.

Bibliography: Dale Hoak, *The Reign of Edward VI*, 1991; J. G. Nichols, ed., *Literary Remains of King Edward VI*, 2 vols., 1857.

Dale Hoak

Elizabeth I (1533-1603). Queen of England, 1558-1603, this daughter of HENRY VIII and his second wife, ANNE BOLEYN, was born 7 September 1533 at Greenwich Palace. Henry at first proclaimed Elizabeth princess of Wales and heir to the throne, as he had earlier done for his first daughter MARY. Before Elizabeth was three years old, however, Henry had her mother Anne executed for adultery and treason, and Elizabeth, along with Mary, was declared illegitimate.

Henry immediately married JANE SEYMOUR, who gave Henry the son that he craved, the future EDWARD VI. Henry subsequently married three more times. It was his sixth, and last, wife, KATHERINE PARR, who strongly influenced Elizabeth. Katherine gathered her stepchildren about her at court and arranged for Elizabeth's excellent education under such men of New Learning as William Grindal and, later, Roger Ascham. In her teens Elizabeth became proficient in Latin, Greek, French, and Italian.

When Henry died in January 1547, he left a will that placed Mary and then Elizabeth back in the succession should Edward die without heirs. Elizabeth went to live with her stepmother, Katherine Parr, who soon made an imprudent marriage with her former suitor, THOMAS SEYMOUR, maternal uncle to the new king. In the early summer of 1548 the then pregnant Katherine Parr suggested that Elizabeth leave Sudeley Castle to set up her own household, because of a flirtation between Thomas Seymour and Elizabeth. After Katherine Parr's death in childbed at the end of August 1548, Seymour engaged in increasingly wild schemes to gain power, one of which included marriage to Elizabeth. Seymour was finally executed for treason, and Elizabeth herself was touched by scandal; rumors abounded that Elizabeth was pregnant. During the rest of her brother Edward's reign, Elizabeth lived quietly, and she regained her reputation as a model of the Reformed faith.

At Edward's death there was a dynastic crisis. Edward disinherited both his sisters in favor on his cousin, LADY JANE GREY, fortuitously married to the youngest son of the most powerful man of the realm, JOHN DUDLEY, duke of Northumberland. Edward's device, without the force of Parliament, was patently illegal; it was also highly unpopular, and Elizabeth's sister Mary succeeded to the throne without a battle. Elizabeth joined Mary in her triumphant procession through London but soon fell out of favor with her Catholic half-sister, and many people saw Elizabeth as a Protestant alternative. WYATT'S REBELLION of 1555 against Mary's marriage to her cousin, Philip of Spain, caused Mary and her council to decide to have Elizabeth lodged in the Tower and examined. Nothing could be proven against her, however, and her life was spared. Upon Mary's death Elizabeth peacefully ascended the throne 17 November 1558.

The English people, disheartened by Mary's religious persecution and losing war with France, were delighted with their new young queen. Elizabeth began her reign by emphasizing the theme of national unity. One of Elizabeth's first acts was to appoint WILLIAM CECIL, later Lord Burghley, as her PRINCIPAL SECRETARY. It was to be a long and fruitful partnership. Other advisers of the queen who served her for many years included Sir FRANCIS WALSINGHAM, Sir CHRISTOPHER HATTON, and Sir ROBERT DUDLEY.

The returned MARIAN EXILES, a number of them serving in Elizabeth's first Parliament, pushed Elizabeth into a more Protestant church settlement than she originally wanted. The 1559 Acts of Supremacy and UNIFORMITY made the celebration of mass illegal and established fines for those who stayed away from the Church of England. Elizabeth, however, looked only for outward conformity, for, as Francis Bacon put it, she did not wish to make "windows into men's souls."

Besides religion, one of the other pressing matters of Elizabeth's reign was the succession. Most of the English hoped the succession, as well as the problem of a woman's ruling, would be solved by Elizabeth's marriage and the birth of a son. Elizabeth, however, while she adored courtship and perceived its use as a political tool, refused all behests to marry. Nor would she name an heir. Certainly her experiences with her father, mother, and stepmothers would hardly have convinced Elizabeth that marriage was an enviable estate. Elizabeth had many political suitors: her former brother-in-law, Philip II; the Habsburg archduke Charles; JAMES HAMILTON, the earl of Arran; Charles of Sweden; and the sons of Catherine de Medici, especially the duke of Alençon. Elizabeth also had a forceful suitor in her favorite, Robert Dudley, whom she eventully created earl of Leicester. For years rumors swept around the queen in terms of her relationship with Dudley, particularly after the mysterious death of his wife, Amy Robsart, in 1560.

The problems of religion and the succession intertwined, especially with Elizabeth unmarried and refusing to name an heir. Many people saw Elizabeth's Catholic cousin, MARY, QUEEN OF SCOTS, as the next heir. In fact, for some Catholics she was the legitimate queen since the pope had never recognized the nullity of Henry VIII's marriage to CATHERINE OF ARAGON, thus making Elizabeth a bastard. The situation became far more serious for England in 1568 when Mary Stuart fled Scotland and put herself into her cousin's hands. Since the Scots refused to take Mary back and allowing her to go on to France or Spain might mean her returning to Scotland with an army, Elizabeth kept Mary in confinement for the next nineteen years. Her presence in England undermined the delicate religious balance and led to the NORTHERN REBELLION in 1569 and to Elizabeth's excommunication by papal bull (see REGNANS IN EXCELSIS) in 1570. During Mary's captivity there were three major plots involving Mary Stuart to assassinate Elizabeth, free the Scottish queen, and place Mary on the English throne with the aid of foreign invasion. The last of these, the BABINGTON PLOT of 1586, led to Mary Stuart's execution 8 February 1587 after Elizabeth agonized for several months over signing the death warrant.

The problems with Mary Stuart were one example of the interconnectedness of religion and international politics and the fear of invasion. There were others. Elizabeth's aid of the Protestants in the Netherlands infuriated Philip II of Spain. After the execution of Mary Stuart, Philip finally committed himself to the invasion of England and the restoration of Catholicism; in the summer of 1588 he sent his SPANISH ARMADA.

One of the draamtic moments of Elizabeth's reign came in August 1588 when she went to Tilbury Camp to encourage the assembled troops. In a statement that perhaps most clearly summarized her sense of self, Elizabeth proclaimed that while she might have "the body of weak and feeble woman, I have the heart and stomach of a king, and a king of England too, and think foul scorn that Parma or Spain, or any prince of Europe, should dare invade the borders of my realm." The invasions never happened; the armada was defeated by a combination of English naval skill and bad weather.

In some ways, the final fifteen years of Elizabeth's reign after the defeat of the armada were an anti-climax. The economy suffered from the drain of the long and expensive struggle in Ireland, as well as from the continued support of the Netherlands. There were also continued struggles with PURITANS over the religious settlement. Some of the younger men at court did not take Elizabeth, an aging female ruler, as seriously as she deserved. This attitude was particularly true of her last favorite, ROBERT DEVEREUX, earl of Essex. Alternately he cajoled and threatened the queen in an effort to gain power. After making a fiasco of the campaign in Ireland, Essex led a rebellion against the queen in 1601. It failed, and Essex was executed.

The later part of Elizabeth's reign was also marked by an incredible renaissance in literary cultural development. The work of such men as EDMUND SPENSER and WILLIAM SHAKESPEARE certainly drew inspiration from the extraordinary woman who ruled England both as a Virgin Queen and mother of her people. While literature, especially drama, was most remarkable, architecture, music, and portrait painting were also flourishing. Overseas trade was expanding, and there was the beginning of interest in expansion and colonization.

Though visibly affected by the ESSEX REBELLION and the earl's execution in 1601, Elizabeth continued in good health and held her final Parliament of her reign that same year. At the beginning of 1603, however, her health began to fail. She died in the early morning of 24 March 1603 at the Palace of Richmond.

Elizabeth's most impressive achievement as monarch was the survival of England as an independent power. Though she had been pressured to marry, her decision to "live and die a virgin" had proved wise. England was not dominated by a foreign power. Her religious settlement was as broadly based as possible, and England did not suffer through the religious wars of her continental neighbors. Elizabeth, bragging that she was "mere English," cared most of all about the love of her people, and the people as a whole did love her throughout her forty-five-year reign. Many consider her one of England's greatest monarchs and one of the greatest women rulers in all of history.

Bibliography: John Neale, *Queen Elizabeth*, 1934; Lacey Baldwin Smith, *Elizabeth Tudor*, 1975.

Carole Levin

Elizabethan Settlement of Religion, or the ANGLICAN settlement, is a term generally applied to the combination of parliamentary and ecclesiastical actions in the early years of the reign of ELIZABETH I that ultimately defined the governmental structure of the established church in England and made a compromise theological settlement possible. This settlement came to be known as the *via media*, the middle way between the Catholicism of MARY I and Rome on the one hand and the church of EDWARD VI and the varieties of Protestant thought in contemporary Europe on the other. The Elizabethan settlement comprehended all but the most zealous Catholics and at the same time gave the more radical Protestants hope that change would occur in the future. Comprehensiveness was its greatest virtue. This middle way, while difficult to maintain, served England well in an age when faith was ideological and religious bigotry and war dominated European politics.

The two parliamentary actions that set the stage for the development of the middle way in 1559 were the Act of Supremacy (1 Eliz. I, c. 1) and the Act of UNIFORMITY (1 Eliz. I, c. 2). After Parliament had concluded, the church hierarchy began the process of enforcing Protestant practice at the parish level through the visitations of 1559, but the statement of essential doctrine, contained in the THIRTY-NINE ARTICLES, was not agreed upon by CONVOCATION until 1563. Still, the politics and actions in Elizabeth's first Parliament had paved the way for that subsequent theological statement.

Religious stability and the peaceful resolution of the future of the church in England were prerequisites for Elizabeth's successful rule. First of all Elizabeth, the symbol of her father's break with Rome, had to be Protestant. The real question was what degree of Protestantism Elizabeth wanted personally and what was suitable for her realm. Elizabeth's exact theological and liturgical preferences were not then and are not now clear. Whatever her personal preference may have been, Elizabeth and her advisers knew the circumstances at the moment dictated a cautious, even conservative approach to the religious settlement, at least at first. Elizabeth seemed to want the church to remain as outwardly like the old as possible to avoid disturbing her more conservative, Catholic subjects, but when parliamentary politics revealed that the Marians could not be satisfied, a more Protestant settlement became possible. By the end of the 1559 Parliament, the settlement was more Protestant than many had expected initially, but it was what the queen and her close advisers wanted. The politics of the first Parliament and the so-called sudden, mysterious changes in the government's legislative posture, which occurred over the Easter recess, were not so much a response to the pressure of the MARIAN EXILES and the Protestant chorus in the House of Commons as a reaction to the stunning opposition to the settlement bills in the House of Lords by the remaining Marian bishops and some of the Catholic lay lords like Anthony Browne, Viscount Mountague. Elizabeth's advisers had recognized the dangers, and the anonymous "Device for the Alteration of Religion" had urged the queen to disarm her conservative bishops and to imprison some ecclesiastical and lay lords until a settlement could be achieved. This more drastic and potentially disruptive action was rendered unnecessary by the conclusion of peace with France, which gave the government enough latitude to establish Elizabeth as the supreme governor of the church and to incorporate the more radical Edwardian form of worship into the Prayer Book.

Defining the role of the Crown was the first priority for Parliament. Although Henry VIII's supremacy had been personal, the supremacy of 1559 was clearly a parliamentary one. Since 1534 some Protestants and more Catholics had objected to a lay person's exercising authority over the church, and in 1559 the proposition that a lay woman could exercise that authority seemed even more offensive. Apologists soon developed the supporting arguments for the right of a woman to rule England and, under limited circumstances, the church as well. The 1559 Act of Supremacy altered the role of the Crown in English ecclesiastical affairs; not only did Elizabeth take the title of supreme governor, but the act stated that ecclesiastical supremacy had been annexed to the Crown by the authority of Parliament. The act also assigned Parliament some functions in terms of the definition of doctrine. Thus after 1559, supremacy in England was exercised by the Crown and Parliament.

The settlement of the form of worship was more difficult to obtain. The Act of Uniformity, which revived the Edwardian Prayer Book of 1552 with some significant differences and prescribed its use throughout England, contained the liturgical settlement, although many did not realize that at the time of its passage. By 1559 Edward's second Prayer Book seemed conservative to the returned Marian exiles after their experiences in Frankfurt and Strasbourg; yet to her Catholic subjects it seemed all too radical. To conciliate these potentially loyal Catholic subjects, Elizabeth insisted on the addition of two sentences to the communion service in the second Prayer Book. The phrase "the body [or the blood] of our Lord Jesus Christ which was given for thee, preserve thy body and soul unto everlasting life" was added to the statement in the 1552 prayer book "take and eat this in remembrance that Christ died for thee." These insertions made it possible for individuals, including some Catholics and some conservative Protestants, to believe in the real presence of Christ and still use the Prayer Book and receive communion. The so-called BLACK RUBRIC of 1552, which declared kneeling at the Sacrament must not imply adoration of the elements, was also omitted. Although the 1552 Prayer Book no longer satisfied many Protestants, they did not believe that the new Prayer Book theology and liturgy were carved in stone, and the Act of Supremacy had provided the mechanism for peaceful change through Parliament.

While the queen and her advisers succeeded in achieving a comprehensive settlement, not all debate had been eliminated. The compromise on vestments inserted in the Act of Uniformity caused considerable trouble. While the queen regarded many questions of liturgy and ritual as matters of indifference in terms of essential doctrine, that is, adiaphora, many Protestants had now adopted more Continental ideas and found some so-called indifferent matters struck at the heart of their theology. The ambiguous statement on clerical garb, that such ornaments and vestments as were used in Edward VI's reign were to be retained, gave rise to the VESTIARIAN CONTROVERSY. This controversy became so heated it threatened the settlement. Still, the settlement legislated in the first Parliament established a means for gradual change, which could accommodate the majority of the queen's subjects within the established ecclesiastical order. Time, shrewd politics, and sensible compromise made the continuation of this type of settlement possible through the Thirty-nine Articles in 1563 and other disputes and debates later in Elizabeth's reign. By that time the conservative, comprehensive settlement had given the church the chance to win the hearts and minds of most of the queen's subjects.

Bibliography: W.S. Hudson, *Cambridge and the Elizabethan Settlement of 1559*, 1980; N. L. Jones, *Faith by Statute: Parliament and the Settlement of Religion 1559*, 1982.

Ann Weikel

Eltham Ordinances (1526). The Eltham Ordinances, which took their name from the royal palace where the COURT happened to be celebrating the holidays, were promulgated by Cardinal THOMAS WOLSEY and HENRY VIII in January 1526. Their 79 chapters specified reforms in the royal HOUSEHOLD in three areas: economy, conduct befitting the king's service, and a restructuring of the Privy Chamber.

Ostensibly the prime concern was insuring that the king was well served and expenses reduced. The recent failure to gain compliance to the AMICABLE GRANT and the cost of the recently concluded ANGLO-FRENCH WAR OF 1522-1525 left the Crown in straitened circumstances, and the ordinances promised relief. Savings were expected by reducing the official size of the royal Household and court. The ordinances envisioned an even greater saving by reducing the large numbers of unofficial hangers-on, who somehow found ways to circumvent the rules and dine at the court's expense. The ordinances also prohibited such practices as dining "in corners and secret places," which drove up the already high cost of provisioning the court. If everyone ate together, the rules argued, there would be less waste of provisions and duplication of effort. Although these provisions would undoubtedly have lowered expenditures, they were seldom enforced, and all later reforms repeated them, a sign that they were largely ignored.

Equally well-meaning, but equally futile, were the rules governing the conduct of those around the king. Such provisions as those prohibiting wiping greasy fingers on the tapestries and excluding dogs aimed at cleanliness and economy as well as etiquette. Provisions that tried to curb boisterous behavior were intended to protect the king as well as instill decorum. But courtiers probably followed the king's example, not his rules, and there is no evidence the court was more sedate.

Although economy and proper behavior were always in need of improvement, and Wolsey may have used them to influence Henry, there can be little doubt that Wolsey's chief motive was political: the removal of his personal enemies from the king's Privy Chamber. Wolsey distrusted and feared Henry's highborn boon companions who had assumed the position of gentlemen of the Privy Chamber. Wolsey purged some of them in 1519, but in the intervening years he was content with neutralizing them by sending his rivals on embassies abroad. In 1526, with peace at hand, he repeated the tactic of 1519. In the name of economy, he reduced the number of gentlemen from twenty-two to fifteen and pensioned off those he did not want to share the king's confidence.

The Eltham Ordinances mark the height of Wolsey's power. He was able to purge even the groom of the stool, Sir William Compton. After that, the rise of ANNE BOLEYN marked the decline of Wolsey and the political effect of the Eltham Ordinances. They also contained a provision to streamline the PRIVY COUNCIL, but if Wolsey was serious, he never had the opportunity to put these portions into effect. However, by specifically mentioning the Privy Chamber, the Eltham Ordinances give explicit recognition to it as a third unit of the royal Household.

Bibliography: David Starkey et al., *The English Court*, 1987.

                                                                    Robert C. Braddock

Empson and Dudley, Affair of. Sir Richard Empson (c. 1450-1510) and Edmund Dudley (before 1472-1510) were councillors of HENRY VII and were arrested and executed early in the reign of his successor. They rose to prominence among Henry's ministers from the years 1505-1506, when Empson became chancellor of the duchy of Lancaster and Dudley president of the council. Empson was of minor Northamptonshire gentry stock and Dudley was the grandson of a baron, but they shared conspicious legal skill and the patronage of Sir Reginald Bray, Henry's influential minister.

Empson served as attorney-general of the duchy of Lancaster from 1478 to 1504, with an interruption under Richard III, and as keeper of the duchy seal in 1504-1505, while Dudley was a Gray's Inn reader in the 1490s and under-sheriff of London from the end of that decade. Each acted as speaker of the Commons, Empson in 1491, Dudley in 1504. Each turned his talents readily to the enforcement of the king's rights, and Dudley chose royal service in preference to the lucrative and honorable position of a serjeant-at-law. Empson followed Bray and his short-lived successor as the chancellor of the duchy, Sir John Mordaunt, in running the duchy's estates efficiently and in chairing the council learned in the law. This offshoot of the king's council sometimes functioned as a court of equity but more usually pursued and fined offenders against the king in a wide variety of matters, especially those concerning his feudal overlordship. Dudley exercised a more independent authority along similar lines, and surviving transcripts from his accounts show that he collected large sums on the king's behalf from those fined for various offenses; from aspirants for appointments to office, for royal favor in lawsuits, or for licenses to marry widows of tenants-in-chief; and from clerics compounding for restitution of their temporalities. Though they rarely worked as a pair and were by no means the only councillors involved in these exactions, both were very clearly identified with Henry's policy of capitalizing on his PREROGATIVES and with the system of bonds for the payment of fines by installment or the forfeiture of large sums in the cases of disloyalty, with which the king assured his political control over his greater subjects.

On the death of Henry VII in 1509 they were thus well fitted to be scapegoats for the late king's oppressive measures, but they had also made enemies on their own account by their ruthless and rapid self-advancement. All the more urgently because Henry had done comparatively little to reward them directly, both had exploited their position in the government and their legal expertise to build up substantial landed estates and had often bought unquiet titles or the lands of the politically and economically vulnerable. Empson notoriously indulged in wholesale judicial corruption in his attempts to disinherit Sir Robert Plumpton. It is consequently hard to calculate the balance of personal malice, cold-blooded reason of state, and response to genuine and widespread hostility in the decision to arrest Empson and Dudley, a decision taken by HENRY VIII and his council immediately on his accession. Early on 24 April 1509 they were taken to the Tower of London; Dudley was tried for treason at London in July, Empson at Northampton in August. Each was found guilty of summoning armed followers to London in April in an attempt to control or remove the new king. Though these charges have usually been dismissed as convenient but baseless fabrications, it is quite possible that they reflect measures actually taken in self-defense. These might have involved a summons to retinues licensed under Henry VII's retaining legislation, either for protection against potential disturbances in London (where Dudley seems to have been especially resented for his role in Henry VII's depredations on the merchant community) or for use in a political crisis on the death of the king.

Empson and Dudley were executed on 17 August 1510, apparently in response to complaints about their extortions presented to Henry VIII during the summer's progress. During their imprisonment each took steps to arrange his private affairs, but Dudley was the more active. He planned, but did not attempt, an escape, and his relatives unsuccessfully paid Thomas, Lord Darcy to procure him a royal pardon. He composed a list of those whose outstanding debts to Henry VII should be canceled or reduced and an interesting but unoriginal political treatise, *The Tree of Commonwealth*. Dudley's son JOHN later inherited from his mother the title of Viscount Lisle and went on to become earl of Warwick and duke of Northumberland.

Bibliography: E. Dudley, *The Tree of Commonwealth*, ed. D. M. Brodie, 1948; C. J. Harrison, ed., "The Petition of Edmund Dudley," *English Historical Review* 87 (1972): 82-99; M. R, Horowitz, "Richard Empson, Minister of Henry VIII," *Bulletin of the Institute of Historical Research* 55 (1982): 35-49.

S. J. Gunn

Enclosures. Enclosing was a controversial topic in Tudor England because social critics perceived it as causing depopulation, dearth, military decline, and popular disorder. It was consequently the object of governmental efforts at regulation.

Any discussion of enclosure must begin with a discussion of legal concepts of property and rights of usufruct. No clear doctrine of possessive individualism, or the absolute and unqualified possession of private property, existed before the end of the seventeenth century. All land in England was, at one time, subject to common or use-rights exercised by other members of the manorial community and was held by conditional tenures that imposed certain obligations upon both lords and tenants. Enclosure in severalty was the assertion of exclusive rights of property and always extinguished common rights. The land was usually enclosed in a physical sense by a hedge, fence, wall, or mound and ditch. The enclosure of arable land lying in common or open fields and its conversion to pasture were considered to be especially pernicious because they destroyed houses of husbandry or, sometimes, whole villages and diminished the supply of able-bodied husbandmen who were regarded as the backbone of English ARMIES until well into the Tudor period. The enclosure of arable land for sheep raising during the Tudor period has been much exaggerated, however, and seldom occurred outside the Midlands, where markets remained inaccessible and the heavy clay soils were unsuited to grain production. The more usual type of enclosure involved the encroachment upon or "improvement" of common wastes, which diminished grazing for tenants' plow animals and milk cows. Extinction of common rights on the manorial waste deprived commoners of their sources of fuel and building materials for repairing their houses. The loss of such use-rights made their economic position more precarious. In addition to these profound changes in land use, the enclosure of commons also often led to "impopulation," a phenomenon characterized by an influx of cottagers to whom the manorial lord and other beneficiaries of enclosure subleased land in small plots. This situation usually caused friction between the old tenants and the new tenants and increased the costs of poor relief, which were usually borne by the former.

Enclosure did not always cause contention in the manorial or village community. Enclosed fields were the rule in the west of England. In many pastoral
communities enclosures stood unchallenged for generations as long as the
resources of the common waste remained abundant. Very few enclosure disputes
are recorded before c. 1520, when the POPULATION began to grow rapidly and
pressed hard upon the resources of land. The increased demand for grain and the
rapidly rising prices stimulated technological innovations in agriculture in order
to increase yields and this caused widespread alterations in land use. Landlords
were unlikely to invest capital in the new convertible husbandry, which was the
essence of the Agricultural Revolution, unless they first gained total control of the
land, which meant extinguishing all use-rights such as grazing on the stubble in
the fields after harvest.

The term *encolsure* served as shorthand for a variety of practices associated
with changes in agricultural practice. It was often confused with engrossing, or
the consolidation of two or more tenancies, which always had a more depopulating effect than did simple enclosure. It could also mean "stinting," in which lords
and tenants sometimes banded together to deny access to the manorial waste to
inhabitants who were not tenants. Enclosure was merely one stage in a series of
alterations in land use, but it was the symbolic act upon which government
prosecutions, social criticism, and popular protest focused. THOMAS WOLSEY
appointed a royal commission in 1517 to investigate depopulating enclosures, and
prosecutions in the Courts of CHANCERY and King's Bench followed. The
enclosure commission of 1548-1549 appointed by EDWARD SEYMOUR, the
protector Somerset, and presided over by John Hales was widely blamed for
provoking the enclosure rioting that accompanied the rebellions of 1549. Official
inquiries and prosecutions for decay of tillage followed upon the Oxfordshire
Rebellion of 1596 and the Midland Revolt of 1607, but by the beginning of the
seventeenth century husbandry was becoming too technical a subject to lend itself
to governmental regulation, and subsequent prosecutions for depopulating
enclosures deteriorated into revenue-raising schemes.

Bibliography: Roger B. Manning, *Village Revolts: Social Protest and Popular
Disturbances in England, 1509-1640*, 1988; Joan Thirsk, ed., *The Agrarian
History of England and Wales*, Vol. 4: *1500-1640*, 1967.

Roger B. Manning

Episcopacy, *jure divino* **and** *jure humano.* The English Reformation was
directed from above, by the monarch in Parliament—and with the initial
cooperation of that ancient estate of the realm, the bishops. For this reason, if no
other, episcopacy survived in England when it disappeared in the Protestant
churches of the Netherlands, France, and Geneva. It faced attack from two
quarters: the Roman Catholics, who regarded the English bishops as instruments
of the Protestant state, and (under ELIZABETH) the PRESBYTERIANS, who

saw episcopacy as a lordly tyranny, not founded on Scripture but merely inherited from a corrupt popish past.

Under HENRY VIII and EDWARD VI, the reformers—facing the Roman Catholic threat—did not place any high priority on upholding episcopal rights. The BISHOPS' BOOK of 1537 made no distinction of office between bishops and priests and treated the former as a grade of the latter. In practice, also, the powers of bishops diminished as Henry—acting through THOMAS CROM- WELL—replaced episcopal visitations with royal ones from 1535. This practice continued during Edward's reign, and for a while legislation extended royal power in the appointment of bishops by ending even the purely formal election rights that had been left to the cathedral chapter. Radical Reformers such as John Hooper— who spent two months in the Fleet Prison before he would agree to wear full episcopal dress at his consecration—were not greatly concerned to lay stress on the rights and prerogatives of the bishop's office.

After the MARIAN REACTION, Elizabeth's settlement brought about a climate in government far more conducive to episcopacy. The queen respected the status of bishops as an ancient estate of the realm and, in any case, believed that it was easier to control the church through a few bishops than through the Commons—let alone deal with the numerous local synods that Presbyterians would have set in place. Elizabeth restored episcopal visitations and governed the church in concert with the bishops. However, while royal policy shifted in the bishops' favor, a number of clerics and laymen began to lobby for Presbyterianism—which they believed that Scripture had prescribed as the only proper form of government for the church. In 1570 Thomas Cartwright opened the assault with lectures at Cambridge, and the debate on the best form of church government kept the presses busy until the 1590s, when the scurrilous MARPRELATE TRACTS finally provoked strong government countermeasures.

Two main theoretical defenses of episcopacy were mounted in the Tudor period. According to one approach, episcopacy existed solely by human law (*jure humano*). In this view, bishops and priests were regarded as sharing one office both in Scripture and in the primitive church; the present distinction in their jurisdictional powers resulted solely from the prince's exercise of the ROYAL SUPREMACY. THOMAS CRANMER adopted an extreme version of this position in some of his writings, claiming that the king could make a bishop just as he could make a sheriff and that he could give powers of excommunication as justly to the one as to the other. Cranmer's claim that at least some spiritual powers were derived from the king was extreme ERASTIANISM, and such views grew increasingly rare after the reign of Henry VIII—with whose own high notions of royal power in church matters they accorded well. Elsewhere, indeed, Cranmer himself argued that bishops and priests were divinely instituted and that the Christian prince should merely insure that they exercised their powers properly.

Many Elizabethan defenses of episcopacy argued that the clergy's spiritual powers—including the powers of ordination and excommunication—were derived from God but that the exercise of these powers was subject to regulation by the monarch acting as supreme governor of the church and that for the sake of good order it made sense to confine the spiritual powers of ordination and excommunication to a small group of clerics—namely the bishops—who would supervise the clergy as a whole. In these writings, the distinction between bishops and other clerics was seen as stemming less from any divine prescription requiring episcopacy than from human laws made to facilitate the smooth running of the church.

In the later 1580s and 1590s such writers as Richard Bancroft, John Bridges, Thomas Bilson, RICHARD HOOKER, and especially Hadrian Saravia responded to PURITAN arguments that Scripture required a Presbyterian form of church government by claiming that both Scripture and the practice of the primitive church in fact witnessed the original institution of bishops. Episcopacy, they said, was the form of government chosen by the apostles, who had themselves appointed Timothy and Titus as bishops. They concluded that episcopacy was the best form of church government and that the distinction between bishops and lesser clergy had biblical and apostolic warrant. To combat the view that Presbyterianism was by divine right (*jure divino*) they propounded the theory of episcopacy *jure divino* and argued that there were Scriptural grounds for confining certain powers to the bishops alone and that the bishops derived these powers from God.

The shift in emphasis of late-Elizabethan churchmen on the question of episcopacy was noted with alarm in certain quarters, but the practical implications of *jure divino* episcopalianism should not be exaggerated. Although they argued that episcopacy was the apostolic model of church government, these writers admitted that other forms might be permissible in extreme circumstances—such as those facing Reformed churches on the Continent. In these cases ministers might exercise the powers normally reserved for bishops. Moreover, although bishops derived their powers to inflict spiritual censures from God alone, they could exercise these powers only in accordance with the wishes of the supreme governor of the church, and any purely temporal powers that the bishops possessed were derived solely from the monarch.

Bibliography: E. T. Davies, *Episcopacy and the Royal Supremacy in the Church of England in the XVI Century*, 1950; Peter Lake, *Anglicans and Puritans?: Presbyterianism and English Conformist Thought from Whitgift to Hooker*, 1988.

J. P. Sommerville

Erastianism. Generally defined as the doctrine of the supremacy of the state in ecclesiastical matters. In Tudor England Erastian theories were voiced to justify the break with Rome and the subsequent ecclesiastical settlements. Two of the most important acts in establishing the nature of the Church of England's relationship with the civil authorities were the SUBMISSION OF THE CLERGY

(1532) and the Henrician Act of Supremacy (1534, see ROYAL SUPREMACY). The former embodied the clergy's agreement that no canon of the church would be made without the king's assent and that existing canons would be revised in accordance with royal wishes; the latter recognized the king as the only supreme head on earth of the Church of England. Independence from papal power was gained at the cost of subordination to the state. After the MARIAN REACTION, the Elizabethan Act of Supremacy (1559) replaced the title of supreme head with that of supreme governor, but the state's ultimate legislative supremacy in ecclesiastical affairs was as real as under HENRY VIII or EDWARD VI.

The civil magistrate's ecclesiastical supremacy was a doctrine with strong roots in Lutheran thinking. Martin Luther had argued for the right of the temporal powers to reform the church. THOMAS CRANMER likewise insisted that Christian princes were responsible for the welfare of their subjects in spiritual as well as temporal matters. Cranmer viewed the Christian people as the proper authority in ecclesiastical matters and held that where there was a Christian ruler, this authority was vested in him.

The belief that the whole Christian people constituted the church and therefore were its rightful governors had been expressed forcefully in medieval debates between popes and emperors, not least by Marsilius of Padua (1275?-1342). His *Defensor Pacis* of 1342, based on Aristotelian principles, was designed to show that the ecclesiastical hierarchy should be completely subordinate to the secular authorities. THOMAS CROMWELL recognized its propaganda value in the debate with Rome and commissioned William Marshall to publish a translation; this appeared in 1535, with Marsilius's democratic RESISTANCE THEORY carefully eradicated. This edition did not sell well, but Marsilius's ideas clearly influenced the important Tudor theorist, Thomas Starkey (c. 1497-1538), and echoes of them resound in many later defenses of the Anglican Church.

The role of the Christian prince in regulating the church was famously stressed in the *Acts and Monuments* of JOHN FOXE. This work, better known as the *Book of Martyrs*, was a Tudor best-seller, despite its enormous length. It portrayed the English Reformation—and the crown's decisive role in it—as standing in a long tradition of godly rulership that stretched back through the Christian emperors to the kings of Old Testament Israel. Foxe's book was mainly anti-papal in its intentions, and it contained little formal theorizing on the ecclesiology of the Royal Supremacy, but it provided a convincing historical justification for the part recently played by the state in reforming the church.

In sixteenth-century Europe there were currents of Protestant thought more hostile to the supremacy of civil authorities in ecclesiastical matters than was the Lutheran tradition. John Calvin and his followers in France, Scotland, the Netherlands, and Geneva organized PRESBYTERIAN forms of church government that excluded the civil magistrate from any direct involvement in the ordinary regulation of ecclesiastical affairs. In the German city of Heidelberg during the 1560s, disputes arose as the presbytery attempted to establish control over ecclesiastical affairs. A leading participant in these debates was Thomas

Erastus (1524-1583), physician to the secular ruler of Heidelberg, the Elector Palatine. In response to the Presbyterians' assertion of the church's divine right to powers of excommunication independent of the civil magistrate and drawing on ideas earlier expressed by a number of Swiss reformers, Erastus insisted that the church possessed no powers to punish offenders except those that it derived from the Christian prince. He argued that the Christian magistrate rightfully held all the authority that the Jewish kings had exercised in the Old Testament and that he, like them, was responsible for the whole external order of the church. Some of Erastus's most important writings were published posthumously at London in 1589, possibly with the backing of leading privy councillors and ecclesiastics, who were hostile to the Presbyterian claims that Erastus was attacking. The term *Erastianism* is sometimes used narrowly to describe the ideas of Erastus, in particular his contention that the church draws its powers of excommunication from the civil magistrate. Erastianism in this limited sense was to be important in the debates on English church settlement of the 1640s. But the term is commonly used more widely to denote any theory that gives the state control over the church.

Under Elizabeth, apologists for the queen's religious settlement mounted a defense of the Royal Supremacy against the criticisms of Presbyterians. This defense was based on viewing the Christian commonwealth of England as one community, united in the person of the sovereign. The same commonwealth was viewed as both a church—insofar as its members were Christian—and a state—insofar as they were men. One community, it was argued, needed one government vested in one sovereign power—and this the Royal Supremacy provided. As in Old Testament Israel, the prince led and commanded the whole godly people. RICHARD HOOKER best articulated this case, but its essentials were accepted by all his codefenders of the Elizabethan settlement. Their defense was as Erastian as their church.

Bibliography: Claire Cross, *The Royal Supremacy in the Elizabethan Church*, 1969; John Neville Figgis, "Erastus and Erastianism," in *The Divine Right of Kings*, 2nd ed., 1914, pp. 293-342.

J. P. Sommerville

Essex's Rebellion (1601). The rebellion led by ROBERT DEVEREUX, 2nd earl of Essex, was the culmination of several years of tension between ELIZABETH and the last favorite of her reign. The queen had been very upset over Essex's behavior as lord deputy in Ireland in 1599. Essex, in disgrace and under investigation, was confined to his house. He wrote a humble submission, and the queen canceled his trial before the STAR CHAMBER. By the end of August 1600 Essex could move about freely except to return to COURT. He continued to besiege Elizabeth with letters attempting to gain permission to do so.

Yet at the same time Essex was writing to Elizabeth he was also plotting to seize the court by force. Also involved in this conspiracy were his sister Penelope, Lady Rich; his stepfather, Christopher Blount; and Henry Wriothesley, earl of Southampton. Essex's behavior became far more uncontrolled in November 1600 when Elizabeth refused to renew his monopoly on sweet wines, a financial disaster for Essex. Essex House became a focal point for those discontented with Elizabeth's government.

On Tuesday, 3 February 1601, five of the leaders of the conspiracy met at Drury House, the lodging of the earl of Southampton. In an attempt to avoid suspicion, Essex himself was not present. The group discussed Essex's proposals for seizing the court, the Tower, and the city. Their avowed purpose was to force the Queen to change the leaders in her government, particularly ROBERT CECIL, even if this attempt meant doing violence to the queen's person.

Three days later others of Essex's followers went to the Globe Theatre to ask the Lord Chamberlain's Men to stage a special performance of *Richard II* with the deposition scene included. The company was reluctant to perform such an old play but agreed when promised a supplement of 40 shillings. On 7 February the council summoned Essex to appear before them. He refused. But he had also lost his chance to take the court by surprise, so he fell back on his scheme to rouse the city of London in his favor with the claim that Elizabeth's government had planned to murder him and had sold out England to Spain.

Essex and his followers hastily planned the rising. About 10:00 a.m. the next morning (8 February) Lord Keeper Thomas Egerton and three others came to Essex in the name of the Queen. Essex imprisoned the four messengers and kept them as hostages while he and his followers, about 200 young noblemen and gentlemen, made their way to the city. Meanwhile, Robert Cecil sent a warning to the mayor, and the heralds denounced Essex as a traitor in the streets of London. At the word *traitor* many of the earl's followers disappeared, and none of the citizens joined him as he had expected. Essex's position was obviously desperate, and he decided to return to Essex House. When he got there, he found the hostages gone. The queen's men, under Lord Admiral Charles Howard, earl of Nottingham, besieged the house. By evening, after burning incriminating letters and documents, Essex surrendered. Essex, the earl of Southampton, and the other followers were placed under arrest.

Less than two weeks after the aborted rebellion, Essex and Southampton were brought on 19 February from the Tower to Westminster to be tried for treason. The trial lasted only a day, and the guilty verdict was a foregone conclusion. Though he had burnt incriminating correspondence to save his followers prior to his arrest, in the Tower after his condemnation Essex followed the advice of his chaplain, Reverend Abdy Ashton, who told him he must purge his soul of guilt. Essex's confession was damning against his fellow conspirators and especially placed blame on his sister Penelope.

On 25 February 1601 Essex was beheaded in the confines of the Tower. Southampton, however, survived in the Tower to be freed upon the accession of

JAMES VI AND I. Sir Christopher Blount, Sir Gelli Meyrick, Henry Cuffe, Sir John Davies, and Sir Charles Danvers all stood trial for high treason on 5 March 1601 and were found guilty. Davies was reprieved, but the other four were executed. There were no large-scale executions, however; the other members of the conspiracy were let off with fines. London had refused to support Essex, even though he was the darling of the people. Eighteen months after his execution, however, a German visitor reported he heard only "Essex's Last Goodnight" sung in the streets of the city. In the court, people observed how much the queen had aged since the Essex Rebellion.

Bibliography: Robert Lacey, *Robert Earl of Essex*, 1971; Richard C. McCoy, "'A Dangerous Image': The Earl of Essex and Elizabethan Chivaltry," *Journal of Medieval and Renaissance Studies* 13 (1983, pt. 2): 313-29; Alison Wall, "An Account of the Essex Revolt, February 1601," *Bulletin of the Institute of Historical Research* 54 (1981, no. 129): 131-33.

Carole Levin

Etaples, Treaty of (1492). Treaty concluded by HENRY VII with France during his one expedition to France. Its terms provided for a substantial cash payment to the English king.

The marriage of Anne of Brittany to Charles VIII in December 1491 ruined Henry's attempt to prop up Breton independence and established French control of the whole southern coast of the Channel. The king was much alive to this danger and in the autumn of 1491 revived his claims to France and agreed on 22 November, in an amplification of the 1489 treaty with Spain, to enter a campaign the following spring. His allies' failure to act and Henry's reluctance to go to war delayed the campaign until late in the season (except for an abortive naval descent on the Breton coast in June 1492). Polydore Vergil argues that Henry decided on his belated campaign only out of fear of reactions at home, should his demands for war taxes turn out to have been deceptive. While maintaining diplomatic contact with France throughout the summer, Henry went on with war preparations and finally crossed to CALAIS on 2 October (estimates of his force varied from 10,000 to 25,000 men). While the forward of the army captured Ardres, the king crossed the frontier on 19 October and encamped before Boulogne on the 22nd, and expected a rapid success. The town, stoutly defended by 1,800 men, proved too strong, and the prospects of a siege at that time of year were extremely grim. However, it was clear that the French were also eager for peace and prepared to make offers. It has been argued, in fact, that Henry mounted the invasion partly to stimulate the French into just such offers, which were surprisingly substantial. On 27 October, the king, faced by the discontent of his army at talk of such a rapid peace, took the unusual step of getting his advisers and captains in the field to "ask" him by petition to make peace on the terms offered. The treaty was concluded at Etaples, a few miles down the coast, on 3 November.

While the treaty itself (a perpetual peace rather than a truce as concluded at Picquigny in 1475) provided for the restoration of commercial intercourse and the all-important undertaking that Charles VIII would not shelter Henry's rebels nor Henry aid Maximilian, the main terms were formulated in an annex called "l'obligation du seignuer d'Esquerdes," ratified by Charles VIII on 13 December. By these, Charles agreed to accept the debt that his wife, Anne of Brittany, owed Henry for his "defence" of her duchy after 1489: 620,000 ecus (see TREATY OF REDON), to which was added 125,000 ecus in arrears for the pensions promised to Edward IV in 1475 and interrupted in 1483 (total in sterling, £159,000). All this was to be paid off at 50,000 livres (28,750 ecus) a year (roughly £5,000).

While these terms are often said to reflect Henry VII's astuteness in war policy, Polydore Vergil pointed out that he was primarily concerned with his security in going to war. He had done so at a difficult moment and had been lucky that the French, anxious to be rid of entanglements in the north, had been willing to buy him off. Even so, the deal was an improvement on that of 1475 from the French point of view. Instead of being virtually perpetual, the payments of 1492 would end at a fixed term and the yearly payments were reduced from 50,000 ecus to 28,750. Moreover, whereas the pension arrears were 450,000 ecus, Henry agreed to reduce his demand to 125,000. This was a reasonable price to assure English quiescence. For his part, Henry no doubt recognized the impossibility of reversing the Breton settlement or of conquering France and made the best of a bad job. He could even make the magnanimous gesture of remitting the French pension to help Charles VIII in Italy in 1495.

Bibliography: Y. Labande-Mailfert, *Charles VIII et son milieu*, 1975; J. Molinet, *Chroniques*, 1935-1937.

David Potter

Evil May Day (1517). The most serious urban disorder during the Tudor period and the only riot of any note against aliens was Evil May Day, 1517. London's alien community, consisting mostly of French and Dutch immigrants, was always very small, never exceeding 5% of the city's total population, but at times relations with citizens became strained. According to Edward Hall, the chronicler, tensions mounted during the early months of 1517 and were whipped up by a peddler named John Lincoln, who convinced Dr. Bell to preface his sermon at Paul's Cross on Easter Tuesday with an exhortation to all "Englishmen to cherish and defend themselves, and to hurt and grieve aliens for the common weal." During the next two weeks there were scattered attacks against aliens, and rumors circulated "that on May Day next the city would rebel and slay all aliens."

As it turned out the riot was spontaneous, triggered by the attempted arrest on May Day eve of some youths playing in the street who did not know that a 9:00 p.m. curfew had been imposed by the king's council a short while earlier. Cries of "apprentices and clubs" rang out, and within a couple of hours 1,000 young men had gathered in Cheapside. After freeing men imprisoned for earlier attacks against aliens, the crowd headed for St. Martin le Grand, a privileged "liberty" where many aliens lived. Ignoring Sir THOMAS MORE, under-sheriff of London, who pleaded with them to disperse, the mob proceeded to spoil houses there and in other alien communities. By 3:00 a.m. the riot had spent itself; 300 people were arrested, nearly all of whom were later pardoned, and the rest wandered home. On 4 May thirteen rioters were convicted of treason and executed, and three days later so, too, was John Lincoln, the instigative peddler.

The famed Evil May Day was a spontaneous riot that lasted for about four hours and involved roughly 1,000 people. Not a single life was lost in the riot itself, and property damaged was restricted to the looting and not the destruction of some aliens' houses. One wonders, then, whether Evil May Day, the only large-scale disorder in Tudor London, figures so prominently in the city's history not for its representativeness but because of its singularity.

Bibliography: M. Holmes, "Evil May Day, 1517: The Story of a Riot," *History Today* 15 (1965): 642-50.

Steven Rappaport

Exchequer. The Exchequer, a financial and accounting department of the English government, had been in existence since the mid-twelfth century. As such, it fulfilled a key function in coordinating the daily conduct of government business. Since such matters as the levying of all fines from the law courts, the auditing of the accounts of many royal officials, the recording of transfers of property held in chief, and the supervising of the execution of statute law all came before the court, there is little that may not be found in its surviving records, although frequently what survives is not the materials relating to normal business but rather exceptional matters that required special attention. Historians have frequently represented the Exchequer as slow, inefficient, and weighed down by inflexible, inadequate, and superfluous checks and balances that produced unsuitably complicated and time-consuming processes. This description has been supported by material drawn from the documents of contemporary, internal departmental quarreling over procedure, motivated by interest in income within a user-pays system, whose arguments were often selective and whose examples were exceptional. Recent studies that have systematically examined particular aspects of the Exchequer process suggest that most business was completed in due time. Most accounts were substantially heard, and ninety% of the money paid in within the set time limits and in the manner prescribed. The proportion of difficult or desperate debts on which so much historical attention has been focused does not seem to have exceeded normal business expectations.

The Exchequer was divided into two distinct parts, the Upper Exchequer also known as the Exchequer of Audit, and the Lower Exchequer or Exchequer of Receipt. As a court of record, the Exchequer also heard some common law cases in what was called the Exchequer of Pleas, and in the Tudor period its equity jurisdiction became a significant reality. Both parts of the court were centered at Westminster (after 1536 part of the new palace of Whitehall), the Receipt at the northeast corner at Westminster Hall, the Audit at the northwest corner. Neither premises were adequate, so many officials operated from their own homes, and meetings were often held at the lord treasurer's or the lord chief baron's houses. In the 1560s and early 1570s the premises were partly rebuilt and relocated, but this change still did not produce enough space to enable all officials to conduct all their business centrally. The records were always stored fairly quickly, theoretically in the Tower, but in practice often in less appropriate archives.

The lord treasurer was responsible for both divisions of the Exchequer but had no fixed role. While his name was included in many formal writs and commissions, daily Exchequer routine did not require him. Participation was not essential for a major role in the broader field of government financial decision making. His control over the courts was partly maintained by the number of lesser offices that were in his gift. This fact made the Exchequer a quasi-fiefdom in 1485 but during the sixteenth century the monarchs asserted the right to appoint to many of the more important positions. Nevertheless, the influence of THOMAS HOWARD, the 3rd duke of Norfolk, on appointments insured a body of officials who were also his own long-term clients so that his influence lingered after his departure from office. WILLIAM CECIL also took a close interest in asserting his own rights to appoint. At least among the lesser offices, moreover, money changed hands to secure particular positions.

The principal officers in the Upper Exchequer were the four barons. While the lord chief baron came from a legal background, the lesser (puisne) barons in 1485 were often drawn from the court's own personnel. The changing role of the barons over the course of the century slowly led to the requirement of legal training, and John Sotherton in 1579 was the last baron who had not been a serjeant. Below them were officials with specialized functions, principally the clerk of the pipe, who was responsible for records, the two remembrancers, and the auditors. In the Lower Exechequer, the two chamberlains, who usually exercised their office by deputy, were the first in dignity. The lord treasurer was represented by the under-treasurer. Meanwhile the clerk of the pells and the writer of the tallies, who by 1550 was calling himself the auditor of the Receipt, disputed the right to supervise the four tellers, who handled the receipt and issuing of revenue in the sixteenth century.

The Receipt, as the treasury and pay office, dealt both in coin and in tallies. It was never the only royal treasury, however, and the percentage of revenue it handled varied widely. The duchy of Lancaster had its own treasury, while both HENRY VII and HENRY VIII used the treasury of the chamber for much of their revenue. When the courts of AUGMENTATIONS and FIRST FRUITS were established, they too had their own treasurers. GENERAL SURVEYORS continued to use the treasurer of the chamber. By EDWARD VI's reign perhaps only a third of all revenues passed through the Receipt, but after the reorganization of 1554 the total may have reached 95% (i.e, in 1555 about £265,000).

The Receipt underwent constant change. Henry VII removed responsibil-ity for money from the chamberlains, who intermittently sought to regain it. This change increased the responsibility of the writer of tallies and the tellers for both money and records. While those due payment were sometimes given a tally of assignment (which operated somewhat like a bill of credit) on another revenue source, they were less ubiquitous than they had been in the fifteenth century. The need for regular payment to the big expenditure departments, however, required funds from reliable treasuries to be earmarked for particular purposes by warrants dormant. Particularly from the 1520s to the 1560s there were constant shifts in the departmental organization, sometimes effected by acts of Parliament (e.g. 14 Hen. VIII, c. 19, repealed 1531; 32 Hen. VIII, c. 52; 5 Eliz. I, c. 17). During the 1520s and 1530s many officials bypassed the Exchequer. Its reinstatement as the primary financial department led to further internal changes. The tellers handled large sums of money but did not provide adequate securities and appear to have kept some of the actual coffers of treasure at their own homes. Several of them died or fled leaving, massive debts that opened a long-running argument over departmental procedures. An attempt in 1555 by Edmund Cockrell, clerk of the pells, with the support of Lord Treasurer William Paulet, the marquess of Winchester, to reintroduce the pells process of checks failed when his opponents appealed to Queen Mary. In the first decade of ELIZABETH's reign, Winchester managed to restore some older checks, but they proved inadequate. The bill for tellers and receivers in the Parliament of 1571 tightened procedures, but some later tellers, including Richard Stonley, still got into difficulties over the use of the reserves that had built up. As a result, the clerk of the pells continued to have grounds for maintaining the case for the restoration of a stricter accounting process that would have substantially increased his fees. Throughout most of the century officers of the Receipt produced summaries of accounts related to the state of the treasury, which are a guide to aspects of finance but cannot be equated to a balance sheet.

The Upper Exchequer was not simply a budget office but rather a conglomerate of administrative departments concerned with aspects of the maintenance of law and order, supervision of palatinate jurisdictions such as Chester, the conduct of royal officials such as sheriffs, escheators, customers, and the clerk of the markets, and the auditing of parliamentary taxation. It heard penal cases that related to breach of parliamentary statutes such as the statute against enclosures and, like any other court, could summon cases from lower courts by *certiorari*. In the Tudor period its structure was significantly modified by internal shifts that were not subject to public scrutiny. The act of Mary's first Parliament that resulted in the amalgamation of the Court of Augmentations and the Court of First Fruits and Tenths with the Exchequer was followed by a protracted period of restructuring that was not concluded until the 1570s when William Cecil became lord treasurer. The final result was significantly different in some respects from the intention of its original promoters. The return of most expenditure accounts to Exchequer's supervision required the establishment of a separate office of the auditors of the "prests"—the term used for money paid in advance for which there had to be an account.

The very specific management problems of controlling expenditure on some aspects of military affairs and public works, however, had been partially solved by this date by the establishment of boards that had primary responsibility for daily oversight. Intermittent expenditure accounts such as those of treasurers for wars were commonly assigned to special commissions, while the legal routine for pursuing defaulters and miscreants was absorbed into the remembrancers' offices, and the auditors of the Exchequer (who often had already been auditors in the other courts) were made responsible for land revenue. In this way separate offices for the different forms of revenue developed. The management of the collections of customs and excise was also restructured and equity jurisdiction was formalized.

The lord treasurer principally remembered as such under the Tudors is William Paulet, 1st marquess of Winchester, who held the office in extreme old age from 1550 to his death in 1572. Previously he had served as an officer in the Court of Wards from 1526 to 1554 and held various financial offices in the Household from 1532 to 1550. He has been credited with the single-handed management of finance in the 1550s and is thought to have been principally responsible for the Exchequer reorganization of the mid-1550s although the evidence for both is indirect and ambiguous. Surviving letters show he was both interested and willing to interfere in daily Exchequer business, but his authority in the Exchequer was not absolute, and, as is obvious in the Cockerell affair, he could be frustrated. While he clearly played a part, not necessarily a leading one, in the amalgamation of 1554, his own preference was for the restoration of the old procedures of the Exchequer, for example, making the sheriffs responsible for all land revenue. His suggestions were not implemented. Nevertheless, he had some triumphs such as the customs reorganization. William Cecil took over the lord treasurership in 1572 and ran the reformed Exchequer effectively until 1598.

Bibliography: J. D. Alsop, "The Structure of Early Tudor Finance c. 1509-1558," in *Revolution Reassessed*, ed. C. Coleman and D. Starkey, 1986; W. H. Bryson, *The Equity Side of Exchequer: Its Administration, Procedures and Records*, 1975; C. Coleman, "Reorganisation of the Exchequer of Receipt," in *Revolution Reassessed*, ed. C. Coleman and D. Starkey, 1986; G. R. Elton, "The Elizabethan Exchequer: War in the Receipt," in *Elizabethan Government and Society Essays presented to Sir John Neale*, ed., S. T. Bindoff, J. Hurstfield and C. H. Williams, 1961; D. Hoak, "The Secret History of the Tudor Court: The King's Coffers and the King's Purse 1542-1553," *Journal of British Studies*, (1987): 208-31.

Sybil Jack

Exeter Conspiracy. The arrest in 1538 and execution for treason of Henry Courtenay, marquess of Exeter, his cousin Henry Pole, Lord Montague's brother-in-law Sir Edward Neville, and thirteen others brought to an end what HENRY VIII and THOMAS CROMWELL believed to be a Yorkist conspiracy against the Tudor regime. It was more nearly a confederacy of disaffected courtiers whose opposition to the changes of the 1530s was expressed primarily in imprudent but technically treasonable talk, compounded by their close relation to the king's nemesis REGINALD POLE and the deteriorating international situation. The end result, however, was the ruin of Pole's family and the destruction, for a generation at least, of the White Rose party.

The background to this tragedy lay in Henry's inability to win support for his DIVORCE and the ROYAL SUPREMACY from his former protégé Pole, a cardinal since 1536 and an internationally respected scholar living in exile in Italy under papal patronage. Pole's elder brother Lord Montague, their cousin and friend the marquess of Exeter, and Sir Edward Neville had remained at court, forming the center of a faction supporting the princess MARY and the old religion, which fell into disgrace in the factional wars attendant upon the fall of ANNE BOLEYN. Had they seriously intended to challenge the new regime, their opportunity came with the PILGRIMAGE OF GRACE and the other northern risings. Exeter's power was in the West Country, and Montagu was influential in Hampshire; sympathetic risings in those places would have posed a major threat to the Crown. Instead, through timidity, ineptitude, or legitimate rejection of treason, they supported the crown and remained quiet.

To the uneasy aftermath of the rebellions at home was added danger from abroad. The growing rapprochement between France and Spain allowed both Catholic countries to join the papacy in opposition to England, and in February 1537 Pole was named papal legate and dispatched toward England perhaps—optimistically—to preside over the restoration of the old faith should the northern rebellions succeed. He got as far as France, where Francis I refused to extradite him as Henry requested, and moved for safety to Cambrai and eventually Liege, where his continued presence and an unwise correspondence with his family in England (particularly with his hotheaded younger brother Geoffrey) both angered and worried the king. Cromwell, who thought he had placed a spy in Pole's entourage, was similarly angered to find the man a double agent, working for the cardinal. In this context disaffected talk in the Exeter-Pole-Neville circle (that the king was a beast, that he would die, that he had sent Peter Mewtas to assassinate the cardinal, that knaves ruled about him, that a change would come about in the realm), combined with the knowledge that both Poles and Courtenays were legitimately descended from Yorkist kings (the Poles' mother Margaret, countess of Salisbury, was Edward IV's niece while Exeter's mother was Edward IV's daughter Katherine), took on a more ominous cast.

Sir Geoffrey Pole was arrested in August 1538, and to save his own life he informed on his brothers and associates; Montague and Exeter were committed to the Tower on 4 November, and Exeter's wife, Gertrude, Sir Edward Neville, and others joined them later that month. A quick trial found them guilty of treason by words, under the 1534 statute; no deeds were proven. Exeter, Montague, Neville, and three others were beheaded on 9 December; sixteen in all eventually died, including also Sir Nicholas Carew, master of the horse. An act of ATTAINDER against all of the "conspirators" was passed when Parliament met again in the spring of 1539, and included among the names was that of Exeter's aged mother the countess of Salisbury. She remained in the Tower until Sir John Neville's rising in Yorkshire in 1541, at the news of which she too was beheaded.

As a result of this series of executions the "White Rose" Yorkist court faction (and the Tudor's most likely dynastic rivals) was destroyed; the Pole family (except the cardinal) was ruined; Exeter's death created a power vacuum in the West Country that was eventually filled by John Russell, newly created earl of Bedford; and those who supported the old nobility or the old order, primarily THOMAS HOWARD, 3rd duke of Norfolk, and STEPHEN GARDINER, were more convinced than ever of the need to destroy Cromwell.

Bibliography: Madeleine Hope Dodds and Ruth Dodds, *The Pilgrimage of Grace 1536-1537 and the Exeter Conspiracy 1538*, 2 vols., 1915; G. R. Elton, *Reform and Reformation: England 1509-1558*, 1977.

Mary L. Robertson

Exploration. An ongoing effort throughout the Tudor era that led English mariners or foreigners in the employ of Englishmen to sail to various parts of the world, collect data later used to encourage further exploration, and in some cases establish commercial or colonial footholds that led to mercantile and political imperialism.

Shortly after HENRY VII's succession, he was approached by Bartholomew Columbus, who represented his brother, Christopher. Seeking funding for a voyage of westward exploration, the Columbus brothers found the English king interested, but he proved unwilling to act before Christopher Columbus finalized his monumental agreement with Ferdinand and Isabella of Spain that led to the discovery of the New World. The missed opportunity underscored by Columbus's success soon led King Henry to consider carefully, and eventually authorize, a projected westward voyage by another Italian adventurer, John Cabot, who appeared in England after 1495. Backed by such Bristol merchants as Hugh Elyot and Robert Thorne, who had heard tales of the fabulous wealth of Cipango (Japan) and hoped to establish trade ties with the island, Cabot received royal letters patent for his voyage of exploration in March 1496. King Henry empowered Cabot and his three sons to discover and occupy any lands unknown to Christians, to trade with the inhabitants of those lands, and required that 20% of the profits of the trade be paid to the Crown. John Cabot sailed on 2 May 1497 in one small ship and after a difficult voyage made landfall at Newfoundland on 24 June of that year.

Cabot explored the coast, convinced himself that he had discovered a continent, observed the extraordinary fishery of the Grand Banks, and arrived back at Bristol on 6 August 1497. Certain that he had found Asia, he proposed to lead a trading fleet to Cipango. Both the king and the mercantile community were enthusiastically supportive, and after a frustrating delay Cabot led five ships filled with merchandise westward in the spring of 1498. John Cabot never returned from this voyage. What befell the fleet remains a mystery, but English knowledge of and a connection with North America was firmly established by Cabot's efforts, as can be seen in frequent subsequent references to what he dubbed the "New Found Land." Indeed, in 1501 and 1502 Henry VII issued patents forming the Company Adventurers to the New Found Land with rights of trade and colonization. The company was active until 1505, when it evidently ceased operations.

English exploration was renewed in 1509 with the voyage of Sebastian Cabot, John's son, who hoped to discover a northwest passage to Asia. By this time the English had determined that the New Found Land was a continent quite separate from Asia, so Sebastian's voyage was more focused than his father's. Sailing south of Greenland and across what became known as Davis Strait, Cabot found an opening north of Labrador; it was probably Hudson Strait, which led him to what he characterized as a great sea that he thought would lead to Asia. In reality, it was Hudson Bay. Dangerous ice floes, which frightened his crews and made them mutinous, eventually forced Cabot to turn back, so he spent the rest of the voyage exploring the coast of North America and searching for a more southerly passage to Asia. Upon his return to England, Sebastian Cabot learned that Henry VII had died and that his successor, HENRY VIII, had no inclination to renew the search for a northwest passage.

Although Henry VIII was passionately committed to expanding the NAVY, exploration never ranked high on his list of priorities. It was not, for example, until 1517 that another English voyage of exploration was undertaken, by John Rastell, a brother-in-law of THOMAS MORE, who along with most of More's circle was fascinated by reports about America. Operating out of London and armed with a royal letter of introduction, Rastell quickly ran into trouble with his crew. First, they delayed the voyage several times by claiming that the equipment was defective, then they refused to go farther west than Waterford in Ireland, where they forcibly put Rastell ashore. Upon his return, he dramatized the adventure in a play, *A New Interlude of the Four Elements*, which contained the first English language descriptions of North America.

Two years later, largely in response to reports about Ferdinand Magellan's expedition, King Henry tried to form a company of London merchants that would finance an effort to find a western passage to Asia and establish trade routes. Even though Sebastian Cabot was recruited to lead the venture, the king's proposals met with a rebuff by the Londoners, who declined to subscribe to the company. In 1527, Henry VIII funded a royal venture led by John Rut to find a northwest passage, but it failed. One of Rut's ships ran aground on the Labrador coast, and he proved unable to contend with the ice floes that had so frightened

Cabot's crews. Turning south, Rut explored the American coast and eventually made his way to the West Indies, the first Englishman to arrive there. When he attempted to trade with the Spaniards on Santo Domingo, he was violently repulsed. This royal effort was matched in 1530 by a private one, when William Hawkins of Plymouth undertook to outfit a fleet and establish trade with Africa and the New World. In the course of enriching himself by trading in African ivory and dyewood from Brazil, Hawkins also acquired considerable knowledge about the lands and people of Africa and the New World. Hawkins founded what became known as the Triangle Trade. Like John Cabot's reports a generation earlier, Hawkins's effort served to intensify interest in exploration.

Two of Henry VIII's three children, EDWARD VI and MARY, continued along the lines of English exploration laid down by the first Tudors. Little was achieved during Edward VI's reign, largely because of economic difficulties and the political instability of the Protectorate. During his time in power, however, JOHN DUDLEY, duke of Northumberland, made an important decision. Recognizing that England must have sound information to have any hope of success in exploration and overseas expansion, Northumberland employed as special advisers Sebastian Cabot, by now the elder statesman of maritime enterprise, and the younger JOHN DEE, who had finished his training in 1551. Between Cabot's vast seagoing experience and Dee's scholarly compilations and analyses, the government was provided with sound advice on what should and could be accomplished. The practical manifestation of these assessments was to shift England's interest away from seeking a northwest passage to Asia and turn instead toward discovering a northeast passage. Cabot framed a plan in 1552 for this new thrust in exploration, and England's first joint-stock company was formed to provide the financing. Commanded by Sir Hugh Willoughby and Richard Chancellor, the fleet sailed from London in the summer of 1553.

It was not until Mary had come to the throne, however, that news was received in England about the fate of this search for a northeast passage. A storm off Norway had separated the two squadrons, and Willoughby was forced to spend the winter off the coast of Lapland, where he and his crews perished. Chancellor, in contrast, discovered the White Sea, sailed to Archangel, made his way overland to Moscow, and established a direct English tie with the court of the Russian tsar, Ivan IV (the Terrible). Chancellor's success far overshadowed the concurrent African explorations of Thomas Wyndham and John Lok and proved to be the highlight of Mary's reign, for it laid the foundation for eastern expansion during the reign of her sister, ELIZABETH.

Exploration during the long reign of Elizabeth occurred steadily and on several fronts throughout the era. Virtually from the start of the reign, English knowledge of Africa was expanded by continuations of the Guinea voyages that started in Mary's reign and the beginning, in 1562, of the slave trade by JOHN HAWKINS, which also provided the English with information about the New World. At the same time, Anthony Jenkinson, who succeeded Chancellor as England's representative at the Russian court, undertook a remarkable trek of discovery.

Traveling down the Volga from Moscow to the Caspian, he turned eastward, journeying all the way to Bokhara along the eastern leg of the "silk route" from China to the Middle East. Jenkinson also explored to the south of that route into Persia, where he established a trading connection with England and also provided valuable information about the geography and people of the area.

English attraction to Asia furthermore led to a revival of efforts to find a northwest passage. Richard Eden, for example, wrote so positively about the passage that Sir Humphrey Gilbert was inspired to make his reputation with its discovery. By 1576, Gilbert had published a tract, *A Discourse for a Discovery of a new Passage to Cataia*, which precipitated a voyage by Martin Frobisher, experienced in African exploration, in that year. Frobisher was unsuccessful in his quest to find the passage, but he did discover a broad channel beyond Davis Strait that he assumed would lead to the Pacific, so he returned to England with news of his breakthrough. In 1577, Frobisher sailed again, this time expecting both to find gold and to sail westward to Asia, but both hopes proved in vain. The following year, he led a large fleet to the same area to carry home what Frobisher thought was gold-bearing ore. While the minerals proved worthless, Frobisher did explore another channel, which he called the "Mistaken Strait," that eventually was known as Hudson Strait. Although his voyages did not achieve their goal, Martin Frobisher significantly increased England's geographic knowledge of North America. Humphrey Gilbert, for his part, led two expeditions to North America between 1578 and 1583. Both failed either to find a northwest passage or establish an English colony, and Gilbert died at sea in a storm while returning to England from the second voyage. He nevertheless added to the store of information about the New World and was especially important in stimulating further exploration and colonizing efforts.

Perhaps the most important stimulus to exploration was, however, the writing of Richard Hakluyt. Beginning in 1579 with his *Discourse on the Strait of Magellan*, continuing in the 1580s with *Divers Voyages to America*, an edition of *De Orbe Novo*, and *Discourse on Western Planting*, and concluding in 1589 with his monumental *The Principall Navigations, Voiages and Discoveries of the English Nation*, Hakluyt supplied the most powerful impulse for English exploration and overseas expansion. His influence is perhaps best seen not only in his books but also in his cartographic work for the East India Company and his membership in both the Virginia and Northwest Passage companies. Hakluyt's influence continued on into the Stuart era even after his death in 1616, for in 1625 his friend Samuel Purchas published *Hakluytus Posthumas, or Purchas his Pilgrimes* as an addendum to Hakluyt's 1589 milestone.

Further exploration during the remainder of Elizabeth's reign was seriously curtailed by the war with Spain, but the traditions begun by the Cabots, Hawkins, Gilbert, and the others were carried on by a new generation. John Davis, for example, revived the search for the northwest passage, and his exploits are acknowledged by the naming of Davis Strait in his honor. Humphrey Gilbert's brother, Adrian, continued exploration around Greenland and Labrador, and

Walter Ralegh developed plans for the charting and settlement of North America. In all, English exploration during the Tudor era was not as dramatic as Columbus's discovery of the New World or Magellan's circumnavigation, but Tudor explorers provided a store of geographic and oceanographic information that profoundly affected European understanding of the rest of the world.

Bibliography: D. Quinn and A. Ryan, *England's Sea Empire*, 1983; J. Williamson, *The Tudor Age*, 1979.

Ronald Pollitt

F

Family of Love. A sect founded about 1540 by a German mystic, Hendrik Niclas (c. 1502-1580), who believed in personal religion without state interference, used unorthodox biblical imagery (e.g., being "godded with god"), disdained formal theology, and urged worship in small groups. In 1561 two Familist defectors in Surrey revealed that the sect had been active in England since Mary's reign and that there were Familists in half a dozen other shires. Mostly unlearned artisans, they made good use of PRINTING—1574 saw an influx of tracts, probably translated into English by their leader, a London woodworker named Christopher Vitel. Efforts to suppress them began in 1575, culminating in a royal PROCLA-MATION of 3 October 1580 and an anti-Familist bill (dropped) in the House of Commons in February 1581. Thereafter concern diminished, though Familists remained in England for another century. Anti-Familist writers (e.g., John Rogers, John Knewstub, William Wilkinson) accused them of denying the equality of God and Christ; believing they were sinless, capable of miracles, and as perfect as Christ; saying heaven and hell are in this world and that nature rules rather than God; opposing infant baptism, observance of the Sabbath, burial of the dead, and ANGLICAN liturgy in general; electing their own bishops, deacons, and elders; meeting in secret; being pacifists; marrying and dispensing charity only among themselves; lying to non-members and feigning Anglican conformity; and practicing communism and free love. Confusion with other sects explains the exaggerated fears they inspired.

Bibliography: J. W. Martin, *Religious Radicals in Tudor England*, 1989.

William B. Robison

Field of Cloth of Gold (1520). Famous but inconclusive meeting between HENRY VIII and Francis I of France that took place 7-20 June 1520 on the outskirts of CALAIS. Its name derived from the widespread use of the material, cloth of gold, by the participants.

The TREATY OF LONDON in October 1518 had secured a general peace in Europe with England under Henry VIII and Cardinal THOMAS WOLSEY serving as the impartial arbiter of future disputes. With the death of the emperor Maximilian and the subsequent election of Charles V as emperor in 1519, the Habsburg lands surrounded a wary Francis I. Conflict between the two powerful rulers loomed, particularly in northern Italy. Both monarchs wanted England as their ally when war eventually broke out.

As these events progressed, England maintained the outward pose of being impartial, although Henry VIII and Wolsey were actually leaning toward an alliance with the emperor. They also, however, wanted to secure the best possible terms from him. Therefore they continued to honor their previous commitments to meet with both parties. It is significant that Henry VIII hurriedly had a brief meeting with Charles V in late May and promised him a second meeting soon on the eve of his long planned meeting with the French.

The long awaited meeting between the English and French kings took place at the border of the English enclave at Calais 7-20 June 1520. Its final arrangements were made in an atmosphere of suspicion as the French feared, correctly as it turned out, that the English were moving into the imperial camp. But, in spite of their misgivings, the meeting came to pass with great pomp and exhibited all the accoutrements and conventions of late medieval chivalry. Thousands of people attended on both monarchs. No expense was spared, costly gifts were freely exchanged, and a great tournament was held. Outwardly, a spirit of friendship based on the Treaty of London prevailed between the two rulers. The only blot on the proceedings occurred when Francis I easily and decisively bested Henry VIII in a wrestling match. Despite that incident, the meeting ended cordially.

In terms of improving Anglo-French relations, the meeting of the Field of Cloth of Gold quickly proved to be meaningless. No further progress followed. Henry VIII and Wolsey's true objective was to secure the best possible terms of alliance from Charles V in the approaching war. Therefore, the more significant negotiation took placed a few week later and resulted in the Anglo-Imperial TREATY OF CALAIS of 10 July 1520, which marked England's first definite move toward a firm imperial alliance.

Bibliography: Susan Doran, *England and Europe 1485-1603*, 1986; Joycelyne G. Russell, *The Field of Cloth of Gold: Men and Manners in 1520*, 1969.

Ronald Fritze

First Fruits and Tenths, Court of. Clerics in the later Middle Ages had paid a number of different taxes to the pope. First fruits or ANNATES represented the first year's revenues of an ecclesiastical benefice that had to be paid by the newly appointed incumbent either immediately or by composition over a number of years. Tenths were annual payments from the benefices of a fixed percentage of the income every year. When HENRY VIII completed his breach with the pope in 1534, the Act of Annates gave these revenues to the king. The precise return from this source would vary depending on the turnover in benefices. In the late 1530s it may have brought in as much as £40,000, but this fell to an average £20,000 thereafter. The VALOR ECCLESIASTICUS compiled in 1535 provided a basis for assessing what was due from the different benefices. THOMAS CROMWELL as vicegerent for ecclesiastical affairs was responsible for the revenues among other ecclesiastical affairs and managed them through a variety of departments and individuals until his execution in 1540.

The money was given to Sir John Gostwick, who was appointed treasurer, receiver general, and commissioner of first fruits and tenths in 1534. Cromwell passed over about £130,000 in 1535, possibly the fine for PRAEMUNIRE. Responsibility for collecting tenths had fallen upon the bishop with occasionally disastrous results when his collector proved dishonest. The bishops' accounts for the money during this period were heard in the EXCHEQUER by baron and auditor. Other individuals involved included Sir William Petre, Cromwell's deputy for administration of testimonies, and Thomas Argall, Petre's assistant, who had legal experience as a clerk in Doctors Commons, was a notary public in Winchester diocese, and in 1534 became registrar of Cranmer's prerogative court of Canterbury.

An act of Parliament passed (32 Hen. VIII, c. 45) after Cromwell's death formally established a court to handle first fruits and other matters pertaining to royal patronage of clerical benefices. Sir John Baker became its chancellor; Gostwick remained treasurer. Thomas Argall, who had been acting in the office, formally became the keeper of the records of first fruits in March 1542, and Baker's clients, Alexander Courthop and Thomas Godfrey, became successive clerks of the court. The exact location of the office at Westminster is uncertain, but it was near the Exchequer.

The court necessarily had regular communication with the bishops both to ascertain what inductions were being made and to supervise the collection of moneys, since the bishops were now part of the tax-collecting machinery. The routine clerical work was done by Argall and Godfrey. By delegated power, they arranged all those cases that did not involve disagreements or require royal decisions about patronage. They negotiated the composition for first fruits, sent out commissions, made the indentures, and took sureties. Formal meetings of the court handled the problems that inevitably arose over arrears from major policy matters such as whether diocesan estates were liable for debts an individual bishop incurred over tenths, to minor matters such as "Has the college of Higham Ferrers surrendered or not" and routine orders to apprehend the recalcitrant.

The Conservative religious views of the main administrators of the court and their background in ecclesiastical administration probably made the transfer of rights and power from church to state more tolerable for the clerics. When the court was dissolved on 23 January 1554 and annexed to the Exchequer on 24 January 1554, it remained a largely independent office in the Upper Exchequer, and the significant personnel were little changed. Baker was already chancellor and under-treasurer of the Exchequer. Thomas Argall and Thomas Godfrey became the two remembrancers of first fruits until either died, at which point there was to be only one. MARY returned the first fruits to Rome by act of Parliament while requiring the church to pay the monastic pensions. ELIZABETH took them back, and the revenues continued to be a useful part of royal income. The office of first fruits in the reconstituted Exchequer continued to function much as it had as an independent court, remaining fully responsible for the affairs in its charge and the care of its own records, which continued virtually unchanged until its abolition in the nineteenth century.

Bibliography: J. D. Alsop, "Thomas Argall, Administrator of Ecclesiastical Affairs in the Tudor Church and State," *Recusant History* 15 (1980): 227-38; F. Heal, "Clerical Tax Collection Under the Tudors: The Influence of the Reformation," in *Continuity and Change*, ed. F. Heal and R. O'Day, 1976.

Sybil Jack

Fisher, John (1469-1535). Bishop and saint, John Fisher was born at Beverley in Yorkshire in 1469 and was sent to study at Cambridge in the 1480s. On his election as a fellow of Michaelhouse in 1491, he was ordained priest. In 1495 he was the university's senior proctor and in that capacity made the acquaintance of HENRY VII's mother, Lady Margaret Beaufort. While continuing his academic career (he became vice-chancellor of Cambridge in 1501), he entered her service and became her confessor. He directed her patronage toward Cambridge, where she not only endowed a lectureship in divinity and a preachership but also founded two colleges, Christ's and St. John's. In 1504 the king appointed Fisher bishop of Rochester, and that same year he was elected chancellor of Cambridge. He retained both offices until his deprivation in 1535. A zealous pastor, despite his commitments at court and university, he usually resided in his diocese. He preached frequently, although most of his surviving sermons were for special occasions, such as the funeral of Henry VII. His sermons on the penitential psalms, however, were among the most popular devotional writings of the time.

As a scholar and patron Fisher showed himself open to HUMANIST influences. A friend of Erasmus and Reuchlin, he took up Greek and Hebrew in his fifties. He persuaded Erasmus to teach Greek at Cambridge (1511-1514), and his statutes for St. John's (1516) were the first to stipulate the study of both Greek and Hebrew in an English college. But in 1519 Fisher showed that he could not accept the possibility of conflict between humanism and church tradition. He argued voluminously against the contention of Lefevre d'Etaples that Mary Magdalene had been wrongly identified by the church with Mary, the sister of Martha. In the 1520s, Fisher continued his polemical career in several works against the Protestant Reformers. These influential writings secured for him a lasting reputation in Europe as an orthodox theologian. He was perhaps the first Catholic author to appreciate the full significance of justification by faith alone in Martin Luther's teachings. And his *Assertionis Lutheranae Confutatio* (Antwerp, 1532) was one of the weightiest and most widely read anti-Lutheran writings of the decade. Besides treatises on the Mass and the priesthood and a vindication of St. Peter's ministry and martyrdom at Rome, he also published *De Veritate Corporis et Sanguinis Christi in Eucharistia* (Cologne, 1527), a defense of the real presence that heavily influenced subsequent Catholic discussions of the Sacrament.

The final phase of Fisher's career began in 1527, when he concluded that HENRY VIII's marriage to CATHERINE OF ARAGON was valid under divine law. He became Catherine's leading theological adviser, composing seven or eight books on her behalf. As Henry exerted pressure on the pope through the English church, Fisher was driven into opposition. Having spoken against the anti-clerical legislation of 1529, he was briefly imprisoned next year for appealing against it to Rome. He led the limited opposition at CONVOCATION in the years 1531-1533 and urged Charles V to consider taking military action against Henry. In 1533, shortly after THOMAS CRANMER annulled Henry's marriage, Fisher preached a sermon in protest—and was again briefly imprisoned.

Later that year he was included in the ATTAINDER of the HOLY MAID OF KENT, although he escaped with a mere fine. His refusal to take the oath to the succession in April 1534 brought him to the Tower for his final imprisonment. Attainted a second time, he was deprived of his see on 2 January 1535. He denied the ROYAL SUPREMACY in May, and he was given a few weeks to reconsider his position. During that time, news arrived of his appointment as a cardinal by Pope Paul III. This only stiffened Henry's resolve, and Fisher was tried for treason on 17 June. His defense, that he had not denied the supremacy "maliciously," was overthrown by a judicial ruling that any denial was ipso facto malicious. He was beheaded on Tower Hill on 22 June 1535. Catholic Europe instantly acclaimed him a martyr, although this was not ratified by papal decree until his beatification on 4 December 1886 and his canonization on 19 May 1935.

Bibliography: B. I. Bradshaw and E. Duffy, eds., *Humanism, Reform and the Reformation: The Career of Bishop John Fisher*, 1989; E. E. Reynolds, *St. John Fisher*, rev. ed., 1972.

Richard Rex

Fitzgerald, Gerald, 9th Earl of Kildare (1487-1534). Son of Garret More, the so-called great earl of Kildare, Gerald succeeded him as 9th earl and lord deputy of Ireland on his death in 1513. The power of the Geraldines lay in a network of alliances with the most powerful families of Gaelic Ireland outside the English Pale and the right to use state powers and prerogatives inside it. The office of deputy had become almost hereditary in the family, and the Irish Parliament and administration were Kildare tools. However, HENRY VIII had more time and more resources for Irish affairs than his father did, and the death of Garret More liberated a movement of reformist, anti-Kildare sentiment in the Pale among nobles and gentry who had long resented the financial and other exactions the Kildares had been able to lay upon them by virtue of their control of the deputyship. Henry was ever alert to complaints about "over-mighty" subjects, and a stream of complaints and schemes for the reformation of Ireland crossed the Irish Sea to an interested readership in the king's two great chief ministers, Cardinal THOMAS WOLSEY and THOMAS CROMWELL.

From 1520-1524 and 1528-1532 Kildare's rule was replaced by either Englishmen (THOMAS HOWARD, earl of Surrey and later 3rd duke of Norfolk, as lord lieutenant 1520-1522 and William Skeffington as lord deputy 1530-1532) or the Butler earl of Ossory, Piers Butler (deputy, 1522-1523 and 1528-1529). Though he was detained in England in the years 1519-1523 and 1526-1530, the country was next to ungovernable even in the absence of Kildare without the commitment of men and money on a scale that Henry was neither willing nor able to contemplate, and all the experiments in alternative methods of administration failed. They had been neither well thought out nor adequately supported by either men or money and demonstrated only that Ireland could not be governed without the Geraldines unless the king was willing to dispense with them altogether, a prospect too expensive and dangerous to contemplate.

In explaining the final break with the Kildares that precipitated the rebellion of Silken Thomas, the opportunism of Henry's new chief minister, Thomas Cromwell, was central; with the intention of curtailing Gerald's powers (though not with the intention of removing him), appointments to vacant offices were filled by Englishmen or known anti-Kildare partisans like Ossory. Cromwell harbored deep suspicions of the earl, and there was no shortage of informants in Ireland willing to detail the earl's high-handed proceedings. In September 1533 he was summoned to England with Ossory and others, and the Irish council, dominated by his opponents, asked for an English governor to be sent over in his place. William Skeffington, an English official with extensive experience of Ireland, was decided upon as deputy, but he was to have a retinue of only 150 men and little financial backing, and it seems to have been supposed (naively) that the earl would tamely accede to his replacement, though experience had amply demonstrated that this would not be so. Kildare was deeply resentful of this latest attempt to downgrade him and suspicious of Cromwell's intentions. He put off as long as possible his departure for England and moved the royal ordinance out of Dublin Castle to his own castles. Momentarily reassured by a commission that allowed him to choose a deputy to replace him, he appointed Thomas Fitzgerald, his eldest son, as lord justice and left for England in February 1534. After questioning by the royal council, he was ordered not to leave England in May

1534, and preparations were continued for Skeffington's dispatch. Upon his detention, Gerald sent Thomas a secret message, ordering him not to come to England. It is probable that he dictated the sequence of events that followed (see KILDARE REBELLION, 1534-1535), and he certainly approved of his son's defiance of the king and the murder of Archbishop John Alen, leader of the anti-Kildare faction on the Irish council, which precipitated defiance into rebellion in July 1534. Imprisoned in the Tower of London in June 1534 and seriously ill of a gunshot wound sustained in 1533, Gerald died on 2 September. In circumstances far less favorable than those his father had faced, Gerald had maintained the power and status of the Geraldines up to the moment when a series of miscalculations by the king and by himself brought about a crisis undesired by both parties and led to the downfall of the mighty house of Kildare.

Bibliography: T. W. Moody, F. X. Martin, and F. J. Byrne, eds., *A New History of Ireland* 10 vols, 1976-. Vol. 2: *Medieval Ireland, 1169-1534*, 1987.

Anthony Sheehan

Fitzmaurice Revolt (1569-1573). The Fitzmaurice revolt was a response by the old Anglo-Irish nobility of Munster to a series of English actions that were perceived as a threat to their long-standing power in that province. During the 1560s English activities in Munster such as colonization schemes, the attainder of Gaelic nobles, and the planned installation of a royal official known as the lord president led the Catholic "Old English" to believe that the Crown would allow them to be displaced by largely Protestant "new" English, usually adventurers or land hunters bent on exploiting Ireland for a quick profit. This revolt of English-descended families was particularly unusual, in that it involved the rejection of English cultural ties and religious innovations, as well as opposing the English government's attempt to establish direct rule over Munster and Connaught.

The revolt of James Fitzmaurice Fitzgerald (d. 1579) was only one of a group of five revolts that occurred among the Anglo-Irish nobles in the period between 1569 and 1575. It is probably the best known because it was undoubtedly the most radical of these uprisings. Fitzmaurice and his ally, MacCarthy Mor, earl of Clancare, not only resigned their English titles in favor of Irish ones but also declared their actions to be in defense of the Catholic faith, an overt attempt to attract the support of the Catholic powers of the Continent. This was the first attempt to introduce the Counter-Reformation to Ireland and as such constituted a grave threat to Elizabeth's precarious religious settlement in the British Isles.

Fitzmaurice's rebellion took such a strident tone primarily because he was not only attempting to prevent the installation of an English government in Munster but also attempting to usurp the earldom of Desmond from his cousin, Gerald Fitzgerald. Since the earl of Desmond had been detained in London since 1567 and would remain so until 1573, Fitzmaurice encountered little opposition, when, in 1568, he assumed the leadership of the Fitzgerald clan and began to raise troops. Soon thereafter, MacCarthy Mor began to raise troops in support of Fitzmaurice's cause, and many younger scions of Anglo-Irish families flocked to their banners.

In June 1569, the revolt began in earnest as Fitzmaurice destroyed the English settlement at Kerrycurrihy and laid siege to the town of Cork. The greater part of the Anglo-Irish nobility of Munster revolted following this success, with even some younger members of the Butler family (traditional rivals of the Fitgeralds) launching their own revolt against the English authorities.

The lord deputy in Dublin, Sir Henry Sidney, reacted quickly, naming Sir Humphrey Gilbert a colonel and dispatching him in August to raise the siege of Cork. The earl of Ormonde, Thomas Butler, was called home from London to help dismember the fragile coalition that supported Fitzmaurice. In this he played a decisive role, ordering his younger brothers and kinsmen to abandon the revolt. Many others were persuaded to the same by the actions of Gilbert, who was empowered to establish martial law in September 1569. He approached his task energetically, slaughtering all who resisted, including women and children. On 4 December, Gilbert received the submission of MacCarthy Mor and deprived Fitzmaurice of his last supporter. Despite the fact that Fitzmaurice remained at large and continued occasional raids, such as the infamous pillage of Killalmock in March 1568, his power was effectively broken. Sir John Perrot was installed as the lord president of Munster in February 1571. It required two more years to capture the last of the rebels, but on 23 February 1571, James Fitzmaurice Fitzgerald made his humble submission to Perrot and officially ended his first revolt.

Bibliography: Nicholas Canny, *The Elizabethan Conquest of Ireland*, 1976.

John Nolan

Fitzroy, Henry, duke of Richmond and Somerset (1519-1536). This illegitimate son of HENRY VIII was born in mid-1519 at the Priory of St. Lawrence at Blackmore, Essex, to Elizabeth Blount, the king's mistress and daughter of Sir John Blount. Cardinal THOMAS WOLSEY stood as one of his godfathers. On 7 June 1525, he was elected to the Order of the Garter and on 18 June was created earl of Nottingham and duke of Richmond and Somerset with precedence over all dukes except the king's lawful issue and with estates and other profits that amounted to about £4,000 a year. He was also appointed lord high admiral of England, lieutenant-general north of the Trent, warden of all the Marches toward Scotland, and other offices.

His new status was no threat to the claims of his half-sister, MARY, who became princess of Wales in 1525. The king may have wanted to make it possible for his natural son to provide enhanced family support for the legitimate line and to make him more attractive in royal courtships, for his name was bruited about as a mate for Catherine de Medici and other noble ladies. As Richmond moved to the north in 1525, the king may also have hoped that the council of the new duke, as a representative of royal power, would be more effective in controlling that region.

While in Yorkshire, he studied English, Latin, Greek, and French, developed an excellent penmanship, and learned to sing and play on the virginals, to the disgust of some advisers, who thought he ought to spend more time on horsemanship. In 1529 when he journeyed south to be appointed lord lieutenant of Ireland, imperial envoys voiced the fear that the island, which he never visited, would be reserved as a kingdom for him. His education was then entrusted to THOMAS HOWARD, 3rd duke of Norfolk, whose son, Henry, earl of Surrey, lived with Richmond at Windsor. In October 1532, Richmond and Surrey joined the king at his CALAIS meeting with Francis I and then resided at the French court until September 1533. On 26 November, with the support of Queen ANNE BOLEYN, Richmond married Mary, Norfolk's daughter, a union that was never consummated.

Richmond witnessed the executions of the CARTHUSIANS in 1535 and of Queen Anne in 1536. In the subsequent redistribution of offices, he became chamberlain of Chester and North Wales. On 8 June, he attended the Parliament that enacted the Second SUCCESSION Statute (28 Hen. VIII, c. 7), declaring ELIZABETH illegitimate. Whether in 1544, when both of his half-sisters, though remaining illegitimate, were restored as heirs to the Crown, Richmond would also have been named, had he still been alive, is problematic, for, unlike them, he had never been recognized as legitimate.

The duke died of acute pulmonary tuberculosis on 22 July 1536, at St. James' Palace and was buried at the Cluniac Priory in Thetford, Norfolk. Despite having ordered a quiet burial, the king, whom Richmond seems to have resembled physically, protested the meager tribute Norfolk provided him. After the DISSOLUTION, his remains were removed to St. Michael's Church, Framlingham, Suffolk.

Bibliography: See the entry in *Dictionary of National Biography*, 1908-1909, rpt. 1938; Michael Joseph Lechnar, "Henry VIII's Bastard: Henry Fitzroy, Duke of Richmond," Ph.D. diss., West Virginia University, 1977.

Retha Warnicke

Flodden Field, Battle of (1513). This English victory over the Scots of 9 September was occasioned by the determination of JAMES IV to discomfort the English and aid his French allies when HENRY VIII invaded France on 30 June 1513. Even then James tarried after summoning the host to Ellem in Berwickshire for 24 July. He did not cross the border until 22 August to confront Norham Castle, which surrendered six days later. Advancing into the Till Valley, the castles of Etal and Wark were subdued, and on 4 September, Ford Castle surrendered—a leisurely progress indicative of a demonstration of strength rather than a full-scale offensive. Nevertheless, THOMAS HOWARD, earl of Surrey (later 2nd duke of Norfolk), mobilized troops at Pontefract and landed others at the Tyne. By 4 September these forces arrived at Alnwick, where Surrey was assured that James would await him until noon on 9 September. Thereafter the Scots crossed to the western bank of the Till and positioned themselves among three hills approached by a narrow gully defended by an entrenchment, behind which the artillery was placed. Surrey countered these tactics, favoring the Scots, by marching northward along the eastern bank of the Till on 8-9 September and crossing the river with his rear-guard at Heton, while his son Admiral THOMAS HOWARD (later 3rd duke of Norfolk) took the vanguard and the artillery over Twizel Bridge, five miles north of the Scottish position and out of the range of the Scottish guns. Why the Scots did not attack during these maneuvers, which barred their retreat, is unanswerable. Too late, the Scots retired to the edge of Branxton Hill, a potentially strong position near Flodden, and denied the high ground to the English. This advantage was lost in the ensuing artillery duel, which forced the Scots to attack in stormy conditions (which rendered archery ineffective) over irregular and slippery ground that prevented the Scottish pikemen from making a headlong charge. In the hand-to-hand fighting the Scottish pikes were no match for the English bills. The Scottish left wing dispersed their opponents, but their right was quickly routed, leaving the outcome to the center battalion, led by their impetuous king, who perished in the thick of battle with the majority of his followers. If the aftermath proved no immediate threat to the Scots and failed to alter their anti-English stance, their losses threatened their domestic stability, and in time the memory of their defeat would undermine the Franco-Scottish alliance.

Bibliography: W. M. Mackenzie, *The Secret of Flodden*, 1931; J. D. Mackie, ed., "The English Army at Flodden," *Scottish History Society, Miscellany* 8 (1951): 33-85; M. Wood, ed., *Flodden Papers*, 1933.

Ian B. Cowan

Flushing and Brill. Two ports on the coast of the Netherlands, now known as Vlissingen and Brielle, these towns assumed a far greater significance in Elizabethan and Jacobean foreign affairs than their small size would imply. Located approximately seventy kilometers apart on a northeasterly axis, the towns are important in part because of their strategic location but primarily because of their connections with the SEA BEGGARS and the Revolt of the Netherlands.

The Sea Beggars (Gueux de mer or Watergeuzen) came into being in May 1568, when Louis of Nassau, William of Orange's brother, required naval protection of his supply line through the Eems estuary after his invasion of Friesland. Recruiting some ships in Emden and contracting for others with a Dutch pirate, Louis soon raised a fleet that was capable both of protecting his communications and of carrying out offensive operations. Despite Nassau's defeat at Jemmigen in July 1568, which deprived the Sea Beggars of a safe port, William of Orange saw them as a valuable instrument in his war against Spain, so he worked to enlarge the fleet. Unfortunately for neutral shipping, the Sea Beggars proved ill-disciplined, spending more time in privateering under Orange's letters of marque than in adhering to his strategic plans and obeying his commands. In time, the Sea Beggars became a semi-independent force that ostensibly worked for the rebels but more often than not plundered to enrich themselves. They quickly became the scourge of the North Sea.

By early 1571, the depredations of the Sea Beggars had so aroused merchants in neutral states that they complained bitterly to ELIZABETH I, who had allowed them to operate out of English ports in tacit support of the rebellion. Eventually, the queen reluctantly acceded to the merchants' demands for action and officially expelled the Sea Beggars from English ports on 1 March 1572. Lacking any secure refuge, the Beggars sailed purposelessly around the Channel and North Sea and were soon considered a spent force by all parties interested in the Revolt of the Netherlands. That estimate proved premature.

Coincidentally with the expulsion of the Sea Beggars from England, the Spanish commander, the duke of Alva, determined to strengthen the defenses of Holland and Zealand by garrisoning or reinforcing several towns, Brill and Flushing among them, in anticipation of an attack by William of Orange. He acted too slowly, however, for on 1 April the Sea Beggars arrived off Brill to find the town undefended. They quickly seized the port, sacked the churches, and proclaimed dire threats against Roman Catholics. A few days later they were reinforced by other Beggars and thus were able to repulse a desperate attempt by Count Bossu and his Spanish troops to recapture Brill. Within two weeks after seizing the town, the Sea Beggars there numbered some 2,000 fighting men, and ejecting them was beyond Alva's power.

Spanish woes increased when, coincidentally with the loss of Brill, a Spanish officer, Hernando Pacheco, arrived in Flushing bearing a commission to build a new fort and collect increased taxes. Flushing's population, declaring their loyalty to Philip II but refusing both to accept a Spanish garrison and to pay new taxes, demonstrated their vehemence when they hung Pacheco and expelled the garrison of fifty Walloon soldiers. A few days later, on 22 April 1572, part of the Sea Beggars' fleet was welcomed in Flushing harbor. Quickly fortified and garrisoned, the town joined Brill as both a secure haven for the rebel navy as well as a beachhead for William of Orange.

Flushing and Brill remained important towns throughout the reign of Elizabeth and well into that of JAMES VI and I. In 1585, for instance, when the TREATY OF NONSUCH was concluded, the English agreed to send troops to support the rebellion, and the Dutch agreed to surrender Flushing, Brill, and Enkhuisen to the English as a token of good faith. In the 1598 restructuring of that treaty, Flushing and Brill, which had come to be known as the "cautionary towns," were left in English hands as security for the £800,000 owed to Elizabeth by the rebels. Upon his succession, James I determined to end the war with Spain and withdraw

English forces from the Netherlands. His efforts, however, to settle the Dutch debt and return Flushing and Brill proved frustrating. In 1616, an agreement was finally concluded that enabled the English to return the towns in exchange for a Dutch payment of only £215,000 of the original debt.

Bibliography: Geoffrey Parker, *The Dutch Revolt*, 1977.

Ronald Pollitt

Forty-two Articles (1553). The first of two official attempts to define the religious principles of the English church during the turbulent days of the mid-sixteenth century and the only formulary of the reign of EDWARD VI.

The Reformation era was characterized by attempts to delineate authoritative positions for national communities of believers throughout Britain and Europe. In England, the process of finding an acceptable doctrinal perspective may be said to have begun during the 1530s, being reflected in such measures as the TEN ARTICLES OF RELIGION (1536), the BISHOPS' BOOK (1537), and the ACT OF SIX ARTICLES (1539). The work of definition continued into the next decade with the production of the KING'S BOOK (1543), although the direction of the church was never securely established during the lifetime of HENRY VIII, as Conservative and Reformist factions engaged in constant jockeying for influence and royal support.

The Edwardian changes brought the Protestant cause in England to its most advanced state in the nation's history. The ascendency of EDWARD SEYMOUR, duke of Somerset, was a time of moderate, though sincere, reform, as reflected in the first BOOK OF COMMON PRAYER (1549). The subsequent regime of JOHN DUDLEY, duke of Northumberland, was even more fervent in its Protestant tone, moving from what might be seen as a temperate Lutheran flavor to a more Zwinglian or Calvinist stance—probably reflecting the concurrent personal struggles and progress of THOMAS CRANMER, archbishop of Canterbury, whose evangelical leanings had been held in check initially by the difficulty in determining Henry VIII's bent, Cranmer's own moderate personality, and his desire for greater concord among the European Protestant community. Cranmer's strategy was to reform the worship and liturgy of the church before focusing on a definitive doctrinal stance that would contain the potential to cause severe division at home and abroad.

With the work of liturgical reform essentially completed (the revised Prayer Book being issued in 1552), Cranmer undoubtedly felt the mounting pressures to codify the church's ideological position. Influenced deeply by the Augsburg Confession, Cranmer had been involved in the production of the Thirteen Articles back in 1538 during discussions with Lutheran divines on the question of agreement. In addition, as early as 1549 he was utilizing a series of articles to assist in the examination of candidates for preaching licenses. In 1551, the PRIVY COUNCIL directed the archbishop to deal with the issue of a formulary in earnest. Though hesitant, Cranmer had a draft version of forty-two articles ready to be submitted for episcopal scrutiny later that same year. The council asked to see them in May 1552, after which they were handed back to Cranmer for further work. By September they were forty-five in number and were thus delivered to WILLIAM CECIL and John Cheke, whereupon the council sent the whole to the royal chaplains.

Following further work that brought the number of articles back to forty-two, Cranmer made a final submission. Over six months lapsed before the articles were promulgated by royal directive on 12 June 1553. The young king survived the date by a number of weeks. It is likely that the articles were to have received some further form of official sanction—either parliamentary or through CONVO-CATION—for, although the title page made reference to episcopal agreement, they were evidently not formally presented to that body. The issue is confused, however, by the fact that convocation records were destroyed in the great fire of the next century and by the possibility that the articles had been initially produced by a commission appointed by convocation in 1551. At any rate, it would appear that some form of the articles were at least reviewed by the bishops at some stage beforehand. Given the council's preoccupation with other matters at the time, coupled with the demise of the unfortunate Edward and the eventual accession of MARY, the articles could not be expected to have had much more than passing impact on the life of the nation. They were later modified, however, to form the basis of the THIRTY-NINE ARTICLES—the definitive statement of the Church of England—in the first phase of the reign of ELIZABETH I.

In terms of content and tone, the Forty-two Articles reflect a preoccupation with what were considered to be erroneous medieval teachings and contemporary deviations. With respect to the former, one must not forget that this was the era of Trent, when the Catholic church was engaged in tightening its own ranks and reasserting traditional dogma. In the English articles, however, the pope is given short shrift as simply the bishop of Rome, while judgment is passed upon works of supererogation, purgatory, the invocation of saints, and the adoration of relics. Within the latter orb (that of the so-called sectaries), Anabaptism was clearly perceived as the most dreaded enemy to national well-being. The authorities (both lay and ecclesiastical) continued to be plagued by the spectre of Munster well into Edward's reign and saw the radicals not only as threats to theological harmony but also as seditionists. Thus, as many as eighteen of the articles have been seen as at least partially aimed at this diverse body of nonconformists, who served such a valuable role to mid-Tudor officials (both Protestant and Catholic alike) as targets for approbrium and vengeance.

The moderately Reformed nature of the articles is particularly evident in the treatment of man in his natural condition. Though permeated by an awareness of the implications of the Fall, the articles stop well short of the extreme Continental posture associated with the doctrine of total depravity and avoid deterministic overtones. The most contentious of the issues treated in the articles, however, was the nature of the presence of Christ in the Sacrament. While the stated formula is clearly Protestant in intention, it is equally obvious that compromise had been necessary to balance the disparate spirits vying for ultimate control. The denial of the bodily presence of Christ in the Sacrament was meant to reinforce the finality of the Cross. While acceptable to many Protestants, the sense could also be reflective of LOLLARD convictions along the same lines. As intimated, Cranmer's own position on such matters had not been immutable, and the pressures from opinionated individuals such as John Hooper, bishop of Gloucester and Worcester, and JOHN KNOX to embrace a thorough, vigorous Protestantism based upon a Swiss Reformed model were undoubtedly considerable. Yet Cranmer was not likely to be swayed from a centrist position by the likes of Knox, who would unquestionably violate his sense of propriety and moderation. He was, moreover, thoroughly committed to the principle of adiaphorism at the national church level and believed that one should not go further in the area of definition than the Scriptures themselves, and this commitment, together with his ability to see shades of truth and merit in various approaches, insured that the articles that bore the imprint of his character would closely mirror his own perspectives.

Bibliography: E. J. Bicknell, *A Theological Introduction to the Thirty-nine Articles of the Church of England*, revised by H. J. Carpenter, 1955; Charles Hardwick, *A History of the Articles of Religion*, 1904; W. K. Jordan, *Edward VI: The Threshold of Power*, 1970.

Andrew Penny

Foxe, John (1516-1587). The author of the famous "Book of Martyrs," chronicling the persecutions of Queen MARY's reign, was born in Boston, Lincs. He matriculated at Brasenose College, Oxford, in 1533, where, among other men, he met Alexander Nowell, later dean of St. Paul's. A diligent student, he obtained a B.A. in 1537; the following year he became probationer fellow of Magdalen College, and he was elected a fellow in 1539 but resigned in 1545 over the issue of clerical celibacy, of which he disapproved. In 1547, he married Agnes Randall and shortly after accepted a position as tutor to the children of the recently executed Henry Howard, earl of Surrey (1517?-1547), including Thomas Howard, later 4th duke of Norfolk (1536-1572).

In 1552, Foxe began work on a history of the LOLLARD martyrs from Wyclif to his own time. His tranquil life was interrupted by the succession of Mary to the throne in 1553. Early in 1554 he fled with his family to the Continent and eventually made his way to Strasbourg, where he arranged for the publication of his unfinished Latin history. From Strasbourg he moved to Frankfurt, where he attempted unsuccessfully to mediate between moderate and radical factions among the MARIAN EXILES. Upon the defeat of the radicals, led by JOHN KNOX, Foxe withdrew from Frankfurt early in 1555 and went to Basel; there he worked as a proofreader for the printer Johannes Oporinus, an experience that left him with a lasting belief in the enormous power of the press.

By this time, news of the burnings in Smithfield had reached the exiles, and Foxe resolved to continue his ecclesiastical history. The result of his labors was the publication, in August 1559, of an expanded Latin history, entitled *Rerum in Ecclesia Gestarum*, ending with the martyrdom of Archbishop THOMAS CRANMER in 1556. In the same year, at the invitation of his former pupil, Thomas Howard, now duke of Norfolk, Foxe returned to England to be ordained priest by EDMUND GRINDAL, bishop of London, in 1560. Until 1564 he lived with Norfolk, whom he accompanied to the scaffold on the duke's execution for treason in 1572.

The language of international scholarship, the language in which Foxe had written the early editions of his history, was Latin. But Foxe, no doubt with the encouragement of churchmen like Grindal, saw that the way to reach a much broader audience was to present English Protestants with an account of the history of their church in their own language. Wishing to expand his earlier volume, he examined episcopal registers, primarily from London and southern England; he pored over the papers of Ralph Morice (d. 1570), Cranmer's former secretary; and he conversed with survivors and eyewitnesses. The first English edition of Foxe's history appeared in 1563 under the title *Acts and Monuments of These Latter and Perilous Days*. Providing an account of church history since the Crucifixion, but focusing primarily on the previous 300 years, it was an instant success, and he set to work on expanding it further. For the next 24 years, until his death, Foxe worked tirelessly on updating and revising his accounts, adding new martyrs, and providing the reader with more detail, supported by the inclusion of lengthy transriptions from the correspondence of martyrs and from the episcopal records of their trials. The last edition to be published in his lifetime appeared in 1583 and was reissued several times, with additions by later writers, throughout the seventeenth century. Though Foxe never received high ecclesiastical office, his work, soon known popularly as the Book of Martyrs, won for him great fame. In 1571, CONVOCATION ordered that a copy of the 1570 edition of the *Acts and Monuments* be placed in every cathedral church. Many parish churches also acquired copies, thus insuring that Foxe's book became one of the most widely read in England.

Foxe was the author of several other works, including two Latin comedies, several sermons, and a manual of Latin grammar, but it is for the Book of Martyrs that he is best remembered. The success of Foxe's book is attributable to a number of factors. By covering virtually all of English church history and, more cursorily, much of that of the rest of Europe, from a Protestant viewpoint, he was able to provide the Elizabethan church with a strong propaganda weapon against Catholic polemicists. He gave his many individual stories an overall shape by setting them within the widely accepted apocalyptic framework, according to which the period of greatest suffering had occurred under the reign of Antichrist, after the "loosing of Satan" in the tenth century. His stories offered readers examples not only of how the faithful should die but of how they should live; it thus became a popular book in gentle households. His inclusion of a large number of martyrs from the lower orders of society, the artisans, fishermen, and apprentices who were the principal victims of the MARIAN REACTION, gave the book an appeal that cut across the lines of social hierarchy. Foxe illustrated his stories with a large number of woodcuts, so that the illiterate could understand them. Often the same woodcut was used to represent several different martyrs, a common device for the reduction of printing expenses.

Foxe is often criticized as an uncritical and bigoted enemy of Catholicism who deliberately distorted the facts, or at best failed to criticize his sources, in order to paint Catholicism in the worst possible light. An enemy of popery he certainly was (though his book holds out the hope that one day the Roman church would purify itself and open the way for a reunion of Christianity), but he was no more and no less biased than any other religious writer of his day. He was evenhanded in the relation of some stories and often admitted that his sources were incomplete or contradictory. It would be going too far to say that he represented the type of critical historical study being pioneered by contemporaries such as William Camden (see HISTORICAL THOUGHT), but because he recorded the memories of witnesses and used sources that have since disappeared, his work remains an important source for the history of the church. Ultimately his purpose was not to write history as such, nor even to attack Catholicism, but to commemorate the Protestant "saints," high and obscure alike, who had given their lives for the preservation of Protestantism in England.

Bibliography: William Haller, *Foxe's Book of Martyrs and the Elect Nation*, 1963; V. N. Olsen, *John Foxe and the Elizabethan Church*, 1973; Warren W. Wooden, *John Foxe*, 1983.

D. R. Woolf

Foxe (or Fox), Richard (c. 1448-1528). This high-ranking clergyman served prominently in the governments of HENRY VII and HENRY VIII but later retired to devote his energies to the pastoral care of his diocese of Winchester.

Richard Foxe was born into a yeoman family of Ropesly, Lincolnshire. He was a student at Oxford, most likely Magdalen College, and appears by 1477 to have been the master of a grammar school at Stratford-on-Avon. Traveling to Paris for further study, he earned the degree of doctor of canon law. It was at Paris that he entered the service of Henry Tudor, earl of Richmond.

When Henry Tudor won his victory at BOSWORTH FIELD in 1485 and became Henry VII, he created a council that included Foxe and his fellow-exile JOHN MORTON. On 29 January 1487 Foxe was provided to be bishop of Exeter and later appointed lord privy seal on 24 February. He served on various diplomatic missions for his king and in 1491 baptized the future Henry VIII. Henry VII further rewarded Foxe by translating him to be bishop of Bath and Wells on 8 February 1492. He justified the king's trust in November 1492 by negotiating the TREATY OF ETAPLES with France. On 30 July 1494 Foxe became bishop of Durham, a post where his diplomatic skills could be better employed on Scottish affairs. During April 1496 he participated conspicuously in the formulation of the treaty with Philip of Burgundy known as INTERCURSUS MALUS. Later in 1497 he cleverly defended Norham Castle against JAMES IV's invasion of England in support of PERKIN WARBECK. When peace was restored with the Scots, Foxe helped with the successful negotiations of 1499 that lead to the marriage of James IV and Margaret, the daughter of Henry VII, in 1503. Meanwhile Henry VII further rewarded Foxe with translation on 20 August 1501 to be the bishop of Winchester, the richest diocese in England.

During the last years of Henry VII, Foxe, along with Morton, acquired a reputation for ruthlessly promoting the royal PREROGATIVE and even violating the secrecy of the confessional. In his will, Henry VII made Foxe his executor along with Foxe's client JOHN FISHER, bishop of Rochester.

Foxe retained a prominent place in the government of the young HENRY VIII and supported the king's marriage to CATHERINE OF ARAGON against the opposition of Archbishop WILLIAM WARHAM. Diplomatic duties continued to fall on Foxe, but the new government's affairs were soon dominated by the ANGLO-FRENCH WAR OF 1512-1514. This enterprise brought the previously obscure THOMAS WOLSEY, another protégé of Foxe's, to the forefront in Henry VIII's council, thanks to his organizational abilities. Meanwhile Foxe's influence waned. During early 1516 he resigned as lord privy seal and stopped regularly attending meetings of the king's council. It was felt at that time, and still is widely thought, that Wolsey ruthlessly pushed his mentor Foxe aside to become Henry VIII's chief minister. Considerable evidence, however, also exists that indicates that Foxe actually stepped down willingly and maintained cordial relations with Wolsey up to his death.

After leaving an active role in Henry VIII's government, Foxe devoted himself to his pastoral duties as bishop of Winchester. He also promoted humanistic learning in England through his foundation of Corpus Christi College, Oxford, in 1515-1516. It included the provision for a lectureship in Greek, the first official recognition of that subject by either Oxford or Cambridge. Blindness afflicted him during the last ten years of his life. On 5 October, Foxe died and was quickly buried in a special chapel inside Winchester Cathedral. He was a classic example of the late medieval ecclesiastical statesman who also promoted reform and renewal within the church.

Bibliography: P. S. and H. M. Allen, eds., *Letters of Richard Fox 1486-1527*, 1929.

Ronald Fritze

G

Gardiner, Stephen (c. 1497-1555). Statesman and bishop of Winchester, Stephen Gardiner was born about 1497 into a family of cloth makers at Bury St. Edmunds. In 1511 he entered Trinity Hall at Cambridge University. Besides gaining a working knowledge of humanistic subjects and Greek, he earned the degrees of bachelor of civil law in 1518, doctor of civil law in 1521, and doctor of canon law in 1522. From 1521 to 1524 he lectured at the university and was elected master of Trinity Hall in 1525. During these years Gardiner also became a tutor for a son of THOMAS HOWARD, the influential 3rd duke of Norfolk. Cardinal THOMAS WOLSEY, the lord chancellor and HENRY VIII's chief minister, soon noticed his talents and made him his secretary in late 1524.

After two uneventful years of service, Wolsey sent Gardiner during 1527, 1528, and 1529 on three lengthy diplomatic missions regarding Henry VIII's wish for an annulment of his marriage. Later he served ably as the king's counsel during his matrimonial trial in June and July 1529. A grateful Henry VIII appointed him PRINCIPAL SECRETARY on 28 July 1529, from which post he was able to avoid the fall of his master Cardinal Wolsey in October 1529.

Unfortunately, Henry VIII's marital problem remained unresolved, and Gardiner could envision no solution outside of the authority of the papacy. Although the king further rewarded him with the rich diocese of Winchester in 1531, Gardiner was even favoring the abandonment of the quest for an annulment of the royal marriage by the spring of 1532. As a result, a radical and largely Protestant faction led by THOMAS CROMWELL pushed him aside and offered Henry VIII a way out of his marriage by substituting ROYAL SUPREMACY for papal control of the English church. Since Gardiner opposed both Protestantism and any reduction of clerical privilege, he became a leader of the Conservative opposition to Cromwell's policies. This stand cost him the king's favor, and along with it he lost appointment to the archbishopric of Canterbury in 1533 and the post of principal secretary to Cromwell in 1534. In 1535, Gardiner partially rehabilitated himself with the king by publishing *De Vera Obedientia* (On True Obedience) which provided a strong intellectual defense of the Royal Supremacy over the Church of England. Henry VIII's dubious reward for this achievement was to make him resident ambassador to France. There he remained from October 1535 until September 1538, when Henry VIII and Cromwell became so unhappy with his performance that they recalled him.

Upon returning to England, Gardiner retired to his diocese, where he opposed Cromwell's policies at the local level, including the publishing of the Great Bible in English in 1539. Meanwhile, Henry VIII's basic religious Conservatism had begun to recoil from the increasing Protestant influence in the English church. This allowed Gardiner and the Conservatives in Parliament to secure the passage of the doctrinally Conservative ACT OF SIX ARTICLES in June. The Conservative offensive continued in the spring of 1540 and combined with the fiasco of the king's marriage to ANNE OF CLEVES to bring about Cromwell's fall in June 1540. Gardiner's triumph brought him little profit. During the spring of 1542, a suspicious Henry VIII named him as his chief minister, although he never allowed Gardiner the same authority as Wolsey or Cromwell.

Henry VIII's will excluded Gardiner from the regency council of EDWARD VI. Instead Protestants led by EDWARD SEYMOUR, the young king's uncle, took control of the government when the new reign began in January 1547. Gardiner doggedly resisted their reforms of the Church of England and soon found himself imprisoned in September 1547 and for most of the reign. Briefly released from confinement in the spring of 1548, Gardiner publicly proclaimed his adherence to traditional Catholic doctrines during a sermon he delivered at Paul's Cross in London on 29 June. The next day he was placed under close confinement in the Tower of London, which lasted until August 1553, during which time a trial deprived him of the bishopric of Winchester.

With the death of the sickly Edward VI on 6 July 1553, the Catholic MARY came to the throne, and Gardiner soon regained political power and his diocese of Winchester. On 23 August 1553, Mary appointed him lord chancellor. During the first Parliament of Mary's reign, he helped to secure the repeal of the Edwardian Protestant statutes and later a revival of medieval heresy laws in late 1554. More positively, he recruited an effective bench of bishops for the Marian church who later fiercely resisted the ELIZABETHAN SETTLEMENT OF RELIGION in a way unheard of from their Henrician predecessors. Although he opposed Mary's plan to wed Philip II of Spain, he swallowed his pride and married the couple at Winchester Cathedral during November 1554. In January 1555 he tried and burnt five prisoners in the hope that a few such examples would break the Protestants' will to resist. Instead, he discovered that the burnings were creating revered martyrs. Because of that realization he tried unsuccessfully to persuade Queen Mary and the new archbishop of Canterbury REGINALD POLE to abandon persecution. But time was running out for Gardiner, and his overexertions caused a decline in his health that eventually resulted in his death on 12 November 1555 at Whitehall Palace in London.

Bibliography: G. R. Elton, *Reform and Reformation: England, 1509-1558*, 1977; J. A. Muller, *Stephen Gardiner and the Tudor Reaction*, 1926, reprint 1970.

Ronald Fritze

General Surveyors, Courts of (1542). Under the Yorkists, the Crown demesne lands that were scattered across England and Wales were not left to the EXCHEQUER but were administered more directly by the monarch himself with the assistance of his council. These estates included the duchies of Cornwall and Lancaster, the county palatine of Chester, and lands that escheated to the Crown by failure of heirs or attainder. In Edward IV's reign the revenues amounted to £10,000 a year. After a brief period at the beginning of his reign, HENRY VII, following a review of his lands by a commission headed by John Lord Dynham, the treasurer, also found it convenient to keep the management of land revenue separate as part of what some historians have called the chamber system of administration, since the treasury of the chamber came to handle the greater part of the royal money, including revenue accruing from the general surveyors. As Henry kept most of the lands escheating through treason in his own hands instead of granting them back to the families of their original proprietors, the lands accounting in this way increased and at various times included the principality of Wales, the duchy of York, and the earldoms of Chester, March, Pembroke, Richmond, Salisbury, Suffolk, and Warwick, plus lands in wardship. By the end of his reign they brought in about £42,000.

After 2 March 1493 land revenue receivers and other specified accountants declared their final account not in the Exchequer but before king and council after a local accounting taken before perambulating "foreign" auditors. The central officials, effectively a committee of the council, came to be called the king's general suveyors and were granted the necessary powers to act as a revenue court, although they were not formally established as a court and their records did not therefore have the unquestionable status of a court of record. Nonetheless, they adjudicated on all matters pertaining to the lands and maintained a consolidated annual summary of these accounts. From at least the years 1493-1494, the general surveyors also took the declared accounts of a number of the expenditure departments including the King's Works, CALAIS, Butlerage, the Staple, the Wardrobe, and the Hanaper.

At the beginning of HENRY VIII's reign there was renewed disquiet about this procedure. Because the surviving records were not unimpeachable as evidence, the monarch's rights might not be assured, or the subject might be harassed for an account already rendered. In June 1510 therefore, Robert Southwell, previously the principal general surveyor, was installed as an additional auditor in the Exchequer with responsibility together with Bartholomew Westby, baron of Exchequer, for the accounts previously rendered to general surveyors, but with restricted powers. In July 1514 an additional auditor was appointed to be responsible for all accounts other than those of the receivers of land revenue. The power of the general surveyors was further extended during the next sittings of Parliament so that the office became effectively independent within the Exchequer. The right of the traverse in the Exchequer court was the last line of appeal for the accountant. The moneys due from these accounts continued to be paid to the treasurer of the chamber, but the actual sums appear to have diminished, in part at least because Henry was more openhanded than his father.

In 1523 by act of Parliament (14 Hen. VIII, c. 19) the whole system was again reorganized, and the role of the Exchequer was altered. The treasurer of chamber was made responsible for Household assignments while the cofferer and with the masters of jewel house, great wardrobe, and works were formally constituted as "foreign" accountants of general surveyors. In 1531, however, this act was repealed. On 15 April 1536 the office of general surveyors was finally established by a statute in perpetuity. In the division of work between AUGMEN-TATIONS and general surveyors the office kept control of lands that fell to the Crown by ATTAINDER; thus they handled those monasteries, like Glastonbury, that came to the king for the treason of their abbots. The problem of their inferior legal status, however, remained until in 1542 a statute at last established them as a court of record with all the inherent powers that implied.

During their early years the general surveyors of Crown lands met in the "Prince's Council Chamber." In 1542 a new office was built for them by Westminster Hall in the Fish Yard. The accommodation included a council chamber and a study house over the stairs. In the office itself the principal article of furniture was a great table covered with 23 yards of green cloth. In 1547 the court was amalgamated with Augmentations.

Bibliography: H. M. Colvin et al., *The History of the King's Works*, Vol. 4 *1485-1660* (Part II), 1982; G. R. Elton, *The Tudor Revolution in Government*, 1953; W. C. Richardson, *Tudor Chamber Administration*, 1961; B. P. Wolffe, *The Crown Lands 1461-1536*, 1970.

                                                                                    Sybil Jack

Geraldine League, War of the (1539-1540). The name given to the loose alliance of Irish and Anglo-Irish lords that protected Gerald Fitzgerald, half-brother of Silken Thomas and the claimant to the earldom of Kildare, after the end of the KILDARE REBELLION and the execution of Thomas and his five uncles. Too ill with smallpox to be sent to England in February 1536, he was smuggled away by his tutor to his aunt, Eleanor Fitzgerald, widow of MacCarthy Reagh, the former chief of Carbery in County Cork. With the energetic assistance of many clerics, who traveled the country denouncing HENRY VIII as a heretic and urging armed resistance to him, Eleanor secured the patronage of James Fitzjohn, the claimant to the earldom of Desmond, and in June 1538 she married Manus O'Donnell, the chief of the O'Donnells of Tyrconnell (modern County Donegal) in Ulster. He was on good terms with Conn O'Neill, the chief of the most powerful family of Ulster, and several other of the chief families of that province and of Munster then banded together to save the young earl. Envoys were sent to the Continent, to the Holy Roman Emperor, Charles V, and to the king of France, Francis I, to secure assistance. The defeat of O'Neill and O'Donnell during a raid into the English Pale in August 1539 put an end to any military ambitions the league might have had, but Gerald was smuggled to France in March 1540 and raised in the household of Cosimo de Medici, duke of Florence. In 1554 Queen MARY restored him to the title and lands of the earldom, and he became the 11th earl (1554-1585), concentrating on rebuilding the fortunes of the Kildares, a task he had accomplished by the end of his life in spite of the suspicion and hostility of the Irish council.

Bibliography: Richard Bagwell, *Ireland Uunder the Tudors*, 3 vols., 1963.

Anthony Sheehan

Greenwich, Treaty of (1543). The peace treaty between England and Scotland signed on 1 July 1543. In fact it consisted of two treaties, one for the settlement of the war and border problems and the other for the terms of the projected marriage between Prince EDWARD and the infant MARY, QUEEN OF SCOTS. Mary was to be held in custody of men appointed by the Scottish Parliament (HENRY VIII had wanted immediate custody), and she was to be handed over to England at the age of ten. Hostages from the Scottish nobility for the accomplishment of this were to be handed over in two months. Scotland was to retain its ancient laws and the union of Crowns was to be dissolved should Edward have no heirs. Meanwhile, JAMES HAMILTON, earl of Arran, next heir to the Scottish Crown, was to be governor of Scotland.

The treaty was the culmination of Henry VIII's policy after his victory at Solway Moss and the death of JAMES V in December 1542. He needed peace with Scotland to start his war with France. The terms emerged from a lengthy and confused period of bargaining. Henry had at first sought to use a number of Scottish noble prisoners captured at Solway to press for the marriage, while ten of these actually signed a secret agreement to back Henry VIII's succession to the Scottish Crown should Mary die. The problem here was that this group never constituted more than a small minority of the nobility. English policy depended on the triumph of an extreme and unstable faction.

At the center of the stage stood the earl of Arran, who had his own plans and tended to shift his stance from time to time. In view of all this, it is surprising there was a treaty at all. Much of the credit should go to Henry's envoy, Sir Ralph Sadler, sent to Scotland in February 1543. On 1 January Arran had been proclaimed governor and next heir to the throne. This event seriously undermined English policy. Arran was at first hostile to Cardinal David Beaton and detained him, while showing hostility to French plans for intervention on behalf of the queen mother, Mary of Guise. He thus gravitated to the pro-English lords like

George Douglas. However, even though the Scottish Parliament declared itself willing to accept the marriage on Scottish terms, Sadler reported that Arran could count on putting off execution of the agreement until after the death of Henry VIII, while hoping for the marriage of his own son to the young queen. He thus neatly sidestepped Henry's superficially attractive offer of the hand of the lady Elizabeth for his son. He could not afford to look too pro-English.

A treaty was made possible when George Douglas brought back from England in May draft terms that allowed Mary to be kept in Scotland until the age of eight and married at the age of twelve at the latest, with the inclusion of Englishmen in her entourage in the meantime. These terms were accepted by the Scottish Parliament early in June with the modification that Mary was not to be sent until the age of ten and should be allowed to return to Scotland should Edward die. These terms were signed by the Scottish commissioners at Greenwich.

The treaty gave Henry VIII the necessary freedom for his war with France, but the latter had already begun to send arms and money to Dumbarton with Matthew Stewart, earl of Lennox, in April, with a promise of military help in the event of another English invasion. Within two months of the treaty, its terms were seriously undermined by the rising power of Beaton and his friends and his reconciliation with Arran. In December, the Scottish Parliament nullified the treaty on the grounds that it had not been ratified within the stipulated time and renewed the old treaties with France.

Bibliography: M. Merriman, "The Assured Scots," *Scottish Historical Review*, (1969); M. Sanderson, *Cardinal of Scotland: David Beaton 1494-1546*, 1986.

David Potter

Gresham College (1575). London college founded by Sir Thomas Gresham. In 1575, despite pressure from an expectant University of Cambridge, Gresham wrote his will endowing Gresham College. His widow was to have Gresham House, in Bishopsgate, and the rents from the ROYAL EXCHANGE. Upon her death, the properties would go to the city and the Mercers' Company, his guild. The governing committee was mandated to choose seven professors, one each in divinity, astronomy, music, geometry, law, medicine, and rhetoric, to lecture each on a different day of the week. The professors would have apartments in Gresham House and salaries paid by income from the Exchange.

Gresham and the committee intended the college to serve the merchant community. Each lecture was directed to be delivered twice, in Latin at 8:00 a.m. and in English at 2:00 p.m. The Latin lectures may have been intended for foreigners (though merchants, English and foreign, generally knew little Latin). The astronomy lectures emphasized navigation; the geometry lectures, mensuration and trigonometry; the law lectures, commercial and contract law. Professors were required to make themselves available in chambers at set hours for consultation, and the bell at the Royal Exchange rang the approach of lectures.

Gresham died in 1579 and his wife died in 1596. Immediately, Gresham's heirs sued the city and the Mercers. The professors, chosen with the assistance of the UNIVERSITIES and their friends at COURT, moved into Gresham House in 1597, then refused to be governed by the Gresham committee. In January 1598 an agreement between the professors and the committee set the schedule, length, and content of lectures. The professors then ignored the agreement. In resolving the challenge to the will, Parliament effectively stripped the committee of power over the professors. As a result, Gresham College became more like the universities, supporting scholarly research. Lectures were sparsely attended, and professors commonly neglected to keep in chambers as required.

From 1658, before its official incorporation, the Royal Society held meetings at Gresham College. However, it was displaced to Arundel House when the Great Fire destroyed the Royal Exchange in 1666. Built, like the Exchange, around a central courtyard, Gresham House was the Exchange's home until the New Exchange opened in 1669. The expense of rebuilding the Exchange reduced the college's endowment, and by 1686 Gresham House was quite dilapidated. It was pulled down in 1768, and Gresham College lectures were thenceforth delivered in a room in the Exchange.

Bibliography: I. R. Adamson, "The Administration of Gresham College and Its Fluctuating Fortunes as a Scientific Institution in the Seventeenth Century," *History of Education* 9 (1980): 13-25; J. W. Burgon, *The Life and Times of Sir Thomas Gresham*, 2 vols., 1839.

Mark Heumann

Grindal, Edmund, (c. 1519-1583). Second Elizabethan archbishop of Canterbury, Grindal was born in Cumbria about 1519. His father was a poor tenant farmer. At Pembroke Hall, Cambridge, which had a reputation for Protestantism, he gained his B.A. (1538), M.A. (1540), and B.D. (1549). During EDWARD VI's reign, he became Lady Margaret preacher at Cambridge but spent more time in London where he assisted Bishop NICHOLAS RIDLEY. Edward's death forestalled Grindal's elevation to the episcopate.

At the accession of the Catholic MARY, Grindal fled to Strasbourg. At Frankfort he mediated between those who used the Edwardian service of 1552 and those who favored Calvinistic practices. He collected information concerning the Marian martyrs and helped JOHN FOXE with his important work.

On Mary's death, Grindal returned home. His staunch supporter WILLIAM CECIL wanted him as bishop of London. Grindal was uncertain about aspects of the ELIZABETHAN SETTLEMENT OF RELIGION of 1559 but accepted, lest the position be filled by some "semi-papist," Lutheran, or time-server. A conscientious bishop of London, Grindal tried to staff his diocese with enthusiastic Protestants. He worried when he had to ordain inferior candidates because there were so few suitable Protestants. This made him sympathetic to moderate nonconformists, and this sympathy exasperated Archbishop MATTHEW PARKER. Grindal urged conformity "for order's sake and obedience to the prince," but he shared the nonconformists' dislike for the surplice and kneeling at communion. Until the VESTIARIAN CONTROVERSY OF 1566, he allowed nonconformists to dominate London's pulpits. However, he dealt firmly with the SEPARATISTS apprehended at Plumbers Hall in 1567.

In 1570 Grindal became archbishop of York. The religiously Conservative north was a sensitive area for the government after the rebellion of the northern earls and ELIZABETH's excommunication (see REGNANS IN EXCELSIS), so this was no "moving upstairs." Grindal and his fellow on the COUNCIL OF THE NORTH, the "puritan earl" of Huntington, Henry Hastings, introduced Protestant ministers and tried to combat RECUSANCY.

Huntington and Cecil wanted Grindal to succeed Parker in 1575. He was one of the few Englishmen with an international reputation. Grindal hestitated, as did Elizabeth, but in November he became primate, amid hopes for reform of the clergy and CHURCH COURTS and cooperation with the more moderate PURITANS against the Catholics. During 1576, Elizabeth queried the wisdom of allowing meetings in which the clergy preached and discussed the gospel, often with the laity. Grindal made inquiries and was satisfied by his bishops' reports. There was evidence that nonconformists had used these "prophesyings" as a platform, but Grindal, convinced of their value, believed they could be controlled and refused to order their cessation. His December 1576 letter to Elizabeth shows he saw their preservation as his God-given duty, which took precedence over obedience to her. Grindal would not believe that all clerical nonconformity endangered the Elizabethan settlement. This attitude caused his downfall, although some contemporaries suggested he was also the victim of some antagonized courtier, possibly ROBERT DUDLEY, earl of Leicester, or the religious Conservative Sir CHRISTOPHER HATTON.

In May 1577 Grindal suffered formal sequestration. He refused to compromise over his defense of prophesyings, despite meetings with the PRIVY COUNCIL and a threatened STAR CHAMBER trial. Grindal's exact ecclesiastical powers during his years of disgrace are difficult to ascertain. He was absent from the Ecclesiastical Commission (see HIGH COMMISSION), and much of his more important work devolved upon Bishop John Aylmer of London. Resignation on grounds of ill-health was discussed, but the legal position was dubious, and Grindal feared financial problems. He died in July 1583. He had never married, a fact that had probably commended him to Elizabeth, who favored episcopal celibacy.

Grindal cared deeply for the church, but his suspension damaged it. He could never accept certain crucial features of the 1559 settlement, including, ultimately, Elizabeth's supreme governorship. She erred in promoting him and would have deprived him had her councillors not dissuaded her. He erred in accepting the promotion.

Bibliography: P. Collinson, *Archbishop Grindal, 1519-1583: The Struggle for a Reformed Church*, 1980.

V. C. Sanders

H

Hamilton, James, Earl of Arran (c. 1517-1575). James Hamilton, son of the first earl, was also grandson of Lord Hamilton and Princess Mary, sister of James III, and consequently an heir to the throne. He succeeded as a minor to the earldom in 1529 but proved to be a rather unstable person in his relationships and policies. In 1536 he went to France with JAMES V, who was married to Mary of Guise. At that time he may have been reputed to be in favor of Protestantism. Later, when James V died in 1542, leaving a week-old daughter, MARY, QUEEN OF SCOTS, as his heir, a regent had to be appointed. Cardinal David Beaton opposed Arran's appointment. But in spite of this opposition, the earl became governor and was declared next in line to the throne by Parliament. There were, however, questions about his mother's marriage to the first earl that raised doubts about his legitimacy. His marriage to the daughter of JAMES DOUGLAS, earl of Morton in 1532, no doubt helped him to overcome any opposition.

At the commencement of Arran's regency he was apparently influenced by Henry VIII of England. In 1543 Parliament passed an act permitting Scots to have copies of the BIBLE in English. Then shortly afterward Arran agreed that Mary, at the age of ten, should marry Edward, the English heir apparent, and at the same time signed the TREATY OF GREENWICH with England. These moves naturally brought opposition from the pro-French, Roman Catholic party, which put pressure on Arran so that a week after signing his agreements with England he suddenly changed sides, returned to Rome, broke the treaties with England, and became an ally of France. This break with England resulted in the English attacks known as "the rough wooing." They brought Scotland and France closer together with the result that in 1548 the young Princess Mary was sent to France, where she married the Dauphin. At the same time, in order to persuade Arran to surrender the regency to Mary's mother, Mary of Guise, Arran was granted the duchy of Chatelherault by the king of France, although he did not surrender the regency until 1554.

By that time, Arran was apparently moving back to a Protestant, pro-English position, so that he appeared as a leader of that party at the Scottish "Reformation Parliament" of 1560. After Queen Mary's return to Scotland in 1561, he gave her his support but opposed her marriage to HENRY STEWARD, Lord Darnley, with the result that he was exiled until 1569. On his return to Scotland, however, he demonstrated his opposition to Mary's abdication by leading the Marian forces. Arran felt that as the noble next in line to the throne he ought to be regent, rather than JAMES STEWART, earl of Moray, Mary's half-brother, a fact that may help to explain Moray's assassination at Linlithgow in 1570 by another Hamilton in collusion with James Hamilton, archbishop of St. Andrews. The result was continuing civil war until the Pacification of Perth in 1573. During a part of this conflict Arran had been imprisoned in Edinburgh Castle, until he agreed to acknowledge Queen Mary's young son, JAMES VI, as king. With James Douglas, earl of Morton, now as regent, a relative peace reigned, but Arran did not enjoy it for long, dying on 22 January 1575.

Bibliography: J. Balfour Paul, ed., *The Scots Peerage*, vol. 1, 1904.

W. Stanford Reid

Hatton, Sir Christopher (c. 1540-1591). Sir Christopher Hatton was one of the most prominent courtiers in Elizabethan England. Born the second son of a minor Northamptonshire family, he was educated at St. Mary's Hall, Oxford, and the Inner Temple, although he did not take a degree, nor was he called to the bar. This was typical of a man preparing to make his way at COURT and not in one of the professions. The only noteworthy aspect of his failure to complete his formal studies was his later appointments as lord chancellor (1587) and as high steward of Cambridge University and chancellor of Oxford University (1588).

Hostile critics claimed that Hatton "danced his way" into court, and if one allows for exaggeration, for once they may have been correct. Hatton's biographers conclude that he did not enjoy the kind of patronage that it normally took to gain a post at court and that he probably first came to ELIZABETH I's attention when he performed in a masque presented in her honor at the Inner Temple. Since he received a coveted place in the Band of Gentlemen Pensioners within two years of this legendary performance, it is likely that he was granted access to the Privy Chamber in 1562, after performing for the queen.

Membership in the Band of Pensioners routinely brought the opportunity to gain royal favor, but he was one of the few to earn promotion to a position of responsibility. The queen appointed him to captain of the Guard and also gentleman of the Privy Chamber in 1572. Five years later he also was named vice-chamberlain, a post that the most prominent courtiers coupled with the captaincy of the Guard. But as was typical of most Tudor officials, it was royal favor, not specific office, that conferred prestige and power. Hatton received other signs of the Queen's favor on his rise to the top: grants of land and office, which added to his prominence and his income. As symbols of his status, he built a substantial city residence at Ely Place, to which the queen paid several long visits, and a magnificent seat at Holdenby.

Hatton may have earned his initial post by his skill at dancing, but Elizabeth did not give positions of responsibility to those who did not merit them. He sought and followed expert advice whenever he obtained a post that might be considered above him. In Parliament he skillfully and painstakingly represented the queen's interest and earned the respect of both houses. As privy councillor (from 1577), he participated in most of the important decisions of the middle third of Elizabeth's reign. He was suspected of being a secret Roman Catholic and as such was the target of an assassination attempt by a PURITAN fanatic, but although he supported individual Conservatives, his religious inclinations, like his politics, were to follow the queen's example.

As befitted one of Elizabeth's favorites, Hatton was the patron of several authors, but aside from his reputation as being a "lover of learned men," there is no evidence that he had an unusual interest in letters. Along with other courtiers he invested in DRAKE'S CIRCUMNAVIGATION OF THE WORLD, during which FRANCIS DRAKE renamed his flagship, the *Pelican*, the *Golden Hind*, after Hatton's coat of arms.

Alone of Elizabeth's reputed lovers, Hatton never married. His life at court and his building projects consumed all his income, and at his death he owed the Crown over £42,000. Elizabeth visited him in his final illness and is reported to have fed him with her own hands. Befitting of the great man he had become, Hatton was buried with great pomp in St. Paul's Cathedral.

Bibliography: E. St. John Brooks, *Sir Christopher Hatton*, 1946; A. G. Vines, *Neither Fire Nor Steel*, 1978.

Robert C. Braddock

Hawkins, Sir John (1532-1595). This famous seaman and naval administrator's father, William Hawkins, was a substantial Plymouth merchant who began to trespass upon Portuguese trading monopolies in West Africa and Brazil in the 1530s. In 1532, the year of John's birth, he was mayor of the town. Both of his sons took part in these voyages as soon as they were of an age to do so. By the time that John began trading in his own right, soon after his father's death in 1554, he was an experienced seaman. In 1562, having identified a new and lucrative market, and after careful preparation, he descended upon the Guinea coast with three ships and seized over 500 slaves. These he shipped across to the semi-deserted north coast of Hispaniola, where, with the connivance of the local planters, he bartered them for colonial produce. Encouraged by his success, in 1564 he equipped another voyage of a similar nature. This time, however, he managed to attract the favorable notice of ELIZABETH I. Not only did she contribute a fully armed ship as her investment in the venture, but she also took

Hawkins into her service and instructed him to sail under the royal arms of England. This apparent favor may have been intended to impose some restraint upon his freedom of action, but it did not prevent him from making a very large profit or from provoking the extreme annoyance of both the Portuguese and Spanish authorities. In 1567 the same successful formula was applied to a third voyage, and again the queen's contribution was the large but elderly *Jesus of Lubeck*. FRANCIS DRAKE captained one of the smaller vessels in the fleet. This time, however, before facing the voyage home, Hawkins was compelled to enter the unsatisfactory harbor of SAN JUAN D'ULLOA to make emergency repairs to the *Jesus*. There he had the misfortune to be trapped by the coming *flota*, bearing the new viceroy of the Indies, Don Martin Enriquez. The subsequent action, which resulted in the loss of the *Jesus* and the narrow escape of Hawkins and Drake, was regarded by the English as a gross example of Spanish treachery. It certainly had the effect of exposing Elizabeth's semi-clandestine support of her seamen and inspiring them to further acts of provocation upon the pretext of revenge.

At some time before 1570, Hawkins had married a daughter of Benjamin Gonson, the treasurer of the navy, and in 1577 he succeeded to his father-in-law's office. He may well have had some share in the work before that date, for he regarded his service to the queen as continuous from 1564 onward, but his exact function is not clear. He was deeply interested in the design of ships, and it seems that his experience with the *Jesus* convinced him that the traditional "Great Ships" were fundamentally unseaworthy. Alternative designs already existed, notably the *Great Bark*, which had been launched in 1515 as an oared galleass and had been rebuilt in 1540 as a flush decked sailing ship. Hawkins preferred this design and may have been responsible for the building of the *Foresight*, with similar specifications, in 1570. After 1577 he was certainly responsible for an extensive naval rebuilding program, prompted by the ever-increasing threat from Spain. In collaboration with the master shipwright, Matthew Baker, he refined and improved the lines of these ships and made them faster and more weatherly than any other contemporary warship. He also mounted more guns and improved the quality of the powder used. His best-known ship was the 441-ton, 34-gun *Revenge*, which was Drake's flagship against the SPANISH ARMADA and was lost in the celebrated action off the AZORES in 1591. Hawkins himself commanded the *Victory* in the armada campaign and was knighted at sea by the lord admiral on 25 July 1588.

In 1589 he also became the controller of the navy and thus combined the two more effective and responsible posts in the Council of Marine. The last phase of his career, until his death in 1595, was beset by controversy. He regarded himself as a reformer, combatting corruption in naval administration, but was also accused of practicing similar abuses. He defended his own integrity with energy and twice offered to resign. The fact that his offers were not accepted suggests that the charges against him were not believed, at least by the queen. After a long struggle, he was at last successful in getting the seaman's basic wage raised to ten shillings a month, and in 1590 he founded (jointly with Drake and Lord Howard of Effingham) the Chatham Chest, a fund for the relief of sick or disabled sailors. In 1595, when he was really too old for active service, he was appointed jointly with Drake to mount another raid upon the Caribbean, but they found the Spaniards well prepared and were repulsed with loss. On 12 November in that year, Hawkins died of dysentery off Puerto Rico and was buried at sea.

Bibliography: C. R. Markham, ed., *The Hawkins' Voyages During the Reigns of Henry VIII, Queen Elizabeth and James*, 1878; J. A. Williams, *Hawkins of Plymouth*, 1969.

David Loades

Henry VII (1457-1509). The founder of the Tudor dynasty, Henry VII was born at Pembroke Castle, WALES, on 28 January 1457. His father, Edmund Tudor, earl of Richmond, a half-brother of Henry VI, died of plague two months before his birth. His mother, Lady Margaret Beaufort, was one of the leading heiresses of the period, being the only child of John Beaufort, 1st duke of Somerset, a great-grandson of Edward III (d. 1377). During his earliest years Henry Tudor resided in the household of William, Lord Herbert of Raglan, an important Welsh Yorkist. After Lord Herbert's execution by Warwick the Kingmaker in July 1469, Henry passed into the custody of his uncle Jasper Tudor, earl of Pembroke, a man of considerable ability and a staunch Lancastrian.

Both Henry and his uncle supported Henry VI's restoration to the throne during the autumn of 1470. However, the rival Yorkist king, Edward IV, returned in triumph from his Continental exile during the following spring. After the battle of Tewkesbury on 10 May, Prince Edward Lancaster, the only son of Henry VI, was killed, while Henry VI himself was murdered in the Tower during the night, 21-22 May. With those two deaths the direct line of Lancaster became extinct, and their claim to the throne devolved on Lady Margaret Beaufort and her son Henry of Richmond. Because England had never been ruled by a woman, Lady Margaret's chances were discounted, so that her son Henry emerged as the leading Lancastrian claimant. As such his existence was a threat to the Yorkist ruler, and Jasper Tudor therefore decided to take his young nephew abroad to safeguard his life.

Between 1471 and 1483 Henry lived in exile with his uncle at the court of Francis II of Brittany. Duke Francis gave them shelter in the hope that they would later assist him against the French Crown, which was attempting to increase its authority over all semiautonomous regions within France. During the 1470s Henry grew to manhood in Brittany, developed a preference for French manners and customs, and lost almost all contact with his homeland. Gradually he sensed that he might spend the remainder of his days in exile and never wield the political power exercised by his illustrious forebears.

During the spring and summer of 1483, Henry's prospects changed dramatically after Edward IV died and his younger brother, Richard of Gloucester, usurped the throne. To become king, Richard of Gloucester deposed his nephew Edward V and imprisoned him and his brother Prince Richard in the Tower of London (see PRINCES IN THE TOWER). When both boys later disappeared and were presumed dead, public opinion turned sharply against the new ruler, who had been crowned on 6 July as Richard III. It thereby became possible for the Lancastrians to reemerge and assert Henry Tudor's claim to the throne. Although there was an unsuccessful rebellion in Henry's favor in October 1483, it was not until 22 August 1485 that Richard III was defeated and killed during the battle of BOSWORTH FIELD, and the Tudor claimant was then hailed as King Henry VII.

After his coronation in Westminster Abbey on 30 October 1485, Henry held his first PARLIAMENT and won quick recognition as the rightful monarch. Thereafter he ruled England with great success until his death on 21 April 1509.

Henry's success on the throne can be attributed to three general factors. First, there was a widespread desire for the reestablishment of peace and stability after the thirty-year conflict generally remembered as the Wars of Roses. Most of the English people were willing to support any monarch who made a serious effort to rule the country fairly and impartially to heal the bitter feud between Lancaster and York. Because Henry was obviously making such an effort, the great majority of his subjects rallied to his banner and assisted him in whatever ways they could. Of course, there were periodic Yorkist disturbances after 1845 and moments of extreme tension that caused Henry himself considerable worry. But in retrospect, those conspiracies had little popular support and only slight chance of toppling him.

Second, Henry enjoyed great success on the throne because, despite his lack of formal education, he was an excellent judge of other men and their motives. During his first months as king, he appointed an unusually capable group of councillors who, with one or two exceptions, served him loyally for many years. He generally relied on well-trained bishops and lawyers, who brought considerable expertise to their appointed tasks. Moreover, he strove from the outset to create what is today known as a bipartisan administration and appointed a substantial number of ex-Yorkists to high office. As a consequence the Yorkists had no reason to believe that he was ruling solely in the interests of the Lancastrians, particularly after his marriage on 18 January 1486 to Elizabeth of York, eldest of five daughters of Edward IV. Once Elizabeth gave her husband several children, who carried the mingled blood of Lancaster and York in their veins, Henry found it easier than ever to win the support of all his subjects.

Third, there were a number of underlying conditions that contributed to Henry's success on the throne. POPULATION was increasing steadily at the time after the demographic decline of between 1325 and 1400. As a consequence the national economy was growing, since there was a widening demand for clothing, shelter, foodstuffs, and services of all kinds. Moreover, the pool of cheap peasant labor was expanding, making it possible for landowners to raise rents whenever leases were renewed and to offer lower wages for spot labor. Although the peasantry's standard of living was declining as a result, the upper classes were prospering and becoming contented with their situation, which indirectly helped Henry to maintain peace and order. Furthermore, England's wool sales to western Europe had grown steadily since the 1470s, and with every decade there was a greater demand for English wool in Continental markets. In 1489 Henry even concluded a commercial treaty with Lorenzo de Medici by which he committed English suppliers to provide as much raw wool as Florence's many workshops needed each year.

The prosperity of the wool trade led to increased receipts from the export taxes (which were collected until the 1720s) and also indirectly triggered an expansion of the import duties, since merchants who sold more wool on the Continent tended to import larger quantities of European merchandise for resale in England. As a consequence the proceeds of the customs taxes grew substantially while Henry was on the throne and gave him the financial resources to maintain a strong and stable government.

Henry also raised money for his needs by using Edward IV's methods to manage the Crown lands effectively: by appealing periodically to Parliament and CONVOCATION for special grants of taxation; by insisting on the effective administration of justice and imposing heavy fines on lawbreakers; and by resorting to benevolences and forced loans, which he had no intention of repaying. In all those ways he managed to raise the total income of the Crown from only £52,000 during his first year on the throne to approximately £142,000 during his final year. In addition he accumulated a cash surplus of more than £275,000, which he bequeathed to his heir HENRY VIII. By many historians Henry VII is therefore remembered as the best businessman ever to occupy the English throne, although his financial exactions led to a resurgence of political tensions during the second half of the reign.

Henry could never have developed his large cash reserve had he followed an aggressive foreign policy. A quiet and taciturn man, he was content to avoid foreign adventures and was never tempted to intervene in the Italian Wars, as the Holy Roman Emperor Maximilian I repeatedly pressed him to do. Only twice during the reign did he engage in combat. In 1492 he fought a brief war against France in an effort to assist Anne of Brittany, the daughter of his older protector Francis II (d. 1488). In 1496 and 1497 he found himself at war against JAMES IV of Scotland, owing to that ruler's support of PERKIN WARBECK, a Yorkist impostor. But those two conflicts were minor affairs that involved little actual fighting. Because Henry successfully appealed to his subjects for funds with which to conduct them, he managed to turn a handsome profit on both occasions.

During the years after 1497, Henry concentrated on winning the friendship of the king of Scots by repeatedly urging him to accept the hand of his daughter Margaret in marriage. In 1503 Margaret went north to Edinburgh and became the wife of James IV. Exactly a century later their great-grandson JAMES VI came south and mounted the English throne as James I, thereby uniting the Crowns of the two countries. Because the union of the Crowns of 1603 was a crucial step toward the realization of British unification, Henry VII's successful Scottish policy must be considered one of his most enduring achievements.

Henry's policy in regard to IRELAND was not as constructive, although it accomplished the goal he set for it. Because Irish conspirators were deeply involved in Yorkist plotting against him, Henry appointed a new lord deputy, Sir Edward Poynings, in 1494 and sent him to Dublin with specific instructions to strengthen the ties between the two countries. Under Poynings' domination, the Irish Parliament of December 1494 passed a series of laws that established undisputed English control. Henceforth no Parliament could meet in Ireland until the lord deputy requested the king's leave and submitted a list of proposals he intended to introduce. Those proposals would be considered by the king and his English advisers, and, if deemed acceptable, a license under the Great Seal would be issued for an Irish Parliament, but only for the ends set forth and approved in advance at Westminster. Equally important, Poynings' Laws stipulated that henceforth all measures enacted by the English Parliament would apply in Ireland, despite specific declarations by the Irish Parliaments of 1409 and 1450 that the Dublin assembly alone could legislate for Ireland. With the passage of Poynings' Laws, a new era in Anglo-Irish relations opened that led in time to the deplorable circumstances, both political and economic, of the Irish people by the beginning of the eighteenth century.

Although the long-term effects of Henry's reign were mixed, the short-term consequences of his rule were positive and beneficial. He brought peace and stability to England, accustomed the upper classes to greater respect for the law, and raised the financial position of the Crown to the highest level it would ever attain. Because of the various ways he strengthened royal authority, his successor Henry VIII was able to sever all ties between England and Rome and to dissolve the monasteries and nunneries without fear of unleashing revolutionary forces.

Bibliography: M. V. C. Alexander, *The First of the Tudors*, 1980; S. B. Chrimes, *Henry VII*, 1972.

                                                                    Michael V. C. Alexander

Henry VIII (1491-1547). Born the second son of HENRY VII at Greenwich on 28 June. He lacked the prospects of Arthur, Prince of Wales (1486-1502), whose name and title symbolized a glorious past while his marriage to CATHERINE OF ARAGON signaled greatness in Europe. But Arthur lacked stamina and his father's wiry strength. He died within a year of marrying Catherine.

There was little remarkable about Henry's education, which mixed the scholastic and Renaissance strains of the age. He was good at music and languages. A huge, bluff, and passionate man, Henry exuded raw power and intimidated his court. He was carnal, like his grandfather Edward IV. Tall, with red hair and small, piercing eyes, he was also avid in his pursuit of pleasure.

What distinguished Henry at his accession on 22 April 1509 was a strange combination of great physical vigor, cold realism, and a passionate devotion to the chivalric and feudal elements in their last flowering. He liked the applications of mathematics in the design of ships and buildings. Everything military fascinated him. He was deeply moved by jousting and blood sport. From early in his reign he developed imperial ideals and ideas. Those young men who shared these interests formed his court and practiced display, play, and the politics of intimacy on a scale to match Henry's ego.

Poets, misreading the first signs of renewal, hailed his accession as the return of an Age of Gold. Acting under council pressures to consolidate the alliance with Spain, Henry married his brother's widow on 11 June 1509. He sacrificed his father's ministers Richard EMPSON and Edmund DUDLEY. His 1510 Parliament reacted against their methods of government without relaxing Henry VII's pressures on the nobility or abandoning his use of special inquests and courts. Henry tightened chamber government but did not pursue details in his father's manner.

His early care was for foreign policy. Henry was determined to renew war in France. This determination gave scope to his first dominant minister, THOMAS WOLSEY, a royal almoner sworn to the council in 1510. In 1512 a joint venture with Spain failed to recover Aquitaine. Wolsey recouped this failure in the invasion of France in 1513, while THOMAS HOWARD, later 2nd duke of Norfolk, defeated the Scots at FLODDEN in September. Henry directed peace with France in 1514, but Francis I's 1515 victory at Marignano drove Henry toward a new reading of the Spanish alliance. The TREATY OF LONDON of 1518 provided for English arbitration of differences between France and Spain, a pacific pose masking a secret pact with Charles V. Its purpose was to dismember France—a plan confirmed in 1522, two years after Henry had been humiliated by Francis I at the FIELD OF CLOTH OF GOLD.

Henry allowed Wolsey to combine the offices of chancellor, cardinal legate, and archbishop of York by 1515 and gave him scope to pursue policies of reform. He pressed innovations in parliamentary taxation, law reform, and the use of the Court of STAR CHAMBER and the nascent Court of REQUESTS. In 1515, the king had intervened to check a violent outburst of anti-clericalism but in the process proclaimed his own imperial powers. Wolsey's use of special commissions to inquire into ENCLOSURES in 1517 proved unpopular among the landholding classes. In 1519 king and minister came into conflict over Wolsey's attempted purge of the minions from chamber and council. The massive inquest of 1522 into military resources also drew resentment, and the multiple subsidies and forced loans for the ANGLO-FRENCH WAR OF 1522-1525 led to revolt in East Anglia against the AMICABLE GRANT. Wolsey came into conflict with Norfolk and other nobles as a result.

There were other storms looming. Martin Luther's revolt against Rome caused the king to enter the lists in 1521, with his *Defense of Seven Sacraments*. This won Henry the title "DEFENDER OF THE FAITH," but his papalism quickly proved embarrassing. In 1526 Francis I and Pope Clement VII allied against Charles V in the League of Cognac, a year after the emperor's decisive victory at Pavia. Charles V occupied Rome in May 1527 and in effect held the pope prisoner.

Henry then gave scope to Wolsey's critics, especially Sir Thomas Boleyn, earl of Wiltshire, the father of ANNE BOLEYN. She had been at court since 1522, and by 1527 the king was deeply in love with her. Already distressed because of the absence of a male heir and fearing the danger to his dynasty from the accession of Princess MARY, Henry expressed his concern in a theological scruple. His text was Lev. 20:21, which forbade marriage with a brother's wife. Despite the contrary text in Deut. 25:5 commanding such a marriage, Henry meant to untie the Spanish knot by annulment at Rome (see DIVORCE, ROYAL).

He quickly challenged the papal power and guided the work of a team of theologians and lawyers in making two arguments, that the pope lacked power to dispense any dictate of God's law, and that the king enjoyed all the powers of an imperial Crown, among them exemption from summons before any court foreign to his own realm.

Between 1527 and 1531 Henry's purpose expanded, and the convening of a new Parliament on 3 November 1529, after Wolsey had failed to secure an annulment decree from a legatine court at Blackfriars, sealed the cardinal's fate. He was stripped of his office, exiled to Yorkshire, and then indicted on praemunire charges. He was succeeded by an opponent of the divorce, Sir THOMAS MORE—one of Henry's many quixotic moves.

These events initiated the second great phase of the king's reign, in which the king's marriages and domestic policy dominated. The chief parts were played by two Thomases—CRANMER, who became archbishop of Canterbury in 1532, and CROMWELL, who succeeded to Wolsey's unique place of confidence with the king—and by two queens, Anne Boleyn and JANE SEYMOUR.

Cranmer had risen to influence in the divorce crisis after advising Henry to gather support in the universities of England and Europe. Cromwell, Wolsey's factotum, was sworn of council in 1531. He had collected reform proposals from all quarters, including the parliamentary drafts of the common lawyer Christopher St. German. St. German seems responsible for a radical set of legislative proposals among Cromwell's papers, attacking the church and setting forth the doctrine that English regal power was complete and independent, combining secular imperium with spiritual supremacy (see ROYAL SUPREMACY).

Henry then carried forward a constitutional revolution with tremendous speed, in a succession of statutes devised chiefly by Cromwell. These further defined the king's powers, outlawed papal authority in England, and began the inquests by which the vast endowments of the regular religious later fell to the Crown in the DISSOLUTION OF THE MONASTERIES (1536-1539). Cromwell had secured three crucial statutes in 1534: a new SUCCESSION Act, which put Elizabeth in and cast out Mary; the Act of Supremacy, which required an oath acknowledging royal claims and refusing papal ones; and a new TREASONS Act, under which any denial of the king's titles as newly defined, or any claim that he was an infidel, heretic or usurper, was punishable by death (26 Hen. VIII, cc. 22, 1 and 13). This caeseropapism reached its acme in 1536, in the Act Extinguishing the Authority of the Bishop of Rome (28 Hen. VIII, c. 10).

Cromwell went beyond merely giving effect to the royal will. He tried to lead Henry on paths the king was more than reluctant to tread. The Royal Injunctions of 1536 and the 1537 BISHOPS' BOOK began to redefine church doctrine and practices in a moderately evangelical way. Cromwell pressed Henry to make a formal alliance with the Lutheran princes in northern Europe, after managing the coup against Anne Boleyn in May 1536 that ended in her execution and led to the king's marriage to Jane Seymour. In the winter of 1536-1537 the great PILGRIM-AGE OF GRACE challenged Henry's "reformation" and showed serious concerns for the "heretics" about the king. Henry feigned conciliation and denied that Cromwell and Cranmer were his councillors. He then struck hard at the rebels and executed many of their leaders.

In 1538, the remnants of the Yorkist families fell to Henry's wrath, as, earlier, More and Bishop JOHN FISHER had. In that same year Cromwell's leadership was seriously compromised by his close dealings with radical Reformers. Henry moved quickly, issuing a ROYAL PROCLAMATION in November 1538 condemning all eucharistic heresies (see SACRAMENTARIANS) and launching trials in which he took an active role. Cromwell had never effectively recovered from the setbacks of that year, nor had he monopolized power in court, council, and chamber. The birth of Prince EDWARD in 1537 brought to prominence Jane Seymour's brother Sir EDWARD SEYMOUR. Later noted as a Lutheran, he struck an interesting and secret working alliance with the Henrician Conservatives, finding common ground against Cromwell. Bishop STEPHEN GARDINER and THOMAS HOWARD, 3rd duke of Norfolk, took the lead in 1539, with an Act Abolishing Diversity of Opinion (31 Hen. VIII, c. 14). This enacted orthodoxy on the Sacraments and put on hold any further moves by Cromwell in support of religious reforms.

Foreign policy also worked to weaken Henry's trust in his chief minister, in particular the Franco-Habsburg peace of 1538 and the papal bull of deposition issued in 1538. Cromwell's efforts to balance accounts misfired when the king found the doctrinal demands of the German Lutherans as repugnant to his tastes as was ANNE OF CLEVES. She had been urged upon the king by Cromwell after Henry's nearly three years as a widower. He would not consummate the marriage, and in June 1540 Cromwell fell from power.

This victory of the Henrician Conservatives had the king's support and was led by Gardiner and Norfolk. It ushered in the final and least well-understood phase of the king's long reign. In court, chamber, and council, factions with ideological bases vied for power. Cranmer and the military men, Seymour and JOHN DUDLEY, Viscount Lisle, were the chief movers on the one side. Gardiner and Norfolk led the Conservatives, who used the king's weakness for women, his hatred for the French and the Scots, and his loathing for radical religion as the basis for seeking control. They advocated an imperial alliance and the renewal of war with Scotland and France. They even attacked Cranmer in his own diocese, in the 1543 PREBENDARIES PLOT.

These moves failed. Henry reposed unique trust in Cranmer. The war policy all but destroyed the fiscal and financial integrity of the Crown by 1545. Attempts to blunt the thrust of religious reform misfired in 1546. Henry's main concern then seemed to be to secure for his son Prince Edward a trustworthy council and workable regency arrangement. Parliament had allowed the king to devise the Crown by will (35 Hen. VII, c. 1). One of Henry's last deliberate acts of state was to give the signal for the overthrow of the conservatives. In December 1546 Sir WILLIAM PAGET took charge of a paper coup, altering the king's will to reshape the inner council. Gardiner was excluded. Norfolk escaped execution for treason only because of the king's own death on 28 January 1547. Seymour aimed at a protectorship, ably seconded by Paget and other Protestant-leaning or politique men who controlled the Privy Chamber and the Privy Purse.

Henry's reign ended in paradox. He authorized the hunting of heretics and remained Catholic on the eucharist. But he had entrusted his heir to a group of eager careerists who altered his will to suit their own purposes. Bluff Harry's efforts to arrest the revolution he had begun failed.

Bibliography: G. R. Elton, *The Tudor Revolution in Government*, 1953; J. J. Scarisbrick, *Henry VIII*, 1968; D. R. Starkey, *The Reign of Henry VIII*, 1985.

Arthur J. Slavin

Hepburn, James, 4th Earl of Bothwell (c. 1535-1578). James Hepburn succeeded to the border earldom of Bothwell in 1556. But until the last two years of MARY, QUEEN OF SCOTS's personal rule, 1565-1567, this most notorious of her subjects had a low-key political role. Despite his Protestantism, he had remained loyal to Mary's mother, Mary of Guise, during her struggle with the Protestent Lords of the Congregation 1559-1560; but if this loyalty endeared him to the new queen, it was to little effect, for his penchant for taking an independent line meant that he fell foul of the leading Protestants, notably JAMES STEWART, earl of Moray, and in 1562 a lunatic scheme supposedly hatched with JAMES HAMILTON, the lunatic earl of Arran, to kidnap Mary resulted in exile. He returned three years later, in 1565, after Moray's fall from power, became an assiduous attender at Mary's council, and, though still strongly Protestant, rapidly emerged as one of the queen's principal supporters, despite her pro-Catholic leanings of 1565-1566. He was prominent in the aftermath of the RIZZIO MURDER and her recovery of power and was a major beneficiary, being given the important castle of Dunbar. Her dash to his remote border castle of Hermitage in October, while on a judicial business at Jedburgh, to visit him when wounded produced both inevitable scandal and, for Mary, a near-fatal nervous and physical collapse. This "[vain]glorious, rash and hazardous young man," a womanizer and something of a bully, was now the magnate on whom Mary entirely relied. His rigged trial and acquittal after the Darnley murder convinced no one. Nor did his supposed "abduction" of Mary in April 1567, when he intercepted her en route from Stirling to Edinburgh and took her to Dunbar; Mary's connivance was not doubted. At Dunbar, there almost certainly occurred the famous rape, so beloved of Mary's detractors at the time and of historical novelists ever since. Their romantic view is quite misplaced; it was done to force the queen to marry him, with the same calculation as had already led him to force the leading nobles to subscribe to the "Ainslie Tavern Bond," promising their support for the marriage before the "abduction" took place. There remained the need to end his marriage to Lady Jean Gordon, the woman he wed for money, to free him to marry the woman who could bring him power. The Catholic archbishop John Hamilton annulled this Protestant's marriage, whereupon on 15 May the Catholic Mary married him according to Protestant rites. Exactly one month later, it was all over; a substantial coalition of the nobility who would not tolerate rule by Bothwell—including some of the Ainslie Tavern signatories—defeated Mary and Bothwell at CARBERRY.

It has been suggested that Mary's agreement to marry Bothwell was politically wise; he was the one man strong enough to create order out of the chaos following the Darnley murder. It was not so. Mary had once again misjudged the time and the man; personal strength was not enough to outweigh deep aristocratic hostility to this individualist of huge personal ambition nor the popular revulsion against the queen's marrying her husband's murderer. Yet Bothwell remained loyal to Mary and fought on for her after Carberry, but he fought hopelessly because of lack of adequate support. In September 1567, he was captured in Norway and remained in prison for the rest of his life; his death in 1578 in the fortress of Dragholm, insane and chained to a pillar, was the most horrible of the fates of those embroiled with Mary, Queen of Scots.

Bibliography: Gordon Donaldson, *All the Queen's Men*, 1983; Antonia Fraser, *Mary Queen of Scots*, 1969.

                                                                  Jenny Wormald

High Commission, Court of (Also known as the Ecclesiastical Commission). The Act of Supremacy (1559) recognized the right of the supreme governor to delegate her authority in ecclesiastical matters to commissioners (1 Eliz. I, c. 1). The act empowered the commissioners to punish crimes against ecclesiastical law, to settle ecclesiastical disputes, and to enforce religious uniformity.

Elizabeth's first ecclesiastical commission of 1559 was empowered to deal with the usual causes that came within the sphere of the ecclesiastical courts, such as adultery. More important were its dealings with uniformity. The first members included ecclesiastics (led by MATTHEW PARKER and EDMUND GRINDAL), privy councillors such as Sir Francis Knollys, common lawyers, and several gentlemen. The laity outnumbered the clergy. These commissioners could fine or imprison offenders, powers that the ordinary ecclesiastical courts lacked. From this kind of commission, the permanent Court of High Commission developed.

Ecclesiastical commissions established by royal authority were not new—examples can be found from long before the Reformation, while Elizabeth's first commission was very similar to one employed by her Catholic sister in 1557. Constitutionally, the exact origins of this royal power to delegate ecclesiastical authority were unclear. No doubt Elizabeth believed these powers emanated from the ROYAL PREROGATIVE, but it could be claimed that, at least in her reign, their origins were statutory. A 1580 council letter to Grindal spoke of the queen's "Commission Ecclesiastical warranted by the laws of this realm."

The relatively recently discovered records for the northern ecclesiastical Court of High Commission show that the court sat as a formal court in York from soon after Elizabeth's accession. Probably something similar happened in the south at London, although the loss of the records makes it difficult to ascertain when the southern court became permanent. What is certain is that alongside a series of temporary commissions, two permanent courts came into being in Elizabeth's reign, one northern, one southern.

The Northern High Commission concentrated upon the Catholic threat in that conservative province. Before the 1581 act, only the High Commission could fine and imprison RECUSANTS, so the court was politically important, and its membership was virtually interchangeable with that of the COUNCIL IN THE NORTH. At first the majority of the Northern High Commissioners were laymen, but lay participation decreased later in the reign when recusants could be tried in the COMMON LAW courts. The importance of the Northern High Commission gradually declined, and by the early seventeenth century it was a very ordinary ecclesiastical court, although speedier and cheaper than its inferiors.

In contrast, the Southern High Commission became increasingly powerful, especially under the leadership of Archbishop JOHN WHITGIFT and Bishop John Alymer of London. As its power grew, so did its unpopularity. It was from the first an important weapon against nonconformity, both Catholic and Protestant. It was in their capacity as ecclesiastical commissioners that Parker and Grindal dealt with the nonconformist London ministers in 1566. The Plumbers Hall SEPARATISTS (1567) and religious radicals such as John Field (1571) also came before this most powerful of the church courts. Nonconformist ministers could and did suffer deprivation at the hands of the High Commission.

The Court of High Commission reached its apogee under Whitgift. He used it in his campaign against PURITANS. In the subscription crisis of 1584, the High Commission administered 24 articles to the hard core of nonconformists, who refused even limited subscription to Whitgift's three articles of the previous autumn. In the second great conformity drive of his primacy, 1588-1591, Whitgift again used the High Commission against extremists such as Thomas Cartwright and John Udall. Significantly, Whitgift transferred these proceedings to STAR CHAMBER in May 1591. Whitgift's own privy councillorship and closeness to the lord chancellor, Sir CHRISTOPHER HATTON, enabled him thus to use Star

Chamber. This constituted an admission that the secular prerogative court was more effective than the "supreme court" of the church. The High Commission's weakness—although initially its strength—lay in the hated ex officio oath. The laity could not attack the High Commission itself; that attack would mean attacking the supreme governorship. However, they could attack its procedure.

The ex officio oath was used by the Northern High Commission from 1562 at least. Procedure in the court began with articles put in by the plaintiff or by the court itself. Persons summoned before the High Commission did not know the charges but still had to swear to answer any questions truthfully—before they knew what those questions were. This ex officio oath was a civil law procedure, already hated by recusants and, once Whitgift used it against puritans, increasingly loathed by common lawyers. Puritan lawyers pointed out that the procedure was against common and ecclesiastical law. They produced many proofs of its irregularity in common law and cited Henrician legislation that abrogated any canons and ecclesiastical constitutions contrary to common law. The strength of the ex officio oath was that it could get out of a conscientious puritan minister incriminating evidence against himself and his fellows. Its weakness was that a person could refuse to take it. The High Commission could then punish that person for contempt, and imprison him, but that action in effect constituted stalemate. The oath was much discussed. WILLIAM CECIL, Lord Burghley, told Whitgift that he found it "Romish," while in December 1590 Hatton had to deliver a royal command to the judges, to forbid any discussion of the matter. It was the refusal of men such as Cartwright to take the oath that led Whitgift to transfer proceedings to Star Chamber in 1591. The principal legal officers of the Crown had been members of the High Commission during 1590, but even their presence and experience had had little effect on this concerted puritan refusal to take the oath. When Cartwright refused the oath, the High Commission refused to hear his unsworn answers. He could have been kept in prison indefinitely or fined for contempt, but these actions would not have secured a conviction. The whole affair illustrates that Elizabeth's desire to rule the church through her powers as supreme governor and her ecclesiastical servants was impracticable; she needed the support of her secular prerogative and her lay servants, both councillors and judges, as in Cawdray's case. Robert Cawdray, a puritan cleric, was deprived for nonconformity by the High Commission. He brought a Queen's Bench action for trespass against his successor in the benefice. It essentially claimed that the High Commission had exceeded its powers under the Act of Supremacy, and invited the judges to claim a supervisory power over the High Commission in this purely spiritual matter. Cawdray lost. The judges said the 1559 act was declaratory, confirming the royal power; the queen created the ecclesiastical commission by her prerogative and the High Commissions powers were as great as she wanted them to be.

Cawdray's case was a hollow victory, as lay dislike of the High Commission and other ecclesiastical courts steadily increased. From the 1580s onward, the common lawyers had withdrawn from the work of the High Commission, while the jurisdiction of the other ecclesiastical courts was eroded by the secular courts and the use of writs of prohibition starting in the 1590s. These writs of prohibition first became available in the twelfth century to parties in certain kinds of disputes who wanted to prevent determination of their case by ecclesiastical judges. The writs were used to take from the church courts certain cases relating to property. By Elizabeth's reign, it was held that a prohibition would lie in a cause that although spiritual, could not be entertained by the church courts, for example, a suit for tithes on products exempt from tithe. By 1600, 75% of these prohibitions were issued in tithe cases, the remainder mostly in testaments.

Bibliography: C. Cross, *The Royal Supremacy in the Elizabethan Church*, 1969; G. R. Elton, *The Tudor Constitution*, 1982.

V. C. Sanders

Historical Thought. The Tudor period witnessed a great increase in consciousness of the past, much refinement in the methods brought to study it, and the development of a variety of new literary genres for the representation of history. Most medieval historical writing consisted of chronicles, primarily written by the clergy (especially those in religious orders). These works, which stressed the role of divine providence in all events, recorded recent occurrences for the benefit of posterity and were intended primarily for a clerical audience. The expansion of lay literacy in the later Middle Ages stimulated wider interest in the past, and the advent of the PRINTING press made mass reproduction of history books possible. William Caxton (1422?-61) was the first to print a history book in England and chose the medieval *Polychronicon* by the monk Ranulf Higden (d. 1364).

In the early sixteenth century the chronicle tradition was modified, rather than eclipsed, in the writings of humanist historians like Sir THOMAS MORE and Polydore Vergil (1470-1555). More's unfinished *History of Richard III* is a dramatic, powerful piece, which, by focusing on the character of the Yorkist king, created the definitive tyrant of Tudor propaganda. Polydore Vergil's *Anglica Historia* was a much larger work, which was published at Basel in three editions between 1534 and 1555 and reprinted several times in ensuing decades. Vergil was an Italian who came to England in 1502 as a minor papal official and stayed for nearly fifty years. Although his work still shows some resemblances to the chronicle, it was the first full-scale humanist history, emphasizing the role of random elements like fortune as a determinant of events, and critically examining some cherished English myths, such as the almost universally held belief that Britons were descended from Brutus, a Trojan fugitive. Vergil also dared to criticize the twelfth-century imaginative historian Geoffrey of Monmouth (d. 1154) and thereby incurred the wrath of his more learned English readers for the next fifty years. Most subsequent historical writers mimicked Vergil's idea of dividing his history by reigns rather than simply proceeding year by year as the medieval chroniclers had.

The DISSOLUTION OF THE MONASTERIES merely completed a decay of the monastic chronicle that had been taking place for some time. As a genre, however, the chronicle was still far from dead, and the printing press gave it new life. Edward Hall (d. 1547), a London lawyer, borrowed from Vergil to produce a work that was very like the chronicles but that nevertheless had a central theme: the division and reunion of the two great houses of Lancaster and York between 1399 and 1509. Hall dwelt on the great disorder caused by rebellion in history (especially the Lancastrian deposition of Richard II) and the restoration of peace and stability by HENRY VII, which was perfected in the person of his son, HENRY VIII, in whom the two houses were rejoined; this became a connecting theme of much subsequent Tudor historiography. Although chronicles continued to be written until early in the next century, the printing press ultimately proved to be the genre's undoing; it made possible, in the second half of the century, the proliferation of a number of types of historical writing (the plays of WILLIAM SHAKESPEARE, for instance) that made the chronicle itself superfluous. In 1578 a printer's helper named Raphael Holinshed (d. 1580), continuing a project begun by his deceased employer, Reyne Wolfe (d. 1573), published a huge chronicle, partly based on Hall and Vergil but also employing the talents of contemporary writers. Holinshed's *Chronicle* is the largest and last of the Tudor chronicles; in its second edition (1587), which was revised by a group of scholars led by the antiquaries Francis Thynne (1545-1608) and John Vowell, alias Hooker (1526-1601), it summarized a century of historical writing since Caxton, and provided a principal source for the emerging history play.

Providence remained at the center of historical writing in post-Reformation England. The greatest historical work to emerge from the Reformation was the *Acts and Monuments* of JOHN FOXE (1517-1587). Foxe, a MARIAN EXILE, recounted in 2,000 folio pages the martyrdom of saints from antiquity to the reign of MARY. His work was thus both a full-scale history of the church, which traced the Reformation back to medieval heresies, and a record of the recent persecutions in England, to which a large part of the book is devoted. Popularly known as the "Book of Martyrs," it was easily the most widely read book of history in the sixteenth and seventeenth centuries.

In the second half of ELIZABETH's reign, two new types of historical writing emerged. One was the "politic history," a narrative history generally restricted to a short time span (such as a single reign). This differed from the chronicle in a number of ways. It was based on classical models, such as Livy, Polybius, and especially Tacitus (the ancient Roman historian whose works became very popular across Europe at the end of the sixteenth century), and its authors concentrated on character as a principal cause of events, though they certainly continued to admit the power of supernatural forces such as providence. The politic historians studied the past specifically to draw parallels for the present, often with a view to advising a patron or the queen. This practice could be dangerous; when Sir John Hayward (1564-1627) dedicated his account of the deposition of Richard II to the rebel ROBERT DEVEREUX, 2nd earl of Essex, he was thrown in the

Tower. Tudor readers conceived of the past as a stream of historical patterns that were frequently repeated, and Elizabeth I read Hayward's work as approving of rebellion in the past and encouraging it in the present, by implicitly comparing her with Richard II.

The second new type of work was the antiquarian "survey" or "chorography." Antiquarianism in England dated from the late fifteenth century. In the 1540s, John Leland (1506?-1552) had scoured the country for manuscripts and books in the collapsing monasteries, many of which he saved. He recorded the antiquities and oral traditions of the places he visited in two long works, the *Collectanea* and *Itinerary*. Neither was published in his lifetime, but both became an inspiration and a source for later antiquaries. Other antiquaries, such as Leland's friend, John Bale (1495-1563), and the Cambridge scholar John Caius (1510-1573), wrote tracts on ancient British history and used the humanist philological techniques pioneered by Continental scholars in an attempt (futile, as it turned out) to defend legendary figures such as Brutus the Trojan and King Arthur. This "literary" type of antiquarianism continued in Elizabeth's reign, though redirected to the Middle Ages with the Anglo-Saxon scholarship of a group of scholars patronized by Archbishop MATTHEW PARKER (1504-1575) and the legal studies of the Kentish lawyer William Lambarde (1536-1601).

It was Lambarde himself who revived Leland's variety of antiquarianism, which involved the description of England by geographic area. Lambarde's *Perambulation of Kent* (1576) was the first of the chorographies, and it inspired several successors. Various Elizabethan and Jacobean antiquaries soon completed descriptions, not all of equal value, of their counties, described contemporary life and customs, took note of landscape and mineral wealth, transcribed church documents and inscriptions on tombstones, and often recorded the traditions of the common people. It is worth noting, however, that most people did not in fact consider the antiquaries to be writing history, since history had traditionally (following classical guidelines) always consisted of a narrative account of great men and great events. Thus even Camden, who much later wrote a politic history, the *Annales* of Elizabeth's reign (1615), did not view his *Britannia* primarily as a work of history but as a chorography.

The two greatest works of the Elizabethan antiquarian movement were William Camden's *Britannia* (1586) and John Stow's *Survey of London* (1598). Camden (1551-1623) was a London schoolmaster who, inspired by the Continental scholars with whom he corresponded, set about composing a complete description of the Roman antiquities in England. The result was the *Britannia*, a topographical description of the entire island, county by county. This was the most complete description of the remnants of the Roman empire, but it went well beyond that to take note of more recent antiquities and to record the descents and accomplishments of the leading noble and gentle families of the kingdom. Camden relied extensively on the researches of others (including Leland's *Itineraries*) and thus made his work more superficial than some of the county chorographies, but it was a huge success nevertheless and became an indispensable reference tool for antiquaries for the next century, and it was expanded and reissued several times. In 1597, Camden became a herald. From that position he was able both to continue his studies and to help others with theirs, in part by helping to establish a Society of Antiquaries, consisting of the heralds and of other interested scholars, such as Holinshed's reviser, Thynne. The society met from 1586 throughout the rest of the reign, and its members discoursed on subjects ranging from the origins of sterling money to the beginnings of Christianity in England. Among the occasional members of the society was John Stow (1525-1605), a London tailor who already had a string of successful chronicles to his name and who devoted his own last years to a parish-by-parish description of the city of London and its antiquities, the *Survey*, which, despite Stow's lack of a humanistic education, is so detailed and readable that it represents Tudor antiquarian writing at its peak.

Historical writing and historical thought were not entirely coterminous, since much thought about the past took place outside the boundaries of formal historical writing, for example, in polemical discussions of the antiquity of the Reformed church and in nationalistic arguments for England's "imperial" independence from foreign powers, such as that which prefaced the Act of Appeals (1533). Perhaps the greatest mark of the development of historical thought in the Tudor period is not the flourishing of historical writing as such but the fact that history was rapidly becoming a common language among the educated, a shared vocabulary understood by most literate men. Historical examples were increasingly used in political debate, and in the early Stuart period, many members of Parliament would use their antiquarian knowledge to criticize the court; they also appeared with increasing frequency in sermons, as preachers used tales from the past to illustrate their lessons; the success of the history play in Elizabeth's reign showed that it was suitable for public performance as well. Consequently, a much broader section of the populace continued to "hear" history in speech or performance than would read it, though it is also clear that the number of literate men who owned historical works was steadily growing.

By the end of the sixteenth century, English historical thought had changed as dramatically as the types of writing it produced. Legends such as Brutus the Trojan, while by no means completely rejected, were at least now open to debate and criticism. Scholars had also developed a sense of anachronism, which allowed them to date documents more accurately by examining their language and comparing it with the language in contemporary works. This sense of anachronism slowly spread to the public; whereas late medieval thought conceived of figures like Alexander or Julius Caesar as knights or nobles, and depicted them in fifteenth-century garb, scholars, readers, and patrons of the Tudor history play eventually came to realize that these comparisons were not historically valid, though aspects of anachronistic thought remained well into the seventeenth century and beyond.

Bibliography: A. B. Ferguson, *Clio Unbound*, 1979; F. J. Levy, *Tudor Historical Thought*, 1967; May McKisack, *Medieval History in the Tudor Age*, 1971.

D. R. Woolf

Holy League (1496). The League entered into by HENRY VII of England in July 1496. The Holy League consisted of Maximilian I, the Holy Roman Emperor, Pope Alexander VI, the republic of Venice, and Ferdinand II of Aragon, who were ranged against Charles VIII of France. The French king's early successes in Italy (he invaded the peninsula in September 1494) encouraged the other European powers to form defensive alliances (of which the Holy League was a part). Henry's entry into the Holy League marked the culmination of his policy of allying England with the emerging great power, Spain, and maintaining commercial ties with the Netherlands and supported his effort to abandon the old enmity with France in hopes of detaching Scotland from the Auld Alliance. Henry joined the league only after obtaining from Ferdinand a confirmation of the TREATY OF MEDINA DEL CAMPO, one provision of which would unite the two monarchs through the marriage of Arthur, Prince of Wales, and CATHER-INE OF ARAGON, the daughter of Ferdinand and Isabella of Castile. The king was careful to join the league only after it had begun negotiations with Charles VIII. Thus his adherence to the league was conditional upon England's not being required to enter into war with Charles VIII, with whom he had composed differences over the status of Brittany at ETAPLES in November 1492. In the same month Henry entered the Holy League, JAMES IV of Scotland abandoned his support of the Yorkist impostor, PERKIN WARBECK, and the groundwork was laid for the truce of AYTON (September 1497) and the subsequent marriage of James to Margaret Tudor in 1503. The INTERCURSUS MAGNUS, the commercial treaty negotiated between Maximilian (acting on behalf of his son, the archduke Philip) and Henry Tudor, had been concluded in February 1496; this agreement cemented the connection between the empire and England through a mutually recognized economic interest. Henry VII, who had obtained commitments from the emperor, archduke, and James IV that Warbeck would receive no succor in their lands, was now freed from any serious danger posed by the usurper; the king was poised to appear as the leader of a great European power. The Holy League thus permitted the English Crown to assume the posture that it had been denied since the battle of BOSWORTH FIELD, while posing no risks to the carefully calculated policy of the first of the Tudors.

Bibliography: R. B. Wernham, *Before the Armada: The Emergence of the English Nation, 1485-1588*, 1966.

Douglas Bisson

"Holy Maid of Kent" (Elizabeth Barton, c. 1506-1534). Elizabeth Barton first enters history in 1524 as a seriously ill servant in the household of Thomas Cobb of Aldington (Kent). In the throes of her sickness (perhaps epilepsy), she rightly foretold the imminent death of her master's sick child. Thenceforward, she regularly experienced trances and revelations and enjoyed a widening reputation as a seer. Richard Master, rector of Aldington, reported her case to Archbishop WILLIAM WARHAM, who established an investigative commission. This commission, led by Dr. Edward Bocking of Christ Church Cathedral Priory, concluded in 1526 that her experiences were authentic and that her revelations—mostly exhortations to Catholic belief and devotion—were orthodox. That same year, having been cured of her illness in accordance with her own predictions, Elizabeth joined the Benedictine convent of St. Sepulchre's at Canterbury. Her significance for English history derives from her opposition to the matrimonial and ecclesiastical policies of HENRY VIII. From 1528 she foretold disaster should Henry divorce CATHERINE OF ARAGON. She revealed this prediction to Warham, THOMAS WOLSEY, JOHN FISHER, and even Henry himself. Her popular repute as a saintly prophetess made her dangerous to Henry's cause and useful to his opponents. In the 1530s her sphere of influence embraced most of the leading figures in the "Aragonese" connection—not only Fisher and some of the nobility but the Observant Franciscans, the CARTHUSIANS of London and Sheen, and the Bridgettines of Syon. In 1532 she seems to have predicted that Henry would soon die, or at least cease to reign, if he divorced Catherine (the sources are a little unclear on the precise nature and date of the fate she envisaged for him). Late in 1533 Elizabeth and her associates were arrested and interrogated. She irretrievably compromised her credibility by publicly confessing herself a fraud at St. Paul's on 23 November and again at Canterbury on 7 December. The sermon preached at her recantation rehearsed her alleged crimes and hinted at sexual misconduct, to blacken her reputation further. But Henry wanted fuller revenge, and her collapse offered a chance of dealing a heavy blow to the "Aragonese" connection at the same time. As no plausible case of TREASON could be made out against her, recourse was had to the legally valid but morally dubious expedient of a bill of ATTAINDER, which was drawn up to condemn not only her close associates but also John Fisher, THOMAS MORE, and several others. Because More had always been circumspect in his dealings with her, he was able to persuade the House of Lords to exclude him. The act passed in late March and condemned Elizabeth and six priests to death for high treason and Fisher and five others to imprisonment for misprision of treason. One of those condemned to die, Richard Master, was pardoned. Elizabeth and the other five—Dr. Bocking, John Dering (a fellow monk of Christ Church), Henry Gold (parson of Aldermary, London), and Hugh Rich and Henry Risby (Observant Franciscans, wardens, respectively of Richmond and Canterbury convents)—were executed on 20 April 1534.

Bibliography: A. Neame, *The Holy Maid of Kent*, 1971; L. E. Whatmore, "The Sermon Against the Holy Maid of Kent and Her Adherents, 1533," *English Historical Review* 58 (1943): 463-75.

Richard Rex

Hooker, Richard (1554-1600). Richard Hooker was born near Exeter in 1554 and was educated at Corpus Christi College, Oxford, graduating M.A. in 1577. He was made a fellow of the college, lectured in Hebrew at the university, and in 1581 took holy orders. In 1585 he was nominated by Sir Edwin Sandys to the Mastership of the Temple and, with the patronage of Archbishop JOHN WHITGIFT, obtained it in preference to Burleigh's candidate, Walter Travers. Travers, who had been lecturing at the Temple for three years, was a dedicated CALVINIST and the anonymous author of a handbook of PRESBYTERIAN discipline, which was approved and seen through the press by Whitgift's arch-puritan enemy, Thomas Cartwright. As Travers's lectures continued when Hooker was appointed, the two soon clashed in their preaching on predestination and grace and on the status of the Roman Catholic Church; in the words of Fuller, "The pulpit spake pure Canterbury in the morning and Geneva in the afternoon."

These debates with Travers were crucial in shaping the ideas and arguments that Hooker later developed in the *Laws of Ecclesiastical Polity*, the masterly and immensely influential defense of the Church of England for which Hooker is chiefly remembered. To have leisure to write this massive work, Hooker obtained from Whitgift a quiet country church in Wiltshire in 1591 and in 1595 a better one in Kent. He held both livings until his death in 1600. By then, only five of the eight books of the *Laws of Ecclesiastical Polity* had been published; the sixth and eighth appeared in 1648 and the seventh in 1662. These last three books were all edited from Hooker's manuscripts and although very probably authentic, were clearly in the process of revision and are incomplete.

The *Laws of Ecclesiastical Polity* was aimed at justifying the constitution of the Church of England. In part this aim involved repelling the PURITAN attack—in particular by undermining the puritans' claim that Presbyterian government was prescribed by Scripture and that the ceremonies commanded by the Prayer Book were ungodly remnants of popish corruption. Hooker's patrons, George Cranmer and Sandys, helped to insure that this refutation appeared in 1593 in time to influence the debate in Parliament over proposed legislation against Protestant nonconformists. Unlike most of the writings of the episcopal party, however, the *Laws* is a great deal more than an anti-puritan tract for the times.

The *Laws* is a systematic treatise of philosophy. It defends the English church by moving step-by-step from the most fundamental assumptions of the Elizabethans about man and God, nature and grace, law and government to the conclusions Hooker wished to see accepted. The foundations of Hooker's thought are laid in Book I, where he expounds the crucial doctrine of a God-given law of nature, known to all men by the exercise of reason. This belief in natural law had found its most systematic exposition in Thomas Aquinas's synthesis of Aristotelian and Christian thought, and it had dominated much medieval political and ecclesiastical thought. Renaissance HUMANISM and Protestant theology were both hostile to many aspects of scholastic thought, but the belief in the law of nature was so deeply rooted that when Hooker came to analyze the laws of church and state, he could still confidently use it as the cornerstone of his philosophy.

Having reasserted the role of natural law and reason, Hooker accepted that Scripture provided the rules for man's direction in supernatural matters. However, he attacked the puritan claim that Scripture should be the only rule for conduct in all matters, and in particular he dealt specifically with whether the proper form of church government is set down in Scripture. Hooker rejected the puritan claim that the Bible prescribes one immutable church polity and argued that church government is a matter indifferent. That is, Scripture set down unchanging rules for the church's polity, and it was therefore open to men to use their reason to devise any form of government that they found convenient and appropriate.

Much of the *Laws* dealt in detail with the ceremonies and practices imposed by the Church of England. Again, the pivot of Hooker's defense was that these matters are indifferent and therefore that the proper authorities could command whatever they judged fitting. Hooker also repudiated the Presbyterians' demand for lay elders in every church and defended episcopacy. Although Hooker insisted on the antiquity of bishops and on their apostolic origins, he never argued that God had made them necessary to the church. His defense of the ROYAL SUPREMACY was based on contractualist political philosophy that also stood squarely in the central tradition of scholastic natural law theory.

Bibliography: W. Speed Hill, ed., *Studies in Richard Hooker: Essays Preliminary to an Edition of his Works*, 1972; Peter Lake, *Anglicans and Puritans?: Presbyterianism and English Conformist Thought from Whitgift to Hooker*, 1988.

Johann Sommerville

"Household Government." "Household Government" is a term used to describe the method of rule in the medieval world whereby, in the absence of a national bureaucracy, the king's personal servants—members of the Royal Household—also performed national duties because there was little distinction between the public and private nature of kingship. Thus, for example, in medieval England it was common for the king's personal treasury to collect and spend money not only for his personal food and clothing but also for the expense of the royal army.

In his many volumes, the early twentieth-century medievalist T. F. Tout described how this Household system worked and how a national bureaucracy evolved from it. As the needs of the monarchy grew, various Household officials and departments took on increasingly specialized tasks and adopted increasingly complex rules. In time they ceased to perform personal service and no longer followed the court. In Tout's phrase, they had gone "out of court." The great institutions of state, CHANCERY, EXCEHQUER, etc., all began this way. As old officials went out of court, new ones were appointed to cater to the king's personal needs, as the older institutions, now distant from the king, were no longer able to do. The Privy Seal, for example, was set up to provide a quick way for the king to issue instructions after the Chancery had gone out of court. In time it too would become less responsive to the king's wishes and be supplanted by other Household officials. Therefore medieval England saw the evolution of a bureaucracy, but this bureaucracy never completely supplanted the royal Household in the government of the kingdom.

The resilience of the Household was due to its flexibility: it could respond quickly to the king's needs in ways the increasingly formalized departments could not. Therefore, faced with declining revenues, Edward IV and later HENRY VII turned to the treasury of the chamber as the kingdom's principal treasury in their struggle to restore solvency quickly.

According to Sir Geoffrey Elton, the Tudor kings relied on their Households for the government of the realm until THOMAS CROMWELL's administrative "revolution" of the 1530s succeeded in establishing the distinction of personal service to the monarch and bureaucratic service to the state (see TUDOR REVOLUTION IN GOVERNMENT). Henceforward, he argued, the Household would revert to its primary task of feeding and housing the king. While acknowledging that after Cromwell's fall, HENRY VIII occasionally reverted to using his private servants in national causes, such as when he went to war, Elton maintained that Henry VIII's use of the bureaucracy made him modern and made his father the "last medieval king."

Elton's interpretation goes beyond the shift from informal Household government to government by formal bureaucratic departments of state. It encompasses, for example, the supremacy of parliamentary statute over proclamation and the use of the PRIVY COUNCIL to be the chief political and governmental organ of the kingdom. This interpretation has been challenged from several perspectives, but the common theme is that it stresses institutions and ignores personalities. If a Tudor monarch wished to use a member of Household on national business, there was nothing to prevent this use. Furthermore no one could effectively separate the public from the private aspects of kingship. Even so bureaucratic a minister as WILLIAM CECIL was also Elizabeth's private secretary.

David Starkey's study of the Privy Chamber reveals the persistence of Household government because of its ability to adapt to the king's wishes and the difficulty in separating personal from public service. Starkey discovered that Henry VII established the Privy Chamber to serve as a buffer from the distractions of the chamber. Here he could retreat to conduct business with a handful of trusted servants, whose humble birth and administrative talent made them ideal royal servants. Since the wellborn courtiers remained in the chamber to provide the ceremonial side of monarchy, Henry VII had thus succeeded in separating the personal and governmental sides of kingship as Elton's thesis required. However, since the king's personal attendants performed the administration of the kingdom, the creation of the Privy Chamber enhanced Household government; it did not end it.

The accession of Henry VIII changed the nature of the Privy Chamber because Henry changed his father's style of kingship. Now intimate with his servants rather than distant, Henry soon took part in court entertainments and contests of arms and admitted his boon companions to the Privy Chamber. At first these "minions" had no official status and merely provided amusement for the king, but a state visit from Francis I in 1518 demanded that they be given status equal to the French king's *gentilshommes de la chambre*.

Henry soon discovered that these personal servants could also perform important duties as special messengers, ambassadors, and soldiers as the occasion demanded. A message carried by a gentleman of the Privy Chamber had authority that it would not otherwise have. Wolsey quickly realized the political significance of the Privy Chamber and moved to neutralize it by purging its ranks on two occasions and by keeping the gentlemen busy with foreign assignments.

The rise of Thomas Cromwell did not change the public nature of the service of the king's personal attendants. Rather than try to remove the Privy Chamber from the government of the realm, as Wolsey had, he sought to control it by packing the Privy Chamber with his own followers. At Henry's death the Privy Chamber was more influential then ever, if only because it controlled the "dry stamp" which, with Henry's declining health, had become his official signature.

Both EDWARD SEYMOUR, the duke of Somerset, and JOHN DUDLEY, the duke of Northumberland, relied on the Privy Chamber to implement their own particular leadership styles. The advent of women rulers did change the nature of Household government through the Privy Chamber, however. The intimate nature of service in the Privy Chamber required that it be staffed with women. But even here the distinction between national and personal—between privy council and Privy Chamber—which Elton's theory requires is illusory. Under Henry VII the same men served the Crown in both the privy council and Privy Chamber. Under his daughters the wives of councillors were appointed to the Privy Chamber.

Perhaps the clearest example of how the king could use his personal servants to perform national tasks is seen in the post of groom of the stool. Because this official assisted the king in his most intimate matters, using the close stool or chamberpot, it was given to his most trusted servants. The groom was, in fact and later in name, the chief gentleman of the Privy Chamber. In time it seemed natural to give other sensitive matters to him: the keeping of the king's spending money or Privy Purse and later the dry stamp. Since the Privy Purse could be expanded to a national treasury and since control of the king's signature conferred great power, the groom of the stool, while technically a menial personal servant, was in reality a powerful royal official and thus a prime example that Household government persisted under the Tudors.

Bibliography: D. Starkey et al., *The English Court*, 1987.

Robert C. Braddock

Howard, Catherine. Catherine Howard was the fifth wife of HENRY VIII. It is uncertain where she was born, though it was between 1518 and 1527, most likely in 1521. She was one of ten children of the undistinguished and poverty-stricken Lord Edmund Howard (c. 1490-1539)—third son of THOMAS HOWARD, 2nd duke of Norfolk—and his wife, Jocasta Culpeper. From about age ten, Catherine was reared by Agnes, dowager duchess of Norfolk (Edmund's stepmother) at Horsham, Sussex, and Lambeth, Surrey. Her education was limited, though she was literate. In 1536 she became intimate with her music teacher, Henry Manox, though he denied having carnal knowledge of his pupil. At Lambeth, between 1537 and 1539, she was involved with Francis Dereham, a young gentleman who frequently visited her in her bed. The two called each other husband and wife and may have been informally engaged; however, they parted in the fall of 1539 when her uncle, THOMAS HOWARD, 3rd duke of Norfolk, got her appointed as maid-in-waiting to ANNE OF CLEVES.

At court Catherine caught the king's eye. Though Henry married Anne on 6 January 1540, by April he was sending Catherine gifts, by June he was visiting her at Lambeth, and by mid-July he had CONVOCATION declare his fourth marriage invalid. Religious Conservatives, led by Norfolk and Bishop STEPHEN GARDINER, used her to end the king's marriage to Anne of Cleves and oust THOMAS CROMWELL from power. Henry married Catherine on 28 July and proclaimed her queen on 8 August, though she was never crowned. Catherine received lands and expensive jewelry and apparel from the king, was a source of patronage at court, and filled her household with Howard adherents; however, she also made enemies among Protestants and those jealous of her, including John Lasells, whose sister, Mary Hall, had been a servant at Lambeth and knew of Catherine's liaison with Dereham. Catherine was also imprudent. Bored with her husband, she became involved in the spring of 1541 with Thomas Culpeper—a young gentleman of the king's Privy Chamber, once rumored to be her betrothed—and during the king's northern progress that summer, she and Lady Rochford arranged numerous meetings with him. In August she foolishly hired Dereham as her private secretary. Perhaps Henry knew something, for during Lent he refused Catherine entry to his Privy Chamber for a week. But he was shocked when—in London, on 2 November—Archbishop THOMAS CRANMER informed him that he, Thomas Audley, and EDWARD SEYMOUR, earl of Hertford, (all opponents of the Howards) had learned about Catherine and Dereham from Lasells.

Lasells's sister told the same story, Manox and Dereham confessed, and on 6 November Henry received proof of Catherine's intimacies with the two. Catherine confessed on 8 November concerning Dereham (refusing to say they had been engaged, which would have allowed a divorce without charges of treason) and on 11 November admitted seeing Culpeper, though she denied carnal knowledge and blamed him and Lady Rochford. But Rochford deposed that her mistress had known Culpeper carnally, and he was arrested and confessed. On 14 November Catherine was taken to Syon monastery for more questioning, and on 22 November was proclaimed to be no longer queen. Dereham and Culpeper were executed on 10 December. Lord William Howard, the dowager duchess, and the countess of Bridgewater were put in the Tower and on 22 December found guilty of misprision of treason for concealing Catherine's offenses, but all were later pardoned. Catherine went to the Tower on 10 February, and Parliament passed a bill of attainder condemning her and Rochford of treason on the 11th. On 13 February Catherine and Rochford were beheaded.

Bibliography: Lacey Baldwin Smith, *A Tudor Tragedy: The Life and Times of Catherine Howard*, 1961.

William B. Robison

Howard, Thomas, Earl of Surrey and 2nd Duke of Norfolk (1443-1524). This prominent noble and military man was born in 1443, the only son of an East Anglian, Sir John Howard, and his wife, Catherine Moleyns. Educated at Thetford grammar school, he became Edward IV's henchman in 1466, supported him against the earl of Warwick, became esquire of the body in 1471, fought the French in 1475, and was knighted on 18 January 1478. In 1472 he married Elizabeth Tylney (widow of Humphrey Bourchier, Lord Berners), who bore him THOMAS, the future 3rd duke of Norfolk; Lord Edmund; and Elizabeth, mother of ANNE BOLEYN. After his first wife's death in 1497, he wedded her cousin, Agnes Tylney, and fathered Lord William of Effingham and five others.

The Howards supported Richard III in 1483, and on 30 June he made John the first Howard, duke of Norfolk, and Thomas, the earl of Surrey. Thomas carried the sword of state at Richard's coronation, was steward of his Household, a councillor, and a knight of the Garter, besieged Bodiam Castle during the rebellion of October 1483, and became steward of the duchy of Lancaster's Norfolk lands in 1484. But after BOSWORTH FIELD, where his father died, he was imprisoned in the Tower by HENRY VII and attainted.

Pardoned in March 1486, Thomas remained in the Tower until January 1489, when Henry restored his title. But not until 1501 did he recover the bulk of the Howard lands. After suppressing the YORKSHIRE REBELLION in May 1489, he became lieutenant of the north and deputy warden of the marches for Prince Arthur and defended the border against PERKIN WARBECK and JAMES IV in 1496-1497. Made treasurer of the EXCHEQUER and a privy councillor in 1501, he helped negotiate Prince Arthur's marriage to CATHERINE OF ARAGON that year, Princess Margaret's to James IV of Scotland in 1502, and Princess Mary's to Charles, duke of Burgundy, in 1508—Henry's death prevented the last. He was also an executor of the king's will.

Surrey was earl marshal at HENRY VIII's coronation in 1509. He helped with the Anglo-French treaty of 1510, then the Anglo-Spanish treaty of 1511, which led to war with France. In 1512 he strengthened England's northern defenses and in 1513 remained in England with the queen while Henry led an army to France. While the king won the Battle of the Spurs, Surrey outdid him and defeated the Scots on 9 September at FLODDEN FIELD, where James IV died. Lionized by the poet, John Skelton, he became duke of Norfolk on 1 February, 1514, and his son, Thomas, became earl of Surrey. In 1514 he assisted in arranging a marriage between Princess Mary and Louis XII of France and the next year was involved in negotiating peace with the new French king, Francis I. Surpassed by THOMAS WOLSEY, Norfolk learned to cooperate and remained active. He witnessed the creation of the Holy League in 1517, helped suppress the EVIL MAY DAY riots, saw Wolsey adopt his pro-French policy with the TREATY OF LONDON in 1518, was at the FIELD OF CLOTH OF GOLD in 1520, and sadly served as high steward at the duke of BUCKINGHAM's treason trial in 1521. Resigning as treasurer in December 1522, he last appeared in public at the 1523 Parliament. He died at Framlingham Castle in Suffolk on 21 May 1524 and was buried on 22 June at Thetford Priory.

Bibliography: Melvin J. Tucker, *The Life of Thomas Howard, Earl of Surrey and Second Duke of Norfolk, 1443-1524*, 1964.

                                                                William B. Robison

Howard, Thomas, 3rd Duke of Norfolk (1473-1554). Prominent noble, statesman, and military man born in 1473 to THOMAS HOWARD, 2nd duke of Norfolk, and his wife, Elizabeth Tilney. The Howard family enjoyed a close alliance with Richard III and cultivated one with HENRY VII; the result was the marriage in 1495 of Thomas to Lady Anne Plantagenet, a daughter of Edward IV. By 1498 the younger Howard had accompanied his father on military expeditions to the north and initiated a long career as one of the Crown's most trusted and relied upon commanders. In 1513 he again served under his father in battle; he fought as a captain in the vanguard at FLODDEN FIELD. Each was rewarded for his successes in the field; in February 1514 the son was created earl of Surrey while HENRY VIII elevated his father to the rank of duke. Henry VIII employed Surrey in several military campaigns in the early 1520s. Sent to IRELAND in 1520 as the king's lieutenant and charged with keeping order there, but lacking sufficient troops and financial resources to pacify the Irish, the earl accomplished little and was recalled in 1522. The king then ordered Surrey to France, where he carried out a few skirmishes with the French. His efforts failed to defeat the enemy, and in December 1522 Henry called Surrey and his forces back to England. Upon his return Surrey succeeded his father to the position of high treasurer, marking his first significant foray into national politics and officehold-ing. Still, his main value to the Crown at this time was in military service—in 1523, as warden-general of the Scottish marches, he successfully repelled the Duke of Albany from the border region.

Surrey succeeded his father to the dukedom of Norfolk on 21 May 1524 at his father's death. Although he may have supported Cardinal THOMAS WOLSEY's controversial financial policy, the AMICABLE GRANT, there is no doubt over his role in successfully suppressing the rebellions and resistance in East Anglia provoked by the financial scheme. Afterward, Norfolk and several other noblemen actively reentered court and concilliar politics and aimed mainly to undermine the cardinal's policy of rapprochement with France. Norfolk's role in the subsequent fall of Wolsey is debatable; what is apparent is that in 1529, following the cardinal's departure from London, Norfolk and other sympathetically minded peers joined forces to control the council. A religious Conservative who rejected radical Protestantism, Norfolk nevertheless acquiesced to Henry's DIVORCE. As ANNE BOLEYN's uncle, coupled with his deserved loyalty to the king, Norfolk adroitly accepted the situation. Though he administered his offices competently, Norfolk was no great statesman; as a result Henry relied upon him for military skills foremost.

Thus, during the PILGRIMAGE OF GRACE in 1536 and 1537 the duke lead the Crown forces that suppressed the rebellion in the early months of 1537. High in the king's graces on his return from the battlefield, Norfolk reentered high politics and headed the Conservative faction opposed to THOMAS CROMWELL. By late 1539 or early 1540 this group dominated the PRIVY COUNCIL, exemplified by the passage of the religiously Conservative ACT OF SIX ARTICLES (1539). After a diplomatic trip to France in February 1540, during which time he set the agenda for Cromwell's demise, Norfolk benefited from Henry VIII's marrying his niece, CATHERINE HOWARD, in August 1540. For some eighteen months afterwards Norfolk dominated the council and had the inside track to the king. His ascendency, however, was short-lived: in November 1541 Catherine was accused of adultery and subsequently found guilty, and she brought down her uncle with her. Norfolk and the Conservative faction in the council were ruined. The duke lost the king's unquestioned loyalty. Still, Henry employed Norfolk again in military actions; in 1542 the duke led an invasion of Scotland that achieved nothing, and in 1544 he accompanied his ruler to France in the great enterprise of that year.

Henry VIII's death and the succession of EDWARD VI marked the virtual end of Norfolk's career in national politics. Norfolk and other Conservatives sought unsuccessfully to control the protectorship of the minor king and prevent the side led by EDWARD SEYMOUR, earl of Hertford, from gaining ultimate rule. Furthermore, Norfolk suffered attainder, and he faced execution for his son's folly of illegally displaying the Howard family arms at that critical time—only the death of Henry VIII during the night before the duke's scheduled execution saved Norfolk's head. Somerset chose not to kill his enemy; instead, Norfolk was imprisoned in the Tower, and a power vacuum was left in East Anglia, his sphere of domination.

Norfolk remained a prisoner throughout Edward's reign. On Queen MARY's accession he was released and soon after had his attainder reversed. Mary swore him to her privy council, but the aged duke's political and administrative influence had been eclipsed. The queen, however, remembering his military exploits of past, appointed him to suppress WYATT'S REBELLION in January 1554. He failed, and instead the rebellion was stopped in London by loyal troops not under the command of the duke. Some 81 years of age now, Norfolk retired to his Kenninghall estate, where he died on 24 August 1554.

Bibliography: D. Mathew, *The Courtiers of Henry VIII*, 1970; John Martin Robinson, *The Dukes of Norfolk: A Quincentennial History*, 1982.

Eugene Bourgeois III

Humanism. In the context of early modern history, humanism denotes an educational system founded on the moral and intellectual value of studying the literature of classical antiquity. Its distinguishing features were the pursuit of an authentically classical style on written Latin; the search for lost classical Greek and Latin texts; and the introduction of the widespread study of Greek in the West for the first time in almost a millennium. The origins of the humanist movement lay in fourteenth-century Italy; and in the fifteenth century, migrant scholars spread humanist concerns throughout Europe. By the mid-sixteenth century, humanists had taken over the basic curriculum of European schools and the arts course in most UNIVERSITIES. The origins of English humanism are traditionally traced to the patronage of Humphrey, duke of Gloucester (1391-1447), who employed Italian humanists as his secretaries and amassed an impressive collection of classical and humanist manuscripts (many of which still survive in the library named after him at Oxford). From around 1450, English scholars began to visit Italy to study the humanities. Soon afterward, Italian humanists arrived in England to teach in the new style: Stefano Surigone and Cornelio Vitelli at Oxford; Lorenzo Traversagni and Caio Auberino at Cambridge; and Pietro Carmeliano at the court of Henry VII. Nevertheless, the first important English humanists, such as William Grocyn, Thomas Linacre, John Colet, and Cuthbert Tunstall, owed most of their progress in humanist scholarship (especially in Greek) to studies in Italy. The greatest scholar of this group was the one who spent longest in Italy, Thomas Linacre (c. 1460-1524). Traveling to Italy around 1458, he studied under Poliziano and Chalcondylas in the Medici household at Florence. Later, he worked at Venice for the humanist printer Aldo Manutio and also studied medicine at Padua. Returning to England, he practiced as a physician and devoted himself to the translation from Greek of Galen's medicinal treatises. Of this first generation of English humanists, only THOMAS MORE was entirely "home-grown," and even he owed his formation to men who had studied abroad.

Humanism was above all an educational program, making its earliest and deepest impressions in the schools and universities. It soon altered patterns of educational patronage and practice. From Duke Humphrey onward, patrons inclined more and more toward the humanist fashion in their foundations and benefactions—whether or not they themselves showed any proficiency in the humanities. The first landmark in the reception of humanism by grammar schools was the appointment around 1481 of John Anwykyll as the grammar master of Magdalen College School, Oxford. Shortly afterward, Anwykyll published his *Compendium Totius Gramaticae*, a handbook of Latin grammar, which was strongly influenced by such contemporary Italians as Lorenzo Valla and bore ample witness to Anwykyll's own humanist accomplishments. Under Anwykyll, Magdalen School became a seedbed of humanism, numbering THOMAS WOLSEY among its alumni. Another teacher there was John Stanbridge, author of a highly popular grammar book. Equal in importance to Magdalen was St. Paul's School, London, founded in 1510 by John Colet (c. 1467-1519), dean of St. Paul's Cathedral. Colet's statutes for the school prescribed the study of "good litterature both laten and greke," although they emphasized less the pagan classics than the Christian authors of late antiquity and contemporary humanists such as Erasmus. Colet's humanist aims also emerged in his appointment of William Lily (c. 1468-1522) as the first high master of St. Paul's. Lily, a friend of More and Grocyn, wrote a Latin grammar that became in 1542 the royally authorized standard textbook for use in English schools. Finally, Colet persuaded Erasmus to write for the school his *De duplici copia verborum ac rerum*, perhaps the most popular rhetorical handbook of the century. The influence of these schools, not only through their pupils but through their textbooks and their example to other founders, combined with the humanist inclinations of the king and other social leaders to insure that HENRY VIII's reign saw the triumph of humanism in English schools.

The progress of humanism at the universities was evident from about 1450. Oxford in particular showed increasing interest in humanist scholarship and tuition. William Grocyn (c. 1446-1519) acquired not only a sound grasp of classical Latin but also the rudiments of Greek while at Oxford in the 1460s and 1470s. Cambridge lagged behind, but not far. In the 1480s, the arts curriculum was reformed to lay more emphasis on the humanities, although Greek was probably not available until 1511, when Erasmus was persuaded to come and teach it. At both universities, the later fifteenth century saw a proliferation of classical and humanist texts in both manuscript and print. Especially noteworthy was the gradual replacement of medieval translations of Aristotle by new humanist versions, which culminated in the early sixteenth century in the widespread adoption of the editions produced by the French humanist, Lefevre d'Etaples. The new colleges founded around this time provide further evidence for the reception of humanism. The statutes produced by RICHARD FOX, bishop of Winchester, for Corpus Christi College, Oxford (founded 1516), expressly preferred humanism to scholasticism and prescribed the study of classical literature for the arts course and of Scripture and the early fathers for theology. Fox's example influenced Cardinal College, Oxford (1524). At Cambridge, these foundations were matched by that of St. John's College (1511), where JOHN FISHER's statutes (1516) recommended the study of not only Greek but also Hebrew. This period also saw the establishment of the first public lectureships at the universities. Fisher persuaded Henry VIII to finance lectures in Greek and Hebrew at Cambridge, and similar projects were set in motion at Oxford. These ad hoc developments were put on a formal footing in 1542 with the endowment at both universities of the Regius Professorship in Greek and Hebrew.

The age of Henry VIII was without doubt the age of Erasmus. Erasmus of Rotterdam (c. 1467-1536) was the leading scholar of the time and not only produced in flawless Latin original works of grammar, rhetoric, satire, moral philosophy, and devotion but restored and edited classical, scriptural, and patristic texts in both Latin and Greek. During several visits to England he made friends with many prominent scholars and patrons, including Henry, WILLIAM WARHAM, More, Colet, and Fisher. Erasmus helped shape the studies and patronage of his friends, although he would hardly have enjoyed their esteem had not English tastes already become attuned to the modish scholarship he represented. But though he spent some time at Oxford in 1499 and later taught at Cambridge (1511-1514), his influence on most English students was through his books—he was by far the best-selling author of the period.

With the full integration of humanist principles into English schools and universities, England soon produced a generation of native humanists comparable, at least on technical grounds, to the best any country could offer. Chief among these was Roger Ascham (1515-1568), of St. John's, Cambridge, whose book *The Scholemaster* (London, 1570) encapsulated the values of English humanist education. St. John's also produced Sir John Cheke, who convulsed Cambridge in the 1540s with his novel views on the pronunciation of Greek; and John Seton, whose *Dialectica* (London, 1545), modeled on the humanist dialectics of Rudolf Agricola (once Erasmus's teacher), became the standard English handbook on logic. From this time, the tradition of humanist scholarship at the universities remained secure, and the names of the humanists they sent forth become too numerous to mention. However, the most productive humanist of this generation received no formal instruction after the age of twelve. Sir Thomas Elyot (c. 1490-1546) largely taught himself from the study of classical and contemporary authors. He is notable as the first English humanist to make major use of the vernacular for serious writing (though Thomas More had used the vernacular, his greatest work, *Utopia*, was of course written in Latin). Elyot's best-known work, *The Boke of the Governour* (London, 1531), was a typically Erasmian treatise on education and politics with which he hoped to attain the very un-Erasmian objective of political advancement.

Many claims have been made about the wider significance of humanism for English (and, indeed, European) society and have attached it under such titles as "civic" or "Christian" humanism to republicanism, Protestantism, or programs of social and ecclesiastical reform. Recent research has become skeptical of such claims. With the stripping away of modern philosophical connotations from the sixteenth-century concept of humanist studies, it has become plain that there was no simple affiliation between humanist scholarship and any particular political philosophy or religious denomination. The classical heritage was diverse enough to permit humanists to support whichever political system prevailed locally, though it was also capable of permitting the circle of humanists associated with Eramus to elaborate a telling critique of their contemporary society. In the religious sphere, "Christian humanism" has been awarded the paternity of Protestant, Catholic, and Anglican brands of ecclesiastical reform, while it has also been argued that it was in fact destroyed by denominational antagonisms. Perceptions of the relationship of humanism to the English REFORMATION in particular have varied widely. Some have seen humanism as a high road to Reformation. Others have supposed that the Reformation arrested the progress of English humanism with the execution of More. Each view is a caricature. The cases of More and Erasmus, which can be matched by a host of lesser humanist lights, are enough to demonstrate that humanism did not necessarily lead to Protestantism. And the employment of humanists in the church and state of post-Reformation England, not to mention the continued humanist dominance of education, is adequate rebuttal of the contrary thesis. These extravagant theories can be explained by the readiness of humanists then, and historians now, to overestimate the importance of the humanist in society. Inspired by the importance of a rhetorical education in the politics of the classical world, humanists hoped that their education would secure them political advancement. But early modern governments looked to humanists mainly for education and propaganda. Thus, Linacre was hired to teach Prince Arthur and Princess Mary; Richard Croke to teach HENRY FITZROY; Cheke and Ascham to teach ELIZABETH and EDWARD. Such men as Cuthbert Tunstall, Richard Pace, and Richard Morison were recruited by the government to draft letters, make speeches, or produce pamphlets. If such men went on to higher things, as some did, it was because of their administrative or diplomatic talents, not their facility in iambics or panegyrics. As for the various ideals that humanists might have imbibed from their studies, these, as More recognized in *Utopia*, were only too likely to be sacrificed on the altar of dynastic *realpolitik*. In conclusion, it must be emphasized once more that humanism, though enormously influential, was essentially an educational and literary fashion.

Bibliography: A. Fox and J. Guy, *Reassessing the Henrician Age*, 1986; J. K. McConica, *English Humanists and Reformation Politics Under Henry VIII and Edward VI*, 1965; R. Weiss, *Humanism in Fifteenth-Century England*, 3rd ed., 1965.

Richard Rex

Hunne's Case (1514-1515). Richard Hunne was a merchant tailor and freeman of London with a good personal reputation. In March 1511 his infant son died in the parish of St. Mary Malfellow, Whitechapel, and the rector, Thomas Dryffeld (Dryfield), demanded the dead baby's bearing-sheet as a mortuary, or burial fee. Hunne refused on the grounds that the sheet belonged to him and not to the baby. During April 1512 the rector instituted proceedings against Hunne at Lambeth, and there on 13 May 1512 Cuthbert Tunstall, the chancellor of Archbishop WILLIAM WARHAM, later to serve as bishop of London and then bishop of Durham, decided the case against Hunne. Further trouble arose when Hunne brought a charge of slander against Henry Marshall, the rector's assistant, on the grounds that he had refused to conduct Evensong in Hunne's presence. Hunne felt that this action damaged his reputation with his business associates. The slander suit remained unresolved when Hunne began a suit in King's Bench charging Dryfeld and others with violation of the PRAEMUNIRE statutes. His claim was that the CHURCH COURTS, since they were under the pope's jurisdiction, formed a foreign tribunal. Hunne was playing temporal law against spiritual law. But the king's courts decided against Hunne and returned his case to ecclesiastical jurisdiction.

At this point the bishop of London, Richard Fitzjames, a great defender of clerical rights, entered the conflict and had Hunne arrested. The merchant's house was searched, some heretical books, including a Wycliff Bible, were found, and he was imprisoned in the Lollard's Tower (so named on the supposition that LOLLARDS were imprisoned in it) in the southwest corner of old St. Paul's Cathedral. Hunne was accused of heresy. On Saturday 2 December 1514 he was taken to Fulham Palace for examination by Fitzjames. He was returned to prison and on 4 December 1514 was found hanging by a "girdle of silk" from a beam in his cell. A coroner's jury examined the body and dismissed the theory of suicide, since the body and the cell showed signs that Hunne had been strangled before his neck had been broken. The jury then charged Fitzjames's chancellor, Dr. William Horsey, and two of his associates, the summoner Charles Joseph and the bell ringer John Spalding, with willful murder. These three were imprisoned, and there Joseph confessed that he and the others had strangled Hunne.

At that point, Fitzjames appealed to the king's chancellor, Cardinal THOMAS WOLSEY, and begged him to ask the king to have the matter referred to an impartial committee of his council. The king granted the request, and proceedings for perjury were taken against the jury.

Since Hunne had been charged with heresy, Bishop Fitzjames decided to proceed against his dead body with the accusations. A new list of heresies was drawn up based on the Bible found in his home, which had an objectionable prologue and passages marked in Hunne's hand. On Sunday 16 December 1515 the three bishops of London, Durham, and Lincoln along with twenty-five other divines heard the case. Fitzjames found Hunne to be a heretic and had his body handed over to the secular officials for burning. The burning took place at Smithfield on 20 December 1515. Later Parliament took up the case, but Wolsey had it dissolved, and in the remaining fourteen years of his ministry only one more Parliament was called.

The Hunne case is very difficult to solve because of conflicting accounts. The three major primary accounts are by Edward Hall, THOMAS MORE, and JOHN FOXE. Edward Hall, the most important contemporary chronicler of the reign of HENRY VIII, supplies the greatest amount of information. His chronicle is an orderly and, for the most part, accurate record of events. The problem is that he hated the church courts and Thomas Wolsey and held ecclesiastical authority in contempt. Thomas More discussed the Hunne case in his treatise called *A Dialogue*, in which he agreed that Hunne committed suicide. Foxe, in his *Acts and Monuments*, written nearly fifty years after the event, argued against More that Hunne was murdered. Although Hunne's case will never be completely resolved, it does show that there was a strong anti-clerical feeling among the citizens of London.

Bibliography: A. G. Dickens, *The English Reformation*, 1989; Arthur Ogle, *The Tragedy of Lollard's Tower*, 1949.

Don S. Armentrout

I

Intercursus Magnus (1496). Treaty concluded between England and the emperor Maximilian on 24 February 1496. The support given by Maximilian and the dowager duchess of Burgundy to the Yorkist impostor, PERKIN WARBECK, had moved HENRY VII to transfer the cloth staple of the MERCHANT ADVEN-TURERS Company to the English town of CALAIS in 1493. The economic consequences of this embargo for the cloth-finishing industry of the Low Countries and the concomitant need to obtain the support of England for negotiations with France induced the emperor (acting on behalf of his son, the archduke Philip) to negotiate what Francis Bacon called (after Flemish usage) the Intercursus Magnus. Under the terms of the treaty each prince pledged that he would deny succor to the enemies of the other and would expel rebels within fifteen days. Each would assist the other in time of war, though the party making a request for such assistance would bear the expenses incurred by the assisting power. Letters of marque and reprisal were not to be issued by either ruler. English merchants and ships would enjoy free access to the markets and towns of the Low Countries (with the exception of Flanders) while Netherlanders were to enjoy similar privileges in Henry's dominions. The treaty declared that tolls and exactions were not to exceed in value those collected during the last fifty years, promised speedy justice in the archduke's courts, and enjoined merchants to frequent only those marts where customs officials remained available to collect such duties. Provisions also addressed inspection of cargoes, punishments for smuggling and fraudulent dealing, restitution for stolen goods, and the carrying of contraband.

Soon after the ratification of the treaty Philip imposed a new import duty on woolen cloth, the Andreasgulden. Henry once more assigned the cloth staple to Calais to punish this breach of the lately concluded intercourse. Negotiations with the archduke removed the tax in an agreement reached in July 1497, but the Merchant Adventurers, hopeful of obtaining better terms from the towns of the

Low Countries by playing one against the other, refused to limit their traffic to Antwerp and Bergen-op-Zoom, as the new agreement required. The company thus remained at Calais until the fall of 1498. In May 1499 a new agreement confirmed the Intercursus Magnus, withdrew the new duty on English cloth, and lowered the duty charged to the merchants of Netherlands on English wool sold at Calais. Philip also abandoned his attempt to confine the Merchant Adventurers to Antwerp and Bergen-op-Zoom. The Adventurers thus remained free to sell their cloth wholesale in any part of Philip's dominions save for Flanders. Further dissatisfaction regarding imposts led to yet another threat by the Merchant Adventurers to forsake Antwerp for Calais and moved the regent Margaret of Savoy to renew the intercourse in 1502. The Intercursus Magnus remained in effect until new disputes concerning duties led to the conclusion of the so-called INTERCURSUS MALUS in April 1506.

Bibliography: R. B. Wernham, *Before the Armada: The Emergence of the English Nation, 1485-1588*, 1966.

Douglas Bisson

Intercursus Malus (1506). Treaty concluded between Archduke Philip of Burgundy and Henry VII on 30 April 1506. Fresh disputes concerning the duties owed by English merchants in the Low Countries and the desire to obtain the surrender of the Yorkist pretender, Edmund de la Pole, earl of Suffolk, led HENRY VII to transfer the cloth mart from Antwerp to CALAIS in January 1505. The death of Isabella of Castile and Philip's unintended visit to England in January 1506 on his way to claim his wife's Castilian inheritance (the ship was forced into Weymouth during a storm) gave Henry VII unexpected leverage. After enjoying Henry's hospitality for three months, the archduke deputed commissioners to work out the details of a new commercial agreement, one that would modify the INTERCURSUS MAGNUS of 1496. Four days after his departure from England the Intercursus Malus was concluded, so called because it markedly favored English mercantile interests. The new intercourse contained sweeping concessions for members of the MERCHANT ADVENTURERS Company trading in the Low Countries. They now obtained exemption from virtually all duties customarily levied in the Low Countries and also secured the right to sell their cloth wholesale anywhere in Philip's dominions and retail anywhere except in the embattled cloth-finishing province of Flanders. The agreement formally acknowledged the right of English merchants to pay but a single toll when navigating the Scheldt, one of the chief points of contention during the removal of the cloth mart to Calais in 1493. Within a short time, however, the legality of the document became a moot point. While Henry VII ratified the treaty on 15 May, Philip neglected to do so before his death at Bruges on 25 September 1506. The regent for the six-year-old Burgundian heir, the archduke Charles (later Charles I of Spain and Charles V of the Holy Roman Empire), was Philip's sister,

Margaret, dowager duchess of Savoy. Margaret steadfastly refused to ratify the Intercursus Malus; Henry therefore arranged a confirmation of the treaty of 1496 on 5 June 1507. The king showed his good faith by ordering his merchants to forego Calais and return to Antwerp for the Easter mart of 1508. In 1515 Charles attained his majority and began negotiations for improving the standing of his subjects trading in England. He repudiated both the treaty of 1496 and the Intercursus Malus, and argued that both were void because the parties who had contracted them were deceased. The threat of once more moving the cloth staple to Calais persuaded Charles that the time was not ripe for a substantial change in the terms of the "intercourse and amity." In 1520 a treaty was concluded at London that did not address the legality of the Malus but that conceded the single-toll principle to English merchants carrying goods to Antwerp. All legal proceedings emanating from past toll disputes were now abrogated, while subjects of each nation would enjoy liberty of commerce and pay the duties established by the treaty of 1496.

Bibliography: R. B. Wernham, *Before the Armada: The Emergence of the English Nation, 1485-1588*, 1966.

Douglas Bisson

Ireland. At the beginning of the Tudor period, the island of Ireland was divided politically into a confusing mixture of lordships: Anglo-Norman, Gaelic, and a hybrid mixture of both. The relationship of the English Crown with these lordships was complex. Almost all had at some time nominally recognized the king of England as overlord of Ireland, but the fragmentation of political power meant that it was always difficult to turn nominal domination into effective, continuous control. The Tudor Crown's direct influence was confined to the medieval lordship of Ireland, which represented what was left of the Anglo-Norman colony of the early Middle Ages. The main center of the lordship was the area known as the Pale, which consisted of parts of Counties Dublin, Meath, Kildare, Westmeath, and Louth. Here, the authority of the king of England as lord of Ireland was recognized, and English law was observed. In the territories of the Anglo-Norman magnates of Desmond, Kildare, and Ormond the overlord-ship of the king was also acknowledged, but by the later Middle Ages all three earldoms functioned almost autonomously of the government in Dublin. A hybrid mixture of Gaelic and English law operated in the earldoms. The coastal towns in the south and west would also have considered themselves loyal to the king, but most also guarded their medieval royal charters carefully and endeavored to administer their affairs as independently from outside authority as possible. The marcher lordships on the borders of the Pale were controlled by families of Anglo-Norman descent who had over the centuries adopted many Irish customs and legal practices and virtually ignored the jurisdiction of the Dublin govern-ment. The rest of the island was divided into Gaelic lordships where Gaelic customary law was followed. Relations and gradations of power among the lordships in Gaelic Ireland fluctuated and depended on the respective military strength and following of individual lords. Through a system of clientage and tribute the more powerful lords such as the O'Neills in Ulster, the Burkes in Connacht, or the MacCarthys in Munster built up a large military following that enabled them to demand tribute and submission from smaller lordships. It was, however, a highly volatile form of domination that could quickly diminish on the death of a lord. His successor might not be in a position to command the same respect and hence the same military strength. While nominal recognition of the English king's authority was conceded from time to time, Gaelic lords like those of the march usually ignored the authority of the Dublin government.

In the absence of a centralized power base, control of the island involved achieving a balance among the lordships either by keeping the most powerful divided against one another or by establishing as wide a network of alliances as possible. Both strategies were more easily achieved by a governor born in Ireland than a governor appointed from England.

Within the lordship of Ireland, the head of the government was the king of England, who was represented by a lord lieutenant or lord deputy. By the beginning of the Tudor period, the office of chief governor in Ireland was monopolized by the earls of Kildare. From their base in Kildare they were ideally suited to control the Pale and ward off any competitors for the position. Gerald Fitzgerald, 8th earl of Kildare (c. 1456-1513), developed a network of alliances within Anglo-Norman and Gaelic Ireland that gave him authority and influence in most parts of the country. His position in Dublin was virtually unassailable. The main rivals of the Kildares, the Butlers (earls of Ormond), never achieved the same authority. A striking demonstration of Kildare dominance occurred at the battle of Knockdoe in the west of Ireland in 1504. In a military campaign designed to curb the growing strength of the Burkes of Clanricard, Kildare mobilized a large force that included representatives from Anglo-Irish families as well as members of almost all the leading Gaelic families in Ulster and many from the west of Ireland also.

The early Tudor administration had a rather mixed attitude to Kildare power in Ireland. While it suited the monarch financially to leave Kildare in control, the very strength of the Kildare monopoly presented its own problems. Twice in the 1490s the earl of Kildare tried to take on the role of kingmaker in opposition to the Tudors. The response of HENRY VII was to transfer control of the Dublin government to others, either to loyal English officials such as Sir Edward Poynings (lord deputy 1494-1495) or to what were considered the more loyal Butlers. HENRY VIII continued this rather vacillating attitude to the Kildares when he appointed THOMAS HOWARD, earl of Surrey and later 3rd duke of Norfolk, chief governor in 1520. Surrey recommended a rapid military conquest of the whole island as the most effective method of establishing centralized control for the Crown. Surrey's suggestion was attractively simple, but it raised what proved to be a continuing dilemma for the Tudors in Ireland. Henry VIII, like his successors, wanted a peaceful and cooperative country, but he was reluctant to finance a major military undertaking. As a result, the simple solution was rejected in favor of cheaper and more complex ones.

The method devised by Henry's secretary of state THOMAS CROMWELL was to treat the Irish lordship in the same way as he had dealt with other outlying regions of the king's dominions in the north of England and Wales. The excessive powers of local magnates were to be curbed and the regions brought more directly under the jurisdiction of the central authority in London. In Ireland this meant above all that the overriding authority of Kildare had to be reduced. In the early 1530s Cromwell supervised the introduction of reforms into the Irish administration. The Kildares responded by trying to prove that Ireland was ungovernable without their help. But their symbolic display of protest was interpreted as rebellion largely because they tried to enlist papal and Spanish support, a serious act of treason given Henry's precarious international position in the 1530s.

The KILDARE REBELLION in 1533 created two long-term problems for the Tudor administration. First, it left a political vacuum in Ireland. Kildare's disloyalty suggested that Irish-born magnates could no longer be trusted. Although at times tempted to restore an Anglo-Irish magnate to head the Dublin government, the Tudors never again appointed an Irish-born governor. The implication of this change was that the London treasury was obliged to finance an armed retinue to protect the lord deputy. Kildare had had his own private army. The second legacy of the rebellion was that the Kildare lordship had acted as a buffer zone between the Pale and the Gaelic lords of the midlands. When the lordship was abolished, the Gaelic lords began to raid the Pale, and the Dublin government was faced with a serious military problem. The solution was to establish two large military forts at Laois and Offaly, which were later to form the basis of the first plantation in sixteenth-century Ireland. But despite this attempted solution the need to defend the Pale remained a continual theme of Tudor rule in Ireland.

After the Kildare rebellion, the Tudors were, therefore, reluctantly obliged to spend more money in Ireland and to take a more direct interest in governing the country. Much of Tudor policy in Ireland after 1534 can be interpreted as finding an acceptable method of ruling Ireland without the earls of Kildare. The Tudors' Irish problem was compounded by the international situation as Catholic powers recognized the nuisance value Ireland represented and by the migration of thousands of Scottish settlers to northeast Ulster, another potential threat from an alien power.

In the 1540s, Lord Deputy Sir Anthony St. Leger pursued a policy that seemed both cheap and effective. This was the policy known to historians as surrender and regrant. It involved negotiating agreements with the principal Irish lords in which they agreed to recognize the authority of the monarch in return for the king's agreeing to cancel any feudal claims that the Tudor dynasty had to the lords' territories. The Irish lords also agreed to abandon Gaelic lordly titles and obey English law. The agreements formed part of a wider policy that aimed in the long term at the integration of Gaelic Ireland with the area of the old medieval lordship. Henry VIII's assumption of the title of king of Ireland in 1541 has been interpreted as part of the same process. It was a declaration of the king's commitment to govern the whole island and not just the medieval lordship.

Gaelic reaction to St. Leger's policy was mixed. In some lordships the agreements were adhered to, and eventually a process of anglicization was initiated. In most, however, the agreement with the Crown added another potential source of contention to the internecine feuds that often took place on the death of a chief. St. Leger's policy had particularly disastrous effects within the O'Neill lordship of Tyrone and was responsible for much of the unrest in Ulster in the sixteenth century.

Another problem with the policy of surrender and regrant was that the agreements required time to be effective. Several generations needed to observe them before they could be proven to have succeeded. But the continuing Gaelic raids on the Pale and the resistance of the O'Neills, backed up by increasing numbers of Scottish mercenary soldiers, meant that immediate military matters were given a greater priority than was long-term reform. In the reigns of EDWARD VI and MARY the main focus of the government was on defense, and little serious attention was given to the more general aim of assimilating Gaelic Ireland with the old lordship.

By mid-century, therefore, the Tudor administration was committed to spending large sums of money on military campaigns in Ireland but had achieved little in terms of pacifying the country or establishing effective centralized government.

The one positive achievement was perhaps that the position of chief governor had by the 1550s become an attractive prize for young Elizabethan courtiers eager to enhance their reputation in the eyes of Queen Elizabeth with a quick, gloriously successful campaign in Ireland. Both Thomas Radcliff, earl of Sussex (lord deputy, 1556-1564), and Sir Henry Sidney (lord deputy, 1565-1571; 1575-1578), planned to solve the queen's Irish problem quickly and cheaply. Their proposals for reform had much in common. They included the initial pacifying of Ulster, the introduction of a presidential system of government to govern the provinces, and the encouragement of small, private plantation schemes. The plans had much to recommend them. Modeled on the council of WALES and the COUNCIL OF THE NORTH, the provincial presidencies seemed an ideal solution to the decentralized nature of political power in Ireland. They would also help to undermine the overriding authority of some of the larger lords such as the earl of Desmond in the south and the earl of Clancricard (the Burke family) in the west. Scattered colonies of English settlers would introduce loyal communities to remote areas and, if properly armed, would serve as outlying garrisons for the Crown. But although admirable on paper, the plan proved difficult to implement.

It was not until 1569 that the first president of Connacht was appointed. Following some initial resistance, the earl of Clanricard cooperated with the presidential system. By 1585 agreements had been made with all the Connacht chiefs. Known formally as the composition book of Connacht, the agreements were similar to the surrender and regrant arrangements of the 1540s, but they also included an undertaking by the western lords to pay an annual land tax to subsidize the local administration and army. The composition agreements were welcomed by the Irish lords, but in the long term they caused more problems than they solved. The financial burden of paying an annual tax that local officials were authorized to seize by force if it was not paid voluntarily alienated the lords and contributed to their support for the northern chiefs in the 1590s. The peaceful arrangements of the composition book ran counter to the harsh military policy pursued by Sir Richard Bingham, 3rd president of Connacht after the SPANISH ARMADA of 1588.

In Munster, Sir John Perrot was appointed president in 1570. Gerald, 14th earl of Desmond (c. 1533-1583), had a very ambiguous relationship with the new presidential government. Initially the earl (who was returned to Munster in 1573 after six years in London) and the local government officials appeared anxious to cooperate with one another, but gradually the bad behavior of the Crown's representatives alienated many of Desmond's followers. The earl was forced into supporting the FITZMAURICE REBELLION of 1579 in order to retain his position in Munster.

Apart from the establishment of provincial presidencies, the Sussex-Sidney plan also envisaged the establishment of small plantations of English settlers in Ireland. Of the formal plantation schemes undertaken in Tudor Ireland, the plantation of Munster was the most successful. Based on the forfeited lands of the earl of Desmond, it attracted about 4,000 English settlers by 1598.

Plantation had a double role in Tudor Ireland. It provided a cheap means of securing a vulnerable region, but it was also viewed as a civilizing process. Settlers were instructed not to intermarry with the Irish or adopt Irish customs or language. Provision was also made for the building of churches and the appointment of ministers to preach the Reformed religion. In the sixteenth century, however, the success of the Reformation in any part of Ireland was very limited. Government priorities dictated that religious reform took second place to political matters. Clergy appointed by Rome were pragmatically also accepted into the established church. Thus many clergy were not forced to make a choice between the two churches. In the 1590s, however, the Counter-Reformation began to make an impact as Irish clergy educated on the Continent returned to the southern port towns and encouraged a more active resistance to the Reformed church. It was in the 1590s, therefore, that the Reformation could be said to have failed in Ireland.

By 1585, the Tudors had made some progress in bringing outlying parts of Ireland under central control. Only Ulster still had no substantial English presence. In 1585 Sir John Perrot (lord deputy 1584-1588) launched a reform program for the northern province. It failed but his successor, Sir William Fitzwilliam (lord deputy 1588-1594), continued to concentrate government resources on Ulster. Fitzwilliam's attempts to advance English jurisdiction into the north provoked hostility and eventually the TYRONE REBELLION.

The long war that followed won support in the four provinces of Ireland, but it was not a national resistance movement. The Catholic Anglo-Irish community (later known as the Old English) never supported the rebels. The Old English had many grievances against the government. They were alienated by the excessive financial demands of the administration to subsidize the army in Ireland. They resented their replacement in key positions in the Dublin administration by new English officials. And while they accepted the religious reforms of Henry VIII, they rejected the ELIZABETHAN SETTLEMENT OF RELIGION. But despite their hostility to the government, the Old English never identified with the resistance of the Gaelic lords and preferred to express their dissatisfaction indirectly through contacts at court or in the Irish Parliament.

The Irish Parliament was a very insignificant institution by comparison with its English counterpart. Its weakness was partly due to what became known as Poynings' Law. Initially passed in 1494 to curb the influence of the earl of Kildare, the law forbade the enactment of legislation in the Irish Parliament without prior approval from London. The law had an erratic history after 1495. Its suspension could cause as much alarm as its operation because it was viewed as giving too much power to the new English elite in Dublin. Despite the ineffectiveness of the Irish Parliament, the Old English who dominated it (representation being based on the old medieval lordship) used it as a forum to express their opposition to government policy, particularly in the last two Tudor Parliaments in 1569-1571 and 1585-1586. But, while irritating in the sixteenth century, Old English opposition in Parliament did not become a serious source of concern for the government until the seventeenth century.

The defeat of the Gaelic lords at Kinsale in 1602 was a triumph for Tudor rule in Ireland. But military victory did not solve many of the problems that Ireland had presented at the beginning of the Tudor period. Crown authority was still nominal in many parts of the country, and local loyalties were still powerful. It was not until the seventeenth century that centralized government was effectively introduced.

Bibliography: Nicholas Canny, *From Reformation to Restoration: Ireland 1534-1660*, 1987; Steven G. Ellis, *Tudor Ireland 1470-1603*, 1985.

Mary O'Dowd

Islands Voyage (1597). This abortive expedition to Ferrol, Spain, and the Azores was the conception of Sir Walter Raleigh and Robert Devereux, earl of Essex, and was intended as a decisive blow in the war against Spain that had begun with the SPANISH ARMADA of 1588.

Disgraced in 1591, Raleigh had regained a good measure of his standing with the queen due to his participation in the successful invasion and garrisoning of

CADIZ, Spain, in 1596. Philip II, stung by this loss, launched another armada, only to see it dispersed by the English, with the remnants of the fleet taking refuge in Ferrol. Raleigh and Essex saw the Islands Voyage as an opportunity to destroy what remained of the fleet and further wished to commandeer a Spanish treasure fleet in route to Spain from the West Indies through the Azores.

Under the importunings of ROBERT CECIL, Essex, and Raleigh, the queen, reluctant to deplete her already battered resources, agreed to let the voyage take place. Departing in July, both admirals were stalled by storms and were unable to connect with Lord Thomas Howard, who awaited them off Ferrol. Howard, unable to attack Ferrol on his own, returned to Plymouth to join Essex and Raleigh, who petitioned the queen to permit them to capture the treasure fleet at Havana. Elizabeth, wary of the damaged but still potent Spanish fleet at Ferrol, had no intention of letting two of her most experienced admirals play fast and loose with Spanish spoils while the English coast lay vulnerable to attack. She instructed the pair to attack the fleet at Ferrol with fire ships but insisted that someone other than Essex—presumably Raleigh—be in command of this attempt. Essex, disheartened, dismissed the bulk of his land forces and sailed with Ralegh for Ferrol.

Damage to Raleigh's and Essex's ships off Coruna led to confusion in the fleet, as Raleigh misinterpreted orders from Essex and proceeded to Lisbon, instead of Finisterre. Upon arrival at Finisterre, Essex was persuaded that Raleigh's action was that of a traitor or coward and used his absence to go on to the Azores to await the treasure fleet and perhaps draw out the Spanish fleet from Ferrol. While awaiting Essex, Raleigh took Fayal, Spain, in a spectacular coup; an unsuccessful Essex joined him there, threatening to expose Raleigh as a traitor who had deliberately disobeyed orders. Howard mediated the quarrel, and the two admirals then returned to the Azores in search of the treasure fleet. Through a combination of errors, they were unable to take this prize and returned to England in October, their fleet in disarray.

Raleigh's success at Fayal restored his preeminence at court and eclipsed, to a certain extent, the pretensions of Essex, the queen's favorite during Raleigh's years of exile. The Islands Voyage, despite its failure, resulted in a tightening of the alliance among Raleigh, Essex, and Sir Robert Cecil, who saw mutual advantage in protecting each other's interests at court. Essex's betrayal of the alliance in regard to Cecil was to lead, ultimately, to his downfall and execution in 1601.

Bibliography: J. S. Corbett, *The Successors of Drake*, 1933; A. L. Rowse, *Raleigh and the Throckmortons*, 1962.

Connie S. Evans

J

James IV (1473-1513). King of Scots, born 17 March 1473, he became suspicious of his father's intentions over the succession and joined the rebels who encompassed the death of James III at Sauchieburn on 11 June 1488. His coronation was sparsely attended, but his first Parliament showed the new regime had won acceptance. For the next twenty-five years, an undisputed title allowed James to pursue policies designed to stabilize his kingdom and win it international repute. Of noble stature, courageous and intelligent, James ruled in a time of flux that saw the foundation of colleges of learning reinforced by an Education Act (1496) and the introduction of the printing press. If the king's personal concern in these ventures and his reputation as a Renaissance prince are questionable, he patronized the poet William Dunbar, and less commendably, the alchemist Damien. The building work done at the royal palaces was traditional, rather than in the Renaissance style. His principal interest lay in other directions such as the construction of a naval dockyard at Newhaven in which the *Michael* was built as the flagship of a royal fleet, armed with artillery. Such a force was intended as a valuable asset in both national and international terms. Domestically James sought internal peace. Steps were taken to centralize civil justice, while in terms of criminal justice, the king rode the justice-ayres, including an expedition to the Borders. It was, however, the Highlands and Islands that proved most troublesome. The forfeiture of the lord of the Isles in 1493 destroyed one element of stability by creating a vacuum in which unruly chiefs and claimants to the lapsed lordship could operate. Expeditions between 1493 and 1498 served as a preface for a progress throughout the Isles in 1505 designed to quell support for Donald Dubh, a representative of the direct line of the lords of the Isles, who by 1507 was safely in custody.

With domestic peace achieved, international affairs could be accorded priority. Relations with England had been enigmatic since 1488. Initially James, who renewed the alliance with France in 1491, was implacably opposed to HENRY

VII. Antagonism toward England was intensified by the recognition in 1495 of PERKIN WARBECK, but after an expedition on his behalf in September 1496 ended futilely, he became oblivious to Warbeck's fate after his departure in July 1497. After a further abortive raid, peaceful intentions prevailed; a marriage treaty between James and Margaret Tudor, Henry VII's elder daughter, was accompanied by a treaty of perpetual peace, the marriage of the "thistle and the rose" taking place at Holyrood on 8 August 1503. Nevertheless, if the expansion of the Ottoman Empire stimulated plans for a crusade, James's thoughts were diverted to English affairs after HENRY VIII ascended the English throne in 1509 at a time when European affairs were becoming more complex, with a pugnacious pope committed to expelling the French from Italy. To this end a Holy League was formed, which Henry VIII was induced to join in 1511. Prospects of conflict were intensified by incidents at sea and personal animosity between the Scottish and English kings that led to a renewal of the Franco-Scottish alliance in July 1512. As tension mounted, James concluded that he must take action that would discomfort the English and satisfy the French. With Henry VIII's invasion of France on 30 June 1513, that decision became a reality; the host was summoned to meet on 24 July and on 22 August forded the Tweed. Disaster at FLODDEN and the king's death on 9 September were to be the outcome.

Bibliography: N. MacDougall, *James IV*, 1989; R. L. Mackie, *King James IV of Scotland*, 1958.

Ian B. Cowan

James V (1512-1542). King of Scots, born 10 April 1512, he succeeded his father, killed at FLODDEN on 9 September 1513, and was crowned at Stirling. For the next fifteen years, policy was dictated by governors, initially the queen mother, Margaret Tudor, followed by the king's uncle John Stewart, duke of Albany, until 1524, when "erection" of the twelve-year-old terminated Albany's governorship. Arrangements for the king's custody proved unstable, because of the ambitions of ARCHIBALD DOUGLAS, 6th earl of Angus, estranged husband of Margaret Tudor, who seized power with a fresh royal "erection" on 14 June 1526. For two years Angus governed while Margaret plotted for, and in 1528 engineered, James's escape. Briefly under his mother's influence, James's policies soon lay in his own hands.

Financial needs, conditioned by a desire to avoid former financial constraints and his extravagant life-style, exemplified by lavish building works of Renaissance style, characterized his policies. Money was raised in a variety of ways. Marriage plans commenced as early as 1527, but negotiations for the hand of Madeleine, daughter of Francis I, were at first unavailing, and a proposed match in 1534 with Marie, daughter of the duke of Vendome, was unfruitful. Madeleine and James were ultimately married on 1 January 1537 with a dowry of 100,000 gold crowns, but with her premature death, a new bride was quickly found in Mary of Guise-

Lorraine, occasioning an equally handsome dowry. Other means of acquiring wealth were equally at hand, for although James advocated church reform he plundered ecclesiastical resources by exploiting the Crown's right of nomination to major elective benefices, having four of his illegitimate sons placed in rich abbeys. He also played upon the pope's fear of reformation to tax the church on a variety of pretenses, including in 1531 a tax to establish a college of Justice (achieved in 1532) and a levy of one-tenth of Scottish ecclesiastical benefices for three years to strengthen state security. More directly, fines levied at justice ayres grossed considerable sums, as did remissions for the waiving of penalties. Forfeited lands seized by an increasingly acquisitive king were equally rewarding. Personal animosity also played its part in these operations, as kin and supporters of Angus were harried mercilessly by James, whose vindictiveness, ruthlessness, and cruelty compare with those of his contemporary Tudor relations.

Close relationships did not necessarily mean amity, and although James professed friendship with England, his foreign policy was dictated by animosity toward the pro-English policies of Angus and harmony with France promoted by Albany and favored by James's ecclesiastical advisers. Marriage likewise furthered pro-French policies, and if a careful course toward England was initially steered, other councils eventually prevailed. In 1538 and 1539 a European crusade against the schismatic Henry VIII seemed likely, but the proposed coalition disintegrated while Henry advocated neutrality. James was encouraged to follow England's example and break with the pope, a policy unlikely to find favor with the Scottish king, who had condemned heresy and whose pacts with successive popes were financially advantageous. Nevertheless, James agreed to meet the English king at York in 1541 but, to Henry's rage, failed to do so. Thereafter Henry, who had made the journey north, revived claims to English suzerainty over Scotland. Although an English force was routed at Haddon Rig, James determined on retaliation, but when part of his reluctant army, led southward by his unpopular favorite, Oliver Sinclair, was confronted by inferior English forces at Solway Moss on 24 November 1542, many Scots deserted, others surrendered, and the borderers turned on their fellow countrymen and left Sinclair, in the rout that followed, to flee "most manfully." When news of the disaster reached James, he appears to have suffered a total nervous collapse, retired to Falkland to ponder his past mistakes, apparently moaning "Fy, fted Oliver? Is Oliver tane? All is lost." On hearing of his daughter's birth (see MARY, QUEEN OF SCOTS), he reputedly prophesied of the Stewart claim to the throne that "it came with a lass, it will pass with a lass" and turning his face to the wall, died, an apparently unloved tyrant, on 14 December, leaving a kingdom facing another long minority.

Bibliography: G. Donaldson, *Scotland: James V-James VII*, 1965; M. W. Stuart: *The Scot Who Was a Frenchman*, 1940.

Ian B. Cowan

James VI and I (1567-1625). King of Scotland and England, James VI, like his mother, MARY, QUEEN OF SCOTS, came to the Scottish throne as a baby, at a time of great crisis. Unlike his mother, he was intensely interested in the business of ruling. Shortly before his twelfth birthday, he pronounced himself old enough to rule without regents; by his mid-teens, he was impressing English diplomats and driving ELIZABETH I to fury because of his skill in the art of political dissimulation. Comments on his laziness and passion for hunting were also being made before he was twenty; but no one doubted that this "old young man" was a very clever one.

At one level, the political chaos that he inherited was remarkably short-lived. The civil war of 1568-1573 saw the deaths of his first three regents, two by violence, but his fourth regent, JAMES DOUGLAS, earl of Morton (1572-1578), restored peace and order, with the comparative ease resulting from a general weariness with instability and war. Even Mary's continuing existence caused little trouble; it was Elizabeth, not the Scots, who had to deal with that situation. But there remained the underlying and crucial problem of restoring the authority and prestige of a monarchy that had last been effective in 1542; and this problem was not short-lived.

In 1582, James was seized by the "Ruthven Raiders," extreme Presbyterian lords led by William Ruthven, earl of Gowrie. This action was not a novel occurrence. Earlier Stewart kings had been "kidnapped" during their minorities by factions seizing power through the king's person; in this case the Raiders sought to offset the pro-French and suspected Catholic influence of Esme Stuart, duke of Lennox. In 1583, James escaped to the welcoming support of the Ruthven rivals, and his personal rule effectively dates from then. But on 5 August 1600, he was again kidnapped in the mysterious "Gowrie Conspiracy;" William's son (Earl John Ruthven) and his brother apparently kidnapped the king, held him for a few hours and threatened his life, until he was rescued, and the brothers were killed. Who was kidnapping whom remains unclear; James's major critics, the Presbyterian ministers, believed that the Presbyterian Gowries were the victims. One contemporary account unwittingly turns it into farce, with men rushing up and down the stairs of Gowrie House, hurling themselves against locked doors, and charging down the wrong passages. But the event was very frightening—so frightening that it is difficult to imagine James's devising a plot in which he was so much at risk. It looks like a harebrained gamble devised to restrain a king now all too successfully resisting the demands of the extreme Presbyterians. It fits no pattern; it was too individualistic, just like the actions in the early 1590s of the maverick Francis Stewart, earl of Bothwell, another would-be kidnapper of the king, whose antics included bursting in on him when he was half-dressed—an action that disturbed the casual James infinitely less than ROBERT DEVEREUX, earl of Essex's, similar ill-timed intrusion into Elizabeth's chamber before the queen had donned the wig, make-up, and robes that hid the reality. But Bothwell was dangerous because, despite his involvement in the North Berwick witch trials of 1590-1591, he had, like Gowrie, the support of the kirk and therefore survived until 1595.

To these cases can be added the problems caused by the northern Catholic earls, Huntly, Erroll and Angus, involved in treasonable dealings with Philip II of Spain in 1589 and 1592, in Huntly's case, a feud with James Stewart, 17th earl of Moray, which ended with Moray's murder in 1592. "Methinks I do but dream," wrote the frantic Elizabeth, desperately trying to force James to take action against them. It all looks like an aristocracy out of royal control. But James's casual approach suggests something very different. When he chose to act, as he did against the northern earls in 1595-1596, it worked. But inherent in the Bothwell and Gowrie cases was what, to him, was the real problem: the kirk.

The failure of Mary to give any religious direction had meant that for some twenty-five years, the Reformed kirk was free to develop a particularly radical line on the relative powers of church and state. Far more threatening to James's kingship than any magnate were the claims of Andrew Melville and his followers, the extremists who denied the Crown any control over ecclesiastical affairs, while having no scruple about interfering in secular ones and using their great propaganda weapon, the pulpit, against the king. The late 1580s and 1590s, therefore, saw a sustained effort by James to establish his authority over the church, restoration of a clerical estate in Parliament, and diocesan episcopacy. He was visibly winning by 1603. It was done by brilliant management of the supreme court of the kirk, the General Assembly. James had one right, of naming time and place for its meetings, and he used it to full effect. Meetings were held in the more conservative areas of the country, and he turned up in person to manipulate people and business. In the 1590s, he gave the same personal attention to the management of Parliament and thus ensured that his earlier defeat at the hands of the Presbyterian party, with their "Golden Acts" of 1592, would not be repeated. Even the rebellious Catholic earls were pressed into the service of royal policy; they could be used as a bargaining counter with the kirk. James ran a tough monarchy, such as the Scots had not experienced for decades. Its style was made possible by Scottish convention, which allowed James to be present at meetings of Parliament, assembly, and council; and attend he did, assiduously. It entirely suited this man of great skill in debate; the absence of such conventions in England, where the monarch was cut off from these bodies, was to harness adversely that particular ability.

James's tutor had been George Buchanan, humanist, apologist for the deposition of Mary, and leading exponent of the theory of contractual kingship, in which the king was answerable to his people and could be removed by them. James's own theory, divine right kingship, expressed in his books *The Trew Law of Free Monarchies* and *Basilikon Doron* in 1598-1599, was the antithesis of Buchanan's theory. But its primary raison d'être was not as an ideology for secular politics; it was the answer to Melville's separation of the two powers, spiritual and temporal. This fact is why James's theory was, and remained throughout his life, very different from his practice of kingship. He had a high sense of royalty, but he was in no sense an autocrat. He was casual and shrewd, and he knew when to leave problems alone unless—as with the kirk—he was forced to act, in which case he did so to great effect. It was an approach that would have great advantage in England, notably in reducing tensions within a church where paranoia about PURITANS far milder than any Melvillian had become excessive under Elizabeth.

Above all, James was confident about present achievement and future success. Unlike his mother, he was not obsessed about the English throne; he simply waited to get it and occasionally showed understandable irritation about Elizabeth's refusal to die. This attitude put him in a much stronger position with Elizabeth than Mary had been; he was to infuriate her all his life by refusing to listen to her increasingly hectoring advice, and nothing more clearly shows the change in relationships than the £58,000 that this neurotically parsimonious monarch poured out in annual pensions—and the list she had drawn up, detailing her good deeds to Scotland, one for each year like a good girl guide.

James was one of Scotland's greatest kings. No king from Scotland was likely to be regarded by the hostile and xenophobic English as one of England's greatest. Yet despite his failure to bring about his cherished dream of incorporating Union, his reign after 1603 was still remarkably effective. The Scottish experience of this king, an extraordinary combination of intellectual and political realist, explains why.

Bibliography: Maurice Lee, Jr., *John Maitland of Thirlestane*, 1959, and *Great Britain's Solomon: James VI and I in his Three Kingdoms*, 1990; A. G. R. Smith, ed., *The Reign of King James VI and I*, 1973; D. H. Willson, *James VI and I*, 1956; Jenny Wormald, "James VI and I: Two Kings or One?", *History* 68, 1983: 187-209.

Jenny Wormald

Jesuit Mission. The Spaniard Ignatius Loyola founded the Society of Jesus in 1540, an order of priests whose purpose was to work within society rather like secular priest. They rapidly became an important force within the Counter-Reformation and worked in heretic Europe and in the wider world to save souls. There were a number of notable English Jesuits in the Tudor period, but the society neglected England, and it was among the last European nations to receive its own province, or Jesuit department, in 1623.

Henry More, the seventeenth-century historian, says that before 1580 there were sixty-nine English Jesuits. They were sent by the society to work in many parts of Europe and beyond: in Poland, India, Portugal, Hungary, France, Italy, and Germany. In the late 1570s, as the seminary movement developed, the Jesuits became more deeply involved in English affairs. When William Allen founded the English College at Rome in 1579, it was soon placed under the management of Italian Jesuits. In 1580, the great "Jesuit invasion" of England began: an invasion of three men. The Jesuit mission of 1580 was significant since it was highly publicized both by the Jesuits themselves and by the government; it served therefore to put the spotlight on the whole Catholic seminary movement. The two best-known Elizabethan Jesuits were the leaders of the mission of 1580: Robert Persons and Edmund Campion.

Edmund Campion (1540-1581) pursued a successful career as an Anglican in the early years of Elizabeth's reign. His eloquence at school, then at Oxford, led him to deliver two Latin speeches before a sovereign: first Mary and then Elizabeth. In 1571 he decided to convert to Catholicism and fled abroad. He was trained at Douai and then joined the Jesuits and was at first set on a career in Bohemia. Instead, he was sent to England with Persons. His mission lasted only a year (1580-1581), during which time he traveled widely in England, preached and also had printed in secret his pamphlet *Decem Rationes*, ten reasons for being a Catholic. The Jesuits held a meeting at Southwark in which the need for lay recusance was emphasized. They also brought a new instruction from the pope to be communicated to laymen concerning the papal Bull of Excommunication of 1570 (see REGNANS IN EXCELSIS). This papal "faculty" or "rescript" of 1580 declared that Catholics were no longer bound by the Bull of Excommunication in present circumstances: in other words, they could obey the queen. This message was intended as a peaceful gesture, but it only served to alarm the authorities further when they learned of it, since the temporary nature of Catholic obedience seemed almost more sinister than outright disobedience. In 1581, Campion was arrested, tortured, tried with others on a spurious charge of treason, and executed.

Robert Persons, or Parsons, (1546-1610) was also an Oxford convert. When Campion was arrested, he avoided death by fleeing abroad. He never returned to England. Abroad, he was, after William Allen, the most influential Elizabethan Catholic. His greatest asset was his skill as an author. While in England, like Campion, he had published Catholic works; and in exile, he produced dozens more. He wrote history, political theory, controversial theology, works of devotion, and satire. He was among the greatest Elizabethan prose writers. His books had a great impact on Catholics at home, although everything he did excited controversy. His greatest work was political: *A Conference about the Next Succession to the Crown of England* of 1594, in which he defended the idea of popular sovereignty. Persons was also a great educator, founding a school at Eu in France for English Catholic boys and two seminaries in Spain. In the last years of the reign he was principal of the English College at Rome. He was a successful administrator and diplomat, working incessantly abroad to help organize the mission in England and its support services abroad. He urged the cause of English Catholicism at the court of Philip II, with the Guises in France, and in the Vatican. He was also a politician, working at first with Allen and then alone to help expedite a political solution to the English question. He supported the cause of MARY, QUEEN OF SCOTS and then of the Spanish Enterprise of England. His abilities and endeavors won him friends, but also enemies, both among Protestants and among English Catholics. Some Catholics, especially at the end of the reign, blamed Persons for the consequences of the political efforts made to dethrone Elizabeth. This blame was unfair, and Persons was justified—in his own terms—for placing his hopes so firmly in Spain. If Spain failed, it was not his fault.

Most English Jesuit effort before 1603 was expanded abroad, but the mission begun in 1580 continued. Numbers were small, fluctuating at about a dozen in the last decades of the reign. Of these, three further Jesuits were executed. The Jesuit mission was well organized and had some outstanding members. Robert Southwell was a famous poet and prose writer, whose execution almost rivaled that of Campion in pathos and fame. Most attractive of all was the adventurous and commonsensical John Gerard, who succeeded in escaping from the Tower of London and who records his career so delightfully in his autobiography. Such men proved of much value to the English mission, while at times inspiring the jealousy of more workaday secular priests.

Bibliography: F. Edwards, *The Elizabethan Jesuits*, 1981.

P. J. Holmes

Jonson, Ben (1572-1637). After SHAKESPEARE, Jonson is the greatest playwright of the English Renaissance. His comedies command respect for their sharply etched characterizations, vigorous theatrical prose, incisive social satire, and masterful construction. Jonson's work advances the value of self-knowledge; the importance of social harmony established through high ideals and individual integrity; the destructive effects of a slavish devotion to money, power, or status; the vital example that the ancients provided; and the necessary task of the writer to function as social conscience.

Evidence suggests that Jonson was born on 11 June 1572 in London, the son of a minister and the stepson of a bricklayer, to whom he was apprenticed after studying with the antiquary William Camden at Westminster School from 1583-1588. By 1597, having completed Thomas Nashe's *Isle of Dogs*, he had married, soldiered in the Low Countries, and acted. In 1598 *The Case Is Altered* and *Every Man in His Humour*, the first of his comical satires, were staged. He was also imprisoned in Newgate briefly for the murder of an actor. His remaining comical satires appeared shortly thereafter: *Every Man Out of His Humour* (1599), *Cynthia's Revels* (1600), and *Poetaster* (1601). With the accession of JAMES VI and I in 1603, Jonson wrote a Roman play, *Sejanus*, and began composition of his twenty masques and entertainments, many done in troubled collaboration with the great stage designer, Inigo Jones. In 1605 he wrote *Eastward Ho!* with John Marston and George Chapman, and in 1606 his most famous comedy, *Volpone*, was staged, followed by *Epicoene* (1609), *The Alchemist* (1610), *Catiline* (1611)—his second Roman play—and *Bartholomew Fair* (1614).

Two years later appeared *The Devil in an Ass*, along with the first folio of his works, an anthology of nine plays, two collections of poetry (*Epigrams* and *The*

Forest) and several masques (semi-theatrical entertainments with allegorical plots and mythological, fantastic characters). The quality of Jonson's dramas declined in his last decade, though to call his later plays "dotages," as Dryden did, is probably too harsh. His career ends with *The Staple of News* (1626), *The New Inn* (1629), *The Magnetic Lady* (1632), and *A Tale of a Tub* (1633, based on an earlier version). Jonson died on 6 August 1637 and was buried in Westminster Abbey, his tombstone reading, "O rare Ben Jonson."

Jonson's comical satires, an innovative dramatic form influenced by the poetic satires then current, developed "humour comedy," Jonson appropriating the term *humour* from contemporary psychology and reinterpreting it as any affected behavior deserving mockery. From his one-dimensional humour characters spring the more rounded figures of his greatest comedies; such tricksters as Volpone, and Subtle and Face (in *The Alchemist*), compel our interest and amazement, while their rejection of orthodox social morality prompts our laughing condemnation, at times even disgust, as with Volpone's repulsive innuendos to Celia. Volpone's "hymn" to his gold is a masterful monologue of perverted prayer, a revelation of his monomaniacal character and a caricature of Jacobean acquisitiveness and self-aggrandizement. These comedies and *Epicoene* reveal Jonson's skill at tight plot construction inherited from classical dramatists who were, as he stated in his critical work *Timber, or Discoveries*, his "guides, not commanders."

Jonson's poetry and masques praise those virtues whose absence is pilloried in the plays. Many poems celebrate members of the nobility as living symbols of a code seen as central to the English social fabric. In "To Penshurst" he epitomizes this idealistic code in the Sidney's family home, a structure against which other houses are mere symbols of wealth rather than expressions of "the mysteries of manners, arms and arts." His epigrams indict fops and buffoons, his epitaph "On My First Son" is a moving remembrance of "his best piece of poetry," and the songs from the plays combine graceful diction and careful rhythm, which counterpoint the dramatic prose and blank verse. Jonson's spare, disciplined lines, controlled emotional tone, and balanced phrasing place him within the neoclassical tradition. His masques depicted for courtly audiences the interplay of allegorical figures representing what he termed in *Hymenaei* (1606) "the more remov'd mysteries" or exalted ideals of the true nobility: statesmanship, service, devotion to the monarch, marital fidelity, beneficence, and well-ordered, rational life. He also developed the anti-masque, an antic scene of grotesques and debased characters.

Jonson's criticism, the largest body of literary commentary by a Tudor dramatist, records his measured respect for classical models, rejection of an easy imitation of their work, and his belief in literature as an agent of moral and social improvement. His comments praise writing as a disciplined, scholarly craft, not mere hackwork for the ill-educated and unappreciative. His criticisms again reveal his neoclassical outlook by stressing the virtues to be found in Greek and Roman masters, yet he blends their influence with a strong respect for native English tradition and individual originality.

Bibliography: A. Leggatt, *Ben Jonson: His Vision and His Art*, 1981; David Riggs, *Ben Jonson: A Life*, 1989.

Christopher Baker

Justices of the Peace. The justices of the peace (JPs) were the Tudors' principal county officials, and the commission of the peace the most important of a variety of local commissions. Originating as Edward I's keepers of the peace, who assisted the sheriff, these officers became known under Edward III as justices of the peace and were given the power to arrest, imprison, indict, and hear and determine felonies and trespasses. Thereupon quarter sessions—judicial proceedings before a shire's JPs, which met four times a year, usually in the county town—virtually replaced the county court, and by the end of the fourteenth century the JPs had surpassed more ancient local officials—sheriff, coroner, and escheator—to become preeminent in both judicial and administrative capacities. In the fifteenth century JPs were drawn increasingly from among local gentry with an annual income of £20, though this was sometimes waived for persons learned in the law, and their functions including quelling riots, arresting criminals, receiving indictments and trying them by jury at quarter sessions, and administering and supervising local government.

The authority of the JPs was based upon the commission of the peace and on various statutes. The Tudors added greatly to their responsibilities, and though the written commission retained its late medieval form until 1590, substantial statutory changes began with HENRY VII's Parliaments. These enlarged the JPs' role in collecting taxes, increased their power to deal with poachers and to punish riot—especially where maintenance and embracery were concerned—and gave them authority to issue warrants for arrest, to hear and judge all non-felonious statutory offenses, to hold inquests to investigate concealment by other inquests (the *Pro Camera Stellata* statute), to have the sheriff empanel presentment juries and to alter the composition of trial juries empanelled by him if necessary, to punish local officials for extortion and those persons refusing to work at wages fixed by the commission, to audit the collection of fines and estreats, and to regulate beggars, vagabonds, alehouse keepers, weights and measures, and production of certain metals.

Both Henry VII and HENRY VIII had difficulties with corrupt and unruly JPs, and Cardinal THOMAS WOLSEY had to use the power of STAR CHAMBER to administer exemplary justice to some offenders, but by the 1530s THOMAS CROMWELL was able to employ them to enforce the abundant Reformation legislation. Thereafter JPs were frequently involved in enforcing religious laws, notably those against RECUSANCY under ELIZABETH. Statutes continued to add to JPs' duties, and by the end of the Tudor period there were over 300, almost two-thirds passed since 1485. Many of these new duties were essentially administrative, involving among other things the regulation of wages and prices, licensing of alehouses, collection and administration of POOR LAWS, punishment of rogues and vagabonds, enforcement of sumptuary legislation, and maintenance of roads and bridges. There were also important changes in their judicial activities. For example, murder cases were taken over completely by the assizes in Henry VIII's reign, and a Marian law gave JPs a prosecutorial role in trials before the assize judges. Although in EDWARD VI's reign the Crown began appointing LORDS LIEUTENANT to supervise military affairs in the shires, JPs were often deputy lieutenants or served on muster commissions. The increased burden of business made it impossible for JPs to get everything done at quarter sessions. A 1542 act providing for JPs to meet in pairs at petty sessions six weeks prior to quarter sessions was short-lived, but JPs did more and more of their work in small groups or individually as the sixteenth century progressed. In 1590 the outmoded old form of the commission of the peace, which simply gave JPs authority to keep the peace and to inquire by jury into various offenses, was replaced by a new form empowering JPs to enforce legislation for keeping the peace, take sureties from or imprison offenders, hold inquests into a variety of offenses (including malfeasance among local officials), try certain cases on indictment, hear and determine various others (difficult cases were to go before the assizes), and to hold regular sessions.

Commissions of the peace were normally issued annually for each county, though they appeared more frequently if there were changes in the membership. The monarch officially appointed JPs, but the lord chancellor usually chose them. During the Tudor period the commissions of the peace grew spectacularly (from less than ten before 1485 to as many as eighty in some shires during Elizabeth's reign), despite government efforts to hold the size down (notably by WILLIAM CECIL under Elizabeth). Thus it was increasingly necessary for the chancellor to seek advice about appointments from such knowledgeable worthies as the bishops, the assize judges, the local nobility, and even the gentry on the commission themselves. Local men actively sought places on the bench, the ultimate symbol of local status, for themselves and their political allies and thus attempted to influence the Chancellor on their own, through friends and relatives, or with the aid of a courtier patron. Becoming a JP was a complex process. After obtaining the chancellor's warrant for appointment, an individual had to acquire from the Crown Office in CHANCERY a new commission of the peace, which would make his appointment official when proclaimed at quarter sessions, and—following the Reformation—a *dedimus potestatum* authorizing three trusted gentry to give him the oath of supremacy. If he failed to pay the engrossment fee, the commission might remain in the Crown Office for months, and commissions were frequently invalidated by minor clerical errors, leaving JPs unable to take their seats on the bench.

The place one held relative to fellow JPs was extremely important in this status-conscious age. Precedence among the great officers of state, peers, and assize judges was established outside the sphere of county politics, but local status determined the placement of JPs among the successive ranks of knights, esquires, and gentlemen, though for them the procedure was much less cut-and-dried. A prospective JP naturally wished to be placed as high as possible; on the other hand, no established JP wanted a rival or new member to have a position higher than his own. Therefore a great deal of behind-the-scenes effort went into influencing the ranking of active JPs or the removal or demotion of one's enemies on the bench.

The membership of the commission can be divided into three groups. At its head came ex officio members with important national offices, such as the archbishop of Canterbury, the lord chancellor, the lord treasurer, and so on. Occasionally this group included local men who had risen to national prominence, but generally ex officio membership was essentially honorary, and the ex officio members played little direct role in county government and politics. Next came the assize judges and serjeants-at-law, who appeared in the shire at least twice a year for the assizes, which local JPs were required to attend. Finally, ranked in the order of their individual status in the shire, came the active or simple JPs. Not all were genuinely active, because they were prominent enough to be preoccupied with national affairs, were JPs in more than one county, or were simply uninterested or lazy. But it was this group that was expected to do the commission's actual work and from which the men with real local influence usually came.

JPs were essentially unpaid amateurs, so the national government took several measures to insure that there was some legal expertise on the commission of the peace. First, on each a number of men were designated as of the quorum. Prior to its degradation to a mere status symbol in Elizabeth's reign, membership in the quorum required special legal training, and it was expected that at least some members of the quorum would be present whenever any important business was undertaken by JPs. In a well-run, tightly controlled county, it could be expected that attendance at quarter sessions would be dominated by members of the quorum, though not all counties fit that description. Second, one of the leading JPs in each shire was appointed *custos rotulorum*, which made him keeper of the records and gave some supervisory authority over the others. Third, each county had a clerk of the peace to record the commission's activities. There were also a number of manuals for JPs, the most important being William Lambarde's *Eirenarcha* (1581).

The political importance of the JPs can hardly be overestimated. They were essential to the enforcement of the royal will and the implementation of parliamentary legislation in the shires, and their opposition or inactivity could sometimes thwart both. Thus the Crown was reluctant to offend either these "natural rulers" of the shires or the local communities that they governed. Thoroughgoing purges of the commissions were unusual, even at the accession of a new monarch or with the dramatic fluctuations in official religious policy. The civil war that erupted in the 1640s during the reign of a Stuart king less sensitive to local sentiments bears testimony to the wisdom of the Tudors' treatment of local government.

Bibliography: G. R. Elton, *The Tudor Constitution*, 1982; Kenneth Pickthorn, *Early Tudor Government*, 2 vols., 1934; A. Hassel Smith, *County and Court: Government and Politics in Norfolk, 1558-1603*, 1974.

William B. Robison

K

Kett's Rebellion (1549). A term commonly used to describe several violent social and political protests in East Anglia that seriously threatened the regime of EDWARD SEYMOUR, the lord protector for EDWARD VI. Although there were other uprisings in the spring and summer of 1549, the rebellion takes its name from Robert Kett, the leader of the most serious disturbance. ENCLOSURE grievances precipitated the first disorders, but resentment of the gentry and the lack of a powerful magnate compounded the problem in Norfolk and Suffolk. When rioters from the market town of Wymondham started tearing down the hedges of the unpopular lawyer John Flowerdew, he diverted them to his enemy Kett, a prosperous tanner and landholder nearby. On hearing the complaints of the crowd, Kett not only agreed to destroy his own enclosures but joined the rioters. As their leader, he soon gathered a force of 16,000, which established a camp on Mousehold Heath, a hill overlooking the city of Norwich. Almost simultaneously: other "camps" appeared first at Castle Rising and then Downham Market, Norfolk, and also near the two political centers of Suffolk—Bury St Edmunds in the west and Melton near Ipswich in the east. By mid-July, those immediately below the gentry on the social ladder, the townsmen, yeomanry, and minor gentry of East Anglia, had established rebel centers capable of challenging the traditional regional power structure and of ultimately shaking the protector's government to its very foundation.

Most of the other smaller encampments were rather quickly dispersed. The Downham Market group moved on to Norwich, and Sir Anthony Wingfield offered pardons to the men camped at Melton. The government forces, under the command of William Parr, Marquess of Northampton, included local gentry who saw that Bury St. Edmunds was pacified on their way from London to Norwich. The camp at Mousehold Heath was another matter. The mayor of Norwich had cooperated with the rebels out of fear, so the camp was firmly established before Northampton arrived on 30 July, but his feckless behavior made the situation worse. By not taking immediate action, Northampton gave the rebels their opportunity to attack. The subsequent bloody battle killed thirty-six men, including Lord Sheffield. In panic, Northampton abandoned the city, and for the next three weeks Kett and his men virtually governed Norwich. Meanwhile the PRIVY COUNCIL had levied more troops, and with JOHN DUDLEY, the earl of Warwick, now in command, they arrived at Norwich on 23 August. Four days later, Warwick overwhelmed the rebels at Dussindale, and although Kett escaped the carnage that day, he was later captured and executed for treason in December 1549.

Kett's personal reasons for joining and leading the rebellion remain obscure, but the twenty-nine demands drawn up by the men of Mousehold Heath reveal the interrelated political, social, economic, and agricultural problems of mid-Tudor England as well as the particular local difficulties. Resentment of enclosure sparked action, but both Norfolk and Suffolk had two rather different agricultural zones, and each zone had its own set of grievances based on the desire of the tenants to protect themselves and the common lands. Tenants in the sheep-corn zones of pastoral and arable farming resented the foldcourse, the right of the lord to pasture his animals on the tenant's land and the common; while the tenants in the woodland areas reacted to their exclusion from the common pasture. Hedges were a symbol of complicated, intractable, poorly understood conditions that enclosure commissions and Somerset's well-known sympathy for the poorer sort could not begin to solve.

The rebels were also men deeply alienated from the landowning gentry immediately above them in the social order. They wanted a role in the local governing structure. The imprisonment of the Conservative, powerful THOMAS HOWARD, 3rd duke of Norfolk, from the beginning of the reign had created a political and social vacuum in both counties. No other local magnate could replace the duke and control gentry rivalries. When the crisis came, no one was able to rally the gentry to suppress the rebellion before it escalated into a serious problem for the central government.

The rebellion had two immediate consequences; it led to the fall of Somerset, whose economic policies were unpopular with the very landowners whose political support he needed in the privy council and in Parliament, and it also discredited the ideas of the COMMONWEALTH MEN, who had advocated social reform. Hales's commission on enclosure ceased to exist, and the government no longer actively patronized those who preached or wrote about social justice. Edward VI's reign entered a new phase in the autumn of 1549 as different leadership attempted new remedies for England's serious political and economic problems.

Bibliography: A. Fletcher, *Tudor Rebellions*, 3rd ed., 1983; D. MacCulloch, "Kett's Rebellion in Context," in *Rebellion, Popular Protest and the Social Order in Early Modern England*, ed. Paul Slack, 1984.

Ann Weikel

Kildare Rebellion (1534-35). The recall of GERALD FITZGERALD, 9th earl of Kildare, to England in February 1534 was not an immediate cause for discontent among his family and supporters, for he was able to leave his son, Thomas (known to history as "Silken Thomas"), as lord justice in his place. Contrary to the traditional interpretation, Thomas was not an impetuous hothead, deceived by rumors of his father's death in the Tower of London into rebellion; rather, it is now clear that his dramatic repudiation of the king's authority on 11 June 1534, when he laid the sword of state before the Irish council at their meeting in St. Mary's Abbey, Dublin, was done on the instructions of his father and with the intention not of initiating rebellion but of vividly demonstrating the discontent of the Kildares at the king's intention of replacing Gerald as deputy by William Skeffington, an Englishman. When no answer was forthcoming, the rebellion proper may be said to have started with the murder of Archbishop John Alen, the head of the anti-Kildare faction on the Irish council on 27 July 1534. On 29 June, Gerald had been arrested and sent to the Tower, and since he was obviously a dying man by then, having been ill for some time, there was no further reason for restraint on either side.

Militarily, the conflict was a desultory one, for the absence of a royal army left the rebels in charge of virtually the entire country outside the three cities of Dublin, Waterford, and Kilkenny, by default. The failure to take Dublin at the beginning was to prove fatal, and though a halfhearted siege was maintained by Thomas and his supporters until the arrival of Lord Deputy Skeffington in October with a 2,000-man army, the earl (his father having died in the Tower on 2 September 1534) was unable either to take the city or to prevent the English from landing. Outside the city, however, the country was either under the rebels' control or neutral. Only the Butlers of Ormond remained loyal, and they were hard put to maintain their own territories. The earl of Desmond and his allies controlled Munster in support of Thomas, and envoys had been sent to the emperor Charles V seeking his aid against Henry. The prospects of foreign intervention, though in the end coming to nothing but promises and some munitions, seemed real enough to both the rebels and the government to stimulate both to carry on the war relentlessly. Skeffington was plagued by shortages of men and money, and winter campaigning took a toll on him and his army. After a brief campaign that saw several of Kildare's castles fall, only to be retaken by the rebels soon after, the deputy was content to make a truce for the Christmas season, much to the anger of the frightened Irish council, which complained of his delay and reluctance to take the field. By now, only his Gaelic supporters remained with Thomas, fearful of Skeffington's intentions toward them, and even they were insistent on regular payments from him to maintain the struggle. On 23 March 1535, his major stronghold, Maynooth Castle in County Kildare, the hereditary seat of the Kildares, fell by treachery, and the earl became a desperate fugitive, hiding in woods and bogs, still awaiting the foreign aid that had prompted the continuance of the rebellion long after the time when Henry VIII might have been willing to settle on terms.

In July 1535, Lord Leonard Grey arrived in Ireland as marshal of the army, Skeffington's health having deteriorated (he died in December). Grey was Kildare's brother-in-law, and was later to be suspected of being a Kildare partisan, but he was able to persuade the earl to surrender on 24 August on a promise of his life, if not his lands. He was taken to England and imprisoned in the Tower. Henry and his chief minister, THOMAS CROMWELL, were enraged by this leniency, though nothing could be done for the moment for fear of provoking further trouble in Ireland while the "REFORMATION PARLIA-MENT" of 1536-1537 was extending the English ecclesiastical legislation to that country. Once the bulk of the legislation had been passed, Kildare had been attainted (convicted without the need for a trial) of treason in both Ireland and England, and the title and lands had been forfeited to the Crown, there was no cause to hold off any longer. In February 1536, Thomas's five uncles, half-brothers of Gerald, had been arrested and sent to the Tower, though two of them had supported the Crown and one had been neutral, and they too were attainted along with the earl. In February 1537, all six were executed at Tyburn in London. The ramifications of the Kildare rebellion were beyond anything that either Kildare or the king could have imagined at the time, and the modern history of Ireland is conventionally dated from 1534, for the replacement of the Kildares by an administration manned and controlled from England brought Ireland within the ambit of England and English affairs, with drastic consequences for both countries in the centuries ahead.

Bibliography: Laurence McCorristine, *The Revolt of Silken Thomas: A Challenge to Henry VIII*, 1987.

Anthony Sheehan

King's Book (1543). Actually titled *The Necessary Doctrine and Erudition of a Christian Man*. This formulary of doctrine was written during the later Conservative era of HENRY VIII's reign to revise the BISHOPS' BOOK of 1537 and bring it into accord with the ACT OF SIX ARTICLES. The Conservative nature of the work reflected a defeat for Archbishop THOMAS CRANMER, who, along with the conservative bishops Thomas Thirlby of Westminster, Nicholas Heath of Rochester, and John Salcot of Salisbury, appear to have negotiated and written the document. The king himself was involved in the writing, but not all his corrections to the text were incorporated. Nevertheless, unlike the Bishops' Book, this work had the king's official approval and had an introduction provided by him.

In expounding the Creed, seven Sacraments, Ten Commandments, and the Lord's Prayer, the formulary retreated from the movement toward Protestantism reflected in the earlier TEN ARTICLES and Bishops' Book, but condemnations of Lutheran doctrine did not necessarily mean replacement with authentic Catholic or even Anglo-Catholic tenets. Perhaps this substantiates the claim that the king after 1539 was engaged in an attempt at conservative reform rather than in a conservative reaction. For example, while the book upheld transubstantiation and refused communion in both kinds to the laity, it made no mention of the Mass as a sacrifice. It did, however, treat all seven Sacraments as valid and made no distinction between those authenticated in Scripture and those not. Prayers and masses for the dead were continued, albeit with emphasis on their benefit for the whole congregation of Christian people and denunciation of financial abuse, for which the papacy was blamed.

In regard to justification, the work used some Lutheran phraseology but agreed with the medieval schoolmen's description of the individual's role in attaining salvation. The assertion of free will dovetailed with the view that justification was a life-long process that the Sacraments aided. However, while the book rejected solefideism as the route to salvation, it described the transformation of faith into hope and then obedience in a way that did not mesh with Catholic teaching. There also were discussions wherein the Sacraments' meaning or role did not follow Catholic doctrine. For example, while penance was seen as necessary to the sinner's recovery of justification or grace, there was no indication that this action constituted a sacrament of penance. The suggestion that the prayer of priests and assistants produced the Sacramental effect in extreme unction was not Catholic doctrine; nor was the idea that this sacrament was efficacious only to those in the church who, having fallen out of grace by deadly sin, have been restored by penance.

ROYAL SUPREMACY was defended in the discussion that distinguished the church universal, to which all Christians belonged, from its components, the national churches, headed by kings and princes and legitimately maintaining their own traditions and ceremonies. The king's right to nominate bishops was also noted, as was the necessity that clerics exercise their functions in accordance with the pertinent laws made by the prince. This, the last formulary of the reign, died with the king in 1547.

Bibliography: A. G. Dickens, *The English Reformation*, 2nd ed., 1989; Philip Hughes, *The Reformation in England*, 1950-1954.

Martha C. Skeeters

Knox, John (c. 1512-1572). Protestant Reformer; born in Haddington about 1512 and ordained in 1536, he followed George Wishart in 1545 and fully committed himself to Protestantism in April 1547 by joining the murderers of Cardinal David Beaton as their minister at St. Andrews. When the castle fell to the French, Knox was condemned to the galleys but was released in early 1549. Thereafter while living in England, Knox reestablished links with Scottish Reformers. As preacher at Berwick his opinions reached a number of his countrymen. Nevertheless, his interest was largely in liturgical disputes in England. This concern continued after Knox fled to the Continent when England returned to Catholicism in 1553. Knox visited Scotland during 1555 and 1556 but returned to Geneva apparently dispirited and again concentrated on promoting Protestantism in England. It was only after ELIZABETH's accession in 1558 that Knox asserted in purely Scottish terms the people's right to resist blasphemous laws to the death in his *Appelation to the Nobility and Estates of Scotland*.

Knox's cause continued to look bleak in 1557 when his allies, the Scots lords of the "Godlie Band or Covenent," abandoned their resistance. Two years later, however, the political and religious balance changed because of hostility to French influence, and their cause revived. Knox arrived at Leith on 2 May 1559. In his preaching, effectively demonstrated at Perth, Knox not only encouraged the Protestant lords but also engaged the sympathies of the populace. The resultant enthusiasm brought destruction in its wake, but Knox never condoned the conduct of "the rascal multitude." Meanwhile, the inability of the French to provide adequate reinforcements and the intervention of an English task force proved decisive.

Knox then came into his own and principally compiled the Reformers' ambitious program in the "Great Book of Reformation" also styled the "First Book of Discipline." Expressive of Knox's views on education, poor relief, and worship, the sections on the proposed organization of the church are ambigious at all but the congregational level but are indicative of his desire to establish a conciliar form of church government working with the civil magistracy for the creation of a godly commonwealth.

If such hopes were not fulfilled and eventually were redefined in the *Second Book of Discipline* (1578), it was the ideals of Knox that shaped the form of worship adopted by the church. In this respect the Scots Confession of Faith, complemented by sections of the Book of Discipline dealing with worship and belief, constitutes his permanent memorial. Former beliefs were replaced by a new radical CALVINISM, which would accept only usages based on Scriptures.

In personal terms, Knox was less successful; his refusal to become a superintendent because he thought "hys state honorable inoughe" may have stemmed from the belief that as minister of the High Kirk of Edinburgh, he could exert greater influence from his pulpit. If in his *History of the Reformation in Scotland* (1587), it is Knox who emerges triumphant, the one-sided nature of the evidence must be considered. His criticisms of MARY, QUEEN OF SCOTS gained little support from his former allies. For four years Knox remained politically impotent. When from 1565 the Queen committed errors of judgment that led to her abdication in 1567, Knox played no part in these events, for following the murder of DAVID RIZZIO in 1566, Knox was absent, first in Ayrshire and then in England.

Shortly after Mary's surrender, Knox returned to Edinburgh to gloat over his fallen rival, but the factors surrounding Mary's eclipse also encompassed Knox, for following Mary's escape from Lochleven in 1568, her defeat at LANGSIDE, and flight to England, successive Scottish regents had to placate Mary's captor, Elizabeth, to whom Knox was unacceptable, owing to his views on women rulers expressed in *The First Blast of the Trumpet Against the Monstrous Regiment of Women* (1558).

Political impotence, coupled with ill health, meant that while in the years before his death in 1572 his reputation brought him the veneration owing to an elder statesman, few listened to his counsel. Certainly in 1571 at the General Assembly held at St. Andrews, which discussed episcopal appointments, Knox ineffectively "opponit himself directlie and zealuslie" to the making of bishops. Nevertheless, practical considerations prevailed, and in his last letter to the General Assembly in August 1572, Knox compromised and agreed to the proposals outlined in the Convention of Leith. This settlement should have been his zenith, but instead he died disillusioned, embittered that the great men of state had thwarted the full realization of his perfect church by their selfish opportunism. Still, when Knox died on 24 November 1572, these self-same nobles paid him lavish tributes. Whatever his shortcomings, they were richly deserved.

Bibliography: W. S. Reid, *Trumpeter of God*, 1978; J. Ridley, *John Knox*, 1968.

Ian B. Cowan

L

Lady Jane Grey Coup (1553). Lady Jane Grey was born in October, 1537 at Bradgate, Leicestershire, to Henry Grey, marquess of Dorset, and Frances, daughter of CHARLES BRANDON, duke of Suffolk, and HENRY VIII's sister, Mary. Her upbringing was strict, but she was well educated. Early in 1547 Jane joined the household of Henry VIII's widow, CATHERINE PARR, and after her death in September 1548 was the ward of her last husband, Sir THOMAS SEYMOUR (who wanted Jane to marry EDWARD VI), until his fall in January 1549. She returned to court upon her father's creation as duke of Suffolk on 11 October 1551. Suffolk was allied with JOHN DUDLEY, duke of Northumberland and leader of the PRIVY COUNCIL.

Jane's marriage to Northumberland's son, Guildford Dudley, on 21 May 1553 was part of the duke's attempt to keep himself in power and the Catholic princess MARY off the throne. By June he had persuaded Edward VI to overturn Henry VIII's Act of SUCCESSION, replacing Mary and ELIZABETH with Jane and her male heirs, despite the objections of several councillors and judges. Jane had to be bullied into the marriage by her father (she despised her in-laws even more than her parents) and was also reluctant to take the throne. Edward died on 6 July, but the council kept it secret until the eighth. On the ninth it informed Jane that she was queen, and she was so terrified that she fainted. The next day, however, she travelled to the Tower of London, where she issued a proclamation declaring her accession.

Northumberland's scheme soon fell apart. Mary escaped to Kenninghall, where on 9 July she wrote to the council and declared herself the rightful queen. While the council replied on 11 July that Jane was queen, Mary was soon safe at Framlingham Castle in Suffolk, where a growing army of followers joined her. On 14 July Northumberland led an opposing force from London, but Mary was proclaimed queen more and more widely. On the eighteenth the earls of Arundel, Bedford, Pembroke, Shrewsbury, and Worcester, Lords WILLIAM PAGET and

Cobham, and several others abandoned the Tower and agreed to proclaim Mary the next day, as did Suffolk. Not offering battle, Northumberland proclaimed her at Cambridge on the twentieth. Mary entered London on 3 August, with all her enemies imprisoned (against the council's wishes, Suffolk was released).

Northumberland, his oldest son (the earl of Warwick), and the marquess of Northampton were condemned for high treason on 18 August; Andrew Dudley, Sir John Gates, Henry Gates, and Sir Thomas Palmer were convicted the next day. Only Northumberland, Sir John Gates, and Palmer were actually executed, on 22 August. Lady Jane, Guildford Dudley and his brothers, Ambrose and Henry, and Archbishop THOMAS CRANMER were convicted of high treason on 14 November, but their sentences were not carried out. Jane might have escaped but for WYATT'S REBELLION in January and February 1554, in which her father was implicated. She and Dudley were beheaded on 12 February; Suffolk on the twenty-third.

Bibliography: Barrett L. Beer, *Northumberland: The Political Career of John Dudley, Earl of Warwick and Duke of Northumberland*, 1973; Alison Plowden, *Lady Jane Grey and the House of Suffolk*, 1986.

William B. Robison

Lambeth Articles (1595). In 1595 eight Heads of Houses in Cambridge wanted to silence William Barrett, a young chaplain of Gonville and Caius College. Barrett had preached against the CALVINIST ideas of predestination and struck at the heart of the Calvinist certainty of salvation. Calvinist doctrines had been challenged before in Elizabethan England, for example, at Oxford in the 1570s by Antonio de Corro. Now the Cambridge Heads, led by William Whitaker, Regius Professor of Divinity, obviously feared that Barrett was making too great an impact. They sought guidance and support from Archbishop JOHN WHIT-GIFT, who urged moderation. On 10 May 1595, however, the Heads forced Barrett to read a recantation. He did so in a manner many found offensive. The Heads, aware of the primate's uneasiness, appealed again to Whitgift and also to the university chancellor, WILLIAM CECIL, Lord Burghley. Burghley, persuaded by the Heads that university prestige was at stake and probably sympathizing with their theology, affirmed the Heads' right to proceed as they wished against Barrett. Whitgift was furious and wrote, telling both Burghley and the Heads that they were threatening the ecclesiastical authority he exercised under the queen. The Heads were in effect maintaining that their Calvinistic interpretation of the doctrine of the church in England as set out by the THIRTY-NINE ARTICLES was the only correct one.

Whitgift was quite in sympathy with some of Barrett's positions. He agreed with Barrett's interpretation of Article 17 of the Thirty-Nine Articles and so was not convinced of the certainty of salvation in the same way that Calvinists were. Also, Whitgift, Barrett, and Article 18 said that the reprobate contributed somewhat to their own condemnation, while for Calvinists there was no question of individual choice therein. Whitgift pointed out that these were debatable matters over which theologians might justifiably differ.

Barrett, heartened by Whitgift's stance, revoked his retraction on 2 July 1595. His theology was investigated in September, and Whitgift's study of the report revealed that in some points he was in agreement with Barrett. The archbishop now urged the Heads of the Houses to behave with greater circumspection and moderation. In November, Barrett appeared before Whitgift at Lambeth. Whitgift found some of Barrett's opinions "popish" and ordered a second retraction, although it seems unlikely that Barrett ever delivered it.

The most important result of Barrett's case was the Lambeth Articles, November 1595. One of the Heads, Whitaker, had come to Lambeth with nine propositions, to which Whitgift made some minor alterations, in line with Articles 17 and 18 of the Thirty-Nine Articles. Whitgift sent a manuscript copy of his articles to Cambridge. According to the primate, they were "our private judgements" but in line with the true doctrines of the church in England. He wanted nothing contrary to them taught in Cambridge and urged moderation in discussion of such issues.

On 5 December 1595 the queen told Whitgift to stop all discussions of this matter "tender and dangerous to weak ignorant minds." She disliked his allowing disputes over predestination. Some would not be silenced. During December and January, Peter Baro continued the dispute at Cambridge, in spite of Whitgift's vigilance. The Heads accused Baro of speaking against the Lambeth Articles, but despite this accusation it seems that Whitgift was sympathetic to Baro. All this foreshadowed the Arminian controversy of the seventeenth century. It also illustrated ELIZABETH's conception of the role of supreme governor: she, not the primate, was to be the ultimate arbiter of doctrine and whether it was to be debated.

Bibliography: H. C. Porter, *Reformation and Reaction in Tudor Cambridge*, 1956.

V. C. Sanders

Langside, Battle of (1568). After her incarceration in Lochleven Castle in June 1567, MARY, QUEEN OF SCOTS remained out of sight for almost a year. Her son, JAMES VI, was king, and her half-brother JAMES STEWART, earl of Moray, ruled as regent. It was long enough for the passions and the drama that had surrounded her fall to have died down. Unease and regret about her overthrow appeared. The Confederate Lords had appeared a massive and solid group in June 1567. It had very quickly broken up, with ARCHIBALD CAMPBELL, earl of Argyll, one of the earliest to have second thoughts. These were made easier for him and others by the relentless insistence on heaping the blame for the troubles on JAMES HEPBURN, earl of Bothwell; and Moray's government found the consequences dangerous enough to make an open statement in Parliament in December 1567 (which included a highly guarded reference to Mary's private letters) of the queen's guilt in the murder of HENRY STEWART, Lord Darnley, the first time this had been publicly asserted. It failed to have the desired effect.

Thus when Mary, with inside help, escaped from Lochleven in May 1568, she was no longer the isolated figure of the previous year. Moray was in Glasgow, with a small force. Mary moved to Hamilton and then toward Dumbarton. At Langside, outside Glasgow, the queen offered battle. With her superior numbers, she should have won. But she lost. In part, this was due to the skilled generalship of Morton and Kirkcaldy of Grange, in the regent's army. But far more damaging was the fact that her commander, Argyll, simply failed to lead the main part of her army into battle. Afterward, this failure was explained on medical grounds: a faint or an epileptic fit. Such extreme fortune for Moray is perhaps less than convincing; possibly in the moment of decision, Argyll's memory of the past caused him once again to have second thoughts and waver in his support for the queen.

It need not have been fatal. Mary still had a large number of supporters who did not waver, and indeed the war between King's Party and Queen's Party dragged on until 1573. But after Langside, the queen herself effectively doomed her party. She panicked and fled south to Galloway. From there, only two weeks after her escape and wholly against the advice of those with her, she crossed the Solway to England and was apparently entirely confident that Elizabeth would wave some sort of magic wand and restore her. It was the last in a long line of misjudgements.

Bibliography: Gordon Donaldson, *All the Queen's Men*, 1983; Maurice Lee, Jr., *James Stewart, Earl of Moray*, 1953; Jenny Wormald, *Mary Queen of Scots: A Study in Failure*, 1988.

                                                                                    Jenny Wormald

Late Elizabethan Crises. From about 1585 to sometime after the Midland Revolt of 1607 England experienced a series of interrelated economic and political crises accompanied by social tension and popular disturbances. Both contemporary observers and recent historians see this as part of a general crisis observable at the end of the sixteenth century when Western Europe suffered from apocalyptic visitations of famine, plague, war, and disorder.

The last decade of the sixteenth century saw an especially sharp increase in prices. During the period 1594-1597 the price of grain nearly doubled on average and did in fact do so in isolated regions—due in part to the sequence of bad harvests of those years. Longer-range but no less significant forces also pushed prices up; these included demographic pressure (especially in London and in regions characterized by sylvan, pastoral and proto-industrial economies) and the rising costs of war. In England the bad harvests mostly resulted in dearth, a situation in which shortages produced price increases of at least 50%, but some parts of the North and West Midlands actually experienced crises of subsistence, where dearth and famine combined to precipitate a mortality crisis, which is defined as a doubling of the death rate or worse. It is now clear that most of the mortality crises during this period were caused by EPIDEMIC diseases, such as plague and influenza, interacting in a complex way with dearth. These mortality crises had no long-term effect, and demographic pressure upon land resources and chronic underemployment remained greater problems.

Although it is difficult to establish a precise causal relationship between dearth and the incidence of popular disturbances, high food prices often accompanied outbreaks of rebellion and food rioting. Food riots during this period occurred in areas of clothing manufacture in Kent, East Anglia, and the West Country, which were especially vulnerable to a combination of dearth and unemployment resulting from trade depressions. In the Midlands and elsewhere protests against shortages of grain and high prices were more likely to result in anti-enclosure rioting. This was evident in both the Oxfordshire Rebellion of 1596 and the Midland Revolt of 1607. In the areas that gave rise to these disturbances, the protesters perceived that enclosures withdrew land from tillage and thus caused dearth. The leaders of these insurrections were treated with great severity, but the Crown also prosecuted landlords for causing the decay of tillage. The London Apprentices' Insurrection of June 1595 arose more from the harsh administration of justice than from high food prices.

The profits to be made in agriculture from rising food prices led to a whole complex of disputes resulting from alterations in land use, encroachments on commons and wastes, changing concepts of property and use rights, and seigneurial pressure upon tenants for higher rents and rationalized tenures. The peasantry's survival in the 1590s was threatened not only by harvest failures but also by an erratically fluctuating market. Bad harvests from 1594 to 1597 were preceded by a run of good or abundant harvests that glutted the market and depressed prices. Those farmers with adequate storage facilities could profit from the grain shortages and high prices that followed for the next four years, but many smallholders fell behind in their rents, had to borrow money for seed during the years of harvest failure, and were crushed by debt. Consequently, many lost their holdings and were reduced to the status of laborers or forced to seek employment elsewhere. A more obvious causal connection between high food prices and popular protest is to be found in the tendency of rising food prices and rapid population growth together to stimulate agricultural innovations and alterations in land use and to sharpen social conflict as manifested in the greater frequency of enclosure riots and rent and tenurial disputes between, approximately, 1590 and 1610.

The effects of war also heightened the perception of crisis. The last eighteen years of Elizabeth's reign saw increasing mobilization as military expeditions were sent overseas. The first build up came with the army sent to the Netherlands in 1585. The sailing of the SPANISH ARMADA brought a general muster but no fighting by land forces. Military expeditions were sent to France and PORTUGAL in 1589 and to CADIZ in 1596. The TYRONE REBELLION in Ireland in 1596 continued to require heavy recruiting until the end of the reign. Because the recruiting campaigns depended heavily on impressment of vagrants and prisoners, military discipline was bad, and the desertion rate was high. Demobilization exacerbated problems of underemployment and overpopulation—especially in London, where the population doubled in the last quarter of the sixteenth century. Vagrants and discharged soldiers and sailors were difficult to distinguish, and together they tramped the roads of southern England, crowded into London, and participated in disturbances such as the London Apprentices' Revolt of 1595.

In addition to the government's increasing concern about popular threats to public order, there were also indications of a revival of aristocratic unrest in the 1590s. Elizabeth was aging rapidly but refused to name a successor. Several conspiracies were hatched that sought to divert the royal succession. Factional struggles intensified as older patronage systems, headed by magnates such as ROBERT DUDLEY, earl of Leicester, broke up and began to reform in uncertain patterns. ROBERT DEVEREUX, earl of Essex's, followers vied with the clients of Sir ROBERT CECIL to determine who would succeed to the patronage wielded by the aged WILLIAM CECIL. The earl of Essex's inability to obtain rewards for his followers drove him into open revolt in 1601.

Bibliography: Peter Clark, *English Provincial Society from the Reformation to the Revolution: Religion, Politics and Society in Kent, 1500-1640*, 1977; Roger B. Manning, *Village Revolts: Social Protest and Popular Disturbances in England, 1509-1640*, 1988.

Roger B. Manning

Latimer, Hugh (c. 1490-1555). Preacher, bishop, and martyr, Hugh Latimer was born about 1490. He was educated at Cambridge, where he received his B.A. in 1510 and M.A. in 1514 and where, after he took priest's orders, he continued to teach. In 1522 he was named one of a small number of clergy licensed to preach anywhere in England.

During the 1520s he became acquainted with Protestants such as Thomas Bilney and their doctrine and, though he preached against Philip Melancthon, his orthodoxy came under suspicions. In 1525 he was called before Cardinal THOMAS WOLSEY to give an account of his doctrinal beliefs but was cleared of any taint of heresy. In 1529, however, he was preaching openly against certain abuses of Catholic doctrine. By 1530 he was known to favor the DIVORCE and had come to the attention of HENRY VIII, before whom he was called to preach. His increasingly Protestant leanings were becoming public knowledge by this time, but his favor at court spared him from too much trouble. He was brought up before the bishop of London in 1532 and forced to submit but in 1534 became a royal chaplain and a regular preacher at court. In 1535 he was named bishop of Worcester and was becoming such a prominent figure in the drive for religious reform that the rebels of the PILGRIMAGE OF GRACE targetted him and THOMAS CRANMER as clergy who ought to be handed over to them or banished. Instead he ended up as an interrogator of the captured rebel leader Thomas Darcy.

In 1537 he came out openly against the doctrine of purgatory stating that this was the chief reason for supporting the DISSOLUTION OF THE MONASTERIES. His evangelical fervor included the destruction of images and false roods in his diocese and enjoining of his clergy to obtain a Bible or a New Testament.

His career was at a crisis point in 1539. The growing Conservative reaction, as embodied in the ACT OF SIX ARTICLES, prompted him and his fellow bishop Nicholas Shaxton to resign their sees. He was arrested that year but released in 1540 on the condition that he leave London and refrain from preaching. The events of the next six years of his life are obscure, but he seems to have grown more radical in his religious opinions during this time. He was arrested again in 1546 and remained in the Tower of London until his release in 1547 at the accession of Edward VI.

Though he declined to take up the responsibilities of his bishop's office again, the Edwardian era was the high point of Latimer's influence. He was a renowned preacher and was frequently called upon to give sermons before the young king and his court. A favorer of the "COMMONWEALTH" ideal, Latimer used these sermons to lament economic and social ills such as ENCLOSURES, debasement of currency, and the growing intrusion of rich young men into UNIVERSITIES at the expense of poor men's sons. He was responsible in part for the imprisonment and deprivation of EDMUND BONNER, who scornfully called him "that merchant" and took a role in the condemnation of the heretic Joan Bocher. Latimer also spent a great deal of time in Grimesthorpe with the duchess of Suffolk.

At the accession of MARY I, Latimer found himself in trouble with the authorities. Given the opportunity to flee to safety on the Continent, he chose to remain in England and was jailed in the Tower. In March 1554 he was sent, along with Bishop NICHOLAS RIDLEY of London and Archbishop Thomas Cranmer of Canterbury, to Oxford, where he was condemned for heresy and excommunicated. In the autumn of 1555 the Marian government brought the three (to be known as the "Oxford Martyrs") out before a show trial of prominent Catholic theologians. Though Latimer, citing his advanced years and lack of opportunity for study, took little part in the arguments, he was a strong moral presence and encouragement to his fellows. He also made the telling observation that the most powerful argument on the side of his opponents was mere "poena legis." Sentenced to die on 16 October 1555, he told Ridley, his companion at the stake, "We shall this day light such a candle, by God's grace, in England, as I trust shall never be put out."

Bibliography: G. E. Corrie, ed., *The Works of Hugh Latimer*, 2 vols., 1844-1845; D. M. Loades, *The Oxford Martyrs*, 1970.

Gerald Bowler

Leicester's Expedition to the Netherlands (1585-1587). England's first formal military commitment in support of the rebels in the Netherlands, this expedition resulted from the TREATY OF NONSUCH. That agreement between the English and the Dutch called for a specific number of English soldiers, 5,000 foot and 1,000 horse, along with garrison troops for FLUSHING AND BRILL, and the assumption of overall command of English forces by a "gentleman of quality." ROBERT DUDLEY, earl of Leicester, was the "gentleman" appointed by Queen ELIZABETH.

Leicester was the foremost champion of the rebel cause in England, so it was unthinkable to the Dutch that anyone else would assume command.   His appointment officially began on 22 October 1585. From the beginning, concern was expressed about Elizabeth's limitations on Leicester's power as governor general, for she declined to give him absolute control. Eventually, the queen's restrictions complicated an already difficult enterprise.

Leicester landed ceremoniously at Flushing on 10 December and was welcomed by his nephew, Philip Sidney, the popular governor of Flushing, who had strong ties with the Netherlands. Leicester was also enthusiastically greeted by crowds at various towns until his arrival at The Hague, where he soon entered into detailed discussions with Dutch leaders regarding finance, politics, and military strategy. Eager to lock English support irrevocably to their cause, the Dutch urged upon Leicester the authority of governor and captain-general of the United Provinces, which he found tempting despite Elizabeth's limitations on his power. After lengthy conferences at Leiden, where he was advised by his lieutenants, Leicester accepted the new definition of his role. The mistake haunted him for the rest of his life.

Elizabeth was predictably enraged when she learned that the earl had ignored her orders and assumed greater responsibility. To leave no doubt about her displeasure, the queen sent Sir Thomas Heneage to the Netherlands with mortifying letters both to Leicester and the States-General raising the spectre of abrogating the Treaty of Nonsuch. In time, Elizabeth's fury abated sufficiently for her to issue new orders to Leicester, but his stature both in the Netherlands and in England suffered immeasurably from the queen's scornful attacks.

Leicester's expedition was plagued by more than the royal anger. He found himself continually quarrelling with ambitious Dutch politicians, struggling to maintain the supply of his army, and overwhelmed by the expenses that too often were paid from his own purse. At heart, the English commander seems to have believed that if he could wage a successful war and win a firm peace, then the smaller problems would resolve themselves. Accordingly, he concentrated on defeating Parma in the field.

The first English effort came with an attempt to relieve the siege of Grave in Brabant, a key city in the defense of the north. Before Leicester could make any headway, Parma pressed home an attack as he coaxed the surrender of the town with promises of favorable terms, so the English effort failed resoundingly. Throughout the summer of 1586, all attempts by Leicester to turn the military tide against Parma were similarly frustrated. Indeed, not only was Parma undefeated by the English despite the greater numbers at Leicester's command, but he actually improved his position by capturing such towns as Venloo and Neuss while the earl complained and did nothing. By September, Leicester managed to field a substantial army to relieve the siege of Rhineberg, but rather than confront Parma directly, he attempted to lure him into a vulnerable position by first capturing Duisburg and then marching on Zutphen. The threat to Zutphen spurred Parma to counter Leicester's thrust, and on 22 September 1586, a sharp skirmish occurred between some 500 of the earl's men and nearly 5,000 Spaniards. Reluctant to commit more of his troops, Leicester was rebuffed when the Spanish secured Zutphen, and to make matters worse, Leicester's nephew, Philip Sidney, was mortally wounded when a musket ball shattered his thigh. The defeat at Zutphen, combined with earlier setbacks and the death of the popular Sidney, disheartened the English army as much as it depressed the commander. Philip Sidney died of gangrene on 17 October; a few weeks later, Leicester received Elizabeth's permission to return to England and sailed from Flushing.

Robert Dudley's service in the Netherlands was not, however, quite finished. Despite his lacklustre performance, Leicester was sent back in July 1587 with a new army of 4,500 men and a war chest of £30,000. In less than a month, he failed to relieve the siege of Sluys, which fell to Parma on 26 July. Moreover, Leicester found himself once again at odds with the Dutch leaders, strapped for money to sustain his military effort, and discouraged by his inability to contend effectively with Parma. When, in October, an attempted coup by some of the earl's Dutch friends failed to seize Leiden, it was clear to all that it was pointless for Leicester to remain in the Netherlands. On 16 November 1587, Elizabeth sent John Herbert to advocate peace to the rebels, and he also carried a recall order for Leicester, who surrendered his military command to Peregrine Bertie, Lord Willoughby. Having failed utterly in his effort to lead the Dutch rebels to victory, Leicester never returned to the Netherlands.

Bibliography: F. Boas, *Sir Philip Sidney*, 1955; A. Haynes, *The White Bear*, 1987.

Ronald Pollitt

Lollardy. This nonconformist religious movement arose late in the fourteenth century, and John Wyclif (c. 1328-1384) became its chief spokesman. The origin of the word *Lollard* is obscure, but it appears to mean *mumblers*, a term of derision and a common designation for heretics. Archbishop William Courtenay in 1382 used it in denouncing the doctrines of Wyclif.

Lollardy began at Oxford University as a protest of scholars against ecclesiastical corruptions and abuses. Lollards stressed asceticism and the imitation of Christ as proper pursuits of the Christian life, and in doing so they criticized the wealth and opulence of the higher clergy. They denounced the reliance of the church upon the state for protection and enforcement of its laws. Wyclif and his disciples decried compulsory tithes, ecclesiastical fees for baptisms and funerals, and prayers for the dead. They contended that the church had forsaken Christ and the apostles, and Wyclif eventually called the pope Antichrist.

Wyclif and his associates believed that, for a Reformation of England, the BIBLE had to be available in the vernacular tongue. Together with Nicholas Hereford, a doctor of theology from Oxford, John Ashton, fellow of an Oxford college, and John Purvey of Lutterworth, Wyclif supervised the translation of the Lollard Bible from the Latin Vulgate. The first edition appeared in 1384. Even though there was no way to reproduce it mechanically, the Bible must have circulated widely, since over 100 copies are extant.

As they went about, the Lollards preached in any public place where they could get a hearing. They distributed tracts also and thereby spread Wyclif's influence to various parts of England. Despite ecclesiastical opposition, some noblemen protected and encouraged Lollards, and Leicester, London, and the west of England became centers of their strength.

After the CONVOCATION of the clergy condemned Lollard teachings in 1382, William Courteney, archbishop of Canterbury, led the effort to suppress the movement. Oxford expelled professors who supported Wyclif, but sympathy for his cause remained in the university community. King Richard II (1377-1399) at first did not support those prelates who sought to quell the Lollards, and Parliament in 1395 rejected Courtenay's demand that it require destruction of all copies of the English Bible. This encouraged the Lollards to vigorous activity, and sympathetic members of Parliament argued for adoption of the Lollard call for reform. The *Lollard Conclusions* appears to reflect the substance of this appeal. This document states that the Lollards objected to the material possessions and political positions of prelates and that they denied the sanctity of monastic vows, the doctrine of transubstantiation, and extra-biblical rites and ceremonies. They held that the king should reform the church by asserting his rule over the bishops. They wanted abolition of pilgrimages and the worship of images, and they insisted that all true priests preach God's word.

The Lollard appeal of 1395, which asked Parliament to authorize reform, actually provoked Richard II to oppose them, which was a heavy blow to their interests. In 1396 Thomas Arundel succeeded to the see of Canterbury and brought to that position an intense hatred of heretics. In 1399 Henry IV (1399-1413) took the throne and soon began persecuting Lollards with much more intensity than his predecessor had shown. DE HERETICO COMBURENDO, enacted in 1400, provided the legal basis for repression, and many executions followed. Lollardy, however, survived.

The Lollards found support among peasants who despised the financial exactions of the clergy, while Arundel pressed for elimination of nonconformity. The *Constitutiones Thomae Arundel* (1408) became the basis for a systematic assault on heretics. The *Constitutiones* banned preaching without episcopal approval and ordered the burning of all Lollard writings. Oxford University came under close scrutiny and soon ceased to be a place of overt sympathy for Wyclif's teachings.

Some noblemen continued to support the Lollards nevertheless, and Sir John Oldcastle was most prominent among them. He was a friend of Henry V, who became king in 1413. This monarch tried to persuade the nobleman to turn against the heretics. Oldcastle refused, and some of his supporters fought against the royal forces. Sir John was executed in 1417, and his death left the Lollards without an effective leader.

Despite persecution, Wyclif's teachings continued to command a following, as some priests promulgated them in their parishes. Lollard Bibles and other literature remained in circulation. In 1476 Oxford once again purged itself of suspected heretics, but St. Andrews University in Scotland had became comparable to Oxford as a site of heretical activity some time before that. It is clear that Lollardy was growing in its influence in Scotland right up to the threshold of the Protestant Reformation.

Although persecution forced them to become a clandestine movement, the Lollards of England continued their nonconformist activities and thereby prepared their country for the coming of Protestantism. Lutheran reformer ROBERT BARNES sold copies of WILLIAM TYNDALE's New Testament to Lollards from Steeple Bumpstead, and recent research indicates significant Lollard influence upon Tyndale himself. Lollards identified readily with the Protestant principles of *sola scriptura* and salvation *sola gratia*, which they held as legacy from Wyclif, even though the lack of theologians among them may have obscured somewhat the Oxford reformer's soteriology.

The survival of Lollardy into the sixteenth century shows that the English Reformation was not simply the product of an intellectual-theological movement from the Continent imposed by the Crown. When the Lollards contacted the early English Protestants, the experience infused the former with new energy. Practically all Lollards by then were common people without theological learning, and their movement sorely needed effective scholarly leadership, which Protestant Reformers were ready to supply. The Lollard-Protestant amalgamation featured the erection of a Reformed church upon a foundation laid by late medieval dissenters whose sixteenth century heirs progressively absorbed Protestant teachings.

Bibliography: Margaret Aston, *Lollards and Reformers*, 1984; John A. F. Thomson, *The Later Lollards, 1414-1520*, 1965.

James Edward McGoldrick

London. When Henry VII arrived at St. Paul's Cathedral to claim his throne on 3 September 1485, he rode into a city where not quite 50,000 people lived. Though small by Continental standards, London was by far the largest city in the realm, about five times as populous as Norwich, England's second-largest city. Nearly 120 years later when Henry's granddaughter, Elizabeth, lay on her deathbed, the capital's population had more than tripled in size, and by then it was one of only a handful of cities in Europe with at least 120,000 inhabitants. This phenomenal growth was due entirely to immigration, for London's death rate was so high and its overall birth rate so low that its population was unable even to reproduce itself, let alone to generate a net increase that averaged more than 1% per year across the twelve decades that the Tudors reigned.

So strong was the capital's magnetism that one of every eight people born in England who survived to adulthood lived in London for some years. They came in droves. In the mid-sixteenth century about 3,000 immigrants streamed in through the city's gates each year, half of them young people in late teens and early twenties arriving to begin apprenticeships and enter domestic service, though many would stay for only a few years. They came from all over England. Indeed, London's migration field was unusually large: in the 1550s young men travelled an average of 115 miles to apprentice there, one-third coming from places at least 150 miles away. They were young and old, rich and poor. In his famous *Survey of London*, published in 1598, John Stow proudly described London as a melting pot, its people "by birth for the most part a mixture of all counties, by blood gentlemen, yeomen, and of the basest sort without distinction." Some came because wages were higher in London than elsewhere in England, others to take advantage of the capital's liberal poor relief policy, but most probably came for the same reason that draws people to major urban centers to this day: to seek their fortunes in "the big city."

Throughout the realm London's influence was felt. Indeed, what made London unique among Europe's major cities was the extent to which it functioned as a capital city. With the seat of royal government and of Parliament only a mile away in Westminster, London had always played an important role in English politics and government, a status enhanced by developments during the Tudor period that further integrated England politically and administratively and thus increased that power of institutions and places at its center. The city's political influence was also based on the wealth of its citizens; London alone accounted for more than one-half of the revenue from taxes levied upon cities, Londoners loaned Tudor monarchs hundreds of thousands of pounds, and from its trade came more than two-thirds of the Crown's customs revenues. Equally important was London's role as the economic capital of England, the port through which passed as much as three-quarters of the nation's imports and exports, the hub of its domestic trade network, the home of the ROYAL EXCHANGE and other financial and commercial services. London was also England's biggest market. Within a circle of counties that grew larger as domestic trade expanded, the demands of the capital's population stimulated production not only of grain, dairy products, meat, and other foodstuffs but also of coal and raw materials for manufacturing. London was a rich source of capital and leadership for industrial and especially commercial ventures, such as the East India, Levant, and other companies that launched England's quest for an empire overseas.

London loomed so large in the life of the nation because so many roads led there, especially if in "metropolitan" London one includes Westminister and the suburbs nearby. People came in pursuit of power and patronage, of offices and MONOPOLIES; they came to purchase or settle disputes over land, in ever-increasing numbers from the 1540s when the sale of Crown and church lands began in earnest; the gentry and aristocracy flocked to London to see and be seen during its popular social season. London was the legal capital of England. Before King's Bench, Common Pleas, and other courts people pressed suits that multiplied as much as tenfold during the litigious Elizabethan era, and to the Inns of Court young men came to learn the COMMON LAW. London was arguably England's religious capital as well, for though Canterbury was its titular capital, the province of Canterbury was administered from London. One of the ports through which the new religion was introduced into England, London provided a haven for Protestantism in its early years, a base for its conversion of the southeast. The Inns of Court, GRESHAM COLLEGE, and other institutions made London a center of higher education, the only one of any note outside Cambridge and Oxford, and its grammar schools were models for schools founded elsewhere. London was also a center of vocational education, training a significant share of England's non-agricultural labor force. In the mid-sixteenth century more than 7,000 young men were serving apprenticeships in the city at any one time, but more than half of them chose not to finish their terms, emigrating instead to towns and villages throughout the realm and bringing with them valuable skills learned in the capital.

Thus the Tudor decades were a crucial period in London's history, an age of enormous growth and great changes. It is easy, however, to overstate the capital's modernity and to forget that it remained medieval in many respects. Most people lived within its ancient walls, still standing and encircling little more than a square mile, and thus physically London was a small city; one could walk from the Tower in the east end to St. Paul's in the west in half an hour. In many respects the nature and functions of municipal government had changed little since the fourteenth century. London was still divided into twenty-five wards, at least until 1550, when the city purchased the rights to Southwark from the Crown and a new ward was added on the south bank of the Thames. Each ward was administered by an alderman who also served on the court of aldermen, the city's executive body. Aldermen performed important judicial and legislative functions as well, the latter because the powers of the court of common council, the legislature, were limited, though during Elizabeth's reign the 212 common councilmen began to play a larger role in municipal government. The routine work of government was organized throught the 242 precincts into which wards were divided, the 111 parishes, and especially the roughly 100 livery companies, descendants of medieval guilds. Companies not only regulated the economy but also collected taxes, administered courts, provided social services, and organized feasts, processions, etc. As they had been since the early fourteenth century, the companies' powers were based on their control over access to citizenship, "the freedom," for only by joining a company could a Londoner become a citizen and thus exercise the franchise, set up a business, and enjoy other economic and political rights. Freemen were not an exclusive elite, since roughly three-quarters of the city's men were citizens; in practice there were few freewomen in Tudor London.

Londoners were aware that their city was changing, becoming less medieval, more modern, and not everyone welcomed those changes. People elsewhere in England also had mixed reactions to the capital's growth. Many registered their approval by voting with their feet and flocking there in ever-increasing numbers; others resented the concentration of economic power in London, especially outports that complained that it robbed them of trade. Historians too disagree about the consequences of London's transformation from a small city by Continental standards to one of the largest urban centers in all of Europe. Some argue that it produced a massive increase in social and economic problems, while others maintain that the capital was able to accommodate its demographic growth without much difficulty for much of the period, for not until the late sixteenth century do complaints about overpopulation figure in contemporary sources. In the 1580s the Crown first voiced its concerns about the aldermen's ability to govern and provision the capital's burgeoning population, but two decades of statutes and proclamations failed to slow its expansion, and thus it was a resigned JAMES VI and I who predicted wryly that "soon London will be all England."

How did London fare under the Tudors? The growth of population contributed to a near fourfold increase in retail prices in London, as it did elsewhere in England, but more than two-thirds of that increase occurred during two brief periods of severe inflation in the 1540s and 1590s, and thus throughout the bulk of the Tudor period the rate of inflation averaged only 0.5% per year, a modest trend to which most Londoners were able to adapt. London experienced some unemployment as its economy struggled at times to keep pace with demographic growth, but here too the picture was far from bleak. Driven by the demands of an expanding population and a threefold increase in exports of CLOTH, most of which was bound for Antwerp, whence it was reexported to consumers in Western Europe, the economy thrived during the first half of the period, but cloth exports peaked in the early 1550s and then declined, creating unemployment among the one-third of London's men employed in finishing and marketing cloth. The end of the great Tudor boom in cloth exports hurt the economy, but it recovered gradually during Elizabeth's reign. As the national market became more integrated and domestic trade expanded, the city's commerce was sustained and its shipbuilding industry was stimulated by shifting its focus from exports to imports and from overseas to domestic trade. The economy also profited from London's role as the capital of England. Its many functions attracted thousands of people each year, and the money they spent there stimulated employment in the distributive, professional, and service sectors of the economy. London was a manufacturing center as well. Clothing, leather, metal, and other industries, employing three-fifths of the labor force, benefited from the demands of the city's growing population and its emergence as a center of consumption. During the Elizabethan decades, therefore, London's economy responded to the challenges posed by the growth of its population by changing its structure, becoming more diversified and thus less dependent upon commerce, allowing it to keep pace with demographic growth and hence to maintain a degree of economic prosperity for most of the Tudor period.

Many historians see Tudor London differently, arguing that the rise in prices was greater than suggested above, that the gap between demographic and economic growth was much wider, and that as a result as many as two-thirds of its people were impoverished. Unquestionably there was poverty in the capital, but contemporary surveys indicate that in most years people receiving poor relief amounted to no more than 10-15% of the population. The fact that at least two-thirds of all householders were able to pay taxes amounting to several weeks' income also suggests that most Londoners were situated between the extremes of rich and poor, the "middling sort" who, according to Stow, "do far exceed both the rest." Over the issue of London's stability historians are similarly divided. Some claim that the capital was notorious for outbreaks of popular disorder during the Tudor period, its streets filled with turbulence and riot, but there is no evidence of either a pattern of pervasive instability or a single rebellious disorder. Not once did the capital experience a popular rising aimed at overthrowing or even challenging the government or the established social order, and unorganized outbreaks of serious unrest, such as EVIL MAY DAY, were very rare and involved little or no loss of life and minimal destruction of property. Most disturbances were brawls involving small numbers of youths, and even they occurred infrequently.

The reasons for London's stability are many, not the least important of which was the fact that under the Tudors England was a relatively prosperous and remarkably stable country, and consequently the capital did not have to struggle to maintain stability in the midst of rebellion, religious strife, or economic depression. Yet London was not without problems or devoid of tensions, and thus within the walls there were factors that promoted stability. Wards, parishes, and companies provided institutionalized means of resolving conflicts among groups in society, such as journeymen and masters, and between individuals as well. Their courts dealt with civil and quasi-criminal offenses and provided ordinary people with a system of justice that was accessible and capable of settling a wide range of disputes between buyer and seller, employer and employee, mother and son. These components of the urban substructure formed the framework of life in the capital, a network of hundreds of geographical and occupational communities to which men and, in many respects, women belonged and in which they formed important social bonds. Collectively they provided a stable foundation for London society, services, and support for its people, and for those reasons played a crucial role in maintaining stability. Considerable opportunities for social mobility also contributed; after completing their apprenticeships, four of every five men who lived in London for at least a decade (as most men did) eventually set up their own shops, and one-third entered the livery, the elite of their companies. Hence the promise of opportunities for advancement, though clearly not fulfilled for all, united the interests of various social groups and maintained their common commitment to the stability of the society in which they lived. Finally, the attitudes of the capital's people, including its rulers, toward poor relief, foreigners, and other problems the city faced were characterized more by adaptation than inflexibility, by a willingness to undertake remedial action, and thus played a role as well in preserving the stability that was London's signal characteristic during the Tudor period.

Bibliography: I. Archer, *The Pursuit of Stability: Social Relations in Elizabethan London*, 1991; A. L. Beier and R. Finlay, eds., *London 1500-1700. The Making of the Metropolis*, 1986; S. Brigden, *London and the Reformation*, 1990; R. Finlay, *Population and the Metropolis. The Demography of London 1580-1650*, 1981; F. F. Foster, *The Politics of Stability. A Portrait of the Rulers in Elizabethan London*, 1977; S. Rappaport, *Worlds Within Worlds: Structures of Life in Sixteenth-Century London*, 1989.

Steve Rappaport

London, Treaty of (1518). HENRY VIII and Cardinal THOMAS WOLSEY conceived of and promoted this international agreement, which pledged France, England, the empire, Spain, the papacy, and many of Europe's minor powers to keep the peace perpetually and to unite against any aggressor.

Henry VIII had spent the first years of his reign fighting Louis XII in the ANGLO-FRENCH WAR OF 1512-1514 and so maintained England's traditional pattern of alliances and animosities. He was also prepared to continue, at least, indirect hostilities with the new French king Francis I when England's most important ally, the Spanish king Ferdinand of Aragon, died in 1516. His successor Charles I (soon to be Emperor Charles V) made a separate treaty with France at Noyon. The emperor Maximilian followed suit and signed the Peace of Cambrai with France. Henry VIII and his new chief minister Wolsey found themselves diplomatically isolated, with France ominously seeking influence in England's neighbor, Scotland. As a result, Wolsey was forced during 1517 to seek better relations between his master and Francis I.

The entire context of European international relations in 1517 was pushing strongly for a general peace within Christendom. HUMANIST scholars increasingly promoted the medieval ideal of unity and peace among Christians. Practical considerations also dampened the warlike enthusiasms of rulers. The costs of warfare had grown almost prohibitively, and the series of wars fought in Europe during the twenty-five years prior to 1518 had left the belligerents exhausted. But the most telling argument for a general European peace was the need to unite the Christian nations against the renewed threat from the Ottoman Turks.

Pope Leo X had been concerned about Turkish aggression since the beginning of his pontificate in 1514. He had repeatedly urged Christian unity and a renewal of crusading. On 6 March 1518 he began another appeal for a five-year truce and a crusade against the Turks. Legates carried this appeal to the great powers of Europe, including England. Unfortunately for Leo X, Henry VIII and Wolsey managed to take over his effort and make it their own. They began by refusing the papal legate Lorenzo Campeggio admission into England until Wolsey was made a co-legate. From that point, the crafty Wolsey pushed Campeggio aside as chief negotiator of the truce.

England and France quickly reached an agreement on 2 October 1518. They were soon joined by Spain, the pope, the empire, and twenty lesser powers. But instead of agreeing to the five-year truce proposed by the papacy, they made an international agreement under Wolsey's presidency. All the signatories agreed to unphold the peace and to act collectively against any nation that acted an an aggressor. England and France also reached separate agreements that returned Tournai to France in exchange for a pension to England and promised Mary, Henry VIII's duaghter, in marriage to the French Dauphin.

Initially the Treaty of London inspired high hopes among intellectuals, and it did managed to preserve the peace for thirty months. It also greatly enhanced the prestige of Wolsey and his king. The continuing rivalries between the rulers of Europe, however, doomed the treaty to ultimate failure. Charles I of Spain was elected Emperor Charles V of Germany in 1519 after Emperor Maximilian's death. This success made Charles by far the most powerful ruler in Europe and consequently aroused the fears and jealousy of Francis I. It also made the two rulers direct rivals for control of the duchy of Milan. So instead of thinking about peace among Christians and a crusade against the Turks, both Francis I and Charles V began to seek allies for their own looming conflict. There was nothing Wolsey and Henry VIII could do to stave off the conflict.

Increasingly England leaned toward the imperial camp in spite of supposedly impartial meetings with Charles V and with Francis I at the famous FIELD OF CLOTH OF GOLD in June 1520. Francis I grew suspicious and during the fall of 1520 reconquered Spanish Navarre for the Albret family while Charles V's attention was focused on the revolt of the Communeros in Spain. Charles V accused France of breaking the Treaty of London, and war began in 1521, ending the universal peace. Henry VIII continued to claim to be an impartial arbitrator to the French at the conference at CALAIS even as an alliance was concluded with the emperor in the TREATY OF BRUGES, which ultimately resulted in the ANGLO-FRENCH WAR OF 1522-1525.

Bibliography: Susan Doran, *England and Europe 1485-1603*, 1986; Garrett Mattingly, "An Early Nonaggression Pact," *Journal of Modern History* 10 (March 1938): 1-30.

Ronald Fritze

The Lopez Plot (1594) was uncovered amid the suspicions and court rivalries following William the Silent's assassination. After ROBERT DEVEREUX, earl of Essex, failed to have Sir Francis Bacon appointed attorney-general, he sought revenge against his rivals, Sir ROBERT CECIL and WILLIAM CECIL, Lord Burghley.

An agent of the Spanish government, Estaban Ferrera, visited the queen's chief physician, an elderly Jew named Roderigo Lopez. Essex despised Lopez for revealing that Essex had syphilis. Suddenly Essex had Ferrera arrested and had all Spanish mail seized. A smuggled letter addressed to Ferrera, with vague references to payments and jewels, was intercepted. The interrogations of Ferrera and the smuggler revealed plots against Don Antonio of Portugal that included Tinoco, a Spanish agent in Belgium who had recently been arrested by Burghley and who had been carrying an unusually large amount of money, jewelry, and two vague letters addressed to Ferrera.

Essex, Burghley, and Robert Cecil subsequently questioned Tinoco, who admitted that he was sent to bribe Dr. Lopez to serve Philip II. The three had Dr. Lopez arrested and his home searched and they interrogated him. The physician defended himself so well that Robert Cecil immediately informed the queen of Essex's harsh treatment of her personal physician and she severely rebuked Essex.

After fuming for two days, Essex announced that he had discovered a plot centering on Lopez's poisoning the queen. Ferrera and Tinoco were coerced into admitting complicity while Essex's agents stirred up anti-Spanish and anti-semitic hysteria among the populace. Robert Cecil and Lord Admiral Charles Howard interrogated Lopez, who collapsed under their attack and affirmed all of their assertions.

Within forty-eight hours Dr. Lopez was convicted of treason, his recantations were ignored, and his execution sentence was loudly applauded by angry spectators. It is doubtful that Elizabeth or the Cecils believed Lopez guilty. Essex gained favor with the crowds, restored his influence at court, and avenged himself against Lopez without favorably impressing the queen and alerting his enemies to his disquieting ability to stir up the mobs and use them to further his political goals.

Bibliography: Martin A. S. Hume, "The so-called conspiracy of Dr. Ruy Lopez," *Transactions of the Jewish Historical Society of England* 6 (1908-1910): 32-55.

Sheldon Hanft

Lord Lieutenant. Created in the medieval period to be a temporary military position responsible for leading forces raised in the counties, the office of lord lieutenant became a permanent and integral part of local administration during the course of the sixteenth century. This transformation of the nature of the office was accompanied by an increase in its administrative duties, which were expanded beyond the military. Until the last two decades of ELIZABETH I's reign, however, the central government continued to regard the office of the lieutenancy as an ad hoc institution to be used in response to immediate problems of the government. Only during the years 1585-1603 did the office gain true permanence, and only then was it systematically involved in everyday local administration.

Lords lieutenant were employed by HENRY VII and HENRY VIII almost solely to command militia raised to suppress internal unrest. Commissions of array were issued to raise the forces and to authorize the lords lieutenant's command of them. Whether to put down the notorious PILGRIMAGE OF GRACE in 1536 and 1537 or to quell local disturbances in Dorset and Somerset nine years later, these early lieutenants served temporarily and simply as military commanders charged with pacifying specific districts. The Crown appointed noblemen and powerful commoners to the lieutenancy, selecting them for both their allegiance to the monarch and their local prestige.

During EDWARD VI's reign (January 1547-July 1553), EDWARD SEYMOUR, the protector Somerset, issued distinctive commissions of lieutenancy but did not deviate from his predecessors' policies concerning the temporary and predominantly military nature of the office. JOHN DUDLEY, duke of Northumberland, Seymour's successor, significantly altered the nature of the lieutenancy.

Lords lieutenant now took charge of the overall supervision of the county musters: they were to supervise the yearly militia exercises, train the soldiers, and administer the levies. In addition, non-military administrative functions were added to their local powers. The lord lieutenant had to implement martial law within the jurisdiction of his commission and had to enforce the use of the BOOK OF COMMON PRAYER. These new judicial and social duties marked the first stage in the lieutenancy's rise to the top of the local government hierarchy. Northumberland also commissioned a greater number of lords lieutenant for the shires (or groupings of shires) in the last four years of Edward VI's reign. This action provided more regularity and permanency to the office. However, the temporary nature of the lieutenancy remained: the lieutenants were commissioned each summer but were invariably terminated by mid-fall.

The reign of MARY I (July 1553-November 1558) brought a temporary halt to the expansion of the lieutenancy. Marian lords lieutenant continued to carry out their customary military duties—the administration of the general musters and the subduing of rebellious areas. Notably, though, the reign witnessed an increasing opposition by various localities to lords lieutenant's authority. Some corporate towns and chartered liberties claimed that the commissions granting the lords lieutenant jurisdiction throughout specified counties infringed on their customary and Crown-granted independence from outside interference. The Crown and council preferred to seek compromises between these feuding authorities while never relinquishing the right to grant an overriding authority to the lords lieutenant.

Elizabethan policy-makers resumed a slow and gradual expansion of the powers of the lieutenancy. From 1558 to 1585 the Crown and council delegated the general oversight of the county magistracy and their extensive out-of-sessions work to the lords lieutenant. Still, the lord lieutant remained but one of several local administrative officials. Elizabeth's lords lieutenant became the chief link between the central government and the localities. This duality of representation became a unique, although not always a successful or non-contentious, feature of the office. Appointments continued to be ad hoc and with an unstable tenure. Commissions tended to be granted for a single county or two counties joined specifically for a single lieutenancy. Perhaps the most significant development related to the lieutenancy before the years 1587-1588 involved the provision of deputy lieutenants. These special assistants to the lord lieutenant emerged as regular officials in response to the increase in the non-military administrative duties delegated to the lords lieutenant. Technically Crown appointees, deputies in practice were nominated by the lord lieutenant from among the leading local gentlemen. By 1569 the deputy lieutenant had gained formal recognition as a Crown official, and in the following quarter-century rose in status and acquired more political power while undertaking an increasingly larger share of the burden of local administration. Lastly, deputy lieutenants enjoyed the full power and authority of a lord lieutenant whenever their superior was absent from the district.

The years c. 1587-1603 marked the lord lieutenancy's tranformation from being an occasional and temporary appointment to lifelong tenure in office. As this change took place, the lords lieutenant and their deputies also became burdened with more socio-economic and judicial duties. The supervision of religious conformity (particularly RECUSANCY), the regulation of the local grain trade, assessing and collecting subsidies, addmiministering poor relief, and the oversight of regulations concerning the eating of meat during Lent all came under the jurisdiction of the lords lieutenant and particularly their deputies. In addition, as the supreme local military governor, the lords lieutenants received ever more military duties; contributions had to be levied for the supply of arms and armor, for coat and conduct money, and for the salary of the muster master.

By the close of the Tudor era, the lords lieutenant had become the chief local administrative official of the Crown. They clearly headed the hierarchy of county officers that included the deputy lieutenants, JUSTICES OF THE PEACE, other ad hoc commissioners, militia captains and the muster master, and a host of lesser officials. Empowered by Crown commission, directed by the PRIVY COUNCIL, leading the local government—the lords lieutenant truly stood as the key link between central and local government.

Bibliography: W. P. D. Murphy, ed., *The Earl of Hertford's Lieutenancy Papers 1603-1625*, 1969; Gladys S. Thomson, *Lords Lieutenant in the Sixteenth Century: A Study in Tudor Local Administration*, 1923.

Eugene J. Bourgeois II

Lutheranism in England. As the careers of England's major Protestant Reformers illustrate, the importation of HUMANIST ideals and canons of scholarship preceded the appearance of evangelical theology in that country. Erudite humanists, the great Erasmus among them, visited England from the Continent, and English churchmen sometimes went to the European mainland to study with leaders of the New Learning. Such contacts led devout, educated clergymen to apply the humanist methods of research and teaching to the reform of their church. Their objective at first was to overcome clerical ignorance by improving the education of priests, who could then teach laymen the fundamental doctrines of Christianity. In this way English humanist-churchmen hoped to combat ecclesiastical corruption and abuses and to stimulate the piety of the people.

Although learned, concerned scholars sought only moral and administrative reforms, their experiences on the Continent brought them into contact with Lutheran theology early in the sixteenth century. German efforts at reform included correction of ecclesiastical abuses, but they demanded a complete review of traditional dogmas on the basis of *sola scriptura* as well. At the University of Wittenberg the application of the New Learning to the study of the Christian faith had led to a renunciation of papal supremacy and the formulation of a system of doctrine in which salvation *sola gratia* and justification *sola fide* were the keystone. These teachings spread widely, and soon the writings of Martin Luther appeared in England, to which they had been carried clandestinely by German merchants of London's STEELYARD community. In these ways Lutheranism came to England, where the legacy of John Wycliffe and the LOLLARDS had prepared the country for the Protestant Reformation. By the 1520s church authorities were apprehending a number of common people for praising Martin Luther and promoting his teachings.

The initial center of Lutheran activities in England was at Cambridge, where an informal circle of scholars gathered occasionally at the WHITE HORSE INN. Prominent among them were ROBERT BARNES, Thomas Bilney, John Frith, HUGH LATIMER, THOMAS CRANMER, MATTHEW PARKER, and William May, several of whom became martyrs for the Protestant faith. All of them exerted lasting influence upon the development of the Church of England, of which some became bishops. Barnes seems to have been the leader of these "Cambridge Germans," as the group became known. Participants studied and discussed Luther's writings and the New Testament in the version of WILLIAM TYNDALE even after the government proscribed heretical literature.

It appears that at first the White Horse gatherings attracted devout Catholics who sought to correct abuses by overcoming clerical ignorance, as Erasmus advocated. Gradually, however, a rift developed within this circle as the members acquired an understanding of Luther's doctrine of salvation, which featured his belief in the impotency of the human will to seek God. In 1524 and 1525 Erasmus and Luther attacked each other on this point in books entitled *De Liberio Arbitrio* and *De Servo Arbitrio*. Those who, with Erasmus, affirmed the priority of human freedom remained Catholics. Those who adhered to Luther's belief in the total depravity of man's sinful nature and his inability to contribute toward his salvation became Protestant Reformers.

By the time the White Horse scholars became divided, the government had banned importation and circulation of Luther's works, but Bilney, Barnes, and Latimer preached boldly against corruptions and superstitions and thereby encountered episcopal opposition. Barnes may have been the first of the White Horse group publicly to espouse tenets that the ecclesiastical establishment deemed heretical. When he denied that Christians have the right to sue one another in civil court, he incurred the charge of Anabaptism. Barnes was arrested at the same time that Cardinal THOMAS WOLSEY was attempting to destroy all Lutheran books and unauthorized versions of the Bible. Barnes did, in fact, distribute Tyndale's New Testament. After a period of consequent confinement, Barnes escaped to Germany, where Wittenberg was a refuge for English Protestants.

The English New Testament of William Tyndale first appeared in 1526 (see ENGLISH BIBLE). Soon German merchants in London were distributing the English Scriptures, together with Luther's writings. In addition to rendering the New Testament into English, Tyndale composed theological treatises that became effective means to disseminate Luther's doctrines and his own interpretations of the Christian faith. These treatises espoused almost all the major principles of Lutheranism, although Tyndale differed with Luther concerning the Sacraments. That he was a major force in the transmission of Luther's teachings to England is undeniable, even though he shared many concerns with the Lollards and developed views of the Sacraments that became characteristic of the Reformed persuasion.

The third important figure in the transmission of Lutheranism to England was John Rogers (1500-1555), a Cambridge graduate who became chaplain to the MERCHANT ADVENTURERS in Antwerp. There he became acquainted with Tyndale. Rogers was proficient in German and soon settled in Wittenberg and was a pastor there from 1537 to 1547. When EDWARD VI ascended the throne, Rogers returned to England, but he became one of the early victims of the MARIAN REACTION. Rogers completed the translation of the Old Testament that Tyndale left unfinished at his death. This version, known as the Matthew

Bible, contains prefaces and notes that express Lutheran interpretations. It appears that Hans Luft, a Wittenberg printer, published this edition of the Scriptures.

Lutheran dogmatic writings appeared in England through the work of Richard Taverner, who in 1536 translated the *Augsburg Confession of Faith* and Philip Melanchthon's *Apology* for that confession. English and German scholars referred to these documents often during discussions pursuant to an Anglo-German diplomatic agreement that was never concluded. The *Apology* was especially influential when the English compiled the TEN ARTICLES, and Thomas Cranmer's *Institution of a Christiam Man*, commonly called the BISHOPS' BOOK, bears the impress of Melanchthon's *Apology* and Luther's catechisms. Lutheran themes are prominent in the FORTY-TWO and THIRTY-NINE ARTICLES of religion too, despite the growing influence of Reformed theology at the time they were adopted.

The first Protestant textbook on systematic theology to appear in English was the *Common Places* of Erasmus Sarcerius, which Richard Taverner translated from Latin on order of THOMAS CROMWELL. Sarcerius composed *Common Places* to instruct pastors who had little understanding of theology. Taverner translated and edited some postils of Sarcerius to assist English preachers also. The doctrinal character of these homiletical materials is decidedly Lutheran. During the reign of Edward VI (1547-1553) Reformed theology gained ascendency in England, but Cranmer continued to study Lutheran literature, which affected his sermons and catechisms as well as his *Articles of Religion* and the BOOK OF COMMON PRAYER. The order of baptism in the prayer book closely resembles the Lutheran original, as does the ceremony for marriage. Editors of later versions of these documents, however, purged some of the Lutheran elements.

Although translations of Luther's works and those of his co-workers Melanchthon, Johann Brenz, Andreas Osiander, and Sarcerius circulated in England beginning in the reign of Henry VIII, the Lutheran interpretation of the Sacraments did not enjoy broad acceptance there. Zwinglian and CALVINIST views were more popular, and during the reign of Elizabeth I (1558-1603) some translators altered the text of Lutheran books so as to remove their teachings about the Sacraments. This alteration may have occurred because Protestant exiles fleeing from persecution under Mary Tudor (1553-1558) had gone mostly to areas of the Continent where the Reformed version of Protestantism predominated. When some of them became bishops in the Elizabethan church, they brought their Calvinistic persuasion with them.

ANGLICANISM, as it established its doctrinal position under Elizabeth I, became a Reformed body in which Calvinistic teachings achieved great prominence. The foundations of that church are, nevertheless, generally Lutheran.

Bibliography: Henry Eyster Jacob, *The Lutheran Movement in England*, 1890; James Edward McGoldrick, *Luther's English Connection*, 1979; N. S. Tjernagel, *Henry VIII and the Lutherans*, 1965.

                                                    James Edward McGoldrick

M

Marches of Wales, Council in the. The original council in the Marches was formed by Edward IV to rule in the name of his son, Prince Edward. HENRY VII created his son and heir, Arthur, Prince of Wales in 1489, and in late 1501 the prince took up residence at Ludlow but died after five months. In that brief period, and following the precedent set by Edward IV, the council governed the lands of the principality and certain lordships in the Marches and supervised the administration of justice in the borderland. From 1502 the council continued to function as the king's commissioners, an arrangement that was not altered during the principate of HENRY VIII or after his accession to the throne in 1509. The English border shires had been encompassed within the council's jurisdiction from an early stage of its history, and from 1518 it exercised a limited authority over private as well as royal lordships. Its criminal jurisdiction was further enhanced as part of THOMAS WOLSEY's reforms of 1525, when Princess MARY took up residence at Ludlow Castle for two years as nominal head of the council.

Initially THOMAS CROMWELL addressed the problem of lawlessness in the Marches in late 1533 by appointing the ruthless Bishop Rowland Lee as lord president of the council. Abandoning this draconian approach in 1536, Cromwell coordinated administrative reforms for the whole of WALES. However, though the council in the Marches did not feature in the "Act of Union" (27 Hen. VIII, c. 26), it was called on to implement its provisions, and the consolidating measure of 1543 (34 and 35 Hen. VIII, c. 26) conferred on the prerogative court a standing in statute law.

The early Tudors had favored rule by a bishop as lord president, but after 1547 (with two brief exceptions in the reign of Mary) lay presidents were appointed who also acted as LORDS LIEUTENANT for all the Welsh shires. During ELIZABETH's reign, the civil jurisdiction of the council expanded more rapidly than its criminal juristiction. It may well be that the establishment of the rule of law after the "union" increased the litigiousness of the Welsh. Formerly deprived of impartial justices by intimidation or inequality before English law, the Welsh did not hesitate to press their claims before the new courts. As the nearest major court, the council at Ludlow acquired a reputation for cheap and expeditious justice. In criminal matters, it had the power, not shared by other prerogative courts, to impose the death penalty. Feuding among officials and some corruption partially marred the council's record as a court.

In the field of administration, the council acted as a police force, a civil service, and a military headquarters. Its role as an intermediary between the PRIVY COUNCIL and the local communities and courts became more important after the "union." It grew in size in the latter half of the century, but there were many absentees, especially among the lawyer-councillors. As it developed the character of a vice-regal court, it played a significant role in the interaction of local and court factions, particularly those of ROBERT DUDLEY, earl of Leicester, and ROBERT DEVEREUX, earl of ESSEX. Meanwhile, the English border shires had grown restive under the authority of the council and before 1600 were making a common cause with common lawyers of the Westminster courts in their campaign to restrict the jurisdiction of the prerogative court at Ludlow to the Welsh shires.

Bibliography: C. A. J. Skeel, *The Council in the Marches of Wales*, 1904; Penry Williams, *The Council in the Marches of Wales under Elizabeth I*, 1958.

P. R. Roberts

Marian Exiles. When the Marian regime began to restore Catholicism to England, one method it used to neutralize its opponents was to force them out of the country. The European Protestant theologians, such as John a Lasco and Peter Martyr Vermigli, who had flocked to England during the reign of Edward VI, were given notice to leave, and the colonies of foreign Protestant artisans were also quickly driven out. A similar method was employed on domestic Protestants, who were warned of impending arrest but given sufficient time and opportunity to make their escape. By the end of 1553 at least 800 English men, women, and children, laymen and clerics, began making their way to the safety of Protestant enclaves on the Continent. Here they sought not only physical safety and the right to practice their own form of worship but also the chance to define and preserve their national religion for the day of its eventual return to England.

These Marian exiles went first to the Protestant cities of Strasbourg and Frankfurt, where they had contacts and the assurance of a friendly reception. Later colonies were also established at Emden, Zurich, and Wesel while smaller groups emigrated to Worms and Duisburg. At Frankfurt, a quarrel broke out among the exiles that seems to have foreshadowed religious arguments of the Elizabethan period. Many of the Englishmen in that city, led by Richard Cox, dean of Westminster, wished to preserve the ceremonial of the Edwardian English church while others, more radical, wanted to carry out a further, more rigorous

Reformation. Eventually the local authorities had to intervene, and these "Troubles at Frankfurt," as the quarrel came to be known, resulted in the splitting of the colony in 1555, with the hotter gospellers moving to Geneva. The group at Wesel also had to pull up stakes and move as the result of suspicious voices against them; in 1557 these folk moved to the Swiss town of Aarau.

Though there was significant contact among these groups of religious exiles, there was often a lack of unity on important issues, and each colony had its own distinctive nature depending on its members or the temper of its hosts. Strasbourg seems to have had more than its share of Edwardian notables, including John Ponet, bishop of Winchester, Sir John Cheke, tutor to EDWARD VI, and a smattering of former court officials, ambassadors, and wealthy merchants. Future church leaders predominated in Zurich, where John Jewell, John Parkhurst, and James Pilkington, all to become Elizabethan bishops, came to study with Peter Martyr Vermigli. The Wesel/Aarau congregation was notable for being the only colony in which artisans predominated. The Emden group was said to be the richest of the colonies, and its location made it an important center for the production and distribution of exile literature. The largest and most assertive of the exile groups was based in Geneva, where the most uncompromising fighters for further Reformation were found—men like JOHN KNOX, Christopher Goodman, and William Whittingham, all of whom were destined for controversial careers.

Aside from studying with European Protestant leaders such as Vermigli, Heinrich Bullinger, and John Calvin, the most important work of these religious exiles was the writing and smuggling of Protestant literature for readers in England. Using Continental presses, the exiles produced over 100 works (109 survive) to encourage their coreligionists back home, explain Protestant doctrine, or urge them to flight, martyrdom, or rebellion. The most famous works are those with controversial political content like Knox's *First Blast of the Trumpet Against the Monstrous Regiment of Women*, which argued for the overthrow of the Marian regime, but the exiles also produced the first version of JOHN FOXE's *Book of Martyrs* and the enormously influential Geneva Bible.

Not all of the Marian exiles, however, had left their country for religious reasons; a large proportion of them were on the Continent for secular concerns. Some had taken part in failed coups such as WYATT'S REBELLION; others hoped to take part in future risings, aided by money from the French government. These men formed the core of the Dudley Conspiracy of 1556, which sought to combine an invasion with native rebellions to bring about the overthrow of Queen Mary, and the ill-fated landing of Thomas Stafford, whose raiders seized Scarborough Castle in 1557 but whose hopes for a crown ended on the gallows. While this sort of adventurer congregated in Paris or French ports, other political exiles found Italy an attractive location, particularly Padua with its university and Venice with its anti-Habsburg foreign policy. Prominent among exiles in Italy were Edward Courtenay, earl of Devon; Francis Russell, earl of Bedford; and FRANCIS WALSINGHAM. When war broke out in 1557 between England and

France, many of these secular exiles put patriotism above religion and returned home to serve their country.

On the death of the queen in late 1558, the Marian exile ended, and the sojourners traveled home to mixed receptions. Some like Knox and Goodman had, by the dangerous implications of their political writings, made themselves obnoxious to the new government and found themselves unwelcome in England. Lest they be tarred with the same brush, other exiles took pains to distance themselves from these pariahs—John Aylmer felt obliged to write *An Harborowe for Faithfull and Trewe Subjects* to refute Knox's attacks on the subject of female rule. For some, the exile had deepened religious radicalism. Having spent years living in communities that they felt had been more purely and thoroughly Reformed than England, men like Anthony Gilby, William Turner, and Laurence Humphrey would spend years battling the Elizabethan church over matters of ecclesiastical government and ceremonial. Many of the first generation of "PURITANS" were veterans of the Marian exile. Other exiles found a warmer welcome in the Elizabethan church and rose to positions of eminence in it; a dozen prelates, including EDMUND GRINDAL, archbishop of Canterbury, had spent their Marian years in exile. Political refugees also found a place in the Elizabethan regime. Forty-two former exiles became members of Parliament, Walsingham became principal secretary to the queen, and Russell and Francis Knollys were members of the PRIVY COUNCIL. It seems clear that the significance of the exile endured beyond the reign of Queen Mary and the persecution that originally prompted it.

Bibliography: Kenneth Bartlett, "The Role of the Marian Exiles," in *The House of Commons 1558-1603*, vol. 1, ed. P. W. Hasler, 1981; Christina Garrett, *The Marian Exiles*, 1938.

Gerald Bowler

Marian Reaction. The death of EDWARD VI and the failure of the LADY JANE GREY COUP in the summer of 1553 meant the accession of a queen intent on restoring Roman Catholicism to England. Though MARY I seems to have made promises of religious toleration to gain Protestant support during the succession struggle, the daughter of CATHERINE OF ARAGON, who had clung to the old faith in the face of years of hostile pressure, was sincerely bent on the return of the Roman supremacy and the dismantling of twenty years of schismatic and heretical legislation.

Mary gave evidence of her intentions very quickly. Though her brother was allowed to be buried with Protestant ceremonial, Catholics were soon encouraged by the freeing of their imprisoned bishops, the jailing of Protestant leaders such as THOMAS CRANMER and HUGH LATIMER, a purge of the UNIVERSITIES, and the deportation of colonies of foreign Protestants. By the autumn of 1553 English Reformers were in disarray. Many were planning to flee to the

Continent (the beginning of the MARIAN EXILE) while others struggled with the problems of remaining faithful in the midst of persecution.

Mary's wishes to speed the restoration of Catholicism were hampered by the necessity of involving Parliament in the repeal of Henrician and Edwardian religious legislation and the restitution of papal jurisdiction. Parliament, however, was never going to be a totally cooperative tool in the queen's hands—there were too many men who were anxious to protect their ownership of property once seized from the church or who, while not fervent Protestants, were worried for reasons of nationalisn about the implications of a return to the supremacy of the pope. For example, while the Parliament of October-December 1553 passed the Act of Repeal, which rescinded the corpus of Edwardian church law, it balked at reviving the see of Durham, a proposal fraught with questions of jurisdiction and property. The Parliament of April-May 1554 so vigorously opposed plans to revive medieval heresy laws and reintroduce papal jurisdiction that Mary's officials were obliged temporarily to drop their plans. The real sticking point was the tangled question of former church property, a problem that obliged the queen and her new Spanish husband, Philip, to keep the papal legate Cardinal REGINALD POLE out of England until the church felt ready to compromise. Finally Pole was allowed into the country in November 1554 and announced that the pope had given his permission for the present owners to remain in possession of church land (an arrangement that reassured the landholders but did not extinguish the rights of future popes to demand the property back). In Parliament Pole solemnly absolved the nation for its long schism and admitted England back into the fold of the Roman church. Parliament then enacted anti-heresy legislation that opened the way for a drastic policy of persecution.

The persecution began in February 1555 with the first executions of Protestants. The centerpiece of this campaign was the act against the so-called Oxford Martyrs, Archbishop Thomas Cranmer, Hugh Latimer, and NICHOLAS RIDLEY, who were brought to Oxford for a show trial that was supposed to reveal the weakness of the Protestant cause. Instead, the three defended themselves vigorously, with Latimer's pointing out that the best argument against them was merely *poena legis*. Nevertheless they were pronounced heretics and sentenced to be burnt alive, as were hundreds of other English men and women, mostly common people. Though it succeeded in dispersing or killing most leading Protestant clergy, the Marian persecution was a failure, with the executions so unpopular they often had to be held in secret. Rather than crushing the Reformed religion, the burnings served to raise Protestant morale and show that it was a faith for which people were prepared to die. Underground congregations were established, and Protestant services were conducted under the noses of the Marian authorities for the duration of the queen's reign.

Mary's religious plan ran into further trouble when Paul IV became pope in 1555. The new pope was fanatically anti-Spanish and had also long suspected his old colleague Pole of harboring heretical Lutheran views on the theology of justification. Though in 1556 he allowed Pole to succeed Cranmer as Archbishop of Canterbury, in 1557 he revoked Pole's legatine status and summoned him to Rome to answer to heresy charges. The queen refused to allow Pole to leave the country and barred entry to papal messengers—a deeply embarrassing state of affairs for a ruler who prided herself on her devotion to the papacy.

Despite these setbacks Mary and Pole did have some successes in their renewal of English Catholicism. Visitations and commissions travelled the land and sought out heresy and seditious literature. The physical fabric of the church, which had suffered depredation and neglect for decades, was, to some extent, restored. As far as she could afford it (which was not too far) Mary tried to build up church revenues. Monasticism was reintroduced on a small scale—Westminster Abbey, for example, was restocked with Benedictine monks, Carthusians came back to Sheen, and Bridgettine nuns reoccupied Syon House. Competent, if not always inspiring, bishops were named to fill the vacancies on the episcopal bench, and diocesan seminaries were established to train a new generation of priests. Critics of Pole's policy, however, point to the legalism of his schemes and his ignoring the desperate necessity for exciting preaching and teaching, which might have recaptured the hearts, and not just the obedience, of the people. Pole and Mary appear to have seen English Catholicism in terms of setting aside Henrician and Edwardian novelties to restore a glorious past rather than in terms of introducing a revived and reformed Tridentine Catholicism—witness their decision to turn down the offer of a JESUIT MISSION.

But time ran out for the Marian Reaction. The queen and the cardinal died on the same day in November 1558 and, with the accession of Protestant ELIZA-BETH I, the outlook for Catholicism in the country seemed grim. Indeed, Elizabethan Parliaments went on to outlaw Catholicism, with its adherents suffering under restrictions until the nineteenth century. Nevertheless, it can be argued that Mary's actions permitted the long-term survival of English Catholicism. Her short reign produced new leaders for her church, leaders who were not to apostasize under Elizabeth but who kept alive their religion in exile and in families of the faithful for generations.

Bibliography: A. G. Dickens, *The English Reformation*, 2nd ed., 1989; D. M. Loades, *The Reign of Mary Tudor*, 1979.

Gerald Bowler

Marlowe, Christopher (1564-1593). Dramatist and poet, born the same year as Shakespeare, Christopher Marlowe's brief life and violent death had the intensity of his own dramas. Marlowe was baptized 26 February 1564 at Canterbury and at fifteen entered the King's School there. He entered Corpus Christi College, Cambridge, on a scholarship in 1580, earning the B.A. in 1584 and the M.A. in 1587. His translations of Ovid's *Amores* and the first book of Lucan's *Civil War* (published 1600) were done while still at Cambridge, as was *The Tragedy of Dido, Queen of Carthage* (published 1594). Before taking the M.A., Marlowe left the university for Rheims and probably engaged in surveillance of Catholic scholars there; his M.A. was granted with the urging of the privy council, who reported that "he had done her Majesty good service & deserved to be rewarded." By the time he left Cambridge, he had also begun both parts of *Tamburlaine*, Part I having been performed by the Lord Admiral's Men, likely with famed actor Edward Alleyn, in 1587. Parts I and II were published anonymously in 1590 and 1592.

His reputation as a freethinker and dabbler in the occult was also growing. He was known to be friends with a loose association of men—among them Sir Walter Raleigh; Edward de Vere, earl of Oxford; Matthew Royden, the mathematician; and the astronomer Thomas Harriott—who discussed unorthodox ideas. These activities, for which he was criticized in print (Robert Green called him "atheist Marlowe") helped form the background for *Dr. Faustus*, written no earlier than 1592 and issued in 1604. In 1589, when *The Jew of Malta* was composed, Marlowe was jailed as an accessory in the death of a man killed in self-defense by the poet Thomas Watson. He later roomed for a time in 1591 with the dramatist Thomas Kyd, both writing for the stage and sharing avant-garde ideas. Pembroke's Men acted *Edward II* the following year, and Marlowe again spent time in government service, now at Rouen. His final year, 1593, saw *The Massacre at Paris*, concerning the murder of Huguenots by Charles IX, acted by Lord Strange's company. On 12 May Kyd was arrested for heresy based on papers denying Christ's divinity, papers that he testified were Marlowe's; Marlowe was arrested and brought before the privy council on 20 May. Ten days later, in what may have been a political execution, he was stabbed to death during a tavern argument in Deptford, where he was buried. A month later *Edward II* was published. *Hero and Leander*, a unfinished amatory poem (later completed by George Chapman) based on Ovid and Musaeus in which Hero, the aggressive ingenue, pursued the boasting, inexperienced Leander, was registered at the Stationers that September but not published for five years.

The typical Marlovian dramatic protagonist reveals superhuman ambitions expressed in sweeping poetry, but they are aspirations ultimately benefitting only the self. His heroes ironically exemplify a medieval conviction still current in the 1590s that the life of overweening ambition is, as Macbeth discovered, a "brief candle." Marlowe's best plays depict the giddy attractiveness of unlimited human striving—a stereotypical feature of the humanist outlook—and the tragic results of overreaching desires, whether for money, power, or knowledge. His plays employ a strong poetic verse (BEN JONSON called it "Marlowe's mighty line") new to the English stage and possessed an insistent iambic beat, exotic names, and illusions to far-distant places, all of which create an air of expansive power in his three greatest dramas.

Tamburlaine, the Scythian shepherd for whom authority and conquest mean everything and who treats his conquered foes with the utmost humiliation, displays a ruthless grandeur and believes that nature "doth teach us all to have aspiring minds . . . still climbing after knowledge infinite" to reach "the sweet fruition of an earthly crown." *Dr. Faustus*, based on a legendary John Faustus who sold his soul to the devil to gain knowledge, seeks intellectual insights as greedily as Tamburlaine toppled kingdoms. Like Francis Bacon later, Faustus seeks all knowledge as his province but pressed beyond it for godlike powers. Faustus's gripping fear of divine condemnation, his indecision over whether to follow his good or evil angel—the *psychomachia*, or struggle within the soul, of the morality plays—and the tableau of the seven deadly sins show Marlowe's use of medieval elements along with his hero's Renaissance lust for learning. Barrabas, the avaricious Jew of Malta, foreshadows Jonson's Volpone but lacks the rounded humanity of Shakespeare's Shylock. Marlowe's Jew is a "Machiavel," a theatrical stereotype of Machiavellian evil. His antics are at times farcical, but his defiant tone is powerfully dramatic: "I count religion but a childish toy/ and hold there is no sin but ignorance." With Marlowe begins the mature phase of Tudor-Stuart drama.

Bibliography: Paul H. Kocher, *Christopher Marlowe: A Study of His Thought, Learning and Character*, 1946; Harry Levin, *The Overreacher: A Study of Christopher Marlowe*, 1952.

Christopher Baker

Marprelate Tracts (1587-1589). The Marprelate tracts were seven secretly published pseudonymous works that constituted the best body of English prose satire produced during the Tudor period. As the pseudonym indicates, their object was to discredit the prelates and other ecclesiastical officials of the Church of England who had been opposing PURITAN Reformers and defending the ELIZABETHAN SETTLEMENT OF RELIGION OF 1559.

The immediate origins of the Marprelate tracts lay in the religious ideals and personal antipathies of three supporters of the PRESBYTERIAN church polity of Thomas Cartwright. These men were Job Throckmorton, almost certainly the author of the tracts; Robert Waldegrave, the printer; and John Penry, the business manager. Throckmorton, a member of Parliament for the city of Warwick in 1586 and 1587, had been forced into hiding because of his rash speeches condemning MARY, QUEEN OF SCOTS, favoring aid to the Dutch, and supporting Anthony Cope's Presbyterian "BILL AND BOOK" initiative. Waldegrave had had his printing license revoked, his type defaced, and his press destroyed for printing a Presbyterian book entitled *The State of the Church of Englande*. Penry had been jailed for writing *Aequity*, a puritan plea for more preaching of the gospel in Wales. These three wrote, printed, and distributed the first two Marprelate tracts, the *Epistle* and the *Epitome*, in October and November 1588, respectively, as replies to Dr. John Bridges's *Defense of the Government Established in the Church of England for Ecclesiastical Matters*. Next, they produced the *Mineralls* and *Hay Any Worke for Cooper*, in January and March 1589 respectively. Both of these works were responses to Bishop Thomas Cooper's *Admonition to the*

People of England. *Martin Junior* and *Martin Senior*, two further attacks on Cooper and his colleagues, followed in July 1589. The last tract in the series, the *Protestatyon*, was published in September 1589.

All seven of the tracts were printed clandestinely at a variety of locations in England: the *Epistle* at the house of a Mrs. Crane at East Molesey, near London; the *Epitome* at Sir Richard Knightley's home at Fawsley, Northamptonshire; the *Mineralls* and *Hay Any Worke for Cooper* at John Hales's house at Coventry; and *Martin Junior*, *Martin Senior*, and the *Protestatyon* at Roger Wigston's home at Wolston, Warwickshire.

The Marprelate tracts lampooned the bishops by attacking them personally, by ridiculing their learning, and by satirizing their ponderous and pedantic style of writing. They also taunted the bishops for their inability to find and silence Martin. The light, witty, and irreverent contents of the tracts, supposedly authored by a Martin Marprelate, made them popular with the bishops' secular enemies, but they caused rage and consternation in ecclesiastical and governmental circles.

The bishops moved swiftly to counter the threat from the Marprelate tracts. They hired hack pamphleteers who could meet Martin on his own terms. They also initiated a massive search for Martin and his co-conspirators. Finally, on 14 August 1589, Henry Stanley, the earl of Derby's, men arrested the printers at Manchester and destroyed an eighth tract, *More Worke for Cooper*, which was in the press. Although Throckmorton, Waldegrave, and Penry found new equipment and printed the *Protestatyon*, the end was at hand. Waldegrave and Penry fled to Scotland. Waldegrave stayed there and became JAMES VI's printer. Penry returned to England, became a SEPARATIST, and died for his beliefs on 29 May 1593. The authorities accused Throckmorton of writing the tracts, and a Warwick grand jury indicted him in early October 1590. Throckmorton, however, never admitted that he was Martin.

In the spring of 1591, Throckmorton appeared at Westminster to answer the charges against him. His case was deferred and then suspended. Apparently, relatives and friends at court interceded with the queen to have the proceedings stopped. Still, he had to live under the shadow of possible prosecution until his death in 1601.

Ironically, instead of disgracing the bishops and furthering the cause of Presbyterianism and ecclesiastical reform, the Marprelate tracts were instrumental in destroying the *classis* movement of the puritans. The bishops fulminated against their scurrilous tone, and most thoughtful and learned people, including the Presbyterian leaders, also denounced them. More importantly, the government's search for Martin and his accomplices led not only to the discovery of the *classis* structure but also to the revelation that many *classis* leaders were friends and associates of the Marprelate trio. To many in the church and government, this linkage was enough to prove the bishops' assertions that there was a puritan threat to the established order. Accordingly, the *classis* leaders were arrested and prosecuted, and their movement suppressed. The brash Marprelate participants contributed to the ruin of their cause, but they left a literary legacy of enduring value.

Bibliography: Leland H. Carlson, *Martin Marprelate, Gentleman*, 1981; *The Marprelate Tracts, 1588, 1589*, 1911; William Pierce, *An Historical Introduction to the Marprelate Tracts*, 1908.

Michael Moody

Mary I (1516-1558). Queen of England from 1553-1558, Mary was the only surviving child of HENRY VIII and his first wife, CATHERINE OF ARAGON. Born on 18 February 1516, as a young child she was frequently used by her father as a diplomatic pawn, and by the age of nine she had been betrothed both to the Dauphin, Francis, and to the Emperor Charles V. She was given an unusually thorough HUMANIST education, which was directed for a time by the celebrated Spanish scholar Juan Luis Vives, who wrote *De Institutione Foeminae Christianae* for her guidance. Apart from the humanist interests of both her parents, the excellence of this education was largely the result of the fact that, throughout her childhood, she was her father's heir. She was consequently brought up to inherit a throne but was given no practical training in the art of government, because that was not thought (even by Vives) to be within a woman's competence. Both her intellect and her personality were shaped by this training and retained its imprint. Henry's ultimate unwillingness to accept the prospect of her succession was the most important political circumstance of the second half of his reign, leading to the repudiation of papal jurisdiction over the English church, and frustrating all plans for Mary's marriage. Between 1525 and 1528 she was sent to reside at Ludlow as the nominal head of the council in the MARCHES OF WALES but was not created princess of Wales, as that act would have been interpreted as an unequivocal recognition of her right to succeed. During these years, when her household was under the control of Margaret Pole, countess of Salisbury, Mary began to acquire a group of domestic servants who were to serve her over many years with conspicuous loyalty and unselfishness.

Henry's determination to secure the annulment of his marriage to Catherine, as a part of his quest for a male heir, affected Mary profoundly, but at first indirectly. Throughout the years from 1527 to 1533, while the issue was being vigorously and publicly debated, she retained her household, and her life and education continued unchanged. However, her loyalty and affection were given to her mother and, more significantly, to her mother's chief ally and protector, the emperor Charles V, through his ambassador Eustace Chapuys. After Henry's marriage to ANNE BOLEYN and the birth of ELIZABETH in September 1533, Mary, like Catherine, refused to accept her own demotion. As a result her household was disbanded, and a joint household was established for her and Elizabeth, in which she was very much the inferior partner, living with a few servants in what was virtually house arrest. At about that time, and possibly as a result of the stress that her changed circumstances had induced, she developed a severe menstrual disorder, which continued to afflict her for the rest of her life. Her general health also deteriorated, and the royal physicians were in frequent attendance. Catherine's death in January 1536 was a severe blow to Mary, but the fall of Anne Boleyn, which followed in May, raised her spirits and encouraged her to hope for complete and unconditional rehabilitation. To her surprise and great distress the king insisted more emphatically than before, upon her subscription to the statutes of supremacy and succession. This time her refusal was technically high treason, and Henry considered proceeding to extremities. Instead, Mary surrendered, and to everyone's immense relief, was received back into favor. According to Chapuys, she was conscience-stricken by her own weakness and attempted unsuccessfully to obtain a papal absolution. However, there was no outward sign of this; her relations with the emperor and his ambassador became more distant, and for the remainder of her father's life she lived undisturbed, either in her own reconstituted household or at court. Her relations with his third queen, JANE SEYMOUR, and also with CATHERINE PARR, were excellent, and the perils of the PILGRIMAGE OF GRACE (1536-1537) and the EXETER CONSPIRACY (1538), although both ostensibly in her interest, left her position untouched. In 1543 she was restored to the succession (although not legitimated), after Edward, but ahead of Elizabeth. However, the resumption of desultory negotiations failed to produce a husband for her, and she became convinced that she would not be allowed to marry in her father's lifetime. By 1547 she was thirty-one, and this situation caused her great distress.

With the accession of EDWARD VI she again became the heir to the throne, and in accordance with the terms of her father's will received a landed estate, mostly in East Anglia, to the value of nearly £4000 per annum. She thus became a powerful magnate in her own right and built up a numerous affinity among the East Anglian gentry. As Edward's government, guided first by EDWARD SEYMOUR, duke of Somerset, and then by JOHN DUDLEY, duke of Northumberland, became increasingly Protestant, Mary emerged as the most powerful defender of the mass, and of traditional religious practices. Her relations with the emperor again grew close, as she invoked his assistance to protect her from the consequences of increasingly open defiance against her brother's council. She did not, however, repudiate her earlier acceptence of her father's supremacy and justified her action entirely in terms of defending his religious settlement. Edward's illness and his premature death in 1553 precipitated an attempt by the duke of Northumberland to intrude his daughter-in-law LADY JANE GREY (a granddaughter of Henry's sister, Mary) into the succession in Mary's place. This attempt (which failed to stimulate even Protestant enthusiasm) was defeated partly by Mary's popularity and partly by English respect for law.

As queen, Mary suffered in numerous ways from the consequences of her upbringing, and there were subsequent troubles. Inexperience caused her to work too hard at routine business and to withhold her full confidence from even her closest councillors. She relied to an unseemly extent in the first year of her reign upon Charles V and his ambassador, Simon Renard, and found great difficulty in coping with routine disagreements among her advisers. Her health had been permanently undermined, causing her to suffer two phantom pregnancies and at least two hysterical collapses in the space of five years. Acutely conscious of her royal dignity, she was nevertheless unsure of her own capacity to govern and uncertain of the extent to which her power should be exercised by her consort. Nevertheless the early part of her reign was marked by considerable success. Her marriage to Philip, prince of Spain, Charles V's only legitimate son, was negotiated upon the emperor's intitiative but exactly suited Mary's personal requirement. The marriage was highly unpopular in England, but the terms of the marriage treaty were extremely favorable, guaranteeing English autonomy and holding out the prospect of a dynastic union with the Netherlands. After the summer of 1555, however, Mary's failure to bear a child (not surprising in view of her age and medical record), Charles's abdication, and Philip's increasing preoccupation with the business of his other realms undermined their relationship, both personally and politically. Her determination to restore traditional religious practices was both expected and popular, but an equal resolution to restore the papal jurisdiction was neither and required difficult and protracted negotiations during the autumn and winter of 1554 and 1555. One result of these negotiations was the increasing influence of the papal legate, Cardinal REGINALD POLE, who, by the autumn of 1555 had replaced the absent Philip as the queen's principal support and confidant. Another result was religious persecution of unprecedented scope and intensity, which resulted in some 300 deaths, and the flight of over 800 into exile between 1555 and 1558. Protestant defiance was not overcome by these measures (for which Mary herself was primarily responsible), nor was hostile propaganda subdued.

In the last two years of her life, the good fortune that Mary had enjoyed between 1553 and 1555 deserted her. Philip stayed on the Continent and quarrelled with the pope, disrupting the process of Catholic restoration. Three bad harvests in 1554, 1555, and 1556 caused dearth and hardship, followed by a devastating epidemic of influenza in 1557 and 1558. In 1557 Mary allowed herself to be drawn into her husband's war with France, a war that undermined a hitherto successful financial policy and resulted in the deeply felt loss of CALAIS in January 1558. Most serious of all, she failed to remove her sister Elizabeth as heir to the throne and succeeded only in antagonizing her, a situation that Philip recognized but was powerless to alter. When her conscience was engaged, as in religious policy, Mary could be determined to the point of ruthlessness, but in more ordinary political situations she found decisions difficult and dispassionate judgment impossible. In many respects her government was successful, because the English Crown was strong, and as she died after only five years in power, it is impossible to say with certainty how well her policies would eventually have succeeded. What is certain is that her undesirable historical reputation is largely the result of the fact that Elizabeth successfully and permanently reversed all that she stood for.

Bibliography: D. M. Loades, *The Reign of Mary Tudor*, 1979; D. M. Loades, *Mary Tudor: A Life*, 1989; H. F. M. Prescott, *Mary Tudor*, 1952; R. Tittler, *The Reign of Mary I*, 1983.

David Loades

Mary, Queen of Scots (1542-1587). This legendary heroine of a little great literature and a great deal of soap opera is a historical puzzle; her political skills—the real question about her—are only now being seriously investigated. But her accession in 1542, within three weeks of the English victory at Solway Moss, undoubtedly represented a new level of political trauma for the Scots. There was nothing novel about the English defeat of the Scots in battle, or the accession of a minor, or even sending that minor to France to remove her from the English threat, which had its precedent with David II in 1334. But an infant female gave the megalomaniac HENRY VIII the chance for a replay of the megalomaniac Edward I, in the attempt to annex Scotland by marrying its queen to the English heir, and when that plan failed, to turn to very bloody war, the "Rough Wooing" that lasted until 1550. The death of that tough Catholic JAMES V produced a burst of Protestant enthusiasm and success, followed by two decades of religious slog and stalemate.

From the period 1542-1560, government was in the hands of two regents, the dithering JAMES HAMILTON, earl of Arran, and then the highly effective Mary of Guise, the queen's mother, whose rule was maintained by a combination of innate ability and French officials and troops. But minority also shoved power and responsibility onto the leading Scottish nobles, and factionalism was heightened by religious dissension. Meanwhile, Mary enjoyed a prolonged French holiday as petted darling of the French court, dauphiness, and then queen of France when her husband became Francis II in 1559. Her Scottish kingdom was very remote. It was forced back on her attention not by the death of her husband in December 1560 but by her failure in the next eight months to find another husband who would enable her to remain on the Continent. With no options left, she returned to Scotland in August 1561, where she at least had the wit to exercise her undoubted personal charm and pretend she was pleased about being there. But the fog that surrounded her arrival was symbolic of her rule. She came back to a kingdom where the Protestants were in the ascendent—but only just. The religious stalemate of the 1540s and 1550s had been broken by 1559, when ELIZABETH rejected Catholicism and the Scottish Protestants began to take the offensive against the regent. Meanwhile French internal problems distracted their attention from Scotland and—crucially—Mary of Guise died and the English sent in troops in the summer of 1560. The Protestant lords, Mary's bastard half-brother, James lord Stewart, Archibald Campbell, earl of Argyll and others, backed by a substantial number of lairds, could now act decisively; in August, the Scottish Reformation Parliament abolished the Mass and the power of the pope. In France, their queen shouted treason and refused to ratify these acts. But she then left the "rebels" in control—with her authority—and gave them a year in which to build on their initial victory.

What consolidated that victory was Mary's policy when she returned. Catholic restoration, hoped for by the pope, the kings of France and Spain, and Catholics everywhere, desperately feared by the English, and still entirely possible in 1561, did not happen. Instead, the Catholic queen became the principal financier of the struggling Protestant kirk. Uniquely in Reformation Europe, she treated her faith as a purely private matter and utterly refused what all other rulers recognized as a fundamental burden of monarchy, be they *politique* or devout— responsibility for the religious disposition of their subjects. Her interests were quite different. She wanted to marry—and came up against the irony that she, so keen to adopt the acceptable solution for a queen regnant, could not find a willing suitor, while Elizabeth, who rejected that solution, was surrounded by them. So the queen of Scots dangled after the lunatic Don Carlos of Spain and entertained the entirely reluctant ROBERT DUDLEY, earl of Leicester. She passionately wanted the English throne. Her lack of attention to the business of ruling Scotland meant that the Protestants, Lord James Stewart, created earl of Moray, and others favorable to Elizabeth, who dominated Mary's council, provided the impetus of government. Meanwhile the Queen sat apart from the political center, surrounded by a more Catholic and French household, her preferred but politically weak group. This was not royal government as the Scots had experienced it under Mary's formidable predecessors. It suited the Protestants, but it was an unstable and unimpressive compromise.

What blew it apart was that in 1565 the worm turned. HENRY STEWART, Lord Darnley's attack of measles produced passionate love in Mary. But it was the attempt to assert herself—far too late—that produced the marriage in July 1565, a shake-up in the political establishment, and an effort to do something for the Catholics, even if it is not entirely clear what that was, for it fell far short of determined Catholic restoration. A temporary victim was her half-brother, driven out of Scotland after the CHASEABOUT RAID of 1565. A more permanent one was her Italian secretary, DAVID RIZZIO, subject of scandal, but far more seriously, a sacrificial object of four years of the lack of a royal policy and nine months of an inept one. The reign was spiralling down out of control. Forced to restore the Protestant lords and still saddled with the drunk and irresponsible Darnley, Mary's only achievement in this period was to give birth to a son, JAMES VI, who would have nothing of the weakness of his parents, in June 1566. The murder of Darnley in February 1567 might also have been an achievement, for it eradicated a menace. But the rush into the arms of JAMES HEPBURN, earl of Bothwell, ensured that the murder ushered in disaster: defeat at CARBERRY by the Confederate Lords in June, enforced abdication in July, and imprisonment in Lochleven Castle.

In May 1568, she escaped. But her defeat at the battle of LANGSIDE forced her into flight to England and eighteen years of whining, demanding, and cheerfully plotting to kill the English queen. It lasted so long partly because of

Elizabeth's refusal to put to death an anointed sovereign, despite the periodic frenzy of her subjects, but also because nothing would persuade the Scots to have Mary back. The attempt to reach a settlement in 1568 and 1569 produced no result; Elizabeth proclaimed the honor of both Mary and Moray, now regent, and Mary remained in England. But it did produce the famous Casket Letters—eight letters, a sonnet, and two marriage contracts between Mary and Bothwell. The letters made clear her complicity in the Darnley murder, and the sonnet had all the hallmarks of the Barbara Cartland woman, masochistic and male-dominated. The Confederate Lords had found this damning evidence in 1567, but it was only Elizabeth's insistence that brought it into the open; the letters disappeared in 1584, when they passed to James VI, and have never been seen since. They have been a wonderful subject for speculation, forgeries in the eyes of her defenders, genuine for her detractors. Probably they were genuine. The woman they portrayed was not a familiar sixteenth-century literary image, and the Scots' desire to suppress them, contrasted with Elizabeth's enthusiasm for them, may point to the handwriting having been genuine; even Mary's Scottish opponents, and certainly her son, stopped short of having her actions portrayed beyond a doubt to the world. But they matter little; if the letters were genuine, she was "guilty," if forged, she was not necessarily "innocent." More to the point, if she knew nothing about the Darnley murder, she was virtually alone among the political nation of Scotland, which would be a more telling comment on her political awareness than any question of their authenticity.

Her other attempt to get her throne back, the "Bond of Association," whereby she would rule jointly with James, foundered by 1584 on the rock of James's understandable lack of enthusiasm. All that was left was ever more foolish plotting, culminating in the BABINGTON PLOT of 1586, known to the government from the beginning, and so finally in February 1587 a conspirator's death, which she met with great courage and all the trappings of martyrdom.

Bibliography: Antonia Fraser, *Mary Queen of Scots*, 1969; Maurice Lee, Jr., *James Stewart, Earl of Moray*, 1953; Michael Lynch, ed., *Mary Stewart: Queen in Three Kingdoms*, 1988; Jenny Wormald, *Mary Queen of Scots: A Study in Failure*, 1988.

Jenny Wormald

Medina del Campo, Treaty of (1489). An Anglo-Spanish treaty of alliance brought about because the French kings had been expanding royal power throughout the fifteenth century. In the 1480s, Louis XII began to move against Francis, duke of Brittany. HENRY VII, in an effort to maintain his position in Brittany and to protect England's Breton ports, began a policy of building alliances with the neighbors of France.

Completed on 27 March 1489, the Treaty of Medina del Campo stated that, in the event of war with France, England would come to the aid of Spain. It further stipulated that England could withdraw from such a war only after taking Normandy and Aquitaine –a very unlikely possibility–whereas Spain could make peace anytime after Roussillon and Cerdagne were recovered.

Because both monarchs later contended that the treaty had never been fully ratified, Medina del Campo was primarily important for reasons other than the military alliance. As a commercial agreement it gave the merchants of England and Spain the rights of natives in their commercial dealings in the other's country. It reduced customs duties to the rates used in 1459. The treaty also instituted regulations for the issue of letters of marque and reprisal, and it established a guarantee for good behavior whereby ships, upon leaving port, would leave a bond or surety from which any damage claims could be paid. The agreement also closed Aragon and Castille to Yorkist pretenders. The most noteworthy clause of the compact, however, was the betrothal of Arthur and CATHERINE OF ARAGON.

Bibliography: S. Doran, *England and Europe, 1485-1603*, 1986.

Brian Christian

Merchant Adventurers. The regulated company that controlled the export of woolen cloth in sixteenth-century England. The Merchant Adventurers, a company in London, asserted that their privileges derived from a charter granted by Henry IV in 1407, although this charter did not distinguish between Londoners and other Englishmen. Though the Adventurers of Southampton had conducted a lively business with Italy and Spain, and those of Hull plied a bustling trade between their port and Scandinavia in the late Middle Ages, the London merchants (chiefly freemen of the Mercers Company) soon engrossed the trade in woolen cloth to Antwerp. The trade of the other ports decayed steadily during the first half of the sixteenth century while that of London increased dramatically. The Adventurers carried not only woolen cloth but also leather, hides, tin, lead, and other goods. CLOTH, however, was by far the most important English trade item, accounting for 80% of the value of of the nation's exports by 1542. Since the export of unwrought cloths to be dyed and dressed by the more sophisticated craftsmen of the Low Countries jeopardized the nascent cloth manufacturing industry in England, statutes were enacted that prevented the export of both undressed and dyed cloths above a set price (which aimed at having the cloths finished in England rather than in the Low Countries). During the first half of the sixteenth century the company thus regularly petitioned the Crown for relief from the operation of laws that required cloths above a certain price to be fully manufactured in England. When the soaring price of cloth (fueled by the debasement of the COINAGE, which began during the last years of HENRY VIII's reign) outstripped the price limit set by the statute of 1542 (33 Hen. VIII, c. 19) the Crown authorized the export of cloth under license only, a practice that prevailed during the reign of ELIZABETH.

The London Company of Merchant Adventurers (incorporated as the Merchant Adventurers of England in 1564) established control over its membership in both the English House in Antwerp and the Mercers' Hall in London through the election of a governor and a Court of Assistants. These men arranged the four annual marts to which the Adventurers "trafficked," regulated the admission of new members, judged peccant apprentices and other erring members of the fellowship, and punished interlopers who sought to engage in the cloth trade without benefit of membership. The chief rivals of the Londoners for the woolen cloth trade remained the men of the outports, often merchants of the STAPLE who saw a formerly profitable trade in wool vanishing with the increase in English draperies, and the once-mighty German Hansa. During the course of the sixteenth century the London company either excluded the merchants of the outports from the lucrative cloth trade as interlopers with the assistance of the Crown or admitted them to membership in the company for an entry fee (but with the inferior status of "redemptioners"). With the contraction of trade after the collapse of the Antwerp cloth market in 1551, the redemptioners (also known as the men of the New Hanse) found themselves excluded from the trade altogether by the London oligarchs (the Old Hanse).

The Hanseatic League proved a more formidable adversary. Drawing their privileges from a charter extracted from Edward IV in 1474, the Hansards enjoyed a favored status not extended to other merchant strangers or to native merchants. These "Easterlings" paid only three pence poundage on goods carried into England (Englishmen paid twelve pence) and a charge of twelve pence upon each exported cloth (compared to the fourteen pence due from natives). Their liberties included access to Blackwell Hall in London, where they could trade directly with the country clothiers, a privilege denied to other strangers. The most frequent accusation concerned the "coloring" of the goods of other merchants, that is, carrying the goods of denizens or native interlopers who thereby benefitted from the lower customs duties paid by the league. Though Edward IV predicated the grant of privileges upon a vaguely worded promise of reciprocal rights for English merchants in Hansa towns, especially Danzig, this pledge went unfulfilled during his reign and those of the Tudors. The London Company's usefulness to the Crown in standing surety for Crown loans negotiated by Thomas Gresham in the Low Countries and their assistance in maintaining the price of sterling at an acceptable rate led an appreciative Crown to suspend temporarily the Hansa's privileges in 1552 and then revoke them totally in 1560.

The Adventurers conducted their trade to the Low Countries under the terms of the INTERCURSUS MAGNUS, a treaty negotiated by Henry VII with the emperor Maximilian in 1496. This treaty established the trade largely on the terms that had prevailed for the previous fifty years. Though the vagaries of dynastic politics and the course of the English Reformation produced interruptions of the "intercourse," mutual economic interest maintained the London-Antwerp trade nexus for most of the sixteenth century. In 1564, however, the Adventurers petitioned the Crown for a charter of incorporation as they prepared to abandon

Antwerp and establish the staple at Emden. Despite the reservations that some councillors had regarding the monopoly that the charter conferred upon the company (notably WILLIAM CECIL, who retained sympathy for the Staplers), a worried Crown now acted to protect the company's position during a time of worsening relations with Philip II and a decaying cloth market. Although the company returned to Antwerp in January 1565, the company sought safer haven for their precious cargoes when the Dutch revolt endangered the mart at Antwerp. The Adventurers transferred the staple to Hamburg in 1567, but the enmity of the Hansa drove them back to Emden in 1579. They later settled at Middelburg in the United Provinces in 1598 but moved to Hamburg again in 1611.

Bibliography: G. D. Ramsay, *The City of London in International Politics at the Accession of Elizabeth Tudor*, 1975.

Douglas Bisson

Monopolies. It was an undoubted PREROGATIVE of the Crown to regulate trade by the grant of monopolistic rights, which were issued under letters patent. The recipients were licensed to export prohibited goods or were exempted from statutes that regulated the manufacture of important commodities. From the mid-sixteenth century the government also issued patents to foreign inventors and entrepreneurs to lure them to England. The commendable objective was to achieve economic self-sufficiency. To this extent monopolistic patents were justifiable. They attracted new skills to England, protected inventors, and enabled the Crown, when circumstances warranted it, to inject an element of flexibility into an economy that was rigidly controlled by statutory regulations. Although the practice raised a constitutional question—whether the prerogative could dispense with statute in particular cases—there were few complaints so long as it was not abused. However, in the 1580s and 1590s ELIZABETH exploited the practice to excess. She was in financially straitened circumstances and found in monopolies a cheap form of patronage. They were granted not to regulate trade or encourage foreign skills to England but as favors to officials, courtiers, and servants. Others were sold for sorely needed cash. Patentees received a monopoly in the manufacture, sale, or import of specified commodities or were empowered to issue licenses to others. Such patents were exploited in the interest of the recipient and to the detriment of the public, which usually had to pay higher prices during a period of soaring inflation. It was the enforcement of the patentees' rights, however, that caused the most widespread resentment, because they enjoyed extensive powers of search and punishment against interlopers. Furthermore, victims of the monopolists' activities had no legal redress against actions proceeding from the royal prerogative.

The mounting discontent was voiced in the House of Commons in 1597, when it debated the grievance, only to be disarmed by Elizabeth's promise to reform the misuse of monopolistic patents. Yet nothing was done during the next four years, while abuses and grievances multiplied. When Parliament met in October 1601, the Commons was in an uncompromising mood. Neither Elizabeth nor her council had translated her promise into positive action. It was only in January 1601 that the solicitor-general, Thomas Fleming, received a commission to proceed against harmful patents. Not only did he fail to act on it, but, just two months before Parliament assembled, the PRIVY COUNCIL was defending Edward Darcy's playing-card monopoly. Darcy was a notorious patentee who, on one occasion, struck in the face Sir George Barne, a London alderman, during negotiations with the City's governors over his patent for searching and sealing leather.

The Commons' anger was directed against both monopolies and the council's inaction. The list of patents for both luxuries and necessities was long and growing: currants, iron, steel, glass, vinegar, sea coal, lead, salt, and many others. A lawyer caustically suggested that bread would soon be included. Elizabeth acted belatedly but opportunely, informing the House that she had learned of the grievous harm done to her loving subjects by monopolies. She promised to cancel the most harmful, suspend others, and allow the rest to be challenged in the common law courts. Three days later a royal PROCLAMATION duly cancelled some of the most obnoxious grants, promised the punishment of those who had been guilty of abuses in the execution of their patents, allowed aggrieved subjects to seek remedy at law against the rest, and forbade the privy council to assist monopolists in the execution of their patents. However, it also asserted Elizabeth's prerogative right to issue patents and threatened severe punishment of those who called it in question. She had been obliged to make concessions, but the grants of some patentees remained unimpaired—among them Edward Darcy's right to import and manufacture playing cards. It was not until 1624 that a statute limited monopolies to inventions.

Bibliography: H. G. Fox, *Monopolies and Patents*, 1947; J. Thirsk, *Economic Policy and Projects*, 1978.

M. A. R. Graves

More, Sir Thomas (1478-1535). Statesman and humanist, Thomas More was born in 1478. Little is known of his earliest years, but after spending some time in the household of Archbishop JOHN MORTON, he studied at Oxford in the early 1490s before enrolling at New Inn and then at Lincoln's Inn (1496) to study law. Still unsure of his calling, he lived for a while at the London Charterhouse and considered the contemplative life. At the same time he pursued literary interests and mixed with such prominent scholars as John Colet, Erasmus, William Grocyn, and Thomas Linacre. His early literary productions, including translations of Lucian and of the life of Giovanni Pico della Mirandola, place him in the mainstream of English humanism. However, his flirtation with the contemplative life was decisively ended by his marriage to Jane Colt in 1505 and by his subsequent choice of a career in the law. Over the next decade he held a series of important offices at Lincoln's Inn, built up a lucrative private practice, and embarked on his public career as under-sheriff of London (1510-1518). This period also saw in 1511 the death of his first wife (who had borne him four children) and his immediate remarriage to a wealthy widow, Dame Alice Middleton. More's talents so impressed the government that in 1515 he was sent with an English embassy to Flanders to renegotiate a trade treaty. During this mission he composed his greatest work, *Utopia*. This complex and ironical account of a fictitious transatlantic island society was set within an equally complex debate about the role of the intellectual in politics. His personal position in this debate, already indicated by his choice of a public career, was clarified in 1517 when he accepted a place on HENRY VIII's council. Holding office as under-treasurer of the EXCHEQUER (1521-1525) and chancellor of the duchy of Lancaster (1525-1529), More was near the center of the political stage throughout the 1520s. Though active in STAR CHAMBER justice and in diplomatic work, More probably had little to do with the formulation of policy. But he was often in personal attendance on the king, providing stimulating company and performing secretarial duties. Trusted by both Henry and THOMAS WOLSEY, he was a vital intermediary between them.

Thomas More was involved from an early stage in the English campaigns against heresy of the 1520s. He helped Henry with the *Assertio Septem Sacramentorum* and defended it a few years later with his own pseudonymous *Responsio ad Lutherum*, one of the bitterest attacks Luther ever faced. In 1526 he organized a raid on the premises of the London Hanseatic merchants, in search of heretical books. And with the emergence of WILLIAM TYNDALE as England's leading Reformation propagandist, More was drafted by Cuthbert Tunstall to write againt him—a task he performed over the next five years with every sign of enthusiasm.

Wolsey's fall in 1529 brought More to the peak of his political career, for he replaced the cardinal as lord chancellor on 25 October 1529. Yet he had already declared himself unable in conscience to promote the policy dearest to the king's heart—obtaining a divorce from CATHERINE OF ARAGON. Although he refrained from public dissent, his position was an open secret, and he was soon excluded from meetings of the council concerning that issue. Despite his lack of sympathy with the DIVORCE, he remained consistent to the principle he had espoused in *Utopia* of not abandoning the ship of state merely because the seas were rough. In compensation he threw himself into his judicial duties and into the fight against heresy. The first six burnings of the English Reformation occurred under his chancellorship. He himself played an active part in the investigation of three of those cases, although the allegations of cruelty and illegality levelled against him then and since can be discounted.

As Henry's policy became more anti-clerical in the 1530s, More's position became untenable. He swallowed his distaste for the anti-clerical agitation and legislation of 1529-1530, but overt attacks on the liberties of the English church soon led him into closer alliance with the "Aragonese" faction, which he probably informed about the council's plans. His literary output from 1529 to 1532 (replies to the anti-clerical writings by Simon Fish and Christopher St. German) was barely coded opposition propaganda. The last straw was the SUBMISSION OF THE CLERGY on 16 May 1532. Within hours, More tendered his resignation. In retirement, More continued his polemical campaign against anti-clerical and heretical literature and endeavored to avoid political entanglement. Yet even his "private" life offended Henry. He refused to attend the coronation of Anne Boleyn in 1533. When he found himself included in the bill of attainder laid against the HOLY MAID OF KENT in 1534, he persuaded the House of Lords to insist on his omission from it. He was not, however, able to escape the Act of SUCCES-SION. He refused the oath to that act on 13 April, and on 17 April he was committed to the Tower, where he began to prepare for death. Abandoning polemical theology, he turned to devotional writing with the *Dialogue of Comfort Against Tribulation*. But the pressure to conform was still intense. Later in 1534 an act of attainder declared him guilty of misprision of treason. On 4 May 1535 the CARTHUSIAN priors were executed, the first victims of the acts of supremacy and TREASON, which made it treason to deny that the king was supreme head of the English church. Shortly after this object lesson, THOMAS CROMWELL tried in vain to elicit from More an opinion for or against the supremacy. On 12 June, Sir Richard Rich came to take away More's books and attempted to trap him into denying the supremacy. He probably failed, but when More was brought to trial on four counts of treason on 1 July, the one based on Rich's recollection of this conversation was upheld. Despite a brilliant defense, More was found guilty. He made a final speech in arrest of judgment that made it clear that he was dying for papal supremacy and the unity of the church. This speech did not prevent his condemnation, and he was executed on 6 July 1535.

Bibliography: A. Fox, *Thomas More: History and Providence*, 1982; J. A. Guy, *The Public Career of Sir Thomas More*, 1980; R. Marius, *Thomas More*, 1984.

Richard Rex

Morton, John, Cardinal (c. 1420-1500). Clerical statesman, born in Dorset, John Morton attended Balliol College and Peckwater's Inn, Oxford, and received a doctorate in CANON LAW in 1452. He took holy orders about that time, obtained several rich benefices, and launched a successful career in the Court of Arches. In 1456 Morton was appointed chancellor to Prince Edward of Lancaster (1453-1471) and became active in politics. For the next fifteen years he was a staunch Lancastrian and actively opposed the rival claims of York. After Edward IV's triumph at Towton (29 March 1461), he fled to the Continent and was attainted by Parliament. In September 1470 he returned to England in the company of Richard Neville, the earl of Warwick, and helped to restore Henry VI to the throne. During the following spring, after Prince Edward's death at Tewkesbury and Henry VI's murder in the Tower, he made overtures to Edward IV, who granted him a full pardon in July 1471. Well aware of Morton's great abilities, the Yorkist ruler named him to the council and appointed him Master of the Rolls in March 1472. For the remainder of the reign, Morton was one of the most influential men in the realm and assisted the king in conducting foreign policy. In August 1478 Edward IV arranged for him to become the bishop of Ely, his consecration occurring on 31 January 1479; just before Edward's death on 9 April 1483, he was named one of the executors of the king's will.

Loyal to Edward IV's memory and the interests of his two sons, Morton opposed Richard of Gloucester's efforts to usurp the throne. During the fateful council meeting on 13 June 1483, which preceded the execution of William, Lord Hastings, Morton was arrested and imprisoned in the Tower. Within a few weeks Oxford University petitioned for his release, and he was placed in the custody of Edward Stafford, duke of Buckingham, at Brecknock Castle. During September 1483, after Richard III's coronation and the suspected murder of his two nephews, a conspiracy against the new ruler began, which Morton encouraged. That conspiracy led to a premature attempt to overthrow Richard III and bring Henry Tudor, earl of Richmond, the residual Lancastrian heir, to the throne. In late October Buckingham was caught and beheaded, but Morton escaped to Flanders. Attainted by Richard's only Parliament in January 1484, he lived in exile on the Continent until Henry of Richmond's victory at BOSWORTH FIELD enabled him to return in safety to his homeland. Meanwhile at the papal curia in Rome, he began a process during the first half of 1485 by which Henry received a dispensation permitting his marriage to Elizabeth of York, eldest daughter of Edward IV.

Before the first Tudor ruler's coronation on 30 October 1485, Morton was one of five prelates chosen to officiate.

During the following March he succeeded to the lord chancellorship, and in December 1486 the king arranged for him to become archbishop of Canterbury as well. In September 1493, HENRY VII prevailed on Pope Alexander VI to elevate him to the College of Cardinals. During his final years of life, Morton also served as chancellor of both English universities.

Until his death on 15 September 1500, Morton was the most influential of Henry VII's ministers and councillors. His duties were numerous and varied, although they have just begun to receive adequate historical treatment. He was a leading adviser on foreign affairs and often met with ambassadors from other countries. He assisted Henry in making administrative and ecclesiastical appointments, and he presided over the House of Lords and the upper house of convocation whenever those institutions were in session. Likewise, he directed the proceedings of the council in the king's absence until March 1497, when poor health disabled him and a new official, the lord president, appeared to take his place. Most of his time, however, was given over to the affairs of CHANCERY, since he often held that "no one who came to Chancery should leave the Court without remedy."

Because of the obvious need for greater royal revenue after the troubled reign of Richard III, Morton was a strong supporter of Henry VII's financial policies.

He argued energetically on behalf of the benevolences of 1491 and 1496; and although he did not invent the arguments that later became known as "Morton's Fork" (those who lived comfortably could obviously afford to give, while those who lived simply must have hidden savings from which they could contribute), he proposed that the wealthier inhabitants of London should be assessed sums of up to £60 each, a proposal that caused him to become extremely unpopular in the capital. During the Parliament of January 1497 he addressed the Lords and Commons on the perilous diplomatic situation and the various misdeeds of JAMES IV; in that way he helped build support for the generous grants made by Parliament and convocation. As a result of those grants, the Crown made a profit of more than £100,000 on the Anglo-Scottish war of 1496-1497; so Morton deserves partial credit for Henry VII's success in reordering the royal revenues after the troubled reign of Richard III.

Although Morton made periodic efforts to reform the monasteries, which he believed guilty of religious, moral, and financial infractions, it does not appear that his actions brought any improvement. His most enduring legacy was the series of building projects he completed. At Canterbury Cathedral he financed the construction of the central (Bell Harry) tower, while at Lambeth Palace he is primarily remembered for Morton's Gateway. At Oxford he made extensive repairs to the school of canon law and helped rebuild St. Mary's Church. At Cambridge he was commissioned by the king to supervise the vaulting of King's College Chapel; and at Hatfield, which, like Knowle, was an episcopal palace before the Reformation, he made considerable improvements. Perhaps his greatest contributions in this regard were in the Isle of Ely, where he made renovations to Wisbech Castle and built Morton's Dyke, a great drainage trench through the fens from Wisbech to Peterborough.

Bibliography: C. S. L. Davies, "Bishop John Morton of Ely, the Holy See, and the Accession of Henry VII, *English Historical Review* 102 (1987): 2-30; Christopher Harper-Bill, "The Familia, Administration, and Patronage of John Morton," *Journal of Religious History* 10 (1979): 236-52.

Michael V. C. Alexander

Music. When HENRY VII became the king of England in 1485, the music of that society was old-fashioned and poised for new directions. While not much music from that reign is extant, it is obvious that many later trends were already nascent.

Tudor music developed in the confluence of several historical trends that were at once both creative and reflective of the greater society they occupied. Especially important among them were (1) increased intercultural contact in both the commercial and religious sectors, (2) the Protestant Reformation, (3) HUMANISM, and (4) the acceptance of English as a literary language. Every major Tudor musical trend had its roots in at least three of these nurseries.

The popularity of metrical psalm singing in sixteenth-century England well illustrates this process. The already flourishing Continental metrical psalmody provided models. CLOTH merchants transported texts and tunes, especially those of French dances whose sense of forward motion made them practical for amateur group singing. The rising number of alehouses and taverns provided a place to sing psalms before one could do so in church. An increased vernacular vocabulary made metricization easier. The intellectual climate furnished by humanism nurtured lay religious efforts. The standardization of the English language caused by the widespread distribution of an official BIBLE text in English made printing of devotional texts such as metrical psalters commercially feasible—one could now sell the same edition throughout the country. Religious Reformers encouraged literacy to enable Bible reading and sight singing so that psalms could be sung—all ostensibly to edify but in reality to entertain as well. As a result, by the end of his reign, HENRY VIII could complain that "the word of God, is rhymed, sung and jangled in every alehouse and tavern in the land." By the end of ELIZABETH's reign, metrical psalms were being sung in church as well.

Another lasting contribution of Tudor religious music was the English anthem. At first only a vernacular version of its Latin predecessors, it evolved into a unique genre in its own right. The mature "verse anthem," as it was called, consisted of a series of solo verses, usually with instrumental accompaniment, alternating with choral sections, usually unaccompanied. The anthem's texts were almost always drawn from Scripture, collects, and metrical paraphrases of them. From early in the reign of Henry VIII all sacred music texts tended to emphasize Jesus and the Book of Psalms at the expense of more traditionally Roman Catholic subjects such as the Virgin Mary.

The standards for both religious and secular musical establishments were set by the court. The Chapel Royal was a choir maintained by the Crown for its various chapels. The chapel was able to command the finest musicians in the realm, the adults by choice, the boy trebles sometimes by choice and sometimes by impressment. In general, to be a Boy of the Chapel Royal meant, at the most, upward mobility and, at the least, lifelong economic security. At one point, over 85% of the bishops in the English church had begun their ecclesiastical careers as choirboys. At voice change, those who retained a pleasing sound were guaranteed musical employment through royal patronage. The rest were to be sent to a university or otherwise provided for.

The Chapel Royal was paralleled by a secular vocal and instrumental company. At least during the reigns of Henry VIII and Elizabeth, several of the secular musicians appear to have been foreigners, including Jews. They variously provided music for COURT entertainments and ceremonies, built and maintained the royal instrument collection, and provided some measure of tutelage. The chapel and secular musicians performed together only on grand ceremonial occasions such as coronations and royal funerals when every able-bodied musician was pressed into service.

Music making in the home was an important part of Tudor social life. Even a minimal education included music sight reading and improvisation. Every gentleman was expected to be able to hold a part and play at least one instrument and to do so when called upon at private gatherings. Improvised popular harmony was sung by the lower classes, as well. Women did not generally play instruments in public, but many of them were accomplished musicians. Among their social intimates, they seem to have occasionally participated in music making. Certainly, they acted in private plays, which almost always included music and dancing as did the masques and disguisings.

The new urban gentry joined the court and aristocracy as patrons of music, kept musicians in hire, commissioned works and purchased manuscripts and the occasional piece of printed music. Similarly, cities, towns, colleges, and wealthier guilds maintained waits and minstrels to provide music for various events. Often these doubled as watchmen and criers. At the bottom of the spectrum were less skilled hacks, performing mostly improvised music in alehouse and street. Satirical political songs, ballads, and tunes based on traditional melodies and street cries supplied their stock-in-trade.

Vocal music reflected changes taking place throughout Europe at the time. Melodies tended to be underlayed one note per syllable of text, except occasionally on penultimate notes. Rhythms became more defined. Harmonies increasingly inclined in the direction of diatonic tonalities. Music and text felt a much more intimate relationship; one result of this was text painting, that is, the musical expression of the text, which became popular in such genres as madrigals. For instance, "Rise up O King" might be set to four upward notes; tragic sentiments, to low, descending, or static melodies. Rhythm and tempo were similarly employed to illustrate a text. The solo song as a composed piece came into its own during the Tudor period and blossomed especially during the reign of Elizabeth.

While a wide variety of instrument makers and players flourished during the Tudor period, English keyboard music must take pride of place. Early Tudor keyboard music was closely related to its vocal cousins. Much, especially for organ, grew from plainsong melodies of the liturgy, often played in alternation with choral sections—some, like the "In nomine," even becoming the basis of secular pieces. Keyboard transcriptions of vocal and non-keyboard instrumental music were also popular as were pieces based on a repeated bass pattern, called a "ground."

In time, keyboard genres became more independent of their vocal heritage. This trend was helped by the Protestant Reformation, which made the old plainsong melodies obsolete. The new liturgical genre was the "voluntary," played at meditative times during the liturgy and as intonations before choral pieces such as anthems. In the secular realm, keyboard works were most often built on ground bases and on snatches of popular tunes and street cries. A favorite form was the fancy, a highly imitative piece, its longer specimens having sectional changes in meter and tempo. Also, English composers created the earliest extant keyboard duets beginning in the late sixteenth century. English keyboard music rose to such heights that it even began to influence Continental composers, the only medium in which that influence was the case.

Other instruments were generally played in standard groups. These might consist of a consort of viols, several recorders of differing ranges, or a group of flutes. Of course, necessity occasionally sanctioned other combinations, but one rule was firm: certain instruments were to be played indoors, and others outdoors. Flutes, viols, recorders, and most keyboards belonged indoors; shawms, cornetts, and sackbutts belonged outdoors. Taken in terms of timbre and volume, the division is eminently sensible. The only exception to this rule was the use of outdoor instruments for indoor ceremonies in large spaces such as cathedrals.

Printed music was not an important product during this period. In general, the available technology made it much too costly to be commercially viable until the seventeenth century. Printed blank manuscript paper was more profitable, however, and was produced under a monopoly owned jointly by William Byrd and Thomas Tallis. There were two situations in which printing music made good business sense. One was the small run production of music for pride and reputation's sake, especially those works intended to enhance a composer's international reputation via Continental distribution. The other was such music books as noted metrical psalters, which could have large press runs and multicopy sales. Typically, these contained only a few tunes to which a larger number of texts could be matched.

Musicologists agree that Tudor music did not end with the Tudors in 1603. Most would place the end of that era at the death of William Byrd in 1623 or Orlando Gibbons in 1625. Some would even include the work of Byrd's student and successor as Chapel Royal organist, Thomas Tomkins, who died in 1656.

Bibliography: D. W. Krummel, *English Music Printing*, 1975; Sadie Standley, ed., *The New Grove Dictionary of Music and Musicians*, 1980; David Wulstan, *Tudor Music*, 1986.

Ann E. Faulkner

N

Navigation Acts. This series of statutes attempted to promote the growth of English maritime industries. The first such action occurred during the reign of Richard II when, in 1381, an act was passed that sought to force subjects of the king to use English ships when transporting goods either into or out of England. The following year it was amended so that it would be enforced only if there were English ships available to carry a merchant's wares. Similar acts with the same general aim were passed in subsequent regimes; however, the difficulty of enforcing them became a recurring problem, and they had little effect on bringing about an expansion of the English NAVY until the time of the Tudors.

At the beginning of the Tudor era England had little in the way of either a merchant marine or a royal navy. Most of the trade of the island nation was carried in foreign vessels, and what little English shipping that did exist was confined to relatively small craft that were limited to the coastal trade or short voyages across the Channel. Even at the time of the SPANISH ARMADA the English navy was still relatively small in comparison to the great naval powers of the day. Yet, it was under the Tudors and primarily during the reign of ELIZABETH that England truly became a maritime nation.

Whereas earlier navigation acts had affected only English merchants, during the reign of HENRY VII the government began to turn its attention toward foreigners. In the first year of Henry's reign (1485), an act was passed forbidding the importation of Gascon or Guienne wines in any but English vessels. This act was replaced by that of 1489, which added Toulouse woad to the list of products to be carried only in English ships, and, in addition, taking a cue from Richard II, it required that English merchants transport their goods in English vessels when they were available.

The first navigation act of HENRY VIII's reign, passed in 1532, confirmed earlier statutes, fixed the price of wine, and prohibited its importation during the stormy season. The Act of 1540 greatly reduced privileges Henry VIII had granted the previous year by which foreign merchants had been charged the same duties as English subjects. To be able to take advantage of these reduced rates after 1540, foreign merchants had to ship their goods in English vessels.

In an attempt to protect fishermen, an act of EDWARD VI (1548) replaced the religious prohibition against eating meat on certain days (which had been removed by the Reformation) with a legislative restriction that made the serving of fish on Friday and Saturday mandatory, though the government made certain to point out that such was a political and economic measure and not a spiritual one. The number of "fish days" was expanded to include Wednesdays during the reign of Elizabeth I by an act of 1563. To further protect and encourage England's fishing industry, this same act also allowed fishermen to export fish for the first time and prevented fishermen from being impressed into service in the army or navy. The most important provision of this act, however, was that it reserved the coastal trade to English ships. An earlier act of Elizabeth's (1558) levied foreign duties on all goods shipped into or out of England unless carried in English vessels. The act also attempted to encourage the building of larger English ships by prohibiting the smaller craft from trading with foreign countries. Though there is still debate about the impact of this legislation on the growth of the English navy, the fact that appeals were made to the government for exemptions from these laws indicates that they were enforced and had some effect on the merchants.

Bibliography: Lawrence Averell Harper, *The English Navigation Laws*, 1939.

Brian Christian

Navy. The medieval English navy was, like the ARMY or the PARLIAMENT, not an institiution but an event. The king summoned his fleet when he was going to war, usually for the purpose of transporting an "army royal" across the Channel to France. Part of this fleet was assembled by a regular system of feudal service; for example, the Cinque Ports enjoyed their privileges and immunities in return for providing fifty-seven ships for the king's service for fifteen days. The remainder of the fleet were similarly merchant ships taken up by indenture with their individual owners and paid for at a contracted rate. Such ships were converted for fighting purposes by the simple expedient of building portable wooden castles onto their stems and sterns, which could then be easily removed once the campaign was over. The king normally had no more than a handful of his own ships and a single officer, the clerk or keeper, who was responsible for them. Henry V build up a fleet of over 30 ships during his war with France, but it proved enormously expensive to maintain and was sold or dismantled within a few years of his death. By 1435 Henry VI had only two vessels fit to go to sea. It was in protest against this situation that the *The Libel of English Policy* was written, urging upon the Crown its responsibility to "keep the seas" and to protect the lawful activities of merchants and fishermen.

Although he never had more than seven ships of his own, HENRY VII took this duty seriously and took the first steps toward that permanant transformation of the navy that was to take place over the next 50 years. Using the long-distance Portuguese carracks as his model, he built two new vessels in the early years of his reign, the *Sovereign* and the *Regent*. These were both large (600-700 tons) and were custom-built warships, with high permanant castles and mounting large numbers of small guns. Their purpose, and that of three or four smaller vessels like them, was to "keep the seas" during the summer in time of peace and to form the nucleus of the "navy royal" in the event of war. In 1496 he also built for their maintenance the first dry dock in norther Europe at Portsmouth, not far from the earlier anchorage in the Hamble estuary. Henry encouraged his subjects to engage in long-distance trade, patronized the Bristol voyages across the north Atlantic, and paid a subsidy for all private vessels built of more than 80 tons displacement. His son HENRY VIII built dramatically upon this modest but significant achievement. In the course of his 38-year reign, from 1509 to 1547, he built 47 new ships, many of them large warships, and acquired another 35 by capture or purchase. By the end of his first war with France, in 1514 the "standing navy" numbered about 20 vessels, and by the time of his death, 53. The deliberate policy to keep at least a proportion of the fleet at sea every summer for the "repressing of rovers" had been adopted by about 1535 and led to a significant increase in the provision of docks, storehouses, and other service facilities. Henry experimented with ship design and built not only great carracks like the *Mary Rose* and the *Henry Grace a Dieu* but large galleasses, such as the *Great Galley* and the *Tiger*, and a number of nimble but fragile row-barges. He also experimented with naval gunnery, which was both more innovative and more far-reaching in its effects. The Italians and the Portuguese had mounted heavy guns broadside on in the waists of their ships before the end of the fifteenth century, but more than a very small number constituted a hazard to the stability of the ships. Henry adapted what appears to have been a French invention: he mounted heavy guns to fire through ports cut in the side of the vessel and thus gave the guns a more effective bearing and enabled a larger number to be mounted without any risk of capsize. In the course of his reign these batteries were steadily improved in range and muzzle velocity, and by the end of the reign synchronized broadsides were being attempted for the first time, which were shortly to revolutionize naval tactics. By the early part of ELIZABETH's reign, English warships had ceased to be bases for hand-to-hand fighting and had become primarily floating gun platforms. These developments, of both scale and technique, were supported and facilitated by the creation of a body of experienced and highly paid officers who, by 1545, constituted the Council of Marine (later known as the Admiralty Board)—the vice admiral, the controller, the surveyor, the surveyor of the ordnance, and the treasurer. To their number in 1550 was added a controller of victuals, completing the most professional and effective naval administration in Europe.

Between 1540 and 1560 the direction of strategic thinking also began to change. Medium- and long-distance trade had contracted after 1520, as the MERCHANT ADVENTURERS had concentrated upon shipping cloth from London to Antwerp. But in 1550 a crisis in the Antwerp market swiftly reversed that trend, and English merchants began an energetic search for new and diverse markets. This took them back not only to the Levant and West Africa but also to Russia, the Caribbean, and the south Atlantic. EDWARD VI's council actively encouraged this enterprise and loaned royal ships to the adventurers, a policy that was continued under MARY, when legitimate hopes were also entertained of being allowed to trade in the American dominions of Philip II, briefly king of England as Mary's husband. These hopes were disappointed, and considerable resentment resulted, but the English were admitted to share the navigational technology of the Casa de Contratacion and soon began to develop their own innovative and sophisticated methods. Elizabeth continued to encourage commercial adventure and developed a policy of using her ships as investments in cooperative (and sometimes piratical) expeditions. Her objective was profit rather than "blue water" strategy, but by 1570 English royal ships were appearing in all waters, and the concept of the navy as being exclusively a home defense force was gradually abandoned. Henry VIII's navy never went farther than the Bay of Biscay or the Firth of Forth. Elizabeth's royal standard was flown at SAN JUAN D'ULLOA and borne across the Pacific by FRANCIS DRAKE.

Mary overhauled her father's Council of Marine in 1556 and 1557, placed control in the hands of the lord treasurer, and allocated an "ordinary," or peacetime budget of £14,000 a year for naval purposes. After her war with France, in 1559, Elizabeth decided to maintain Woolwich as her principal base, with Portsmouth as an operational headquarters in time of war. The standing navy was fixed at 24 warships, and a regular policy of rebuilding and renewal was determined upon. On the whole this was maintained throughout the long years of peace that followed, although the ordinary budget was reduced, first to £12,000 per annum, and then to £10,000. In 1577 when Benjamin Gonson, the long-serving treasurer of the navy, died, his place was taken by his son-in-law JOHN HAWKINS, an experienced captain and privateer, who set about the task of persuading the queen to raise the level and tempo of the naval activity. In this task he was largely successful, particularly because the threat from Spain became so obvious after 1580 that not even Elizabeth could ignore it. In ten years after taking office, Hawkins caused some 18 ships to be built, five of them "capital ships" of 500 tons or over. He also adapted the galleass design of Henry VIII's *Great Galley* to produce fast, flush-deck sailing galleons, such as the *Revenge*, which were more maneuverable, more seaworthy, and better armed than any other warships in service. With these ships the English were able to sustain war with Spain after 1585 and raided the Spanish American colonies in that year and Spain itself in 1587. Although the great SPANISH ARMADA of 1588 was defeated as much by the weather and its own tactical mistakes as by the English fleet, the speed and flexibility of the English naval response was nevertheless impressive.

Over 30 royal ships formed the core of the 140 that put to sea in three main squadrons, harried the armada successfully up the Channel, and finally outgunned and outsailed it at Gravelines.

Thereafter, the story was one of anticlimax in terms of military achievement. The PORTUGAL EXPEDITION of 1589 was a failure, and that to CADIZ in 1596 was only a qualified success. A few great prizes, such as the *Madre de Dios* in 1592, were taken, but most of the profits of privateering went to the merchant captains rather than the queen's ships. Hawkins and Drake both died at sea in 1595, and the navy fell victim to the general creeping corruption of late sixteenth-century administration. Nevertheless the navy that Elizabeth bequeathed to JAMES VI and I in 1603 was unrecognizable from the handful of small merchantmen that her grandfather had inherited. The royal navy of England was a Tudor creation.

Bibliography: K. R. Andrews, *Elizabethan Privateering*, 1964; W. Laird Clowes, *A History of the Royal Navy*, 1897; C. S. L. Davies, "The Adminstration of the Royal Navy under Henry VIII," *English Historical Review* 80 (1965): 265-86; T. Glasgow, "The Maturing of Naval Administration, 1556-1564," *Mariner's Mirror* 56 (1970); M. Oppenheim, *The Administration of the Navy*, 1896; G. Parker and C. Martin, *The Spanish Armada*, 1988.

David M. Loades

New Bishoprics, Act Authorizing (1539). (32 Hen. VIII, c. 9). Henrician attempts at reforming the administration of the English church while simultaneously putting to good use the vast royal windfall of monastic wealth resulted in a bill introduced into the House of Lords by THOMAS CROMWELL on 23 May 1539. It was hurried through all readings in both houses and enacted the same day. An elaborate preamble, in the drafting of which HENRY VIII had taken a personal role, expressed traditional HUMANIST concern for education and social welfare in addition to needed reforms in the religious community. The enacting clause empowered the king to create and endow by his letters patent an unspecified number of new dioceses and bishops.

Similar reforms, aimed in part at streamlining the administration of unwieldy and heavily populated dioceses, had been planned in THOMAS WOLSEY's day; they were given added impetus now by the vast wealth accruing to the Crown through the DISSOLUTION OF THE MONASTERIES and accompanying concerns that such wealth be used properly to benefit the religious and social welfare of the realm. The 1539 act gave no specific plan for implementation, and in the following months the king, Cromwell, THOMAS CRANMER, and a number of bishops (principally the Conservatives STEPHEN GARDINER and Richard Sampson) proposed various schemes for financing as many as twenty-one new sees. While Gardiner favored any increase in the influence of the clergy;

Cromwell's main concern seems to have been achieving all necessary reform at a minimum cost to the Crown.

In the end six new bishoprics were established: Westminster in 1540 (it lasted only ten years, being suppressed and merged with London in 1550); Bristol, Chester, Gloucester, and Peterborough in 1541; and Osney (moved soon to nearby Oxford) in 1542. They were financed out of revenues from the larger monastic houses at a total cost of slightly more than £5,000; the suppressed abbey buildings at those sites took on new dignity as cathedrals and were accordingly spared demolition. The endowment was woefully inadequate during the inflation of the mid-Tudor decades, and such shortcomings contributed to the increasingly severe economic problems of the Tudor episcopate.

The new bishops were an undistinguished lot; only Thomas Thirlby at Westminster had national stature, primarily from his diplomatic career. Paul Bush at Bristol, the only strong Reformer in the lot, was a royal chaplain and former provost of the House of Bonhommes at Edington; John Bird was translated to Chester from Bangor; John Wakesman (or Wiche)at Gloucester, John Chamber(s) at Peterborough, and Robert King at Osney/Oxford were the former abbots of Tewesbury, Peterborough, and Isney, respectively.

The principal benefits from the act were in increased administrative efficiency and in education; the new dioceses were charged with supporting grammar schools and university scholars, and during its brief existence Westminster financed readerships at Cambridge and Oxford in Greek, Hebrew, the law, divinity, and medicine.

Bibliography: G. R. Elton, *Reform and Reformation: England 1509-1558*, 1977; Felicity Heal, *Of Prelates and Princes: A Study of the Economic and Social Position of the Tudor Episcopate*, 1980.

Mary L. Robertson

"No Peace Beyond the Line." This phrase comes from the Treaty of Cateau Cambresis (2 April 1559) among England, France, and Spain; the treaty states that beyond "the lines of amity" French ships would defend themselves from the Spanish. There was no mention of the English—they may not have even known about this section of the treaty—since, at that time, they had just begun to venture beyond their own waters.

This clause of the treaty was clearly intended by the Spanish to maintain their monopoly on trade to the New World and protect their convoys, especially the treasure fleet. Thus, if a ship were attacked beyond the "lines of amity," there could be no reasons for complaint or claims for damages, though, on occasion, the French issued letters of marque and reprisal good only beyond the line. It would be several decades before this clause of the treaty had any impact on the English, and they, like much of the rest of Europe, ignored the Spanish claims. Indeed, as relations between England and Spain deteriorated during the 1580s, not only was there "no peace beyond the line," but there was very little before it as well.

The primary historical problem has been determining what these lines were since the science of cartography was still in its infancy. Using the intentions of the Spanish as a guide—the desire to protect their shipping and trade in the Americas—it can be determined that only one well-known and easily identifiable line of latitude need be used. This boundary would be the Tropic of Cancer, which runs through the Straits of Florida. Thus, there were not two "lines" as the treaty suggests but, rather, just one since no line of longitude was involved.

Bibliography: Garrett Mattingly, "No Peace Beyond What Line?" *Transactions of the Royal Historical Society*, 5th series, 13 (1963): 145-62.

Brian Christian

Nonsuch, Treaty of (1585). Anglo-Dutch alliance concluded in August 1585 between ELIZABETH I and the Netherlanders rebelling against Philip II of Spain. In the aftermath of the assassination of William the Silent in 1584, the subsequent death of the Duc d'Anjou, and the refusal of Henri III of France to accept the sovereignty of the provinces in rebellion, the Dutch found themselves facing a constitutional crisis. As each Dutch province sought an advantage and the English fretted about the influence of the French and Spanish in the Netherlands implied by the evolving alliance between Philip II and the Guise family, some political leaders concluded that ROBERT DUDLEY, earl of Leicester, might be able to unite the quarreling factions and guide the rebellion to a successful conclusion. Paul Buys, advocate of Holland and an influential politician, was one of the more prominent of those leaders. He found a keen ally in WILLIAM CECIL, who had opposed intervention in the rebellion for years but by 1584 had concluded that direct English aid of the Dutch was inevitable. Between them, they made it possible for the rebels and the English to conclude a formal alliance.

Late in March 1585, Dutch representatives arrived in London to begin what proved to be tortuous negotiations for a formal treaty. Subsequently, William Davison, English ambassador to the United Provinces, met with rebel leaders in the Netherlands and specified that the towns of FLUSHING, BRILL, and Enkhuisen be surrendered to the English as a token of good faith. This meeting produced the arrival in England of a Dutch delegation empowered to negotiate a treaty with Elizabeth I. After weeks of discussion, the negotiations were hurried to a conclusion by the prospect of a successful siege of Antwerp. Initially, the English queen agreed to support direct intervention in the rebellion by sending 400 horsemen and 4,000 infantry for a three-month period ending late in November, but diplomacy and events altered this agreement. In the end, a treaty was signed in August 1585 that proved to be the basis of relations between England and the Netherlands for the remainder of the century. Elizabeth agreed to provide and support 5,000 foot and 1,000 horse, along with garrison troops for Flushing and

Brill, commanded by a "gentleman of quality" who, with two aides, would sit on the Dutch Council of State. The rebels, for their part, promised to surrender the two towns to the English queen as security. Much was left unspecified that eventually returned to haunt both the English and their Dutch allies. The "gentleman of quality's" role, whether viceroy or not, remained unclear. So, too, did the question of which side would pay for the English troops, an issue destined to cause misunderstanding between the allies because some soldiers were already paid by the rebels and others were supported by the queen. Concluded under stress and in haste and shaped grotesquely by events, the Treaty of Nonsuch of August 1585 left both parties confused about their commitments and eventually precipitated misunderstanding and hostility between the principals.

Bibliography: Alan Haynes, *The White Bear*, 1987.

Ronald Pollitt

Norfolk Conspiracy (1569). In 1568 MARY, QUEEN OF SCOTS arrived in England, so becoming the catalyst for factional politics in the PRIVY COUNCIL. The two major issues that influenced the contending courtiers and privy councillors were the safeguarding of the succession and the extent of WILLIAM CECIL's influence in government. So long as ELIZABETH remained unmarried, Mary was the strongest claimant to the throne of England in the event of Elizabeth's death. ROBERT DUDLEY, earl of Leicester, Sir Nicholas Throckmorton, and Thomas Howard, 4th duke of Norfolk, agreed that Mary had the right to succeed. This was a grim prospect for Cecil, who feared that Mary's succession would lead to the extirpation of Protestants. Meanwhile, Conservative nobles proposed that Norfolk would use his influence to settle her succession to the English throne and that he would at the same time secure the interests of the nobility and effect a reconciliation with Philip II of Spain by replacing Cecil as chief minister. Leicester and Throckmorton were prepared to cooperate with this scheme, believing that Mary would agree to a Protestant and Anglophile domestic and foreign policy if she were restored to the Scottish throne.

Leicester and William Herbert, 1st earl of Pembroke, wrote to Mary to propose the match and detail the political terms to accompany it. Norfolk sent letters and tokens of affection to Mary and received letters back from her. He spent the summer of 1569 building up support in the north. Letters were sent to Thomas Radcliffe, 3rd earl of Sussex, lord president of the COUNCIL OF THE NORTH; Thomas Percy, 7th earl of Northumberland; and Charles Neville, 6th earl of Westmorland—all of whom did not disapprove. Only Edward Stanley, 3rd earl of Derby, dissented. Two conditions were necessary for the scheme's successful implementation. The Scots had to agree to the restoration of Mary; a convention held in Scotland in August refused to hear of Mary's return. Second, Elizabeth had to agree to the marriage. Norfolk lacked the courage to tell her of the proposals but on 6 September Leicester confessed all he knew. Norfolk was summoned by Elizabeth and acknowledged the plans for the marriage, which he defended as sound policy. Elizabeth insisted that the matter be dropped. His support at court collapsed. Ten days later he left the court for London without leave.

On the way to London there were discussions with Pembroke and Lumley about seizing the Tower. Elizabeth took steps to secure Mary and ordered Norfolk to the court at Windsor. He suddenly fled to Kenninghall, his country house in East Anglia. There were rumors that a rising was imminent; Mary urged him to arms, and the northern earls expected to be summoned to assist. In fact there is no evidence of any plan for a concerted rising at this stage. Norfolk gave no lead to the local gentry and did not raise his own tenantry. On 1 October he sent a message to Westmorland to instruct him not to rise and set out for the court. On the way he learned that he was to be confined in Burnham in Buckinghamshire. Within a week he was moved to the Tower. His other confederates—Pembroke; Henry Fitzalan, earl of Arundel; and John Lord Lumley and Throckmorton—were detained. Leicester, who had already confessed all he knew, emerged unscathed and was quickly restored to royal favor.

In the north the earls of Northumberland and Westmorland, afraid to obey the queen's summons to court, went ahead with their own rising, known as the NORTHERN REBELLION. Pembroke was soon discharged to his house at Wilton and was restored to office in December. Arundel was detained until December and dismissed to enforced residence at Nonsuch, and Throckmorton had to live in seclusion. Norfolk remained in the Tower, but his confinement was relaxed. In August 1570 he was allowed to leave the Tower for Howard House in London but was still under restraint. The revelations of the RIDOLFI PLOT, an offshoot of the Northern Rebellion, implicated Norfolk, who was rearrested, tried, and convicted of treason; on 2 June 1572 he was executed.

The result of the Norfolk conspiracy and its failure was to weaken the representatives of the old nobility at court and to strengthen the power of Cecil. Opposition to a strong anti-Catholic policy was no longer politically viable. Elizabeth was reluctant to take the life of a fellow queen, and so Mary lived in prison until 1587, a focus of plots.

Bibliography: Wallace MacCaffrey, *The Shaping of the Elizabethan Regime*, 1968.

D. J. Lamburn

Northern Rebellion (1569-1570). The Northern Rebellion had its origins in the factional squabbles of the PRIVY COUNCIL. These were linked with the proposal for a marriage between Thomas Howard, 4th duke of Norfolk, and MARY, QUEEN OF SCOTS (see NORFOLK CONSPIRACY). Thomas Percy, 7th earl of Northumberland, and Charles Neville, 6th earl of Westmorland, backed Norfolk's objectives and felt that they and their supporters had been slighted by the Tudors. The Percys and Nevilles had traditionally played a key role in the government of the north, but their prominence had been increasingly threatened during the 1560s. When Norfolk was sent to the Tower and Westmorland and Northumberland were summoned to London, they were afraid to comply and mustered their forces, and they took refuge in the pretext that the queen had been misled by evil councillors.

On 14 November 1569 the earls and their supporters marched to Durham Cathedral, where Mass was celebrated and Protestant symbols were removed. Durham was the center of the rebellion. The following day they began a march south and took Ripon, where the emblem of the PILGRIMAGE OF GRACE was raised alongside the Percy and Neville standards. Large numbers were raised from Richmondshire and the North Riding, and proclamations were made on the way. Support was mainly from the earls' estates and numbered almost 5,000 men, but it was not wholehearted, and some commons were forced to join.

Thomas Radcliffe, 3rd earl of Sussex, lord president of the COUNCIL OF THE NORTH, was ill-equipped to oppose the rebels, although an army from the south was being prepared. One original aim had been to rescue Mary, Queen of Scots, but the government moved her to the Midlands. There was no support for the earls from Cheshire and Lancashire, and appeals to the Catholic nobility failed. On 24 November the rebels began to retreat, reaching Brancepeth on 30 November with some desertions. Barnard Castle was besieged and taken early in December, and Hartlepool was captured in the hope that Spanish troops might land there to support the rebels. By 16 December the royal army was near the Tees; the earls disbanded their infantry and fled to Hexham. There was a skirmish between scouts of the opposing forces on 19 December, after which the earls retreated to the Dacre stronghold of Naworth before fleeing to Scotland. Westmorland eventually escaped to the Netherlands, where he lived as a pensioner of Spain. Northumberland was put to death in York in 1572, having been sold by the Scots to Elizabeth for £2,000. Eight of the leaders were executed at Tyburn, but many of the gentry purchased their lives by handing over their possessions to the Crown. Elizabeth ordered that 700 of the rebels should be killed, but it seems that these orders were not fully obeyed.

Although the inspiration for the rising came from events at the court and sympathy for the cause of Mary Stuart, it was as much the result of a regional as of a national crisis. The earls had personal grievances, including poverty and loss of office resulting from the extension of Tudor authority in the north. They were strengthened by those of a militant group of Durham gentry. The new Protestant clerical establishment at Durham, led by Bishop James Pilkington, campaigned to recover alienated ecclesiastical lands and attacked the property rights of the gentry. There is evidence that Catholic survivalism led by a group of priests created a popular revival of Catholic ritual and practice. Although allegiances based on BASTARD FEUDALISM and tenant loyalty is a partial reason for support for the earls, this explanation is not sufficient not all Northumberland's tenants joined the rebellion, and the leaders relied on religious propaganda, force, and the offer of wages and spoils to recruit support.

After the collapse of the rebellion and the reprisals that followed there was a comprehensive redistribution of northern patronage, lands and offices being given only to those loyal to the government and forfeited castles handed only to Crown officials. The Council in the North was reconstituted and put in the hands of Henry Hastings, 3rd earl of Huntingdon, who attacked noble retaining, instructed JUSTICES OF THE PEACE to enforce the laws against RECUSANTS, remove illegal ENCLOSURES, and relieve the poor, and promoted the appointment of Protestant preachers to further the Reformation. The failure of the rebellion led to the strengthening of Tudor authority in the north.

Bibliography: David Marcombe, "A Rude and Heady People: The Local Community and the Rebellion of the Northern Earls," in *The Last Principality: Politics, Religion and Society in the Bishopric of Durham, 1494-1660*, ed. David Marcombe, 1987: 117-51.

D. J. Lamburn

Nowell's Catechism (1570). Authorized by CONVOCATION in 1562, this work by Alexander Nowell (1507?-1602), dean of St. Paul's Cathedral, served as the official catechism of the Church of England in the wake of the ELIZABETHAN SETTLEMENT OF RELIGION of 1559.

Though the Catholic church had long espoused the catechetical method to instill the faith in its new members, such instruction was haphazard and disorganized in the years before the Reformation. Throughout Europe, the Reformers felt the need to set down an exposition of their beliefs and practices, not only to instruct but also to delineate the theological differences between Protestantism and its rival. With their church reconstituted along Protestant lines, the English responded to this need and led CONVOCATION to commission an eminently qualified Nowell for the task; the catechism that emerged in 1570 was the outgrowth of a smaller version prepared by Nowell under the auspices of EDWARD VI in 1549.

Composed of four parts, the catechism detailed Protestant creed and practice in England, with separate sections on the ANGLICAN Sacraments and the Lord's Prayer. As a MARIAN EXILE, Nowell was strongly CALVINISTIC in his religious outlook and emphasized the doctrines of predestination and election in his catechism; he also denied transubstantiation and was vehement in forbidding the use of images.

Nowell was, however, quite ERASTIAN in his adherence to monarchical supremacy in ecclesiastical matters; absolute obedience to those in authority is a hallmark of the Catechism, and this loyalty formed the bedrock upon which the ecclesiastical settlement and the Anglican church rested. Despite its official replacement during the interregnum, Nowell's catechism served as the standard exposition of English Protestantism for more than a century after its publication.

Bibliography: Frank V. Occhiogrosso, ed., *A Catechisme or First Instruction and Learning of Christian Religion (1570)* by Alexander Nowell, 1975; G. E. Corrie, ed., *Nowell's Catechism*, 1853.

Connie S. Evans

Nymegen, Treaty of (1573). Agreement reached between ELIZABETH I and the duke of Alva in April 1573 that ended the trade embargo begun in January 1569 after the English seizure of Alva's payships in the preceding December. Overshadowed by the better- known treaties of BLOIS (April 1572) and BRISTOL (August 1574), this pact tentatively resolved the differences between England and Spain that arose from the first major breach in Anglo-Spanish relations since Elizabeth's accession in 1558.

In December 1568 and January 1569, two events occurred that accelerated the decline in relations between England and Spain that had begun with Elizabeth's tacit support of the rebels in the Netherlands. When, in December 1568, five Spanish ships carrying specie to pay Philip II's troops in the Low Countries were chased into ports on England's south coast by Huguenot privateers, Elizabeth seized the opportunity to disrupt Alva's campaigns against the Netherlanders while simultaneously improving the Crown's financial position. Acting on advice of her PRIVY COUNCIL, the queen ordered that the treasure be impounded and transferred to London. When challenged on the legality of her action by Guerau de Spes, the Spanish ambassador, the queen replied that she was within her rights to borrow the money, which was technically the property of Genoese bankers.

An incautious man, de Spes reacted rashly, portraying the episode in such an exaggerated way to the duke of Alva that early in 1569 he conformed to de Spes's recommendation to arrest all English goods and subjects in the Low Countries. The English, angered by news that came in January 1569 of the Spanish attack on JOHN HAWKINS at SAN JUAN D'ULLOA in Mexico, responded by impounding Spanish goods, and a trade embargo between the two nations soon followed. Discussions to restore normal trade relations took place both in 1570 and, with more intensity, in 1571, but political and military developments made it impossible for the two sides to agree. Finally, in the early months of 1573, Alva reopened negotiations with the English on his own initiative, largely because he was worried that Elizabeth might increase her aid to William of Orange, who had sent representatives to London, and thus worsen Alva's precarious military position. Consequently, the discussions, which took place at Nymegen, were brief and ended in April 1573 with a pact that favored the English. Both sides agreed to lift the embargo and support each other against mutual enemies for two years, and Alva conceded what had been the sticking point in earlier talks: a formula, authored by Elizabeth and her advisers, for restoring the property seized four years earlier. In August 1574, this Treaty of Nymegen was superseded by the Treaty of Bristol, which normalized relations between England and the Spanish Empire until English troops were sent to the Netherlands in 1585.

Bibliography: W. S. Maltby, *Alba*, 1983; R. B. Wernham, *Before the Armada*, 1966.

Ronald Pollitt

O

O'Rourke's Revolt (1590-1591). An early attempt by Brian na Murtha O'Rourke to prevent the extension of English conquest into Ulster, one of the last bastions of Gaelic Ireland.

Despite resistance to the establishment of direct English government throughout Ireland, by 1590 the process had been generally completed with the exception of Ulster, which proved the most difficult province to incorporate into the system by virtue of its terrain and the power of its Gaelic lords. Inroads had been made to achieve control, most notably in the division of the strongest lordship in the province, Tyrone, between its earl and Turlough Luineach. Other lords had been induced to cooperate through the lowering of composition rents and by having their Gaelic titles to land regularized by the English government.

Several lords proved more intransigent, among them Hugh Roe MacMahon, lord of Monaghan, who proved resistant to English governmental interference. Monaghan's repeated border raids led the deputy, Sir William Fitzwilliam, to arrest, try, and execute him in 1592. His actions, however, inspired O'Rourke, on the northern border of the English-held Connaught province, to defy the government as well. Refusing to pay composition rents and preventing a duly appointed sheriff from taking up his post, O'Rourke also permitted Scots and Spaniards to reside in his holdings. In March 1590, Fitzwilliam began a campaign against O'Rourke, who fled to Scotland. JAMES VI, eager to conciliate ELIZABETH, turned him over to the English, who hung him at Tyburn in November 1591. O'Rourke's rebellion proved to be one of the opening salvos of the TYRONE REBELLION (the Nine Years' War), which engulfed Ulster in a struggle against the English government from 1593 to 1603.

Bibliography: S. G. Ellis, *Tudor Ireland*, 1985.

Connie S. Evans

P

Paget, William (c. 1505-1563). Statesman and administrator, William Paget was typical of the men who rose from humble origins to prominence by their political agility and administrative talent. Although from humble origins, he was educated at St. Paul's School and Trinity Hall, Cambridge, where he met many other future royal officials. Paget's patron at Cambridge was Thomas Boleyn, but it was under the patronage of the former master of Trinity, STEPHEN GARDINER, that he first entered the king's service.

Skilled in languages, Paget was sent on several diplomatic missions, most notably to gain the support of foreign courts and universities for HENRY VIII's proposed DIVORCE; his success earned him a permanent government appointment as clerk of the Signet by late 1531. Once established in the king's service, he jumped from Gardiner, now losing favor because of his opposition to the king's proposed divorce, to the rising THOMAS CROMWELL. Cromwell rewarded him with the post of secretary to Queens JANE SEYMOUR, ANNE OF CLEVES, and CATHERINE HOWARD. He became the first full-time clerk to the PRIVY COUNCIL and clerk to the Parliament shortly before Cromwell's disgrace. By now a seasoned bureaucrat, he had no trouble remaining in office and continued the Cromwellian revolution after his patron's execution.

After another successful embassy to France, Paget was sworn of the privy council in April 1543 and appointed one of the two PRINCIPAL SECRETARIES. By the end of the reign, Paget had become the chief secretary, in fact, and he was one of Henry's most trusted advisers. But at the king's death he was able to switch masters once again. He helped EDWARD SEYMOUR, earl of Hertford, overturn Henry's will, which he had partially drawn up, and establish the Protectorate. It was he who remembered the "unfulfilled gifts clause," by which Hertford rewarded his fellow conspirators. Hertford, now the duke of Somerset, rewarded him with the Garter and the posts of comptroller of the royal HOUSE

HOLD and chancellor of the duchy of Lancaster, posts of prestige and considerable potential profit.

Despite his alarm at Somerset's increasingly high-handed manner, Paget remained one of his chief officials, but he was able to change loyalties quickly once Somerset's support vanished. He convinced Somerset that he ought to resign and then turned around and arrested him on behalf of the new regime. For his part in bringing down his former patron, he was named baron of Beaudesert. However, once JOHN DUDLEY, duke of Northumberland, was safely in control, he dropped Paget and sent him to the Tower. After a trumped-up charge of abusing the office of chancellor of the duchy, he confessed, lost his offices, and was fined £8,000 (later reduced). He was eventually released without ever having his case brought to trial.

Paget's temporary disgrace stood him in good stead after EDWARD VI's death, when MARY interpreted suffering at the hands of Northumberland as a sign of loyalty to her. Back in favor, he instinctively championed the Spanish marriage and earned Mary's trust and that of her future husband. However, he never regained the prominence he had enjoyed under Somerset, because he refused to support the extreme religious settlement Mary favored. Instead she appointed him lord privy seal, a post with considerable prestige, but little power.

Elizabeth's accession completed Paget's political demise. The new queen did not reappoint him as lord privy seal, and though he was nominally on the council, he had assumed the role of elder statesman, playing little part in the new regime. Paget died in 1563. He had been a true bureaucrat, faithfully serving whoever seemed likely to hold power. In his three decades of service he used office and influence to amass a considerable fortune.

Bibliography: S. R. Gammon, *Statesman and Schemer*, 1973.

Robert C. Braddock

Pardon of the Clergy, Act for (1531). This statute (22 Hen. VIII, c. 15) pardoned all the clergy of the province of Canterbury for having shared, however indirectly, in Cardinal THOMAS WOLSEY's crime of PRAEMUNIRE. Collaterally, it established the monarch as "sole protector and supreme head of the church and clergy in England," with the qualifier, "so far as the law of Christ allows."

Following Wolsey's indictment (October 1529), confession, and pardon for violation of the Statute of Praemunire, HENRY VIII enlarged the attack and held that all the clergy of the realm had participated in Wolsey's guilt by virtue of having accepted the cardinal's authority as papal legate. Subsequently, they were accused of acting "contrary to the form of the Statutes of Provisors, Provisions and Praemunire." These blatantly concocted charges doubtless served as a means of forcing the clergy to take sides in the ensuing jurisdictional struggle between church and Crown. The CONVOCATION of Canterbury prudently chose the latter. In January 1531, they rushed to seek the king's good graces in a petition that offered him £100,000 for a full pardon.

Wishing to have the substantive principle of the matter publicly affirmed, Henry demanded that the petition's preamble contain the phrase noted above, "sole protector and supreme head of the church and clergy in England." Convocation negotiated the addition of "so far as the law of Christ allows," ostensibly to protect themselves from excommunication by Pope Clement VII but also to retain some semblance of territory. The northern convocation of York followed suit and received a similar pardon the following year for £18,840 (23 Hen. VIII, c. 19). Money itself was not a major issue as the clergy soon would have been asked to grant another subsidy, which payment the pardon preempted.

In the course of the parliamentary debate over Canterbury convocation's pardon, the Commons noted the praemunire statute's broad compass. Fearing for their own purses, the Commons tried to get themselves included in the pardon, for which the clergy were already due to pay by intimating to the king that they might otherwise hesitate to enact the statute. Henry refused to be coerced, but later "of his mere notion, and of his benignity, special grace, pity and liberality" agreed to An Act for the Pardon of the Laity (22 Hen. VIII, c. 16).

The pardon made exceptions for high treason, sacrilege, felonies, "carnall ravishments of Women," outlawries worth more than 20s., and certain other matters that primarily related to questions of property. It concluded with a proviso making the pardon contingent upon actual payment of the subsidy.

Bibliography: G. W. Bernard, "The Pardon of the Clergy Reconsidered," J. A. Guy, "The Pardon of the Clergy: A Reply," and G. W. Bernard, "A Comment on Dr. Guy's Reply," *Journal of Ecclesiastical History* 37 (1986): 258-87.

Ann E. Faulkner

Parker, Matthew (1504-1575). The first Elizabethan archbishop of Canterbury was born into a lesser gentry family from Norwich in 1504 and studied at Corpus Christi College, Cambridge, in the 1520s. There he met radicals such as ROBERT BARNES, John Bilney, and Miles Coverdale. Parker was awarded his B.D. in 1535 and his doctorate in 1538. He became chaplain to Queen ANNE BOLEYN (1535) and to the king (1538). With HENRY VIII's support, he became master of Corpus Christi College and vice-chancellor of Cambridge (1545).

Under EDWARD VI's Protestant regime, Parker married (1547) Margaret Harlestone, the daughter of a Norfolk gentleman. He was vice-chancellor of Cambridge again (1549) and a frequent court preacher. In 1552 he became dean of Lincoln. At the accession of the Catholic MARY in 1553, Parker lost all his preferments. He and his family stayed quietly in Norfolk.

After ELIZABETH I came to the throne in 1558, Parker soon received appointment as archbishop of Canterbury. He maintained that it was his promise to Anne Boleyn that he would look after her daughter's spiritual welfare that made him accept the primacy. For Elizabeth, Parker represented a link with her mother. He was a proven administrator and had remained in England under Mary, whereas others with respectable Protestant pedigrees had returned from the MARIAN EXILE to promote a church more radically Protestant than Elizabeth considered politic.

Parker's consecration took place in December 1559. His was an unhappy primacy. He was not made a royal councillor and had to use WILLIAM CECIL as a sympathetic intermediary when communicating with the queen and her council. The queen was often unhelpful. In 1563 Parker steered his Articles of Religion through a suspicious CONVOCATION, but in 1566 Elizabeth halted attempts to gain statutory confirmation for this clarification of the doctrines and practices of her church. Parker finally attained parliamentary support for the THIRTY-NINE ARTICLES in 1571, after Elizabeth's excommunication (see REGNANS IN EXCELSIS) had confirmed her alienation from Rome.

Parker's problems with the council began in 1565 and 1566. Some of the clergy found the ELIZABETHAN SETTLEMENT OF RELIGION in 1559 insufficiently Protestant. They rejected certain things, such as the wearing of the surplice and kneeling at communion. In January 1565 Elizabeth wrote Parker a letter complaining about this. Possibly this letter was at his suggestion, because despite a similar letter of March 1566, she gave him no further support in his campaign for clerical conformity (see VESTIARIAN CONTROVERSY). She would not authorize his orders, which were then issued as "advertisements" rather than the usual "injunctions." Nevertheless, Parker persevered, until at one point one third of London's parishes were deprived of their ministers. By July 1566, however, only a handful held out, and few were deprived. These nonconformists often had the support of far weightier political figures than the primate. The deprived dean of Christ Church, Sampson, soon acquired a rectory and a prebend under the patronage of ROBERT DUDLEY, earl of Leicester, and Henry Hastings, earl of Huntington. Some bishops were equally unsupportive; the primate bemoaned the laxity of Bishop EDMUND GRINDAL of London, while Bishops Edwin Sandys of Worcester, John Parkhurst of Norwich, and James Pilkington of Durham were unenthusiastic. Pilkington sought and obtained Leicester's encouragement.

Many nonconformists now blamed their troubles on bishops. This position, coupled with further deprivations (1571-1572), led to increasing attacks on episcopacy. A worried Parker warned Cecil that councillors' support for these "PURITANS" would ultimately subvert the whole established order. In 1573 Parker's relations with the council temporarily improved, after a puritan fanatic tried to stab CHRISTOPHER HATTON, but Parker's acceptance of incredible accusations of a puritan plot against Cecil (1574) destroyed the archbishop's credibility. When in 1574 he told Bishops Parkhurst and Sandys to halt prophesyings, which were often dominated by nonconformists, Sandys asked the council if the queen really wanted to end these theological discussions between the clergy and the laity. On their advice, he ignored Parker's instructions. In 1575, Parker received a public scolding from Elizabeth for his enforcement of conformity in the diocesan visitation of Winchester, which had annoyed Leicester.

Parker sought consolation in his household, which was a virtual ministry of propaganda. He collected written ammunition for members of his household, who wrote books against Catholicism and, reluctantly, extreme Protestantism. He published works such as *A Testament of Antiquity*, which "proved" the Elizabethan church had an ancient Anglo-Saxon pedigree. His manuscripts were at the disposal of men such as JOHN FOXE, whose influential *Acts and Monuments* owed much to the primate. Parker masterminded the 1568 Bishops' Bible, although this never attained the popularity of the Geneva edition. His splendid household was meant to improve the image of church and primate, but it was unpopular. For some Protestants it recalled Catholic pomp and pretension.

Parker died in May 1575, a conscientious primate who tried to maintain and strengthen the church established in 1559. He worked hard to attain a better educated, preaching, and conforming clergy. Elizabeth I failed, however, to give him sufficient authority and support. In dealing with Catholics, the political establishment was more united, but in dealing with "puritans," Parker faced councillor opposition. Possibly Elizabeth felt her regime could not yet weather a full-scale attack on the "puritanism" supported by so many of her leading advisers.

Bibliography: V. J. K. Brook, *A Life of Archbishop Parker*, 1962; J. Bruce and T. T. Perowne, eds., *Correspondence of Mathew Parker*, 1853; V. Sanders, "The Household of Archbishop Parker and the Influencing of Public Opinion," *Journal of Ecclesiastical History* 34 (1983): 534-47.

V. C. Sanders

Parliament. The early Tudor Parliaments were the product of over 200 years of historical development. Their original and continuing function was to enable the king and the great men of the land to consult on important and urgent affairs and to adjudicate on pleas and petitions brought before them. Thus the earlier medieval institution had a curial character and indeed was styled "the high court of Parliament." By 1485, however, this description did not reflect contemporary realities, because Parliaments had moved from judicial to legislative solutions of the problems before them. Moreover the newer house, the Commons, had arrived as a full member of Parliament. It alone could initiate taxes, whilet its law-making role had been transformed gradually from a mere petitioner to a coequal partner with the House of Lords. Therefore Parliament had become truly bicameral: an upper chamber consisting of nobles, whose peerage status was becoming equated with lordship of Parliament, twenty-one bishops, and abbatial heads of some monasteries; and a nether house comprised of 296 knights of the shire and burgesses.

Parliament was, as it always had been, a royal creature, activated by the king whenever he needed it and dissolved or prorogued when it had fulfilled its purpose. Nor did that fact change under the Tudors. Sessions remained short, irregular and, apart from the Reformation years (1529-1559), infrequent—no more than an occasional supplement to royal government. Within the bicameral institution the older chamber, the Lords, remained more powerful, prestigious, and efficient. When the two houses assembled, they did so in order to confer with a king who remained outside and apart from Parliament. Each occasion was a "coming-together" or "parley" between king *and* Parliament. Therefore much that was characteristic of its medieval character survived. By 1529, however, one fundamental change had rounded off earlier developments. The Crown had become an integral part of a parliamentary trinity, and so king-and-Parliament was transformed into king-in-Parliament.

Despite the monarch's incorporation into the institution, its legislative competence remained strictly limited. In particular it could not tamper with property rights or meddle in matters spiritual. But the REFORMATION PARLIAMENT (1529-1536) removed those restraints. Initially, it was called to assist HENRY VIII in the annulment of his first marriage. By the time of its dissolution it had reduced the English clergy to obedience, enacted a schism with Rome, and recognized Henry as supreme head of a national Catholic church. Parliament was also utilized to dissolve the monasteries and transfer their property to the Crown, while the king's chief adviser, THOMAS CROMWELL, enlisted its assistance in his state-building schemes: abolishing franchises (semiautonomous territories, especially on the Welsh borders), incorporating WALES and its marches into the English administrative and judicial system, and enfranchising them, together with the county palatine of Chester and CALAIS. In the process, the earlier limits on Parliament's competence disappeared. King-in-Parliament emerged as the constitutional sovereign, whose statutes were omnicompetent, capable of handling anything, including property rights and matters spiritual. When the monarch met with the Lords and Commons, he wielded far more authority than when he acted alone. Henry VIII acknowledged this when he informed the lower house in 1542, "we be informed by our judges that we at no time stand so highly in our estate royal as in the time of parliament." So long as king and governing class remained in general harmony, as they did for most of the century, Parliament's new power simply augmented the Crown's ordinary authority. Indeed, Henry VIII seemed able to get almost anything he wanted. Parliaments repeatedly delegated legislative authority to him—to implement the act in restraint of annates (payments to the pope) in 1532 and the union of Wales with England (1536) and to dissolve chantries when he saw fit (1545). They gave statutory authority to the enforcement of PROCLAMATIONS (1539). After a seven-year campaign, in 1536 Henry obtained the act of USES, which ended the widespread evasion of feudal dues by landowners, another statutory incursion on property rights. When, four years later, its rigorous terms were moderated by the statute of WILLS, the change was sponsored by the Crown, which recognized that concessions had to be made in the interest of Crown-governing class harmony.

The increasing confidence with which Parliament legislated in previously forbidden pastures was demonstrated also by the enactment of the Edwardian Reformation (1547-1552), the Marian restoration of Roman Catholicism (1553-1555), and finally the ELIZABETHAN SETTLEMENT of 1559. This ended the era of dramatic parliamentary development. Thereafter Elizabeth's conservative government used Parliaments to protect the status quo against Catholic threats and, after the years 1584-1585, to fund its military machine in the long war with Spain. However, in several respects her privy council proved to be adventurous. Building on the precedents of Thomas Cromwell's experiments, which, in 1534 and 1540, introduced the novel principle that TAXATION was justified in peacetime as well as in war, it regularly applied to Parliaments for subsidies. Second, parliamentary pressure, orchestrated by the council, wrung from Elizabeth her assent to an act that gave statutory sanction to a limited form of lynch law and that made possible the trial and execution of an anointed monarch, MARY, QUEEN OF SCOTS.

Institutional changes in the privileges, procedures, records, organization, and membership of Parliament accompanied the far-reaching changes in its authority. The history of members' privileges and "liberties of the house" chiefly concerns the commons—a simple consequence of the consolidation and organization of a relatively new coequal legislative chamber (see PARLIAMENTARY PRIVILEGE). The same was true of procedural developments. Initially the older House of Lords led the way. However, during a century in which an unprecedented volume and range of business were transacted, the Commons rapidly systematized its techniques of lawmaking, while the upper house continued to refine its own procedures. The most important development was the regularization of the three-reading procedure. It was already taking shape before the Tudors, but during the sixteenth century inconsistencies disappeared, and it became the only recognized way to enact statute: a literal first reading of the bill to inform members of its contents; a discussion of its substance at the second reading; committal for scrutiny and possible revision; engrossment of the paper bill onto parchment; and a third reading at which the priority was textual precision. By 1601 procedural uniformity was an accomplished fact.

Parliament's records also underwent significant changes. Its medieval record repository had been CHANCERY, but from 1479 the clerk of the Parliaments retained the new acts in his possession. The old master record, the Parliament roll, became merely a copy of the text of statutes, and its place was taken by the clerks' journals of proceedings. As befitted the older house, the Lords' activities were being recorded by the mid-fifteenth century, whereas the Commons' journals were an innovation of Edward VI's reign. At the same time, the lower house moved from the chapter house of Westminster Abbey to St. Stephen's Chapel. This lay within Westminster Palace, which for centuries had housed the Lords, the historic nucleus of the institution, in the Parliament chamber. The Commons' change of venue belatedly confirmed its "arrival" as a coequal partner of the upper house.

This occurred during a time of change in the composition and size of Parliament's membership. The dissolution of the larger monasteries (1539-1540) removed the regular clergy, reduced the Lords' size to between 70 and 80, and left it with a permanent lay majority, despite the creation of six NEW BISHOPRICS in the years 1540-1542. Meanwhile, between 1529 and 1601 the Commons' membership expanded from 296 to 462. This was partly the consequence of state-building in the 1530s, when outliers of the English kingdom were incorporated into it and enfranchised. The Crown also exploited its undoubted right to create new parliamentary boroughs to strengthen its support network in the Commons. More important was the growing attraction of parliamentary service to the country gentry. The county seats, a maximum of ninety, could not satisfy their appetite and so carpetbagging gentry, assisted by noble patrons, ignored residential qualifications and invaded the boroughs. By 1601 they numbered four-fifths of the Commons.

Harmonious relations between the two houses—essential to successful Parliaments—were the norm, although they did disagree over points of privilege, procedure, and, occasionally, political issues. Their parliamentary relations with the Crown also varied according to political circumstances. For example, in the Reformation Parliament, in Mary's early assemblies, and in 1559, the center of anticipated or actual resistance to royal policies was the Lords. When that occurred, the monarch went into alliance with the Commons. More important in the longer term was the placement of his chief adviser. When Thomas Cromwell and WILLIAM CECIL were ennobled, in 1536 and 1571, respectively, the parliamentary initiative too shifted to the Lords. Such swings in the political pendulum, however, had little effect on the general configuration of Parliament's business record. The Lords was consistently better equipped to service the Crown and satisfy private interests with beneficial laws. They were a small elitist assembly of men with life membership and intimate connections with court and government. They enjoyed the services of Parliament's senior bureaucrat, the clerk of the Parliaments, and especially of the legal assistants: royal judges, solicitor, attorney, and king's sergeants. The assistants, seated on woolsacks in the center of the chamber, advised the house on points of law and assisted in the scrutiny and revision of bills. As a consequence, the upper house was usually more efficient and productive. In contrast, the Commons was plagued with inefficiency, an unwieldy and growing membership, many inexperienced knights and burgesses, endemic absenteeism among its legislative specialists, the lawyers, and an inundation of business.

Parliament, however, was not only a legislative institution. It was also a national political forum, in which the monarch discussed urgent affairs, and, at the same time, his governing class took the opportunity to air its grievances—a legitimate parliamentary function. Disharmony, disagreements, even conflict sometimes occurred when important issues and complaints were discussed. Few

Parliaments passed without contentious debate or outspoken criticism: objection to excessive or unwarranted financial demands; the politicking of the "Aragonese faction" in the Reformation Parliament; obstinate resistance to the religious changes between 1529 and 1559; and PRESBYTERIAN attempts to change the "halfly-reformed" Elizabethan church into a godly institution based on the best Continental models. However, not all parliamentary disputes involved the Crown. Many of them were provoked by competing private interests, while others were tetchy border skirmishes over the respective privileges and precedence of the Lords and Commons. Even the attempts to persuade Elizabeth to marry, name a successor, execute Mary Stuart, or make war on Spain were not expressions of parliamentary resistance to royal policies. They were campaigns orchestrated by the privy council and designed to compel her to take action. It is clear that there were no rise in the Commons' political power, no growth of parliamentary conflict, and no emergence of a persistent, organized, radical Protestant opposition to the Crown. Elizabethan Parliaments were not staging posts on the high road to civil war and revolution in the mid-seventeenth century.

Although Parliament had undergone significant changes by 1601, harmony between the members of the trinity, which was the guarantee of its success, had neither disappeared nor even appreciably diminished. It is true that, as the century progressed, the Crown had to refine its managerial techniques. Instead of the earlier overt, even intimidating control and direction by councillors, both during elections and sessions, it adopted more discreet practices. So it prompted the Commons to choose its preselected speaker and operated through a broad network of loyal men-of-business. Its concern was not to overcome opposition, which for the most part did not exist, but to push its business through a rather undisciplined, inefficient lower house. Even during the economic and social dislocation of the 1590s, the escalating faction conflict at COURT, and the swelling discontent over monopolies, Elizabethan Parliaments continued to be productive to the end.

Bibliography: G. R. Elton, *The Parliament of England, 1559-1581*, 1986; G. R. Elton, *The Tudor Constitution*, 1982; M. A. R. Graves, *The Tudor Parliaments. Crown, Lords and Commons, 1485-1603*, 1985.

M. A. R. Graves

Parliamentary Privilege. The history of Tudor Parliaments concerns not only the special rights of individual members of both houses but also the "liberties" of the Lords and Commons. Both were intended to enable the two houses to fulfill their parliamentary functions. If the House of Commons figures more prominently, that is because it had only recently been fully incorporated into the institution as a co-equal partner of the Lords. Its concern with privilege was not symptomatic either of an assertive rivalry with the older upper house or of a growing political challenge to royal authority but simply part of the process of rendering itself more efficient.

Privilege exempted members from normal rules during a Parliament: most notably, freedom from arrest by the order of inferior courts. Although this particular privilege excluded treasons and felonies, it did encompass civil actions, including debt. Members' servants, whose service was regarded as necessary to the parliamentary activity of their employers, were similarly protected. The decisive steps in the consolidation of this privilege were taken in HENRY VIII's reign. When a burgess, Richard Strode, was arrested by the stannary courts for promoting a bill hostile to the tin interest, he secured an act (4 Henry VIII, c. 8) that not only personally indemnified him but, more important, also protected members from inferior courts. Then, in 1542, another burgess, George Ferrers (c. 1510-1579), was arrested for debt. The significance of his case was twofold. The Commons acted on its own authority to secure Ferrers's release, instead of applying, as in the past, for a writ from the lord chancellor. Second, as a member released by parliamentary privilege could not be re-arrested for the same debt, he escaped scot-free. Ferrers's case set a precedent for abuse of this privilege (see Smalley's case below).

More contentious was the Crown's removal of members for political offenses. The official sequestration of William Strickland (d. 1598) for presenting a bill to reform the Prayer Book in 1571, was a tactical blunder that engendered much heat in the Commons. Thereafter Elizabeth was careful to proceed against offending members only for extra-parliamentary activities, as she did with Anthony Cope (1550-1615) and Peter Wentworth (1524-1597) in the years 1586-1587. Meanwhile the house displayed a willingness to extend privilege. In 1585 it attempted to prevent Richard Cooke (1561-c. 1616) from being summoned by subpoena into a law court. However, the lord chancellor not only rebuffed its pretensions on this occasion but also, in 1593, upheld the arrest of Thomas Fitzherbert (c. 1550-1600), because he was a royal debtor. Against the Commons' generous interpretation of the privilege of freedom from arrest should be set its willingness to imprison its own members and their servants for a variety of transgressions. Thomas Copley (1532-1584) in 1558 and Peter Wentworth in 1576 were incarcerated for offensive speech against the monarch, while Dr. William Parry (d. 1585) was sequestered and obliged to beg forgiveness for outspoken opposition to the proposed new law against Jesuits (1584). A further illustration is provided by the complicated affair of Arthur Hall (1539-1605), burgess for Grantham. In 1576 he and his servant, Edward Smalley, engineered the latter's arrest for non-payment of £100 damages arising from an assault charge and then resorted to parliamentary privilege to secure his release. The Commons, unconvinced, imprisoned Smalley and compelled Hall to pay the damages. Hall counterattacked with a pamphlet that was offensive to both the liberties and dignity of the house. For this the Commons expelled, fined, and imprisoned him in 1581.

The House of Lords was equally sensitive about privilege. In 1572 it rallied to the unworthy cause of Henry Lord Cromwell (1538-1592), who had been arrested for contempt by the Court of CHANCERY. It over-ruled the lord chancellor and decided that there was no precedent for the "attachment" of a noble who had "place and voice in parliament." On the other hand, in 1584 it denied privilege to the imprisoned Robert Finnies, because he was not, strictly speaking, a servant of Viscount Bindon (1542-1590), who had attempted to secure his release. This response was sensible, because peers had so many servants of various kinds and degrees that a liberal interpretation of parliamentary privilege might have enabled many debtors to escape their obligations.

The liberties of the two houses, like the privileges of their members, were designed to enable them to carry out their tasks properly. The most important of these liberties was freedom of speech. In 1523 the Commons' speaker, THOMAS MORE, petitioned Henry VIII to allow members to voice their opinions freely, though only on matters placed before them, and even then without "licence" (excessive language). Although this petition was the first recorded formal request, it probably had an antecedent history, and it was certainly repeated and granted regularly thereafter. Such repetition gradually transformed the grant from an act of royal grace to a customary right, if only in the minds of many members. ELIZABETH's strict application of the terms of the grant, however, caused difficulties, especially when she prohibited discussion of religion and PREROGA- TIVE matters. This frustrated ardent Reforming Protestants. So in 1566 Paul Wentworth (1534-1594) and his brother Peter (in 1576 and 1587) were driven to demand the right to speak freely on any subject and, in the process, to challenge the constraints imposed by the queen. But the Wentworths, Peter in particular, enjoyed little parliamentary support; they were easily outmaneuvered, and Elizabeth did not have to retreat from her position.

The Commons could be sensitive, even tetchy, about its liberties in its dealings with the upper house too. When, in 1576, it amended the restoration in blood of Lord Stourton (1553-1588), in a bill from the Lords endorsed with the queen's signature, the upper house questioned the propriety of its actions. The Commons leapt to the defense of its liberties and declared its right to reject or alter any bill, whatever its provenance. This vigorous kind of response was in tune with its increasingly confident management of its own internal affairs. Not only did it discipline members and their servants for misconduct, but it also began to monitor membership qualifications; so in 1550 it allowed the heir of the newly created earl of Bedford to remain, but three years later it declared ineligible Alexander Nowell (1507?-1602), a clergyman. During Elizabeth's reign it extended its supervision of membership to disputed elections and, after a clash with Chancery over the election of the knights for Norfolk in 1586, it effectively asserted control over electoral returns.

Such extensions of the Commons' liberties and privileges were not milestones on the upward path of its political rise but rather the consolidation of rights that were necessary for the efficient functioning of a relatively new chamber. Occasionally hotheads, such as the Wentworth brothers, injected a political dimension when they attempted to enlarge liberties as a means to their particular religious ends. Their opinions were not those of the majority, which responded with indifference and even hostility. On the other hand Elizabeth created problems when she imposed strict constraints on Parliament, one of the prime functions of which was consultation on great and urgent affairs of the realm—and from the 1530s onward these invariably included religion.

Bibliography: G. R. Elton, *The Tudor Constitution*, 1982.

M. A. R. Graves

Parr, Catherine (1512-1548). Catherine Parr, the sixth wife of HENRY VIII, was the daughter of Sir Thomas Parr, master of Henry VIII's Household. She was twice widowed before attracting the king's notice, and was being courted by THOMAS SEYMOUR (brother of JANE SEYMOUR) when Henry decided to marry her. She was a pious and scholarly woman and a devoted Protestant. She married the king on 12 July 1543, and set about to form a family for his children, who responded with loyalty and affection. She also fostered the New Learning and drew to her court Renaissance scholars and learned clergy. She herself combined a religious tolerance with Erasmian piety and wished to avoid the extremes of either religious faction. Besides supervising the education of her stepchildren, she carried out scholarship of her own, and wrote devotional works such as *The Lamentation or Complaint of a Sinner*.

  She readily achieved the king's trust and affection so that when he campaigned in France in 1544, he appointed her his regent. Unfortunately, her religious views and scholarly mind led to a marital and political crisis in 1546. The Conservative faction, led by Bishop STEPHEN GARDINER and the lord chancellor, THOMAS WRIOTHESLEY, hoped to discredit the queen and thereby bring the downfall of the Reformed faction at court; the notorious ANNE ASKEW AFFAIR resulted from their attempts to implicate Catherine in heresy. Being warned that her theological arguments had angered the king and had placed her in danger, she humbled herself, declaring that she had offered disputatious arguments only to divert the ailing Henry from the pain of his ulcerous leg. When Wriothesley came to arrest her, he found her and the king "perfect friends as ever at any time before."

  She remained in Henry's favor until his death in 1547. In April of that year she married her former suitor, THOMAS SEYMOUR. She died in April 1548, after bearing him a daughter.

Bibliography: Paul Rival, *The Six Wives of King Henry VIII*, 1971.

Mary G. Winkler

Peter's Pence, Act Concerning (1534). This statute (25 Hen. VIII, c. 21) of the REFORMATION PARLIAMENT dealt with Peter's Pence, also called Peter Pence, Peterspence, *denarius S. Petri*, "Romefeoh," "Romgesceot," "Romescot," and "hearthpenny," which had originated during the Anglo-Saxon period as a freewill offering to the Roman pontiff. Gradually it became an annual contribution (originally of a penny from each householder holding land worth thirty pence or more) paid to Rome by various peoples of Christendom. Its origin is obscure, but it is clear that it began as a gift and later became a tax collected in midsummer, that is, the five weeks between St. Peter's and St. Paul's Day, 29 June and 1 August, the feast of St. Peter's Chains.

Traditions regarding its origin are confused. It has been attributed to King Ini (Ine, Ina) of Wessex, who paid it for the first time in 725 to support the Schola Saxonum, an educational institution in Rome for English clergy. The earliest clear documentary mention of it is in a letter of Canute (1031), sent from Rome to the English clergy and laity. There was great irregularity in the payment of Peter's Pence, and Pope Gregory VIII in 1074 in a letter to King William demanded that it be paid. William agreed to the claim and promised that the arrears would be paid.

Some confusion seems to have existed between Peter's Pence and the tribute paid by King John. The tribute, or cess, of 1,000 marks (700 for England, 300 for Ireland), which John bound himself and his heirs to pay to the Roman see, in recognition of the feudal dependence of his kingdom was wholly distinct from Peter's Pence. In 1366 Parliament abolished this tribute, but Peter's Pence of 300 marks annually was paid at least intermittently down to Henry VIII's break with Rome.

The Act in Absolute Restraint of ANNATES (1534, 25 Hen. VIII, c. 20), had legally outlawed Peter's Pence payments to Rome without specific mention. The DISPENSATIONS ACT (1534, 25 Hen. VIII, c. 21), prohibited the payment of "such intolerable exactions of great sums of money as have been claimed and taken . . . by the Bishops of Rome, called the pope . . . as well as pension, censes, Peter-pence" etc.

Bibliography: H. Gee and W. J. Hardy, eds., *Documents Illustrative of English Church History*, 1910.

Don S. Armentrout

Pilgrimage of Grace (1536-1537). The Pilgrimage of Grace is usually viewed as an armed rising of the backward and quasi-feudal north of England against the religious policies of HENRY VIII and THOMAS CROMWELL. In fact the motivation was far more complex; social and economic grievances were never wanting, but the religious focus made the movement more formidable and lent a cohesiveness that would have been lacking otherwise. The DISSOLUTION of the lesser monasteries was already under way and aroused fears of the further despoliation of the greater religious houses as well as treasures of parish churches. Although the presence of aristocratic retainers and tenants among the rebels savored of the BASTARD FEUDALISM of the fifteenth century, in fact most of the participants were mustered by hundredal and township levies from among a populace inured to arms and frequently called upon to serve in Henry VIII's wars on the Scottish border and in France.

Something like five revolts may be distinguished within the Pilgrimage of Grace, and these disturbances affected seven different counties—roughly the northern third of England. The first rising in Lincolnshire in early October 1536 revealed an incoherent attempt at a coalition of gentry, parish priests, monks, and local communities, which collapsed before the other rebellions began. It was also the most violent of the protests. By contrast, the main revolt in the East Riding of Yorkshire was disciplined and non-violent. The leader was a charismatic lawyer named Robert Aske, who almost certainly had prior knowledge of anti-Cromwellian aristocratic conspiracies at court; he called the rebellion a "pilgrimage" to emphasize its religious character and provided it with an ideology of resistance based upon the defense of traditional piety. The Pilgrim army mustered 30,000 men and controlled Doncaster, Pontefract, York, and other strategic points in the north. Since this was a much larger army than the king could field, Henry VIII resorted to deception; he promised to negotiate with Pilgrim emissaries in London and persuaded the Pilgrim army to disband in the meantime. Most of the gentry took this opportunity to detach themselves from Aske and availed themselves of the royal pardon. Thomas, Lord Darcy, Aske's second-in-command and one of only two peers to give the Pilgrimage unqualified support, remained loyal to Aske until the very end. Otherwise the great magnates of the north, such as Henry Percy, 6th earl of Northumberland, Henry Clifford, 1st earl of Cumberland, and William, Lord Dacre, remained neutral or hostile, while the earl of Derby raised an army to defend Lancashire against the Pilgrims in the West Riding of York and to preserve his own dynastic influence. When popular disaffection spread to the Lake Counties in the latter part of October 1536, there was evidence of agrarian grievances and hostility toward the gentry. As much as one-third of the total population may have sworn the Pilgrims' oath. A second rebellion in the East Riding in January 1537, led by Sir Francis Bigod, a Protestant who distrusted the king's promise of a pardon, gave THOMAS HOWARD, 3rd duke of Norfolk, and his provost-marshals the pretext that Henry VIII needed to begin hanging rebel leaders. The newly constituted COUNCIL OF THE NORTH, with its headquarters at York, replaced the power of the Percies and other marcher lords. The king and Cromwell also believed that they had sufficient proof of papalist disaffection in the monasteries and proceeded to dissolve the greater houses in 1539.

Bibliography: C. S. L. Davies, "Popular Religion and the Pilgrimage of Grace," *Order and Disorder in Early Modern England, 1500-1700*, ed. Anthony Fletcher and John Stevenson, 1985, pp. 58-91; G. R. Elton, "Politics and the Pilgrimage of Grace," in *After the Reformation*, ed. Barbara C. Malament, 1980; M. E.

James, "Obedience and Dissent in Henrician England: The Lincolnshire Rebellion, 1536," *Past and Present*, no. 48 (1970): 3-78.

Roger B. Manning

Plague and Epidemics. Tudor England suffered chronically from plague and other epidemic diseases. Poor sanitation, the absence of effective medical treatment, the tendency to lump all diseases together as a single phenomenon, and the government's inability to control the movements of infected people during most of the period all contributed to create a dangerous situation. Plague and other epidemics were seen as manifestations of God's wrath toward sinful humanity. There was no germ theory of disease. Instead, outbreaks of plague were blamed on comets and miasma or bad air arising from rotting corpses or other organic matter. The various epidemics that occurred were a major brake on sustained POPULATION growth in sixteenth-century England.

Three major epidemic diseases existed in Tudor England: "sweating sickness," influenza, and bubonic plague. Also known simply as "the sweat," the sweating sickness's exact nature remains a mystery. Large-scale outbreaks occurred in England during 1485, 1507-08, 1517, and 1551. At the time people were impressed by the disease because it killed so suddenly (in less than twenty-four hours) and because it struck the prosperous and powerful, for example, Cardinal THOMAS WOLSEY, who was stricken in 1517 but survived. In terms of its overall rate of mortality, however, the disease was not particularly deadly in spite of the high proportion of people who appear to have contracted it during the various outbreaks.

Influenza struck England at the beginning of ELIZABETH I's reign and contributed significantly to the worst mortality crisis of the early modern era. Harvest failures in 1555 and 1556 resulted in the appearance of famine-related fevers during 1556 and 1557. It was at this point that the "new ague" appeared. This disease was a form of influenza, and it created a national epidemic on top of the localized famine fevers. Both rich and poor people and both urban and rural areas suffered. Between 1556 and 1560 England lost at least 6% of its population.

The bubonic plague was the most persistent and serious form of epidemic disease in Tudor England. Outbreaks always originated outside of England, although once it established itself, the plague could remain endemic for up to a decade. The Tudor plague formed a declining phase in the European-wide wave of the plague that began with the arrival of the Black Death in 1348. Serious recurrences followed, although after 1479 outbreaks became more localized and less frequent. In spite of this weakening of its virulence, widespread occurrences of the plague took place in 1498, 1535, 1543, 1563, and 1603. The plague remained a major check on population growth and struck the poor and the younger segments of the population particularly hard. Urban areas were far more affected than the rural communities of the Tudor period. Local appearances of the plague could be found somewhere in England in almost any year during the sixteenth century. Bubonic plague appears to have caused or at least to have been a contributor to every major mortality crisis of the era. Its ravages continued into the seventeenth century until increasingly effective public health measures brought about its final disappearance after the Great Plague of London 1665-1666.

Bibliography: Paul Slack, *The Impact of Plague in Tudor and Stuart England*, 1985.

Ronald Fritze

Pole's Plot (1562). Devised by Arthur Pole, a Catholic descendant of Edward IV's brother, the duke of Clarence, this conspiracy had as its intent the replacement of ELIZABETH I with MARY, QUEEN OF SCOTS on the English throne.

In the aftermath of Elizabeth's accession, many English Catholics, alienated by the official Protestantism of the country, sought to depose Elizabeth, whom they regarded as an illegitimate usurper. Pole collaborated with his brother and other Catholic sympathizers to solicit military aid from the Guises (the Scottish queen's powerful French relatives) to dethrone Elizabeth. The astute Guises declined to participate, although the French and Spanish ambassadors to England made vague promises of support. Alvarez de Quadra, the Spanish ambassador and an inveterate plotter, had long used his embassy as a gathering site for the disaffected English Catholics and was suspected by the queen's secretary, WILLIAM CECIL, of subscribing to the plot. As a result, Cecil authorized raids on the French and Spanish embassies to flush out English Catholics and discredited De Quadra in the process.

Pole and his associates were arrested in October 1562, and Cecil held up the plot as an example of the continuing Catholic threat to Elizabeth's security. The Parliament of 1563 attainted the plotters and passed an act that made non-subscribers to the Oath of Supremacy guilty of treason after a second refusal; it also excluded Catholics from serving in the House of Commons. Elizabeth tempered the act to prevent persecution of the Marian bishops, but it marked the beginning of a concerted campaign against English Catholicism.

Bibliography: W. MacCaffrey, *The Shaping of the Elizabethan Regime*, 1968; C. Read, *Mr. Secretary Cecil and Queen Elizabeth*, 1955.

Connie S. Evans

Pole, Cardinal Reginald (1500-1558). Humanist, cleric, and statesman, Pole possessed considerable intellectual gifts and unswerving integrity, but his distinguished career can be almost entirely attributed to his ancestry. He was born in March 1500, his father being Sir Richard Pole, a cousin of HENRY VII through a common descent from Margaret Beauchamp, and his mother Margaret, the daughter of George, duke of Clarence. He was thus of royal blood on both sides and as a younger son was from the first destined for a career in the church. At the age of seven (when his father was already dead) he was sent to the school of the Carthusian house at Sheen, and the influence of that order remained with him for the rest of his life. His mother was favored by both Henry VII and his son, and in 1512 Pole became a king's scholar, first at school and the following year under the care of the prior of St. Frideswide's at Oxford. From there he proceeded to Magdalen College, where he was for some time under the tutelage of the celebrated humanist, William Latimer. He proceeded B.A. in 1515 and received a number of ecclesiastical preferments from the king but remained at his studies in Oxford until in 1521 HENRY VIII sent him to the University of Padua, with a generous allowance of £100 a year. In Padua he certainly studied, but he also maintained a semi-princely state and was treated as a personal representative of the king of England. At this stage his studies were mainly literary, and he assembled around him a distinguished and devoted group of young scholars, both English and Italian, including Thomas Lupset, Richard Pace, Alvise Priuli, and Giovanni Morone. In 1526 he returned to England, having acquired a reputation for humanist learning, virtue, and extreme taciturnity. He continued to enjoy ample means, thanks to the king's generosity, but had no career, either lay or clerical. He took up residence close to (but not in) the Carthusian house at Sheen, but in spite of his numerous benefices he had not, as yet, taken orders. In 1528, however, the onset of the king's "Great Matter" (the annulment of Henry's marriage to CATHERINE OF ARAGON) saw him called upon to earn the support that he had been receiving for the previous sixteen years. The issue was rapidly becoming an academic as well as a political controversy, and the king called upon the services of his learned men. Although his personal sympathies and family connections all prompted him to side with the queen, Pole could not, in the circumstances, fail to respond.

For two years he travelled back and forth to Paris, accompanied by Lupset, Thomas Starkey, and Edward Fox; in 1530 he assisted Fox in securing a favorable judgement from the Sorbonne—a great achievement since it was the most prestigious and conservative theological faculty in Europe. However, the strain upon his conscience became too great, and he told the king frankly where his sympathies lay. Henry was understandably angry but merely sent him back to Italy with a generous pension to resume his studies. By the end of 1532 he had returned to Padua and resumed his former life-style, together with many of his earlier friendships. His interests were now turning to theology, and his circle included many leading Reformers who had taken refuge in Venice after the sack of Rome in 1527, among them Gregorio Cortese, Gasparo Contarini, and Gian Pietro Carafa. He seems to have been respected by all these friends but was something of a mystery to them, as he was extremely uncommunicative about his own opinions. The problem with which he was struggling was a common one at the time—whether to devote his life to scholarship and personal piety or whether to join his friends in the arena of active reform. He made his decision in the summer of 1536, when the reforming Pope Paul III (elected 1534) made Contarini a cardinal and invited him to set up a commission for the reform of the church. Pole was one of those whom Contarini recruited, and by the end of the year he had become a Cardinal. The commission's report, the *Consilium . . . de emendenda ecclesia*, was submitted in the following year, proposing drastic and far-reaching changes. Pole was now a marked man. In 1541 he was appointed papal governor of the *Patrimonium Petri* and took up residence in Viterbo, where both his position and his reputation made him the center of a reforming humanist group, known as the *spirituali*. The development that had finally motivated him to active involvement had been an attempt in 1535 to recruit his support for Henry VIII's claim to the title "Supreme Head of the Church." Coming immediately after the executions of JOHN FISHER and THOMAS MORE, this tactless approach had stung him into action. He wrote and sent to the king a bitterly worded tract, *Pro Ecclesiasticae Unitatis Defensione*, which was subsequently (1537) published in Rome without his consent. Henry was furious, denouncing Pole as an ingrate and a traitor. He made a number of unsuccessful attempts to have him extradited or murdered and took revenge on his family over the so-called EXETER CONSPIRACY in 1538.

After the failure of the unification talks with the Lutherans at Regensburg and Contarini's death in August 1542, Pole became the leader of the increasingly beleagured *spirituali*. Regensburg had handed the reforming initiative to those who wished to counterattack heresy on all fronts—the *zelanti*, led by the increasingly fanatical Carafa. Carafa made no secret of his doubts about Pole's orthodoxy, and it seems that the latter did have some sympathy with the Lutheran position on justification. Nevertheless, in 1545 Pole was appointed, along with Cardinals Del Monte and Cervini, to preside as a legate over the opening of the Council of Trent. During the first sessions, between 1545 and 1547 every position that he sought to defend was defeated, and he eventually resigned, pleading ill health. In all probability he had had a nervous breakdown. At the same time he resigned his office in Viterbo and moved to Rome. In spite of these setbacks his personal standing remained high, and when Paul III died in 1549 it was generally expected that he would be elected pope. This hope was frustrated, partly by the suspicions of the *zelanti* but more by the opposition of the French, who regarded him as too close to the Habsburgs—a legacy of his English associations. When Henry VIII's Protestant heir, EDWARD VI, died in July 1554 and was succeeded by Catherine of Aragon's daughter, MARY, Pole sought and was granted a legatine mission to England. Ironically, the emperor Charles V prevented him for fifteen months from going to England, while he installed his only son, Philip, as king-consort. Thereafter only a protracted negotiation between Philip and Pope Julius III over the future of secularized church property in England finally opened the door to Pole in November 1554, and he was able to return to England after 23 years. For the next four years Pole presided over the restoration of the Roman Catholic church in England. But the election of his old enemy Carafa as Pope Paul IV in the spring of 1555 spelled danger. After a bitter political quarrel (and a brief war) with King Philip, Paul recalled all his legates from Philip's lands in April 1557 and specifically summoned Pole to Rome, where charges of heresy were threatened. Since 1556 Pole had also been archbishop of Canterbury (having finally taken priest's orders on the eve of his consecration), and Mary refused to allow him to answer the summons. He remained in England, a bitterly disillusioned man. He had resolved his theological problems by putting his trust in the authority of the pope, only to have that turned against him by a personal enemy. As legate he gave priority to discipline and organization after the long and disruptive schism and was not enthusiastic for Catholic evangelism. Whether this strategy might have succeeded in time will never be known, because Mary and Pole died within hours of each other, on 17 November 1558, and Elizabeth I destroyed the labors of both of them. It is hard now to appreciate the qualities that made Pole respected in his lifetime, for he wrote little and seldom spoke clearly on any issue except the wickedness of Henry VIII.

Bibliography: J. G. Dwyer, ed., *Pole's Defense of the Unity of the Church*, 1965; Dermot Fenlon, *Heresy and Obedience in Tridentine Italy*, 1972; R. H. Pogson, "Reginald Pole and the Priorities of Government in Mary Tudor's Church," *Historical Journal* 18 (1975): 3-21.

D. M. Loades

Political Thought. Tudor political ideas owed much to medieval thought. Few English theorists of the sixteenth century were startlingly bold or original thinkers. The whole age produced less in the way of truly novel theorizing than the two decades from 1640 to 1660, and no Tudor political philosopher can compare in stature with Thomas Hobbes. Yet the Tudor period did witness the first use of the printed word as political propaganda, and the controversies of the age led thinkers to give new twists to old theories and to adapt Continental modes of thought to English circumstances.

Throughout the period, sermons and books emphasized the divine origins of political authority and the subject's duty of obedience. Lacking a police force and standing ARMY, the Tudor state placed much reliance on the pulpit to insure that the mass of the population remained obedient. Perhaps the commonest theme in Tudor political sermons is the wickedness of rebellion—a theme made the more urgent because rebellion was a constant threat (and an occasional reality) in a century of rapid social, political, and religious change. Typical treatises condemning rebellion are Sir Richard Morison's *A Remedy for Sedition* (1536), Sir John Cheke's *The Hurt of Sedition, How Grievous It Is to a Commonwealth* (1549), and Bishop John Christopherson's *Exhortation to All Men to Take Heed and Beware of Rebellion* (1554). Tudor teaching on rebellion was given classic expression in the famous homilies on obedience (1547) and rebellion (1571) incorporated in the Church of England's BOOK OF HOMILIES.

A variety of attitudes underlay the claim that rebellion was sinful. There were passages in the Bible to prove its wickedness, and of these the most important were the fifth commandment (which was seen as enjoining obedience to magistrates and monarchs as well as to natural parents) and the assertion by St. Paul in the thirteenth chapter of his epistle to the Romans that "the powers that be are ordained of God. Whosoever therefore resisteth the power, resisteth the ordinance of God: and they that resist shall receive to themselves damnation." The universe was commonly regarded as an ordered hierarchy in which each created being had its allotted sphere and role. To resist one's governors, it was held, was to invert the natural order of things, and the inevitable consequences would be social disruption and disaster. The state—or "body politic"—was commonly compared to the human body, and both were seen as governed by a monarchical head. Other analogies were frequently used to illustrate the need for order and obedience in political life. For instance, the state was often compared to a hive of bees, ruled over (so it was supposed) by a king.

Coercive political authority was seen as necessary to the stability of society, given the sinfulness of fallen human nature. To resist authority was in effect to destroy stability and to court divine punishment, for God's providence would be sure to inflict calamity upon those who infringed His laws. The civil magistrate was God's deputy on earth and as such could never actively be resisted. God remained superior to his deputy, and if the king commanded things that were contrary to God's laws, it was necessary to obey God and disobey the king. Such disobedience, however, could never take the form of active resistance. Only passive resistance was lawful, and subjects were bound meekly to suffer whatever penalties the king might inflict upon them for disobeying his evil commands (see RESISTANCE THEORY).

Though it was widely agreed that rebellion against authority was evil, there was no universal consensus on precisely what persons or institutions held authority. Under HENRY VIII, the Reformation threw into high relief the question of the relationship between royal and papal power, and the same question lay at the center of much debate between Protestants and Roman Catholics under ELIZABETH, especially after the bull of excommunication of 1570 (see REGNANS IN EXCELSIS). For Roman Catholics, the clergy—led by the pope—possessed God-given authority in ecclesiastical matters and were divinely empowered to exercise this authority independently of the civil magistrate. Many also argued that the pope could give binding commands on temporal matters if he thought that by doing so the spiritual welfare of Christians would be enhanced, and it was on these grounds that Elizabethan Roman Catholics justified the pope's claim to be able to depose temporal sovereigns, in particular the queen.

Among the best-known works to vindicate the Roman Catholic position were REGINALD POLE's *Pro Ecclesiasticae Unitatis Defensione* of 1536 and writings of the Elizabethans William Allen and Robert Parsons. In opposition to papal claims, a great many writers argued that the civil magistrate was supreme in both the temporal and ecclesiastical spheres and that the clergy's powers were purely spiritual. Two of the most famous treaties that put forward such ideas were the *De Vera Obedientia* (1535) of STEPHEN GARDINER, and the *True Difference Between Christian Subjection and Unchristian Rebellion* (1585) of Thomas Bilson.

All Protestants agreed with Bilson in denying that the church could depose monarchs. But not all agreed in granting the monarch ecclesiastical supremacy. Under MARY, John Ponet, JOHN KNOX, and Christopher Goodman argued that the commonwealth was authorized to remove ungodly rulers and in the reign of Elizabeth PRESBYTERIANS argued for the autonomy in ecclesiastical matters of the church's officers and councils. The supremacy of the civil magistrate over church government was asserted against Presbyterians in a number of works published in the 1590s, and these books include RICHARD HOOKER's great *Laws of Ecclesiastical Polity* (books 1-5, 1593-1597; books 6-8, 1648-1662).

Though Hooker saw the magistrate as supreme in both temporal and ecclesiastical matters, he held that this supremacy was located not in the monarch alone but in the monarch-in-Parliament, and he argued that the queen could act only in accordance with the law of the land. The idea that England was a limited monarchy features strongly in Thomas Starkey's interesting *Dialogue between Pole and Lupset* (c. 1529-1532) and received added impetus from the publication of *De Laudibus Legum Angliae* (1537; in English translation 1567) by the fifteenth-century judge Sir John Fortescue. Most members of the Elizabethan House of Commons seemingly regarded the queen as a limited ruler, and Fortescue's constitutional theory underlay the political attitudes expressed in the reports of the great lawyer Sir Edward Coke, which began to appear at the end of the sixteenth century. Higher claims were made for royal power in the works of some churchmen, including the Henricians WILLIAM TYNDALE and Stephen Gardiner. In the 1590s some well-placed ecclesiastics attacked Presbyterian and Roman Catholic ideas by asserting that the monarch was an absolute sovereign who derived power from God alone, who alone made law, and who could rule outside the law of the land if he judged this necessary. Such absolutist views were given very clear expression in the *De Imperandi Authoritate* (1593) of Hadrian Saravia. Saravia's theory was close to that of the famous French absolutist, Jean Bodin.

A great deal of Tudor political thinking was concerned with the rights and duties of rulers and subjects and with the relationship between secular and ecclesiastical power. A rather different tradition also flourished in the shape of humanist calls for social reform based on a rational analysis of the practicalities of political life. Many works were produced advising rulers on how they might govern well by promoting the common good (for instance, Sir Thomas Elyot's *The Book Named the Governor*, 1531) and giving detailed suggestions for improving English society—for example, by discouraging idleness, promoting education, and reforming the law. Easily the greatest of such writings was THOMAS MORE's *Utopia* (1516), and another excellent example of the genre is Starkey's *Dialogue Between Pole and Lupset*.

In the latter half of the century, political thinking became increasingly concerned with the issues raised by religious division and by the consequent threats of rebellion and invasion. Calls for moral and social reform continued to be made by Protestant preachers, and lay writers became increasingly interested in humanistic analysis of society and attempted to draw general laws and maxims from a study of the past and present practices of England and other countries. In 1584 Machiavelli's political works were printed in London, and among those who fell under the spell of the Florentine's empirical approach to politics was Sir Francis Bacon. His *Essays* (first edition 1597; final, enlarged addition 1625) typify one strand of the humanists' approach in concerning themselves primarily with what men do and not what they ought to do.

Bibliography: Christopher Morris, *Political Thought in England: Tyndale to Hooker*, 1953; Quentin Skinner, *The Foundations of Modern Political Thought*, 2 vols., 1978.

J. P. Sommerville

Poor Laws. Changing socio-economic conditions in sixteenth-century England increased the extent and depth of poverty and the number of vagrants and prompted apprehension and concern among England's ruling elite and later in the century also among the middling classes. While a variety of initiatives dealing with poverty, beggary, and vagrancy came from the central government, local corporate governments, and PARLIAMENT, it was the statutes or poor laws passed by Parliament that formed the basis of a nationally uniform, parish-based system of relieving and regulating the poor.

Several factors propelled the sixteenth-century increase in poverty and vagrancy. A rising POPULATION brought an oversupply of labor and thus unemployment, while inflation effected a rise in the price of consumables twice that of wage rates. The plight of smallholders forced off their land by ENCLO-SURE and other developments also contributed to migration and vagrancy, as did warfare, which especially after c. 1560 involved the greater use of men from the poor and criminal classes, at least for overseas duty. While both the number of poor and the intensity of poverty grew, the government eradicated facilities for poor relief with the DISSOLUTIONS of religious houses and the elimination of many hospitals, almshouses, and religious guilds related to CHANTRIES. These changes particularly affected towns, which first introduced some measures for relief and regulation of the poor and elaborated others.

Although institutional changes during the Reformation affected poor-relief, Protestantism itself does not appear to have been an ideology crucial to the development of Tudor poor laws. Motivation came rather from other directions such as fear of disorder and rebellion among the ruling elite, the belief among the so-called COMMONWEALTH thinkers that any idle or decaying elements in society threatened the whole body politic, and the staunch belief of Renaissance

HUMANISM in the possibility of human and societal improvement, a view that implied that poverty was not inevitable. In the latter sixteenth century a desire for both social welfare and the reform of manners or behavior among the lower orders was widely voiced, with enthusiastic Protestants or PURITANS taking the lead in concrete endeavors.

Poor laws dealt with controlling and punishing the healthy idle (sturdy beggars and vagabonds, masterless men and rogues) and with relieving the disabled or "impotent" poor while curtailing, and finally prohibiting, begging. A vagrancy act of 1495 (11 Hen. VII, c. 2) repeated medieval concerns with wandering poor and provided a less rigorous and less expensive punishment for able vagabonds: stocking rather than imprisonment. In 1531 whipping superseded stocking (22 Hen. VIII, c. 12) and remained the rule, although other corporal punishments, which were also means of identifying offenders, were later introduced, such as branding on the chest with a "V" for vagabond (1547), burning through the ear (1572), and branding with an "R" for rogue on the shoulder (1604). Provision in 1531 for returning vagabonds to their place of settlement continued throughout the period.

Loss of freedom and even felony charges were other punishments decreed for sturdy beggars and vagabonds, although sometimes it is difficult to distinguish between loss of freedom and provision of employment, as in the statute of 1536 (27 Hen. VIII, c. 12), by which able beggars were to be put to labor and charged with felony if persisting in begging or vagabondage. It should be pointed out in regard to this act that it was a substitution for a preceding draft with far-reaching concerns that emanated from THOMAS CROMWELL's circle and that recognized a myriad of reasons for unemployment, both voluntary and involuntary. The draft was much too radical to receive parliamentary support, and even in its much modified form the law probably did not remain in effect beyond 1536. Still it offered guidelines for the future with its provisions for employment, organized relief, and prohibition of begging.

The concept of curtailing vagabonds' freedom reached impracticable proportions in an act of 1547 (1 Edw. VI, c. 3) which made possible two years of enslavement for sturdy beggars or even lifetime slavery if they ran away. There is no evidence that this act was enforced, however, and it was repealed in 1549 (3 and 4 Edw. VI, c. 16). The act of 1572 dictated that felony charges would follow second and third offenses for vagabondage (14 Eliz. I, c. 5). When in 1576 the law ordered every town official to gather stocks of wool and such to set the poor to work, it also decreed that persons refusing to work should be committed to houses of correction, which were to be established in all counties and supported by rates (18 Eliz. I, c. 3). This development had been anticipated in London (Bridewell being its most famous house of correction) and other towns, but with little success, given the mixing of the unemployed and incorrigibles. The measure was repeated in 1598 in a statute that repealed all previous acts (39 Eliz. I, c. 4). This law included a new definition of vagrants, including, as before, masterless men and dangerous occupations such as bearward, minstrel, peddlar, etc., but also persons refusing to work for statutory wages. These vagabonds were to be whipped and returned to parishes of birth or last residence. This action could be taken by the constable and minister of a parish without the approval of even a single JUSTICE OF THE PEACE. Only the punishment of dangerous and incorrigible rogues involved Quarter Sessions.

Besides the threat of wandering, masterless men to public order, open begging also was thought to imperil society's health. The law of 1495 allowed the disabled poor to return to home parishes, where they were permitted to beg, but not to leave their hundreds. In 1531 the statute provided for the licensing of beggars by justices; leaving the areas where they were licensed would bring whipping or stocking. Begging was further circumscribed, at least briefly, in 1536 when indiscriminate doles to the poor were forbidden. In 1552 the law prohibited any to sit openly begging, but in 1555 this was modified to permit licensed begging in areas where the poor were too numerous to be relieved otherwise (2 and 3 Ph. and Mary, c. 5). This modification was retained in the Elizabethan statute of 1563 (5 Eliz. I, c. 3). In 1572, however, an act prescribed that beggars' children aged five to 14 might be bound out to service (5 Eliz. I, c. 5). In spite of all these measures, of course, unlicensed begging was never completely eradicated any more than was vagabondage.

The curtailment of begging, however, necessitated the organization of collections for the relief of the deserving poor. At first the contributions were voluntary, but gradually the law moved toward a compulsory poor rate. The law of 1536 called for voluntary alms to be collected by churchwardens or two others. That of 1547 decreed that collections would be made weekly after exhortation by a preacher and that, in addition, cottages would be erected for the disabled poor. The statute of 1552 brought yet more organization to the system and went a step further toward compulsory giving. Two collectors were to make the weekly collections, now specifically to be made on Sundays. Those who refused to contribute were to be exhorted by ministers and, that exhortation failing, by bishops. Furthermore, records were to be kept of the names of the poor and the contributors. Under Elizabeth this trend continued. In the statute of 1563 those refusing to contribute to poor relief after exhortation before the bishop were to appear before justices who could imprison them if they still refused. Moreover, officials who neglected their poor-relief duties were to be fined, and imprisonment awaited collectors who failed to produce quarterly accounts. This system was sustained in the law of 1572, although provision was made for persons who considered themselves overtaxed to appeal to Quarter Sessions. As the voluntary nature of contributions declined, the law also developed the notion of putting the poor unemployed to work, as shown in the statutes of 1572 and 1576. An act of 1598 (39 Eliz. I, c. 3) took the compulsory element of collections further; overseers of the poor were required in all parishes and given a variety of responsibilities, including the power to distrain the goods of any refusing to contribute to poor rates.

By 1598 the poor law, as modified slightly in 1601 (43 Eliz. I, c. 2), had a clear shape. Vagrants were to receive summary punishment; the disabled poor were to collect outdoor (noninstitutional) relief financed by compulsory poor rates; and employment was to be provided for the deserving, able poor. The latter was the weakest element for local officials found it much easier to pay cash doles than supervise work, and it was not always easy to find masters willing to take on poor apprentices. Nevertheless the statutes of 1598 and 1601 established a poor law that was well suited to small rural communities and adaptable to large urban areas, and it decreed national uniformity. The poor law alleviated poverty, though not as well as pre-Reformation institutions would have done had they remained. It combatted disorder, though probably not directly. Rather it demonstrated the benevolence of the privileged and powerful and thus encouraged deference and maintenance of the status quo. It was a major, if unplanned, achievement, which lasted without significant change until 1834 and can be said to have laid the foundation of the modern welfare state.

Bibliography: A. L. Beier, *The Problem of the Poor in Tudor and Early Stuart England*, 1983; E. M. Leonard, *The Early History of English Poor Relief*, 1900; Paul Slack, *Poverty & Policy in Tudor & Stuart England*, 1988.

Martha C. Skeeters

Population. The population of England during the early fourteenth century was approximately 6 million people. By the middle of the next century, however, the population had declined sharply due to the spread of epidemic diseases like the bubonic PLAGUE, a fall in the average temperature, and an increase in the average age at marriage. As a result of these factors the population fell to around 2 million by the 1450s. The number of people stabilized by 1470, and the country began to see a population increase in the mid-1510s and 1520s. This trend continued virtually without interruption until the 1620s. By 1520 the population had grown to 2.3 million people and by 1541 to over 2.7 million. But England faced bad harvests, plague epidemics, and a series of local crises in the 1550s that resulted in a slight decrease in the country's population. From 1550 to 1560 the national population decreased by approximately 6,000 people. Following this latter date, the population again increased due to a surplus of births over deaths, as England was relatively free from the ravages of the plague and other epidemics. During the reign of ELIZABETH I (1558-1603) serious outbreaks of the plague occurred only in 1563, 1592-1593, and 1603. The virtual absence of serious epidemics outside the major cities and mild rates of mortality contributed to higher life expectancy (40 years) and a rapidly growing population. By 1580 the English numbered over 3.5 million. At the end of Elizabeth I's reign there were over 4.1 million people in the country.

The rapid growth in the English population over the period of the sixteenth century had numerous effects upon the country. There was a close link, for example, between the rising population and increasing prices for foodstuffs. Population increases precipitated rising prices, already driven up by inflation, war, and periodic harvest failures. The growing population also increased the demand for industrial goods and increased their price as well. During the twenty-five years from 1571 to 1606 real wages declined significantly. This decline had a major impact upon delayed marriages, which, in turn, affected fertility and new births. The population of the country was also influenced somewhat by immigration from France, the Netherlands, and Germany as people fled from religious persecution. The increased population also contributed to growing rates of unemployment and underemployment. In addition, as unemployment rates increased, so did the numbers of vagrants. Wages would also decline as employers had a ready availability of workers at hand.

The population of England was distributed relatively evenly throughout the country, with southern counties having a slightly greater population density. In general, people settled on the most fertile soil and along the coasts and inland rivers and streams. Northern regions were relatively uninhabited. Although England remained an overwhelmingly rural country, its towns absorbed the excess population of the countryside. In general, the population drifted from the north and west toward the south and east, with LONDON drawing people away from the country. Few large towns existed in England during the sixteenth century. London and its suburbs grew from approximately 75,000 in 1500 to a population of 200,000 in 1600. No other town, however, matched the size and influence of that city. Norwich held around 12,000 people in 1500. Residents of Newcastle, Exeter, Winchester, Salisbury, and Coventry numbered about 5,000. By 1600 about 10% of the population lived in towns, with London being largely responsible for this change.

Population figures are relatively accurate for the period after 1538 because in that year THOMAS CROMWELL required all English parishes to accrue and maintain records of births, marriages, and deaths within their areas of jurisdiction. The accuracy and completeness of figures improved after 1558 because Elizabeth I's government provided parishes with parchment on which they could record their demographic information.

Bibliography: E. A. Wrigley and R. S. Schofield, *The Population History of England, 1541-1871: A Reconstruction*, 1981.

David B. Mock

Portugal (Don Antonio) Expedition of 1589 was initially proposed by WILLIAM CECIL in the preceding August as an enterprise to capture the damaged remnants of the SPANISH ARMADA on its return voyage. ELIZABETH combined this project with an attack, near the Azores, on the unprotected treasure fleet from America as a way to refill her treasury and respond to the armada's insult. Her

PRIVY COUNCIL's conservatism, a shortage of seaworthy ships, and rough seas through March postponed the implementation of her scheme.

After her privy council decided that land forces were needed to capture the forts protecting Lisbon, it was proposed that these forces also be used to restore Don Antonio to the Portuguese throne, from which he had been deposed in 1580. The expansion of the project brought support from the Dutch, from English merchants, and from a flood of 23,000 volunteers who joined Sir John Norris and Sir FRANCIS DRAKE with dreams of profit, revenge and glory.

In March, Norris and Drake secretly arranged with Don Antonio that if the reconquest failed, they would establish him in one of his territories in return for permission to capture former Portuguese possessions in the East Indies. Thus while the government primarily sought the destruction of Spanish shipping and the capture of the silver fleet, the leaders of the expedition had different priorities. The unwieldy expedition with too few fighting ships, 60 Dutch flyboats, and inadequate supplies departed England in April.

Drake's fleet sailed to Coruna and destroyed one ship while 52 of the armada's damaged vessels lay anchored at Santander and San Sebastian and were unarmed and vulnerable. Although English forces took the town and defeated a counterattack, they failed to take the upper fortress or to carry off the 60 pieces of ordnance they captured. During the occupation, large quantities of food and wine were captured. Much wine was consumed abusively and contributed to the spread of dysentery, which later devastated the expedition. The Coruna raid inflicted little damage on shipping and weakened Drake's fleet because 2,000 men returned to England with their plunder.

As the expedition sailed to Lisbon, its leaders developed a plan for a coordinated land-sea attack, strongly favored by Don Antonio and Norris, which was poorly conceived and ineptly executed. The army was landed at Peniche, 45 miles northwest of Lisbon, and had a debilitating march. Torrid heat, difficult terrain, and disease reduced the army that captured Lisbon's suburbs to less than 10,000, a third of whom were incapacitated. The harsh treatment of Don Antonio's supporters by Spanish authorities after 1580 was effective, and no Portuguese rebelled when Don Antonio returned. Lacking sufficient artillery and local support, the expeditionary forces retreated as Drake's fleet, delayed by weather, sailed up the Tagus. While the commanders blamed each other for the failure to take Lisbon, Norris's insistence on landing at Peniche was the pivotal misjudgment.

Before they departed, the arrival of a fleet of 60 Hanseatic League ships loaded with grain and contraband provided a new opportunity. Drake seized the supplies and prepared to go to the Azores to ambush the treasure fleet. After a brief raid in which Vigo and the surrounding countryside were plundered, Drake despaired of reaching the Azores and returned to England.

While the expedition embarrassed Spain and brought £30,000 in prize money and 150 cannon, the queen was disappointed by the unpopularity of Don Antonio, by the fleet's inability to capture the remnants of the armada, and by the lack of an attempt to intercept the silver fleet. The failure of the enterprise to achieve its political objectives led to Drake's retirement, made merchants reluctant to support subsequent joint-stock, military ventures, and guaranteed a continuation of the war.

Bibliography: R. B. Wernham, *The Making of Elizabethan Foreign Policy, 1558-1603*, 1980.

Sheldon Hanft

Praemunire. The medieval praemunire statutes of 1353, 1365, and 1393 aimed at protecting rights of jurisdiction claimed by the English Crown against papal encroachment. They were accompanied by four statutes of Provisors made from 1351 to 1389, which were passed to prohibit papal "provisions," or appointments to vacant English benefices without respect for the rights of ordinary patrons. The term *praemunire* can denote the statutes, the offense, the writ, and the punishment.

Though THOMAS WOLSEY was known to threaten opponents with praemunire in his capacity as chancellor, the offense first became a prominent issue in the sixteenth century in 1513 in Richard HUNNE'S CASE. Next in 1515 the Crown threatened CONVOCATION with praemunire charges for questioning Dr. Henry Standish, warden of the London Greyfriars and a vocal supporter of limitations on benefit of clergy. A far more significant use of praemunire, however, occurred in October 1529, when Thomas Wolsey, failing to get papal dispensation for HENRY VIII's DIVORCE, was indicted for illegally exercising his papal powers as legate.

The king's attack on the church continued in the summer of 1530 when fifteen clerics were cited in the King's Bench under praemunire for abetting Wolsey. By January 1531 charges of praemunire were extended to the whole of the English clergy for exercising their ecclesiastical jurisdiction. After negotiations between convocation and the Crown, the clergy purchased the king's pardon for over £118,000. The king, however, refused to define actions prohibited under the praemunire statutes and left the clergy in the vulnerable position of not knowing just what actions might bring praemunire charges. While penalties also remained unclear, they could include forfeiture of lands and goods and imprisonment at the monarch's pleasure as well as loss of benefices and preferments. The king had seized a powerful weapon to intimidate the clergy as he sought his divorce and then began the establishment of ROYAL SUPREMACY.

Penalties under praemunire were contained in a number of acts contributing to the royal supremacy, but these were eradicated by the first Marian Parliament. Another offense under praemunire was created, however, when Parliament established in 1554 that all suits relating to titles to church lands were to be tried at COMMON LAW; anyone who sought to challenge them in the CHURCH COURTS was made liable to praemunire (1 and 2 Ph. and Mary, c. 8).

When ELIZABETH came to the throne, the Act of Supremacy of 1559 (1 Eliz. I, c. 1) restored the monarch's power over the church and included penalties of praemunire for offending against the act (see ROYAL SUPREMACY). They were also included in the harsher act of 1563, an act for the assurance of the Queen majesty's royal power over all estates and subjects within her highness's dominions (5 Eliz., c. 1) Other Elizabethan acts against Catholics also carried penalties of praemunire.

Bibliography: A. G. Dickens, *The English Reformation*, 2nd ed., 1989; G. R. Elton, ed., *The Tudor Constitution*, 2nd ed., 1982.

Martha C. Skeeters

Prebendaries Plot (1543). In the 1540s THOMAS CRANMER was subjected to a number of attacks that reflected the religious divisions and revealed the precarious position of the archbishop in the last decade of HENRY VIII's reign. The Prebendaries Plot, which originated in his own Cathedral Chapter, occurred in the spring of 1543. It was the result of hostility to Cranmer among Conservative clergy in his diocese and the concern of some Kentish gentry about his failure to enforce the law against radical Protestants.

Cranmer had little influence in the reorganization of the Chapter of Canterbury after the DISSOLUTION OF THE MONASTERIES, and seven of the twelve prebendaries were hostile to him. Five of them, William Gardiner, Arthur St. Leger, Richard Parkhurst, John Miles, and William Hadleigh, eventually became involved in the Prebendaries Plot. Three of the six preachers were also religious Conservatives. Two of them, Robert Serles and Edmund Shether, as well as John Willoughby, the vicar of Chilham, were also involved. The gentry plotters included prominent figures like Sir John Baker, one of Cranmer's opponents on the PRIVY COUNCIL, as well as seven Kentish JUSTICES OF THE PEACE.

The divisions between Cranmer and his Cathedral clergy were accentu-ated by his actions against Conservative clergy and his perceived failure to deal as severely with Protestants. In 1541 Serles was summoned to appear before Cranmer for statements made in his sermons. Although he appealed to the privy council, Cranmer's jurisdiction was upheld, and Serles was sentenced to a short term of imprisonment. Complaints about Cranmer's tolerance of Protestant preachers and his persecution of religious Conservatives were made to STEPHEN GARDINER when he passed through Canterbury, and, although he may not have been involved in the plot from the beginning, he became the leading supporter of the plotters' cause on the council.

In March 1543, Serles joined with Willoughby to bring charges to the council and accused Cranmer of heresy. They received the support of Dr. John London, warden of New College and dean of Christ Church. Charges were now drawn up in legal form with signatures of witnesses appended. With Gardiner's support they were presented to the council, which resolved to set up a commission of inquiry to investigate the charges.

Cranmer might have been in serious trouble had not Henry VIII intervened after the articles were given to him in April. According to the account of Cranmer's secretary, Ralph Morice, the king showed the articles to Cranmer and appointed him to the commission of inquiry to investigate "how this confederacy came to pass." Cranmer was reluctant to accept, because he would be considered a biased judge, but the king insisted. The investigation was eventually delegated to Thomas Legh, who discovered evidence that led to action against the plotters. Dr. London was convicted of perjury and died in prison, but other clergy received only short prison sentences and were ordered to write Cranmer to ask forgiveness for their actions against him. Although the plot reveals the king's continuing support for his archbishop, it also served as a warning to Cranmer that policies that were considered too favorable to Protestantism could pose a serious threat to his position.

Bibliography: Jasper Ridley, *Thomas Cranmer*, 1962; Michael Zell, "'The Prebendaries' Plot of 1543: A Reconsideration," *Journal of Ecclesiastical History* 27 (1976): 241-53.

Rudolph W. Heinze

Prerogative, Royal. The prerogative consisted of those privileges and powers reserved by law to the Crown that enabled it to conduct the business of state and effectively govern the realm.

The most specific manifestations of the "ordinary" prerogative in the Tudor era were the feudal fiscal rights relating to royal property and royal PROCLA-MATIONS. On the other hand, the evolving concept of an "absolute" prerogative was a broad, yet imprecise recognition of the Crown's discretionary authority to insure justice and provide security to the nation. However, even the absolute prerogative was limited by law for the Tudors because they always sought the sanction of law for their actions. Hence, PARLIAMENT was utilized by HENRY VIII to justify and legally strengthen the dissolution of the Roman church and the creation of the Church of England.

Sixteenth-century legal authorities distinguished the Crown's position in the modern state from the feudal relationships. They envisioned the monarch as the head of the state, a duly constituted entity, and therefore part of a traditional constitutional system. A popular contemporary illustration was the concept of the monarch's two bodies, one natural and one political. Disabilities or limitations of the monarch's natural body could not limit the authority of the politic body to establish policies, administer government, and rule the nation. The monarch, together with the royal subjects, was part of the national body politic. Because of this modern view, the description of the Crown's authority in medieval documents such as the *Prerogativa Regis*, which listed specific feudal rights of the Crown, was no longer sufficient or complete to describe the royal prerogative.

Tudor lawyers believed that some prerogative powers were inseparable and inalienable from the person of the monarch. For example, the Crown alone could make certain appointments or issue pardons. The general notion of inseparability was capable of expansion so that there were no clear limits placed on what powers ought not to be included as "inseparable." The Crown's dispensing power over acts of Parliament also was without a definable restriction. While imprecision was not a problem for the Tudors, it was under the Stuarts. Even though the Crown was expected to act within the law, the monarch had wide discretion as to how actions might be implemented and interpreted. There were several areas in which the Crown's authority was deemed to be broad, including ecclesiastical governance, foreign policy, and maintenance of law and order. The term *absolute prerogative* did not imply that the monarch might ignore or subvert the law; he merely could determine when and how the law would be enforced.

The question of sovereignty was not much debated during the sixteenth century as it was in the following century. The Tudors did not claim that the monarch was the sole sovereign authority in the state. There was no apparent need for a divine right theory of kingship because the Tudors did not create the archetype of absolute monarchy. In the sixteenth century, as in previous centuries, the king-in-council-in-Parliament paradigm was accepted universally. Neither the Tudors nor members of Parliament conceived of independent authorities and institutions (Crown and Parliament) that might clash on the question of sovereignty. Ideas of jurists and royal officials were shaped by medieval English commentators such as Henry Bracton and John Fortescue rather than by Continental contemporaries such as Jean Bodin. In short, the Tudors only modified the medieval structure of the state and did not create a new abstract entity.

Elizabethan publicists refined the constitutional role of the monarch without eliminating entirely the ambiguity of the absolute prerogative. Sir William Stanford's *Exposition of the King's Prerogative* (1568) summarized the medieval notions of prerogative, reviewing the ordinary rights of the Crown such as fiscal privileges. Thus, Stanford essentially recounted Robert Constable's 1495 lectures on *Prerogativa Regis*. Sir Thomas Smith's *De Republica Anglorum* (1583) was a comparison of England's government with Continental systems. Smith stressed that the English system was peculiar in part because of the COMMON LAW, compared to the Continental reliance on Roman civil law. While the Roman legal tradition exalted executive supremacy, English common law placed the monarch in the constitutional structure as a partner with Parliament and the judiciary. Therefore, while retaining extensive powers, the monarch was part of a larger constitutional entity with definite boundaries. RICHARD HOOKER's *Ecclesiastical Polity* (1590) focused upon a most important responsibility of the Tudors—the headship of the church. More than just defending the Elizabethan THIRTY-NINE ARTICLES, however, Hooker discussed the principles that supported the Crown's constitutional authority in the state as well as the church. Hooker argued that theological doctrines harmonized with the political prerogatives of the executive. Similar to other commentators, Hooker emphasized the supremacy of the law and the fact that royal authority was subject to the laws of the realm. The source of laws was the whole body politic within which the monarch functioned. These and other Elizabethan writers demonstrated the Tudors' practical adaptation of medieval tradition to accommodate the demands of modern government.

At the end of the sixteenth century, Tudor polity continued to recognize the common law as the basis of the legal system. However, transformations in ecclesiastical, financial, social, and foreign affairs forced alterations to allow the monarch sufficient flexibility and discretion to govern the changing nation. The prerogative courts (CHANCERY, REQUESTS, and STAR CHAMBER) allowed the Crown to promote administrative efficiency and to guarantee equity for its subjects even though those courts occasionally encroached upon the common law courts. Tudor governance remained within the confines of the king-in-council-in-Parliament, a corporate relationship responsibility. Still, the importance of the Crown role in the system definitely increased over the century. Even if the ill-defined nature of the prerogative provided the potential for abuse and set the stage for historic constitutional clashes in the seventeenth century, the Tudor monarchs and most of the English people were satisfied with their particular understanding of the royal prerogative.

Bibliography: W. S. Holdsworth, "The Prerogative in the Sixteenth Century," *Columbia Law Review* 21 (1921): 554-571.

Daniel W. Hollis III

Presbyterianism. The distinguishing features of Presbyterianism in Elizabethan England were a pronounced adherence to the cardinal tenets of Calvinist theology (the sovereignty and providence of God, the divine act of predestination upon which the salvation of the elect is dependent, the importance of preaching and the Sacraments of baptism and the Lord's Supper, and the importance of discipline in upholding godly precepts), the parity of ministers and congregations, a hierarchy of representative assemblies ("classes," provincial synods, national synods), and the enforcement of discipline at the congregational level through a consistory comprised of the pastor and popularly elected elders. Within English Presbyterianism there was considerable disagreement about the respective authority of the consistory and the congregation, especially the question of the former's accountability to the latter.

The first major treatise expostulating Presbyterian polity was Walter Travers's *A Full and Plaine Declaration of Ecclesiastical Discipline*, originally written in Latin and first published in 1574. Travers, who had been forced to relinquish his fellowship at Trinity College, Cambridge, by JOHN WHITGIFT, developed his Presbyterian views at Geneva in the company of Theodore Beza, John Calvin's successor and the primary architect of Presbyterianism. The Latin edition carried a preface by Thomas Cartwright, who may have been responsible for the English translation that appeared later the same year.

The English Presbyterian movement originated in London, where its earliest proponents adopted tenets known to them from the experience of the MARIAN EXILES in Geneva, acquaintance with the Reformed congregations of Dutch and French refugees in London (the "stranger" churches), and probably the lectures on Acts for which Cartwright had been ousted from Cambridge in late 1570. Against a background of mounting dissatisfaction with the bishops and the seemingly stalled progress of further reformation, radical Protestants such as John Field and Thomas Wilcox openly avowed Presbyterian polity after Queen ELIZABETH blocked an attempt in the House of Commons to pass a bill empowering bishops to exempt ministers from using controversial portions of the BOOK OF COMMON PRAYER. Work on their *Admonition to the Parliament*, however, had almost certainly been under way before the queen acted on 23 May 1572, for the *Admonition* appeared in print the following month and ignited the celebrated ADMONITION CONTROVERSY, in which Cartwright and Whitgift became the principal protagonists.

The early Presbyterian community in London included a number of illustrious ministers, such as Christopher Goodman, one of the English architects of an advanced theory of tyrannicide, and Edward Dering, infamous in court circles for his willingness to call even the highest personages in the realm to account for their actions. Laity too were active, including the scholar Laurence Tomson, a translator of the New Testament, and Anne Locke, a disciple and correspondent of the Scottish Reformer JOHN KNOX. From Newgate Prison, where he had been incarcerated for his part in writing the first *Admonition*, Field proposed a conference to draft a confession of faith and a form of discipline, but more cautious heads prevailed. Instead the Presbyterian cause was advanced through illegal publications, including collections of the first and second *Admonitions* and other pamphlets, and the establishment of a Presbyterian network that extended into the Midlands and Shropshire. By the summer of 1573 Field and his colleagues had won the support of various London aldermen and wealthy citizens, and Richard Crick and Arthur Wake proclaimed the Presbyterian message from the influential Paul's Cross pulpit in the city. The government responded in November by appointing inquisitorial commissions to force the Presbyterians to conform or be deprived of their pastorates. A wanted man, Cartwright fled to the Continent, where he shortly helped to publish Travers's *Full and Plaine Declaration*. Field too may have fled abroad, but Wilcox visited colleagues in the Midlands and then settled in London. With its key leaders abroad or intimidated, the Presbyterian movement temporarily stalled.

Impetus for the next stage of Presbyterian development came at Norwich in 1575 during the hiatus between the death of Bishop John Parkhurst in February and the confirmation of Edmund Freke as his successor in November. During this period the Norwich clergy operated their "exercises"—meetings to improve preaching—on a Presbyterian basis, according to which all ministers were deemed equal and the role of moderator rotated. In October 1582 three of these ministers (Crick, Edmund Chapman, and Richard Dow), having relocated along the Sussex-Essex border, launched the Dedham conference. Because lay elders did not participate, this was not a Presbyterian classis in the proper sense, although a 1586 assembly in London referred to Dedham and similar conferences as classes. Such groups regarded their members as equal and expected them and their congregations to heed the advice rendered by the conference. The conferences dealt with a wide variety of ministerial and casuisitical issues, sought advice from Cambridge divines, and furthered discipline. The membership was PURITAN rather than narrowly Presbyterian, for a number of participants favored the reform rather than the abolition of the episcopate. Unquestionably, however, the classes were useful to the Presbyterians in advancing their message.

The primary goal of the classical movement in the late 1580s was the imposition of godly discipline in the churches. To this end Presbyterian ministers meeting in London during the winter of 1584-1585, disillusioned by the House of Commons' refusal to consider Dr. Peter Turner's bill to place the government of the state church in the hands of ministers and elders, determined to establish such discipline even in the absence of a parliamentary statute. Such action would convert their conferences into proper classes and synods, but first they needed to settle on a Book of Discipline. A book was ready at the beginning of 1587, and copies were distributed to supportive clergy with instructions for its immediate implementation. On the heels of this action, Anthony Cope, presumably acting for the Presbyterians in Parliament, offered a bill in February 1587 that would abrogate all extant religious legislation and replace the Book of Common Prayer with a revised version of the Genevan liturgy. As in 1584, the queen quashed the new "BILL AND BOOK."

The classical movement retained its commitment to the Book of Discipline, although Presbyterians were divided as to whether the work should proceed without parliamentary approval. General synods were convened at Cambridge (September 1587), in Warwickshire (April 1588), and again at Cambridge (September 1589), but Field's death in 1588 robbed the movement of perhaps its strongest voice. Militant Presbyterians, such as John Udall, lecturer at Kingston, the Welshman John Penry, and especially Job Throckmorton, anonymous author of the vitriolic MARPRELATE TRACTS, strongly denounced their religious enemies and thereby further divided the movement. The Presbyterian cause, notwithstanding its internal divisions, the ignominy cast on it by the Marprelate episode, and the repressive work of the Court of HIGH COMMISSION, did not perish, but another fifty years passed before Presbyterians could realistically hope to revolutionize the polity of the state church.

Bibliography: P. Collinson, *The Elizabethan Puritan Movement*, 1967; S. J. Knox, *Walter Travers: Paragon of Elizabethan Puritanism*, 1962; P. Lake, *Anglicans and Puritans? Presbyterians and English Conformist Thought from Whitgift to Hooker*, 1988.

Richard L. Greaves

Princes in the Tower. The sons of Edward IV and Elizabeth Woodville, Edward V and Richard, duke of York, were aged twelve and nine, respectively, at their father's death on 9 April 1483. Lodged in the Tower of London by their uncle Richard, who usurped the throne as Richard III on 28 June, they disappeared from view and are generally held to have then perished about this time. Despite much speculation and scholarship, their exact fate remains a mystery. Richard III's responsibility for their deaths is a matter of continuing contention.

Edward, the eldest son, was born in SANCTUARY at Westminster late in 1470. His parents' clandestine marriage in 1464 and his father's alleged pre-contract to another woman provided grounds for challenging his legitimacy in 1483. The marriage brought problems from the outset. The advancement of the queen's kinsmen was a factor in Richard Neville, earl of Warwick's, seizure of power in 1470-1471, when Edward IV was forced into temporary exile, and in the alienation from court of the king's brothers, George, duke of Clarence, and Richard, duke of Gloucester.

Created Prince of Wales and established in his own household at Ludlow, Edward was a promising child, whose daily routine can be reconstructed from guidelines laid down for his education. His governor was his maternmal uncle, Anthony Earl Rivers, a man of learning and refinement, and his council was made responsible for the government of Wales and the Marches. His brother Richard was born at Shrewsbury in 1473, created duke of York in 1474, and married in 1478 to Anne Mowbray, heiress of the Mowbrays, dukes of Norfolk. Though his child-bride died in 1481, he was confirmed in her inheritance, to the chagrin of other heirs, notably Lord Howard, who, raised to the dukedom of Norfolk on Richard III's accession, clearly profited from the princes' bastardization.

Edward V succeeded his father unchallenged. A regency council was established, but contention soon surfaced between the dowager queen's party and William Lord Hastings, a major issue being the role of the king's uncle. Neither the new king nor Gloucester was as yet in London, and when the two parties met at Stony Stratford on 30 April the uncle took Edward under his protection and purged his household of Rivers and other alleged traitors. Though Edward was lodged in the Tower and the Woodvilles took sanctuary, preparations for the boy's coronation continued through May. Tension mounted, however, as Gloucester amassed troops and struck at opponents. On 13 June he sent Hastings to the block and arrested other councillors, and three days later he committed Prince Richard to the Tower. Allegations impugning the legitimacy of Edward IV's children were made by Henry Stafford, duke of Buckingham, and others, and on 26 June Gloucester was formally petitioned to take the throne.

Rumors of the princes' demise soon spread. According to an Italian report, they rapidly disappeared from view, and people believed the worst. Their deaths were widely assumed by autumn, when there was a major rebellion in southern England involving the dowager queen, many of the old king's friends and retainers, Lancastrian diehards, and the renegade Buckingham. Originating in a conspiracy to liberate the princes, its scale and momentum and in particular, its novel focus on Elizabeth of York, Edward IV's eldest daughter, can be explained only by this assumption.

Richard III did not scotch the rumors and may have been content for people to believe them dead. More troubling, presumably, were the allegations of murder most foul. Apart from a hint of a move to inculpate Buckingham, however, there is no evidence of any denial of the charge. Richard certainly had the means and the motive for the murder. It would have been folly to allow the princes to remain a focus of opposition, and there were doubtless others who desired their deaths. Richard's responsibility may, nonetheless, have been limited. The princes could have died of the plague, through starvation or neglect, or at the hands of over-zealous jailers. Perhaps their bodies were hurriedly and inadvisedly concealed. A hypothesis of this sort may help explain the dowager queen's willingness to come to terms with Richard in 1484.

The princes' fate was a mystery from the outset. The early reports, which variously aver that they were poisoned, drowned, or suffocated, lack credibility. More surprisingly, Richard's overthrow brought no new revelations, nor indeed any charge more specific than the shedding of infants' blood. HENRY VII clearly had no sure knowledge of what had happened. The bodies of his brothers-in-law were not recovered, and his regime was plagued by pseudo-princes, whose claims were not always easy to refute. Later on an "official line" was perhaps deemed necessary. In 1501 Sir James Tyrell, condemned for treason, allegedly made a confession to the murder, which was inspiration for THOMAS MORE's, and thus WILLIAM SHAKESPEARE's, reconstruction. Tyrell was a plausible scapegoat, but the circumstances related by More, including the suffocation and burial of the boys, are problematic and unconvincing.

Given the lack of evidence and the many oddities in the case, alternative theories have abounded. Many seek to exonerate Richard and cast Henry VII, Buckingham, or Norfolk as the villain. While most accounts assumed the princes died in 1483 or soon after, some speculate about their escape or concealment. Earlier conjecture of this sort apparently ended with the unmasking of PERKIN WARBECK, whose claim to be Richard of York was taken seriously in some surprising quarters.

The discovery in 1674 of two skeletons in the Tower of London promised hard evidence. Hailed as the missing princes, the remains were buried in Westminster Abbey. Medical examination in 1933 indicated that the childern were roughly the ages of the princes when first incarcerated. Doubts have been cast, however, on these results, and the hope remains that further examination with modern techniques will be more conclusive.

Bibliography: P. W. Hammond, ed., *Richard III: Loyalty, Lordship and the Law*, 1986; C. Ross, *Richard III*, 1981.

Michael J. Bennett

Printing. Though print culture in England can be said to have begun with the earliest importation of printed materials, a more conventional point of departure is the establishment of William Caxton's press at Westminster in late 1475 or early 1476. An English woolen mercer who prospered in the Low Countries, Caxton learned printing at Cologne and set up a press at Bruges before returning to England. *The Recuyell of the Historyes of Troye*, which he translated into English from the French and printed while abroad (late 1473 or early 1474), is generally deemed the first of his efforts and the first book printed in English. His earliest publications at Westminster were undated; recent studies suggest that he began book production in England well before the fall of 1476 and that he started with a few small quartos and perhaps a book of hours before taking up the folio edition of the *Canterbury Tales*.

By his death, probably early in 1492, Caxton had published, in addition to indulgences and other ephemera, about 100 books—educational aids, encyclopedias, moral and religious instruction, allegories, works of chivalry, histories, poetry, romance, satire, and so on. About three-quarters of these were in English, roughly one-quarter his own translation. Caxton's success has been ascribed to his specialization in vernacular texts, his familiarity with what was fashionable on the Continent, his fortune in having cultured and well-placed patrons, his shrewd assessment of an elite or aspiring English clientele, and his affinity for books that were best-sellers in script and/or unavailable through overseas trade.

Printing at Westminster continued under Caxton's Alsatian assistant, Wynkyn de Worde, until late 1500 or early 1501, when de Worde moved operations to Fleet Street in London, nearer the hub of the book market. Though he reprinted some of Caxton's folios and produced some costly commissioned books, de Worde favored smaller, cheaper works for a wider audience—for example, domestic instruction, popular romances, primers, jest books, sundry pamphlets. One of the most prolific publishers in early English printing history, he is believed to have produced over 800 titles.

Whereas Caxton and his successor turned the new technology of moveable type to a flourishing enterprise, most pioneer printers of the late fifteenth century had modest success, at best. Around 1478, Theodoric Rood of Cologne set up a press at Oxford, where he and his sometime partner, stationer Thomas Hunte, are thought to have issued fewer than twenty scholarly works; the latest dated publication is imprinted 1486. A second provincial press, credited with eight titles, was in operation from about 1479 to 1486 at the Benedictine Abbey at St. Albans, long known for manuscript production.

Printing was introduced to the city of London around 1480 by John Lettou, presumably a Lithuanian, who appears to have published two books on his own before joining forces with the Flemish printer William de Machlinia, with whom he produced at least five law texts before vanishing from historical view. Machlinia, who continued to publish until about 1490, managed a reasonable business in legal studies, which comprised roughly a third of his thirty-odd publications. Around 1496, another collaborative press began printing in London, a partnership of Julian Notary of Brittany and two other men, both of whom had evidently left the business by 1499. Before the end of his publishing career, about 1520, Notary issued close to fifty books, many of them liturgical.

Some of the finest examples of early English printing are by Richard Pynson, a Norman who seems to have assumed Machlinia's law trade after 1490. First located outside Temple Bar, Pynson moved to Fleet Street in 1500 and became printer to the king in 1508. By his death, c. 1530, he had published some 400 works, mostly legal and liturgical.

The early sixteenth century saw an increase in number and a more general prosperity among both printers and publishers. As markets took shape, the business heirs of the major printer-publishers stood to inherit well-established lines and customer groups, as well as costly press equipment—a situation that permitted more stability and continuity. Pynson's legal printing trade, for example, passed to his rival Robert Redman; after Redman's death in 1540, his business was assumed by his widow, Elizabeth Pickering; at her remarriage, the trade was taken up by William Middleton, who continued to issue chiefly legal texts. Kin and countrymen of alien printers, we may gather, inherited the liabilities as well as the tools and markets of their predecessors, as native resentment toward foreign artisans was both widespread and strong. Assuming in 1508 or 1509 the business of the highly skilled Norman printer William Faques (apparently first to be officially appointed printer to the king, c. 1504), Richard Faques initially printed under his French name but later substituted the anglicized "Fawkes." Legal records indicated that some alien printers and their employees were physically attacked by angry citizens.

The flowering of the printing industry is a development both reflective of and, in part, responsible for a series of edicts regulating foreign craftworkers in England. Whereas the Act of 1484 (1 Ric. III, c. 9), designed to inhibit alien commerce, had exempted the book trade so as to foster its domestic growth, the acts of 1523 (14 and 15 Hen. VIII, c. 2) and 1529 (21 Hen. VIII, c. 16) did not spare foreign printers and booksellers from increasing proscription. In 1534, both printing and retail bookselling became the exclusive privilege of English subjects, and the importation of bound books was forbidden (25 Hen. VIII, c. 15). Until this time, historians suggest, under a third of those employed in the book trade in England were native.

Not merely a protection for enterprising citizens, the Act of 1534 was also part of a continuing campaign to check religious and political heresy. A PROCLAMA-TION of 1538 required that all English books be licensed by the PRIVY COUNCIL or its designee before printing or distribution, and this surveillance, orginally intended to ensure HENRY VIII's particular brand of Reformation, was endorsed by both EDWARD VI and the Catholic MARY I. In 1557, business interests and state censorship converged in the royal charter accorded the Worshipful Company of Stationers of London, a document that restricted printing to company members or holders of royal patents, bestowed kingdom-wide rights of search and seizure, and granted powers of self-governance. The company's practice of requiring all licensed titles to be entered in the Stationers' Register before printing, intended to establish exclusive but transferable rights to copy, may have seemed an effective means of reinforcing Crown control. The charter most certainly facilitated both royal scrutiny and the regulation of competition through its virtual confinement of printing to London, where production could be easily monitored by state and corporate authorities.

The implicit ban on provincial printing may have been, at least momentarily, a pro forma measure, as most printers outside London seem to have failed or fled by the date of the charter. Though a number had hoped to service outlying centers of learning, local markets were small and orthodoxies unstable. Before 1520, three printers at York and two at Oxford appear to have come and gone. John Siberch, presumably invited by resident humanists, printed in Cambridge only from about 1520 to 1522. (The university obtained royal license to print in 1534, but this privilege was not exercised.) Two extant books dated 1525 and 1534 indicated sporadic production at Tavistock Abbey; a 1528 breviary issued by John Scolar, earlier at Oxford, is the only evidence of printing at the abbey near Abingdon. At St. Albans, John Herford turned out perhaps seven books between 1434 and the abbey's closing in 1539. At Canterbury, there is evidence for heretical publication in the mid-1530s, and John Mychell printed there in the early forties, returning, after time in London, to produce an estimated seventeen titles between 1549 and 1556. Anthony Skolokar and John Oswen allegedly printed books in Ipswich, consecutively, between 1547 and 1548, but these strongly Protestant works may bear false imprints. Doctrinal turbulence made artful dodging a necessity for those who could suddenly be found seditious; Oswen, by privilege of Edward VI, printed religious texts for Welsh distribution in Worcester from about 1549 to the accession of Mary, then disappeared from record.

In 1559, ELIZABETH I confirmed the Stationers' charter and extended deputy licensing to selected church officials; in 1566, an order of the privy council strengthened penalties for illegal publication. Prohibited works continued to surface despite grim displays of royal justice. The Catholic printer William Carter, executed in 1582 for producing heretical texts with bogus imprints, published at least eleven titles in four years of clandestine printing. (An estimated 250 RECUSANT works in England, from underground or abroad, circulated during Elizabeth's reign.) Tudor attempts to regulate the press culminated in the

STAR CHAMBER decree of 1586, which empowered government officials to limit the number of presses and employees and which expressly restricted printing to the London area, except for the two university presses at Oxford and Cambridge. (The first official university printers—Joseph Barnes, at Oxford from 1585, and Thomas Thomas, at Cambridge from 1583—were thus reconfirmed.) Additionally, the Stationers' Company was newly authorized to investigate all printing sites and to confiscate illegal copy and equipment. Both Crown and company vigorously enforced the new and reiterated sanctions, but illicit printing persisted, most notably with the PURITAN pamphlet attack on the bishops in 1588-1589 (see MARPRELATE TRACTS).

Within the realm of orthodox printing, the proliferation of royal patents became a vexed issue over the course of the century. Some of the earliest exclusive rights to copy were those granted the king's printers for all official or royally owned text. As can be inferred from the receipts of Thomas Berthelet and Richard Grafton, who held the title 1530-1547 and 1547-1553, respectively, they secured short-term privileges for specific religious and educational titles, including the Bible. Upon appointing John Cawood as queen's printer, Mary I trimmed incumbent rights so as to grace other favorites, and Elizabeth I was quick to ascertain that book patents, like other MONOPOLIES, could be parlayed for political and financial gain. After her accession, in addition to appointing Cawood and Richard Jugge jointly as life printers to the queen, Elizabeth extended life monopolies to Richard Tottel for all law books and to William Seres (and son) for all psalters, primers, and prayer books. Long-term patents for other lucrative genres were to follow—for example, to John Day for the *ABC* and catechisms, to Thomas Marshe for Latin grammars, to James Roberts Watkins for almanacs and prognostications. Book patents were not restricted to printers or publishers; Sir Thomas Wilkes, a diplomat, acquired the privilege of queen's printer of England in 1577 and sold the office to Christopher Barker for a hefty sum. These grand monopolies, in combination with miscellaneous title and author assignments, had predictable market effects; unprivileged printers could find themselves without work while patentees or their designees underproduced to create artificial shortages and high prices.

Piracy was a logical and continuing response to this concentration of profit, but by the 1570s the excluded printers were openly protesting the existing monopolies and organizing to block injurious new ones. One insurgent leader, John Wolfe, began to print in volume with no regard for privilege whatsoever, claimed it lawful for all men to print lawful books, and defended his actions with the argument "I will live." Wolfe was pacified in 1584 or 1585 with a piece of John Day's patent and became himself a ruthless hunter of pirates, but his more steadfast associate, Roger Ward, remained a dedicated offender well into the 1590s and produced about 10,000 illicit copies of the *ABC* and large runs of other protected works despite serial press seizures and prison terms. The militant pirates succeeded in publicizing inequities within the industry and thereby necessitated concessions, which included more shared monopolies, more shared production, and the release of some patented copies to the Stationers' Company for the assistance of poorer members. These changes had small effect, ultimately, on the distribution of wealth. Rather, they opened the way for a more efficient organization of privilege, whereby the company held and leased patents as a purveyor of corporate "stock."

The history of printing in sixteenth-century England, as taken from extant records, is a history of increasing censorship and centralization. But the repetition of prohibitions also reveals a continuing failure to stem the flow of materials that challenged current dogma. About one-third of printed books surviving from this period were not entered in the Stationers' Register, which suggests a remarkable casualness toward, or circumvention of, regulatory practices. Additionally, as is made explicit in an order of the archbishop of Canterbury and the bishop of London in 1599, apparent compliance with regulation did not always mean actual compliance; the order forbids further publication of satires and epigrams, requires that histories and plays be approved in advance by authorized agents, and stipulates that authorizing signatures be authenticated before the printing of books in problematic genres—all of which point to previous chicanery. Restriction of public expression was, under the Tudors, frequently met with creative subversion, and this conflict was to continue in the seventeenth century.

Bibliography: Colin Clair, *A History of Printing in Britain*, 1965; John Feather, *A History of British Publishing*, 1988; Marjorie Plant, *The English Book Trade*, 1839, rev. 1965.

Janis Butler Holm

Privy Council is the name conventionally reserved for the select board of royal advisers that came into existence about the period 1536-1537; it was a smaller body of more exclusive membership than councils appointed earlier. Although contemporaries employed *council* and *privy council* interchangeably before and after the 1530s, "the king's council" is a historically accurate designation for the period before Mary I's accession (1553), "the queen's council" thereafter.

Tudor privy councillors combined three functions in membership of one body: they advised the sovereign on all matters of policy; they enforced that policy and administered the realm in their capacities as great officers of state and the royal HOUSEHOLD; they adjudicated disputes and acted quasi-judicially as a board of arbitration. Privy councillors routinely considered so many different kinds of business that nothing, it seems, fell outside their competence. In this scope they were unique; none of the councils serving kings in France, the empire, or Castile, for example, exhibited the fullness of power or discharged the responsibilities of the Tudor privy council.

The size, composition, and procedures of HENRY VII's council closely resembled those of the Yorkists. Edward IV employed 188 councillors after 1471; 227 served Henry VII. Twenty-two of Edward IV's men (of the 40 still alive in

1485) and 20 of Richard III's could be counted among those active in Henry's reign. In composition Henry's council was still "medieval" in that a fourth (61) were clerics and another fifth (45) nobles; the remainder included lawyers (27), officers (49), and a group of knights and esquires best described as courtiers (45). At Henry's accession some 15 or 16 attended meetings at court; attendances sometimes grew to 40 and even 50 and included as many as 8 bishops and a sprinkling of lesser clergy (the dean of the chapel royal, the king's almoner, etc.). At Westminster this council met regularly during the sixteen weeks of the law terms and discussed whatever the king put before it, including private suits; Henry himself frequently attended, characteristically dominating the meetings. A clerk recorded attendances and noted the business concluded.

Out of term, when the king went on progress or moved to another palace, a smaller "council attendant" moved with the court and left a residual group in London. Neither group formed a separate institution; on the king's return to Westminster both merged in the one (and only) whole council. Although in theory all councillors were equal, the council attendant nonetheless enjoyed paramount political influence, since within the whole council it constituted an active inner ring, as it were, of the king's most trusted advisers, most of them officers of his Household.

Henry VII's death effectively increased the importance of councillors attendant, as HENRY VIII was content to leave the conduct of affairs to the members of the inner ring, but THOMAS WOLSEY's rise checked their influence: Wolsey essentially usurped the functions of both king and council. Although the council continued to meet as it had under Henry VII, its proceedings under Wolsey were much less political and far more curial, or judicial. It was during Wolsey's tenure as lord chancellor that the judicial sessions of the council in Star Chamber (a room at Westminster with gilded stars on the ceiling) became, properly speaking, the sessions of a judicial court, the Court of STAR CHAMBER. By 1530 the Court of Star Chamber and the king's council were separate institutions. At any rate, when Henry VIII complained that he lacked sufficient councillors about his person, Wolsey, already overburdened with work, proposed the creation, in the terms of the ELTHAM ORDINANCES of 1526, of a reduced council of twenty members attendant upon the king.

Although the council of the Eltham Ordinances remained merely a proposal, it was obviously the model for the later privy council, but just how this reconstituted council of the 1530s came into being is something of a mystery. Was it, as Sir Geoffrey Elton maintained, the product of THOMAS CROMWELL's "revolutionary" program of administrative reform? Or did circumstances and events—in particular the rebellion known as the PILGRIMAGE OF GRACE (1536)—force Cromwell and the king to reorganize the traditional board? Like Wolsey, Cromwell (Wolsey's protégé) apparently aimed at reform: he may have projected a scheme "for the establishment of the Council" in June 1534, though exactly what he meant by "the Council" remains unclear. Ever since Wolsey's fall (1529), "select" councillors, that is, insiders of the sort who would have constituted the earlier inner ring—men like Cromwell, the dukes of Norfolk and Suffolk, and the earl of Wiltshire (ANNE BOLEYN's father Thomas)—had met secretly, if irregularly, in the king's Privy Chamber at court. The subject of their deliberations was almost exclusively political—the king's divorce proceedings, the break with Rome, etc.—and left to other councillors in Star Chamber (whose number included various judges and lawyers) the judicial work that Wolsey had supervised earlier. The rebellion of 1536 drew attention to the distinctive, politically influential nature of the "select" council; the rebels attacked several of its members, including Cromwell, as lowborn and unfit to rule. In his published response to the Pilgrims, Henry VIII reaffirmed the integrity of this circle of select appointees by identifying its nineteen members; here is the evidence of a privy council of restricted, exclusive membership. (Compare the 120 who served during Wolsey's ascendency.) Other lists, as well as letters from the council to captains in the field, corroborate the formation of the privy council at this time (the autumn of 1536-the spring of 1537). Politically, however, it cannot have been a council wholly of Cromwell's making, since among its members his religiously Conservative opponents outnumbered him, and his attempts after 1536 to reassert his control of the king's affairs brought them out against him. In retrospect, the reconstituted privy council of 1536-1537 became permanent only after his fall (10 June 1540); the recorded proceedings (published between 1890 and 1907 as *The Acts of the Privy Council*) date from 10 August 1540, when the reorganized body acquired a formal register and a salaried professional staff.

Constitutionally, EDWARD VI's minority (1547-1553) made manifest the council's recognized competence: the privy council, not the king, was empowered to govern the realm, an authority the council (consisting initially of Henry VIII's sixteen executors) relinquished to one of their number, EDWARD SEYMOUR, duke of Somerset, whose patents as lord protector authorized him to appoint and summon councillors at will. Political necessity persuaded him to revive a privy council of traditional size (twenty to twenty-two members) and composition, that is, one composed of the great officers of state (chancellor, treasurer, privy seal, great chamberlain, high admiral) and the king's Household (great master, chamberlain, vice-chamberlain, comptroller, treasurer, master of the horse, secretary). To these were added two prelates (the archbishop of Canterbury and the bishop of Durham), a diplomat (the dean of Canterbury and York), and various courtiers and officials (including two gentlemen of the king's Privy Chamber, the chancellors of augmentations and the Exchequer, and the master of the king's wardrobe).

In the making of policy, however, Somerset's attempt to circumvent his colleagues precipitated within the council a coup (October 1549) organized by JOHN DUDLEY, duke of Northumberland. Once in power, Northumberland employed the latent powers of the heretofore honorific office of president of the council to purge the board of his enemies and pack it with his friends and to expand membership (to 32) chiefly by the addition of nobles who doubled as LORDS LIEUTENANT charged with the suppression of revolts in the shires. A larger council was not less efficient, however; the system of government by a small working group of the larger board, sometimes described as an Elizabethan development, was actually established by Sir WILLIAM CECIL under Northumberland's direction in the period 1550-1553. The presumed evidence of Edward VI's reform or direction of council business—his council memoranda, etc.—is a student's exercise; the king was following, not leading, his councillors' work. Sir WILLIAM PAGET's "Advice to the King's Council" of March 1550 codified the ideal procedures governing the conduct and administration of business.

The history of MARY's council is the story of two councils that became one. At Kenninghall (9-12 July 1553) Mary appointed eighteen personal adherents and Catholic coreligionists—most of them officers in her Household—to lead her rebellion against "the false Queen Jane." However, none of the Kenninghall men (save one) had held high office; her accession secured, she turned increasingly to men of experience and of a second group of twenty-two appointees (added between 20 July and 4 September 1553), fully seventeen had served in the councils of her father and brother—the very men, that is, who had helped make the Reformation. At Westminster these men assumed the direction of business of state, and effectively replaced the short-lived Kenninghall "council." Of Mary's fifty privy councillors only nineteen were really active. Among the various committees organized by Paget was the eight-member "council of state," an ad hoc group so styled to make King Philip think he was addressing the real men of power, a diplomatic deception, no doubt. The myth of "factions" in Mary's council has obscured the reality of institutional stability and administrative continuity, the latter explained by the presence of Henrician and Edwardian careerists like Paget.

Under ELIZABETH the council actually grew smaller; at one time numbering eleven and never more than nineteen, it stood at thirteen in 1601. Clerics had almost vanished; JOHN WHITGIFT, archbishop of Canterbury, was Elizabeth's sole ecclesiastical appointee (1586). Rarely present in council, the queen left the conduct of affairs to a working group of four or five of her most trusted men; between six and nine were typically present at meetings at Greenwich, Whitehall, and Hampton Court. Until 1588 the following eight were most often present in council: William Cecil, Lord Burghley; ROBERT DUDLEY, earl of Leicester; Sir Francis Knollys; Sir FRANCIS WALSINGHAM; Sir Thomas Smith; Thomas Radcliffe, 3rd earl of Sussex; Charles Lord Howard of Effingham; and Sir James Croft. On great questions of policy, councillors were supposed to offer their best advice (no matter what Elizabeth's views) and then implement the queen's decisions, but Elizabeth's characteristic indecision, procrastination, and delay frequently forced them to adopt covert tactics of manipulation to secure her support for their policies, policies she hated or resisted; the proposed alliance with foreign Protestants is a case in point.

If the forging of such policy was very often a game of political maneuver, Elizabethan councillors routinely discharged an extraordinary range of administrative responsibilities. In their own persons (as officers of state or lords lieutenant) or in their letters to local officials they ordered the defense of the realm; regulated industry, prices, and trade; managed the queen's and England's finances; enforced the ELIZABETHAN SETTLEMENT OF RELIGION of 1559 (a task requiring the detection and punishment of RECUSANTS); gained control of warrants under the Great Seal (action unimaginable under Henry VII); managed the business of Parliament; supervised the work of sheriffs, judges, and JUSTICES OF THE PEACE; and, with characteristic Tudor paternalism, occasionally inquired into morals public and private. The Elizabethan privy council was relatively the most powerful, flexible, and efficient instrument of royal government in early modern Europe.

Bibliography: G. R. Elton, ed., *The Tudor Constitution*, 2nd ed., 1982; John Guy, *Tudor England*, 1988; Dale Hoak, *The King's Council in the Reign of Edward VI*, 1976; Dale Hoak, "Two Revolutions in Tudor Government: the Formation and Organization of Mary I's Privy Council," in *Revolution Reassessed*, ed. C. Coleman and D. Starkey, 1986; Michael Pulman, *The Elizabethan Privy Council in the Fifteen-Seventies*, 1971.

Dale Hoak

Proclamations, Royal. A legislative order, administrative regulation, or formal announcement issued by the Crown by authority of the ROYAL PREROGATIVE and intended for public reading and posting throughout the realm. The right of Tudor monarchs to legislate in this way was unquestioned throughout the sixteenth century, although theories about the proper scope, authority, and enforcement of proclamations so made varied from time to time.

Issued by the Crown ostensibly with the advice (but not consent) of the council, expiring at the death of the monarch, and made without recourse to PARLIAMENT, proclamations were distinctly inferior in authority to statute law, which they could neither alter or contradict. Nor could they create felonies or treasons, touch property rights protected under the common law, or deprive the subject of life or limb. They were nevertheless an effective tool of Tudor government, for they provided a quick and flexible solution to specific problems during those times when Parliament was not in session or when emergency conditions required an immediate response. Thus proclamations were used extensively in military and diplomatic affairs (to announce war or peace or quell a rebellion), in economic or social regulation (controlling trade and industry, prices and wages, and particularly the COINAGE or dealing with poverty, famine, or PLAGUE), in announcing changes (through birth, marriage, or death) in the royal estate, in the legal and administrative fine-tuning necessary to implement a parliamentary statute (often by virtue of authority granted to them in the act itself), and—beginning with the 1530s—in implementing the religious policies set by the government.

The initiative for proclamations came usually from the government working through the council and—from THOMAS CROMWELL's time, aside from a brief Marian respite—primarily from the PRIVY COUNCIL working through the PRINCIPAL SECRETARY, but also from the monarch himself and not infrequently from a private party or corporate interest group moving the government to address some issue of concern. Once a proclamation had been drafted, the fair manuscript copy was engrossed on parchment and signed by the monarch. It was then delivered to CHANCERY, which issued a writ under the Great Seal ordering the text (sometimes rehearsed in the body of the writ and sometimes attached separately) to be proclaimed and posted throughout the country. Most proclamations were then delivered to local officials through the sheriff. By ELIZABETH's reign the printed format was distinctive, headed "By the Queen," sometimes including a content title, and concluding with the formula "Given at...," the invocation "God Save the Queen," and the identification of the printer. Once distributed, the text was read and then posted at customary places throughout the country (at market crosses, in front of guildhalls or churches, at town gates, and—in London and other principal cities—sometimes at various stages in civic processions). Not all texts have survived, and no comprehensive, official collection was printed during the sixteenth century.

Enforcement was a problem. Under HENRY VII and the early years of HENRY VIII, proclamations had no force in the COMMON LAW courts, and insuring compliance was left to the council sitting as the Court of STAR CHAMBER. Although fines, forfeitures, and imprisonment were all possible, their use was seldom specified and usually inadequate. It was to solve this problem, and perhaps to confirm an already existing prerogative right by basing it on parliamentary authority, that Thomas Cromwell introduced into Parliament in 1539 a bill that became the Statute of Proclamations (31 Hen. VIII c. 8). The preamble stressed the value of proclamations, particularly during those times when Parliament was not in session, and noted the need for better enforcement. The act itself confirmed the king's right to make proclamations with the advice of his council, restated existing legal limitations on their power, and—the principal point—declared that they were to be obeyed "as though they were made by act of Parliament." It also established a cumbersome new subset of the council with powers of enforcement. This last provision may not have been in the original bill, which has not survived. Certainly the bill provoked substantial opposition in both the Lords and Commons for reasons that are no longer clear, and the end result must have been a compromise with Cromwell's original aim, which was perhaps to make proclamations enforceable in the common law courts. The act, which changed little in practice, was revised in 1543 and repealed in 1547 after Henry VIII's death. Opponents of early absolutism and some later historians saw in the statute an attempt to bypass Parliament and establish a Tudor despotism, but this interpretation is now largely rejected.

Individual Tudor monarchs or their ministers used proclamations in varying degrees and for varying purposes, but none overstepped the basic boundaries already laid down by the beginning of the dynasty. Henry VII issued at least 67, primarily for military and diplomatic matters; Henry VIII at least 243, most widely under THOMAS WOLSEY, who was impatient with Parliament. After the 1539 act; EDWARD SEYMOUR, duke of Somerset, who, like Wolsey, preferred proclamations to statutes, and JOHN DUDLEY, duke of Northumberland, issued at least 127 in Edward VI's name; Mary only 64; and finally Elizabeth, the most active of them all, at least 382.

Bibliography: Since not all proclamations have survived, there is some disagreement over the total number in the Tudor canon; the vast majority have been published in a modern 3-volume edition by P. L. Hughes and J. F. Larkin, *Tudor Royal Proclamations*, 1964-69. Also see R. W. Heinze, *The Proclamations of the Tudor Kings*, 1976; F. A. Youngs, *The Proclamations of the Tudor Queen*, 1976.

Mary L. Robertson

Puritanism. Apparently first used in the mid-1560s, the word *Puritan* was originally a term of opprobrium, as was its synonym *precisionist*. By the end of the sixteenth century *puritan* had acquired a wide range of connotations, some of which were political or social. The problem of meaning was compounded when modern historians (e.g., W. Haller, M. M. Knappen, A. Simpson) created assorted definitions of puritanism and contrasted this ideological construction, however formulated, with ANGLICANISM, the views and practices of non-puritans in the Church of England. A large body of historical literature was written around the theme of an Anglican-puritan rivalry in religion, politics, and society. This confrontational model was challenged in the 1970s and 1980s by "revisionist" historians (e.g., P. Collinson, M. Finlayson, C. M. Dent), who played down Elizabethan controversies over vestments, the BOOK OF COMMON PRAYER, ecclesiastical discipline, and polity and focused instead on an alleged doctrinal consensus among Protestants. Reflecting the dominant mood of the 1980s, revisionist historians concomitantly discarded the prevailing view of puritans as protorevolutionaries and depicted them instead as respectable conservatives and members of the "moral majority." Blame for destroying the peaceful Protestant consensus was then shifted to William Laud, bishop of London, and, beginning in 1633 archbishop of Canterbury. Some revisionists went so far as to deny the importance of religious factors in what had once been known as the Puritan Revolution. Rejecting revisionist views as extreme, other historians (e.g., D. D. Wallace, R. L. Greaves, W. Hunt) recognized both the substantial degree of theological unity within the established church and the characteristic piety and religious concerns of the puritans that distinguished them from other members of the state church (typically referred to as Anglicans, conformists, or formalists).

Puritans can usefully be defined as those Protestants in the Church of England who sought to purge both ceremony and liturgy of Catholic accretions and who shared a distinctive religious experience. They explained the latter in terms of a spiritual reorientation with a particular emphasis on purity of heart and mind. Their sense of spiritual warmth was the core of their shared experience of the godly community. Concerns about predestination and demands for holy living created anxiety in some puritans, especially during the early stages of their religious life, but ultimately most of the godly seem to have acquired assurance of salvation and a sense of belonging in their respective fellowships. Puritans were stricter than Anglicans with respect to matters on which the Bible offered no specific advice (i.e., adiaphora); such practices were acceptable only if they were not offensive, if they were orderly and edifying, and if they glorified God. The puritans tended to see their religious life in terms of the duty to do only what God had commanded, whereas Anglicans tended to focus more on their liberty to do whatever the Bible had not prohibited. Their outlooks differed as well with respect to worship; the puritans, with their aniconic tendencies, urged major liturgical reform, partly to expunge allegedly "popish" ceremonial, partly to place greater emphasis on the sermon. Puritans also tended to distinguish themselves by their interest in experiential predestinarianism, as opposed to the more common credal variety, and in covenant theology.

Much of the time the differences between puritans and Anglicans pertained to emphasis or degree, not conflicting beliefs. As Protestants and as members of the Church of England they concurred on much, and in this general sense it is appropriate to speak of an Elizabethan consensus; one must, however, also remember the significant matters on which they disagreed. Important too is the fact that puritans, like Anglicans, differed among themselves and thus complicate efforts to formulate working concepts of puritanism and Anglicanism, both of which are perhaps best eschewed in historical discourse.

Although puritan origins are to be found in the disputes over the Book of Common Prayer among the MARIAN EXILES at Frankfurt and in the subsequent withdrawal of advocates of further reform to Geneva, the first substantive controversy in England commenced in 1565, when the government attempted to force the clergy to wear the prescribed vestments (see VESTIARIAN CONTRO-VERSY). Most Elizabethan puritans had no desire to abrogate episcopal polity, although many wanted reforms in the bishopric. When it became increasingly apparent, however, that the bishops, as royal servants, were reluctant to anger Queen ELIZABETH by supporting major reforms, the more extreme puritans, such as John Field, Thomas Wilcox, and Thomas Cartwright, began espousing a PRESBYTERIAN polity. This issue exacerbated the fissures within the puritan camp and led to attempts to persuade Parliament to enact legislation effectively terminating episcopal authority. The advocates of this view, known as Presbyterians, themselves disagreed in the late 1580s over the wisdom of implementing a Book of Discipline and thus Presbyterian polity without parliamentary approval. SEPARATISTS—Protestant extremists who so despaired of reforming the state church that they left it to establish their own congregations of believers—shared many puritan ideals but should be distinguished from the puritans.

The importance attached by puritans to preaching attracted them to lectureships as a principal means to spread the gospel. While the antecedents of lectureships predated the puritans and though a number of Anglicans supported this institution, lectureships were utilized most effectively and most extensively by puritans–so much so that King JAMES VI and I (ruled England, 1603-1625) later regarded them as a dangerous innovation. In fact, lectureships represented a practical response to the Church of England's unwillingness or inability to provide adequate numbers of qualified preaching clergy. Most lectureships were endowed by parishes or town corporations, with the funds coming from contributions or bequests. Considerable control, therefore, was in lay hands, causing some ecclesiastics to fret, especially when the lectures were given by independent ministers rather than more easily regulated beneficed clerics. The historian of the lectureships, P. S. Seaver, has underscored the extent to which they reveal the laity's desire to control the church at the parochial level. This desire was, of course, particularly true of the puritan laity.

The emphasis on preaching also accounted for the puritans' prominent involvement in prophesyings–ministerial conferences designed to improve preaching through biblical exposition and constructive criticism. As in the case of lectureships, prophesyings were not exclusively puritan; their origins, in fact, go back at least to Zurich in the 1520s, during the early period of Reformed Protestantism. Yet in their Elizabethan context, prophesyings were dominated by the puritans. For the most part, participation was limited to clerics and divinity students, although the laity were often allowed to listen and tended to debate the religious issues once the conference had concluded. In the early 1570s the bishops of Chichester, Exeter, and Lincoln promoted the prophesyings, and the movement reached its zenith between 1574 and 1576. Not until 1574, when Elizabeth ordered Archbishop MATTHEW PARKER to terminate the prophesyings at Norwich, did the institution become controversial. Parker's successor, EDMUND GRINDAL, unsuccessfully opposed the queen's order to halt prophesyings in the province of Canterbury, but the ensuing repression only prompted more militant puritans, including those in Norwich, to meet illegally. The Norwich prophesying, which had been controlled by the ministers themselves rather than an episcopal appointee, was an important step in the emergence of the Presbyterian classis. As an institution the prophesyings not only sharpened the pulpit skills and expanded the knowledge of ministers but also increased the number of committed laity, whose belief rested on comprehension rather than mere ecclesiastical authority.

The intensity of puritan convictions was increasingly evident as well with respect to their attitude toward the fourth commandment. The puritans, of course, were not alone in honoring the Sabbath, but by the late 1570s they had taken the lead in calling for stricter Sunday observance, especially by making the Sabbath binding as part of the moral law, a view not shared by some Anglicans. Not until the 1590s did the puritan Richard Greenham raise the argument that Sabbath observance made good business sense (the unbroken rhythm of the six-day work week); however, most Elizabethan writers confined their exposition of the Sabbath to religious considerations.

Controversy erupted in the 1590s when some puritan ministers, including Nicholas Bownde, treated the Sabbath in a distinctly legal fashion and provoked a strong reaction in some Anglican quarters. In 1599 Thomas Rogers, for instance, repudiated Sabbatarianism, and JOHN WHITGIFT, archbishop of Canterbury, confiscated Bownde's treatise. In so doing they misleadingly identified Sabbatarianism, the origins of which were actually medieval, with the puritans. Mounting puritan concern with Sabbath violations, however, was an unmistakable indication of the zeal with which they approached their religious calling. Without a full appreciation of the source and extent of this spiritual fervency, an accurate understanding of the puritans is impossible.

Bibliography: P. Collinson, *The Elizabethan Puritan Movement*, 1967; R. L. Greaves, "The Puritan-Nonconformist Tradition in England, 1560-1700: Historiographical Reflections," *Albion* 17 (1985): 449-86; P. S. Seaver, *The Puritan Lectureships: The Politics of Religious Dissent 1560-1662*, 1970.

Richard L. Greaves

Q

Queen's Safety, Act for (1585). One of the most pressing concerns of the Parliament of 1584-1585 was enacting legislation to provide defense of ELIZABETH. In December 1584 the bill for the queen's safety was discussed in committee and then debated in the House of Commons. Though it was inspired by the BOND OF ASSOCIATION, the Act for the Queen's Safety dealt specifically with someone's making an attempt on the queen's life in order to advance a claimant to the throne, and anyone's then supporting this claim would be considered TREASON. A further clause authorized people to pursue and kill both culprits and the claimants, an echo of the Bond of Association. A difference, however, was that the claimant's heirs were not included in this latter aspect, and the queen would be able to restore the title of the heir, if she saw fit. The clear implication was that this act was aimed thoroughly against MARY, QUEEN OF SCOTS, while her son JAMES VI was potentially exempt from it.

Sections of the bill provoked a great deal of debate. Critics fastened onto a significant problem: if the queen were killed and all authority lapsed, how could effective action be taken? Having run its course in committee, the bill was brought into the House of Commons for a first reading 14 December. There was little debate, though the members were not happy or united on the bill.

Elizabeth then intervened. On 18 December Sir CHRISTOPHER HATTON rose to inform members that her majesty appreciated their care of her safety and expressed her approval of the bill; however, she believed her safety was in God's hands, and she could not consent that anyone should be punished for the fault of another. Particularly she did not wish the penalties to extend to the offender's issue—obviously James VI—unless he was also found at fault. The committee met that afternoon and struck out that proviso and revised the bill. One of the members said that he could not give his consent to the bill as it was now constructed. At this point, Elizabeth's own misgivings caused her to decide to delay, and at this point she commanded her councillors to proceed at this point no further. The bill was to be shelved until after the Christmas recess.

During the recess, WILLIAM CECIL, Lord Burghley, and others worked hard to transform the bill for the queen's safety into a measure that would be both effective and acceptable. Burghley proposed a draft bill that would provide, in the event of Elizabeth's murder, that all officials would continue in office "in the name of the Crown of England" and an executive body, a "Grand Council," would be temporarily set up with the authority to govern the realm until those concerned with the queen's death were indicted, tried, and executed, and a Parliament was called to hear and determine all claims to the succession of the Crown. This plan was never placed before the House of Commons because Elizabeth refused to accept it.

When Parliament took up the question of a bill for the queen's safety in February, the committee, in a deadlock, decided to ask the queen's advice about what they should do now. Burghley drafted a new bill in consultation with the queen. The committee met on 27 February, and then on 3 March Sir Christopher Hatton introduced the bill into the House of Commons for a first reading.

The text of the bill was based on the earlier one but took into account Elizabeth's concerns. In the event of a rebellion, invasion, or plot against the queen, a set of commissioners would investigate and pronounce judgment. The act then stated that all subjects could pursue to the death anyone the commission declared had known about the offense. Were there to be a successful attempt on the queen's life, only those for whom the assassination was effected were to be killed—their heirs would be included only if it could be proven they had also known. Should the queen be killed, Mary Stuart would suffer for it, but James VI would be exempt unless he too were involved. Instead of Burghley's plan for an interregnum, the commission was solely to investigate and destroy the guilty. This version of the act was passed and the Bond of Association was amended to conform with the act; it was repealed only centuries later in the reign of Queen Victoria.

Bibliography: John Neale, *Elizabeth I and Her Parliaments, 1584-1601*, 1957.

Carole Levin

R

Rationale of Ceremonial (1543). A Conservative explanation of the ceremonies employed by the English church that was never officially adopted due to royal and Protestant opposition.

During the Middle Ages, the religious ceremonies of the English church had evolved in a haphazard and unsupervised manner. By the early sixteenth century, the various ceremonial observances in use had become too numerous to keep track of, suffered from excessive formalism, and were insufficiently understood by most participants. Furthermore, many foreign practices had infiltrated the English ceremonies, a situation that HENRY VIII and many nationalistic leaders of the English church in the 1530s found offensive. As a result, the king appointed a committee on 12 April 1540 for reforming and rationalizing the religious ceremonies of the English church. This committee consisted of the Protestant bishops Thomas Goodrich of Ely and Robert Holgate of Llandaff and the Conservative bishops John Clerk of Bath and Wells, John Capon (Salcot) of Salisbury, Richard Sampson of Chichester, and John Bell of Worcester. An act of Parliament (32 Hen. VIII, c. 26) quickly confirmed the committee's existence. Most of its work appears to have been done by Goodrich, Capon, and Bell. Basically they tried to explain the existing Latin services, to revise and to reform those practices, and finally to reproduce them in English. As the work progressed, it became more and more complicated and so less and less useful. It also assumed a definite Conservative stance that was not congenial to either Henry VIII or Archbishop THOMAS CRANMER. As a result, they secured the suppression of the resulting document, the *Rationale of Ceremonial*. In its place, Cranmer quickly produced his own alternative English litany in May 1544, which was adopted by royal command by the Church of England. Although the preparers of the Edwardian service book studied the *Rationale of Ceremonial*, its Conservative approach had little impact on subsequent developments in the English liturgy. So the suppression of the *Rationale of Ceremonial* during the seesawing religious situation of the early 1540s was a defeat with serious long-term consequences for religious Conservatives in the Church of England.

Bibliography: C. S. Cobb, ed., *The Rationale of Ceremonial, 1540-1543*, 1910.

Ronald Fritze

Recusants. Recusants were those who refused to obey the religious laws enacted especially in the reign of ELIZABETH I. Even without the epithet *popish*, the term tended to apply particularly to Roman Catholics, and their chief act of recusancy was the refusal to attend ANGLICAN churches. A series of penal laws was passed by Elizabeth's Parliaments, especially in the second half of the reign, to punish recusancy. The ACT OF UNIFORMITY of 1559 (1 Eliz. I, c. 2) followed the Edwardian example in punishing absence from church most mildly, with a shilling fine every week payable to the churchwardens. Far severer punishments were reserved for priests who used an unauthorized form of service and, by the Act of Supremacy, for those who denied the ROYAL SUPREMACY. Elizabeth made sure that these severer penalties were seldom resorted to early in the reign. It is clear that the goverment did not at first expect many Catholics to avoid churchgoing. Attempts in PARLIAMENT to pass harsher laws were blocked by the queen until foreign and domestic developments in the 1570s and 1580s led to a series of laws aimed to crush the developing Catholic community. By the act of 1581 "to retain the Queen's Majesty's subjects in their due obedience" (23 Eliz. I, c. 1), it became treason to persuade or to be persuaded to the Romish religion with intent to withdraw the queen's subjects from their natural obedience, while to refuse to go to church was punishable by a fine of £20 a month. By the Act Against Popish Recusants of 1593 (35 Eliz. I, c. 2), all such people were confined to within five miles of their "place of usual dwelling" unless they had a license from a bishop or justice of the peace to travel. Disobedience was punishable by forfeiture of all goods for life, but those who publicly abjured Catholicism were free of the restrictions.

The figure usually given for the martyrs in the reign of Elizabeth is 183, of whom 59 were laymen. Torture was used to extract confessions, and the method of execution gruesome—in effect, death by evisceration. In addition, large numbers of laymen and priests were imprisoned; in 1583 the London prison lists show 103 prisoners. Many died of prison fever (typhus) and other complaints—at least 42 in the whole period, according to one estimate. Others were forced into exile to avoid persecution. The recusancy fines were intended to hit the rich, who alone could afford them, but yielded large sums to the EXCHEQUER, especially after the legislation was refined in 1585. Between 1581 and 1592, £45,000 was collected from fewer than 200 individuals in all. This persecution was justified in political terms by the government; Catholics were seen as a threat to the political stability of the realm at a time when England was at war with Catholic Spain (which had papal support) and at a time of plots against the queen's person by a minority of Catholics. But the aim of the persecution was not solely political, since the religious observances of the Catholics were punished and their attendance at Protestant churches enforced. In the end, the persecution failed in religious terms, although the government might argue that it succeeded politically. Catholicism survived, but so did the queen.

Between 1558 and 1603 Roman Catholicism changed from the official religion of the whole nation to a nonconformist sect, underground and hunted. How many Roman Catholics there were by the end of the reign is almost impossible to say. A survey taken in 1603 shows an active Catholic community of perhaps 40,000. Such a number seems trivial, but the government's anxieties can be explained if we take into account two factors. First, Catholicism was concentrated in certain areas: Lancashire, Yorksire, and the northern counties especially but also Staffordshire, Herefordshire, and parts of Wales and pockets in other counties—Norfolk, Hampshire, and Sussex, for example. The most Catholic areas were generally well away from London and hence not of great strategic importance, although their very distance from the center made them worrying. Second, the number of the gentry involved in recusancy was disproportionately high. In some areas—around Northallerton and in Nidderdale in Yorkshire and in coastal Lancashire—the majority of landed gentry families contained Catholic members. So, the natural leaders of Tudor society were strongly affected.

The history of Catholicism in Elizabeth's reign has been the subject of learned disagreement. The traditional Catholic historiographical view was that there was a clear continuity between the old medieval church and the recusant Catholicism of Elizabeth's reign. Many Englishmen may have abandoned the church or been forced into heresy by persecution and propaganda, but a small body continued to keep the faith. A. G. Dickens's study of Yorkshire began to question this view by looking at the area where recusancy was strong in the middle years of Elizabeth's reign and seeking to find a correlation between that strength and signs of Catholic activity there at the time of the queen's accession. He found little such correlation. John Bossy and Hugh Aveling developed a complete theory from Dickens's suggestions and drew support also from an old, largely JESUIT tradition that seems also to agree with this view. Bossy and Aveling see the Catholic church as thoroughly routed by the events of HENRY VIII and EDWARD VI's reign. Even under MARY I there was no really strong revival, and the first fifteen years of Elizabeth's reign showed a progressive Catholic decline, especially in the face of the queen's studied moderation. The revival came in the 1570s and 1580s when missionary priests, imbued with Counter-Reformation spirit (and some of them converts from Protestantism) came back to England to create a new church. This new Catholicism had, perforce, to become something nearer to a mission than a church, indeed something very like a nonconformist sect. In the last ten years, Christopher Haigh has questioned the Bossy-Aveling thesis. Haigh studied Lancashire first—the great "sink of Popery" under Elizabeth—and found that there were considerable signs of revival there in Mary I's reign, which continued into Elizabeth's time. More broadly, Haigh has argued that in the early years of the latter's reign, much of the old Catholicism survived. The English Reformation took considerable time to gain support and by 1558 few Englishmen can have been converted to Protestantism. Catholic "survivalism" was a strong force under Elizabeth. There is much evidence to support this statement, records of visitations and church court proceedings show frequent efforts by parishioners to keep Mass goods and Catholic relics safe for a future Catholic restoration. Protestant clergy report despairingly of rustic superstition and ingrained Catholics habits of their flocks. Clergy deprived at the beginning of the reign of Elizabeth began a missionary effort long before the SEMINARY PRIESTS returned to England. Indeed, the revival of the 1570s and 1580s was the work in part of men who had left England soon after the ELIZABETHAN SETTLEMENT OF RELIGION. Clearly, as Patrick McGrath has shown, there is something to recommend both the revivalist and survivalist theses. Haigh is doubtless right to emphasize that the Protestant Reformation was a long, difficult process, but the superstitions of a country population did not necessarily imply anything more than simple, rural folk beliefs. There was more to Counter-Reformation Catholicism than that. The careful, parochial preservation of vestments and ornaments may also be explained in more prosaic ways than as evidence of deep-rooted love of the Catholic church; peasant parsimony may be nearer the mark. On the other hand, the differences between the seminarists of Bossy-Aveling's revival and the Catholic remnants they ministered to from 1574 onward cannot have been very great. It was not until the reign of Charles I that we begin to read in Catholic literature a real appreciation that the Ecclesia Anglicana may never be restored. The seminarists of Elizabeth's reign came not to found a new sect but to keep alive a survivalist mentality until political action or divine providence should restore a Catholic ruler. Their long-term aims were those that would easily coincide with the objectives of the survivalist Catholics of the early years of the reign. Recusancy as a form of religious protest was most fully and strongly advocated by the seminary priests and Jesuits, especially in Robert Persons's *Brief Discourse Containing Certain Reasons Why Catholics Refused to Go to Church* (1580). Nevertheless, writers of the period of "survival" early in the reign had also advocated recusancy, and at the Council of Trent in 1562 a definitive instruction in favor of recusancy had been issued. On this crucial issue, therefore, the old and new generation of Catholics were in agreement. But recusancy was a dangerous practice throughout the reign, both before and after 1581, and both the old survivalist priests and the new missionaries were prepared to accept church papists or those who practiced occasional conformity as good Catholics. The casuist literature of the period shows clearly that in the confessional Catholic priests were to make very little fuss about attendance at Protestant churches and indeed about other subterfuges necessary to save a Catholic from persecution. In this respect, the seminary priests showed as much common sense as Catholics had in the days of uncertainty at the beginning of the reign.

Bibliography: J. C. H. Aveling, *The Handle and the Axe*, 1976; J. Bossy, *THe English Catholic Community 1570-1950*, 1975; C. Haigh, "Revisionism, the Reformation and the History of English Catholicism," *Journal of Ecclesiastical History* 36 (1985): 394-406.

P. J. Holmes

Redon, Treaty of (1489). The Treaty of Redon was concluded between HENRY VII and Duchess Anne of Brittany on 10 February 1489. Henry's negotiators, commissioned on 11 December 1488, were Richard Eggecombe and Henry Aynesworth, and those of the duchess were Philippe de Montauban, Guillaume Guegen, and Roland Goujon. The terms established a firm alliance, aid in the case of invasion of Brittany, support from Brittany for any English invasion of France, and no sheltering of rebels. Specifically, Henry undertook to aid the duchess with 6,000 men for the space of a year but entirely at her cost and against the concession of two fortresses out of a list of five named in the treaty. In addition, Anne promised not to marry without Henry's agreement and only to conclude alliances otherwise with Ferdinand of Aragon and Maximilian.

Henry VII gained his throne with substantial French military aid and was reluctant to contemplate war in his first years. But no matter how reluctant to become involved in foreign war Henry VII might be, it was widely recognized that England could not accept with equanimity the effective incorporation of Brittany into the French kingdom. That incorporation seemed to be a distinct possibility because of the sonless Francis II, duke of Brittany's signing the treaty of Sable on 20 August 1488. It promised the French Crown wardship and control of the marriage of his heiress and daughter Anne.

In the months following Francis II's death, therefore, there was a period of hectic diplomatic activity, which led to the formation of, in effect, a triple alliance among Maximilian, king of the Romans, Henry VII and the Iberian sovereigns. The Treaty of Redon formed the centerpiece of this structure, complemented by the TREATY OF MEDINA DEL CAMPO, concluded with Ferdinand and the Isabella in March 1489 and the treaty of Dordrecht with Maximilian on 14 February 1489.

Duchess Anne's hand in marriage was now a matter of sharp competition. Charles VIII of France could not advance his own case immediately without jeopardizing French control of Artois and Franche-Comte, held through his betrothal to Maximilian's daughter, Margaret. The duchy was torn by faction struggles, and Henry VII was drawn into the support of the marshal de Rieux, whose candidate for the duchess's hand, d'Albret, was repugnant to her. The first English troops arrived at Guerande in March but were drawn into confused skirmishes between local contenders for power. Maximilian deserted the triple alliance in the Treaty of Frankfurt (22 July 1489), which had as one of its objects the removal of English troops from Brittany. Ultimately Henry's policy in Brittany was left completely ruined by the fall of Nantes to French forces

(February 1491) and the consent of the young duchess to her marriage with Charles VIII on 6 December 1491.

Bibliography: J. S. C. Bridge, *History of France From the Death of Louis XI*, 5 vols., 1921-1936; R. B. Wernham, *Before the Armada*, 1966.

D. L. Potter

Reformation Parliament. The extraordinary legislative program enacted during this Parliament (1529-1536) gave legal validity to the changes in church and state rising out of the Henrician Reformation, set new precedents for government regulation of the social and economic affairs of the nation, and—by resting these sweeping changes on parliamentary statute—created a new and broader role for the institution of Parliament itself as central to the government of the Tudor state.

On 6 August 1529 writs of summons were sent to the Lords, and elections were ordered for the Commons, for a Parliament to be held at Blackfriars Monastery in London on 3 November. In the six years since Parliament had last convened, the king's financial condition had worsened, his hopes for a DIVORCE from CATHERINE OF ARAGON were stalemated by delays from Rome, THOMAS WOLSEY's failure in this had caused his own disgrace, and the cardinal's enemies had taken new strength from the nation's growing anti-clericalism. HENRY VIII and his ministers hoped to find in Parliament financial relief through new taxes and some solution to his marriage crisis; his subjects welcomed the opportunity to reopen grievances tabled in 1532 and to introduce the private bills and other business for which parliamentary authority was necessary. The first session convened as scheduled, elected Sir Thomas Audley as speaker of the House of Commons (he moved into the Lords in 1532 as keeper of the Great Seal and then chancellor, and was replaced as speaker in 1533 by Humphrey Wingfield) and immediately removed to Westminster, where it remained for seven sessions over the next seven years.

Membership in the Commons consisted of 74 knights of the shire elected from 37 counties and 236 burgesses from 117 parliamentary boroughs for a total of 310. While the counties usually returned members from among the landowning gentry, that group had not yet invaded the boroughs; municipal corporations elected members from among their own circle of politically active merchants. Complaints that the government "packed" the Commons with its own men were heard but are unjustified; the Parliament was broadly representative of the politically active nation, and the large number of members with ties to the government merely reflects the growing number of such men within the larger group.

Of the 107 members of the House of Lords, 57 were temporal peers led by THOMAS HOWARD, 3rd duke of Norfolk. The remaining 50, Lords spiritual, were divided between 21 archbishops and bishops and 29 abbots and priors and led, initially, by the archbishop of Canterbury WILLIAM WARHAM and, then, with far greater effect from 1532, by his successor THOMAS CRANMER. The chief legal officers of the Crown were also present in the Lords. When the DISSOLUTION OF THE MONASTERIES removed abbots and priors from the scene, the secular nature of the upper house was permanently settled.

That this Parliament was neither packed nor controlled by the Crown was clear from the experience of the first session (November-December 1529), when lack of direction from the government allowed the strongly anti-clerical Commons to set its own agenda for reforming ecclesiastical abuses. Petitions against excessive probate and mortuary fees resulted in acts regulating both (21 Hen. VIII, cc. 5 and 6), and a bill limiting pluralism and non-residence, though toned down by substantial opposition from the Lords spiritual, passed after revisions in a compromise committee of both houses (21 Hen. VIII, c. 13). The only official measure of the session released the Crown from repaying Wolsey's forced loans of 1522 and 1523 (21 Hen. VIII, c. 24), and no solution was offered for the king's divorce.

The government's program was still uncertain when the second session convened in January 1531, and the principal stage for attempts to control the English church shifted to CONVOCATION. There the clergy, under threat of PRAEMUNIRE indictments, voted Henry VIII a subsidy of £100,000 and recognized him as supreme head of the church in England with the compromise qualifier "so far as the law of Christ allows." This paved the way for Parliament to pardon the clergy for their praemunire offenses (22 Henry VIII, c. 15). It also took up several private and local bills, discussed proposals for social and religious reform, tinkered with laws concerning poisoners, SANCTUARIES, and pleadings, passed a harsh act against beggers (22 Hen. VIII, c. 12; see POOR LAW), and adjourned in March.

By 1532, under THOMAS CROMWELL's control, the government's management of Parliament became more consistent and assured, if not always successful. The king's divorce continued to overshadow all religious matters in the third session (January-May); twin needs for independence from Rome and for royal control over the English church generated an Act in Restraint of ANNATES (23 Hen. VIII, c. 20) made conditional after much opposition in both houses. Remaining anti-clericalism in the Commons, however, coincided with Cromwell's aims to produce a further attack in the COMMONS' SUPPLICATION AGAINST THE ORDINARIES; this, combined with more royal threats, led to the Submission of the Clergy, by which convocation abandoned all claims to legislative independence. The government also proposed enough other legislation (for new taxes, improving navigation and river drainage, regulating trade and industry, reforming some aspects of the land laws) to show that Parliament was becoming the Crown's perferred instrument for extensive social engineering in the Tudor Commonwealth. Not all officially sponsored bills passed, but it is clear that Parliament was now being used to implement royal and ministerial policies.

The fourth, fifth, and sixth sessions (February-April 1533, January-March 1534, and November-December 1534) finally settled the "King's Great Matter"

by establishing the independence of the English church in the ACT IN RE-
STRAINT OF APPEALS (24 Hen. VIII, c. 19), the DISPENSATIONS ACT (25
Hen. VIII, c. 22), and the Act of Supremacy (26 Hen. VIII, c. 1; see ROYAL
SUPREMACY), and enforcement of these policies by the TREASONS Act (26
Hen. VIII, c. 13). An act of ATTAINDER was used to destroy the HOLY MAID
OF KENT Elizabeth Barton, and to attaint Bishop JOHN FISHER of misprision
of treason.

The legal and religious deadlock broken, Parliament turned with renewed
energy to tackling other problems in the Commonwealth, and their failure to solve
such complex matters as poverty, unemployment, and inflation should not
overshadow the signficance of the attempt. Both government-sponsored bills and
those proposed by private interest groups addressed wide-ranging social,
economic, and legal issues. In 1533 statutes fixed prices for staple foodstuffs,
encouraged the cattle industry by regulating the slaughter of calves, encouraged
the CLOTH TRADE by supporting the growth of flax, and passed sumptuary
laws; 1534 saw acts attempting to limit sheep farming, regulate ENCLOSURES,
preserve dwindling numbers of fish and wildfowl, and fix prices on more staples.
The government also at last succeeded in enacting new taxes; FIRST FRUITS
AND TENTHS now came to the Crown along with a new lay subsidy, establishing the precedent that TAXATION need not be limited to times of war or national
emergency.

Parliament did not sit during 1535. The seventh and final session convened in
February 1536 and passed an extraordinary series of 63 acts dealing with virtually
every aspect of English government and society. By parliamentary statute, the
SECOND ACT OF SUCCESSION (28 Hen. VIII, c. 7) rearranged the descent
of the Crown; the lesser monasteries were dissolved and their wealth turned over
to a new COURT OF AUGMENTATIONS; English shire organization, the
COMMON LAW, and parliamentary representation were given to WALES by the
Act of Union (27 Hen. VIII, c. 26); other jurisdictional franchises were abolished;
the STATUTE OF USES (27 Hen. VIII, c. 10) limited evasions of the Crown's
feudal revenues; the cloth trade helped by standardizing sizes; harbors and rivers
were dredged and repaired; laws regulating enclosures were strengthened; a new
Poor Law, watered down though it was from the government's original ambitious
proposal, nevertheless distinguished for the first time between the able-bodied
poor and those unable to work for whom parish relief was necessary; and finally,
as in every Parliament, a raft of private bills allowed the land transfers and other
legal remedies so necessary to the politically elite classes.

After seven long years the Reformation Parliament was dissolved on 14 April
1536. Its extraordinary range of activities and its use by the Crown as the chosen
instrument of constitutional change established the omnicompetence of parliamentary statute. The active partnership of king, Lords, and Commons had become and
would remain the ultimate sovereign authority in the English modern national
state.

Bibliography: G. R. Elton, *Reform and Reformation: England, 1509-1558*, 1977; Standford E. Lehmberg, *The Reformation Parliament 1529-1536*, 1970.

Mary L. Robertson

Reformation, English (Interpretations). Revisions in the interpretation of the English Reformation derive, to a large degree, from the growing influence of social history in the last generation. Social historians generally deny that the Reformation came about because of abuses in the medieval church and are more interested in investigating the changing spiritual attitudes of ordinary people and local communities. They show a sensitivity to the historical context of the Reformation that was often wanting in the confessional concerns of older church historians, who tended to follow JOHN FOXE's *Acts and Monuments* in assuming that the Reformation restored pristine Christianity following the centuries of corruption and superstition that had characterized the medieval church. Revisionist historians such as Christopher Haigh instead argue that the late medieval church generated a popular religious revival, especially noticeable in the north of England, which culminated in the plans of MARY and Cardinal REGINALD POLE to introduce the Catholic Reformation into England. Assuming that the Protestant Reformation was inevitable, historians of the Protestant-Whig tradition had regarded Mary's reign as a sterile period. Whereas the older church historians tended to see the Reformation as a specific event or a monolithic movement, which could be fitted into a precise chronological period, the revisionist historians stress the idea of a complex series of movements and a protracted struggle.

A. G. Dickens (*The English Reformation* 2nd ed. London, 1989) helped to clarify the distinction between on the one hand, the "official Reformation," that is, the establishment of the ROYAL SUPREMACY in ecclesiastical affairs, the enactment of the various religious settlements, and the promulgation of official liturgies and articles of religion, which had absorbed the attention of the older ecclesiastical historians, and, on the other hand, the "popular Reformation," which occurred when individuals and communities began to display Protestant attitudes. Dickens argued for a rapid popular Reformation deriving from late medieval Lollardy as well as from Continental Protestant sources. G. R. Elton, on the other hand, insisted upon a rapid Reformation imposed from above by THOMAS CROMWELL's vigorous policies of enforcement in the 1530s. Dickens was one of the first to do a local study of the origins of Protestantism, and while he never espoused the new social history, he was forced to conclude that outside of London and the southeast, "Protestants with strong convictions were still thinly spread at the midcentury". Yet Dickens seemed unable to accept the consequences of his own conclusion. Although he implicitly accepted the idea that the Protestantization of England was not accomplished until the second half of the sixteenth century, he continued to regard the reign of Elizabeth as merely an epilogue to the Reformation.

In a number of books and essays, Christopher Haigh has propounded the view that the English Reformation was a slow process, sustained by both official patronage and popular support but, at the same time, characterized by real struggle between Catholic and Protestant. Until the government had purged Catholics from among the local JUSTICES OF THE PEACE and the UNIVERSITIES began to graduate trained preachers in the 1570s and 1580s, popular Protestantism could make little headway. PURITANISM, once viewed as a deviant form of English Protestantism, was depicted by Patrick Collinson as the mainstream of that movement and the instrument of Protestant reform. If the impact of a dynamic Protestantism is removed from the mid-Tudor period to the reign of ELIZABETH, then it becomes difficult to explain the Protestant Reformation in terms of an inexorable reforming movement or medieval Catholicism in a state of collapse. David Starkey and others suggest that the causation and subsequent direction of the Henrician and Edwardian religious settlements depended upon a fortuitous interaction of factionalism at court and in the PRIVY COUNCIL as well as historical accident.

Bibliography: A. G. Dickens et al., *The Reformation in Historical Thought*, 1985; Christopher Haigh, ed., *The English Reformation Revised*, 1987.

Roger B. Manning

Regnans in Excelsis (1570). Pius V (pope 1566-1572) promulgated the bull "Regnans in Excelsis" against ELIZABETH in February 1570. After a "trial" of Elizabeth, in her absence, before the judicial authorities of the Apostolic Chamber, Pius declared that he was the successor to St. Peter and possessed plenary authority over the church; that Elizabeth had seized the kingdom and declared herself supreme head of the church in England and thus infringed on papal authority; that she had filled her council with heretics, abolished Catholic rites and ceremonies, and, as a follower of John Calvin, had compelled her subjects to abjure papal authority and encouraged heresy; that true Catholics were being persecuted; and that she had required her subjects to swear an oath of obedience to her supremacy over the church. As a result of these actions Pius excommunicated her, deprived her of her pretended title to the kingdom and absolved her subjects from their allegiance; any subjects obeying her were similarly included in the sentence of excommunication.

The purpose of the bull was to assist and encourage the rebels in the NORTHERN REBELLION (which had already collapsed) by assuring them that their actions were lawful and justified. Catholic powers were not consulted and Philip II of Spain and the Emperor Maximilian II expressed strong disapproval. Neither was there any papal attempt at that time to encourage Catholic powers to invade England and put the bull into effect. The effect of the bull in England was to accelerate ideological confrontation since it gave the government grounds for seeing all Catholics as potential traitors. Severe penal legislation against Catholics was passed in the next Parliament. The bull added to the difficulties of Catholics who wished to remain obedient to both pope and queen, and by no means all Catholics recognised this power of the papacy in the temporal sphere.

Bibliography: Claire Cross, *The Royal Supremacy in the Elizabethan Church*, 1969; A. O. Meyer, *England and the Catholic Church under Queen Elizabeth*, 1916, reprint 1967.

D. J. Lamburn

Requests, Court of. Also known as the Court of Poor Men's Causes, this court of equity developed out of the king's council and drew its authority from that body. Its jurisdiction competed with the COMMON LAW courts, particularly the Court of Common Pleas and made it unpopular with the common lawyers.

The most remote origins of the Court of Requests date, perhaps, to the year 1349; however, the reign of HENRY VII marked a turning point in the history of the court. Its records begin in 1493 and show an increasingly active participation by members of the council under the presidency of the lord privy seal. At first the court travelled with the king on progresses; then in 1516 it established a permanent seat in London at Whitehall. Known as the Court of Requests from 1529, it acquired two permanent professional judges about 1550. They were known as masters of requests and eventually eclipsed the amateur members of the council. The masters of requests formalized the simple rules of the court, which did not meet in fixed terms but was accessible throughout the year.

The rules of the court provided that litigation commenced with the plaintiff's petition to the king, which the defendant was required to answer. Evidence was gathered through interrogatories administered to compelled witnesses. Because the Court of Requests functioned as a court of conscience, its users could avoid much of the complicated and expensive procedure of the common law. Requests had extensive equitable jurisdiction over property, contracts, family, law, forfeitures for crime, fraud, and violent torts.

By 1590 the common law courts launched an attack on the Court of Requests, claiming that it lacked a proper grant of authority. Its existence was not based on a royal grant, a statute, or immemorial custom. The Court of Common Pleas began to enjoin against the hearing of cases by the Court of Requests. These attacks continued into the seventeenth century, and Edward Coke in 1628 concluded that the Court of Requests lacked jurisdiction. Continuing to function until 1642, it was not included in the statute abolishing the Court of STAR CHAMBER. In spite of that oversight, the Court of Requests was not revived at the Restoration.

Bibliography: I.S. Leadam, ed., *Select Cases in the Court of Requests, 1497-1569*, 1898; L.M. Hill, ed., *The Ancient State: Authority and Proceedings of the Court of Requests by Sir Julius Caesar*, 1975.

J. V. Crangle

Resistance Theory. Resistance theory is the body of thought that seeks to justify the violent overthrow of tyranny. The sixteenth century was the golden age of resistance theory, and the English contribution to it was considerable.

The many armed uprisings of the Tudor period that took place before 1553 were conducted without the benefit of resistance theory. The participants did not claim to be in revolt against the king but rather announced they were taking part in a demonstration of discontent whose aim was not a revolution but redress of grievance. It was not until the reign of MARY I that rebels openly stated that the goal of their opposition was the overthrow of the ruler.

Though the Edwardian clergy had taught that disobedience to government was a sin, many Protestants changed their mind when the Marian persecutions began. From secret presses English Protestants began to follow European examples and advocate resistance to religious tyranny. The earliest reistance tract of the MARIAN EXILE was John Bale's 1554 *Faithful Admonition of a Certain True Pastor*, a translation of Martin Luther's call to violence in defense of Protestantism. To Bale and all exile writers who followed him, resistance was not rebellion but a truer form of obedience, as one chose to heed God rather than a tyrant. Another European Reformer whose writings influenced English Protestants was Peter Martyr Vermigli. The 1555 *Cohabitation of the Faithful with the Unfaithful* called on "inferior magistrates"—officers of the state—to lead resistance to a government that commanded ungodly actions.

Marian exiles also justified their resistance on grounds other than religious. To the author of the 1555 *Certain Questions* the queen was a usurper who did not deserve to rule because she was an illegitimate child and had broken the rules of royal succession. Worst of all, she was a traitor who sought to betray the realm into hands of foreigners. Xenophobia was a theme played on by almost every advocate of resistance. *A Warning for England* (1555) pointed to the atrocities the Spaniards had committed, while both John Bradford's 1556 *A Copy of a Letter* and the anonymous *Lamentation for England* (1557) accused Spain of plotting to invade the country. These sorts of arguments seemed to have some effect—the men of the Dudley and Stafford conspiracies used issues raised in exile tracts to justify their actions.

The tract that best united religious and secular justifications was John Ponet's 1556 *A Short Treatise of Politic Power*. Ponet complained of both imposition of Catholicism, which he equated with idolatry, and the extortion, murder, and injustice undertaken by Mary. Government, said Ponet, was ordained for the well-being of the people, who could change their government whenever it abused them. If nobles and inferior magistrates could not be counted on to carry out the resistance, then private citizens could imitate biblical and classical examples and assassinate tyrants and enemies of the people. When Ponet wrote, his ideas on resistance were the most comprehensive and sophisticated of any mainstream Protestant and outstripped European Reformers, who restricted resistance to the inferior magistracy and for religious causes only.

The last years of Mary's reign produced writings by authors who emphasized the religious dimension of tyranny. The clearest examples are JOHN KNOX's *First Blast of the Trumpet Against the Monstrous Regiment of Women* and Christopher Goodman's *How Superior Powers Ought to Be Obeyed*. Both rejected secular excuses for resistance, and both claimed to draw their guidance on political affairs from Scripture, which demanded that the people as well as inferior magistrates overthrow an ungodly government. Moreover, the very concept of a female ruler violated God's laws; Mary was thus doubly damned as a queen and as an idolater.

Unfortunately for Knox and Goodman, Mary's successor was ELIZABETH I, who naturally resented their arguments against women's rule. Elizabeth's displeasure served to alert her authorities to the hazards of resistance theory, and they compelled returning exiles to foreswear such dangerous ideas. This fact does not mean, however that resistance writings disappeared under Elizabeth—in fact, for a time they thrived.

Throughout Elizabeth's reign, English Protestant writers found resistance theory useful in defense of the faith. It could be used to justify the rebellions of foreign Protestants and also to act as a bulwark against the claims to the English throne made by the Catholic MARY, QUEEN OF SCOTS. The 1572 Parliament saw the resurrection of Marian resistance theory by members who sought to justify the death of the Scottish queen as a usurper and idolater. Arguments for religious resistance and tyrannicide could also be found in the marginal notes of Protestant Bibles until well into the seventeenth century.

Though Elizabeth's church often persecuted the hotter sort of Protestants known as PURITANS, none of them, unlike the English Catholics, ever tried to use resistance theory against her. Bolstered by a papal bull that called for the overthrow of Elizabeth (see REGNANS IN EXCELSIS), the English Catholic leadership in exile abandoned their earlier policy of non-violence. Nicholas Sanders, who was to die accompanying a Spanish invasion of Ireland, trumpeted the power of the papacy to depose errant kings. Cardinal William Allen's 1588 *Admonition to the Nobility and People of England*, meant to be distributed following the success of the SPANISH ARMADA, declared Elizabeth a usurper and tyrant worthy to be overhrown by papal sanction and force of Spanish arms. But the most widely read of the English Catholic theorists was the Jesuit Robert Persons, whose 1594 *Conference about the Next Succession to the Crown* was so comprehensive a statement on resistance that it was reprinted several times in the seventeenth century by Protestants. It ignored arguments about papal power and instead claimed, as Ponet had, that the people had a constitutional power to rid themselves of evil rulers.

By the end of Elizabeth's reign resistance theory was in retreat. The diminished threat to England from foreign Catholicism meant that Protestant talk of resistance was no longer the necessity it had been. Attempts by English Catholics to win toleration demanded an end to their threats to overthrow the queen. The political crises of the seventeenth century, however, saw a revival of English resistance theory.

Bibliography: Gerald Bowler, "Marian Protestants and the Idea of Violent Resistance," in *Protestantism and the National Church in Sixteenth-Century England*, ed. P.G. Lake and Maria Dowling, 1987; P.J. Holmes, *Resistance and Compromise*, 1982.

Gerald Bowler

Restraint of Appeals, Act in (1533). The explicit purpose of this act (24 Hen. VIII, c. 12) was to terminate the pursuit of appeals to Rome in certain types of cases. Its immediate, though unstated, objective was to reserve to an English church court the power of final decision in HENRY VIII's Great Matter—the annulment of his marriage to CATHERINE OF ARAGON.

Until the summer of 1530 Henry had accepted papal jurisdiction in the matter, although he had uttered vague threats against the pope's authority. But from September onward came evidence of a new approach. He put forward two related claims: first, to an English privilege conferring immunity from citation to courts outside the realm and second, to an imperial power in the Crown that would enable him to prevent appeals to such tribunals. Could Parliament authorize the archbishop of Canterbury to determine the case, the pope's prohibition notwithstanding? A meeting of common and canon lawyers in October 1530 rejected this idea. A substantial shift of opinion in England, particularly on the part of the church, was essential to the implementation of the new claims. Qualified acceptance of the ROYAL SUPREMACY by the CONVOCATIONS (early 1531), the SUBMISSION OF THE CLERGY (May 1532), and the appointment of THOMAS CRANMER as archbishop of Canterbury (January 1533) secured the compliance of the church.

Preparation of a parliamentary bill to give effect to the royal claims was probably begun by THOMAS CROMWELL and other councillors in September 1532, shortly after the death of the Conservative archbishop WILLIAM WARHAM. By this time the idea of a broad attack on papal jurisdiction had already superseded the original notion of a measure concerned with the settlement of the King's Great Matter alone. Revision of successive drafts (eight of which survive) continued during the following months. The bill was introduced into the Commons on 14 March 1533. After facing some strong initial opposition there, it passed swiftly through both houses in April.

The preamble to the act contains one of the most famous statements of English national sovereignty. This realm is an empire, as "old authentic histories and chronicles" show, and accepted as such in the world, "governed by one supreme head and king," to whom a "body politic, compact of all sorts and degrees of people," divided into spirituality and temporality, owe obedience next to God. God has given the king full power to determime finally all causes arising within this realm without any foreign interference. The Church of England has always been competent to interpret matters of divine law or spiritual learning, while the temporal laws have been executed by temporal judges; both these jurisdictions join together in the due administration of justice. Under the king's predecessors, sundry Parliaments have passed legislation to preserve the PREROGATIVES of the imperial Crown of this realm and its jurisdictions from papal and other foreign encroachments. Yet this legislation has not prevented abuses arising from appeals to the remote court of Rome: great delays and difficulties in producing relevant evidence. The act goes on to command that all testamentary and matrimonial causes and rights to ecclesiastical revenue arising within the king's dominions be henceforth determined there, any external processes or censures notwithstanding. The final court of appeal is to be that of the appropriate archbishop, save in cases touching the king, where appeal may lie to the upper house of the appropriate convocation. (In 1534, the Act for the Submission of the Clergy provided for the hearing of appeals from the archbishops' courts by commissions appointed by the king in Chancery.)

The framers of the preamble invoked the testimony of the past to conceal its radical character. Extracts from the "histories and chronicles" to which it refers were included in a corpus of texts, some of them spurious, known as the *Collectanea satis copiosa*. Probably compiled by Edward Foxe, the king's almoner, and Thomas Cranmer, this collection was the chief basis for the arguments about jurisdiction and sovereignty employed in royal propaganda from September 1530 onward. To some extent the appeal to the past rested on solid ground; papal jurisdiction in England had indeed been limited by late medieval Parliaments. But neither church nor Crown had claimed full authority in matters of divine law and spiritual learning (which necessarily included the interpretation of God's word revealed in the Scriptures)—here was the revolutionary nub of the act.

The measure paved the way for the final judgment of the King's Great Matter by Archbishop Cranmer, which swiftly followed (May 1533). Despite the radical claims advanced, the break with Rome was not complete. The act, presumably by design, does not specify all the causes in which the pope might have claimed jurisdiction. Furthermore, some other papal powers and revenues were not finally abrogated until the following year. Yet the biggest step on the path from loyalty to schism had been taken.

Bibliography: G. R. Elton, "The Evolution of a Reformation Statute," in his *Studies in Tudor and Stuart Politics and Government*, vol. 2, 1974; J. Guy, "Thomas Cromwell and the Intellectual Origins of the Henrician Revolution," in *Reassessing the Henrician Age: Humanism, Politics and Reform 1500-1550*, by

A. Fox and J. Guy, 1986; G. Nicholson, "The Act of Appeals and the English Reformation," in *Law and Government in Tudor England, Essays Presented to Sir Geoffrey Elton on his Retirement*, ed. C. Cross, D. Loades and J. J. Scarisbrick, 1988.

Ralph Houlbrooke

Richmond, Articles (Treaty) of (1562). Also known as the Treaty of Hampton Court, this shadowy agreement was reached at Richmond Palace by WILLIAM CECIL for ELIZABETH I and the representatives of the prince of Conde, the leader of the Huguenots, on 19 September 1562. It was an intervention intended to help the beleaguered Huguenots against the ultra-Catholic forces under the leadership of the Guise family. Queen Elizabeth agreed to supply Conde with 100,000 crowns to aid "the Prince against the hate his enemies bear to the word of God." There were thus overtones of support for international Protestantism, which Cecil; Sir Nicholas Throckmorton, the English ambassador to France; and ROBERT DUDLEY strongly advocated. It was also agreed that English troops would besiege Newhaven (Le Havre) and aid in the defense of Rouen and Dieppe. Elizabeth primarily hoped that she would be able to exchange Le Havre for CALAIS at a later date. She also hoped to prevent the threat to England posed by the resurgence of a militantly Catholic France under the domination of the Guise family. Unfortunately the English intervention was a complete failure, and by 29 June 1563 Rouen, Dieppe, and Le Havre had all fallen.

Bibliography: P. S. Crowson, *Tudor Foreign Policy*, 1973; R. B. Wernham, *Before the Armada: The Emergence of the English Nation, 1485-1588*, 1966.

Gary Bell

Ridley, Nicholas (c. 1500-1555). Bishop of London during EDWARD VI's reign, he was a leading Protestant Reformer and one of the earliest Marian martyrs. Nicholas Ridley was born at Willimotesewick in Northumberland. He went to Pembroke Hall Cambridge, in 1518 and received his B.A. in 1522. In 1524 he became a fellow of Pembroke Hall. A year later he obtained his master's degree. In 1527 he went abroad to read divinity at the Sorbonne and Louvain. After returning to Cambridge in 1530, he was appointed public orator and chaplain to the university in 1534. During this period he built a reputation as a student of the classics and a master of logic. He also spent much of his time reading and memorizing the Bible.

He seems to have adopted Protestant beliefs gradually. He may have already been identified with the Reformers when he was appointed chaplain to THOMAS CRANMER in 1537 and instituted to the living of Herne in Kent in the following year. During the last years of HENRY VIII's reign Ridley continued to receive honors and preferments. In 1540 he was appointed one of the king's chaplains and master of Pembroke and was awarded a doctorate in divinity. He became a prebend of Canterbury in 1541 and a prebend of Westminster in 1545. During these years he resided mainly at Herne, where he studied the treatise of the ninth-century monk Ratramnus, *De Corpore et Sanguini Domini*, which argued against the doctrine of transubstantiation. His reading of Ratramnus led him to a study of the Scriptures and the Fathers, which convinced him that transubstantiation was not taught either in the Bible or by the early church. By 1545 Ridley had come to a Protestant understanding of the eucharist, which he presented to Cranmer in 1546.

After Henry VIII's death, Ridley was consecrated bishop of Rochester in September 1547. Working with Cranmer, he became one of the principal figures involved in the Reform of the English church and the revision of its liturgy and doctrine. He was a member of the commission that compiled the first English Prayer Book; however, when the new Prayer Book came out in 1549, he felt the eucharistic doctrine lacked adequate clarity. Ridley was enthroned as bishop of London in April 1550 after EDMUND BONNER was deprived. He used his new position to bring both reform and Reformation theology to London. He preached regularly throughout the see and appointed known Protestants to high positions in London. In May 1550 he carried out a visitation that sought to bring both moral and doctrinal reform. He insisted on the abolition of any ceremonies not provided for in the Prayer Book and ordered the substitution of communion tables for altars. His defense of the action reveals his eucharistic theology. He argued that since an altar was used for sacrifices and a table for eating and the eucharist involved spiritually feeding on Christ's body and blood rather than sacrificing Him anew, a table was more fitting than an altar. Despite his clear commitment to Protestant doctrine, he was critical of those who made an issue of what he considered nonessentials. When John Hooper refused to be consecrated bishop of Gloucester in the prescribed vestments, Ridley was not prepared to dispense with them, because he did not believe in violating the law in matters of adiaphora.

Ridley also had an active social concern. He fought against the misuse of confiscated church property by greedy politicians. He helped prevent the spoliation of Clare Hall, Cambridge, and on his advice Edward VI founded sixteen grammar schools for boys and a number of London hospitals. Upon Edward's death Ridley initially supported LADY JANE GREY and preached at St. Paul's Cross against Mary's claims. When MARY became queen, he was deprived and imprisoned in the Tower with his friends Cranmer and HUGH LATIMER. In 1554 he was taken to Oxford for trial. After a public disputation, long imprisonment, and a second trial he was burnt at the stake in October 1555.

Although Ridley's writings are few in number, he was a first-rank theologian who was well acquainted with Continental theology. His main work, *A Brief Declaration of the Lord's Supper*, written during his imprisonment, is a carefully constructed, moderate presentation of his eucharistic theology.

Bibliography: J. Ridley, *Nicholas Ridley*, 1957; Nicholas Ridley, *Works*, 1843.

Rudolph W. Heinze

Ridolfi Plot (1570-1571). This plot ended the English negotiations to restore MARY, QUEEN OF SCOTS to the throne of Scotland and eventually led to the execution of Thomas Howard, 4th duke of Norfolk. Roberto Ridolfi was a Florentine banker who had lived and done business in London since 1555. He was also a secret agent for the pope, and it was to him that the Bull of Excommunication (see REGNANS IN EXCELSIS) had been secretly sent. Ridolfi was also secretly in the pay of both France and Spain, and his business dealings were a convenient cover for dealings with Don Guerau de Spes, the Spanish ambassador, John Leslie, bishop of Ross, Mary Stuart's chief agent, and other potential conspirators against ELIZABETH.

One such conspirator was the duke of Norfolk, who had already been warned of the dangers of involvement with Mary Stuart. In 1570 Norfolk signed a submission binding himself to forego the idea of marriage to Mary or any other cause relating to the Scottish queen. Yet Norfolk had hardly taken this submission seriously; he had shown it to Mary before he signed it and continued afterward to correspond with her. Ridolfi found it easy to draw Norfolk into a conspiracy against Elizabeth.

Ridolfi's plot, as it finally evolved in discussion with de Spes and other conspirators, called for the duke of Alva to send over a force of at least 6,000 men (Ridolfi preferred 10,000), along with money and arms for the English insurgents. The men were to land at Harwich or Portsmouth and march on London. Meanwhile the duke of Norfolk and his friends would rise in revolt. Norfolk would either rescue Mary or secure Elizabeth as a hostage against anything happening to Mary. Catholicism would be restored to England, and Mary and Norfolk would be queen and king not only of Scotland but of England as well.

At the end of March 1571 Ridolfi left England to meet with the duke of Alva, the pope, and Philip II. In the Netherlands Alva was unimpressed with Ridolfi and his ideas, but Ridolfi received a warmer welcome both in Rome and in Madrid and added to the plot the possibility that Elizabeth would be murdered. Philip agreed that if Elizabeth were assassinated, the duke of Alva would lead an invasion of England. Ridolfi foolishly sent word back to his conspirators in England that all was going well, and his messenger, Charles Baillie, was arrested as he returned to England and made a full confession. WILLIAM CECIL, Lord Burghley, thus discovered part of the plot.

In August more was discovered when Norfolk was found to be sending money to Mary's supporters in Scotland. Norfolk's servants were arrested, and his house was searched. The incriminating documents found there allowed Burghley to figure out the entire plot, including the complicity of de Spes, who was expelled from England in January 1572. On 16 January 1572 Norfolk was tried before his peers at Westminster Hall for treason and found guilty. Elizabeth, however, kept postponing the execution of her cousin and the only duke of the realm.

Inevitably, as a result of the plot, Elizabeth's attitude toward Mary Stuart changed. Ridolfi's messenger had been arrested just after Elizabeth had sent commissioners to Scotland to try to obtain Mary Stuart's restoration as queen of Scotland. When Elizabeth learned what Mary's involvement actually was, she abandoned the policy of restoration or liberty for Mary Stuart under any circumstances. Another indication of how much Elizabeth changed her attitude toward Mary as a result of the Ridolfi plot is the fact that she for the first time allowed Burghley to have George Buchanan's *Detection*—the story of Mary; HENRY STEWART, Lord Darnley; and JAMES HEPBURN, earl of Bothwell from the point of view of the Scottish Protestant lords—translated and published together with the Casket Letters. When Parliament met in May 1572, the House of Commons insisted on the execution not only of Norfolk but also of the Scottish queen. Elizabeth spared Mary Stuart, but Norfolk was executed 2 June 1572. Ridolfi was luckier. Unable to return to England, he spent the rest of his life in Florence. Outliving both Mary Stuart and Elizabeth, he died in 1612 at the age of eighty.

Bibliography: Francis Edward, *The Marvellous Chance: Thomas Howard, Fourth Duke of Norfolk, and the Ridolfi Plot, 1570-1572*, 1968.

Carole Levin

Rizzio, Murder of David (1566). On 1 March 1566, HENRY STEWART, Lord Darnley, pronouced his intention of ridding the country of those who abused MARY, QUEEN OF SCOTS' kindness, especially "a stranger Italian called David," who might be killed "in the presence of the Queen's Majesty or within her palace of Holyroodhouse." Darnley was a fool. But on 9 March, that event was precisely what happened when he, Patrick Lord Ruthven, JAMES DOUGLAS, earl of Morton, and others burst in on the queen's private supper party and killed her Italian musician and secretary. It was the first of two spectacular murders of Mary's reign.

The immediate cause was Mary's summons to the CHASEABOUT rebels to return to Scotland and stand trial in Parliament on 12 March. They did not wait; their associates, loyal to Mary the previous summer but now much less convinced of the benefits of her rule, forced a trial of strength in which the sacrificial victim was Rizzio, but the real target was the queen. The physical threat to a woman six months' pregnant cannot be discounted; but at the very least, they would strike at her through her servant. Why, then, was a little hunchbacked Italian of such political importance?

In the short term, the answer lay in Mary's increasing isolation. At the time of her success against JAMES STEWART, earl of Moray, she had considerable support. But by September 1565, the English envoy Thomas Randolph was already commenting on her increasingly dangerous withdrawal: "To be ruled by the advice of two or three strangers, neglecting that of her chief councillors, I do not know how it can stand." Her recognition that Darnley was a liability rather than an asset pushed her firmly toward Rizzio as her principal confidant, with total indifference to the hostility that this move would inevitably arouse. In the past, Mary had leaned on Moray and William Maitland of Lethington and maintained a Protestant status quo. Now, having broken with Moray, she flirted with a Catholic policy, encouraged by a Catholic Italian who was a wonderful target for sexual scandal and xenophobia. But behind that lay the longer-term error. Even in the more peaceful days, Mary's main associates had been those in her private royal apartments, her household, which included Catholic friends and foreign ones. The presence of foreigners had caused offense at the time of Mary of Guise; Mary, Queen of Scots continued it. Meanwhile, she had left a largely Protestant council to get on with the business of government. Indeed, she had made virtually no new appointments to the council she had found on her return in 1561, a sign of remarkable royal indifference. But in December 1563, Patrick Lord Ruthven had become a member. Just over two years later, his views were at last expressed, with a force and murderous brutality that reflect the extent of the frustration created by a monarch who had allowed a dangerous level of separation between council and household.

After it was over, Moray returned, intending to take charge. But Mary, with considerable personal courage, detached Darnley from the rebel lords, escaped, and fled to Dunbar to build up support. She returned to Edinburgh in some strength. She and the son born in June survived the Rizzio murder, but her preemptive strike against the Protestant lords had failed. She lived with them in an uneasy truce for a further year. Then the third great crisis of these two short years overwhelmed her.

Bibliography: Julian Goodare, "Queen Mary's Catholic Interlude," in *Mary Stewart: Queen in Three Kingdoms*, ed. M. Lynch, 1988; Jenny Wormald, *Mary Queen of Scots: A Study in Failure*, 1988.

Jenny Wormald

Roanoke. The pioneers of English colonization in the New World, Sir Humphrey Gilbert and his half-brother, Sir Walter Raleigh, argued that English colonies in America could serve as bases of operation against the Spanish. After two unsuccessful attempts, one in 1578 by both Gilbert and Raleigh and another in 1583 by Gilbert alone, Raleigh secured a six-year grant from ELIZABETH in 1584 to establish a colony in the New World.

A small exploratory mission was sent out that same year. After the transatlantic voyage, the group coasted up the Carolina Banks looking for a suitable harbor. Eventually, they came to the inlet between Roanoke and Hatarask islands. They landed on Hatarask on 13 July and took possession of the region in name of the queen. Several days later, they made contact with the Carolina Algonquin Indians, with whom they established good relations. They brought two of the local Indians, Manteo and Wanchese, with them on their return to England. Unfortunately, the company only made a cursory examination of the nearby waters and land.

On the expedition's return to England, Raleigh named the region Virginia in honor of the virgin queen, Elizabeth, hoping that she would give him financial aid in return. When none was forthcoming, he began to search about for private investors. Raleigh used the double inducement that a colony in Virginia, because of its Mediterranean latitude, could provide commodities similar to those obtained from southern Europe. In addition, as he had explained to the government, its location would provide an excellent base of naval operations in the Caribbean, especially for privateering ventures against the Spanish.

To lead the first colonial expedition, Raleigh picked his cousin, Sir Richard Grenville. Six vessels carrying 600 men left Plymouth in April 1585. Though separated by storm, the ships rejoined by July and, at the end of the month, were anchored in Port Ferdinando on Hatarask Island. With the use of Manteo and Wanchese as intermediaries, friendly relations were reestablished with the Roanoke chief, Wingina, who agreed to let the English settle at the north end of Roanoke Island.

Because much of the food supply had been destroyed when one of the ships had run aground earlier, it was decided to establish a colony of only about 100 men, much smaller than had originally been planned. After installing Ralph Lane as leader of the colony, Grenville departed for England in August. Lane set about exploring the region in earnest and, later in the year, discovered Chesapeake Bay. In the spring of the following year, while scouting Albermarle Sound, Lane heard reports from the local Indians of metal that sounded like copper or gold further inland and a bay to the north where pearls might be found.

Lane began preparations to move the colony north to Chesapeake as soon as reinforcements arrived from England. In the meantime, relations with the local Indians began to sour. Because the colonists had arrived too late in the year to plant their own crops, they had bartered for food with the Indians. This situation was fine as long as the Indians had a surplus, but when their own supplies began to dwindle, they refused to continue trading with the English. In March 1586 hostilities erupted between the colonists and the Indians. In June, a relief fleet under Sir FRANCIS DRAKE finally arrived, and Lane soon decided to end the colony and take passage back to England. Meanwhile, Sir Richard Grenville had set out from England with fresh supplies and reinforcements, only to find the settlement abandoned. Unfortunately, he decided, rather than risk losing claim to the country, to leave fifteen men to retain possession. These men were never seen nor heard from again.

Raleigh made another effort to establish a colony in 1587. This settlement, however, was to be founded on Chesapeake Bay, not Roanoke, and would involve planters, not soldiers and gentlemen as in the previous colony. On 8 May the colonists, including eighteen women and nine children, left England under the command of John White. As would often be the case in the future, relations between the sailors and the colonists were poor, and, on arriving at Hatarask on 22 July, the planters were forced to go ashore at Roanoke rather than Chesapeake so the sailors could sooner sail to the Caribbean and plunder the Spanish.

Though the colony started on a happy note—White's daughter, Elenora Dare, gave birth soon after their arrival in the New World to Virginia, the first American-born child of English parents—the situation quickly deteriorated. The Indians, remembering their previous experiences with the English, eluded attempts to restore contact and soon began to attack the colonists. When the ships that had brought them over left on 27 August, it was decided that White would return to England in an effort to obtain more supplies and additional settlers. Unfortunately, by the time of his arrival back in England the threat of the SPANISH ARMADA prevented any reprovision of the colony. The following year also saw no action taken. Not until 1590 was White able to return to Roanoke, and there he found the settlement deserted. The only clue left behind was the word "Croatoan" carved into one of the trees. This signal indicated that the colonists had moved to Croatoan Island. Before they could investigate, however, foul weather forced them to abandon the Carolina shore, and that was the last that was ever heard of the ill-fated colonists.

Bibliography: David N. Durant, *Raleigh's Lost Colony*, 1981.

Brian Christian

Rouen Expedition (1591-1592). After Spanish armies relieved the siege of Paris and landed in Brittany in 1590, England's Queen ELIZABETH, fearing that the defeat of the Protestant Henry IV would give Spain control of France's channel ports and desiring repayment of earlier loans, a diversion for her ambitious courtiers, and British occupation of CALAIS or Le Havre, sent several expeditions to assist the French king.

The third and largest of these was organized and led by her favorite, ROBERT DEVEREUX, earl of Essex, who raised 4,000 troops and personally spent £14,000 equipping them. They landed at Dieppe on 1 August with orders not to depart until Henry had signed a formal treaty with Elizabeth and aggressively besieged Rouen. Two weeks later Sir Roger Williams and the original force of 600 men joined Essex at Dieppe.

After Henry IV invited Essex to meet at Compiegne, halfway between them, Essex and 100 well-dressed men made the 130-mile dash through occupied territory. The meeting proved counter-productive, and Henry vacated the area to seek German assistance. Elizabeth's anger at Essex's failure to get Henry to visit England or besiege Rouen was tempered by the news that Essex suffered from the fever that afflicted his troops, whose strength was halved by mid-September. Essex's suffering was increased by the death of his brother in a skirmish on 8

September and by Elizabeth's "Declaration of the Causes that Move her Majesty to Revoke her Forces in Normandy," issued on 24 September.

To try to placate Elizabeth, Henry sent Marshal Biron and 12,000 troops to besiege Gournay, and Essex joined the siege, which captured the city on 27 September. On his arrival at Rouen on 8 October, Essex knighted twenty-four officers and further antagonized Elizabeth, who ordered him home and received him coldly. Asking to be replaced, Essex effected a reconciliation and an extension of his commission. When he returned on 18 October, he found that half of his army had succumbed to dysentery, malaria, typhoid, disillusionment, or desertion. By early November he complained of having only 1,000 able-bodied men. He returned to London to request more assistance but his stay was shortened by news that the duke of Parma was moving toward Rouen with a large force from the Netherlands. Essex returned with 600 seasoned troops from the Netherlands and found that Parma was slowed by winter weather, the French were abandoning the siege, and the weather had increased the ravages of disease.

The futility of an assault and the realization that no serious combat would resume until the spring prompted Essex to challenge Rouen's governor, Villar, to a duel or tournament to settle the conflict. Villar declined, citing the obligations of his office, and Essex departed on 8 January 1592 and left Sir Roger Williams in command. Williams departed Rouen in April when Parma relieved the siege. But although the futile expedition's costs caused the sale of royal lands and fueled discontent in England, it did successfully divert Spanish forces from the Netherlands and helped deny the Spanish a French base from which to attack Britain.

Bibliography: R. B. Wernham, *After the Armada: Elizabethan England and the Struggle for Western Europe 1588-1595*, 1984.

Shelton Hanft

Royal Exchange (1566). The London Stock Market, built 1566-1567 on Cornhill by Sir Thomas Gresham. In 1538, soon after the opening of the Great Bourse in Antwerp, such a building was proposed for Lombard Street. Originally dominated by Italian ("Lombard") merchants who traded in bills of exchange, the street was commonly used for open-air commercial bargaining, with meeting times set traditionally at noon and evening. Landlords would not sell, and the proposal died.

In 1565 Sir Thomas Gresham offered to build the exchange if the city would provide the land. Once it was finished, he promised, he would give it to the city and to his guild, the Mercers' Company. The Cornhill site was purchased, and on 7 June 1566 Gresham ceremonially laid the first brick of the foundation. Gresham employed a Flemish architect to design and build the Exchange. Materials came from Flanders and Gresham's Suffolk estate and workmen came from Antwerp, a fact that offended the London bricklayers. Completed in 1567, the Exchange looked very much like the Antwerp Bourse. A square, paved central court was surrounded by a covered walkway or piazza. Above the columned arches facing the square were niches with statues, including one of the queen. Within the building itself, above the piazzas, were 100 shops. The main entrances were to the north and south. Immediately east of the south entrance was a bell tower; the bell struck at noon and 6:00 p.m. to summon the merchants. Atop each corner of the building was a grasshopper, the Gresham family emblem.

The Exchange took two or three years to thrive. However, its success was confirmed on 23 January 1571, when Elizabeth visited and proclaimed it the Royal Exchange. A fanciful account is given in Thomas Heywood's play *If You Know Not Me, The Second Part* (1606). The Exchange became a favorite resort for citizens and, locals complained, a place where boys, children, and young rogues spent Sundays and holidays "shoutinge and hollowinge." The upper shops were occupied by milliners, haberdashers, armorers, apothecaries, booksellers, goldsmiths, and glass sellers, all appealing to an upscale clientele. News sellers and orange and apple sellers frequented the gates. As early as 1580, however, there were complaints about unsound construction.

Gresham did not immediately fulfill his promise. When he died in 1579, his will gave the income from the Exchange to his widow during her life. Upon her death in 1596, the property was deeded to the city and the Mercers, but with the income assigned as the endowment of GRESHAM COLLEGE. During the Great Fire of 1666, the Exchange was wholly destroyed, except for the statue of Sir Thomas standing near the north end of the western piazza. The rebuilt Exchange opened in 1669; it was demolished in 1838.

Bibliography: J. W. Burgon, *The Life and Times of Sir Thomas Gresham*, 2 vols., 1839.

Mark Heumann

Royal Supremacy. In the early years of HENRY VIII's reign, criticisms of clerical and ecclesiastical power were heard from many corners. From the king's perspective, clerical liberties and immunities (e.g., BENEFIT OF CLERGY and SANCTUARY) disrupted law enforcement and were inconsistent with a strong centralized state. During Henry's campaign for a DIVORCE from CATHERINE OF ARAGON, he was presented with the *Collectanea satis copiosa*, a compilation of ancient sources that had been made to support his legal case. In it, Henry discovered the argument that he would use to strip the clergy of their independence and have himself acknowledged as the supreme head of the church in England. The sources in the *Collectanea* suggested that in the past, by divine right, the king of England had had no earthly superior. Henry used this argument to demand that the pope relinquish his claim to try the divorce case; he also began looking for a way to recapture his rights over the church, which the *Collectanea* showed him had been lost. Additions to the *Collectanea* showing rulers summoning and dominating synods and confirming their edicts helped Henry expand his claims even further.

PARLIAMENT was not ready to accept the claim that all laws spiritual and temporal took effect from the king, the "allonly Supreme emperyall hede" of the church; the clergy would have to recognize his supremacy first. Henry tried to achieve that recognition when he charged the clergy with PRAEMUNIRE in 1531. They offered him money in return for recognizing their immunities and existence as a community outside his jurisdiction, but Henry demanded instead that they recognize him as supreme head of the English church. This novel claim was conceded only "as far as the law of Christ allowed," which rendered it virtually meaningless. Under intense pressure, the clergy finally accepted Henry's supreme authority over them in May 1532. Parliament then enacted that all ecclesiastical cases, including appeals, be heard in English courts (ACT IN RESTRAINT OF APPEALS [24 Hen. VIII, c. 12]).

In the next parliamentary session, the revolution begun in 1532 was completed by formally severing ties with Rome and subjecting all aspects of the church to the king. First, Parliament gave statutory form to the SUBMISSION OF THE CLERGY (25 Hen. VIII, c. 19), forbade the clergy to make laws except by license from the Crown, and submitted all existing canons to review by a committee appointed by Henry, as intended in the 1532 Submission. Next, the Act in Restraint of ANNATES (25 Hen. VIII, c. 20) reenacted unconditionally the provisions of the conditional statute of 1532 (23 Hen. VIII, c. 20) and rewrote the rules for selecting bishops. Bishops were to be nominated by the king, and cathedral chapters would be required to elect the royal nominee; the pope was removed from the process of consecration. The DISPENSATIONS ACT (25 Hen. VIII, c. 21) transferred the authority to issue dispensations from Rome to the archbishop of Canterburyand established the rules by which they would be issued. The aAct gave ultimate authority to the king, to whom people could appeal if the archbishop refused to grant a dispensation. Since the king received his authority from God, Parliament could not grant it to him, but the Act of Supremacy (26 Hen. VIII, c. 1) formally acknowledged the king's supremacy over the church, made it possible to punish those who denied it, and recognized the king's right to conduct periodic visitations of the church to identify and reform abuses. Finally, the Act for FIRST FRUITS AND TENTHS (26 Hen. VIII, c. 3) established a new scheme for clerical taxation in place of the abolished system of annates.

This statutory package maintained considerable continuity with the past. CANON LAW remained virtually unchanged, since Cromwell's new code of canons (c. 1535) was never considered and Henry never appointed the commission that Parliament had authorized. The church still sold dispensations, and the clergy still paid taxes to the head of the church, although the levies created by the Act for First Fruits and Tenths were much higher than previous papal taxation.

Control of the church was partially secularized. While Henry did not claim that he could administer Sacraments, he did formulate law and doctrine, discipline the clergy, and impose bishops. Henry delegated much of his power to another

layman, THOMAS CROMWELL, who occasionally presided over CONVOCA-
TION, and was made one of the lords spiritual with precedence over all of the
bishops by act of Parliament in 1539 (31 Hen. VIII, c. 10).

Henry's appointment of Cromwell as vicar-general and vicegerent in spirituals
gave him the power of visitation and acting as supreme judge over ecclesiastical
cases. He established a vicegerential court, which functioned from October 1535
to February 1540, and began a general visitation of the church in 1535.
Traditionally, after a visitation uncovered abuses, injunctions were issued to
remedy them. Cromwell issued his first injunctions in 1536. Most of them are
unoriginal, such as those that order the clergy to catechize the young, administer
the Sacraments properly, and avoid taverns. Signs of the changes in the church
are orders to preach against the pope's usurped power and to encourage people
to perform charitable works rather than waste money and time on relics and
pilgrimages. The clergy were enjoined to observe and support the new laws and
to set forth and explain the TEN ARTICLES and the new calendar of holy days
to the people. In 1538, Cromwell issued additional injunctions, which encouraged
everyone to read and study the ENGLISH BIBLE, now to be placed in every
church. Images that were the objects of superstitious practices were to be
removed, and the people were to be taught that images were nothing more than
"books of unlearned men," showing the examples of saints' lives for them to
learn. All parishes were to begin keeping registers of baptisms, marriages, and
burials. The remaining clauses enjoined regular gospel preaching by licensed
preachers, quarterly reading of the Injunctions, and conformity with the new
order. Resistance was to be reported to the king, PRIVY COUNCIL, vicegerent,
or JUSTICES OF THE PEACE. On Cromwell's order, sheriffs and justices of
the peace also began serving as government watchdogs over the bishops and
clergy.

Parliament's position was ambiguous. Although God gave Henry his title,
Parliament had enacted the new church order and showed increasing interest in
church matters, partially eclipsing the authority of convocation. In the ACT OF
SIX ARTICLES (31 Hen. VIII, c. 14), Parliament established doctrine without
consulting convocation, and in 1540 it began to confirm clerical taxation granted
by convocation.

Implementing and enforcing these changes were entrusted to Cromwell, who
orchestrated a multifaceted campaign. He began England's first deliberate,
sustained government propaganda campaign. In 1534, Edward Foxe and Richard
Sampson, both of whom were rewarded with bishoprics, wrote Latin defenses of
the supremacy for a learned audience. At the same time, a highly successful
anonymous piece, *Little Treatise Against the Muttering of Papists in Corners*,
reached a much wider audience. Cromwell also sponsored the first English
translations of anti-papal works by Lorenzo Valla and Marsiglio of Padua.
STEPHEN GARDINER helped without Cromwell's prompting and published *De
vera obedientia* in 1535 to regain the favor he lost after his impolitic response to
the COMMONS' SUPPLICATION. Controlling the pulpit was a key element of

his campaign. Preaching was carefully monitored, and the bishops were ordered to lead a pro-supremacy preaching offensive; prepared texts allowed even unlearned clergy to use the pulpit constructively.

Resistance was a continual problem, and Parliament provided measures that could be taken against the disaffected. All adult males were required to swear an oath in support of the First Act of SUCCESSION (25 Hen. VIII, c. 22) and other acts "made in confirmation or for the execution of the same." This requirement was, in effect, to swear people to a rejection of papal authority, since that had been the necessary prelude to the ANNE BOLEYN marriage. There was virtually no opposition to that oath. Additional oaths of some sort renouncing the jurisdiction of Rome and supporting the Royal Supremacy came to be demanded of parish clergy, new officeholders, those suing livery of lands, and those taking holy orders or a university degree.

The supremacy was also protected by expanding the definition of TREASON to include committing any act or writing or publishing anything that criticized the marriage or interfered with the succession. Verbal attacks and refusing the oath of succession were only misprision, punishable by imprisonment at pleasure and loss of possessions. The Treasons Act of 1534 (26 Hen. VIII, c. 13) extended treason still further to include calling the king a heretic, schismatic, tyrant, infidel, or usurper or depriving him of any of his titles by spoken or written words. Finally, the Act Extinguishing the Authority of the Bishop of Rome (28 Hen. VIII, c. 10) closed a loophole and provided punishment for those who maintained the authority of Rome without directly attacking the king; they could be imprisoned at pleasure and forfeited all possessions. In April 1535, instructions went out to those in authority to order the arrest of anyone suspected of supporting the papacy. Cromwell did not begin a reign of terror. He investigated each case, and those he seriously suspected of guilt were held over for jury trial. Over five years, he considered at least 400 cases, and over half of them were abandoned; only about 65 people were executed for opposing the supremacy.

Bibliography: G. R. Elton, *Policy and Police: The Enforcement of the Reformation in the Age of Thomas Cromwell*, 1972; G. R. Elton, *The Tudor Constitution*, 2nd ed., 1982; Stanford E. Lehmberg, *The Reformation Parliament 1529-1536*, 1970.

Eric Josef Carlson

S

Sacramentarians. A term applied in the sixteenth century to English religious nonconformists, including Anabaptists and Zwinglians, who denied the real presence of the body and blood of Jesus Christ in the eucharist.

Once the jurisdictional portion of the English Reformation was accomplished, doctrinal disputes began to arise in the latter years of HENRY VIII's reign. Dating from the late fourteenth century, there had been a number of followers of John Wycliffe (d. 1384), the LOLLARDS, who had advocated the eucharist as a Sacramental (memorial) act only. This tradition was grafted onto the religious nonconformists of the mid-sixteenth century, whose belief systems took several forms. As these groups shared certain doctrines, the definitions of the groups became blurred, a fact that allowed the English government generically to label all of them as Sacramentarian in nature. The most important groups in this regard were the Anabaptists and the Zwinglians.

Since Henry's Reformation was jurisdictional, not doctrinal, he was determined to preserve the Mass in its traditional practice; on no point was he more intransigent than that of the nature of the eucharist. A firm believer in the real presence, Henry was adamant that any argument to the contrary was heresy of the highest order. This doctrinal heresy, with others, was harshly punished under the second Tudor king.

The Anabaptists, fleeing persecution on the Continent, started appearing in England during the 1530s, where they hoped to be welcomed by the followers of Wycliffe and WILLIAM TYNDALE. Their central doctrine, opposition to infant baptism, was coupled with the Sacramentarian view of the eucharist. This doctrinal heresy drew the ire of Henry's government, which issued an edict against them in March 1535 and again in November 1538. Though English Anabaptists were pardoned by Henry in 1539, their persecution continued for the balance of his reign. Under EDWARD VI, who oversaw the doctrinal divorce from Rome, the Sacramentarian aspect was accepted by the English church, and

Anabaptists were persecuted for other heresies that the mainstream church rejected. MARY I persecuted all Protestants, regardless of affiliation, while ELIZABETH I, her successor, generally returned to the policies of Edward VI in her treatment of the Anabaptists.

Huldreich Zwingli (d. 1531) and his followers adhered to the Sacramental nature of the eucharist but, unlike the Anabaptists, practiced infant baptism. Zwinglians were considered radical on the Continent, since Martin Luther's brand of Protestantism firmly embraced the doctrine of consubstantiation. In England, Zwingli's creed, with its Sacramental definition of the eucharist, was accepted by the Lollards, and Tyndale's writings show evidence of Zwinglian influence. The main appeal of Zwinglianism in England was in its emphasis on the personal freedom to believe as one chose and its advocacy of toleration. Though equally persecuted for their Sacramentarian views, the Zwinglians were more conservative in their Protestantism, allowing for their assimilation into the English church as designed by the Elizabethan settlement.

Bibliography: A. G. Dickens, *The English Reformation*, 2nd ed., 1989; I. B. Horst, *The Radical Brethren*, 1972.

Connie S. Evans

San Juan d'Ulloa (1568). This port of landing for Mexico City has been described as a "wretched makeshift" in relation to its important function. It was not a deep water port, and the anchorage was protected by a shingle band about 220 meters long, which in the late sixteenth century mounted a number of gun batteries to command the harbor. The nearest city of residence was Vera Cruz, about fifteen miles up the coast, and except when the silver fleet was expected or present, there was little activity at San Juan.

On 15 September 1568 JOHN HAWKINS commanding a fleet of six English ships was forced to seek refuge there to effect necessary repairs to his flagship, the *Jesus of Lubeck*. Hawkins had been engaged in illegal slave trading, and his position was extremely vulnerable, except in situations in which he could command superior force. He had left Cartagena about four weeks earlier to sail home but had been trapped by contrary winds. By the middle of September he no longer had sufficient victuals to cross the Atlantic, and the *Jesus*, which was royal ship, had become too leaky to be risked further. Warned that the incoming fleet from Spain was expected at the end of the month, Hawkins decided that the risk of encountering it was less than the risk of remaining any longer at sea and, flying the royal banner of England, sailed boldly into the harbor at San Juan. Because they were expecting the silver fleet and because English ships normally carried the red cross of St. George, the Spanish garrison did not identify him until it was too late and Hawkins had secured control of the strategic batteries on the shingle bank. Negotiating from a position of strength, he then secured an agreement with Antonio Delgadillo, the captain of the port, to purchase his victuals and carry out repairs unmolested. The authorities in Mexico City were duly notified of his presence and peaceful intentions. Next morning, 17 September, the silver fleet arrived, much earlier than expected, and bearing the new viceroy of the Indies, Don Martin Enriquez, the son of the marquess of Alcanizes. Since his intentions were supposed to be peaceful, Hawkins had no option but to allow the fleet to enter, in spite of his command of the batteries. An agreement was reached whereby the English were to remain in control of the guns but were to depart peacefully as soon as their repairs were completed. Hostages were exchanged, and the Spanish ships duly entered.

Don Martin, regarding the English as heretics and enemies of his king, seems never to have intended abiding by his word and began to plan an attack as soon as his ships were anchored. He secreted soldiers from Vera Cruz in several merchant ships anchored close to the batteries, with the intention of taking them by surprise, and ordered the gun crews of his warships to prepare their pieces for action. The attack was launched on the morning of 23 September. A confused action then ensued, lasting from ten in the morning until four in the afternoon. The Spaniards quickly seized the shore batteries but even with their aid were unable to do much damage to the English ships. The *Judith* got away at an early stage, and of the smaller vessels, one was sunk and two were captured. Soon after noon, only the *Jesus* and the *Minion* were still holding out, having sunk two Spanish ships in the process. The larger ship was immobilized, and for some time Hawkins concentrated his attentions on trying to salvage the profits of his voyage by transferring his goods to the *Minion* and using the *Jesus* as a shield. Late in the afternoon, he decided to cut his losses and escaped in the smaller ship, with his remaining able-bodied men. Out of range of the shore guns, and sure that no Spanish ship was in a fit condition to follow, he anchored near the *Judith* for the night. The following morning the *Judith* had gone, and Hawkins had no option but to follow, leaving the *Jesus* and her guns (and some of his profits) in Spanish hands. Protracted recriminations followed on both sides. Hawkins blamed FRANCIS DRAKE for desertion but reserved his main fury for the treachery of the Spanish viceroy, a flame that burned fiercely for over twenty years and from which many other Englishmen took fire. The Spanish commanders blamed each other for having bungled the operation and allowing so notorious a pirate to escape, having inflicted far worse damage than he had suffered. Each side drew the conclusions that it wished, but the effect upon the English was both deeper and longer-lasting.

Bibliography: Edward Archer, ed., *The Third Voyage of Sir John Hawkins, 1567-8*, 1895; M. Lewis, "Fresh Light on San Juan d'Ulloa," *Mariners Mirror* 22 (1936): 324-45.

David Loades

Sanctuary. The doctrine of sanctuary allowed persons accused of crime to take refuge on consecrated property such as church buildings and thereby to avoid the ordinary operations and penalties of criminal law and eventually to remove themselves under the church's protection to safety in a foreign territory.

Papal bulls of the early thirteenth century noted the protection of fugitives, and Henry III of England ratified existing rights to protection from the church in 1253. In essence, sanctuary, as implemented in England, allowed the accused criminals to take refuge on consecrated properties of many types. The accused could there confess his guilt to a public official, such as a coroner, and then abjure the kingdom by formal oath and promise to leave the country. Thereafter, the accused would be allowed to proceed to a border or port town in safety and from there go to live in a foreign land. Tardy departure and absence of good cause, cancelled the immunity from arrest and prosecution that protected the party claiming sanctuary. The procedure was not without its punitive and deterrent features. Persons claiming sanctuary were required to adopt the humiliating dress of one condemned to death, to travel without shoes or headdress, and to wear only a simple shirt while carrying a cross. Their goods were forfeit, their lands could be seized, and their wives were treated as widows.

Sanctuary posed certain practical difficulties. Many accused took refuge on consecrated soil and remained there rather than abjuring the kingdom. Others abjured but did not leave as promised due to lack of transportation or a desire to remain in their homeland. Still others pretended to leave but escaped custody. Such fugitives were hung, if caught.

Critics argued that sanctuary allowed criminals to avoid punishment and to escape the jurisdiction of secular authorities at the expense of public order and security. Efforts to undermine the doctrine of sanctuary from 1378 onward failed repeatedly in the face of powerful clerical opposition. English judges finally lost patience with the protection of felons in 1487 and created a major exception in the case of Humphrey Stafford; they ruled that sanctuary could not be invoked by individuals accused of high treason. HENRY VII also obtained a papal bull in 1487 that authorized the seizure of the property of those in sanctuary, the diminution of sanctuary authority in cases of treason, and the removal of sanctuary's protection from recidivists. In 1511 the rights of sanctuary and BENEFIT OF CLERGY were withdrawn from defendants accused of murder.

The reign of HENRY VIII marked a radical reduction of the right of sanctuary. A statute of 1529 provided that a fugitive claiming sanctuary for felony or murder should be branded for identification. Royal courts demanded that places of sanctuary needed to prove their status by means of a royal grant. Papal bulls were considered invalid for establishing the legitimacy of a sanctuary. Parliament abolished abjuration in 1531. The accused was no longer required to leave the kingdom but instead could remain for life at an appointed location in England, with death as the penalty for escape. Further controls were placed on sanctuary in 1536 when embezzlers were excluded from protection and those claiming sanctuary were prohibited from carrying weapons or leaving the sanctuary at night. A statute of 1540 drastically abridged the properties defined as sanctuaries and left only churches, churchyards, and certain locations indicated in the act. It also excluded from protection those accused of murder, rape, burglary, arson, or sacrilege. France abolished sanctuary in 1539 while the pope excluded people charged with assassination, heresy, and treason, highwaymen, and others from protection in 1591. England legally abolished sanctuary in 1623. Even so, certain sanctuaries for debtors survived until 1727.

Bibliography: Isobel D. Thornley, "The Destruction of Sanctuary," in *Tudor Studies*, ed. R. W. Seton-Watson, 1924.

J. V. Crangle

Science. The investigation of the natural world in Tudor England was carried out by diverse men with different goals and expectations. What we might now call science encompassed both the more traditional academic discipline of natural philosophy (owing its classical heritage to Aristotle) and the practical mathematical and mechanical arts. The dynamic interaction between the quest for a more complete theoretical understanding of the world and the practical and often patriotic drive for power over nature made the sixteenth century a period of scientific expansion and transformation. By combining rigorous scholarly investigation with the quest for knowledge for the sake of utility, a "new science" was born that developed into the scientific revolution of the seventeenth century.

Natural philosophy had long been integral to the UNIVERSITY curriculum in England. From the twelfth century, students studied both trivium (grammar, rhetoric, and logic) and quadrivium (arithmetic, geometry, music, and astronomy). By the fourteenth century, Oxford had established a significant school of physics at Merton College and developed a mean-speed theorem unequaled until the sixteenth century. With the Tudor succession, however, the supremacy of the quadrivium and of scholastic education in general began to be called into question. The introduction of Christian HUMANISM, especially at Cambridge, and of Reformed ideas initiated a battle concerning the relative merits of humanism and Aristotelianism. Though natural philosophy seemed at first to be a casualty of this war, both scholarly systems helped change and expand the natural philosophical horizons in the sixteenth century.

Although more concerned with understanding the books of the Bible and of Cicero in their original languages than in predicting the paths of planets, humanism helped infuse new life into natural philosophy. It did this in three ways. Humanists translated classical scientific sources from the original Greek; humanist methodology treated written sources in a completely new and more skeptical manner; and humanism introduced a new purpose for and mode of scientific discourse. But probably most important, humanism instilled new life into its opponent, Aristotelianism, by forcing scholastics to make their arguments and methodology more rigorous. Thus Aristotle's system did not give way before the humanist onslaught; rather, it incorporated much of the methodology and rigor of the new humanistic studies, while retaining Aristotle's basic framework. The Aristotelian system had proven extremely fruitful as a research program; it was all-encompassing, including the study of the physical world—physics, astronomy (using the Ptolemaic geocentric universe), and biology—and the study of the spiritual and social world—metaphysics, logic, and politics. Until a similarly sophisticated paradigm could be established in the seventeenth century, Aristotelianism remained useful and necessary. Thus, the history of natural philosophy throughout the Tudor period is one of the refinement and triumph of Aristotelianism, rather than of its defeat. When blended with the practical concerns of mechanical and mathematical practitioners, it developed into a science uniquely English and ultimately fruitful.

In the early sixteenth century, England lagged behind Continental contemporaries in scientific sophistication. Englishmen interested in mathematical topics struggled to understand and translate Continental ideas for a largely non-Latinate audience. Humanists like Thomas Linacre (1460-1524), Roger Ascham (1515-1568), and Richard Eden (1521?-1576) translated Continental works on medicine, mathematics, and geography and struggled with a language that lacked technical sophistication. Robert Recorde (1510-1557) and Cuthbert Tunstall, bishop of Durham (1474-1559), both wrote manuals of elementary mathematics and attempted to understand and explain Euclid and Ptolemy to readers unfamiliar with these concepts and with Latin.

By ELIZABETH's accession in 1558, a foundation of mathematical knowledge had been established. As more gentry and merchants' sons began to enter the universities, the orientation of scientific studies changed. Since these same men played important roles in government and at court, as well as investing in mercantile activities, a dynamic and symbiotic relationship began to develop between theoretical and practical investigations. University training and philosophical knowledge remained of prime importance, but the impetus for determining which questions would be asked and which modes of explanation would be acceptable came from economic, social, and political concerns, rather than merely from theoretical curiosity. Therefore, utilitarian pursuits such as navigation, fortification, ballistics, geography, and surveying formed the nucleus for English scientific investigation in this period. In these areas, Tudor scientists established some originality and competence, which aided them in their growing definition of themselves as separate from the Continent—with works often written in English, promoting English superiority and separateness. Richard Hakluyt's (1552?-1616) *The Principal Navigations of the English Nation* (1589) and Edward Wright's (1527-1615) *Certaine Errors in Navigation* (1599) are important examples of this growing trend.

The most famous of the second generation of Tudor scientists (combining natural philosophy and practical interests) was the mathematician and necromancer, Dr. JOHN DEE (1527-1608). Dee advised navigators and investors concerning most of the important Elizabethan voyages of exploration. As well, he was a respected mathematician and Elizabeth's court astrologer. Dee's library at his estate at Mortlake was probably the most important scientific library in England, and his publication, with translator Henry Billingsley (d. 1606), of Euclid's *Elements* in English was one of the most ambitious projects of the period. This publication (1570) was a masterpiece of translation and printer's craft. The audience for this expensive and weighty tome is unclear, contributing to our recognition of the tension between esoteric knowledge and English practical art. Dee himself claimed that the publication of Euclid and the advancement of the mathematical arts in general would promote the practical knowledge and abilities of English craftsmen, but it is likely that the book was owned and used by fellow scholars rather than by men in mechaniacal fields.

This generation of Tudor scientists produced a few men who contributed to the advancement of scientific knowledge on the Continent as well as in England, especially the physician and herbalist William Turner (d. 1568), the astronomer and mathematician Thomas Harriot (1560-1621), the magnetical theorist William Gilbert (1540-1603), and the mathematician and geographer Edward Wright. The publication of Gilbert's *De Magnete* (1600), which introduced the theory that the earth was a large magnet, and that of Wright's *Certain Errors*, which introduced a geometrical method of plotting a map using the Mercator projection, placed England for a time in the forefront of scientific discourse.

As well as these few luminaries, the community of investigators of the natural world increased generally during Elizabeth's reign and included many lesser-known but equally committed English scientists. Thus, by the death of Elizabeth, English science had established both a firm theoretical framework and an eager community of scholars and practitioners.

By 1603, a truly "English science" had been created. No longer merely the natural philosophy of the schoolmen, this new science was based on utility and practical experience, later to be defined by Francis Bacon. This science had a strong theoretical and mathematical basis, which came from the universities and the mathematical studies that had such practical applications. As well, Englishmen had begun to define science as neutral and value-free—a study that could be pursued by scholars and craftsmen alike and that existed outside the political, economic and religious strife of the day. These elements—utility, theory, and ideology—were necessary ingredients for the establishment of the "new science" that developed in the seventeenth century. It was from this slow definition and refinement of science in Tudor England that the Royal Society and Isaac Newton would spring.

Bibliography: M. Feingold, *The Mathematicians' Apprenticeship. Science, Universities, and Society in England 1560-1640*, 1984; C. Schmitt, *John Case and Aristotelianism in Renaissance England*, 1983.

Lesley B. Cormack

Scotland. The accession of HENRY VII of England found Scotland under James III (1460-1488) in turmoil. Domestically the king was at odds with his magnates and even with his own family. Anglo-Scottish relations were at a low ebb after the loss of Berwick in 1482 and attempts at reconciliation were uncertain. Events after BOSWORTH allowed for a fresh approach; a Scottish delegation attended Henry's coronation, and negotiations brought a new stability to the relationship between the two kings. Not all Scots favored this, while internal dissension distanced many magnates from a king who became increasingly suspicious of their loyalty and even that of his son and heir, James, duke of Rothesay. The upshot was a rebellion in which their two opposing armies met at Sauchieburn, near Stirling on 22 June 1488. Although defeated, James might have rallied had he not fled the field, fallen from his charger, and thereafter been stabbed by an unknown assassin; his son succeeded to his crown.

The reign of JAMES IV (1488-1513) is one of marked contrast, although this view, fostered by contemporary historians, is questionable. However, in personal and domestic terms his rule not only encouraged new attitudes in which learning flourished and the spirit of inquiry advanced but also produced an era of internal peace in which justice, law, and order were maintained even in remote parts of the kingdom. In foreign affairs, although heavy expenditure was incurred on naval and military developments, James's record was less impressive. Accord with Henry VII was shattered through support for PERKIN WARBECK, but although hostilities were replaced by a treaty of Perpetual Peace (1502), symbolized by the marriage in 1503 of James and Margaret Tudor, Henry VII's elder daughter, that peace was a fragile one. With the accession of HENRY VIII in 1509, the true nature of Anglo-Scottish relations was revealed amid a web of international tension that eventually led James to his defeat and death at FLODDEN in September 1513.

His successor JAMES V (1513-1542) experienced a long minority in which factions, including the queen mother and her second husband, ARCHIBALD DOUGLAS, 6th earl of Angus, vied for power with the governor, John Stewart, duke of Albany, and James Hamilton, 1st earl of Arran. With the overthrow of Angus in 1528 James finally assumed personal kingship, which, if characterized by vindictiveness and avarice, maintained domestic law and order through justice ayres in criminal cases, and, in civil affairs, the erection of a College of Justice in 1532. If finance gained through fines, forfeitures, and remissions was as important as the desire for justice, these profits, supplemented by dowries from two French marriages, allowed the king not only to conserve assets but also to indulge in his passion for artillery and Renaissance palaces. Financial considerations likewise muted his concern for church reform which was subordinated to a material policy of mulcting its wealth through commendation and taxation, although he strenuously opposed heresy. Internationally, he consistently supported the French alliance, reinforced by marriage and financial subsidies. Nevertheless, James tried to maintain friendly relations with England, but these attempts failed through James's reluctance to follow English ecclesiastical policies, exemplified by his failure to meet Henry VIII at York in September 1541. The breakdown of negotiations led to an invasion of Scotland in August 1542 when Sir Robert Bowes was defeated by the earl of Huntly at Haddon Rig. Another invasion and claims to suzerainty over Scotland goaded James into action. With the support of Cardinal David Beaton, archbishop of St. Andrews, his pro-French advisor, the king led part of his army to Lochmaben while the remainder under Oliver Sinclair advanced on a more easterly route to be driven back in disorderly rout after the borderers turned against their fellow Scots; many magnates preferred capture to death. A dispirited king retired to Falkland where, turning his back on his lords, he died.

The heir to the throne, MARY, QUEEN OF SCOTS, (1542-1567), was only six days old, and authority passed to the earl of Arran as governor on 3 January 1543 despite a challenge from Cardinal Beaton. Reinforced by support from magnates released from English custody and the return of the earl of Augus, Arran's position was confirmed with his recognition as second person of the realm, heir presumptive, and governor until the queen's "perfect age." Negotiations immediately commenced for the marriage of Mary and Henry VIII's son Prince EDWARD, while ecclesiastically possession of the Scriptures in the vernacular was authorized. Beaton's opposition to these moves was neutralized by his temporary detention, but support from the queen mother, Mary of Guise, and the return from France of Matthew Stewart, earl of Lennox, strengthened his hand while weakening that of Arran, for Lennox was heir presumptive, if doubts about the governor's legitimacy were upheld. Nevertheless, Arran concluded the TREATY OF GREENWICH on 1 July 1543, arranging for Mary's marriage by proxy and her domicile in Scotland until the age of ten. However, Henry's demands for her custody and an end to the French alliance brought increased opposition which the treaties' ratification heightened. The pressure upon Arran was effective; he quickly came to terms with the cardinal, and on 11 December Parliament abrogated the agreement. This *volte-face* occasioned upheavals in party alignments. Thereafter, Lennox sided with Angus and the pro-English lords, and for a time civil war seemed inevitable, but after a few skirmishes the Angus-Lennox forces capitulated, Lennox retired to England, and Angus was warded.

Henry's reaction was predictable; he ordered EDWARD SEYMOUR, earl of Hertford, to invade Scotland, a task accomplished in May 1544 with burning and looting on both sides of the Forth and throughout the Borders. The raid threw the Scots into confusion, with an attempt in June to supersede Arran by Mary of Guise, leading to further infighting occasioned by the earl of Lennox. Ultimately two rival Parliaments in November made an appeal for unity against "our auld inymeis of Ingland," and reconciliation was achieved, with the cardinal emerging as a dominant figure in a triumvirate with Arran and Mary. A further invasion in early 1545 again devastated the Borders but met defeat at Ancrum Moor. The "Rough Wooing" had proved counter productive to English interests, which were further weakened with the arrival of French forces and bribes that outbid Henry's attempts for support.

If in political terms Beaton's policies had triumphed, these political upheavals weakened ecclesiastical dominance and encouraged heretical opinions, a result illustrated in the career of George Wishart, who came to Scotland in 1543 with the commissioners who negotiated the Treaties of Greenwich. In 1544 and 1545 he preached in Ayrshire, Dundee, and Montrose but was less enthusiastically received in the neighborhood of Edinburgh, near which, after a brief association with JOHN KNOX, he was apprehended and burnt as a heretic (1 March 1546). Revenge, compounded by personal animosity, followed on 29 May, when a band of lairds broke into St. Andrew's Castle and murdered Cardinal Beaton. During the subsequent siege, the lairds, who hoped for English intervention, were joined by Knox as their minister, but in the event it was a French force who took the castle on 31 July 1547. Only then, with Knox condemned to the galleys, did the expected English invasion materialize, led, following the death of Henry VIII, by the protector Somerset at the head of 16,000 men. They met the numerically superior Scottish army at Pinkie, near Musselburgh, but the Scots, deficient in cavalry, abandoned their dominant position and amid the ensuing confusion suffered an overwhelming defeat. Although the English withdrew, they returned in 1548 to garrison various centers, including Haddington. The queen, following the arrival of a French fleet and troops, was taken for safety to France while Arran received the duchy of Chateauherault for arranging Mary's marriage to the French Dauphin.

Thereafter, English and French forces held various vantage points; Haddington was eventually abandoned by the English in 1549, and a general peace was negotiated in the following year. Although Arran was still nominally in charge, Mary of Guise and her French advisers became increasingly prominent. The approach of Mary's twelfth birthday furthered the removal of the governor, who was persuaded by a mixture of bribes and threats to resign office and facilitate the appointment of Mary of Guise as regent in April 1554; links with France had never been closer.

While this relationship was welcome to orthodox churchmen, it was less so to those who favored Protestantism, even if the new regent adopted a policy of appeasement toward political opponents and heretics alike. Nevertheless, concessions were counterproductive, and opposition grew as attempts toward Reformation from within failed. The impending marriage of Mary, Queen of Scots to the Dauphin Francis increased fears that Scotland would become an appendage of France. In consequence many magnates and lairds aligned themselves with the pro-English Reforming party who, in December 1557, published the "First Band," a pledge to work for the recognition of a Reform church. Initially this attracted few supporters, but by early 1558 there was increasing support from the lairds and barons, who authorized proposals for Reformed worship. The marriage of Mary on 24 April 1558 added strength to their cause, which was encouraged by the accession of ELIZABETH in England. The revolution did not, however, gain momentum until the arrival of John Knox on 2 May 1559 and his subsequent sermon in Perth, which brought together magnates, lairds, and their supporters to form the so-called army of the congregation, a title signifying their commitment to the Protestant cause. Nevertheless, in the marching and countermarching that characterized the ensuing skirmishes with the forces of the queen regent, emphasis was laid on the struggle against French domination. For a time in August 1559 when "fower ensignes of Frenchmen" arrived at Leith, the outcome remained uncertain. Two factors were decisive, English intervention in March 1560, followed by the fortuitous death of Mary of Guise in June. Thereafter, the TREATY OF EDINBURGH between France and England in July 1560 ended French influence in Scotland, and in the subsequent Parliament the victorious lairds on 17 August accepted a Reformed Confession of Faith. This was followed by enactments abrogating papal authority and forbidding the saying of Mass. However, as early as 29 April the great council of Scotland commanded certain ministers to compile a book containing their "judgements touching the reformation of religion" which in a revised and expanded form was considered by convention of nobility and barons in January 1561. The program for Reform, now termed a "Booke of Dyscipline," although never officially approved, not only presented the ideas of the Reformers on worship, organization, and discipline in the church but also envisaged liberal advances in both school and university education and provision for the poor. Practical considerations and the return, following the death of Francis II, of Mary, Queen of Scots in 1561 did, however, prevent its implementation, and compromise on matters of finance and ecclesiastical organization was initially all that could be achieved. Concessions to the Reformed church and a degree of statutory recognition were not conferred until the collapse of her political policies in 1566. Nevertheless, Mary's downfall, encompassed in her abdication (1567), defeat at LANGSIDE (1568), and flight to England, brought little respite to the Reformed church as a series of regencies during the minority of JAMES VI (1567-1625) led to civil war between the king's and queen's men. However, before that ended, the regent John Erskine, earl of Mar, had reached an agreement with the church at a convention at Leith in 1572 by which the existing ecclesiastical structure was retained, with bishops nominated by the Crown but subject to the authority of the General Assembly, a stipulation that Mar's successor, the regent JAMES DOUGLAS, earl of Morton, encouraged bishops to ignore. In such circumstances the Leith agreement could not be expected to endure. In its search for solution the church redefined its position in the *Second Book of Discipline* in 1578. Leadership for this course of action was undertaken by Andrew Melville, a former student of St. Andrews, Paris, and Poiters who taught at Geneva before returning to Scotland in 1574 as principal of Glasgow University. With the status of a doctor, he became a leading figure in the General Assembly and principal compiler of the *Second Book of Discipline*. In content the program is not, however, as innovative as sometimes claimed; the redefinition of the principles that governed the polity of the Scottish church led to some departures from the organizational plans of 1560, but 'innovations' were, with the exception of the claim for the full restoration of the church's patrimony and the concept of life-elders, clarification of existing practice. In essence the two Books of Discipline diverged little on basic issues and are particularly consistent in their unanimous belief that church and state were separate and distinct entities.

The development of this doctrine made conflict between both parties inevitable; the regent Morton refused to ratify the book, but his displacement as regent in 1579 and final fall from power in 1581 facilitated the introduction of presbyteries. Morton's fall also precipitated a struggle for control of the young king, who had spent his formative years at Stirling tutored by the eminent humanist and Renaissance scholar, George Buchanan. Initially on friendly terms with Mary, Queen of Scots, he had acquired his culture in exile in France and Portugal. Alienated from Mary by the death of his kinsman HENRY STEWART, Lord Darnley, he formulated her adversaries' case, the *Detecio*, used at her "trial" at York in 1568. In charge of James's education from 1570, he was a strict disciplinarian who was responsible for much of the king's erudition, although the views expressed in his *De Jure regni apud Scotos and Rerum Scoticarum Historia* were contrary to the king's belief in divine right.

The hopes of the kirk were boosted with James's abduction by the Ruthven Raiders in 1582. However, with his escape in the following year, the king under the direction of James Stewart, earl of Arran, passed the Black Acts, reaffirming episcopal authority and abolishing "that form lately invented in this land called the presbytery." Nevertheless, the king's political instability led to a compromise in 1586 that allowed the continuance of presbyteries in association with bishops. Presbyterian dominance was gradually established, and final victory seemed to have been secured by the Crown's acceptance of the new ecclesiastical organization in the so-called Golden Act of 1592. At this stage James, who had acquired personal command of policy in 1587, the year of his mother's execution, was still insecure, but events turned in his favor as he successfully defused problems ranging from threats posed by his Catholic earls in northeast Scotland to disorder in the Borders. If his policy for similar peace in the Highlands and Islands was more difficult to achieve, law and order were maintained throughout his realm. Relations with his magnates also became more harmonious, partially through the creation of new lordships based upon former church lands, which also enriched the royal coffers and enabled James to recover some of his lost influence over the church with an agreement in 1597 that the king might appoint parliamentary bishops. Nevertheless, much of James's success at the end of the sixteenth century was aided by the increasing certainty that he would succeed Elizabeth. On 24 March 1603 that dream became a reality; the Tudor era had given way to that of the house of Stuart.

Bibliography: G. Donaldson, *Scotland: James V–James VII*, 1965; R. Nicolson, *Scotland: The Later Middle Ages*, 1974.

Ian B. Cowan

Sea Beggars (Gueux de mer, Watergeuzen). An informal naval force, nominally loyal to William of Orange and varying in power and size according to the fortunes of war, that played a vital role in the success of the rebellion in the Netherlands as well as the defeat of the SPANISH ARMADA in 1588.

The Sea Beggars first appeared in May 1568, after Count Louis of Nassau, William of Orange's brother, invaded Friesland with a powerful army. His location required naval protection of his communication line through the Ems estuary to the Calvinists in exile in England, so Count Louis hurriedly created a navy from the available resources. Some of his ships were equipped and their crews hired in Emden; others were added to Louis's squadron by a Dutch pirate, Jan Abels, who acted as a broker. Partly because of the irregular way in which the fleet was created and also because of the appearance and behavior of the ships and crews, these rebel sailors were dubbed the Sea Beggars. Throughout their existence, the Sea Beggars were predominantly Netherlanders, and most of the captains and crews came from northern provinces, particularly Holland and Friesland. Some had broad experience in piracy and privateering, and many were drawn from the ranks of unemployed fishermen; all were excellent seamen notable for their courage, resourcefulness and independence.

Shortly after the fleet's creation, the Sea Beggars were dealt a setback when Nassau was defeated at Jemmigen in July 1568. Deprived of a safe home port, the Sea Beggars began operating independently as privateers, using letters of marque issued by William of Orange. Welcomed in English ports and encouraged by Orange, the Sea Beggars soon became a formidable and elusive naval force that seriously disturbed Alva's efforts to contain the revolt in the Netherlands. Unfortunately for neutrals, the Sea Beggars cavalierly chose their targets; they quickly became a menace to shipping in the Channel and the North Sea.

Indiscriminate marauding by the Sea Beggars reached such an extent that by early 1571, victimized merchants, especially those of Emden, complained to Elizabeth. Despite her desire to aid the rebels, the queen felt constrained to satisfy the protesting merchants, so she expelled the Sea Beggars from English ports on 1 March 1572. Having lost their last secure refuge, the rebel navy cruised aimlessly in the Channel and North Sea. Understandably, the Sea Beggars were dismissed as a military force by all parties interested in the revolt of the Netherlands. They still, however, had much to contribute to the rebellion.

When the Sea Beggars were ejected from England, the duke of Alva coincidentally decided to prepare for an offensive by William of Orange by strengthening the defenses of Holland and Zeeland. Specifically, Alva planned to garrison or reinforce some forty towns, FLUSHING AND BRILL among them. He acted too slowly. On 1 April, the Sea Beggars appeared in force off Brill and found the port undefended. They occupied the town without opposition. Shortly thereafter, on 22 April 1572, some of the Sea Beggars were welcomed in rebellious Flushing. They soon garrisoned the town, erected secure defenses, and joined Brill as both a sanctuary for the rebel navy as well as a beachhead for William of Orange in the northern provinces.

The Sea Beggars' hold on Flushing and Brill proved to be too much for Alva and his successors, for the rebels continued to hold the towns until the English occupied them in 1585. Even afterward the Sea Beggars operated freely out of Flushing and Brill to attack Spanish shipping and keep control of the coastal waters in the hands of the rebels. Although they had their triumphs and defeats over the years, they were instrumental in winning all of Holland for the Orangists, an unsurpassed contribution to the success of the rebellion. Militarily they worried the Spanish flank and disrupted trade to an alarming degree, and financially they supported the war effort by continually capturing prizes. Strategically, the Sea Beggars' most important activity came in 1588 when, with their shallow-draft vessels and renowned seamanship, they intimidated the duke of Parma so much that he never seriously undertook to fulfill his role of providing troops and barges for Philip II's complicated scheme to invade England.

Bibliography: G. Parker, *The Dutch Revolt*, 1977; D. Quinn and A. Ryan, *England's Sea Empire*, 1983.

Ronald Pollitt

Secretary, Principal. During the sixteenth century the principal secretary of state gradually replaced the lord chancellor as the chief administrative officer of Tudor govennent and—in the hands of a really capable politician like THOMAS CROMWELL or WILLIAM CECIL—was the single most powerful official in the realm.

The office originated in the late fourteenth century as the keeper of the signet seal, the third and least in a hierarchy of initiating and authenticating seals used to conduct the business of the realm. As the Privy Seal and Great Seal went "out of court" and acquired fixed bureaucratic offices (the Privy Seal Office and Chancery) at Westminster, the signet remained the monarch's private seal and its custodian was a personal servant in the royal HOUSEHOLD. The signet was used as a warrant to the Privy Seal (which in turn warranted the Great Seal) and as authentication for the king's own correspondence and for some minor administrative orders. By Edward IV's reign the principal secretary (so named to distinguish him from the secretaries for the French and Latin tongues) had no little personal influence because of his daily proximity to the monarch and was increasingly active in diplomatic affairs and even embassies. This pattern was continued under HENRY VII and in the first two decades of HENRY VIII's reign under such secretaries as Richard Pace, William Knight, and STEPHEN GARDINER.

When Thomas Cromwell succeeded Gardiner as principal secretary in April 1534, the role of the office was revolutionized; he made of it the central administrative and executive post in the king's government and used it to control virtually all aspects of both foreign and internal affairs. This change was possible in part because the powers and limitations of the position had never been fully defined—its influence depended on the abilities of the current incumbent.

Cromwell exploited the triple assets of control over the approach to all three seals, a newly created role in the emerging PRIVY COUNCIL, and the political influence that came from personal proximity to the monarch. He also took the principal secretary's office out of the royal Household and gave it an independent existence as an organization, including not only the four regular signet clerks but also his own private secretarial staff. Meanwhile, all three seals lost influence in initiating administrative activity; instead, "mere" letters from the secretary took on a greater role in the routine governance of the realm. When Cromwell's political skill gained him control over the privy council that came into being in the late 1530s, the technical details of such control became associated with his place as principal secretary: setting the agenda, speaking first to present the government's position, keeping records, and acting as principal channel between councillors and monarch. Cromwell's final contribution to the office was to divide it into two coequal positions in April 1540 and give them to his own two assistants, Ralph Sadler and THOMAS WRIOTHESLEY. The immediate purpose was to place one secretary in attendance on the king and the other on Cromwell. This division survived Cromwell's fall and continued, with few discontinuities, until the latter eighteenth century.

Mid-Tudor secretaries such as Sir William Petre and Sir WILLIAM PAGET lacked Cromwell's skills, and the political power of the office diminished during Edward VI's minority and Mary's return to a larger council. William Cecil's appointment in 1553 (interrupted by Mary's reign but reinstated by Elizabeth in 1558) signalled the return of a first-class statesman and politician capable of exploiting fully the potential of the office. Under Cecil (1558-1572), FRANCIS WALSINGHAM (1573-1590), and ROBERT CECIL (1596-1608), the principal secretaries were once again preeminent in Elizabethan goverment and administration. This was now even more than in Cromwell's time based on the secretary's control of the privy council but, as in the earlier periods, depended also on the right to dispense much of the Crown's patronage. Two of Walsingham's private secretaries, Robert Beale and Nicholas Faunt, wrote treatises on the office of principal secretary of state and on the organization of their private secretariats, in which can clearly be seen the origin of the two great departments of state that governed England during the seventeenth and eighteenth centuries.

Bibliography: G. R. Elton, *The Tudor Revolution in Government*, 1953; Florence M. Grier Evans, *The Principal Secretary of State*, 1923.

Mary L. Robertson

Seminary Priests. During the reign of ELIZABETH I, upward of 800 Englishmen were trained as Catholic priests abroad, and many of them were sent back to England to administer the Sacraments and preach the Catholic faith there. There were two principal seminaries: one at Douai, which removed to Rheims for a time, and another at Rome. The first of these was established by William Allen in 1568.

William Allen (1532-1594) came from a Lancashire family of the minor gentry. He studied at Oriel College, Oxford, and became principal of St. Mary's Hall in the reign of MARY I and also a university proctor. Like many other Oxford dons he left the university after the accession of Elizabeth I and went to Louvain in the Spanish Netherlands, where in the company of other expatriate intellectuals, he published works of religious controversy to be smuggled back to England to strengthen Catholic resistance there. He returned to England in disguise in 1562, where the problems of Catholics under the new regime were made clear to him. In 1568, on the advice of a Netherlander, Jean Vendeville, he opened the seminary at Douai. This was the first training college established after the Council of Trent had suggested such foundations be made, although it is likely that the intention at first was merely to found an English hostel attached to the University of Douai, where Allen was a teacher. Soon the idea of sending the graduates of this college back to England developed, perhaps especially after the failure of the NORTHERN REBELLION, late in 1569, had shown that Protestantism was likely to last for a number of years yet, and hence the Catholics in England needed immediate spiritual help before a permanent Catholic restoration came about. The college was forced by the Dutch Revolt to leave Douai for Rheims in 1578, and it received the patronage of the Guise family while there, until it was safe to return to its old home in the Netherlands in 1593. The college was funded largely by a papal pension and by the generosity of the king of Spain. The teachers at the seminary continued to publish religious works, and in 1582 the first Catholic translation of the New Testament into English was printed in Rheims, largely the work of Gregory Martin. The Old Testament, also completed by Martin at the time, was not printed due to lack of funds until 1609.

The other great seminary was at Rome. There had been a hostel or "hospice" for English pilgrims to Rome since Saxon times, and on the accession of Elizabeth this began to function as an asylum for dispossessed English priests and academics. Men drawn from this group were instrumental in having Elizabeth excommunicated in 1570 but did little else. From 1576 Allen was sending students to the hospice to relieve pressure on numbers at Douai, and in 1579 by papal bull it became a seminary in its own right and was soon placed under the management of the Jesuits. By 1585, 33 students from the English College, Rome, had returned to England. In the last years of the reign Robert Persons also founded two more seminaries in Spain itself. The first was at Valladolid, where English students began to study from 1589, and the second was at Seville, founded shortly afterward. Persons also set up in 1582 a school in Eu in France to prepare young men for the seminaries. By the end of the reign the school had removed to St. Omer and had 100 boys on the roll.

The first seminary priests returned to England in 1574. Of the 800 priests trained abroad roughly 180 did not return to England at all, and a further 140 are not known to have worked there in Elizabeth's reign. Hence only 471 priests are certainly known to have worked in England, a figure lower than some authorities have suggested. Between 1580 and 1603 it is probable that in any one year only an absolute maximum of 150 (and at times as few as 100) were actually at work in England. Of the priests who returned, 60% had ceased to operate five years after landing, and 62% of the 471 known to have worked in England are known to have been captured at one time or another by the authorities. The first missionary priest to be executed was Cuthbert Mayne, hung in 1577 for bringing a (religious) bull into the country, contrary to a law of 1571 that, following the papal bull of excommunication of Elizabeth, had forbidden this act. The government saw the arrival of the seminary priests as a threat to its political safety, and a persecution began, reaching its height in 1588, the year of the SPANISH ARMADA. At first priests were accused of real treason on the basis of alleged conspiracies abroad, with their political opinions being used as evidence of their treasonous intent. This process was not satisfactory, since so many of the priests were genuinely opposed to direct political action against the queen. As a result in 1581 an act was passed making it treason to reconcile a person to the Catholic faith with intent to withdraw him from his allegiance to the queen; in 1584 it was made treason simply to be found to be a priest ordained abroad. In all, Elizabeth executed 123 priests (and one unordained friar); all but 3 of these were seminary priests and only 4 were Jesuits (although 6 more were received into the society while in prison).

The seminary priests lived a dangerous life. While abroad they were stalked by English spies, some of whom infiltrated the seminaries themselves. They had to return to England in disguise, but often carrying incriminating evidence of their priesthood in the form of books and Mass goods. A number of routes were established: across the Channel to the Kentish ports; from Spain to the Devon peninsula; or from the Low Countries to Northumbria. None of these passages could be secure. Once in England, the priest was often very much on his own, and much depended on his own intiative and the contacts he had. Half of the seminarists claimed to come from the gentry, and this helped them, since they commanded respect and might return to their locality in reasonable safety. Little in the way of an organization seems to have been set up by the priests themselves to run the mission, and the lay structures established to support priests seem perforce to have been informal and temporary; we do not really know, however, since they were, of course, secret. The successful priests depended above all on the support of Catholic upper classes, but also—clearly—on the sympathy of their servants, tenants, neighbors, and tradesmen. The most visible evidence of the hunted life of a priest is the priest holes which exist still in many country houses: hiding places in chimneys, false walls, and ceilings. The historian can also study the casuist manuals used by the seminaries to train their students to see how the priests were encouraged to adopt all necessary subterfuges to avoid arrest. The seminary movement, combined with the work of "old" Marian priests at first, whose role is sometimes neglected, was a success. It built up a sizeable kernel of committed Catholicism in some parts of the country, and it struck a significant blow in England for freedom of conscience. No doubt the seminarists are open to criticism; Robert Persons himself saw that some parts of the country were neglected by the priests, while in other areas there were too many. This fact and their dependence on the gentry are explained by the severity of the Elizabethan persecution, which was directed—understandably enough—at Catholic centers in the north, and which depended on the gentry for its enforcement. What is surprising is that in the face of the threat of the gruesome death, imprisonment, and exile, so many young men were prepared to sacrifice all hope of a comfortable family life and a successful career to serve their fellow Catholics in hiding and on the run.

Bibliography: P. J. Holmes, *Resistance and Compromise*, 1982; A. Morey, *The Catholic Subjects of Elizabeth I*, 1978; P. McGrath and J. Rowe, "Anstruther Analysed: The Elizabethan Seminary Priests," *Recusant History* 18 (1986): 1-13.

P. J. Holmes

Separatists. Tudor Separatists were radical Protestants who rejected the legally established Church of England as hopelessly Romish, non-scriptural, and antichristian. Like the radical PURITANS from whose ranks they came, they represented an extreme response to the two principal pillars of the ELIZABETHAN SETTLEMENT OF RELIGION of 1559. The first was that the Church of England should be national in scope and subject to the authority of the queen, the PARLIAMENT, and the episcopal hierarchy. The second was that the church liturgy, polity, and discipline should be determined with reference to a *via media* position based primarily on the Prayer Book of 1552, tempered by the queen's conservative religious opinions, rather than on strict adherence to the Scriptures as seen from the Reformed Protestant positions held by some returning MARIAN EXILES. However, unlike the puritans, who abhorred schism, the Separatists drew the logical conclusion that the established church must be abandoned and a new church faithful to God's word founded in its place.

As part of their struggle to create this new church, Separatists sought to revive the life and practice of the New Testament through the careful gathering of outwardly holy, professing Christians into covenanted, self-governing congregations. Within these congregations, the word of God would be faithfully preached, the Sacraments sincerely administered, and the lives of all members rigidly regulated by a discipline that was drawn directly from the Scriptures and enforced by popularly elected church officers with the consent of the congregation.

During the 1560s and 1570s, groups of London Separatists were modeling themselves on the patterns of secret association and worship employed by Protestants in England during MARY's reign. Probably never more than 200 to 300, these dissatisfied worshipers withdrew from their parish churches and formed clandestinely gathered congregations so that they could worship without the "idolatrous" vestments, rites, and ceremonies that offended their consciences. The official response to these withdrawals was prosecution, for refusal to attend the legally authorized parish services was an offense against the queen's government. Imprisonment, coupled with intransigence on both sides, hardened attitudes. The secular and ecclesiastical authorities looked on these Separatists as subversive to both the spiritual and the secular hierarchies. The Separatists, in turn, increasingly came to view the established church as corrupt, contrary to the Scriptures, and no longer Christian. Thomas Cartwright's controversial Cambridge lectures on church polity in 1570 further estranged both Separatists and puritans from the establishment by declaring episcopal government non-scriptural and therefore inappropriate to any rightly constituted church of God.

By the spring of 1581, the focus of Separatist activity shifted to East Anglia, where Robert Browne and his coworker, Robert Harrison, were attracting followers. Both of these men had become so frustrated with the open and unchecked sinfulness in the Church of England that they resolved to organize their own congregation, which would included only those whose lives outwardly conformed to God's biblical pattern. Browne was soon imprisoned for his beliefs, but WILLIAM CECIL, Lord Burghley, a distant kinsman, repeatedly intervened to prevent more severe punishment. Both in and out of jail and later in exile with his brethren at Middelburg in the Netherlands, Browne continued to elaborate and refine his ideas. He, Harrison, and their group agreed to covenant with the Lord and to live and worship under His laws and government as set forth in the Bible. Their mission was to edify one another and to watch carefully over each other to detect and root out sin and to "judge all thinges by the worde of God." After the initial covenanting, the congregation chose Browne as pastor and Harrison as teacher. Discipline was based directly on Matt. 18: 15-17. These verses prescribed private, personal admonition for sins, followed by group admonition, and finally, if necessary, a trial before the whole congregation. If the offended remained obstinate, a majority of the church could vote to excommunicate him.

Browne hoped that his small company would prosper under his system, but poverty and personal bickering among members wrecked his experiment. Disillusioned, he returned to England and rejoined the English church in 1586.

While Browne and Harrison were abroad, Separatist agitation in East Anglia again came to the notice of the queen's government. The authorities dispatched two judges of assize, Sir Edmund Anderson and Sir Christopher Wray, to restore order and conformity. Anderson and Wray hung two men for distributing Brownist books in July 1583. These harsh judicial penalties were followed by the promulgation of the Three Articles on 29 October 1583. These articles, together with the subscription that the government required to them, greatly angered both puritans and Separatists. Within this context of controversy, Separatism continued to exist in parts of East Anglia throughout Elizabeth's reign. Thomas Wolsey, a former Anglican clergyman, probably provided at least some of the continuity of leadership that kept the movement alive.

One of the best proofs of the ongoing character of Separatist activities is in the conversion of Henry Barrow, the greatest of the Elizabethan Separatists, about

1585. Son of a Norfolk squire, Barrow had been deeply affected by Cartwright's works and puritan preaching. However, according to Stephen Ofwod's *Advertisement* (p. 40), Barrow had been a puritan scarcely 18 months when one of Browne's books came into his hands. Barrow undertook to refute the work; but instead, he was himself converted through the additional influence of Thomas Wolsey's persuasion and his own Scriptural reading.

Although he was arrested on 19 November 1587, Barrow, assisted by his collaborator John Greenwood, managed to write the most vehement and convincingly polemical tracts that Elizabethan Separatism produced. In almost all respects, Barrow agreed with Browne. He believed that the Church of England had fallen into total apostasy, and his solution to this situation was to "reduce all things and actions to the true ancient pattern of God's word."

During the last months of Barrow's life, in 1593, a new Separatist congregation was organized in London. Francis Johnson was elected pastor, and John Greenwood was chosen teacher. From its beginning, this new church was beset with crises. Thoroughly alarmed by the earlier discovery of the puritan classis movement and angered by the jests of the MARPRELATE TRACTS, the government more than ever perceived extreme Protestant dissent to be a serious threat. Accordingly, Barrow, Greenwood, and John Penry, a recent convert to Separatism, were tried and hung in the spring of 1593. Johnson and other imprisoned members of the London church also feared death, but they were not executed. Instead, on 7 April 1593, the Parliament passed a new statute entitled an "Acte to retayne the Quenes Subje[c]tes in Obedience" (35 Eliz., c. 1). This statute stipulated that all "sedicious sectaries" older than 16 years who refused to conform within three months were to be banished from the realm. Those who also refused to go into exile or who were convicted of a second offense were to be treated as felons and hung. Many of the London church chose banishment, and they sailed for the Netherlands in the summer of 1593. Johnson and three other leaders were released from prison in the spring of 1597, and, after an abortive colonization voyage to Newfoundland, they joined their banished brethren at Amsterdam in September 1597.

While incarcerated, Johnson had written *A True Confession of the Faith*, which was printed at Amsterdam in 1596. This *Confession* codified Brownist-Barrowist beliefs in 45 articles and represented the first published attempted to set forth Separatist positions systematically. It was also the first of a large number of tracts published by the Johnsonian church as part of a continuing Separatist effort to win converts among puritans at home. These tracts were printed on the church's own press and, together with letters and other messages, were smuggled into England by messengers known as "wandering stars." Nevertheless, by 1596, Tudor Separatism had already passed its peak. Although Separatist congregations and individuals remained active in East Anglia, London, and elsewhere, they appear to have made little headway in gaining additional converts until the early years of JAMES I's reign.

Bibliography: Stephen Brachlow, *The Communion of Saints*, 1988; B. R. White, *The English Separatist Tradition*, 1971.

Michael E. Moody

Seymour, Edward, Duke of Somerset (c. 1500-1552). Best known as the lord protector of the realm during EDWARD VI's early years and as a Reformist in religion whose government initiated the Protestant Reformation.

The eldest son of a Wiltshire knight, Seymour, like his father, Sir John (d. 1536) and paternal grandfather (John, d. 1491) was trained for war and honorable service in the royal HOUSEHOLD. Sir John's soldiering in France (1514) and position as knight of the body doubtless explain young Edward's appearance as *enfant d'honneur* to Mary Tudor after her marriage to Louis XII (1514). A matriculant at both Oxford and Cambridge, he was knighted in France in the course of Suffolk's campaign (1523). THOMAS WOLSEY's subsequent favor won him appointment (1525) as the duke of Richmond's master of horse and a member (with Wolsey) of an embassy to France (1527).

An esquire of the body (from September 1530), he became a royal favorite, sleeping (as his official duties required) in the king's chamber and gambling with HENRY VIII on tennis, backgammon, bowls, and cards, which the two regularly played together. Henry frequently lent him money—£1,000 in 1532—which explains how Seymour was able between 1530and 1532 to invest more than twice his income in mortgages and so expand the landed base he had acquired from the estate of his deceased first wife, Katherine Fillol of Dorset. By April 1531 he had married Anne Stanhope, a notoriously sharp-tongued woman with connections at court (her cousin was Sir Francis Bryan).

Seymour's extraordinary rise to power and influence followed immedia-tely upon his sister's marriage to the king (May 1536); JANE SEYMOUR's unforeseen death (October 1537) checked neither his career nor his fortunes. Created Viscount Beauchamp of Hache at the time of her wedding and earl of Hertford at the birth of Prince Edward (October 1537), he was sworn a privy councillor (by 7 April 1536) and granted so many estates by the king (chiefly those of former monasteries in Wiltshire) that by 1540 he enjoyed an annual income in excess of £3,900, of which about £2,550 was derived from land, acquired with the help of his patron, THOMAS CROMWELL, whose son Gregory married his sister Elizabeth. Cromwell's disgrace (1540) left him unscathed, and CATHERINE HOWARD's demise—he conveyed the charges against her—only served to enhance his standing. By temperament ill-suited to political maneuvering, he had never tried to manage the king; politically circumspect, he became in dignity (as knight of the Garter, 9 January 1541) and office (great chamberlain, January 1543) one of the king's great men.

Henry's wars of the 1540s paved the way for his climb to supreme authority. Appointed warden of the Scottish Marches (26 October 1542), he was given command of the van of THOMAS HOWARD, 3rd duke of Norfolk's, army in

Scotland. He was certainly no military genius; his promotion to commander in the north (12 February 1544) and, in place of Norfolk, commander-in-chief of all armies overseas (March 1546) is explained by Norfolk's blunders and the deaths of other, more seasoned generals (such as Suffolk and Rutland). The burning of Edinburgh (May 1545) and his lieutenancy at Boulogne, as much as the fortification of Guisne and Calais, testified to his energy and ruthless efficiency. By contrast, his diplomacy in this period—at Brussels with the Emperor in 1544, for example—failed miserably.

Of greater moment politically in December 1546 was Henry VIII's illness and impending death (28 January 1547); at court the downfall of the Conservatives (STEPHEN GARDINER and the Howards) opened the way for Seymour and his allies (the Reformists) to dominate the circle of those named (in Henry's will) to King Edward's council. Precedent and his status as Edward's elder uncle also recommended him as the boy-king's governor. Seymour aimed higher; with WILLIAM PAGET he had plotted in Henry's last hours to have Edward commission him (12 March and 24 December 1547) governor and protector; as duke of Somerset (from 16 February 1547) he was empowered to act as de facto king. When his brother, THOMAS, challenged this in Parliament (hoping to become governor himself), Seymour (through the council) charged him with treason. Thomas's execution (March 1549) on trumped-up charges revealed the depths of the duke's heartless severity.

As protector (and high treasurer from 10 February 1547), Somerset often circumvented a council whose membership he had expanded; though impolitic, such circumvention was not illegal. But an imperious will and an inability to delegate authority to others—especially in financial matters—crippled his government: his methods as much as his policies doomed him. His chief policy centered on the Scots, whom he meant to punish for refusing an offer of union, but by 1549 his costly strategy of garrisoning Scotland had almost bankrupted England and cancelled the effects of the victory at Pinkie (10 September 1547). His debasement of the COINAGE might have enabled him to write off such debts had it not been for the French, who, favoring the Scots, declared war on England (8 August 1549). The timing of this declaration could not have been worse, as it coincided with widespread domestic rebellions. Contrary to the contemporary legend—the "good duke" who championed the poor—Somerset did not hesitate to use force against the commons in 1549; his mistake was to have alienated his colleagues, who finally overthrew him (11 October 1549).

An earlier historiographical tradition ascribed to Somerset the visionary outlook of a modern liberal; in reality his values were very much those of the Tudor aristocracy. The income from dissolved chantries, which he had promised to charity, underwrote instead an adventurist war policy. By repealing Henry VIII's laws against heresy—supposed evidence of his religious "toleration"—he escaped the penalties of statutes that proscribed his own religion. Somerset was a Protestant zealot who for international, political reasons—the threat of an imperial invasion—was forced to mask in ambiguities the radical theology of the first BOOK OF COMMON PRAYER (1549). The book was supposed to heal religious divisions; rejected by both Reformist and Conservative divines, it helped spark rebellion. In religion perhaps his greatest legacy was the almost overnight destruction of a popular culture—the images and rituals associated with "superstitious" traditions. On balance, his official Reformation was essentially negative; it outlawed Catholic practices but was too short-lived to convert the nation.

His release from the Tower (February 1550) and readmission to the council—the work of JOHN DUDLEY, earl of Warwick, who needed Somerset's support against factious Conservatives—tempted him to think that he might yet recover his former power, which that Dudley now wielded as president of the council. But ambition had made rivals of the two men, and by 1551 Somerset (as he himself admitted) "contemplated" Dudley's apprehension. Dudley, superior at this game, struck first, engineering Somerset's arrest (11 October 1551), trial (1 December), and beheading (22 January 1552) on fabricated charges.

Somerset's attractive qualities—his patronage of music and architecture, his religious idealism—were overshadowed by his failures as a politician. In office he was myopic, inflexible, and proud, the victim of his own shortcomings and Dudley's greater cunning.

Bibliography: M. L. Bush, *The Government Policy of Protector Somerset*, 1975; Dale Hoak, *The Reign of Edward VI*, 1991.

Dale Hoak

Seymour, Jane, Queen of England (1509-1537). The third wife of HENRY VIII, Jane was the eldest daughter of Sir John Seymour and descended from Edward III on her mother's side. She first attracted the king's attention in 1536 when he had become disenchanted with ANNE BOLEYN. Jane's brother, EDWARD SEYMOUR, had been in the king's favor since he had accompanied the king to Boulogne in 1532, and Edward convinced Jane to leave the court of CATHERINE OF ARAGON and attach herself to the court of the new queen, Anne Boleyn. There, her modest piety proved an attractive alternative to the mercurial personality of the queen. Her brothers encouraged her to display these appealing qualities, and soon the king fell in love with her. On 8 January 1536, Catherine of Aragon died, and in mid-January, following Henry's serious accident in a tournament, Anne Boleyn miscarried what those in attendance believed to be a boy. Henry became convinced that he saw the hand of God again depriving him of a male heir. He began his courtship of Jane Seymour in earnest as he appointed a commission to discover evidence against his second wife. Anne was subsequently accused of adultery, tried, and beheaded. On the day of Anne's execution, Archbishop THOMAS CRANMER issued a dispensation allowing Henry to marry Jane, who was his cousin. The following day the couple were betrothed, and they were married on 30 June, Jane choosing as her motto, "Bound to obey and serve."

The marriage had important consequences for the Seymour family. Edward Seymour was created Viscount Beauchamp and, as brother-in-law of the king, wielded great influence. Jane clearly understood that it was her role to produce a male heir and to secure his succession. Under her influence the princess MARY was reconciled with her father when Mary agreed loyally to serve any of Henry's future children.

Jane became pregnant early in 1537 and on 12 October gave birth to the long-awaited male heir, who would become EDWARD VI. Jane, however, succumbed to puerperal fever and died twelve days later. Henry remained loyal to her memory and requested at the end of his life to be buried with her at St. George's Chapel, Windsor.

Bibliography: William Seymour, *Ordeal by Ambition: An English Family in the Shadow of the Tudors.*, 1973.

Mary G. Winkler

Seymour, Thomas, Baron Seymour of Sudeley (c. 1509-1549). Lord high admiral of England, naval commander and courtier, executed in 1549 on fictitious charges of treason. Seymour was the fourth son of Sir John Seymour (1473/4-1536), a prominent Wiltshire knight, groom of the chamber to HENRY VIII, and veteran of two English invasions of France (1513 and 1522). Nothing certain is known of Thomas's upbringing and early education. His fluency in French and his father's preferment—Sir John had given attendance on Henry at the Valois court—probably explain his appointment (by 1530) as a royal messenger in Sir Francis Bryan's embassy to Francis I.

Seymour's rise to power and influence dates from 1535 when Henry VIII began to court his sister, JANE; when Henry married Jane in May 1536, Seymour, then 25, was advanced to the office of gentleman of the Privy Chamber, an obvious sign of royal favor. He was also entrusted with military command and ambassadorial duties. When Henry declared war on France in 1543, Seymour saw active duty in the Netherlands as a marshal of the field, assuming command of the army that finally captured Boulogne. For his bravery at Boulogne the king promoted him to admiral and made him master of ordnance for life (1544). In 1544, as admiral and captain of the *Peter*, Seymour's failure to victual Boulogne sparked the council's rebuke but not Henry's wrath; his standing at court remained intact. To the various offices and former abbey lands granted him since 1536, he added Hampton Place in 1545 and renamed it Seymour Place.

As the senior knight for Wiltshire in Parliament (1545) and one who had taken a prominent part in the ceremonies of the Henrician court (ever since the christening of his nephew, Prince Edward, when he himself was knighted, 18 October 1537), Seymour by 1545 stood well placed to share with his elder brother, EDWARD (the future duke of Somerset), supreme authority during the anticipated minority of Edward VI. Appointed to Henry VIII's privy council on

23 January 1547, only five days before the king's death, Seymour expected in the new reign to be appointed governor of Edward VI's person and (with Somerset) dominate the members of Edward's regency council, which was council composed of the executors of Henry VIII's will. When Henry died on 28 January 1547 Somerset seized for himself the office of governor as well as that of protector of the realm. Shocked by his exclusion (in Henry's will) from the council of regents—Henry had named him but an "assistant" to the executors—Seymour demanded on 2 February 1547 that the protector surrender to him the office of governor, an arrangement the earl of Warwick duplicitously alleged the council had earlier accepted.

Somerset's refusal produced a compromise whereby Seymour was admitted to the council (2 February 1547), elevated to the peerage (as a baron on 16 February), invested a knight of the Garter with promotion to high admiral (17 February), and (according to WILLIAM PAGET's testimony regarding Henry VIII's dying wishes) rewarded with £500 in land. Yet resenting Somerset's retention of the governorship of the king, Seymour refused to join the protector's invasion of Scotland (August 1547). As a gesture of appeasement, Somerset appointed him in his absence one of Edward's custodians, an opportunity Seymour exploited by launching a campaign to win the governorship by statutory means. Aiming to use the parliamentary session of 4 November-24 December 1547 as a forum for abolishing Somerset's rule, Seymour created an uproar in a Commons speech attacking the constitutionality of the Protectorate. Although he finally dropped his ill-considered bill "to have the king better ordered," he was able to force a revision of Somerset's tenure; henceforth the protector served at the boy-king's pleasure.

After December 1547 Seymour endeavored to persuade young Edward that in order to bear "the honor and rule of his own doings" he must revoke Somerset's commission. This action was essentially the "crime" that sent Seymour to the block. He was arrested on 17 January 1549 and charged in a council "decree" with thirty-three articles of treason. Under examination he accepted three of the charges encompassing his attempts to instill notions of self-government in Edward's head—he had drafted letters to that end that he had intended for Edward to copy and sign—and knew that none of those acts constituted treason. The other articles, most of them hastily drawn and repetitious, were either fabricated (imagining the king's death) or based on hearsay; none was indictable. His secret marriage to CATHERINE PARR (May 1547), for example, was impolite but not illegal; following Catherine's death (September 1548) he had also hoped to marry Princess ELIZABETH, but with the council's consent and not secretly, as rumor had it. After examining the evidence in the case, the council's lawyers concluded that Seymour's "fault was not treason"; fearing future prosecution if they falsified a case tried "by order of the common law," they recommended proceeding by a parliamentary bill of attainder, thereby allowing the government the convenience of decreeing Seymour's guilt rather than having to prove it. The Commons consented to the bill on 5 March 1549.

There is no evidence that Seymour suffered from paranoia or was otherwise mad. A willful man of "great pride" and occasionally reckless behavior, he was (as contemporaries averred) a victim of his own ambition and driven by envy of his brother's position. He was beheaded on 20 March 1549.

Bibliography: S. T. Bindoff, ed., *The House of Commons 1509-1558*, vol. 3, 1982; Dale Hoak, *The Reign of Edward VI*, 1991.

Dale Hoak

Shakespeare, William (1564-1616). In his prefatory poem to Shakespeare's first folio of 1623 (the first collected edition of the plays), BEN JONSON said the playwright was "not of an age, but for all time." The fame of William Shakespeare, a son of the middle class like Chaucer, has proven the truth of Jonson's comment; he is the greatest playwright in the English language, able to convey the spirit of his own era as well as the enduring variety of human nature. He was baptized in Stratford-on-Avon on 26 April 1564, son of Mary Arden and John Shakespeare, a glove maker and dealer in grain and timber who rose to be high bailiff of the town but who later fell into debt. Shakespeare attended the free grammar school in Stratford. He married Anne Hathaway when he was 18 and she was probably about 26 and likely pregnant. In 1583 a daughter, Susanna, was born, followed by twins, Hamnet and Judith, in 1585. Between their births and his first activity in London around 1592, little is known of him; suggestions as to his activities can only be conjecture. Evidence of his early impact on the London stage appears in Robert Greene's *Groats-worth of Wit* (1592) which parodies a line *Henry VI*, part 3. Greene chides "an upstart Crowe, beautified with our feathers, that with his *Tygers heart wrapt in a Players hide* . . . is in his own conceit the only Shake-scene in a countrie." After the reopening of the theaters in 1594 following a two-year hiatus due to plague, Shakespeare established a firm link with the lord chamberlain's acting company, later known as the King's Men when its patronage changed. When Richard Burbage built the Globe Theater in 1599, Shakespeare became a principal playwright and shareholder and acted a bit in minor roles such as, legend has it, the ghost of Hamlet's father. By this time he apparently was able to assist his debt-ridden father and in 1597 had bought a comfortable home, New Place, in Stratford. While residing in London he retained his link to Stratford, inherited his parents' holdings, and purchased land and rental property. He moved from London to Stratford around 1610, two years after his father's death, and probably completed some plays there. Hamnet died in 1596, and Shakespeare's one granddaughter died childless; he thus left no direct descendants. He died on 23 April 1616, his will of 25 March bearing one of only six known, genuine signatures by him.

Unlike controversial CHRISTOPHER MARLOWE or cantankerous Jonson, Shakespeare's life was free of outward disturbance, and his last years especially were those of a comfortable gentleman. Attempts to derive biographical background from the plays are foiled by his consummate skills at "losing" himself in the infinite variety of his characters. The relative scarcity of biographical facts and his lack of any postgrammar school education have made the question of authorship a perennial topic for non-scholars, yet the extant evidence and the irrefutable reputation he gained in his own day make other claimants for authorship—for example, Francis Bacon, Marlowe, Edward de Vere, the earl of Oxford—finally unconvincing.

Shakespeare gained his earliest reputation as a poet as well as a dramatist. When Francis Meres praised him in *Palladis Tamia* (1598), he listed twelve plays plus two amatory poems: *Venus and Adonis* (1593) and *The Rape of Lucrece* (1594). Shakespeare also had begun his sequence of sonnets by 1599; the entire group of 154 (the final two are spurious) was published in 1609. The degree to which these poems depict biographical events is debatable. The identities of "Mr. W. H." (to whom they are dedicated) and the "dark lady" of the poems, for example, have not conclusively been resolved. This sequence represents the highest example of the English sonnet form. In 1601 appeared his elegy *The Phoenix and the Turtle*.

The dates of final completion for the thirty-seven plays are not precise; no manuscripts exist, and dating must be based on internal and external evidence such as style, publication dates, the Stationer's Register, or contemporary notices. Harbage offers the following chronology: *Comedy of Errors* (1590); the three parts of *Henry VI* (1590-1592); *Richard III* (1593); *Taming of the Shrew* (1593); *Titus Andronicus* (1594); *Two Gentlemen of Verona* (1594); *King John* (1594); *A Midsummer Night's Dream* (1595); *Richard II* (1595); *Love's Labor's Lost* (1596); *Romeo and Juliet* (1596); *The Merchant of Venice* (1597); *1 Henry IV* (1597); *2 Henry IV* (1598); *As You Like it* (1598); *Henry V* (1599); *Julius Caesar* (1599); *Much Ado About Nothing* (1599); *Twelfth Night* (1600); *Merry Wives of Windsor* (1600); *Hamlet* (1601); *Troilus and Cressida* (1602); *All's Well That Ends Well* (1603); *Measure for Measure* (1604); *Othello* (1604); *King Lear* (1605); *Macbeth* (1605); *Timon of Athens* (1606); *Pericles* (1607); *Antony and Cleopatra* (1607); *Coriolanus* (1608); *Cymbeline* (1609); *Winter's Tale* (1611); *Tempest* (1611); *Henry VIII* (1613).

Four broad stages appear in the growth of Shakespeare's plays. Those written before 1595 demonstrate a fairly obvious reliance on sources, especially Roman comedy, relatively narrow character development, and a beginner's concern for the development of a poetically dramatic language. *The Comedy of Errors* and *Two Gentlemen of Verona* display the confused-identity plot common to the comedies of Plautus and Terence, while *Love's Labor's Lost* and *The Taming of the Shrew* employ extensive rhyming, puns, and self-conscious wordplay. *Richard III*'s character is rather one-dimensional, a stage villain in historical dress. However, *The Merchant of Venice* signals a greater pathos and sense of character in Shylock, and comedies in the second phase display a sharper realism in such figures as Rosalind in *As You Like It*, the tone at times even darkly sinister in such "problem comedies" as *Measure for Measure* or *Troilus and Cressida*. The histories of this phase, which like all his history plays are not always factually precise, depict more rounded personalities confronting complex situations, as in *Henry IV*. The dark comedies and *Hamlet* reflect the introspective and morally confused world common to Jacobean tragedy and usher in the third period of the great tragedies. Figures such as Lear, Othello, Macbeth, and Hamlet himself are poignant and evocative explorations of the individual confronting conflict on personal, social, and spiritual levels; to many these are the greatest dramatic works ever composed. Their language is often colloquial, not artificially poetic, yet Shakespeare's insights are conveyed in masterfully symbolic terms. The final period's romances or tragicomedies (*Pericles, Cymbeline,* and *The Winter's Tale* and the *Tempest*) offer themes of reconciliation rather than conflict and are usually read as the poet's artistic farewell to his craft. In *The Tempest*, Prospero, the wise father and magician, is able to transform the crude, destructive forces on his island (probably modeled on the newly discovered Bermuda), to educate those around him in self-knowledge and to relinquish willingly his magical power and accept his life's end. Shakespeare's work thus ends on a note of fulfillment and acceptance.

Bibliography: Kenneth Muir and S. Schoenbaum, *A New Companion to Shakespeare Studies*, 1971; S. Schoenbaum, *William Shakespeare, A Documentary Life*, 1975.

                                                          Christopher Baker

Shane O'Neill, Rebellions of (1560-1567). Shane O'Neill (1530-1567) was the eldest legitimate son of Conn Bacach O'Neill, earl of Tyrone. As the eldest son, Shane was the tanist or heir in the Celtic tradition. In 1541, however, Conn Bacach had chosen to legitimatize an adult son, Ferdogah or Matthew O'Neill. Matthew was openly recognized by the English government as Conn's heir to the earldom and in fact was created Baron Dungannon in recognition of this fact.

In 1558, however, Shane murdered his half-brother and drove his dying father to the English-controlled Pale. Shane was subsequently accepted as chieftain by the Celts of Ulster. He assumed the title of The O'Neill, indicative of the Ulster sovereignty following the death of his father in 1559.

Though Queen ELIZABETH and her lord deputy in Dublin, Thomas Radcliffe, earl of Sussex, denied Shane's claims in Ulster, he quickly established his authority over the MacMahons, Magennises, Maguires, O'Hanlons, and O'Cahans, as well as the O'Neills. In 1561, he increased his power by seizing Calvagh O'Donnell, who held the title earl of Tyrconnell on English authority. This action, which made Shane master of practically all Ulster, also made him a rebel against the English Crown.

Sussex's response included the strengthening of Shane's enemies within Ulster, the O'Donnells of Tyrconnell, and the Scottish clan Macdonnell in Antrim. Direct military action was also taken against Shane by Sir George Stanley, commanding English troops. Shane showed his military skill by turning back this expedition in July 1561. This embarrassment persuaded the queen of the ineffectiveness of military solutions to the Irish problem, and Shane was invited to London to negotiate a settlement.

Shane, who arrived in London in January 1562, apparently made a good impression at Elizabeth's court. Confessing his rebellion and signing a submission, Shane proceeded to defend his position regarding his inheritance. During Shane's stay in London, another of his rivals at home, Brian O'Neill, the son of Matthew, met a violent end at the hand of Shane's kinsmen. Despite this disturbing news, the queen had by 30 April decided to send Shane back to Ireland with the lordship of Tyrone. In effect, Shane had been recognized as the ruler of Ulster in exchange for his taking the oath of obedience.

During the next four years, Shane was supreme in Ulster. He had barely returned when he began raiding the O'Donnells in violation of his oath. A 1563 raid against Shane by English forces failed to subdue the stubborn chieftain, and Sussex lacked the resources necessary to repeat this effort. In contrast, Shane's power was at its height. Tyrone was prosperous and possessed a greater population than any other Irish county during these years. Shane armed numerous field workers, a move toward militarization that no previous Irish chieftain had dared to undertake. In May 1565, Shane defeated the Antrim Scots at Glenshek and so subdued his last local opposition.

By the time Sir Henry Sidney succeeded Sussex as lord deputy in 1566, it was clear that something had to be done about Shane, who was now corresponding with the king of France. Sidney brought new energy and a renewed financial commitment on the part of the queen to the task. Sidney promptly launched an expedition intended to break Shane's power by garrisoning Derry and restoring the O'Donnells to Tyrconnell.

Though the Derry project failed, Hugh O'Donnell was re-established, and he finally toppled Shane. Attacked by Shane in May 1567, O'Donnell successfully launched a surprise assault on Shane's large army with only 400 warriors. Defeated, Shane inexplicably sought haven among another of his enemies, the Scottish clan MacDonald in Antrim. Welcomed by his foes with a feast, on 2 June 1567 Shane was hacked to bits by his hosts after a bout of drinking. His head was sent to Dublin, where it was displayed over the castle gate for several years.

Bibliography: C. Falls, *Elizabeth's Irish Wars*, 2nd ed., 1970.

John Nolan

Sidney, Philip (1554-1586). Known as the author of the first English-language sonnet cycle, Sidney was the model Elizabethan courtier excelling in languages, diplomacy, fencing, and horsemanship. He was born 30 November 1554 to Sir Henry Sidney, lord deputy of Ireland and lord president of Wales, and Lady Mary

Dudley, sister of ROBERT DUDLEY, earl of Leicester. In 1563, Sidney entered Shrewsbury School, and in 1568, he entered Christ Church, Oxford, but was forced to withdraw before matriculation because of a serious outbreak of the plague.

From May 1572 to May 1575, Sidney traveled and lived abroad (by favor of Queen ELIZABETH) to continue his education in languages and governance. During this time, Sidney made the acquaintance of many important Protestant leaders and their representatives, including Hubert Languet (1518-1581), the agent of August, elector of Saxony. Languet became a close friend and correspondent of Sidney. Upon his return to England, Sidney was appointed cup-bearer to the queen (August 1575), one of the several honorary posts he would hold in the COURT.

On 7 February 1577, Sidney was made ambassador to Emperor Rudolf, and through his diplomatic position, Sidney sought support for the Protestant League. Within five months he was recalled, and sensing his mission was a failure, he retired to his sister Mary, the countess of Pembroke's, estate in Wilton, where he remained until 1581.

Sidney's first Wilton composition was a masque for the queen entitled *The Lady of May*, which was followed by *Arcadia*. *Arcadia*, dedicated to his sister upon its completion in 1580, contains 77 poems connected by a fictional narrative of courtly life and divided into five books separated by four pastoral eclogues. As a model, Sidney may have used Jacopo Sannazaro's *Arcadia* (1502), which employs elements of Virgil's and Petrarch's poetry. Two unique features of the *Arcadia* (known as the *Old Arcadia*) are the first double sestina and epithalamium written in the vernacular.

By January 1581, Sidney was a member of Parliament, despite his letter to the queen in 1579 urging her to abandon her plans to marry the duke of Anjou, and he had completed *Certain Sonnets*, a collection of thirty-two poems that reflect his skill with meters and his interest in the relationship between musical and poetical rhythms. Most of the sonnets were original compositions in English, although there are some translations from Spanish and Italian.

In November 1581, Sidney began the first sonnet cycle written in English, *Astrophil and Stella*, which was completed in March 1582. These 108 sonnets and 11 songs are arranged as a narrative to tell the story of the love of Astrophil, a courtier, for Stella. Although influenced by Petrarch's *Sonnets to Laura*, Sidney infused the character of Astrophil with recognizable emotions and created a persona that reflects the period's interest in the psychology of action. The dispute lingers among scholars' interpretation of the sonnets concerning the extent of Sidney's interest in Penelope Devereaux, Lady Rich.

During the Wilton period, Sidney also wrote *The Defense of Poetry*. Since some of the ideas in the *Defense* are executed in the sonnets, it is assumed the *Defense* preceded *Astrophil*. Regarded as the first English-language debate about poetry, the *Defense* addresses the charges leveled against poetry by Stephen Gosson, whose *School of Abuse* was dedicated to Sidney. In his *Defense*, Sidney delineates the types of poetry and the uses of history and poetry, reviews the history of English verse, and adduces an impressive list of arguments by classical scholars to support his central claim that poetry has a positive influence on man's life and actions.

Sidney became "Sir Philip Sidney of Penshurst" in January 1583 so he could act as a proxy for Prince Casimir, brother of the elector Ludwig, at the latter's confirmation as a knight of the Garter. On 21 September 1583, he married Frances, daughter of Sir FRANCIS WALSINGHAM, who had long considered Sidney as a "son."

Sidney's work on the revision of the *Arcadia* (known as the *New Arcadia*) was interrupted in 1584 as the Spanish became more aggressive against England's allies, the Dutch. In 1585, Sidney returned to court as the cohead of the Ordnance, and he was responsible for forming a naval battalion as well. Sometime during this year, he also began reducing the *Psalms* into English verse and finished forty-three in forty-one different forms of varying quality. The remaining psalms were completed by the countess of Pembroke and published in 1599. By November 1585, Sidney was appointed governor of FLUSHING, and in July 1586 he led the first successful campaign by English forces against the Spanish in the Netherlands. His prowess with horse and sword, as well as his courage, attention to duty, and concern for the well-being of the troops, was admired and remarked upon at home and abroad.

On 22 September 1586, Sidney was fatally wounded in the left leg at the battle of Zutphen, and on 17 October he died, attended by his wife. His regal funeral in February reflected the love and esteem his peers felt for this promising soldier and statesman. From his funeral and subsequent accounts of his life and deeds as written by his contemporaries much of the legend of Sidney was derived: Sidney as a courtier of near-mythical grace and intellect. The first edition of his poetical works was published in 1589, edited by the countess of Pembroke.

Bibliography: Jan van Dorn, et al., eds., *Sir Philip Sidney: 1586 and the Creation of a Legend*, 1986; James M. Osborn, *Young Philip Sidney 1572-1577*, 1972.

Beverly Schneller

Simnel, Uprising of Lambert (1487). Even after HENRY VII's easy victory over the YORKIST RISINGS of 1486, some still hoped to reverse the verdict of BOSWORTH FIELD. The safest way to proceed now seemed to lie in promoting an impostor, who could be unmasked at a later time and a rightful Yorkist heir proclaimed. Such was evidently the thinking of John de la Pole, earl of Lincoln, the favorite nephew of Richard III and the latter's intended successor. Although Lincoln had made his peace with Henry VII, he continued to be dazzled by the glittering prospect of the throne, and during the winter of 1486-1487 he became involved in a complex conspiracy.

The plot of 1486-1487 revolved around a ten-year-old Oxford boy named Lambert Simnel. Although a trademan's son, Simnel had been tutored by an ambitious priest, Richard Symonds, who hoped to acquire a bishopric one day. Under Symonds's tutelage, Simnel had acquired a cultivated and aristocratic manner. Although the details are obscure, Symonds was evidently in contact with Robert Stillington, bishop of Bath and Wells, a Yorkist stalwart for many years. Together Symonds and Stillington decided to have Simnel impersonate Edward, earl of Warwick, a grandson of Richard, duke of York (d. 1460). Aside from a few individuals close to Henry VII, no one knew for certain whether Warwick was still alive. Accordingly Symonds and Stillington felt they could safely parade their protégé as that Yorkist pretender to the throne. Should they actually capture the crown for Simnel, they would be entitled to great rewards. But to have a fair chance of success, they felt compelled to bring the earl of Lincoln into the plan. He agreed to cooperate in the expectation of later divulging Simnel's real identity and acquiring the throne for himself.

By January 1487 Lincoln had contacted his aunt Margaret, widow of Duke Charles the Bold (d. 1477). A resident of the Low Countries, Margaret had an enormous yearly income and was ready to support any conspiracy against the hated House of Tudor. She at once agreed to provide 2,000 men under the command of Martin Schwartz, a distinguished military leader from Augsburg. Once assured of Margaret's assistance, the conspirators sent Simnel to Ireland, where Yorkist feeling was still strong. Richard of York had been a popular deputy of Ireland during the 1440s, since he permitted the Irish a considerable measure of self-rule; because Warwick was Duke Richard's grandson, he had a claim to Irish assistance. It therefore seemed likely that a boy posing as Warwick and thus as the rightful claimant to the English throne would receive a warm welcome in Ireland, which in fact proved to be the case.

However, reports from English agents in Ireland soon reached HENRY VII's desk. After convoking an emergency Great Council, Henry paraded the real earl of Warwick through the streets of London on 19 February. On that occasion he was recognized by a large crown that included the earl of Lincoln.

Although the element of surprise had been lost, Lincoln was too deeply involved to turn back. He eluded the watch on the ports, caught a ship to the Low Countries, and convinced his aunt Margaret that the plan must go forward. The dowager duchess ordered that the outfitting of a large force continue, and in late April it embarked for Ireland. After a voyage of nearly a week, it reached Dublin on 5 May, where the impostor and a large group of lords and prelates were waiting. Preparations began at once for a coronation ceremony in Christchurch Cathedral, and on 24 May Simnel was crowned by the archbishop of Dublin and the bishop of Meath. Rebel strength continued to grow, and early in May a flotilla of nearly 5,000 men set forth from Howth for England.

Meanwhile Henry VII had established himself at Kenilworth Castle and alerted his supporters to be ready to join him at any moment. On 5 June he learned of the rebels' landing on the Lancashire coast at Furness; after traveling to Coventry the next day, not knowing where a pitched battle might occur, he headed farther north. Within another nine days the two armies were only six miles apart, and a major battle was all but inevitable.

On Sunday, 16 June, the battle of Stoke began when Henry ordered a charge about 9:00 a.m. The king had about 12,000 men in his command, while the rebel horde was only half as large. Moreover, the Tudor vanguard was entrusted to the best general on the field, John de Vere, 13th earl of Oxford, a veteran campaigner. His rebel counterpart, the earl of Lincoln, was only 25 years of age and had never directed battle forces before. In addition, the rebel army was a disunited and polyglot horde of English, Irish, and German troops. Accordingly, Henry saw no need to commit over half his men to the fray and kept the remainder safely in reserve. Because the battle was fought by armies of approximately equal size, the outcome appeared uncertain at first. But the Irish regiments had no protective armor and were soon cut to ribbons by the English archers. By the time fighting ended about midday, over 4,000 of Henry's enemies lay dead on the field, including Lincoln and Schwartz, while many others were captured during the pursuit that ensued. As for Simnel, he was taken alive and imprisoned briefly. Henry then transferred him to Westminster, where he served for several years as a turnspit in the royal kitchens, although the king ultimately employed Simnel as one of his falconers.

Often called the last battle of the Wars of the Roses, the encounter at Stoke revealed just how strong Henry's hold on his kingdom had become. Waverers rallied to him as a consequence, and Yorkist hopes for the future grew dimmer. Although all conspiracy did not die away during subsequent years, sensible men could see that the monarch was too strong and capable for there to be a reasonable chance for a Yorkist restoration.

Bibliography: Michael Bennett, *Lambert Simnel and the Battle of Stoke*, 1987.

Michael V. C. Alexander

Six Articles, Act of (1539). Formally titled "An Act abolishing diversity in opinions," this statute (31 Hen. VIII, c. 14), containing a statement of traditional belief to which CONVOCATION had given assent, was passed in June 1539. Severe penalties for denial of the articles were attached. While the first article omitted the inflammatory word *transubstantiation*, it affirmed this doctrine of the eucharist. The second held that communion in both kinds was not necessary for the laity. The third article said that priests in orders were not to marry while the fourth maintained that vows of chastity or widowhood by men or women were to be observed. The fifth gave approval to private Masses, and the sixth, to auricular confession. All but the last were held to be ordained by God's law.

Severe penalties for dissension were included. Those who contradicted the first article or who despised the blessed Sacrament were guilty of heresy and to be burnt, with forfeiture of lands and goods. Those who preached, taught, or obstinately held contrary to the other five articles were to suffer a felon's death (without benefit of clergy) while simply holding contrary opinions would bring imprisonment and loss of all property for the first offense and a felon's death for a second. Those who contemptuously refused confession or abstained from receiving the blessed Sacrament at the accustomed time were to suffer imprisonment and pay a fine; a second offense would be a felony.

Any man or woman who married, having advisedly vowed chastity, also was to suffer a felon's death. Marriages of priests and of persons who had vowed chastity or widowhood were declared void, and clergy who failed to put away their wives or who married in the future were declared felons. After 12 July 1539, any priest convicted of concubinage was to suffer imprisonment, forfeiture of goods and benefices for the first offense, and a felon's death for a second; the women involved were to have the same punishment. (An amendment in 1540 removed the death penalty. The deadline probably was related to Archbishop THOMAS CRANMER's plans to send his wife back to her native Germany.)

The act empowered bishops and archbishops given commissions by the king, officials of CHURCH COURTS, and JUSTICES OF THE PEACE to enforce the law. The commissioners were given power to destroy books with material contrary to the act, and parish priests were periodically to read the act in their churches. The act was not systematically enforced, but along with acknowledgment of ROYAL SUPREMACY it remained the foundation of orthodoxy for the rest of the reign.

With the exception of auricular confession, all of the six articles had been anticipated in pronouncements made within six months prior to the Parliament of 1539. While a traditionalist or anti-Cromwellian group of councillors promoted these articles, and they represented a defeat for Cranmer, THOMAS CROMWELL, and others such as Bishops HUGH LATIMER and Nicholas Shaxton, who resigned their sees, the selection of topics also flowed logically from and were consistent with existing expressions of policy. Moreover, this policy reflected the king's own instinctive conservatism, as well as his diplomatic perspectives and his desire to end religious conflict and dissension. His preference for amiable relations with the Catholic French and imperial powers rather than the German Lutherans played a part in the king's articulation of faith as did his new knowledge of the religious unrest in Calais, which highlighted the problem throughout the realm. All of these factors influenced the formulation of the six articles and their institution in statute, but it was the king who sifted the influences, scrutinized the articles, and determined their content.

Bibliography: G. Redworth, "A Study in the Formulation of Policy: The Genesis and Evolution of the Act of Six Articles," *Journal of Ecclesiastical History* 37 (1986): 42-67.

Martha C. Skeeters

Social Structure/Ranks. English society under the Tudors consisted essentially of a diverse assortment of small-scale communities. It was overwhelmingly rural with some 90% of the English residing in dispersed dwellings, villages, or small towns with fewer than 2,000 residents. Nuclear family households were the norm. They were linked to one another by various bonds of kinship, neighborliness, patronage, and clientage. These nuclear households included not simply the members of the immediate family but any other people who were living with them. They were a patriarchal and male-dominated institution, which was exemplified by the basing of population figures on the number of male heads-of-households. The Tudor nuclear family also exhibited all the modern attitudes of domesticity, affections for children, and mutually caring relationships between spouses and between parents and children.

Contemporaries and later historians generally agree that the most fundamental characteristic of Tudor society was its pervasive and high degree of social stratification. Society was divided into various status levels or ranks. While these rankings were supposedly well demarcated, they were still prone to some blurring and confusion. The rankings' origins lay in the institutions of feudalism and manorialism and so no longer accurately reflected the social realities of sixteenth-century England. Social mobility also contributed to the confusion as some people improved their economic status and in turn tried to improve their social rank. All of this uncertainty only heightened English society's attentiveness to status difference. It permeated everyday life, with status distinctions being reflected in clothing, diet, seating arrangements for parish church and the quarter sessional courts of the counties, salutations, and public processions. These social rankings for the most part reflected the unequal distribution of wealth and power.

In Tudor England, a person's rank and status were determined by the possession of a number of social and economic characteristics. The preeminent criterion for membership in the upper ranks of society was the possession of landed wealth. This situation is not at all surprising since England was still a largely rural society and land remained the source of most wealth. At the same time, other things contributed to the determination of social rank: birth, given titles of nobility, the source of wealth, style of life, occupation, positions in and the exercise of authority, legal qualifications, and the respect of the local community. Furthermore, the relative importance of these social traits varied from locality to locality throughout England.

The fundamental social division in English society was between the gentlemen and the commons. Each of these two broad ranks was further broken up into various subgroups based on social status. The royal family occupied the pinnacle of English society. After them came the lay peers. These titled nobles were ranked in descending order as dukes, marquesses, earls, viscounts, and barons. This peerage was distinguished by the possession of hereditary titles, preferential legal status, and the privilege of being summoned to sit in the House of Lords in Parliament. A title of nobility was acquired either by birth and succession or by creation by the monarch. Creation as a titled noble was frequently a reward for significant service to the Crown. These lay peers never constituted more than a tiny fraction of the English population—in 1500 there were perhaps 40; in 1547, 48; in 1559, 61 and in 1603 around 55. Their individual wealth varied greatly but as a group they possessed an average annual income of £1,000. They formed the richest social ranking at the beginning of the Tudor era and maintained their position through the entire sixteenth century.

Just below the lay peers were the gentry, all those gentlemen who lacked titles of nobility. About 2-3 % of the English population belonged to the social rank of the gentry. The gentry were further subdivided into the categories of knights, esquires, and mere gentlemen, the lowest status. Originally the monarch had awarded the status of knighthood for military service. By 1500, the rank was generally given to those gentlemen whose landed estates generated at least £40 of income annually. It was also used as a courtesy title by the untitled eldest sons of the nobility. Valued Crown servants were also commonly elevated to the knighthood. Esquires officially consisted of all the untitled male heirs, along with their descendants, of the younger sons of the nobility, specific local officeholders such as sheriffs and JUSTICES OF THE PEACE, and those ancient families who could prove that previous family members had held the rank. Informal qualifications for the rank of esquire were the possession of appropriate landed wealth, a leisurely life-style, selection for local government, and the respect of the local community. The rank of gentleman originally was used to indicate only the younger sons and brothers of knights and esquires and their male heirs. By the sixteenth century, however, the rank of gentleman was attributed to all those who fulfilled the same informal qualifications used to identify esquires, but to a lesser degree.

All of these ranks of the gentry were entitled to possess a coat of arms, which served as the formal and visible recognition of gentle status. Heralds from the College of Arms visited the counties every generation. Their purpose was to determine all those who truly were members of the gentry and those who were not. The findings were recorded in a document known as a "heralds' visitation," which was basically a collection of genealogical tables. A herald could also grant a coat of arms, including the status of gentleman, to lawyers, university professors, and military officers of the rank of captain or higher as long as they possessed the necessary wealth and leisured life-style. During the sixteenth century it took an income of at least £10 a year or over £300 in goods for a person to be able to live as a proper gentleman.

Taken as a group, the gentry formed an elite of wealth and power in the local communities of Tudor England. While consisting of only about 1,000 members during HENRY VIII's reign, the number of gentry expanded to some 16,000 by 1603. The economic status of the gentry varied greatly from region to region in England. As a result, the ultimate test for gentility was possession of a coat of arms since many self-styled gentlemen claimed the status improperly.

The commons represented the other major social grouping in rural English society. They vastly outnumbered their social betters, the landowning gentlemen, and comprised at least 80% of the total population. Four degrees of ranks divided the commons, which in descending order were yeomen, husbandmen, cottagers, and landless laborers. Ideally, a yeoman had an annual income of at least 40s and farmed freehold land that carried a fixed nominal rent, was not subject to the lord of the manor, and could be passed on to his heirs without restriction. In reality, their landholdings were often mixed and included copyhold (subject to the lord of the manor) and leasehold (subject to a relatively short leasing agreement) lands. It took at least fifty acres of land to maintain the independent status of a yeoman, who also possessed the right to vote in the county's parliamentary elections. The richest yeomen often possessed more wealth than some lesser gentlemen. They stood at the top of the hierarchy of the commons and in the absence of any resident gentry would assume preeminence in many villages.

Husbandmen came after yeomen in social status. They were usually tenants or copyholders and worked farms consisting of between five and fifty acres. After the husbandmen came the cottagers, who worked small holdings of several acres and as a result needed to earn extra money by hiring out to the more substantial farmers. The landless laborers were just that, landless, and so worked for wages to survive. Both cottagers and the landless laborers lived at the subsistence level. Along with the husbandmen they formed the majority of the rural population of England.

Considerable local variation existed in this rural social structure. Lowland areas contained more gentlemen than did the upland regions. Similarly, greater numbers of gentlemen and rich yeomen lived in the sheep-corn regions, which also supported a higher percentage of landless laborers than did purely pastoral areas. Cloth-making areas contained industrial wage earners not found elsewhere.

This basic system of ranks was subject to some blurring of distinctions, which was increased by the growing numbers of lawyers, merchants, and royal civil servants in sixteenth-century England. They, along with the wealthier yeoman, fell into the category of the "middling sorts of men." Their wealth allowed them to adopt the life-style of the gentlemen, and they often held positions of authority in the local and central government. Strongly desiring gentle status, they acquired the landed estates and the necessary bonds of kinship and friendship that went along with it. Often their neighbors considered them to be gentlemen even if the heralds from the College of Arms did not. This sort of social mobility permeated Tudor society.

A few historians, most notably R. H. Tawney and his supporters, have argued that these "middling sorts" represented an emerging middle class that largely accounts for the dramatic increase in the numbers of gentlemen during the sixteenth century. This incipient middle class supposedly usurped the power and prestige traditionally belonging to the peerage. Lawrence Stone subsequently gave support to this hypothesis by suggesting that the Tudor peers had indeed lost status because of land transfers to the "middling sorts." H. R. Trevor-Roper opposed this thesis with the contention that no real decline occurred among the peerage and that only court gentry (royal officeholders) improved their lot while the country gentry did not. This academic debate became known as the "gentry controversy." J. H. Hexter effectively ended it by exposing the myth of any corporate rise of the middle class at the expense of the peerage. While many individuals rose or fell within the two groups, the evidence did not support a rise or decline for either group as a whole. Since, the English POPULATION doubled during the Tudor era, that fact alone partially explained the growth of the "middling sort." Furthermore, the great increase in the market for land after the DISSOLUTION OF THE MONASTERIES also contributed to the same process. Tudor England was dominated by traditional distinctions of social status that increasingly did not reflect reality. That dilemma caused sixteenth-century Englishmen much confusion, and it continues to confuse historians.

Bibliography: W. G. Hoskins, *The Age of Plunder: The England of Henry VIII 1500-1547*, 1976; D. M. Palliser, *The Age of Elizabeth: England Under the Later Tudors 1547-1603*, 1983; Keith Wrightson, *English Society 1580-1680*, 1982.

Eugene J. Bourgeois II

Spenser, Edmund (c. 1552-1599). The foremost author of non-dramatic verse in the Elizabethan age, Spenser is best known for the unfinished epic poem, *The Faerie Queen* (1589 and 1596) and for inventing the rhyming pattern for the sonnet, which he used in *Amoretti* (1595), the second sonnet cycle written in English. Between 1580 and 1598, Spenser served in Ireland as a government official, occupying various posts.

Born in 1552 or 1553 in London, Spenser attended Merchant Taylors' School and Pembroke College, Cambridge (B.A. 1573; M.A. 1576). While at Pembroke, Spenser developed a close friendship with a don, Gabriel Harvey, whose *Marginalia* and correspondence reveal much about Spenser as a young poet and as a student.

Spenser visited Ireland in 1577, and in 1578 he became secretary to John Young, the bishop of Rochester. In 1579, Spenser published *The Shepheardes Calendar*, which through twelve eclogues tells the story of Colin Clouts's love for Rosalind and his friendship with Hobbinol (modeled after Harvey). Spenser's use of fables in select eclogues and the arrangement of the poetry in a calendar form are innovative.

Spenser became secretary to Arthur, Lord Grey de Wilton, lord deputy of Ireland, in 1580. Whle working for de Wilton, Spenser formed ideas about the Irish people as barbarians and his belief in the rightness of the English policy of supremacy in Ireland, which he later developed in *A View of the Present State of Ireland* (1633). Between 1583 and 1585, Spenser acquired lands in County Cork, making him, along with Walter Raleigh, one of the "Undertakers" of Munster, who lived rent- and tax-free on Irish property seized by English settlers and protected by English troops. In 1585, Spenser served as deputy clerk of Munster, and in 1588 he became the Clerk of Munster. On 26 October 1590 he became the official owner of the Kilcolman Castle in Cork, and in 1591 he published two more works, *Complaints* (three volumes) and *Daphaida*. He married Elizabeth Boyle on 11 June 1594, and in 1595 he published *Colin Clouts Come Home Again*, *Astrophel* (on the death of Philip Sidney), and *Amoretti* (89 sonnets with four Anacreontic lyrics), which with the *Epithalamium*, records in verse Spenser's courtship of Boyle and his wedding to her.

Although he published *Prothalamium* and *Fowre Hymns* in 1596, Spenser's most important publication that year was the three remaining books of the projected twelve-book epic, *The Faerie Queen* (Books I-III, 1589). Dedicated to Queen Elizabeth, Books I-III also contained sonnets addressed to eminent members of court and Spenser's letter to Raleigh outlining the poet's methods and intentions in writing an allegorical poem, "a dark conceit," on the virtues required of a gentleman. For the first books, Spenser received a £50-annuity for life from the queen. To Books IV-VI, he added the well-known "Two Cantos on Mutabilitis." Because *The Faerie Queen* is a complex and rich allegory, it continues to generate scholarship on topics ranging from its genre to its influence on other poets, especially Milton and Blake.

Appointed sheriff of Cork in 1598, Spenser fled Kilcolman Castle on 16 October 1598 as rebel forces sympathetic to the earl of Desmond burnt it to the ground. Spenser's estate was largely composed of lands seized and divided after Desmond's death. There is a tradition that an infant Spenser died in the fire.

Spenser, who left his wife in Cork, arrived in London in late 1598 or early 1599. There he strove to contact his former supporters, many of whom were unavailable. For a brief period the poet was ill with influenza, and he died of unspecified causes 16 January 1599. He was buried in Westminster Abbey adjacent to William Chaucer at the expense of the earl of Essex. Although acknowledged today as the author of *The Faerie Queen*, Spenser was best known in his time as the author of *The Shepheardes Calendar*. The posthumously published *A View of the Present State of Ireland* is a valuable historical document, not only for its codification of the English policy of conquest and confiscation but also for its information on Irish practices of husbandry, legal and economic systems, and literature.

Bibliography: E. Heale, *The Faerie Queen: A Reader's Guide*, 1987; T. W. Moody et al., *A New History of Ireland*, vol.3: *Early Modern Ireland 1534-1691*, 1976.

Beverly Schneller

Staple, Merchants of the. This regulated company controlled the export of English wools through the staple (mart) at CALAIS from the fourteenth century until its transformation into a purely domestic trading group in the reign of JAMES I. Properly known as the "Mayor and Company of the Staple at Calais" until the loss of that town in 1558, these merchants became the leading trading company of late medieval England, engrossing the once-lucrative traffic in wools, which was conducted through England's last remaining Continental possession. Charged with the expense of garrisoning and fortifying the town, the company entered into engagements known as acts of retainer with HENRY VII and HENRY VIII. These acts required the payment of fixed sums of money at stated times and seriously depressed the prices that the debt-ridden merchants obtained for their goods. By 1527 the Merchants of the Staple found themselves unable to support the financial burden of Calais as required under the Act of Retainer of 1515; they forfeited both lands and money to the Crown to retain their right to trade. After 1534 the Staplers usually exported cloth under licenses granted on a yearly basis, which allowed them greater freedom than the acts of retainer had. Though the company stubbornly cleaved to the principle of exporting through a mart town, the company's difficulties were exacerbated by the staple system; smugglers were able to avoid the extortionate custom on wool (forty shillings a sack), Italian merchants were free from the obligation to ship through Calais, and individual merchants obtained royal licenses to export wool outside of the Calais staple.

Despite complaints that competition was the true source of their decline, the increase in English CLOTH manufacture, itself stimulated by the high export duty charged on wool, was the most significant factor reducing the volume of wool and woolfells exported by the Staplers. The importance of the Staple Company to the Crown as an agency for the repayment of foreign loans thus diminished with the growth of English cloth manufacture and the rise of the MERCHANT ADVEN-TURERS Company. The development of the native cloth industry deprived the Staplers of the Flemish market for English wool (driving the clothiers of Flanders to seek out inferior Spanish wools) while the London-based Adventurers ruthlessly excluded the Staplers from their monopoly of the cloth trade carried to Antwerp. Thus while the new charter granted to the Staplers in 1561 specifically exempted them from the jurisdiction of the Merchant Adventurers, the charter of 1564 incorporating the latter fellowship as the Merchant Adventurers of England just as clearly confirmed that company's grip on the cloth trade at a time when the Staplers were sorely tempted to encroach upon it.

After the loss of Calais in 1558 the overseas staple was transferred first to Middelburg and then to Bruges. During the middle years of Elizabeth's reign the Staplers divided their dwindling trade in wools among these towns and Hamburg. In 1584, the Staplers, expelled from the cloth trade by decision of the PRIVY COUNCIL, received a valueless MONOPOLY to export wools for the next seven years, which effectively ended the staple system. In 1614 the export of English wools was prohibited by PROCLAMATION, and the Staple Company of England thereafter devoted itself to the domestic wool trade.

Bibliography: E. E. Rich, *The Ordinance Book of the Merchants of the Staple*, 1937.

Douglas Bisson

Star Chamber, Court of. The Court of Star Chamber was simply the king's council operating under the more formal procedure of Roman civil law and dispensing a body of law derived from common and statute law. It took its name from the *Camera Stellata* in the palace of Westminster—so called because of the decorations on the ceiling and walls of the room in which the council met. Older authors were wrong in asserting that the court had its origins in the so-called Star Chamber Act of 1487 (3 Hen. VII, c. 1); the court probably dates back to the time of Edward III, although its judicial function as an equity court was not differentiated from the administrative functions of the medieval council until the reign of HENRY VII. The judicial functions of the council were emphasized by Cardinal THOMAS WOLSEY as lord chancellor, and the business before the court continued to increase in every reign until the court was abolished by an act of Parliament in 1641 (16 Car. I, c. 10).

When the judicial functions of the Court of Star Chamber were separated from the new PRIVY COUNCIL in the late 1530s, the chief justices of the Courts of King's Bench and Common Pleas were joined with the privy councillors in the Court of Star Chamber to provide legal advice. Other judicial officers were added to the Star Chamber bench from time to time. The court also began to confine its sessions to the four legal terms, whereas the privy council continued to sit six and, sometimes, seven days a week. The jurisdiction of the court was limited to misdemeanors and excluded felonies (except for suicides, where the king's almoner sued to recover the suicide-felon's goods), nor could the court hear and determine crimes or employ punishments that touched life or limb. The penalties imposed upon conviction included fines, imprisonment, flogging, the pillory, and, occasionally, mutilation of the ears and nose. Although the court had always concerned itself with breaches of the king's peace (assault and battery, riot and unlawful assembly, and, later, unlawful hunting and dueling) and interference with royal justice (maintenance, subornation, perjury, official corruption, and extortion), most of the early and mid-Tudor cases were civil in nature and usually involved questionable titles to lands (fraud, forgery, trespass, forcible entry, and detainder). After 1558 real property cases were referred to the common law courts, and the court largely concerned itself with the misdemeanors listed above plus the new crime of seditious libel.

Unlike the COMMON LAW courts, which used a mixture of Latin and Law French in indictments and pleadings, with evidence given verbally in English, Star Chamber, in common with other English-bill courts such as CHANCERY and REQUESTS, employed written pleadings and evidence in English. Private parties having a grievance addressed a form of petition known as a bill of complaint to the king or, sometimes, to the lord chancellor and alleged the wrongs committed by the defendants. Prosecutions brought by the attorney general on behalf of the king were properly called informations. The defendants made an answer, and a further exchange of allegations and responses might be made by means of replications and rejoinders. If the court officials thought that the defendants' answers were vague or failed to state the truth, a set of very specific interrogatories would be drawn up and administered to the defendants, who made further answer in the form of sworn depositions. Witnesses were also obliged to answer by means of written depositions. While a good part of the pleadings and evidence of the court survives, the judgments of the court have largely disappeared, although some contemporary abstracts from the entry books of decrees and orders survive. While it is not always possible to determine the outcome of a particular case, the pleadings and evidence afford rich and detailed information for the social historian. Litigants frequently filed cross suits in Star Chamber that never came to hearing or judgment; many of these cases may be traced to a conclusion in other equity and common law courts.

Bibliography: T. G. Barnes, "Star Chamber Mythology," *American Journal of Legal History* 5 (1961): 1-11; J. A. Guy, *The Court of Star Chamber and its Records to the Reign of Elizabeth I*, 1985.

Roger B. Manning

Steelyard. The London establishment of the Hanseatic League (Hansa). A square, walled precinct between Upper Thames Street and the river, in the parish of Allhallows the Great (modern EC4), the Steelyard contained a guildhall, a chapel, storefronts, warehouses, and residences. Its name derives from *STAL*, a merchandise showroom.

The Hansa, a German mercantile confederation that included Cologne, Lübeck, Hamburg, and Danzig, had *Kontore* (merchants' associations) in Novgorod, Bergen, Bruges, and London. Established in 1281, the London *Kontor* held special trade privileges, including reduced customs, by royal charter. It elected an alderman to London's Guildhall and shared guard duties for Bishopsgate. All Hansa merchants coming to London were required to lodge at the Steelyard. The London *Kontor* dominated lesser Hanseatic establishments at Ipswich, Yarmouth, Lynn, Hull, York, Newcastle, and Boston. The merchants sold chiefly timber and wax, and they bought English woolens.

The Steelyard was an important conduit by which Lutheran thought came into England. Lutheran books were banned in England from 1521. However, in the Hanseatic cities Lutheranism spread rapidly. On their trips home, Steelyard merchants obtained Lutheran books for circulation among German and English friends in London. THOMAS MORE's son-in-law William Roper received books by Martin Luther from Steelyard men. In 1526 four Steelyard merchants were prosecuted for heresy, and their books were burned at St. Paul's. Ten years later, Steelyard men were attending sermons at the house of the Reformer John Bale. Ten years after that, they supplied him with the manuscript memoirs of the Protestant martyr ANNE ASKEW.

The hostility of the English MERCHANT ADVENTURERS, tougher trade policy under ELIZABETH, and rivalries within the Hansa spelled the end of the Steelyard. In 1578, when the Steelyard demanded both the renewal of its ancient charters and restrictions on English trade at Hamburg, Elizabeth demanded that English merchants in Hansa cities receive trade privileges similar to the Steelyard's. In 1580 Steelyard merchants were required to pay the same duty as other aliens when exporting cloth. In 1589, the English accused the Hansa of having supported the SPANISH ARMADA, seized sixty Hanseatic ships off Lisbon, and left the Steelyard almost deserted. In 1598, in retaliation against Emperor Rudolph II for barring the Merchant Adventurers from Germany, Elizabeth closed the Steelyard, sequestered its buildings, and expelled Hansa merchants from the realm. In 1606 the property was returned to the Hansa. The Steelyard was destroyed in the Great Fire of 1666 and finally sold in 1853.

Bibliography: S. Brigden, *London and the Reformation*, 1989; P. Dollinger, *The German Hansa*, 1970.

Mark Heumann

Stewart, Henry, Lord Darnley (1545-1567). As the second husband of MARY, QUEEN OF SCOTS, Darnley was one of the unfortunates of history, a man born to high position without the commensurate ability to sustain it. As the son of Matthew, earl of Lennox, he was not only a major aristocrat but also a potential claimant to the Scottish throne. Furthermore, as the son of Margaret Douglas, daughter of James IV's widow, Margaret Tudor, and her second husband, Archibald Douglas, earl of Angus, he also had a claim to the English throne, second only to that of Mary, Queen of Scots herself. Brought up in the English court, where his father had taken refuge when his support for Henry VIII had brought his banishment from Scotland in 1544, his other attractions were his physical appeal—not entirely borne out by the lanky-legged and weak-faced figure portrayed by Hans Emsworth when he was seventeen—his Catholicism, or what passed for it, and his willingness in 1565 to marry a queen who was by then finding it exceedingly difficult to acquire a husband.

It remains a problem why Elizabeth allowed first Lennox in 1564 and then Darnley himself in 1565 to go to Scotland. Mary's envoy James Melville of Halhill, describing the negotiations for the Leicester marriage, indicates that Elizabeth anticipated Scottish enthusiasm for Darnley; "Ye like better of yonder long lad," she said, trying to wrong-foot an intelligent diplomat well able to stand up to her. At one extreme, it has been suggested that Elizabeth, knowing all too well Darnley's character, set him up, with Machiavellian cunning, to Mary's damnation; at the other extreme, the most recent and more plausible interpretation is that she was outmaneuvered. But the damnation certainly happened, admittedly with some help from Mary herself. Her violent enthusiasm for him produced marriage on 29 July 1565 and, on 30 July, her proclamation of him as king, entirely on her own authority, to a stunned and silent audience. In August, JAMES STEWART, earl of Moray, was in rebellion, and the Protestant ascendancy of 1561-1565 shattered, to be replaced by a faltering move toward a pro-Catholic policy, ineffective but nonetheless frightening because of the peace between France and Spain which created fears of an international Catholic league. But by the autumn, the dreadful truth was clear; Darnley's "kingship" was expressed in excessive drinking, public insults to the queen, and total indifference to government. Mary was by now pregnant, and Darnley could be minimalized.

His response was to unite in March 1567 with the rebellious Protestant lords, whose sop to this willing tool was the promise of the Crown matrimonial. Power was regained over the dead body of David Rizzio, but, predictably, there was no Crown matrimonial. The insults to the queen became even more public; the Scottish "king" refused to attend his son James's baptism (thus allowing doubts about his legitimacy) and wrote to the kings of France and Spain, to proclaim Mary's indifference to the Catholic cause. The liability was too great, for Catholics and Protestants alike; as Mary shied away from divorce, death was the only solution. On 10 February 1567, the house of Kirk o' Field, where Darnley lodged, was blown up, and the fleeing Darnley was caught and smothered. JAMES HEPBURN, earl of Bothwell, and Darnley's Douglas kinsmen were certainly there; Moray and other leading politicians certainly knew what was intended; and so, unless she was wholly out of touch with reality, did his wife.

It was her behavior after the murder, not the murder itself, that brought Mary down and turned a violent solution sought by everyone into a cause célèbre. His unspeakable character was rewritten by JOHN KNOX and other opponents of the queen. His ghost walked in 1568-1569, when the murder became the main issue in Elizabeth's effort to settle the problem of Mary in England, with Moray as regent in Scotland. It walked again in 1581, when the murder was used as the excuse to execute the most powerful of James VI's regents, JAMES DOUGLAS, earl of Morton. Darnley, dead, was a far more potent figure than the miserable, short-lived reality.

Bibliography: Simon Adams, "The Release of Lord Darnley and the Failure of the Amity," in *Mary Stewart: Queen in Three Kingdoms*, ed. M. Lynch, 1988; Antonia Fraser, *Mary Queen of Scots*, 1969.

Jenny Wormald

Stewart, John, 4th Earl of Atholl (d. 1579). John Stewart succeeded his father as earl in 1542. There is some uncertainty about his date of birth and whether his first marriage was to Elizabeth Gordon, daughter of the 4th earl of Huntly. But it is certain that he was married to Margaret Fleming, relict of Robert, master of Montrose, and of Thomas, master of Erskine.

Atholl was a staunch Roman Catholic who voted against the Protestant confession and the establishment of the Protestant church in 1560. He was also a strong supporter of Mary of Guise, the regent. On the return of MARY, QUEEN OF SCOTS from France in 1561, he was appointed a privy councillor. He approved of Mary's marriage to HENRY STEWART, Lord Darnley, and took part in the expedition led by JAMES STEWART, earl of Moray, who defeated the earl of Huntly at Corrichie in 1562. During the next two or three years he became one of the leaders of the Marian party and in 1565 was appointed lieutenant in the north.

His support for Mary was withdrawn, however, when after Darnley's murder she married JAMES HEPBURN, earl of Bothwell. He then joined the Protestant lords, who forced Mary to abdicate and established her son, JAMES VI, as king of Scotland in 1567. At that time Atholl was made the provisional regent until the earl of Moray was appointed to that position. He apparently approved of the appointment of Moray, but in 1569 when Mary divorced Bothwell, he gave his approval to that action, although it did not mean that Mary came back to Scotland. During the regencies of Mary; Matthew Stewart, earl of Lennox; and John Erskine, earl of Mar, he seems to have remained in the background as he had given his support to Mary's party. When JAMES DOUGLAS, 4th earl of Morton, from James VI's party was nominated to the position of regent in 1572, he voted against him.

In 1577 Atholl came into conflict with ARCHIBALD CAMPBELL, earl of Argyll, who claimed that Atholl had no right to a commission of justiciary over his own territory, which was illegal, since he, Argyll, held the office of justice-general by hereditary right. This conflict led to a feud between the two men, that the regent Morton tried to heal. He was successful, but for him it was a disaster, for both the earls were very strongly opposed to Morton personally and to his policies. The result was that Morton was forced to demit the regency in March 1578, and in April Atholl was given the office of chancellor of the realm. When Morton returned to power in 1579, he endeavored to bring about reconciliation with the opposition. He invited Atholl to a banquet, but shortly afterward Atholl died mysteriously on 24 April 1579. Morton was accused of poisoning him, but although he denied this, the suspicion still remains.

Bibliography: J. Balfour Paula, *The Scots Peerage*, 1904.

W. Stanford Reid

Submission of the Clergy (1532 and 1534). In 1532, CONVOCATION voted an act known as the Submission of the Clergy. Two years later, in 1534, PARLIAMENT passed An Act for the Submission of the Clergy to the King's Majesty (25 Hen. VIII, c. 19), which confirmed convocation's document as a statute along with certain provisions for its implementation. Both enactments reflected the need to resolve convocation's divided loyalties to pope and Crown for reasons both English and Henrician.

The convocation's measure of 1532 was itself an outgrowth of the 1532 COMMONS' SUPPLICATION AGAINST THE ORDINARIES. HENRY VIII, upon receipt of the Answer of the Ordinaries had taken three important steps. (1) On 30 April, he sent the answer to Commons, accompanied by the following message:

"We think their answer will smally please you, for it seemeth to us very slender. You be a great sort of wise men; I doubt not but you will look circumspectly on the matter, and we will be indifferent between you." (2) He next (10 May) demanded major concessions from convocation regarding their ecclesiastical legislative powers. Basically, he asserted the right of royal review for all past and future legislative actions by convocation. (3) The following day (11 May 1532), Henry met with Commons' speaker, Thomas Audley, twelve other leaders of that body, and eight lords and said: "Well-beloved subjects, we thought that the clergy of our realm had been our subjects wholly, but now we have well perceived that they be but half our subjects; yea, and scarce our subjects; for all the prelates at their consecration make an oath to the pope, clean contrary to the oath that they make to us, so that they seem to be his subjects, and not ours. Copies of both the oaths I deliver here to you, requiring you to invent some order that we be not thus deluded of our spiritual subjects." Appropriate parliamentary action was drafted but did not evolve into statute for two more years.

Meanwhile, Henry turned to convocation and, after much negotiation and heavy political pressure, the upper house of the southern convocation reluctantly succumbed to the king's demands. First among these was the promise to submit to the monarch's legislative oversight. This meant convocation could not even meet except under royal writ, nor could any canons be enacted without royal assent. In addition, a twenty-two-person royal committee was to be appointed to examine all existing canons; consistent with the growing laicization of matters spiritual, half of its members were to be laymen.

It was not a clear victory. The lower clergy refused to concur, and, of the bishops, only three really had supported the capitulation (Archbishop WILLIAM WARHAM and the bishops of Exeter and Ely). Three others had agreed protestingly, and eight were either necessarily or conveniently absent. One bishop, John Clerk of Bath and Wells, courageously voted no. Furthermore, the affair precipitated Chancellor THOMAS MORE's resignation on the following day.

Power based on such weak foundations of legitimacy contained little or no real authority. By 1534 Henry felt it necessary to confirm convocation's surrender by parliamentary statute, which added the right of the king to fine and imprison resisters and completely removed the already diminished right to appeal to Rome in any manner. Also, according to the earlier ACT IN RESTRAINT OF APPEALS (24 Hen. VIII, c. 12), the archbishop had been the highest place of appeal, but now the king or his appointed commissioners (delegates of appeals) would serve as the religious court of last resort. No oath was required by this act.

Bibliography: G. R. Elton, *Reform and Reformation: England 1509-1558*, 1977.

Ann E. Faulkner

Subscription Crisis (1583-1584). In October 1583 the new archbishop of Canterbury, JOHN WHITGIFT, issued the Three Articles dealing with abuses and nonconformity in the church. Anyone exercising an ecclesiastical function had to subscribe to these controversial articles. The first said the queen had, under God, supreme authority in all spiritual matters. It was designed to weed out any Catholics or PRESBYTERIANS who found the supreme governorship unacceptable.

The second claimed the Prayer Book and Ordinal contained nothing contrary to the word of God. A subscriber undertook to use the Prayer Book in its entirety. Some Protestants found parts of the Prayer Book to be offensive. It left scope for belief in the real presence. It required the use of vestments, a practice that recalled the Catholic priesthood, and had already caused a furor in 1566. All this alienated clerical favorers of Continental forms of Protestantism, who had been accustomed to modifying their usage of the Prayer Book accordingly.

The third article required subscription to the Articles of Religion as agreed upon by the CONVOCATION of 1563 and set forth by royal authority. Those articles contained doctrines that those in favor of Continental forms of Protestantism would find suspect. This had been recognized in the 1571 statute, which required subscription only to the "true christian" articles of 1563.

The second article really hurt sensitive consciences. This went far beyond seeking out Presbyterians. It would catch many moderate PURITANS. Whitgift maintained that the queen herself had ordered him to pursue this policy. In his province it provoked a widespread reaction, ranging from the indignant clergy to their lay supporters at the county and at the PRIVY COUNCIL level. Roughly 350 ministers refused to subscribe, risking the loss of their livelihoods. Whitgift dismissed delegations who came to protest as "boys, babes, unlearned sots."

Councillors and gentry sympathized with the ministers. In February 1584 WILLIAM CECIL, Lord Burghley, and Sir FRANCIS WALSINGHAM were ill, and Robert Beale, clerk of the council, summoned Whitgift before the council to explain himself. Whitgift complained that the church was his sphere; he could not operate effectively if answerable to the laity. Orchestrated petitions from clerics and laity submerged the council, while Beale marveled at Whitgift's lordly behavior. During May 1584 a delegation of leading Kentish gentlemen visited Whitgift at Lambeth. One, Thomas Wooton, said Whitgift was the first primate to set himself against the gentry. They threatened to seek redress from the queen and council for Canterbury's 10 silenced preachers (out of a total between 80 and 100).

In the summer of 1584 Whitgift changed his position. He wanted full subscriptions to the first and third articles, but simply a promise to use the BOOK OF COMMON PRAYER. This change brought many ministers back within the fold. It seems Whitgift and the council had agreed to concentrate upon the more turbulent nonconformists. There were very few deprivations. The concerted outcry from the Protestant gentry, upon whom the Tudor government in the localities depended, and from sympathetic puritan councillors such as Burghley, Walsingham, and Sir Francis Knollys had resulted in an apparent defeat for Whitgift. In fact, the resilent primate simply changed tactics.

Whitgift turned to the court of HIGH COMMISSION. There clerics could be forced to answer questions designed to test their nonconformity on the ex officio oath. This new procedure was used against the more extreme nonconformists, the ringleaders of the recent resistance. Whitgift was successfully dividing the "puritan" movement. The more moderate puritans' subscriptions were now advertised as proof that the church was Reformed and comprehensive: anyone agitating for further reform could be accused of factious extremism.

The puritans had repeatedly called for a conference with their opponents, and they finally got their wish with the Lambeth Conference of 1584. ROBERT DUDLEY, the earl of Leicester, requested it and presided over it. Burghley and Walsingham both attended. Walter Travers and Thomas Sparke argued against the bishops Whitgift, Edwin Sandys, and Thomas Cooper. The very existence of this conference seemed a triumph for the nonconformists and demonstrated their apparent equality with the bishops in the eyes of their secular supporters, but the two-day disputation solved nothing. Travers and Sparke would not be lured into attacking the organization of the English church and concentrated upon relatively minor points. This behavior made their complaints seem non-militant but also unimportant. Whitgift's propaganda machine claimed a victory.

Throughout 1584 Whitgift had remained under attack. The complaints centered on the ex officio oath procedure in High Commission, repugnant to those accustomed to COMMON LAW procedures. Knollys talked of a PRAEMUNIRE, supported by other councillors. Burghley told Whitgift that his proceedings smacked of the Spanish Inquisition. Whitgift's opponents then switched their attack to Parliament, despite royal orders to avoid debating religion. Elizabeth, however, made clear her support for her primate and the religious settlement of 1559. She rejected "new-fangledness." Whitgift had won this battle.

Bibliography: P. Collinson, *The Elizabethan Puritan Movement*, 1967.

V. C. Sanders

Succession, First Act of (1534). Passed by the fifth session of the REFORMA-TION PARLIAMENT in March 1534, this act (25 Hen. VIII, c. 22) resolved questions about the marriage of HENRY VIII and the birth of his daughter ELIZABETH to Queen ANNE BOLEYN the previous September. This statute is significant for several reasons. It is the first parliamentary act to define the future succession of the Crown rather than merely registering a past acquisition of it as in the case, for example, of HENRY VII, the first Tudor monarch. Although Parliament was asked to draw out the consequences of principles that it was delegated rather than principles that it was able to proclaim through its own initiative, this statute nevertheless resulted in the succession's becoming for the first time a matter of the COMMON LAW, testable in its courts. Its passage is one of the important signs of the setting up of the sovereign power in the mixed body (king-in-Parliament), one of the major achievements of the early Reformation. Finally, by relying upon a statute to define his inheritance, an issue that was hitherto thought to be ordained by God, Henry would be able to prove to Christendom that his marital decisions had the support of his kingdom. The specific, immediate reason given for this act was the need to avoid controversies, as had occurred in the past, that might arise because of conflicting claims to the throne and the insecurity of the succession.

The marriage of Henry and CATHERINE OF ARAGON was declared invalid on the grounds that she had been "carnally" known by her first husband, Henry's brother, Arthur, Prince of Wales. All unions such as this, which were made within the forbidden degrees of God's laws, were said to be detested by Him. It was clarified that men were forbidden to marry their brothers' widows only when the alliances had been sealed with "carnal knowledge." *De futuro* or unconsummated alliances of widows would not prevent the validity of subsequent marriages with their husbands' brothers.

Despite no mortal's having the power to dispense with divine law, dispensations arising from the authority of men, an indirect reference to the papacy, had occasionally permitted these unions to take place. Any and all annulments of these forbidden marriages were ratified, and the issue of them, thus implicitly including the king's daughter, MARY, were pronounced illegitimate. All couples who had married within the forbidden degrees of God's laws were required to be separated by ecclesiastical sentence.

Henry's marriage to Queen Anne was recognized as "true, sincere, and perfect ever hereafter," and her issue were identified as the king's lawful children and given the right to inherit "according to the course of inheritance and laws of this realm." In order of precedence, the succession was to be settled upon his sons by Anne and their heirs; next, to his sons by future wives and their heirs; then to Elizabeth and his other daughters by Anne and their heirs; and fourth to his daughters by future wives and their heirs. For lack of such issue, the "right" heirs of the king were to inherit. The statute further dealt with problems that would arise if the king died leaving only minor children. If his male issue were under eighteen or his female issue unmarried or under the age of sixteen at his death, their guardian was to be their natural mother and a council, as had been designated by Henry.

Writing, printing, or the committing of exterior deeds that placed the king in peril, prejudiced his marriage to Queen Anne, endangered his heirs, or interfered with their right to succeed were declared acts of high TREASON. The use of words only in committing these acts constituted the lesser crime of misprision of treason. All of the above offenders were to be denied the right to SANCTUARY, and a savings clause was included for people who had interest in the lands forfeited by ATTAINDERS under this statute.

The king's subjects were to be required to swear to uphold this statute, and any who refused were also to be charged with misprision of treason. Since the exact wording of this oath was not specified, a loophole existed whereby individuals could claim that the statements that they were subsequently asked to uphold, such as renouncing the powers of foreign authority, presumably an allusion to the pope, exceeded the statute's requirements. When a few English people did subsequently refuse to take the oath, another statute (26 Hen. VIII, c. 2) clarified Parliament's position by declaring that the king's subjects were not to be faithful or obedient to any foreign power or "potentate."

Although it did not name her, one of the aims of this statute was to confirm the illegitimacy of Mary and the concurrent transference of her title, princess of Wales, to Elizabeth, who actually continued as the royal heir only until the passage of the second succession statute (28 Hen. VIII, c. 7), which pronounced her illegitimate, her mother having been executed on 19 May, two days after the annulment of her marriage to Henry. Ultimately, of course, the third succession statute (35 Hen. VIII, c. 1) restored to the succession both of Henry's daughters, who nevertheless retained their illegitimate status.

Bibliography: Mortimer Levine, *Tudor Dynastic Problems, 1460-1571*, 1973.

Retha Warnicke

Succession, Second Act of (1536). On 17 May 1536, two days before the execution of Queen ANNE BOLEYN, THOMAS CRANMER, archbishop of Canterbury, declared her marriage to HENRY VIII annulled and thus demoted her daughter ELIZABETH to illegitimate status. These actions necessitated a second succession statute (28 Hen. VIII, c. 7) to settle the royal inheritance. Passed in June 1536 by the Parliament called to deal with Anne's fall, she was said, in the preamble, to have confessed to Cranmer about an impediment to the marriage and to have committed treason.

Although this act repealed the first succession statute (25 Hen. VIII, c. 22), Parliament discharged from its penalties only the offenders who had violated the earlier statute since the beginning of this session. Anne and her five accomplices, George, Lord Rochford, Henry Norris, Sir Francis Weston, Mark Smeaton, and William Brereton, who had earlier been executed for treasonable acts, were attainted and their goods were forfeited. A savings clause was included for all people who had interest in the lands forfeited by any attainders under this statute.

The status of the king's three marriages was further clarified. Queen JANE SEYMOUR was recognized as his legal wife. His unions with CATHERINE OF ARAGON, the widow of his brother, and Anne were declared invalid, and the issue of those alliances were pronounced illegitimate and "utterly foreclosed" from the succession. His heirs were to be his sons by his third queen, Jane, and their heirs, then the sons of future wives and their heirs, next the daughters and their heirs of Jane and his future wives. As for the remainder of his heirs, to avoid political strife the king was given authorization to name other heirs in his letters patent or in his last will; all so designated were to be authorized fully to succeed.

They were not identified in the statute for fear that they would be tempted to lead a rebellion against the king and his lineage. Henry was also empowered to list those who would govern in the event he died while his heirs were minors. If at his death his male issue were under eighteen or his daughters unmarried or under sixteen, their natural mother and a council or a council alone, the members of which was to be named in his will, were to serve as their regents.

Like its predecessor, this statute defined treasonable acts, including now as high treason all words, as well as writing, imprinting, or the committing of any exterior act or deed that, among others, imperiled the king or his heirs, prejudiced the new marriage or the new succession, called the former marriages lawful or the issue from the same legitimate, or slandered the judgments that had invalidated the unions. All such offenders were to be denied the right of sanctuary.

An oath to uphold the statute, which recognized the king as supreme head, was detailed and listed all persons, including those who held lands or offices of the king, required to take the oath. Those who refused were to be subject to the penalties of high TREASON, also without the right of SANCTUARY.

Finally, all statutes to the "derogation" of this act were declared void. Like the first succession statute, it was to have short duration, for in the THIRD SUCCESSION STATUTE (35 Hen. VIII, c. 1) his daughters, although retaining their illegitimate status, were restored to the succession.

Bibliography: Mortimer Levine, *Tudor Dynastic Problems, 1460-1571*, 1973.

Retha Warnicke

Succession, Third Act of (1544). In 1544 as HENRY VIII was preparing to invade France, he became concerned about the succession in the event he was to be killed in battle, since Queen CATHERINE PARR and he had no children, and his heir, EDWARD, son of Queen JANE SEYMOUR, was still a minor child with no issue of his own. The king's intentions regarding his heirs were enacted in the Third Act of Succession (35 Hen. VIII, c. 1) by his eighth Parliament.

The succession was set out as follows: if Edward died without heirs, the Crown should descend to the king's daughter Mary and her lawful heirs and then to his daughter Elizabeth and her lawful heirs. By letters patent or his will, Henry was further empowered to set conditions by which his daughters could inherit, and if MARY breached those conditions, then ELIZABETH was to succeed. If she was already dead or also violated the conditions, then the persons named by the king in his will or in his letters patent would succeed. If Henry should decide not to establish any such limitations, his daughters would be able to rule absolutely. He thus chose to restore them to the succession, but not to official legitimate status, an extraordinary action, but it is also true that the unhindered CANON LAW did customarily grant the privilege of legitimacy to children who had been born to couples of annulled marriages but who believed that they had entered into and had a valid union at the time of childbirth. Left unmentioned here were the names of the king's first two wives and the reasons his alliances with them had been invalidated.

The statute, as indicated, gave Henry full authority to designate heirs beyond his children and their issue either in his last will or in his letters patent. This concession was significant for it was a power that he did not possess by virtue of his PREROGATIVE as king. Shortly before his death, he did further limit the succession in his will, establishing the Suffolk line, the descendants of Mary his younger sister, as his heirs and completely ignoring the Stuart line, the descendants of Margaret his elder sister. The terms of his will were effectively ignored in 1603 when James I, the great-grandson of Margaret, became monarch.

This succession statute included an oath, that superseded the oaths authorized by the ROYAL SUPREMACY statutes (28 Hen. VIII, c. 7 and 28 Hen. VIII, c. 10) and that, like that of the second succession statute (28 Hen. VIII, c. 7), recognized the king as supreme head. Henceforth only the oath given here would be required and of the following people: all who held lands and offices of the king, all spiritual persons, all with degrees from the universities, and any others at his pleasure. Anyone who refused to take the oath was to be charged with high TREASON. Parliament also declared it an act of high treason, without the right of sanctuary, to use words, writing, imprinting, or any exterior deed or act to interfere with this statute, to try to obtain its repeal, or to attempt to disinherit any of the royal heirs. As usual, a general savings clause was included for all people who had interest in the lands forfeited by ATTAINDERS under this statute.

Bibliography: Mortimer Levine, *Tudor Dynastic Problems, 1460-1571*, 1973.

Retha Warnicke

Surveyor of the King's Prerogative. The office of Surveyor of the King's Prerogative was created on 19 August 1508 by HENRY VII. Edward Belknap, a trusted royal minister, was the first and only person appointed to the position. The office was suspended by HENRY VIII in 1509 and never reinstated.

Henry VII was increasingly anxious to assert and to extend the royal prerogative during the last years of his reign. He instituted the office of Surveyor (supervisor) of the King's Prerogative to help in that effort. It was intended to be a permanent position. The privy seal appointment of 1508 authorized the surveyor Edward Belknap to exercise broad prerogative authority in the following matters: 1) to make inquiry concerning crimes; 2) to seize property belonging to those apprehended for violating the king's prerogative; 3) to inquire about and seize property of widows in wardship to the king who married without licence; 4) to lease or dispose of seize property; 5) to collect the profits from the lands of outlawed persons; 6) to seize and sell goods and chattels of persons summoned by the sheriff for felonies, murder, or outlawry; and 7) to assess and levy fines for outlawries and for widows marrying without licence.

County surveyors were appointed to assist Belknap and he was also empowered to call upon sheriffs to facilitate the holdings of inquiries and inquisitions and upon justices of the peace to assist investigations. Revenues generated by the Surveyor were paid directly to the king or the king's privy chamber rather than the exchequer. The Surveyor's fee was one ninth of all profits produced by his office and the county surveyors took one tenth of the remainder. The Surveyor operated under bond.

Henry VII died seven months after creating the office of Surveyor of the Royal Prerogative causing a suspension of operations. The new office had quickly become unpopular. Some of the county surveyors appear to have been overly zealous in finding violators in an effort to increase their own fees. Most complaints stemmed from the fact that the new office was simply more efficient in enforcing the king's prerogative and many people, including the personnel of the common law courts, did not like it. As soon as he assumed the Crown, Henry VIII dismissed the county surveyors. But he did not immediately abolish the office. In 1510 he pardoned Belknap and the deputy surveyors for their actions during the operation of the Surveyorship but it was not until 16 May 1513 that he officially released Belknap from the office. Meanwhile the functions of the surveyor had been taken over by other offices in the king's chamber.

Bibliography: W. C. Richardson, *Tudor Chamber Administration*, 1952.

John V. Crangle

T

Taxation and Revenue. In the sixteenth century taxes were raised by rates both for local government and for ecclesiastical needs, but the dominant purpose was for central government. The theory, which was rarely questioned, held that it was the accepted duty of the subject to provide support in time of necessity. Subjects, however, frequently claimed to be willing but unable to pay extraordinary taxes and hoped that the monarch might live on the Crown's recurrent resources. These "ordinary" revenues varied enormously in their value. They included the casual profits of courts, fines, and fees, which were small alongside the profits from Crown estates, which were more or less permanently in royal hands. Also found in this category were lands forfeited for treason, which included some of the biggest holdings, and the lands that came from the DISSOLUTION OF THE MONASTERIES. Had they all been retained, they might have yielded up to £135,000 a year, but they were rapidly and constantly diminished by grants and sales to the long-term royal loss. There were also revenues that came from feudal dues such as escheat and extent or by WARDSHIP (the monarch's right to hold the lands of tenants in chief while the heir was a minor and to dispose of his/her marriage) and livery (a small tax paid by all those who held from the Crown on their accession to the land). The most profitable of these was wardship, which brought in a comfortable return, averaging £14,677 a year over the sixteenth century. A new source of income after the Reformation that brought in at least a comfortable £15,000 a year was the clerical dues of FIRST FRUITS AND TENTHS.

The next important source of ordinary revenue, which was, however, granted by the Parliament, was the customs. Since the reign of Edward IV these were usually granted at the first Parliament of a reign for the monarch's life. Permission to export was governed by regulation; various acts prohibited exports of certain goods such as oxen, livestock generally, and their by-products such as hides and woolfells. Brass, copper, beer, and herring were restricted, and in a famine all export of grain might be suspended at a moment's notice. Customs duties included the general inward customs charge of tonnage and poundage. Tonnage was a fixed charge levied on wine per tun, and poundage was a blanket 12 pence in the pound of assessed value (not actual sale value) of all goods coming into the realm. Customs on goods exported were primarily levied on wool and wool products at a normal rate of so many cloths (depending on the type) per sack of wool but also on tin, through the stannaries. Revenue from customs had been declining in the first half of the sixteenth century, but under MARY, Lord Treasurer William Paulet, 1st marquess of Winchester, introduced reforms that restored the customs to a major source of regular royal income. These included important changes in the administrative practices for collecting the customs, whether they were managed directly or by farming. The Book of Rates, which set the sums to be collected on each item, was also massively revamped in May 1558. While it may have been an inducement to smuggling, raising the duty levied upon a broadcloth from 14d to 6s-8d for Englishmen and to 14s-6d for strangers significantly increased royal revenues.

Customs on cloth from London alone in the early years of Elizabeth's reign brought in about £30,000 a year gross, and total receipts in an ordinary year were £75,000. Customs were not simple to collect, a situation that encouraged governments to settle for a fixed return by "farming" their collection to private individuals. Returns, moreover, fluctuated wildly as an embargo, open warfare, drought, or famine could disastrously affect trade.

A royal privilege that must be considered indirectly as a revenue item is purveyance. This privilege had such potential for abuse that it was one of the great grievances frequently aired in Parliament. Purveyance gave the Crown the right to make compulsory purchases at predetermined rates, in theory those current in the nearest markets as determined by the clerk of the market. Any purchases by the Crown, whether for the HOUSEHOLD or for the needs of the ARMY or NAVY, could be met by purveyance. Every leading minister seems to have attempted to provide a structure that would prevent abuses, but no one succeeded. Bills were proposed, and statutes were passed to little effect. EDWARD SEYMOUR, the duke of Somerset, unsuccessfully sought to replace purveyance by a general tax; the idea reappeared in 1581 and again early in JAMES VI and I's reign. In ELIZABETH's reign compositions in kind at fixed low prices were negotiated with most of the shires. Undertakers, often leading JUSTICES OF THE PEACE, levied a tax known as the composition for the amount of goods and services due from the county. By the end of the period purveyance may have been worth £37,000 a year to the Crown.

In time of crisis such as the 1540s and 1550s the Crown borrowed both on international markets, principally Antwerp, and from the London corporation and livery companies. Such short-term borrowing was only a stopgap and if protracted involved the Crown in serious difficulties. Loans, however, were frequently raised locally in anticipation of taxes to bridge the gap between grant of a subsidy and its collection. Here commissioners dealt with individuals or small groups who agreed to advance a sum, which was entered in an indenture. The money was paid to commissioners or directly to Exchequer, and a bill obligatory or tally from Exchequer recorded the payment. From 1544 to 1552 the government also engaged in a massive debasement of the COINAGE, which brought short-term profits to bridge the gap in government finances. Usually, however, such gaps resulted in appeals for extraordinary assistance to the royal subjects.

This assistance could come only through Parliament. Most Parliaments seem to have granted a tax at the beginning of a reign for the maintenance of the royal estate. Whether this tax was seen as distinct from normal taxes, which were granted in response to the needs of defense or "war finance," is doubtful. Some historians have proposed that there is a shift in the sixteenth century to a more general concept of continuing support for the central government, whose needs even in times of peace could no longer be met from ordinary revenue. Besides, the funds were not kept in watertight compartments anyway, and the normal expenses of the kingdom were met from extraordinary revenue; but a Parliament that did not audit accounts could not know this fact.

The long-established parliamentary grant was the fifteenth and tenth, which was theoretically a tax on moveable property. Its collection had ossified so that each fifteenth and tenth, in practice a fixed charge on a vill, was guaranteed to raise about £29,500 on the laity and £11,000-12,000 on the clergy. To raise larger sums, two, three, or more fifteenths and tenths had to be granted at once, and their collection was often spread over a number of years. Poll taxes were unpopular so the Tudor monarchs were therefore also looking for new forms of tax. They found the subsidy an attractive proposition. This tax offered a graded tax based on land, goods, fees, or wages, theoretically reassessed individual by individual on each occasion and varying in the percentage asked for. Subsidies were mixed with the older taxes from HENRY VIII's reign onward. A subsidy levied on the wealthy at the rate of 2s in the pound or 10% in one year might raise up to £100,000. As the century wore on, however, assessments for the subsidy became less and less realistic so that Parliament had to grant several subsidies at once to raise the sums needed.

Other methods of raising extraordinary revenue, which did not depend on Parliament, were tried from time to time. Despite an act of Parliament against them passed in Richard III's reign, HENRY VIII attempted benevolences, forced loans, and aids, particularly in the early 1520s. A benevolence was theoretically a grant freely provided by the donor at his discretion when he was approached by an itinerant commissioner armed with a letter under the privy seal that alleged an urgent necessity. When the king proposed to lead an army in person as in 1496 and 1522, a benevolence was plausible and accepted. Forced loans, in contrast, were more frequently resisted, although they carried the prospect of repayment. The loan collected in 1522-1523 produced about £200,000 and was finally canceled by act of Parliament in 1529.

In 1525 the AMICABLE GRANT aroused such opposition that it was abandoned. Although THOMAS WOLSEY took the blame, HENRY VIII almost certainly knew and approved it. Much later Henry tried a variety of different devices, a "benevolent" loan, "devotion money," and a "contribution." The most notorious was probably the "free gift" in lieu of service in 1545. Payment was encouraged by the spectacle of one London notable departing for personal service in Scotland because he had refused to contribute.

The protector Somerset attempted a range of new taxes, including a poll tax on sheep, which he hoped might replace some of the older taxes. There was so much resistance that JOHN DUDLEY, duke of Northumberland, reverted to established practices, and neither MARY nor ELIZABETH sought to introduce new taxes but perferred to tighten the screws on revenue that was already well established.

It is very difficult, if not impossible, accurately to calculate the monarch's gross or net income at any point in the sixteenth century. Figures of what was paid into the central treasuries represent only a part of the royal income. For example, the Merchants of the STAPLE paid money directly for the CALAIS garrison. Any figures are thus only a rough approximation and probably an underestimate. Bearing this fact in mind, it has been suggested that Henry VII raised only £280,000 from direct taxation of laity and £160,000 from clerical taxation. His total revenues in the last years of his reign may have averaged £113,000 at most, including £42,000 from landed revenue. Henry VIII's ordinary revenues in 1529 were thought to be £150,000, and in his last years total income reached £400,000 in one year. This figure, however, included money raised by debasement and land sales, which were asset dispersals and could not be continued indefinitely. The effects were felt in the reigns of EDWARD VI and Mary, although the government under Edward raised an average of at least £270,000 a year for war purposes. At the beginning of Elizabeth's reign a near trebling of customs receipts, the recovery of clerical FIRST FRUITS AND TENTHS, and some alienated land combined with parliamentary taxation to give her an income of over £250,000 a year, sometimes double that amount. This level does not seem to have been always maintained in the middle years of her reign, but by the wars at the end of the reign, her income was increased to over £600,000.

Bibliography: J. D. Alsop, "The Theory and Practice of Tudor Taxation," *English Historical Review* 97 (1982): 1-30; F. C. Dietz, *English Government Finance 1485-1641*, 2nd ed., 1964; G. R. Elton, "Taxation for War and Peace in Early Tudor England," in *War and Economic Development*, ed. J. M. Winter, 1975; G. L. Harriss "Aids, Loans, and Benevolences," *Historical Journal* 6 (1963): 1-19; G. L. Harriss, "Thomas Cromwell's 'New Principle of Taxation,'" *English Historical Review* 93 (1978): 721-38; R. S. Schofield, "Tudor Subsidy Assessments," in *Law and Government under the Tudors*, ed. C. Cross, D. M. Loades and J.J. Scarisbrick, 1989; B. P. Wolffe, *The Crown Lands 1461-1536*, 1970.

Sybil Jack

Ten Articles of Religion (1536). The first formulary of faith resulting from the English Reformation, the Ten Articles were written in response to the growing religious divisions within the kingdom and the efforts to negotiate an alliance with the German Lutheran princes. The articles, which are entitled "Articles Devised by the Kinges Highness Majestie to Stablyshe Christen Quietnes and Unitie Amonge Us and to Avyoyde Contentious Opinions" in the edition originally printed by Thomas Berthelet in 1536, were the product of discussions by a committee of bishops under THOMAS CRANMER's presidency, a committee that HENRY VIII had appointed in February 1536 to draw up articles of religion. Although Henry VIII may have made some corrections in the final draft, it is unlikely that he wrote them, as is claimed in the title and in one of Henry's letters. The historian John Strype believed that Cranmer played a major role in drafting them, but Jasper Ridley, a modern biographer of Cranmer, believes they were probably written by Edward Foxe, the bishop of Hereford. Foxe, who was involved in the negotiations with the Lutherans, presented "a book of faith and articles" on the king's behalf to the southern CONVOCATION in July 1536.

The articles were clearly influenced by the discussions with the Lutherans in the early months of 1536. Throughout the negotiations the Lutheran princes had insisted on doctrinal unity before agreeing to a political alliance. Since Henry VIII would not accept the Augsburg Confession, the Wittenberg Articles of 1536 were devised. Although based on the Augsburg Confession and its Apology, the articles made some minor concessions with the hope of making them more acceptable to the English. Although there are important similarities between the Wittenberg Articles and the Ten Articles and the latter have been interpreted as an effort to conciliate the Lutherans, the differences are more significant.

The articles were characterized by a degree of ambiguity on controversial questions. The first article identified the Bible and the three ecumenical creeds as standards of faith. Baptism, in the second article, was defined in the orthodox sense in opposition to Anabaptist teachings. The third article accepted penance as a Sacrament and defined it in the traditional Catholic sense. The fourth article, which dealt with the eucharist in a way that could be understood in a Lutheran sense but that Catholics could also interpret as teaching a doctrine of justification. Although it maintained that the sole cause of our salvation was "only the mercy and grace" of God in Jesus Christ, it also stated that justification was attained "by contrition and faith joined with charity" and stressed the necessity of "good works of charity and obedience" after justification. The next four articles dealt with the use of images and honoring of saints as well as praying to saints and other rites and ceremonies. In each case the practice was upheld, but abuses were condemned. The final article declared that praying for the dead was a laudable practice, but it refused to define the place where they were or the pains they were suffering because it maintained these things were "uncertain by Scripture." Possibly the greatest ambiguity was in what was not said. Although three of the seven medieval Sacraments, baptism, penance, and the eucharist, were discussed and defined as Sacraments, the other four, matrimony, confirmation, orders, and extreme unction, were ignored.

The articles were adopted by convocation in July 1536 and signed by THOMAS CROMWELL, the bishops, forty abbots, and fifty members of the lower house of Convocation. Although the Royal Injunctions of 1536 ordered that the clergy declare them to those under their cure, preaching except by bishops or in their presence was forbidden by the king until Michaelmas. When preaching was resumed, clergy were instructed simply to read the articles and not to interpret them. The articles were superseded by the publication in 1537 of a second formulary of faith, the BISHOPS' BOOK, which, unlike the Ten Articles, was never officially authorized by the king.

Bibliography: Jasper Ridley, *Thomas Cranmer*, 1962; E. G. Rupp, *Studies in the Making of the English Protestant Tradition*, 1947.

Rudolph W. Heinze

Thirty-Nine Articles (1563). The doctrinal formulary of the Church of England promulgated during the ELIZABETHAN SETTLEMENT OF RELIGION of 1559.

The Thirty-nine Articles, or the Articles of Religion, were approved by CONVOCATION in their Latin form in 1563. In essence, they represented an advanced stage of an ongoing process of definition that had begun in the late Henrician era and that had temporarily culminated in the FORTY-TWO ARTICLES of 1553. It was decided that the latter articles should undergo revision and then be presented as the ultimate religious statement of the Elizabethan church. Following further discussion and amendment in 1571 (at which time the English version appeared), they have remained the doctrinal foundation of the ANGLICAN church down to the present day.

The doctrinal posture of the English church presented no small problem to the episcopacy during the early years of ELIZABETH's reign. The Forty-two Articles had been put forth too late in EDWARD VI's reign to have enjoyed enduring acceptance, and the Marian program that followed hard on its heels implied a full return to Catholic standards—though no official, distinct confession of faith was issued during those years. The Elizabethan divines, among whom the returned MARIAN EXILES represented a vociferous minority, thus approached the business of further definition with a certain degree of enthusiasm and relish and perhaps mistakenly assumed that a Continental-style Protestant framework could be imposed with relative ease. The expectations of the zealous wing were disappointed considerably by the outcome, which finalized the policy of moderation and comprehension pursued by THOMAS CRANMER, archbishop of Canterbury, and his circle down to 1553. The wishes of the monarch must also have been crucial in this regard, as well as the personality and persuasions of

MATTHEW PARKER, who had been appointed archbishop of Canterbury and who had approved eleven Articles as a temporary expedient.

The initial episcopal revision of the Edwardian articles also contained forty-two articles, though not corresponding exactly to the original formulary. Only sixteen of the entries of 1553 were left untouched. In convocation, three articles dealing with what were perceived to be radical errors were eliminated. The formulators were careful not to alienate any parties or interests that could be accommodated by a statement built upon concord and consensus. At that point, the Thirty-nine Articles were adhered to by a majority in the Canterbury convocation. By the time the authorized Latin version actually came forth in early 1564, Article 20 (dealing with the question of the church's authority) had been altered, and Article 29 (regarding the presence of evildoers at communion) had been dropped entirely. These changes were in all likelihood instituted by Elizabeth herself in keeping with her policy of conservatism. Though the Council of Trent had now concluded its proceedings, the papal missive that ended hopes of immediate conciliation was not forthcoming until 1570.

Thus, for a relatively long interval, the English church adhered to only thirty-eight authoritative articles. When convocation took a second look at the formulary in 1571, all thirty-nine were approved, including Article 29 on the Sacrament. Elizabeth's willingness to reinstate what she had evidently forbidden in 1563 is perhaps something of a puzzle, though it may be well explained with reference to the papal bull of excommunication (see REGNANS IN EXCELSIS). In any event, the articles were given final approval by Parliament and convocation in 1571.

Analyzing the tenor of the articles has proven prickly if not impossible. The temptation for parties to claim them as being of one particular stripe or another for propaganda purposes has, generally speaking, not been successfully resisted. One can scarcely avoid judging them as Protestant in the first instance, because of their strong commitment to the authority of the Scriptures. At the same time, hermeneutical and semantic skills might conceivably be employed to render them sufficiently close to medieval doctrines to accommodate moderate Anglo-Catholics. This in itself would be rather ironic, since the founders of the Anglican church were convinced that they had departed from a church in error and schism—one that had ceased to handle the Sacraments and preach the word of God in a proper fashion.

As to which brand of Protestantism is most clearly evinced in the articles, one must concede that the extremism that was current in high circles during the last half of Edward's reign is most certainly curtailed (hence the dissatisfaction of the PURITANS within the English church). This fact would suggest a turning away from Zwinglianism together with an avoidance of high CALVINISM. The two critical articles in this respect concern the nature of the presence in the Sacrament and the meaning of predestination. Both give evidence of the spirit of compromise then afoot. Article 28 thus did not stop with a rejection of transubstantiation as unscriptural but also stressed the reception of Christ's body in a spiritual sense alone. The tone was thus not exclusively favorable to any one Continental Reformational tradition, though with respect to the Swiss, it was closer to John Calvin than to Huldreich Zwingli and perhaps nearer to the spirit of Philip Melancthon and Martin Bucer than to either. It was certainly not a Lutheran description, though again, Anglo-Catholics might take considerable comfort from its moderation. At the same time, Article 17 on predestination cannot be said to have favored the full Calvinist interpretation and was more at home with a Lutheran approach in its predestination to life assertion. Certainly the influence of early Lutheran confessional thought was never completely eradicated in the English world. In addition to Continental influences, one could also argue for native evangelical input from LOLLARDY and the example of Cranmer's dexterous use of compromise continuing to influence decisions.

The articles also made a significant statement regarding the role of the monarchy in the governing of the realm. Although it is conceded that the sovereign should have the right to rule in both the civil and ecclesiastical spheres, it is declared in Article 37 that administering the Sacraments and the word of God do not fall within the sovereign's purview. Thus, a distinction was carefully drawn between the queen's general right to supremacy in the ecclesiastical realm and the authority to carry out specific religious and spiritual tasks. Although little attention seems to have been given to developing an adequate doctrine of the church, Article 34 recognized the legitimacy of ceremonial and traditional variations in different settings. Such modifications were tied exclusively to the operation of the national church, thus leaving no room for nonconformists.

The Thirty-nine Articles can best be seen as a reflection of issues and struggles that the English church faced at this crucial juncture in its development in the sixteenth century and, as such, cannot be appreciated apart from an awareness of the original context in which they were born—at the transition point between the medieval and the modern era. Theologically, the primary focus of the English Reformers was Christological, as they sought to emphasize the mediatorial work and position of Christ in opposition to what were seen to be medieval distortions of the primitive Christian tradition. The greatest compromise may have taken place between the royal faction and the Protestant extremists, the latter apparently having no choice but to acquiesce for the moment and hope for better things in the future should the formulary run aground and need replacing—as it might well have appeared at the moment. At the same time, it is easy to exaggerate the strength of the opposition to the articles. Englishmen of most persuasions could boast of the articles as thoroughly biblical without being contentious—a peculiarly English achievement and not a mean one at that, given the stormy realities of the age of confessionalism throughout much of Europe. In short, this was a compromise, a serious attempt to separate essentials from things indifferent, and one that an Erasmus could have devised and approved while his Continental colleagues concentrated upon cudgeling one another with exactitudes and polemics.

Bibliography: E. J. Bicknell, *A Theological Introduction to the Thirty-nine Articles of the Church of England*, rev. H. J. Carpenter, 1955; William P. Haugaard, *Elizabeth and the English Reformation: The Struggle for a Stable Settlement of Religion*, 1968; Oliver O'Donovan, *On the Thirty-Nine Articles: A Conversation with Tudor Christianity*, 1986.

Andrew Penny

Throckmorton Plot (1583). One of the last of the plots to free MARY, QUEEN OF SCOTS and murder ELIZABETH, this conspiracy caused a furor that led directly to the creation of the BOND OF ASSOCIATION. After being educated at Oxford, Francis Throckmorton and his brother Thomas, both Catholic nephews of Sir Nicholas Throckmorton, left England for a prolonged tour of the Continent, where they met exiled English Catholics and learned of plots to restore Catholicism to England. In Paris Francis became involved in a plot with the duc of Guise, financed by Pope Gregory XIII and Philip II for the invasion of England and the overthrow of Elizabeth. Mary Stuart's Paris agent, Thomas Morgan, had put Throckmorton into touch with Bernadino de Mendoza, the Spanish ambassador in London. In 1583 Throckmorton returned to London and took a house, which was the center of communication among Morgan in Paris, Mendoza, and Mary Stuart, with whom Throckmorton corresponded directly. The same year Sir FRANCIS WALSINGHAM intercepted some of Mary Stuart's secret correspondence and learned that Throckmorton was a chief agent for Mary. For six months Walsingham's spies followed Throckmorton; he was eventually arrested in November 1583. When two gentlemen came to arrest him, he rushed upstairs and destroyed a letter to Mary Stuart as he went; he also managed to convey by a maidservant a casket of dangerous documents to the Spanish ambassador before his arrest. What was found in his house was still damning, however—a list of Catholic nobles and gentlemen willing to support the "Enterprise of England" and safe places when foreign armies could land.

Time on the rack broke the captured Throckmorton's endurance, and he disclosed everything to Elizabeth's council. Some of the conspirators, including his brother Thomas, fled when news of Francis's arrest broke; others were arrested and placed in the Tower. Francis Throckmorton was tried at Guildhall on 21 May 1584 and found guilty, condemned to death, and forced to repeat his confession. He was executed at Tyburn 10 July.

The Spanish ambassador, Mendoza, had been so deeply involved in the Throckmorton conspiracy that his participation could not be overlooked. In January 1584 the council summoned him and set forth his misdeeds. Though Mendoza denied any wrongdoing, he was given his passport and told to leave England within fifteen days. As the last resident Spanish ambassador of Elizabeth's reign, he declared as he took his leave that as he had failed to satisfy Elizabeth as a minister of peace, he would see what she thought of him as a minister of war. Elizabeth's government went to the trouble of publishing an account of the Throckmorton conspiracy and Mendoza's role in it to explain his expulsion (*A Discoverie of the Treasons Practiced and Attempted against the Queene's Majestie and the Realme by Francis Throckmorton*, 1584).

Throckmorton's conspiracy alarmed the English. It was revealed soon after that a young Warwickshire Catholic gentleman had been arrested for planning to assassinate Elizabeth, and only a few months later on 30 June 1584 William of Orange was murdered. The fear caused by the Throckmorton plot and what would happen if Elizabeth were killed led directly to the council's issuing the Bond of Association.

Bibliography: A. L. Rowse, *Ralegh and the Throckmortons*, 1962.

Carole Levin

Trading Companies of the Tudor period can be divided into two categories, the regulated companies and the joint-stock companies. After paying an entrance fee, a merchant belonging to a regulated company carried on trade as he normally would have, within certain guidelines established by the company. The main advantage was that it offered the protection of belonging to a large corporate body. With a joint-stock company members purchased shares in the company's ventures and left the trade to be handled by the company's directors and merchants. This type of enterprise allowed a large number of people to pool their resources in more risky enterprises. In addition, since business was conducted by the company's representatives, membership was not limited to merchants, as was the case with the regulated companies.

The company of MERCHANT AVENTURERS of England was one of the greatest regulated companies of the Tudor era. It evolved from an earlier association of London cloth merchants named the Fraternity of St. Thomas à Becket. Though the company first received official recognition in 1486, a royal charter was not granted until 1505. This charter gave the company the exclusive privilege of exporting woolen goods from England. It also set the cost of membership in the company at the low price of ten marks and thus allowed any merchant to join. The company's operations were first centered in Antwerp, where it received special privileges. The vicissitudes of the revolt of the Netherlands and the animosity of the Hanseatic League caused it to relocate several times.

The Russia (or Muscovy) Company was the first of the new joint-stock enterprises. First organized in 1553 under the name Merchant Adventurers for the Discovery of Lands, Countries, Isles, and Places Unknown, its intended purpose was to find a northeast passage to the Orient. The company's first expedition set sail the same year it was organized and succeeded in making contact with Russia later that year. With the return of the survivors of the expedition the company was granted a charter by MARY and Philip in 1555 for an exclusive trade with Russia (EDWARD VI had died in 1553 before letters patent could be issued). Besides being looked upon as a new market for the English cloth trade, Russia was also viewed as a possible path to Persia, and between 1558 and 1580 the company sent seven expeditions to Turkey and Persia with varying success. However, the establishment of the Levant Company in 1581 ended the profitability of such ventures. In addition, Russia became a major source of cordage for the growing English merchant fleet. However, trade with Russia was never extremely profitable. During the first thirty years of trade with Russia, the company had to contend with the whims of Ivan the Terrible, while the last years of the sixteenth century witnessed a decline in the position of the company due to the encroachments of Dutch merchants.

The Eastland Company was granted a charter in 1579 for an exclusive trade with the Baltic countries, except for Russia. The charter was granted, at least in part, because the company was seen as an opponent to the Hanseatic League. However, English merchants had been trading in the Baltic for years, and the sudden closing of these markets to all but the privileged members of this regulated company created problems. The company carried on a trade of manufactured goods for raw materials with varying success.

The Levant (or Turkey) Company was chartered as a joint-stock company in 1581 with an exclusive trade with Turkey. A new charter was issued in 1593, when it merged with the Venice Company and expanded the company's area of operation to include the Venetian Republic and the overland route to India. Two years later the company changed its status to a regulated company. Though there were a number of dangers involved in this trade including the Barbary corsairs and the hostility of the Venetians and, in the last quarter of Elizabeth's reign, the Spanish, the company managed to conduct a profitable trade exporting English linens and woolens and importing spices, fruits, and other products.

The Morocco (or Barbary) Company, another regulated company, was chartered in 1585. Unfortunately, the company was commercially unsuccessful, and it failed within a few years of its founding.

The Guinea (or Africa) Company was granted a charter as a regulated company in 1588 for the exclusive trade to the areas around the Senegal and Gambia rivers. The company carried on a successful trade with the local natives, exchanging cloth and trinkets for Guinea gold. However, the company faced the opposition of the Portuguese, who considered Guinea to be within their sphere of influence. In addition, English merchants who were not members of the company were resistant to the company's exclusive claims.

The East India Company was formed in 1599 because after the Dutch raised the price of pepper and also because the Levant Company had failed to establish an overland trade with India due to the almost continual wars between Turkey and Persia. The company met almost immediate opposition from the Portuguese and Dutch, but it succeeded in the next century in becoming the most successful of the joint-stock companies.

Bibliography: E. Lipson, *The Economic History of England*, Vol. 2: *The Age of Mercantilism*, 6th ed., 1956, reprint 1961.

Brian Christian

Treason, Law of. The fundamental law of treason before the Tudor era, the 1352 statute, made it high treason to compass the death of the king, his queen, or his heir; to rape the king's consort, eldest daughter, or his eldest son's bride; to levy war against the king within the realm or support his enemies; to counterfeit the great seal, the privy seal, or royal coin; and to murder certain royal officials. Between 1352 and 1485 judicial interpretation or "constructive treason" made treason by words possible. The Tudors enacted almost seventy new statutes, though the actual scope of treason law expanded less than this number suggests. They sought to define treason more clearly by codifying COMMON LAW precedent and to handle problems related to the royal SUCCESSION, the ROYAL SUPREMACY, the increase of treason by words in print, and other matters. The Crown could also proceed against traitors by a parliamentary act of ATTAINDER, though ordinarily this supplemented a judicial conviction. Martial law allowed summary trial and execution during a rebellion, though this law was not always employed.

The early Henrician period brought new legislation, judicial construction, and procedural change, but the most important time for expanding the scope of treason law was the meeting of the REFORMATION PARLIAMENT, 1529-1536. The first SUCCESSION ACT in 1534 made it treason to slander HENRY VIII's marriage to ANNE BOLEYN in print, while spoken words were to be misprision of treason, a relatively new and lesser offense. The general treason act of 1534 updated the 1352 statute to protect the king, queen, and heir, made it treason to speak against the Royal Supremacy or withhold the king's castles, ships, and ordnance, and expanded forfeiture to include all of a traitor's goods. The second SUCCESSION ACT made spoken words against Henry's marriage to JANE SEYMOUR treason, as well as refusal to be examined under oath about it. In 1536 the act against the pope's authority made it treason to refuse the oath of supremacy, and another proscribed forging the king's sign manual, signet, and privy seal. While this period is regarded as HENRY VIII's most severe, the years 1536-1547 produced treason legislation less easily justified by the standards of the day, including the PROCLAMATIONS act and laws on royal marriages and the succession. EDWARD SEYMOUR, the protector Somerset, repealed all Henrician treason legislation in 1547 except that denial of the Royal Supremacy remained treason, but in 1552 JOHN DUDLEY, duke of Northumberland, practically restored the 1534 statute. MARY returned to the 1352 statute, though not before convicting supporters of LADY JANE GREY, and after WYATT'S REBELLION the Parliament of 1554-1555 passed acts to punish speech against Mary's marriage and the Catholic restoration and to protect Prince Philip. With Elizabeth treason legislation proliferated, much of it related to religion. The first supremacy act made it treason to defend by deed or written word the ecclesiastical jurisdiction of a foreign ruler or cleric, and in 1563 Parliament made it treason to refuse the oath; however, the 1352 statute remained central. Following Elizabeth's excommunication (see REGNANS IN EXCELSIS), two acts of 1571 made it treason to receive a papal bull, to deny that Elizabeth was queen or that she had the right to devise the descent of the Crown, to declare her schismatic or a heretic, or to claim a place in the succession. Use of attainder died out in the 1570s as the tangle of overlapping statutes grew. Another important act in 1585 was a response to treason instigated by JESUITS or their sympathizers. But by the 1570s the Elizabethan treason code was riddled with inconsistencies, a situation that was made worse by numerous additional acts in subsequent Parliaments, strained interpretations of the law, and pressure put upon judges in cases like those of the ESSEX REBELLION in 1600.

Treason trials were usually held either in King's Bench or at assizes, but a nobleman could be tried in the court of the high steward, like Buckingham in 1521. The Crown often appointed special commissions of *oyer and terminer*, sometimes stacked to guarantee conviction. The accused was not allowed legal counsel, a copy of the indictment, or sworn witnesses on his behalf, and not until Edward VI's reign was the testimony of two witnesses against the defendant required. The prescribed punishment for male traitors was to be hung, drawn, and quartered, though persons of noble estate were often simply beheaded. Executions were orchestrated to convey to observers the horror of the offense against the Crown and the divine order of the universe. Gallows speeches were expected, and subsequent addresses by assize judges, sermons, and pamphlets instructed subjects to avoid treason.

Bibliography: John Bellamy, *The Tudor Law of Treason: An Introduction*, 1979.

William B. Robison

Troyes, Treaty of (1564). This treaty extricated England from the unsuccessful intervention in France resulting from the ARTICLES OF RICHMOND. It also set the stage for closer relations between the two powers.

ELIZABETH had intervened in France during 1562 with the hope of regaining CALAIS, aiding the French Protestants, and preventing a resurgence of French power. The English garrison occupying Newhaven (La Havre) first suffered from the plague. Then their erstwhile Huguenot allies made a separate peace and joined forces with the royal army and eventually forced the English to surrender on 29 July 1563. At this point Elizabeth decided to make peace with France. The resulting Treaty of Troyes began by ending the formal state of hostilities. The French also promised to pay England 120,000 crowns to recompense them for the expenses of their military expedition. They also agreed to continue their recognition of English rights to Calais (first acknowledged after the fall of the town by the Treaty of Cateau-Cambresis). The French and English ambassadors signed the treaty on 12 April 1564, and it was proclaimed in London on 22 April and in Paris on 1 May.

The signing of the treaty and subsequent events marked a significant warming of relations between England and France. Elizabeth's natural caution in foreign affairs had been reinforced by the disastrous results of the expedition to Newhaven. She would no longer attempt to aid the Huguenots of France in their struggle with the Catholic majority. France also made a substantial payment to England that most knowledgeable observers understood ended any lingering English hopes of regaining Calais. A France torn apart by religious civil wars also did not appear to be a great threat to England. Instead both powers realized that it was the domination of Europe by the Habsburg family, particularly the Spanish branch, that posed the greatest threat to them. The growing friendship of England and France was further cemented in 1572 by the TREATY OF BLOIS.

Bibliography: M. Dewar, *Sir Thomas Smith: A Tudor Intellectual in Office*, 1964; R. B. Wernham, *Before the Armada: The Emergence of the English Nation, 1485-1588*, 1966.

Gary Bell

Tudor Revolution in Government. This term first appeared in the title of a book by G. R. Elton: *The Tudor Revolution in Government: Administrative Changes in the Reign of Henry VIII* (Cambridge, 1953). This argued that in the 1530s a deliberate and largely successful attempt was made to change the basic principle of English government from reliance on the royal Household to a structure of organized departments outside the Household. The book ascribed this transformation to deliberate policies adopted by THOMAS CROMWELL; he terminated the ascendency of the treasurer of the king's chamber over the royal resources, equipped old and new agencies of finance with bureaucratic identities, set up the PRINCIPAL SECRETARY as the chief executive minister, and organized a PRIVY COUNCIL of nineteen members out of the large and undifferentiated Council used by the late-medieval kings. At the same time, Cromwell began to provide a better and more positively departmental organization for the administration of the HOUSEHOLD itself. In subsequent studies, Elton elaborated this initial construct to present the 1530s as an age of crucial reconstruction that started the formation of the early modern state—unitary and sovereign—out of its noticeably less structured medieval predecessor.

Though for a time received uncritically, the thesis soon enough led to debate. The subordinate role of HENRY VIII was called in question in R. B. Wernham's review in the *English Historical Review* for 1956. A more searching exchange ensued in the pages of *Past and Present* in 1963-1965. Here G. L. Harriss maintained that nothing new happened in the 1530s; bureaucracy was supposedly the characteristic of medieval government too. P. H. Williams argued, on the other hand, that the change initiated neither amounted to a major transformation nor produced the lasting effects postulated by Elton. Elton replied, and this reply led to a second phase of debate, but in the end the contestants were content to differ.

The first serious modification of the "revolution" thesis sprang from the discovery of D. R. Starkey that just when, in Elton's view, the royal Household withdrew into running no more than the personal concerns of the monarch, it actually produced a new administrative office in the king's Privy Chamber. Starkey demonstrated successfully that this inmost group of the king's entourage became the center of court and national politics; more debatably, he tried to maintain that it also continued the Household's control over the king's finances and patronage, both of which Elton had seen as taken over by such "national" institutions as formal financial departments and the secretary of state. This major revision, which denied that there had been any kind of transformation, let alone a revolution, in the administrative arrangements of Tudor England, was expounded by Starkey in several places but especially in his contributions to a volume edited by himself and C. Coleman: *Revolution Reassessed* (Oxford, 1986). At the same time, other scholars—notably J. A. Guy, who summarized his view in chapter 6 of his *Tudor England* (Oxford, 1988)—cast doubts on both the originality of Thomas Cromwell and his sole control, though they accepted some of the main notions involved in Elton's original thesis. Unlike Starkey, they wished to modify, not demolish. Under the influence of much of this further work, Elton has himself somewhat modified his views, for example in *Reform and Reformation* (London, 1977).

At present, therefore, various positions are tenable with respect to the 1530s and their "revolution." Only Starkey totally rejects the idea of significant change deliberately undertaken by Cromwell's administration. Elton continues to ascribe to Cromwell a general plan of major reform in both the principles and practices of royal government in England; but he accepts that Cromwell inherited and used a good many ideas and in the short time available to him was not able to complete as much transformation as he had intended. Elton now sees more positive achievement than he used to in the reforms by Cardinal THOMAS WOLSEY. In between, other scholars place different emphases on the changes that occurred and on the parts played in bringing them about by Cromwell, other royal servants, and on occasion even the king. However, except for Starkey, whose more uncompromising theories about continued Household government will not stand up to investigation, no one now doubts the vital importance of the 1530s for the development of English politics, government, and constitution, nor does anyone any longer neglect Thomas Cromwell and his role. More particularly, Elton's demonstration in *Reform and Renewal* (Cambridge, 1973) that Cromwell should be seen as a man who based action in the state on a set of intellectual principles closely allied to the tenets of HUMANISM seems to be generally accepted.

G. R. Elton

Tyndale, William (c. 1494-1536). Best known as the first translator of the printed BIBLE in English, he was also an active defender of the Reformed cause. Born at or near Slymbridge in Gloucester, Tyndale came from a well-to-do yeoman family. He entered Oxford University in 1510 as a member of Magdalen Hall and earned his B.A. in 1512 and his M.A. in 1515. Sometime between 1516 and 1519, he made his way to Cambridge University, where it appears that he learned Greek. He stayed there through 1521.

Tyndale returned to his native Gloucestershire in 1522 as the private chaplain of Sir John Walsh of Little Sodbury and the tutor of the family's children. By this time, he was an outspoken critic of the church's doctrine and institutions. According to legend, he became an advocate of the Reformed cause at Oxford as a result of reading Martin Luther, although this story depends on his remaining at Oxford past 1517. Strong circumstantial evidence also indicates that Tyndale's religious ideas, at least partially, had their origin in preexisting LOLLARD beliefs circulating around Gloucestershire. The resulting local clerical harassment convinced Tyndale to move to London and there to translate the Bible into English as the best way to aid the Reform movement.

Arriving in London in 1523, Tyndale sought the patronage of the new bishop of London, Cuthbert Tunstall, by submitting a translation of Isocrates. Although that effort failed, he did manage to attract the support of the merchant Humphrey Monmouth. But because the English clergy were so hostile to the translation of the Bible, in early 1524 Tyndale, subsidized by Monmouth, moved to Europe. On 27 May 1524 he matriculated at Luther's University of Wittenberg but departed in less than a year. By the fall of 1525 he was in Cologne and busily tried to publish a translation of the New Testament with the assistance of William Roye, another English Protestant, and the local printer Peter Quental. Unfortunately Roye bragged about the project to the Catholic polemicist Johannes Cochlaeus, who notified the authorities. They seized most of the work, although Tyndale and Roye escaped to Worms with enough of their materials to publish the English New Testament in 1526.

Tyndale's New Testament proved popular with readers and unpopular with the clerical authorities. Besides trying to suppress the translation, in 1528 Cardinal THOMAS WOLSEY attempted to have Tyndale arrested in Worms. As a result, he moved to Marburg, where he lived under the protection of the Protestant Landgrave Philip of Hesse. It was sometime between 1528 and 1530 that Tyndale adopted the Zwinglian doctrine on communion. Meanwhile on 8 May 1528 he published the *Parable of Wicked Mammon* which discussed the doctrine of justification by faith and the social obligations of Christians. He quickly followed with *The Obedience of a Christian Man* on 2 October. This work defended the Reformers against charges of promoting social instability and insisted that subjects had an absolute duty to obey their secular rulers. Furthermore, Tyndale asserted that scripture was the supreme authority for formulating doctrine. ANNE BOLEYN brought this book to the attention of HENRY VIII, who gave it his hearty approval.

In 1529 Tyndale left Marburg and eventually made his way to Antwerp late that year. There he published a translation of the Pentateuch on 17 January 1530 and his *Practice of Prelates* in the same year. In the latter work he continued his attacks on the leadership of the Roman Catholic church in general and Cardinal Thomas Wolsey's administration in England in particular. Tyndale's principles also led him to denounce Henry VIII's DIVORCE proceedings made him the only English Reformer to do so, and also thoroughly alienated the once favorable king of England.

Meanwhile, the outspoken Tyndale entered an acrimonious debate with Sir THOMAS MORE, who considered him to be England's chief heretic. During the spring or summer of 1531 he published his *An Answer to Sir Thomas More's Dialogue*, a response to More's attack of June 1529 on the Reformed cause in *A Dialogue cocerning Heresies*. More answered Tyndale with two long polemics, but Tyndale declined to reply. Instead he published a translation of Jonah in 1531, wrote several theological tracts and biblical commentaries, and published revisions of his translations of the New Testament in 1534 and 1535 and the Pentateuch in 1534. In addition, he translated but was not able to publish the Old Testament from Joshua to II Chronicles.

Henry VIII, during 1531, at first tried to reconcile with Tyndale through the English envoy Stephen Vaughan. But when that attempt failed the mercurial king attempted unsuccessfully to have the emperor Charles V arrest him for sedition and return him to England. In 1533 Tyndale took up residence in the protected house of the English merchant community in Antwerp as the guest of Thomas Poyntz. On 21 May 1535, Henry Phillips, an English student at Louvain University, lured him out of the English residence into the hands of the ecclesiastical authorities. While he was imprisoned at Vilvorde Castle, Tyndale attempted to continue his translation of the Old Testament. The intercessions of Vaughan and other English friends failed to save him when he was tried and found guilty of heresy. On 2 October 1536, he was strangled at the stake and then burnt. Although his translation of the Bible remained unfinished, Tyndale's work served as a firm foundation for all the Protestant translations that followed.

Bibliography: J. F. Mozley, *William Tyndale*, 1937; D. D. Smeeton, *Lollard Themes in the Reformation Theology of William Tyndale*, 1986.

Ronald Fritze

Tyrone Rebellion (1594-1603). The Tyrone Rebellion, also known as the Nine Years' War, was the most prolonged and widespread Irish revolt of the sixteenth century. The Ulster chief who initiated the rebellion was Hugh O'Neill, the eldest son of Matthew O'Neill, who had claimed the earldom of Tyrone in the 1550s. Despite Matthew's illegitimacy, his branch of the O'Neill family had been supported by the English against SHANE O'NEILL throughout the 1560s. Because both his father and brother had been murdered by Shane's party, Hugh had been raised in the safety of London after 1566. Thoroughly anglicized and educated, Hugh was believed to be loyal to the English Crown and in the 1580s was established in Ulster with English support. In 1593, he was elevated to the earldom of Tyrone, and in 1595, he claimed the Gaelic title of the O'Neill. With this came the claim to sovereignty over Ulster, which had been held by the O'Neills for centuries.

In holding both an English earldom and the Irish chieftaincy, Hugh O'Neill drifted toward alliance with the Gaelic lords of Ulster. The English responded to this shift in their client's loyalties by strengthening their position in Ulster during 1593. Sir Henry Bagenal, the marshal of Ulster, began to garrison strategic locations around the borders of Tyrone's territory. This action not only drew O'Neill further into rebellion but isolated English troops in untenable positions. By 1594, O'Neill had clearly decided to fight, and in search of an ally, he began negotiations with Philip II of Spain.

The war began in February 1595, when Tyrone's brother, Art O'Neill, attacked and destroyed an English fort on the Blackwater River. In May, Tyrone himself defeated Bagenal's army at the battle of Clontibert, and in June he was declared a rebel. Though O'Neill went to Dublin to protest his continued loyalty to the queen's cause to the incoming lord deputy, Sir William Russell, the English government was determined to end O'Neill's pretensions to sovereignty. Sir John Norris, with 3,000 veteran troops from Brittany, was made general of the queen's forces during September. By May 1596, he had convinced Tyrone to come to terms, and an uneasy truce took effect in Ulster.

In 1597 new conflicts broke out, as Gaelic lords in Munster attacked English settlers in that region. At the same time, the English rebuilt the fort on the Blackwater, a move that Tyrone reacted to by blockading the place. Sir Henry Bagenal's attempt to resupply this garrison in August 1598 led to the worst defeat suffered by Elizabeth's forces, the battle of Blackwater, or Yellow Ford, on 14 August 1598. During this fight, Bagenal marched into an ambush and was killed, along with over half of his 4,000 troops. The English narrowly avoided being totally overwhelmed by Tyrone, who used irregular tactics. Tyrone was practically the master of the island for a short period, but fortunately for the English government, he declined to use the opportunity to attack Dublin.

In April 1599, the queen's favorite, ROBERT DEVEREUX, earl of Essex, arrived in Dublin with the largest expedition ever dispatched by Elizabeth's government and was determined to bring Tyrone to battle. Essex proved to be unsuited to the task, as the wily O'Neill led him on a fruitless tramp through the wilderness and whittled Essex's 16,000 men down to 4,000 in a period of twenty-one weeks. This ill-conceived campaign came to an end in September, when Essex agreed to private negotiations with Tyrone. The outcome of this talk was a six weeks' truce. The queen, furious with her general's incompetence and suspecting him of treachery, removed the earl from command.

His successor, Charles Blount, Lord Mountjoy, who arrived in Dublin during February 1600, proved to be the bane of Tyrone. Empowered as both lord deputy and general, he and the new president of Munster, Sir George Carew, devastated the countryside. Although Mountjoy's first battle with Tyrone, at Moyry Pass in October 1600, proved to be inconclusive, it was clear that Tyrone would be worn down if he did not receive help.

The long anticipated Spanish invasion force landed at Kinsale, in Munster, on 21 September 1601. Consisting of 3,500 men, it was commanded by the veteran Don Juan Del Aguila. Mountjoy and Carew quickly laid siege to Kinsale with 7,500 English troops. Under constant fire from Mountjoy's artillery and cut off from supplies, the Spaniards were near surrender by December when Tyrone marched south to relieve them. This situation presented Mountjoy with the opportunity to force the Irish into a battle in the open field. This climactic battle occurred near Kinsale on the morning of 24 December 1601 and resulted in the complete defeat of Tyrone's army. On 2 January 1602, the Spanish in Kinsale surrendered.

With this defeat, Tyrone's rebellion was effectively crushed. Though sporadic skirmishing continued until Tyrone made his submission on 30 March 1603, the rebel cause was hopeless after Kinsale. The rebellion of Hugh O'Neill was the most successful Irish rebellion of the sixteenth century, but in the final analysis, it served only to open Ulster up for future English plantation.

Bibliography: G. A. Hayes McCoy, "The Completion of the Tudor Conquest and the Advance of the Counter-Reformation," in *A New History of Ireland*, vol. 3, 1976.

John Nolan

U

Uniformity, First Act of (1549). The government of the boy-king EDWARD VI, though dominated by men inclined to Protestant views, did not move in an overly hasty manner to change the nation's religious practices. The TREASON Act of 1547 removed much of the medieval and Henrician apparatus of religious enforcement. But the first major element in the attempt by the Edwardian regime to impose a new religious settlement on England was the 1549 Act of Uniformity (2 and 3 Edw. VI, c. 1). Its chief concerns were the adoption of a single order of service and the publication of the first BOOK OF COMMON PRAYER, largely the work of Archbishop THOMAS CRANMER. Hitherto the English church had seen the use of five diverse orders of service: those of Bangor, York, Hereford, Lincoln, and Salisbury (Sarum); Salisbury was the most widespread.

The Book of Common Prayer revolutionized the English church service in a Protestant fashion and emphasized the participation of the congregation as part of the theology of the priesthood of all believers and the communion service as a memorial. This new viewpoint was phrased, however, in such a way that even Conservative bishops such as STEPHEN GARDINER could pronounce themselves willing to accept the doctrine in their own way.

A major novelty was the abolition of Latin in any part of the service, a change that removed much of the mystery from the proceedingsand that was reinforced by the regular reading of Bible passages in English.

The Act of Uniformity provided a range of penalties for clergy who refused to use the new order of service. These penalties ranged from a fine and temporary loss of benefice for the first offense to life imprisonment for the third conviction. The act forbade criticism of the Book of Common Prayer in plays, songs, or speech and penalized those obstructing its use. The act specified that each parish provide itself with the new prayer books but, significantly, did not propose penalties for those laymen who refused to attend services.

The act encountered opposition in the House of Lords from Conservatives such as Bishop EDMUND BONNER of London, who felt that the new view of the eucharist was simply a revival of old heresy. Two lay lords joined eight bishops in voting against the act, but the bill passed the upper house into the Commons, where it was overwhelmingly accepted. Though the new act and book were designed to advance the Protestant cause quietly and without unduly alienating the traditionally minded, they nonetheless drew fire both from Protestant radicals and from Conservative Catholics. To evangelical firebrands, such as John Hooper and the European Protestants, things had clearly not gone far enough, while Catholic sensibilities in the countryside were outraged. The latter culminated in the WESTERN REBELLION of the summer of 1549, sometimes called the "Prayer Book Rising." Angry Catholics of the West Country demanded an end to the new service, which they termed "a Christmas game" and a return to the traditional Latin Mass, images, and prayers for the dead. Though their rebellion was crushed, their actions helped to bring down the rule of EDWARD SEYMOUR, duke of Somerset, a chief supporter of the new doctrines.

The significance of the First Act of Uniformity is both constitutional and religious. For the first time, Parliament, free of the directions of an adult monarch, guided the decision-making process for the doctrine and ceremonial of the English church. As well, the act introduced the Book of Common Prayer, an enduring monument of English prose that remained at the center of English church life for centuries.

Bibliography: A. G. Dickens, *The English Reformation*, 2nd ed., 1989; W. K. Jordan, *Edward VI: The Young King*, 1968.

Gerald Bowler

Uniformity, Second Act of (1552). (5 and 6 Edw. VI, c. 1). The moderate attempt at theological compromise that was embodied in the first BOOK OF COMMON PRAYER was unpopular with both religious extremes. Catholic protest demonstrated itself in the WESTERN REBELLION, and those Protestants who wished to take the English Reformation further soon began proposing amendments to the settlement of 1549. NICHOLAS RIDLEY, the new bishop of London, made his position clear by ordering the removal of altars in his diocese, replacing them with "the Lord's board after the form of an honest table," and forbidding traditional gestures such as elevating the host. Martin Bucer, the Regius Professor of Divinity at Cambridge and one of a number of Continental Protestant theologians who had come to England since the accession of EDWARD VI, prepared a work, the *Censura*, criticizing the 1549 book in some detail. From Geneva John Calvin urged Archbishop THOMAS CRANMER to undertake further Reformation immediately. Cranmer seems to have taken their advice seriously and began work on a new prayer book shortly after the original came into effect. By 1551 a draft version was circulating among the bishops for their comments.

JOHN DUDLEY, soon to be the duke of Northumberland, controlled the government at that point. A man of variable religious opinion, he decided for political reasons to support the evangelical party in the English church and joined in the demand for a clearer expression of an uncompromising Protestantism by the Church of England. In March 1552 a new act of Uniformity and a new Book of Common Prayer were introduced in Parliament. The act did not repeal the First Act of Uniformity but carefully stated that, though in 1549 a very godly order had been set forth, a number of dissidents had been absenting themselves from services and doubts had been raised. Therefore a more perfect act was being presented. This time the penalties were enacted for those who refused to be present at the new order of service or who attended alternate ceremonies. First offenders faced six months in prison, and life imprisonment was ordered for third-time convictions. As was the case in 1549, a minority of Conservatives in the House of Lords opposed the legislation, with three lay lords and two bishops voting against it. The House of Commons witnessed no opposition and passed the bill immediately.

The new Book of Common Prayer was no mild attempt at pleasing both sides but rather set out a liturgy that was unequivocally Protestant. In the preface to the book Cranmer explained that over time certain ceremonial practices had crept into the service and become superstitious hindrances to true worship. The new order of service, he claimed, was clearly grounded in the Holy Scriptures. It changed the very name of the Mass to that of the Lord's Supper; the altar was replaced by a communion table; the priest was now termed a minister, and he was to wear a simple surplice in place of elaborate vestments. The theology of the eucharist moved away from Rome toward the Swiss view. Where the 1549 service had the words "The body of our Lord Jesus Christ which was given for thee, preserve thy body and soul unto everlasting life," the 1552 reading was "Take and eat this in remembrance that Christ died for thee and feed on him in thy heart by faith, with thanksgiving."

While Conservatives were distressed by these changes, the failure of the Western Rising in 1549 evidently dissuaded them from violent resistance. Ironically, protest was strongest among Protestant "hot gospellers," who wished to purge utterly the "popish dregs" from the church. They were still upset that ceremonials such as kneeling during the reception of the Lord's Supper had been retained. While the new Book of Common Prayer wsa being printed, JOHN KNOX, a Scottish exile who had become a royal preacher, voiced his complaints about this lingering "idolatry" in a sermon before the king. The PRIVY COUNCIL, in a move that demonstrated the power of the Edwardian supremacy in religious affairs, asked a furious Cranmer to consider further changes. Despite the archbishop's objections, the council ordered the insertion of the BLACK RUBRIC, an annotation that made it clear that kneeling in no way implied any adoration of the elements of communion or "any real and essential presence there being of Christ's natural flesh and blood."

The Second Act of Uniformity and Book of Common Prayer, along with the rest of Edward VI's religious legislation, had a short life span. The accession of MARY I in 1553 swept them all away, but their legacies lingered in the renewed Protestantism of the ELIZABETHAN SETTLEMENT OF RELIGION.

Bibliography: W. K. Jordan, *Edward VI: The Threshold of Power*, 1970; E. C. Whitaker, ed., *Martin Bucer and the Book of Common Prayer*, 1974.

Gerald Bowler

Universities. The Tudor period experienced many changes in education, most of which can be studied in the changing nature and function of the two universities, Oxford and Cambridge. The university on the eve of the Reformation had changed little since the thirteenth century. The medieval university had arisen initially to provide education to boys of low social background who were seeking a career in the church. Under the direction of regent masters, students attended lectures and participated in academic disputations. Studies centered only initially on the seven liberal arts (grammar, rhetoric, logic, arithmetic, geometry, astronomy, and music); most students would be expected to incept as masters and then study in one of the higher faculties of law, medicine, and divinity. Legal studies at the universities were of particular importance, since the universities were the only training schools in England for the canon and civil laws used by the medieval church.

In terms of their fundamental organization, the modern history of the universities can be said to have begun in 1535 with the abolition of CANON LAW in England and the prohibition of its teaching. At the same time, ROYAL SUPREMACY over the church wrenched the universities from the control of the clergy and placed them directly under the Crown. This secularization continued throughout the sixteenth century and is illustrated by the fact that henceforth the chancellors were, with a few exceptions, laymen; thus Bishop JOHN FISHER, executed in 1535, was succeeded as chancellor of Cambridge by THOMAS CROMWELL, while Oxford had lay chancellors, except for a brief period under MARY I, from 1552 till the end of the century.

Secularization is also clearly evident in the student body. The two universities survived a crisis in the 1530s and 1540s, when they lost their original raison d'être, to emerge in the second half of the century as the principal centers for the education of wellborn youth; the number of students at each university rose from something less than 200 in the 1540s to well over 400 in 1580. Estimates of the average number of freshmen matriculating in each year show similar increases; at Oxford the number rose from 124 in the first decade of the century to 358 in the last, while the average number of B.A.s granted per year rose from 24 in the 1500s to 117 in the 1590s.

This growth has often been attributed to the influence of HUMANISM, but in fact early Tudor humanists did little to promote lay attendance at the universities. Sir Thomas Elyot, whose *Book Named the Governor* (1531) was an early influential tract on gentle education, did not regard university as an essential part of the young gentleman's upbringing, while his younger contemporary, Thomas Starkey, regretted that poor men's sons were being displaced in the schools by the sons of gentry. Nevertheless, the number of laymen with some university experience increased dramatically under ELIZABETH; the number of members of PARLIAMENT with a university education more than doubled during her reign. By 1603, most JUSTICES OF THE PEACE and deputies lieutenant had some university experience, though it is true that many students never took a degree, stayed only two or three years, and then traveled abroad or proceeded to legal studies at the Inns of Court. By this time, the principal connection remaining between the universities and the church was that an increasing number of parish clergy had acquired a degree and in some cases pursued higher studies in divinity; indeed, so much improved was the level of clerical education by the early seventeenth century that the universities soon produced more clerics than the church required and thereby obliged many to seek other types of employment, of which schoolmastering was one.

A second important change was the decline and almost total disappearance of the halls at which undergraduates had lived during the first two and one-half centuries of the universities' existence. By 1550, only eight of these remained; unlike the colleges, the halls had no corporate existence and no landed endowments; they were therefore ill equipped to survive the general decline in student numbers that marked the middle third of the sixteenth century. From the 1540s, a growing number of law students (except those studying civil law for use in the post-Reformation church courts) abandoned the universities for the study of the common law at the Inns of Court in London. The other victors were the colleges, which in the first decade of the sixteenth century had begun admitting paying undergraduates. Enriched in the 1540s by the DISSOLUTION OF THE MONASTERIES, which left many of them much better endowed, the colleges began offering instruction outside the university lectures that had previously comprised the core of the student's education, under the guidance of tutorial fellows and, to a lesser extent, of college lecturers. Meanwhile, the autonomy of the colleges was increased by government statutes granting new, wide powers to the college heads at the expense of the regent masters, who were no longer acknowledged as the core of the university. Lay philanthropy also added to the number and wealth of the colleges, as many new ones were added and old ones refounded. Lady Margaret Beaufort, mother to HENRY VII, endowed Christ's College and St. John's College at Cambridge, while Sir Thomas Pope established Trinity College, Oxford. This pattern continued later in the century as powerful patrons such as Sir Walter Mildmay created further new colleges such as Emmanuel at Cambridge.

The position of the regent masters was further eroded by the appointment, through lay patronage, of a paid professoriate. Lady Margaret Beaufort endowed the chairs in divinity that still bear her name, while her grandson, HENRY VIII, established Regius chairs in divinity, law, medicine, Hebrew, and Greek. These professors, together with paid college lecturers, provided the lectures that were designed to supplement the supervision of college tutors.

The curriculum at Oxford and Cambridge changed much more slowly and gradually than did the universities' organization and social composition. The heart of the undergraduate education remained the seven liberal arts and the three philosophies (moral philosophy, natural philosophy, and metaphysics); a student would study five or six of these subjects in succession during a residency of sixteen terms (four years). During this time he would read prescribed texts under the guidance of his tutor, who was also charged with the boy's moral upbringing; he would also attend set lectures provided by the university and engage in the practice of public debate, or "disputation," on set problems. University and college statutes strictly regulated the course of study and the works to be read, though it is clear from the notebooks of tutors and undergraduates that there was a great deal of variation, both between the two universities and from tutor to tutor; by 1600, most students had their traditional fare of the liberal arts leavened with works on geography, chronology, and history. Sometime in his fourth year the student could petition for "grace" to "determine," that is, for permission from his college and from the university to participate in disputations prior to supplicating for his bachelor's degree. For many students, the baccalaureate remained only a preliminary to later inception as a master and advanced study in one of the higher faculties of law, medicine, and divinity.

Medieval scholars studied grammar and logic from a number of medieval texts such as the *Sentences* of Peter Lombard and Priscian's grammar, which were usually presented in the form of Latin lectures rather than studied from a text. Humanist learning began to infiltrate the curriculum toward the end of the fifteenth century, as scholars such as John Colet and William Grocyn placed new emphasis on the study of Greek and classical, Ciceronian Latin. Thomas Linacre, whose interests included medicine as well as classics, contributed a new Latin grammar, which largely replaced Priscian's work, and visiting scholars like Erasmus, who lectured on Greek at Cambridge from 1511 to 1513, further increased the trend toward humanist study. Rhetoric, the art of elegant oral and written expression, assumed a prominence in the curriculum it had not enjoyed previously, and students began to study original authors such as Virgil and Cicero. Although lectures remained an important method for the presentation of material to students, the increasing availability of standard texts in printed form gradually reoriented the course of study toward private reading under the guidance of tutors; the wills of many deceased students show that the collection of small personal libraries was part of undergraduate life.

Aristotle remained perhaps the single most important author studied, and university statutes specify his works, together with those of Cicero, as the core of liberal arts learning, especially in logic. But in the second half of the sixteenth century, as newer educational treatises became available, the study of Aristotelian philosophy came, at least briefly, into decline. An important influence was that of Ramism, named for Peter Ramus (d. 1572), a prolific French author of textbooks on logic. Ramus had argued that Aristotelian logic, and still more the vast scholastic edifice built upon it, had become unnecessarily complex and difficult to grasp. His simplified logic, illustrated with numerous diagrams, proved particularly popular in the 1570s and 1580s at Cambridge, where students read both his works and those of earlier humanists such as Rudolf Agricola; at Oxford, Ramus was read by the erudite president of Corpus Christi College, John Rainolds. But Ramism never commanded the allegiance of more than a minority of tutors, and before the end of the century, the study of Aristotle was reasserting itself in what can be called a "neoscholastic" revival, illustrated, for instance, in the works of the St. John's College, Oxford, philosopher John Case.

A more dangerous criticism came from outside the universities from former undergraduates who began to doubt the efficacy of their highly abstract education. Such critics included the future chancellor, Sir Francis Bacon, and the Elizabethan explorer, Sir Humphrey Gilbert, one of several men to propose the creation of a royal academy to teach students such practical skills as navigation and geography. Like Starkey a generation earlier, Gilbert believed that the universities were properly the school of the lowborn, pursuing clerical or civil-law careers; the true gentleman and noble, to serve his country fully, needed a different type of education. Though Gilbert's plan, and several similar proposals, were stillborn, the impetus for more training in natural sciences and "mechanic" arts did issue in the establishment of GRESHAM COLLEGE at London in 1595. Together with the Inns of Court and Inns of Chancery, the schools for dancing and defense, and various other institutions providing technical training, London offered enough in the way of higher education to be referred to colloquially, in the early seventeenth century, as the "third university."

Just as the Renaissance had an effect on the structure of university education, so were the universities unable to resist the impact of the Reformation. During the reign of EDWARD VI, both Oxford and Cambridge became centers for religious change under the influence of visiting Continental Reformers such as Peter Martyr Vermigli at Oxford and Martin Bucer at Cambridge. During Elizabeth's reign, Cambridge, traditionally the more conservative junior institution, acquired a reputation for PURITANISM. This was due partly to its location in East Anglia, a region with a high concentration of puritan families, and partly to the fact that many of the early Reformers had been students there rather than at Oxford. But for whatever reason, puritanism continued to flourish under the influence of tutors and lecturers such as Laurence Chaderton and William Perkins, to whom preaching the word and teaching were two sides of the same coin. The foundation of colleges such as Sidney Sussex and Emmanuel, whose statutes prescribe a godly education for their youth, helped further the influence of moderate puritanism. This was largely tolerated by the Elizabethan regime since it promoted godly learning; more radical puritans such as the PRESBYTERIAN leader Thomas Cartwright did not fare so well—Cartwright, the Lady Margaret Professor Divinity, was deprived of his fellowship and his degree and expelled from Cambridge in 1571. Oxford remained religiously more conservative, and in 1581 it imposed the requirement that matriculating students subscribe to the THIRTY-NINE ARTICLES (a requirement that did not apply at Cambridge), though this seems to have been aimed primarily at rooting out Roman Catholics. Though it had not Cambridge's puritan reputation, several leading moderate puritans held great influence at Oxford, such as Laurence Humphrey, president of Magdalen College and Regius professor of divinity, and Corpus's president, John Rainolds. Lay patrons of puritan inclination, such as Sir Walter Mildmay and ROBERT DUDLEY, earl of Leicester and chancellor of Oxford from 1564, helped considerably in the entrenchment of puritanism at both universities.

Though the universities have sometimes been regarded as intellectual backwaters, promoting outdated knowledge, it is clear that this assessment is unjust. While undeniably conservative, they continued to provide a crucial nursery for intellectual activity throughout the late sixteenth century and beyond. More important, by adapting themselves to the changing religious and social environment of the Tudor age, and in particular to the requirements of a newly literate and educated gentry, they were able to emerge from the sixteenth century in a much stronger position than they entered it.

Bibliography: Hugh Kearney, *Scholars and Gentlemen: Universities and Society in Pre-Industrial Britain 1500-1700*, 1970; James McConica, ed., *The Collegiate University*, vol. 3 in *The History of the University of Oxford*, 1986; Lawrence Stone, ed., *The University in Society*, 1974.

D. R. Woolf

Uses and Wills, An Act Concerning (1536). (27 Hen. VIII, c. 10). Better known to contemporaries as the act of "primer seisin" and to posterity as the Statute of Uses, this act played a key role in HENRY VIII's campaign to increase royal revenue from feudal incidents, tenurial obligations owed by those who held land directly from the Crown. It is also a milestone in the history of the land law and one of the principal secular grievances attacked by the rebels at the time of the PILGRIMAGE OF GRACE and related risings of 1536.

During the later Middle Ages and early Tudor period, the legal device known as the "use" was widely employed by landholders for a number of purposes, the most important of which was the intergenerational settlement of land. To create a use, the holder of land transferred the legal ownership of it to trustees ("feoffees") who then held it "to the use of" himself and/or anyone else he nominated (the beneficiary was in either case known as the *cestuy que use*). The popularity of the device lay principally in the fact that it overcame the COMMON LAW rule that prohibited land from being passed to nominated heirs by means of a will. It worked because the testator, who was a *cestuy que use*, passed on the use (occupation and profits) of the property, but not the ownership itself, which remained in the hands of the trustees. With the aid of the use, a landowner could overcome the law of primogeniture and pass his property to whomever he wished.

However, the use also generated a number of problems, all of which lay in the background to the passage of the statute. First, since the beneficiary of the use, the *cestuy que use*, divested himself of ownership of the property but continued to enjoy the profits from it, the nature of his estate in the eyes of the common law was problematic. Second, the creation of uses frequently involved legal instruments, such as the "bargain and sale," which did not require public notoriety, traditionally a necessary part of land conveyancing. Hence uses were associated with secret, informal agreements that were sometimes associated with attempts to defraud creditors or future purchasers. Finally, and most importantly in connection with the passage of the statute, the beneficiary of a use could evade feudal incidents such as WARDSHIP and primer seisin (whereby the lord enjoyed one year's profits of the land), which were due when a lesser tenant died and his heir came into ownership. Since *cestuy que use* had transferred the legal estate of his property to a self-perpetuating group of trustees, the owner of his land never died!

Since it was a major feudal landlord, the Crown had long suffered significant losses of income as a result of uses. Minor attempts to remedy this state of affairs were made in the reign of HENRY VII, but the sustained attack on uses as a means of evading feudal obligations appears to have begun in 1526, when the council ordered the rigorous prosecution of royal rights. Then, in 1529, an agreement was reached and signed by Lord Chancellor THOMAS MORE and thirty members of the peerage in which the king agreed to forego two-thirds of his due from feudal incidents in return for a package deal in which the Crown and all other feudal lords would be guaranteed the other third regardless of whether land was devised by will or held through uses.

Bills based on this agreement were put to Parliament on several occasions in the early 1530s but rejected by the Commons, who apparently saw less for themselves in the compromise than the Lords had. In 1532 Henry was so exasperated by their refusal that he threatened to withdraw the deal and "search out the extremitie of the law." An opportunity to do just this was found in 1535 when the Crown brought a lawsuit against the testamentary settlement that the dead peer Lord Dacre of the South had made of his estate. Under considerable pressure from the king, the judges sitting in Exchequer chamber ruled in this case that uses and a will could not be employed to establish the inheritance of land.

The decision in Dacre's case did not, as is sometimes said, make uses illegal. It did, however, threaten the tenure of anyone who held his land as a result of a will, and this threat was enough to force Parliament to accept a tough bill on uses, which became law in the spring of 1536. The preamble to the statute rehearses a number of the alleged abuses that had long been associated with uses. Land should not be devisable by wills or transferred by other fraudulent and secret methods.

The Crown and other lords suffered a loss of feudal incidents such as wards, reliefs, and marriage. Heirs were disinherited, and women were defrauded of their rights to dower. By contrast, the body of the statute is ingeniously simple. It merely declares that were several persons to hold land to the use of another person, the *cestuy que use*, not the trustees, is deemed to have the ownership. The advantage of this change to the Crown and other feudal lords was that since the beneficiary of the use, and not the self-perpetuating trustees, was henceforth considered the owner of the land, feudal incidents could be collected when he died because ownership would clearly pass to his heir. Wills of land were also in effect abolished. Furthermore, while the statute protects the rights of married women who had an income, or "jointure," settled on them for their maintenance in the event of the death of their husbands, it also stipulates that in those cases where a jointure had been established the woman was to be deemed to have forfeited her common law right of "dower," which entitled her to claim one-third of the estate of her deceased spouse. There was only one major concession to the landowning classes, who must have been suffering considerable anxiety, but it was a vital one. The last clause of the act specifies that wills made before 1 May 1536 were to be considered valid despite anything in the act or any previous judicial decision to the contrary, and thereby the clause protected existing titles to land against the potentially disastrous consequences of the judgment in Dacre's case.

The Statute of Uses opened the way for the Crown to exploit feudal incidents to the full, and by vesting ownership in *cestuy que use*, it firmly placed controversies about uses within the sphere of the common law courts, as opposed to CHANCERY. However, both the full exploitation of feudal dues and the limitation on the testamentary disposition of land were considerably modified by the STATUTE OF WILLS, which was passed in 1540. Finally, since there were still many occasions on which it was desirable to give the beneficial enjoyment of land to someone without conveying ownership, lawyers continued to devise increasingly devious methods of creating uses. In this respect the Statute of Uses contributed significantly to the nightmarish character of subsequent English land law.

Bibliography: J. H. Baker, *The Reports of Sir John Spelman*, Vol. 2, 1978; E. W. Ives, "The Genesis of the Statute of Uses," *English Historical Review* 82 (1967): 673-97.

C. W. Brooks

V

Valor Ecclesiasticus (1535). Following HENRY VIII's statutory assumption of the headship of the church in England but before the systematic DISSOLUTION OF THE MONASTERIES had begun, Parliament turned its attention to the taxation of the clergy. By the Act of FIRST FRUITS AND TENTHS of 1534 (26 Hen. VIII, c. 3) the Crown was authorized to require the first year's income of every ecclesiastical benefice, both secular (from archbishops to parish priests) and regular (headships of all religious communities). In addition each would contribute to royal coffers one-tenth of his or her annual income. Before such a tax could be collected it was necessary to discover the extent and source of clerical incomes. To this end the same act provided for the immediate appointment in every diocese of a body of commissioners, all of them laymen but with the addition of the bishop, to survey the income of every incumbent. It was an enormous task, but the commissioners worked hard and found the clergy remarkably cooperative, no doubt relieved that a threat to confiscate all their property and pay them a fixed stipend had not materialized.

The *Valor Ecclesiasticus*, as the commissioners' returns became known, was complete by the early part of 1536. In it were set down, deanery by deanery, every religious house and some 9,000 parishes. All kinds of income were included, both gross by way of rents and other landed income, and net, after deduction of all fixed outgoings. In the case of the religious houses the latter included fees payable to lay officers and stipends payable to the vicars of parishes whose rectorial tithes had been appropriated. Also included were the so-called spiritual revenues, largely parochial tithes. By and large where direct comparisons with other records can be made, for example leasehold rents, the *Valor* has been shown to be extraordinarily reliable. In cases such as monastic demesne, the commissioners had to put their own valuation on the property, and those figures have been found to be somewhat conservative. This often turned to the advantage of early lay grantees of the former monastic lands, for those whose duty it was to prepare the post-Dissolution valuations resorted only too gladly to the *Valor*. In fact it is difficult to imagine how the Dissolution itself could have proceeded as smoothly as it did without the help of the *Valor*.

Very considerable variations in the income of the bishops were laid bare, from the net figure of nearly £4,000 enjoyed by the bishops of Winchester down to that of just over £400 by the bishop of Rochester. Both figures included both "temporal" income, that is, from landed property, and from various administrative dues. As in the case of all the *Valor* figures, what was now on record was the income due, not what was actually received in any one year. Much clerical income in any case was casual, such as profits of manorial courts, and the commissioners could provide only what they considered to be a fair average figure.

Most of the parochial clergy were found to be very dependent on the active farming of their glebe, that is, their agricultural land, and on parish tithes. Both of these provided, however, a useful hedge against the inflation that was to be a feature of the mid- and later-Tudor English economy. But the parochial clergy were but poorly paid, only about half of the livings of England and Wales being worth over £10 a year, a third being under £5 and nearly a tenth less than £2. However, the *Valor* continued to serve as the basis of royal taxation of the clergy until comparatively recent times.

Bibliography: Felicity Heal, *Of Prelates and Princes*, 1980; R. O'Day, *The English Clergy: The Emergence and Consolidation of a Profession, 1558-1642*, 1979; A. Savine, *English Monasteries on the Eve of Dissolution*, 1909.

                                                                    Joyce Youings

Vestiarian Controversy (1566). This was a conflict during the 1560s between the bishops of the Church of England and more radical Protestants who refused to wear the prescribed clerical dress, which was significant in the emergence of the PURITAN party.

An incident in the Edwardian Reformation presaged the later controversy. In 1550, John Hooper was offered the bishopric of Gloucester but refused rather than be consecrated wearing the required episcopal vestments, which he thought contrary to Scriptural simplicity. Hooper was imprisoned by the council for a few weeks until he acquiesced to Archbishop THOMAS CRANMER's insistence that vestments were an indifferent matter, or adiaphora, and then he was consecrated in the proper attire. Important foreign divines offered opinions on the matter. John a Lasco, then in London, supported Hooper; but Martin Bucer, Peter Martyr, and John Calvin all agreed that while vestments were best set aside, the matter was not of sufficient importance to justify refusal to serve in the Reformed Church of England.

Advanced Protestant impatience with such remnants of the old religious order reappeared with the ELIZABETHAN SETTLEMENT OF RELIGION, and not only among returning MARIAN EXILES, whose influence has sometimes been exaggerated. Nonetheless, the 1559 Act of Uniformity and Royal Injunctions restored the eucharistic vestments as well as a special outdoor habit for the clergy. Protests followed, Thomas Sampson complaining that the bishops were "habited in the golden vestments of the papacy." However, the eucharistic vestments had come to be so tainted by association with transubstantiation and the persecuting Marian bishops that no effort was made to enforce their use in the visitations of 1559, many of them in any case having been destroyed in the iconoclasm of that year. The *Interpretations and Further Considerations* issued by the bishops in 1560 sought the minimal uniformity of the cope at communion and the surplice for other services, but this uniformity was widely disregarded, even by some bishops. In the lower house of the Canterbury CONVOCATION of 1563 a proposal to abandon all vestments received considerable support.

In 1564 Archbishop MATTHEW PARKER urged Sampson and Laurence Humphrey, heads of Oxford colleges and known as opponents of vestments, to set an example by wearing the surplice, but they refused on the grounds that while the surplice was in itself adiaphora, it had been consecrated to idolatry by the papal church. In January 1565, Parker received a letter from Queen ELIZABETH, probably drafted by WILLIAM CECIL, complaining of lack of uniformity and directing the bishops to seek remedy. Parker and four other bishops accordingly drafted and circulated in 1566 some new articles, known as the "Advertisements," which enjoined the use of the cope in cathedral and collegiate churches and of the surplice otherwise; outdoor dress of square cap, tippet, and gown was also required. This document did not, however, receive the queen's backing, her interest being sporadic. Some bishops, including John Parkhurst, James Pilkington, and Edwin Sandys, did not enforce these orders, and EDMUND GRINDAL, bishop of London, who eventually did, told opponents that he would rather not wear the cope or surplice but did so for the sake of order and obedience. Meanwhile at Oxford, Sampson was deprived; at Cambridge there were disturbances. The London clergy were assembled before both Parker and Grindal at Lambeth Palace in March 1566 and told to subscribe their willingness to wear the required dress or else be suspended. Thirty-seven refused, some of them popular preachers whose suspension gave rise to public disorders. But most eventually conformed.

Opponents fought back. Even before the Advertisements, in March 1565, twenty persons, including the Bible translator Miles Coverdale, the martyrologist JOHN FOXE, and Alexander Nowell, dean of St. Paul's, appealed for relief from the use of the hated dress. Months later Robert Crowley, a fiery London preacher, denounced vestments in a Paul's Cross sermon, and in 1566 he attacked them in *A Briefe Discourse Against the Outwarde Apparell and Ministring Garmentes of the Popishe Church.* Anthony Gilby also published several attacks on the "rags of Rome." Opponents argued that vestments, far from edifying the church, scandalized the godly.

The nonconformists sought the opinions of foreign divines, but Henry Bullinger responded that churches should not be forsaken over vestments. Theodore Beza, though more hostile to the vestments, agreed. The bishops defended their case by publicizing these moderating views of foreign divines. As the decade closed, disturbances and the pamphlet war waned, vestments ceasing to be a major issue. But even though the importance of this controversy in the emergence of puritanism can be overstated, it had permanent results; a party dissatisfied with the extent and pace of Reform had taken shape, to which the name puritan was now attached, although this group soon turned to other issues. And thoroughly "radicalized" persons, including some layfolk who had all along been more militant than their pastors, formed underground SEPARATIST meetings, free of the "popish" surplice.

The controversy was not trivial. Religions are symbolic systems, in which matters of dress, gesture, rite, and formula carry multilayered meanings. Retention of such relics of the old ways as the surplice signaled to advanced English Protestants the failure of thorough Reformation as well as opportunity for the subversion of Reformation. These "puritans" carried even further the iconoclastic rejection of idolatry and superstition characteristic of the Reformed tradition and insisted that God must be worshiped as commanded in Scripture (Calvin had argued that knowledge of God led to right worship of God). The bishops also generally followed Swiss theology, but Parker and his supporters in defending vestments gave voice to the adiaphorism of the Lutherans. Other important issues were also involved, such as the extent of Christian liberty and the role of the state in matters of religion.

Bibliography: Patrick Collinson, *The Elizabethan Puritan Movement*, 1967; J. H. Primus, *The Vestments Controversy*, 1960.

Dewey D. Wallace, Jr.

W

Wales (the Union with England). Henry Tudor's invasion of England in 1485 was facilitated by the support he received from Welsh sympathizers who flocked to his banner after he landed at Milford Haven. Long since hailed by the bards as deliverer of the Welsh from English oppression, Henry had a greater claim on their loyalty than other candidates to the throne by virtue of his Welsh name and descent. That connection was exploited to his advantage before the triumph at BOSWORTH, and he was to acknowledge it in calculated acts of generosity during his reign, when Welsh communities and individuals were to benefit from his special, if discriminating, favor.

HENRY VII was the only king of England since the conquest of Wales in 1282 to proclaim himself Prince of Wales on his accession. In 1489 he surrendered the title in favor of his heir, who had been christened Arthur (b. 1486), to endorse the symbolic association of the dynasty with "British kingship." The accession of the first Tudor monarch reconciled the Welsh to English rule, although the country itself was left very much as Henry had found it divided into the principality of five shires in the north and west and the lordships of the Marches. He stamped his authority on the country in two ways with the institution of a council in the MARCHES and in 1490 through the systematic imposition of the "indentures of the Marches," whereby lords and stewards of royal lordships entered into bonds to keep order within their jurisdictions. In each case he built on the precedent set by Edward IV, though in Wales as elsewhere Henry pursued his policies with greater thoroughness than his predecessor had done. The marcher council was originally formed to administer the prince's estates, and after Prince Arthur's death in 1502 the Marches continued to be governed under the general supervision of the king's commissioners at Ludlow.

The downfall in 1521 of the duke of Buckingham, the last independent marcher lord of any consequence, made the king's authority unchallenged in the area and threw into relief the anachronism of the marcher system of government.

Schemes were devised by Crown officials in the Marches for the conversion of the lordships into shireground and the abolition of Welsh and marcher customs. These were finally realized in 1536 with a series of acts of Parliament for the extinction of franchises, the introduction of JUSTICES OF THE PEACE, and the administration of English COMMON LAW throughout Wales. The so-called Act of Union (27 Hen. VIII, c. 26) provided for a systematic overhaul of Welsh local government, and that was finally consolidated in the comprehensive statute of 1543. In the interval Welsh native laws were abolished, and the newly formed Welsh constituencies of shires and boroughs sent members of Parliament for the first time to Westminster in 1542. In 1540-1541 a plan was formulated to institute both a principality for Prince EDWARD (born 1537) and a national judicature headed by a chancery with powers confined to the twelve shires of Wales. This plan was in the event rejected in favor of a settlement that blurred the boundary between the two countries by preserving the provincial character of Tudor rule over Wales and the English borderland as exercised by the king's commissioners at Ludlow. Accordingly, this prerogative court, which continued to be designated the "council in the Marches of Wales" even after the "Marches" had been eliminated, received statutory recognition in 1543. In the making of these constitutional adjustments, royal ordinance and proclamation as well as statute were used as legislative instruments to effect the transformation of laws and government. However, the assimilation of the administration of the king's dominions to that of the realm of England was not complete in every detail. In the final act of 1543 the king retained, in the form of a general enabling clause, a right to legislate for Wales without further reference to Parliament. The special relationship of Crown and principality was thereby retained after the "union," though in the reign of JAMES I this legislative right was considered by the judges to have been personal to Henry VIII. It was repealed in Parliament in 1624.

For all the influence of dynasticism on the settlement of Wales after the birth of Prince Edward in 1537, the guiding principle of the new policy introduced in 1536 was efficient government through the uniform application of English common law. Many of the Welsh gentry had long since opted for English law in preference to the native forms of inheritance. They were now entrusted with judicial and administrative responsibilities in their own localities at the same time as they profited from the distribution of monastic lands. There is evidence from the northern principality that members of this class had taken the initiative in these reforms in law and administration early in 1536. Their proposals were evidently adopted by THOMAS CROMWELL in his formulation of a comprehensive policy of integrating border areas within the realm.

The Reformation, in contrast to the so-called union of Wales with England, was a movement imposed from above and outside. There were few religious Reformers in Wales before the 1540s and no traces of surviving LOLLARDY. In the absence of institutions of learning, Welshmen could not encounter HUMAN-ISM in their own country. Anti-clericalism was less virulent than it was in England, and there was no tradition of satire in the social commentary of bardic

poetry. The factors that aided the spread of LUTHERANISM IN ENGLAND—
regular contacts with the continent and the importation of contraband heretical
books along the trade routes—did not obtain in Wales. The greatest advantage that
the Henrician Reformation possessed there was the strength of loyalty to the
dynasty. The church offered little resistance to the changes; the most gifted Welsh
clerics were beneficed in England, and the higher clergy in the dioceses chose to
be complaisant royal servants. Few churchmen believed they had to embrace
"heresy" or newfangledness in doing the bidding of a sovereign considered to be
of unimpeachable orthodoxy. Early alarms were sounded about latent opposition
to the Reforms, but this did not materialize, for lack of leadership as much as lack
of strong attachment to the old faith. With the decline of the marcher lords, the
families of Herbert, Devereux, and Somerset carved out spheres of influence for
themselves in the south and west as members of a court aristocracy of service,
which was obedient if not always conformist.

These magnates and the majority of the gentry throughout the country
benefited to an even greater degree than their counterparts in England from the
political and economic changes that accompanied the Reformation, and they
managed to hold on to their gains throughout the different regimes and religious
settlements of the century. Although a few bards testified to a lingering hostility
to Protestantism as "ffydd y Saeson" (the Englishmen's faith), there was to be no
rebellion against the Crown in sixteenth-century Wales, prompted by religious or
any other discontent. For the most part, the Welsh were able to identify with a
dynasty of their own race, and the Protestant faith was plausibly represented by
the Reformers as something not altogether alien to native traditions and cultures.

Indeed, Welsh Tudor antiquaries contributed an important strand of argument
to general ANGLICAN apologetics with the claim that the Reformed faith was a
restoration of the pure religion practiced by the early Celtic church before
"Romish impurities" were imported by St. Augustine of Canterbury. Some of the
Protestant humanists went further to assert that the ancient Britons possessed
sacred texts in manuscript and the Scriptures in their tongue. They used these
claims in their campaign to promote new translations for the benefit of their
contemporaries, the heirs of the British traditions. The defense of the British
history of Geoffrey of Monmouth against the revisionism of Polydore Vergil by
Welsh and English writers served to bolster an important attribute of the Tudor
myth—the claim to a restoration of British kingship—and thereby sustained
Welshmen's sense of the historic identity of their nation while at the same time
fostering closer ties with the Crown.

Professor Glanmor Williams, the historian of the Reformation in Wales, has
written that in its religious aspects, "the conflict between the Catholics and
Protestants was to resolve itself with a struggle for the possession of a largely
inert mass of the population between two rival groups of humanists." The first
Welsh printed book, a religious primer compiled by the Henrician politique, Sir
John Price, appeared in 1546, to be followed by a series of publications by
William Salesbury, the foremost Welsh humanist of the age. Salesbury was

largely responsible for the translation of the New Testament and the BOOK OF COMMON PRAYER (1567), which had been authorized by an act of Parliament of 1563. The translation of the whole Bible (1588) was the work of William Morgan. In his dedication to Queen Elizabeth, Bishop Morgan declared that many Welshmen had already read the New Testament and had also learned English by comparing it with the English version placed beside it in every parish church. This was a recognition of the fact that the Tudor policy of assimilating the Welsh to English manners had not been entirely abandoned with the official sponsorship of the vernacular Scriptures. Morgan's Bible is acknowledged to be a classic of Welsh prose that standardized the language and prevented it from disintegration into a patois.

Most of the bishops of the Elizabethan church in Wales were Welshmen, and, for all the abuses that proliferated in the dioceses, the general improvement in pastoral care may have had a greater immediate impact on the quality of the religious lives of the people than did the availability of the Scriptures in their own language. Although Protestant writers boasted of a high level of literacy among the monoglot Welsh, the puritan John Penry lamented the lack of preachers proficient in the Welsh texts. The Bible did not become generally accessible until the publication of the portable edition in 1630. Exile Welsh Catholic humanists on the Continent supplied the campaign of reconversion with original works of piety, and others rendered into Welsh, to vie with the Protestant translations; while the recusants at home absented themselves from the services in which they might have heard the gospel in their own tongue. RECUSANTS were concentrated in areas of the border country, especially in the southeast under the protection of the Somerset family, earls of Worcester. In northeast Wales and the Llyn peninsula, where ROBERT DUDLEY, earl of Leicester, held the lordship of Denbigh and rights over the Forest of Snowdon, backwoods squires were actuated by religious conviction and motives of self-preservation in their resistance to the encroachments of the preeminent patron of puritans. Welsh Catholic exiles claimed that the majority of their fellow-countrymen at home were attached to the old faith. Although contemporary statistics gathered by the bishops of the established church contradicted this view, it is probably true to say that the hold of Protestantism on the country was still a tenuous one at the turn of the century.

Bibliography: P. R. Roberts, "The Union with England and the Identity of 'Anglican' Wales," *Transactions of the Royal Historical Society*, 22 (1972): 31-47; P. R. Roberts, "The 'Act of Union' in Welsh History," *Transactions of the Honourable Society of Cymmrodorion*, 1972-1973 (1974): 49-72; Glanmor Williams, *Welsh Reformation Essays*, 1967.

P. R. Roberts

Walsingham, Sir Francis (c.1532-1590). This staunch PURITAN served as secretary of state and a PRIVY COUNCILLOR from 1573 to 1590. Originally a family of prosperous London vintners, the Walsinghams had established themselves among the Kentish gentry by the time Francis was born. He had good COURT connections; through his mother he was related to the influential councillor of HENRY VIII, Sir Anthony Denny, and his mother's second marriage, when he was a child, brought him into contact with the household of the 1st baron Hunsdon, a Boleyn relative of ELIZABETH I. At the age of sixteen in 1548, he entered King's College, Cambridge, where the Protestant scholar Sir John Cheke was provost. Walsingham did not take a degree there and traveled in Europe before attending Gray's Inn. MARY I's reign provided few advancement opportunities for one related to obvious Protestant families involved in the plot to make LADY JANE GREY queen and in WYATT'S REBELLION, so he studied civil law at Padua and visited Basel, Switzerland.

Returning to England shortly after Elizabeth's succession, he was soon at court working under the direction and benefaction of Sir WILLIAM CECIL. In 1559, Cecil promoted him for membership in Parliament, where he continued to serve throughout his life. The security of his queen and Tudor rule became his primary objective no matter what official position he held over the years; diplomacy and intelligence work were the hallmark of his long political career. He served as ambassador in France from 1571 to 1573, and during the St. Bartholomew's Day Massacre he sheltered Protestants at his house. He returned from France totally distrusting the Catholic Charles IX and his mother Catherine de Medici. This attitude influenced his actions against Catholics in general and against MARY, QUEEN OF SCOTS, "that devilish woman," in particular. While he was secretary and councillor, after his appointment in 1573, Walsingham consistently supported military action in favor of Protestants and against Catholic powers. The queen's frugality in military matters and her infamous tendency to procrastinate frustrated him. He was not as successful at court as others, because while Elizabeth recognized his ability and integrity, she found him too gloomy and pessimistic. He may not have fitted the profile of an Elizabethan courtier, but he was indispensable to her because he had developed an extraordinarily extensive spy network. He began to supply Cecil with information in 1567, and during the development of the RIDOLFI PLOT of 1571 he refined his intelligence gathering into a system by patiently combining information from official sources at home and abroad with information from merchants and undercover agents who served him directly. In 1586, when BABINGTON plotted Elizabeth's murder, he deliberately entrapped Mary, Queen of Scots. While Mary's supporters saw his actions as cruel and lacking in morality, Elizabeth's security justified any means to Walsingham. Fortunately for his career, he was ill when Elizabeth signed Mary's death warrant, and he, unlike his colleague secretary William Davison, escaped the worst of Elizabeth's wrath after Mary's execution.

Walsingham received hundreds of reports about Philip II's plans to invade England, but he was unable to convince Elizabeth or her council to make adequate preparations. He lacked influence with the queen, and his usual alliance with the more persuasive ROBERT DUDLEY, earl of Leicester, had deteriorated for personal and political reasons. Leicester had failed to help with the debts of Sir PHILIP SIDNEY, Walsingham's son-in-law, and had not supported Walsingham for the office of chancellor of the duchy of Lancaster, which he obtained in 1587. Walsingham's more bellicose position on military questions continued to isolate him from Elizabeth's chief advisers in the privy council until after the defeat of the SPANISH ARMADA. He struggled with various physical ailments for the last two years of his life, but he continued to serve on the council until two weeks before his death. Although he did not acquire great wealth during his career and in fact died in debt to the Crown, he had consistently patronized and promoted puritans and contributed to various voyages of EXPLORATION.

Bibliography: C. Read, *Mr. Secretary Walsingham and the Policy of Queen Elizabeth*, 3 vols., 1925.

Ann Weikel

Warbeck, Conspiracies of Perkin (1491-1499). After the SIMNEL Plot of 1487, several years elapsed before HENRY VII was confronted by a new Yorkist impostor. This was Perkin Warbeck (or Osbeck), who had been born in the Low Countries in 1475. Like Simnel, Warbeck had a refined and aristocratic manner, which caused him to attract the notice of Sir Edward Brampton, a Yorkist partisan who had been exiled from England shortly after BOSWORTH FIELD. Three years later Warbeck had taken employment with Pregent Meno, an enterprising Breton clothier who used him to model his expensive garments. During the autumn of 1491 Meno and Warbeck arrived at Cork in southern Ireland, where the latter made a strong impression on the mayor and his associates. Encouraged by a Yorkist schemer from Exeter, John Taylor, the municipal authorities decided that the cultivated Warbeck must be of royal descent; and in November 1491 they paraded him through the city streets as Prince Richard, the younger son of Edward IV, who had probably died in the Tower of London eight years before. From 1491 until his capture by Henry VII in 1497, Warbeck masqueraded as "Richard IV" or the main Yorkist pretender to the throne; and because he received periodic aid from individuals in high places, he caused the Tudor monarch many anxious moments.

As early as December 1491, Henry VII was aware of "Richard IV" and the new conspiracy against him. He immediately sent an army to Cork under Thomas Garth and "Black James" Ormond, which caused Warbeck's supporters, led by the earl of Desmond, to retreat into distant Munster. By that juncture a special emissary from Charles VIII, whose relations with England were far from cordial, had arrived and invited Warbeck to accept French assistance. Thereupon the impostor embarked for Paris, where he was welcomed as the younger son of Edward IV and granted a pension and spacious living quarters.

For the next ten months Warbeck remained as an honored guest in the French capital, since Charles VIII considered him a valuable pawn in his growing difficulties with England. Those difficulties came to a head in October 1492, when Henry VII led an army of more than 12,500 men to the Continent. More concerned about affairs in Italy, the French offered such generous terms that Henry could not refuse them. On 3 November 1492 the treaty of Etaples, restoring peace between the two countries, was signed while Charles VIII expelled Warbeck to the Low Countries.

When Henry VII learned of Warbeck's new whereabouts, he pressed insistently for his expulsion. But the archduke Philip was a stubborn man and refused to oblige. A trade war between England and the Low Countries soon broke out, which ultimately resulted in the emperor Maximilian I, the archduke, and Margaret of Burgundy all agreeing to support an assault on southern England by Warbeck.

In June 1495 Warbeck sailed across the Channel with fourteen ships. However, the 300 men who disembarked on the Kentish coast near Deal were quickly defeated by the local sheriff, who sent them off in chains to the capital. Thereupon the impostor, who had not gone ashore, decided to try his luck again in Ireland. Once again English forces drove him out, and by the end of November 1495 he had arrived at the court of JAMES IV at Stirling.

Regardless of whether James IV believed Warbeck to be a true Yorkist prince, he hoped to exploit his presence to recover the great border fortress of Berwick, which the English had captured in 1482. Accordingly, James gave Warbeck a warm welcome, including an allowance and permission to marry one of his cousins, Lady Catherine Gordon. During the first half of 1496, Henry VII tried to dislodge Warbeck from the Scottish court by repeatedly offering to conclude a marriage agreement between James and his own daughter Margaret. But because Henry would not consider exchanging Berwick for the impostor, James mobilized an army of 1,400 men and invaded northern England in mid-September. The attackers received no popular support, and, threatened by large English forces, they recrossed the border into southern Scotland in less than a week, having accomplished nothing of value.

During the spring of 1497, James IV received additional offers for an eventual dynastic alliance with the English Crown. As a consequence the king of Scots soon expelled Warbeck from his dominions, although he generously provided "Richard IV" with a ship to speed him on his way. Briefly stopping in Ireland, within six weeks the impostor decided that his only chance of success lay in making a sudden descent on Cornwall. There the embers of the recent CORNISH REBELLION might be fanned back to life.

Early in September 1497 Warbeck and over 100 supporters embarked for western England, and on the seventh they landed on the shores of Whitesand Bay, near Land's End. After finding shelter for his wife in a local monastery, the impostor and his followers set out for Bodmin and attracted thousands of recruits along the way. Failing to capture Exeter, threatened by superior forces, and finding his escape blocked, the impostor surrendered to royal agents. He was taken in chains to Taunton, where he made a full confession in the presence of the king and his own wife, who had just been brought in by royal guards.

Despite all the trouble they had caused, Henry VII was unusually merciful to the young couple now in his power. Lady Catherine was allowed to become a lady-in-waiting to Henry's consort, Elizabeth of York. As for Warbeck, the monarch initiated no legal proceedings but placed him under loose surveillance at Westminster Palace. Had Warbeck resigned himself to that arrangement, he would have enjoyed a comfortable existence for the remainder of his days. But he still had hopes for the future and tried to escape in June 1498. Recaptured after traveling less than ten miles, he was imprisoned in the Tower, where he lived for over a year.

Henry VII was determined that nothing should prevent his son's marriage to CATHERINE OF ARAGON. But during the spring of 1499 Catherine's parents, Ferdinand and Isabella, revealed that they would never send her to England as long as any "doubtful royal blood" remained to threaten her safety. Henry correctly interpreted this position as a hint to eliminate Warbeck and another captive in the Tower, Edward, earl of Warwick, the long-imprisoned grandson of Richard, duke of York. Tricked into an escape plan, both men were charged with high treason. Convicted in due course, Warbeck was executed at Tyburn on 16 November, while Warwick was beheaded on Tower Hill thirteen days later.

With his two victims' deaths, Henry VII closed the book on the longest chapter of Yorkist intrigue that ever confronted him. Yet his conscience was clearly troubled by his resort to judicial murder, since a contemporary observer reported that he aged twenty years at the time.

Bibliography: Michael Van Cleave Alexander, *The First of the Tudors: A Study of Henry VII and His Reign*, 1980.

Michael V. C. Alexander

Wardens of the Marches. The northern Marches were adjacent to the frontier with Scotland. The area was divided into three Marches or wardenries, each being under the jurisdiction of a lord warden. The East March, the smallest, extended from the river Aln north to Berwick-upon-Tweed, the warden's headquarters, and west to the Scottish border and the Cheviot. The Middle March took in the remainder of Northumberland, extending westward to the border with Cumberland. The West March was coterminous with the counties of Cumberland and Westmorland, its headquarters being at Carlisle. Across the frontier were the three Scottish Marches, which had the same names as the English, and the keepership of Liddlesdale.

The office of warden had its origins in the wars with Scotland, which began in 1295. From 1309 wardens of the Marches were permanent officials of the Crown charged with the responsibility for defending the March against the Scots. By the Tudor period the wardens commanded men performing border service, maintained fortifications, and kept the peace with the Scots. They had authority to conduct negotiations with their Scottish opposites and enforce March law, the customary laws peculiar to the Borders. Wardens could appoint their own deputies, officials, and clerks, and the warden of the East March was usually governor of Berwick with his own special council. Border administration was governed by March laws, which dealt with offenses for which English and Scots could claim redress from wardens in the opposite March, such as cattle rustling, murder, and destruction of property, and which laid down the procedures in times of truce and for trials of offenders. In times of truce meetings between officials on both sides of the border could be held monthly, although meetings were not always so frequent, to discuss arrangements for trials and to settle accounts of those claiming redress for border infringements and raids.

The choice of those appointed to serve as wardens during the Tudor period reveals three distinct categories and shows a growing trend towards effective central control and the elimination of independent action on the part of important frontier magnates. Up to 1536 the Percy earls of Northumberland dominated border affairs in the East and Middle Marches, a position matched by the Neville earls of Westmorland in the west. Although there were signs of change under HENRY VII it was not until the 1530s that the power of the traditional frontier magnates was consistently challenged. Those appointed thereafter tended to be lesser men who owed their position not to territorial landowning but to the Crown. Men like the Dacres and Thomas Wharton in the West March, Thomas Forster in the Middle March, and Sir William Eure in the East March relied on the Crown for their authority and were more easily controlled by it, even though they still had connections with the locality they governed. Under EDWARD VI the policy of direct assertion of Crown influence was continued, but under MARY, the earls of Northumberland and Westmorland were able to reassert their influence. ELIZABETH reverted to a policy of deliberately excluding them from positions of trust along the border. After 1536 wardens were encouraged to report regularly to the PRIVY COUNCIL to seek instructions and advice and to request assistance. Later during Elizabeth's reign the third type of warden appeared; southerners such as Henry Carey, 1st Lord Hunsdon, and his sons were dependent on the Crown for their position and were prepared to enforce government policies. Similar changes may be seen in the appointment of officers serving under the wardens. As part of the same policy, from time to time the COUNCIL IN THE NORTH was given jurisdiction over the Marches; Henry Hastings, 3rd earl of Huntingdon, the lord president of the council, visited the Borders in 1593 and revealed their parlous condition. In 1598 it was suggested that a council should be established in the Marches, effectively to take over the powers exercised by the wardens.

The effect of these changes was twofold. First, tension in Anglo-Scottish relations diminished, especially after 1586, so that the government became less concerned with border transgressions. The appointment of an ambassador to the Scottish Court reduced the importance of the wardens as a source of information, while officials with special commissions dealt with the international functions previously enjoyed by wardens. Second, there was an increasing tendency for wardens to become non-resident, leading to increased rivalry in the Marches between gentry and officials. When JAMES I came to the throne in 1603, the wardenries were dissolved; March law, with no wardens to enforce it, was abolished by Parliament in 1607.

Bibliography: R. R. Reid, *The King's Council in the North*, 1921; D. L. W. Tough, *The Last Years of a Frontier*, 1928; S. J. Watts and Susan J. Watts, *From Border to Middle Shire; Northumberland 1586-1625*, 1975.

D. J. Lamburn

Wardship and the Court of Wards. The institution of wardship represented a lingering aspect of feudalism in sixteenth-century England. Basically, wardship originated in the monarch's rights over land held by his subjects in knight service, that is, for military duties. Those holding land by such tenures from the Crown were tenants-in-chief. When a tenant-in-chief died, the heir was obliged to seek a regrant of the estate. This involved receiving a grant of livery, which conveyed the right to enter the inheritance by paying a fee called relief, if the heir was an adult male. If the heir was a minor (under twenty-one years of age if a male and generally under sixteen if a female), the Crown assumed wardship and took responsibility for the heirs until they reached adulthood. By 1485 the Crown's PREROGATIVES in wardship had expanded to include control of the wards' lands and the right to arrange for their marriages. The Crown could offer unmarried male wards a suitable bride, and it reserved the right to choose husbands for unmarried female wards. Although these arranged marriages were binding, the wards did have the right to marry a spouse of equal or greater social standing or to reject the proposal. Thus, the monarch reaped extended benefits from this fiscal feudalism, since the revenues from the lands also went to the Crown during the wardship. Ever in need of money, the Tudors energetically exploited this source of potential revenue. The right to arrange the heir's marriage or to manage the estate was often sold to a third party. In this way, fiscal feudalism transformed wardship into a commodity that could be bought and sold.

Since the Tudor dynasty actively participated in the revenue-producing aspect of wardship, it became necessary to develop administrative procedures and eventually a specialized bureaucracy to handle that business. HENRY VII vigorously attempted to gather his feudal revenues more efficiently. With regard to wardship, he first relied on a very personal system of administration. This informality gave way to a more structured approach about 1503, when Henry VII definitely placed the responsibility for managing wardships and the associated revenues within his chamber administration. Simultaneously he created the basic officers of wardship, later formally systematized under HENRY VIII. These officials were the master of wards, a receiver-general of wardship revenue, an auditor, and particular receivers for each county.

Henry VIII built upon this existing administrative structure by further organizing and centralizing it. William Paulet, master of wards from 1526 to 1554, and THOMAS CROMWELL helped to complete the process. Cromwell certainly oversaw the conclusion—the formal foundation of the Court of Wards by statute (32 Hen. VIII, c. 46) in 1540. A subsequent act of Parliament in 1542 (33 Hen. VIII, c. 22) brought livery within the cognizance of the court, now named the Court of Wards and Liveries. These two statutes formally founded the court as a court of record. It was responsible for several basic functions the administration and government of all royal wards and their lands, widows of deceased tenants-in-chief, and the mentally incompetent; the handling of all judicial matters arising from the court's administrative duties; and the financial accounting for all revenues generated by the court's activities. The impetus behind the formal foundation of the court came from several recent developments. As the Crown faced increasing financial difficulties during the 1540s, the need arose for a more efficient and systematic collection of all Henry VIII's feudal revenues. Furthermore, a dramatic increase in the number of wardships and liveries occurred, which was due the Crown's improved knowledge of those estates that were liable. In addition, there was a larger number of estates held by tenancy-in-chief as a result of the provisions of the Statute of Uses (27 Hen. VIII, c. 10) in 1536 and the Statutue of Wills (32 Hen. VIII, c. 1)) in 1540. Both of these statutes were designed to halt the erosion of the king's feudal rights and to increase tenancies-in-chief by linking them to the Crown's sales and grants of former monastic lands.

From 1540 to 1600 Crown appointees filled the nine statutory offices that handled the bulk of business that flowed through the court. The master of wards headed the court and was its principal executive officer. In 1561, WILLIAM CECIL replaced Paulet in the office and held it until his death in 1598. The surveyor-general of liveries ranked second in the hierarchy and mainly looked after the Crown's interests in liveries. Next in rank were the receiver-general and the auditor. Legal matters were chiefly the responsibility of the attorney. These five were the highest-ranking officials of the court and composed its judiciary. This judicial work was not simple, and the court generated a large number of written pleadings in English. A clerk of wards and a clerk of liveries performed much of the daily administrative and secretarial functions of the court. Its final two officers were the minor ones of usher and messenger.

As the years passed, particularly after 1563, additional subofficials and under-clerks swelled the court's bureaucracy. This multiplication of officers and the fees invariably due to them heightened the general public's growing displeasure with the court. The official salaries started out low and actually decreased in their real value during the course of the sixteenth century. These nominal salaries, however, were substantially augmented by the major officers' receipt of bribes, gifts, and various fees on each step of the lengthy administrative procedure used in grants of wardship and livery.

Two officials administered all of the local business of the court. The escheator was appointed annually by the lord treasurer and so actually worked for the Exchequer. The feodary was appointed by and at the pleasure of the master of wards. In fact, by 1540, the feodaries had usurped much of the escheators' work and significance. It was the feodary's survey and valuation of each heir's lands that the master of wards used when pricing a wardship or livery. Further information concerning the geographical location, the extent and value of land, the types of land tenures held by the deceased tenant, and the name and age of the heir(s) was provided by the document known as an "inquisition post mortem," which was drawn up by the escheator and the feodary along with the help of a local jury on the occasion of the death of a tenant-in-chief.

The revenues collected by the Court of Wards and Liveries fluctuated and were never more than a minor source of royal income. The average annual amount brought in by the Elizabethan Court of Wards and Liveries was about £15,000. It is possible that the court's greatest value lay in its provision of a fairly lucrative source of additional income for selected important royal officials. Basically, the court acquitted itself well in its provisions for those wards who were the widows of tenants-in-chief and the mentally incompetent. The same thing, however, cannot be said with regard to the treatment of minor wards.

The Court of Wards and Liveries continued to operate well into the seventeenth century. ROBERT CECIL succeeded his father as master of wards and served from 1599 to 1611. Belatedly, he attempted to reform the court and its policies, particularly by raising the prices for wardships by at least 300%. This policy only served to increase public discontent further. In 1610, he even proposed that the Crown give up its rights to wardship in return for a regular sum of money granted by Parliament that would have been part of the failed Great Contract. The court survived until it was abolished by the Long Parliament in 1645, an action confirmed by the Restoration government in 1660.

Bibliography: H. E. Bell, *An Introduction to the History and Records of the Court of Wards and Liveries*, 1953; Joel Hurstfield, *The Queen's Wards: Wardship and Marriage Under Elizabeth I*, 1958.

Eugene Bourgeois II

Warham, William (c. 1450-1532). He was born at Malshanger in Church Oakley, Hampshire, to Robert and Elizabeth Warham and attended Winchester College in 1469 and New College, Oxford, in 1473. Admitted a fellow, he left New College in 1488 after taking the degrees of B.C.L. and D.C.L. and was later incorporated at Cambridge. His first offices were those of advocate in the court of arches and of principal or moderator of the civil law school, Oxford. He also served Oxford as chancellor from 1506 to 1532.

From 1490 comes evidence of his first mission abroad when he was proctor at Rome of the bishop of Ely and of Christ Church Cathedral priory, Canterbury.

By 1496 and 1497, when he was asked to negotiate a marriage between CATHERINE OF ARAGON and Arthur, Prince of Wales, and to travel to Scotland, he had already served on several embassies, including one to Maximilian, king of the Romans.

From 1493 he held many offices, among them subdeacon of Lichfield, precentor of Wells, archdeacon of Huntington, prebendary of Timsbury in Romsey Abbey, Hampshire, and several rectories. Most of these he resigned upon his election in 1501 to the bishopric of London, from which he was translated to Canterbury in 1503. In 1494 he had become master of the rolls and in 1502 exchanged it for keeper of the great seal, and he won the title of lord chancellor after his election as archbishop. As chancellor, he addressed Parliament and as archbishop promulgated a code of reforming statutes for his court of audience and made visitations of his province.

The royal family often required his assistance. Warham crowned HENRY VIII in 1509 and subsequently officiated at many royal functions at court and in the countryside. He greeted Cardinal Lorenzo Campeggio in 1518 and met with Charles V both before and after he attended the FIELD OF CLOTH OF GOLD in 1520, but he was excused from greeting the emperor again in 1522 because of a "complaint of the head," a recurrent health problem.

By November 1515, when he gave THOMAS WOLSEY the cardinal's hat, his influence at court had begun to wane. The next month he relinquished to him the great seal, reportedly with little regret, as he was displeased with the king's foreign policy. After Wolsey became papal legate in 1518, he encroached upon Canterbury's prerogative. In 1521 Warham had to respond to Wolsey's letter about Lutheran heretics at Oxford University and denied that the heresy was widespread.

Until his death on 22 August 1532, Warham was caught up in the DIVORCE dispute. At first he supported the king, for Catherine received no assistance from him, although he was appointed chief of her counsel. After Wolsey's fall, Warham rebuked Oxford University for delaying its decision about the validity of a man's marrying his brother's widow, signed letters asking the pope to approve the divorce, attended a Hampton Court session about England's relations with Rome, and requested Bishop JOHN FISHER to cease assisting the queen. In January 1531 he accepted Henry as supreme head of the church after his own disclaimer, "in so far as the law of Christ allows," was added, but by February the ailing archbishop, who had made out his will in 1530, decided to protest all parliamentary acts derogatory to papal authority or to Canterbury prerogatives. Despite his brave response in 1532 to the Commons' petition, which complained about the clergy's independent lawmaking power, that if anything amiss were found it would be reformed, the clergy were forced to acquiesce.

He died at St. Stephen's, Canterbury, and was buried in his cathedral on 10 September 1532, having divided his possessions among All Souls' and New College, Oxford, and Winchester. With his considerable income, he had been a valued patron of Erasmus but had been unsuccessful in persuading him to settle in England.

Bibliography: *Dictionary of National Biography*; A. B. Emden, *A Biographical Register of the University of Oxford to A.D. 1500*, 3 vols., 1959; Michael Kelly, "The Submission of the Clergy in 1532," *Transactions of the Royal Historical Society*, 15 (1965): 97-119.

Retha Warnicke

Western Rebellion of 1549. The armed rising that took place in the southwest of England against the regime of EDWARD SEYMOUR, the protector Somerset, stemmed from several causes, but in contrast with other local rebellions of the same year, was primarily motivated by discontent over matters of religious belief and practice. The people of Cornwall nourished a Celtic tradition of devotion to local saints and in this alone felt particularly threatened by the Reformation.

The accelerated pace of reform that followed the accession of EDWARD VI met with little enthusiasm anywhere in the southwest, and the inquiries into church goods, following so soon after the dissolution of the CHANTRIES, aroused deep suspicions of the government's further intentions. In Devon there was also widespread opposition to a new parliamentary tax on sheep, though otherwise there was virtually no agrarian unrest in the southwest, where the fields had long been very largely enclosed.

The immediate cause of the rising in 1549 was undoubtedly the statutory imposition of a new Prayer Book in English. Ordered to be used on and from Whitsunday, it was first actively resisted in the small village of Sampford Courtenay in mid-Devon, remote from the more densely populated and richer south of the country and the urban centers of Exeter and Plymouth. In fact it was on Whitmonday that the villagers forced their priest to say the old Mass in Latin. The failure of local magistrates, one of whom was actually murdered in the village, to quell the disturbance had the effect of arousing neighboring communities, and what had begun as a merely local protest escalated into a widespread commotion. Almost by instinct the country people moved toward the walled city of Exeter, the county's capital. Attempts to halt them at Crediton by the two Carew brothers, local Protestant gentlemen, only aggravated the situation, especially as the news now reached the rebels that the Cornishmen were on their way. They had assembled in Bodmin and came by way of Plymouth, whose civic leaders capitulated without a fight. After some circling of Exeter and the capture of few gentlemen in the course of fleeing the city, the rebels settled down in camps outside the walls and effectively barred all movement in or out of the city for nearly six weeks. In fact there was quite considerable support among the citizens for the rebels' aims but in spite of severe deprivation, the city's traditional loyalty to the powers-that-be prevailed.

The leadership of the rebel army had been assumed by a mere handful of lesser gentlemen, of whom the most important was a notoriously aggressive Cornish gentleman, Humphrey Arundell. By and large the farmers seem to have given way to country tradesmen, but the most effective and enduring leadership was provided by a small number of dissident priests, outstanding among them being Robert Welsh, also a Cornishman, vicar of the parish of St. Thomas just across the river south of Exeter. In due course the leaders hammered out various sets of "articles," that is, demands, which were conveyed to Westminster. Basically these called for a halt to religious changes and for a return to the status quo at the end of HENRY VIII's reign. The only sign of any class conflict was the article calling for a limit to be placed on the number of servants which could be employed by any one gentleman.

Only after the local magistrates had clearly failed to bring peace did Somerset send to the scene John Lord Russell, already a familiar figure locally, not only as president of the short-lived COUNCIL OF THE WEST but as a considerate landlord in the region. At first he was provided with a very small force, but when he failed to recruit additional men locally, he was supplied with an army of foreign mercenaries intended by Somerset for service against the Scots. A preliminary skirmish at Fenny Bridges near Honiton, a few miles east of Exeter, followed by a full-scale battle on Clyst heath, nearer to the city, resulted in all the rebels who fought either being killed or routed. Exeter was relieved, and the remnants of those in arms were finally crushed not far from Sampford Courtenay, where the trouble had started.

The city of Exeter was well rewarded for its loyalty, as also were the few local gentlemen who had been active against rebels. John Lord Russell soon after became earl of Bedford. Although not immediately satisfied in their religious demands, at least the farmers among the rebels had the satisfaction of seeing the sheep tax repealed before the year was out.

Bibliography: A.L. Rowse, *Tudor Cornwall*, 1941; Anthony Fletcher, *Tudor Rebellions*, 3rd. ed., 1983.

Joyce Youings

White Horse Tavern. The initial impact of Protestantism in England is associated with a group of Cambridge scholars who met regularly at the White Horse Inn (or Tavern) in St. Edward's parish. The gatherings were labeled "Little Germany," probably because Martin Luther's writings were being discussed there. We know relatively little about these meetings, because our major source for them, JOHN FOXE, gives us only the barest details.

According to Foxe "the godly learned in Christ" from a number of Cambridge colleges "conferred continually together." They chose to meet at the White Horse because many who came from the colleges of St. John's, Queens and Kings "came in on the back side." We do not know precisely when these meetings took place or even the names of all who attended, and there is no account that specifically tells us what took place. They may have begun even before the first burning of Luther's books in Cambridge in 1520 or 1521. Luther's books were clearly being exported to England in 1519, and, according to Erasmus, important people in England admired Luther's writings. Although it is not clear if the meetings at the White Horse were attended only by a closed group of early Cambridge Protestants or if "the godly learned" included people who were simply interested in discussing Luther's doctrine, it is possible that as many as 50 or 60 leading opponents of Protestantism, like STEPHEN GARDINER, may have attended. In addition among those resident at Cambridge in the 1520s were a large number of people who would take important roles of leadership in the English Reformation. Future archbishops and bishops like THOMAS CRANMER, Nicholas Heath, MATTHEW PARKER, HUGH LATIMER, NICHOLAS RIDLEY, Nicholas Shaxton, and John Bale as well as other early Protestants like John Frith and WILLIAM TYNDALE, who was at Cambridge from 1519 to 1521, were probably among "the godly learned."

The leaders of the group were Thomas Bilney, Hugh Latimer, and ROBERT BARNES. Bilney, who was converted to the Protestant doctrine of justification through reading Erasmus's New Testament and some of Luther's treatises, introduced Latimer and Barnes to evangelical doctrines and is credited with beginning a study group of Cambridge men interested in discussing Luther's ideas. Barnes gradually became the informal leader of those who met at the White Horse, and Foxe mentions those meetings immediately after his discussion of Barnes's sermon at St. Edward's on Christmas Eve 1525, which led to accusations of heresy against him. Barnes, who was urged by the vice-chancellor to make a public recantation, met with Bilney and six or eight others, probably from the White Horse group, and they encouraged him to stand firm. He refused to recant, and in February 1526 Barnes was arrested and called before THOMAS WOLSEY, who had been scurrilously attacked in the sermon. At the same time a search for Lutheran books was carried out by the vice-chancellor with the serjeant-at-arms and the proctors. The authorities may have received information from an informer, since, according to Foxe, they searched the rooms of some thirty suspect persons and went straight to the place were the books were usually kept. However, Dr. Forman, the president of Queens, managed to circulate a warning, and the books were removed before the authorities arrived. This type of harassment and the ban on Luther's books made public discussion of his works considerably more dangerous, and the meetings at the White Horse probably ended after the arrest of Barnes.

Bibliography: William Clebsch, *England's Earliest Protestants*, 1964; A. G. Dickens, *The English Reformation* 2nd ed., 1989.

Rudolph W. Heinze

Whitgift, John (c. 1530-1604). The third Elizabethan archbishop of Canterbury was born of gentry stock in Lincolnshire about 1530 and gained his B.A. (1554) at Pembroke Hall, Cambridge. In 1555 he became a fellow of Peterhouse. Andrew Perne, master of Peterhouse, was his patron and protector during the Catholic MARY I's reign. With ELIZABETH's restoration of Protestantism, Whitgift entered holy orders (1560) and became Bishop Richard Cox of Ely's chaplain. In 1563 he attained his B.D. and the Lady Margaret lectureship in divinity at Cambridge.

Whitgift opposed Archbishop MATTHEW PARKER's conformity campaign in 1565, but Perne rightly predicted Whitgift would conform for the sake of advancement. He was soon a royal chaplain, and in 1567 master of Pembroke Hall and doctor of divinity. He became master of Trinity and in 1570, vice-chancellor of the university and promoted statutes that increased the powers of the senior members. He now opposed nonconformity and the extremists led by Thomas Cartwright.

Whitgift was made dean of Lincoln in 1571. In 1572 Parker persuaded him to answer *The Admonition to Parliament* (see ADMONITION CONTROVERSY). Whitgift's defense of the established church was rewarded with the bishopric of Worcester in 1577. There, his handling of RECUSANTS and temporizing over clerical nonconformity impressed the Protestant gentry. As vice-president of the COUNCIL OF THE MARCHES, he deputized for the frequently absent lord president Henry Sidney.

In 1583 Whitgift became primate. He always enjoyed far greater support than his predecessors, Parker and EDMUND GRINDAL. His archepiscopate began with a campaign against clerical nonconformity in the winter of 1583-1584. Faced with widespread opposition from the clergy, gentry, and PRIVY COUNCIL, he backed down in the summer of 1584 and concentrated upon the more extreme nonconformists, against whom he used the ecclesiastical court of HIGH COMMISSION. The procedures therein aroused great antagonism because of the use of the ex officio oath. Nevertheless, Whitgift was persistent.

Whitgift was the only Elizabethan bishop to become a member of the privy council (1586). This position, coupled with his association with Elizabeth's favorite, Lord Chancellor CHRISTOPHER HATTON, gave him the political power base that enabled him to pursue successfully his drive for conformity. The extremist MARTIN MARPRELATE TRACTS discredited all PURITANS and helped Whitgift to quiet nonconformist threats to the established church by the 1590s. Hatton's death in 1591 still left Whitgift with political support from other members of what contemporaries called the "Little Faction," including Sir Thomas Sackville, Lord Buckhurst, and Sir John Puckering, the new Lord keeper.

Whitgift's drive for conformity led to accusations that his was a negative policy. He was well aware of the other problems of the ministry and tried to solve them, although nonconformity was given equal, if not greater, priority. He reminded laymen that their impropriated tithes aggravated clerical poverty and contributed to pluralism, non-residence and poor quality clergy, but Whitgift was powerless in the face of economic reality. Abuses in the established church were attacked in Parliament, as was Whitgift's conformity campaign. Elizabeth supported her primate. In 1585 she stopped parliamentary discussion of her church and threatened to "uncouncil" privy councillors supporting the agitation, which threatened her supreme governorship. Whitgift monitored parliamentary proceedings so that Little Faction supporters could counterattack, as with Hatton's great speech against Anthony Cope's Presbyterian "BILL AND BOOK" (1587). The speech was prepared by Whitgift's protégé, Richard Bancroft.

Like Parker, Whitgift had a household that functioned as a ministry of propaganda and was staffed by writers and preachers such as Bancroft, William Barlow, and other future bishops. Whitgift had learnedly confuted the "Admonition," but now he countenanced polemic, used smear tactics, and played on lay fears of disorder and theocracy. Against Martin Marprelate he used professional wits. Like Grindal, he encouraged "puritans" to direct their propagandistic energies against Catholics, as with William Whitaker. Whitgift was relatively uninvolved with the one publication that stands out from the contemporary mess of ephemeral polemic, RICHARD HOOKER's *Of the Laws of Ecclesiastical Polity*.

Whitgift had a splendid household. His retinue of 800-1,000 persons equaled THOMAS WOLSEY's. His entertaining of monarch, nobility, and gentry reflected his awareness and his improvement of the social standing of the primate. This anticipated the rise in clerical aspirations that caused tension under the Stuarts.

Seventeenth-century doctrinal disputes over CALVINISM were also anticipated during Whitgift's archepiscopate as the controversy culminating with the Lambeth Articles shows. Elizabeth scolded Whitgift for allowing debate on this sensitive issue. The apocryphal story that she teased her "little black husband" by threatening PRAEMUNIRE probably captures the spirit of their relationship.

Elizabeth's death (1603) worried Whitgift. When the new king summoned a conference to Hampton Court in January 1604, Whitgift and Bancroft feared that JAMES I might prove an impartial umpire between the bishops and nonconformists, but while James recognized the need for improvements, he wanted to preserve the church he had inherited basically unaltered. Whitgift died soon after, assured that the ELIZABETHAN SETTLEMENT OF RELIGION, which he had labored long to preserve, would remain undisturbed—for the moment.

Bibliography: V. J. K. Brook, *Whitgift and the English Church*, 1957; P. Collinson, *The Elizabethan Puritan Movement*, 1967; V. Sanders, "John Whitgift: Primate, Privy Councillor and Propagandist," *Anglican and Episcopal History* 56 (1987): 385-403.

V. C. Sanders

Wills, Statute of (1540). Also known as "An Act of how Lands may be willed by Testament" (32 Hen. VIII, c. 1), it resolved a long-standing conflict between HENRY VIII and his subjects over revenue due to the Crown from feudal incidents, tenurial obligations owed by those who held land directly from the king. It freed landholders from the full exactions to which they had become liable as a result of the STATUTE OF USES of 1536 and legalized the disposition of land by will, a practice that was severely limited by the statute and the judicial decision in Dacre's case (1535).

The preamble of the Statute of Wills is notable for its statement of the king's mercy, love, and benevolence toward his subjects, who in return are said to give him their reverence, obedience, and prayers. The substance of the act is based on the principle that feudal dues such as WARDSHIP and primer seisin would be levied on only one-third of the land technically liable to them. Thus two-thirds of all lands held directly from the Crown (tenure-in-chief) could be devised by will at the "pleasure" of the owner, while one-third would be reserved to cover the interests of the king. Similarly, in those cases in which land was held by military tenure (knight's service) of a lord rather than a king, that lord could collect feudal incidents on a third. Landowners who held land neither from the king nor by military tenures were completely free to dispose of all of their land by will. Thus, in return for a clear obligation to pay a part of their feudal dues, landholders were released from the pressure that the Statute of Uses had put them under to pay all. In addition, although legal devices involving uses had made it possible before 1535 to dispose of land by will, the Statute of Wills marked the first full recognition of the legality of doing so. This was important because it enabled landowners to break the custom of primogeniture and provide for their children as they pleased.

The political circumstances surrounding the passage of the Statute of Wills are not easy to interpret but are of interest nevertheless. The revolution in the land law that had been created by Dacre's Case and the Statute of Uses was attacked by the participants in the PILGRIMAGE OF GRACE of 1536 and would have been intensely unpopular among all ranks of landholders from the gentry down through the yeomanry (who frequently made complex settlements of their land). At the same time THOMAS CROMWELL seems by 1538 to have been aware that the lawyers were busily at work devising legal instruments designed to overcome the restrictions created by the Statute of Uses and thereby opening new loopholes through which feudal incidents might be avoided. Both of these factors might certainly have inclined the Crown to seek a compromise, yet there is little evidence that Cromwell was planning in 1540 to introduce a bill on wills to accompany the measures associated with a closely related matter, the creation of the Court of Wards. In the event, the bill that led to the Statute of Wills was introduced into Parliament only a month after Cromwell's fall from power in the summer of 1540. Furthermore, the provisions of the statute are virtually identical to a package deal on feudal incidents that was agreed to by Henry VIII and thirty members of the nobility in 1529. This suggests that the passage of the act should be seen at least in part as a result of the greater influence of Conservative and aristocratic counsels on the king after the fall of Cromwell.

Bibliography: J. M. W. Bean, *The Decline of English Feudalism 1215-1540*, 1968.

C. W. Brooks

Wolsey, Cardinal Thomas (1472?-1530). With the possible exception of STEPHEN GARDINER, MARY's lord chancellor, Wolsey was the last great ecclesiastical statesman of medieval England. He became a priest, not because he had any vocation or spiritual gift, but because, as a clever boy of relatively humble origins, the church offered the only possible route to wealth and preferment. He was born in Ipswich in late 1472 or early 1473, the son of a wealthy grazier, and was given a sufficiently sound schooling to enable him to proceed to Magdalen College, Oxford, at about the normal age of fourteen or fifteen. He proceeded B.A. and M.A. and became a fellow of Magdalen by 10 March 1498, when he was ordained on the title of his fellowship. In the following year he became senior bursar and was therefore probably a fellow of several years' standing. As bursar he was responsible for the completion of Magdalen College tower, and as master of the college school, for teaching the sons of Thomas Grey, marquess of Dorset, who provided him with his first living.

In 1501, beginning as he meant to go on, Wolsey obtained two other benefices *in commendam* and a dispensation to be absent from all three. In the same year he left Oxford to become chaplain to the archbishop of Canterbury, Henry Deane. By 1505 he had passed from Deane's service to that of Sir Richard Nanfan, the deputy of CALAIS, who was responsible for his first introduction to the COURT. When Nanfan died in 1507 Wolsey was already 35 and held no significant public office. However, on Nanfan's commendation he then became a chaplain to HENRY VII and had been successfully employed on a number of minor diplomatic missions by the time the king himself died in 1509. By the summer of 1509 Wolsey had become dean of Hereford, but he did not become chaplain and almoner to HENRY VIII until December of that year, possibly because his manner and life-style did not commend themselves to the king's austere and powerful grandmother.

Once he had secured the modest but important office of almoner, Wolsey was quick to make himself useful, first to RICHARD FOX, bishop of Winchester, an experienced and influential privy councillor, and then to the king himself. By 1512 it was recognized that this "master almoner" had a flair for administration and a gift for hard work. Both these talents were taxed to the utmost by the outbreak of war. The withdrawal of Henry's ally, Ferdinand of Aragon, and the consequent collapse of the Guienne campaign threatened to turn the king's triumphant martial promenade into a fiasco. That this situation was spectacularly redeemed in 1513 by victories at Tournai and FLODDEN was largely the result of Wolsey's logistical skill and abundant energy. He had found the quickest way (for a man) to the king's heart, and his career blossomed immediately. In 1514 he became bishop of both Lincoln and Tournai and by the end of the year had exchanged the former see for the archbishopric of York, vacated by the death of Cardinal Christopher Bainbridge in July. Henry's enthusiasm for his profitable servant and Wolsey's ambition, stimulated by success, were both at high pressure. The king pressed Pope Leo X to make his new archbishop a cardinal, as there was no English cardinal after Bainbridge's death, and Wolsey pressed his own suit to be named legate *a Latere*. A year later, he was both cardinal and lord chancellor, although he had to wait until 1518 before the somewhat reluctant Leo could be persuaded to name him legate and until August 1524 before Pope Clement VII finally granted him that office for life.

Wolsey remained Henry's chief minister for fourteen years, until his failure to bring about the annulment of the king's marriage to CATHERINE OF ARAGON led to his downfall in 1529. He was widely accused, both at the time and since, of being arrogant, of usurping the functions of the king's council, and even of being *ipse rex*—the real king. Recent research has modified many of these judgments. Wolsey did indeed bear the main burden of administration, but the king remained very much in control, not only of policy, but also of patronage, even down to quite a minor level. He also continued to consult other councillors, although Wolsey's voice was the most dominant and most frequently heard. The cardinal was also a hardworking courtier, who by no means took his ascendancy for granted, and although he endeavored to make sure that the king's most intimate servants—his privy chamber—were sympathetic, he could not control their appointment. The famous "purge," which he is alleged to have carried out in 1519 to remove antipathetic elements, is now thought to have been the work of the whole council. As a diplomat Wolsey was immensely skilled, and his great triumph was the TREATY OF LONDON in 1518. The fact that it collapsed in less than two years did not diminish the credit that both he and Henry derived from it. Contrary to what was once believed, he did not pursue a "balance of power" policy in Europe but rather sought to exploit each situation as it arose for his own and his master's advantage. The fact that he tried not to offend the papacy in the course of these maneuvers probably had more to do with his status as legate *a latere* than with any desire on his part to become pope. The person who raised that possibility was Henry, not Wolsey, and it was not pressed.

In domestic affairs it was through his judicial work as lord chancellor that Wolsey made his greatest and most lasting impact. The Court of STAR CHAMBER (the senior equity court) was very largely his creation, because he formalized the king's prerogative of justice and established both the procedures and the personnel of the court. As primate and legate, however, he conspicuously failed to grasp a unique opportunity for ecclesiastical reform. This failure was due less to the obstructiveness of Archbishop WILLIAM WARHAM of Canterbury than to his own lack of motivation. Although deeply interested in education (and the first founder of Christ Church, Oxford), Wolsey had no reforming zeal and embodied many abuses in his own person, as the career of his son, Thomas Winter, bears witness. He maintained a highly personal style of secular administration and built up the king's authority assiduously, particularly in the north and in the Marches of Wales, but as a manager of Parliament, he was inept and left no significant legacy of legislation. First and last, Wolsey was the king's man, and it was the withdrawal of the king's confidence that destroyed him. As legate and archbishop he could have defended himself in 1529. Instead he chose to surrender to charges of PRAEMUNIRE and thereby performed his last great service to Henry in strengthening his hand for the coming battle with the church.

Bibliography: J. A. Guy, *The Cardinal's Court*, 1977; A. F. Pollard, *Wolsey*, 1929, reprint 1968; G. Walker, *John Skelton and the Politics of the 1520s*, 1988.

David M. Loades

Wriothesley, Thomas (1505-1550). Statesman and administrator, Wriothesley was born in London on 21 December 1505, the eldest son of William Writh (alias Wriothesley) and Agnes Drayton. Her father was a London draper, but it was on the paternal side that important connections to HENRY VII's court existed. Wriothesley's father was York Herald, and his uncle Sir Thomas was Garter King of Arms. Both were sons of Sir John Writh, who had also been Garter King of Arms. Thomas's first cousin was the famous London chronicler Charles Wriothesley, Windsor Herald.

On this foundation it was no accident that THOMAS HOWARD, 3rd duke of Norfolk, stood godfather to the future lord chancellor. Nor can it be any surprise that young Thomas entered St. Paul's, where his young friends included the future Henrician leaders WILLIAM PAGET, Anthony Denny and John Leland. Wriothesley's father died in 1513, but a close family supervised his continuing education and sent him to Trinity Hall, Cambridge, where he became the pupil of the future bishop of Winchester, STEPHEN GARDINER. Gardiner was doctor of both laws, and the decision to study law looked back to Wrioth-esley's great-grandfather, a London lawyer.

When Gardiner joined Cardinal THOMAS WOLSEY's service early in 1524, young Wriothesley followed him. He was on intimate terms with Wolsey's man of all work, THOMAS CROMWELL and addressed that rising star as "master" in 1524. Tradition asserts that Cromwell provided for Wriothesley's entry into an Inn of Chancery a decade before Thomas entered Gray's Inn (1534). This possibility fits well the pattern of Sir Thomas's later career. So, too, does the thick web of family connections linking Wriothesley to several Henrician officials, for example, Sir Edward Peckham, a Gardiner kinsman who was cofferer of the king's Household. They were to become brothers-in-law early in the 1530s, each marrying a daughter of William Cheyne of Chesham Bois, Bucks—Peckham to Anne and Thomas to Jane (1533).

Wriothesley's first official preferments came at the beginning of the 1530s. In 1530 Wriothesley was named a clerk of the signet, presumably because Gardiner was then HENRY VIII's principal secretary. Other posts came rapidly, among them appointment as engraver at the Tower mint. Wriothesley also began to accumulate lands, mainly in the southern counties.

His aspirations to a career in government so solidly grounded, Wriothesley seemed destined for a prominent place in the middle levels of administration when his involvement in the DIVORCE proceedings altered his prospects. In 1531-1532 he went on embassies tied to Henry's marital diplomacy. Henry took in good stead this service, and Gardiner's fall from favor failed to alter Wriothesley's upward movement. Cromwell took him into his own service in 1533-1534. Cromwell made Wriothesley chief clerk of the signet and then of the office of the Privy Seal in 1536. A letter book dating from 1535-1538 shows how completely Wriothesley managed Cromwell's patronage.

In 1538 Wriothesley exhibited the anti-clericalism familiar in Cromwell's entourage and earned Gardiner's enmity for vehemence in the iconoclast campaigns. There are from this time surviving proposals by Wriothesley touching the former monastic endowments and their use for hospitals, poor relief, and also the founding of a standing army. He had served in the Commons in 1539.

In April 1540, just before Cromwell fell, Wriothesley was promoted to the principal secretaryship jointly with Ralph Sadler. Now a knight, Wriothesley emerged as the dominant partner in the divided office, surviving a purge of Cromwellians. His settlement of differences with Gardiner, his friendship with the duke of Norfolk, and his intimate friendships with Paget, Peckham, and others protected his position at court and council. So, too, did his championing of a pro-imperial foreign policy, his active role in the detection of CATHERINE HOWARD's adultery, and the fatal illness of Sir Thomas Audley, lord chancellor.

Wriothesley became lord keeper on 22 April 1544 and then Lord Chancellor on 3 May, having been promoted Baron Wriothesley of Titchfield on 1 January. He belonged to the line of political chancellors, but earlier had served as clerk of the Crown and king's attorney in King's Bench. This service and his education in the law fitted him for his office and cast into disrepute assertions that he was undeserving of his office by virtue of lack of experience at law.

Now established as a leading Hampshire landowner, Sir Thomas had earned Henry VIII's lasting trust for competence in managing the war finances in 1545. He was named an executor of the king's will and on the testimony of Paget received both a gift of £500 and elevation to the earldom of Southampton on 16 February 1547. By then he had arranged marriages for his daughters and also his son and heir Henry with leading Hampshire and Sussex families. He was a power at court, in council, and in the county.

The swiftness of his fall in 1547 therefore seemed to contemporaries all the more inexplicable. Neither of the explanations preferred by historians withstands scrutiny. Charges of usurping the COMMON LAW brought by members of inns of court were moved by EDWARD SEYMOUR, the protector Somerset, in a conspiracy to purge the chancellor and were untrue. But Wriothesley was deprived of his high office by a council decree on 6 March 1547. There is no foundation for the idea that as a Henrician "Catholic" he was purged by the protector to preserve the Protestant succession of EDWARD VI. Wriothesley was at that time a moderate evangelical in religion, firmly anti-papal, anti-clerical, and a protector of Protestants. Moreover, by his own request, the very radical Reformer Bishop John Hooper preached his funeral sermon, when Southampton died after a long illness, amid rumors of melancholy and even suicide.

There had long been a feud between Wriothesley and Somerset, traceable to land disputes, personal enmities, and Wriothesley's frustration of Seymour's scheme to revise the COURT OF AUGMENTATIONS to make easier the granting away of ex-monastic lands. Wriothesley alone among the councillors had opposed Somerset's usurpation of Henry's plan for Edward VI's minority.

After a period of house arrest, the earl was put at liberty and soon returned to the council and took an active role in the 1547 Parliament. He refused to enter Sir THOMAS SEYMOUR's 1548 conspiracy against the protector. But in the general unheaval of October 1549 he joined the coup led by JOHN DUDLEY, earl of Warwick. Warwick had apparently promised to share the government with him, and Wriothesley had been given grants worth more than £6,700. But he received neither honors nor any office, though he had hoped for the vacant post of lord treasurer. By 3 December 1549 Wriothesley had taken to his London house, cast aside, sick, and never to regain either his health or any role in government. He made his will on 21 July 1550 and died on 30 July.

Bibliography: A. J. Slavin, "The Fall of Lord Chancellor Wriothesley," *Albion* 7 (1975): 265-286; A. J. Slavin, "Lord Chancellor Wriothesley and Reform of Augmentations," in *Tudor Men and Institutions*, ed. A. J. Slavin, 1972, pp. 49-69.

Arthur J. Slavin

Wyatt's Rebellion (1553-1554). Sir Thomas Wyatt's rebellion was part of a conspiracy begun in November 1553 combining Protestant opposition to the restoration of Catholicism and general fear of foreign domination caused by MARY I's decision to marry Prince Philip of Spain. WILLIAM PAGET and his allies on the PRIVY COUNCIL joined the imperial ambassador, Simon Renard, in supporting the marriage. Bishop STEPHEN GARDINER, the lord chancellor, wanted the queen to wed Edward Courtenay, earl of Devon, who became involved with the conspirators, placing Gardiner in jeopardy. The French ambassador, Antoine Noailles, also tried to convince Henri II to join. Some insurgents wished only to change Mary's mind, but their leaders and others sought to marry Courtenay to Princess ELIZABETH and make her queen. On 18 March Wyatt was to raise the county of Kent, with Sir Peter Carew doing so in Devon, Sir James Croft in Herefordshire, and Henry Grey, earl of Suffolk, in Leicestershire.

Sir Thomas Cawarden may have intended the same in Surrey, and the rebels had support in Sussex and Hampshire. But word of the plan leaked out.

Three events forced the rebels to act prematurely. First, Carew aroused suspicion by ignoring a council summons of 2 January. Then, on 18 January Renard, hearing rumors about a French fleet, informed Mary of all that he knew. The conspirators heard what he did and decided to act immediately. Wyatt left London for Kent on 19 January. Finally, on 21 January Gardiner forced Courtenay to confess. He suppressed part of what he learned for his own safety, for he had angered Mary and lost influence on the council by opposing the marriage. But the queen learned enough that on the next day she ordered the JUSTICES OF THE PEACE to publicize the marriage terms and suppress sedition and resistance to the Catholic restoration.

In Devon, Carew ran afoul of the sheriff, Sir Thomas Dennis, failed to convince the shire of the Spanish threat, met resistance because of his role in suppressing the insurrection of 1549, and on 25 January gave up and fled to France. That day the council summoned Suffolk from Surrey, but he fled to Leicestershire, and the following day the council proclaimed him a traitor and sent the earl of Huntingdon after him. The shire disliked the Greys, and Suffolk got little support in Leicester on the twenty-ninth and found Coventry's gates closed the next day. He was arrested on 1 February. Croft did not even try to raise Herefordshire. Lord William Howard arrested Cawarden at Blechingley on the twenty-fifth. The next day Gardiner examined and released him, with orders from the council to raise men. But on the twenty-seventh, Howard arrested him again and confiscated his arsenal.

Only Wyatt in strongly Protestant Kent actually raised a force. The council learned of this on 21 or 22 January and tried Gardiner's policy of negotiation, but Wyatt raised his standard at Maidstone on the twenty-fifth anyway. The sheriff, Sir Robert Southwell, and Lord Abergavenny, the only two Kentish magnates actively to support Mary, had difficulty raising men. On the next two days Mary imprisoned the marquess of Northampton and Sir Edward Warner in the Tower of London, appointed Lord William Howard as her commander, gave the aged THOMAS HOWARD, 3rd duke of Norfolk, command of the London "White-coats," and proclaimed the rebels traitors. Meanwhile Wyatt moved to Rochester. The next day at Wrotham, Southwell defeated Sir Henry Isley, whose followers were captured or scattered. But on 29 January most of the Whitecoats deserted to Wyatt at Rochester, and he had 3,000 men, though many poorly equipped, when he set off for London on the thirtieth. Yet he wasted time by detouring to Cooling Castle, where Lord Cobham was captured or joined him. On 31 January Mary tried negotiation again, offering to pardon all who went home within twenty-four hours, but Wyatt demanded custody of Mary and the Tower, the talks ended, Gardiner was discredited, and the rebels were proclaimed traitors anew. Mary now took the initiative, went to the Guildhall, and appealed successfully for London's support. Paget won control of the council, the earl of Pembroke took command of the queen's supporters, and Lord William Howard was left to defend London.

On 3 February the rebels reached Southwark, where the inhabitants welcomed them, and men raised by Howard in Surrey deserted to Wyatt. The rebels fraternized with the locals and sacked Gardiner's palace but could not force the gate. So on 6 February they left Southwark for Kingston, repaired and crossed the bridge, wasted time trying to free cannon bogged in mud and then made for London. Early on the seventh Wyatt attacked, Howard repelled him at Ludgate, and Pembroke's troops routed his weary band. Wyatt was soon in the Tower; most of his men surrendered. Whether the Londoners opposed Wyatt or simply feared a sack is unclear, but their support saved the queen.

The rebellion lasted eighteen days, with three minor skirmishes and no more than 70 killed. Of 480 men tried and convicted, fewer than 100 were executed. All others were pardoned. Wyatt, Suffolk, and Isley were executed, Croftes escaped punishment, Carew was in France, and Cawarden was released. Suffolk's daughter, LADY JANE GREY, and her husband, Guildford Dudley, also died because of Jane's claim to the throne, though not even her father proclaimed her queen in 1554. Courtenay fought against the rebels; no concrete evidence against Elizabeth was found. Gardiner recovered to manage the prosecution and, reversing his previous opinion, to claim religion was the rebellion's only cause. Mary went on to unhappy marriage with Philip, the eventual king of Spain.

Bibliography: D. M. Loades, *Two Tudor Conspiracies*, 1965; W. B. Robison, "The National and Local Significance of Wyatt's Rebellion in Surrey," *Historical Journal* 30 (1987): 769-90.

William B. Robison

Y

Yorkist Risings (1486). After the change of dynasty resulting from HENRY VII's victory over Richard III at BOSWORTH FIELD, there were lingering Yorkist sympathies throughout England. In Yorkshire, Worcestershire, and other countries, small bands of Yorkist diehards voiced dissatisfaction with recent events, which they hoped to reverse in due course. Although 28 Yorkist leaders were attainted by Henry VII's first Parliament in November, many dangerous men remained at liberty, having gone into hiding or taken SANCTUARY in religious houses. Such men caused difficulties for Henry when in the spring of 1486 he made a progress through the midlands to York as a way of consolidating his power over the realm.

During the first week of March Henry left London for Lincoln on a royal progress. On reaching Lincoln, where he spent Easter week, he learned that Francis, Lord Lovell, and the influential Stafford brothers, Humphrey and Thomas, had left Colchester Abbey, Essex, and ridden in opposite directions. Their plan was to raise rebellions in York and Worcester. Refusing to return to London, Henry prudently summoned the duke of Bedford and the earl of Northumberland to join him with several thousand armed retainers.

On 17 and 18 April 1486, the earl of Northumberland and his retinue on their way to meet Henry at York scattered a band of 300 Yorkist partisans. Meanwhile Henry had resumed his march and entered York in state on 21 April. Although he received a warm welcome from the mayor and aldermen, there was an attempt to assassinate him two days later. For two weeks thereafter Henry remained stoically in the city while Northumberland took the lead in apprehending the conspirators, most of whom were executed. However, Lord Lovell managed to escape, ultimately sailing across the Channel to the Low Countries to become a pensioner of Margaret of Burgundy, the widow of Duke Charles the Bold as well as the disgruntled sister of Richard III.

Back in London during the first week of May there were violent protests and demonstrations in Henry's absence. On 5 May a Yorkist band even tried to storm Westminster Palace. When that venture failed, the plotters rode off and attempted to overwhelm a royalist force encamped at Highbury. Defeated a second time, they withdrew and went into hiding.

Doubtless Henry was unaware of the disorders in the capital when he left York for Worcester on 6 May. As he approached the latter place, he and his escort were relieved to see the Yorkist faction collapse and scatter in panic. The Stafford brothers retreated across the border into Oxfordshire and again went into sanctuary, this time with the abbot of Culham. This time the king decided to apprehend the Stafford brothers, even if the sanctuary rights of Culham Abbey had to be violated in the process. On 13 May Sir John Savage entered the monastery, seized the two brothers, and took them in chains to Westminster, where they were tried before the King's Bench at the end of June, convicted, and sentenced to die. Humphrey Stafford was executed at Tyburn early in July, although the king commuted the sentence of Thomas on the grounds that he had been corrupted by his elder brother. Subsequently several dozen other Yorkists were condemned by tribunals at Worcester and Birmingham, over which Henry maintained a careful watch.

Bibliography: S. B. Chrimes, *Henry VII*, 1972.

                                                                    Michael V. C. Alexander

Yorkshire Rebellion (1489). Because of the domestic and international insecurities facing his new regime, HENRY VII instituted some unprecedentedly high taxes in England. These taxes were resented, particularly in Yorkshire. Serious grumblings began there in early 1488, although it was not until 20 April 1489 that an organized resistance movement emerged during a meeting of some malcontent commoners at Ayton. Henry Percy, the 4th earl of Northumberland, gathered some of his retainers and went to meet with about 700 rebels at South Kivington by Thirsk. Negotiations over tax payments broke down, and the rebels managed to murder him when his retainers declined to protect him. Percy was the only known casualty of the rebellion, and his death removed the only significant royal magnate in the north. His death, in turn, gave the rebels further time to organize their movement. On 10 May a royal PROCLAMATION denounced the rebels, but in spite of this, Sir John Egremont, a member of the local gentry, joined the rebellion on 11 May and took command. The rebels advanced to Doncaster by 13 May but turned back and went to York. There about 5,000 insurgents entered the city on 15 May when traitors opened a city gate to them. Meanwhile, royal forces left Cambridge on 12 May to suppress the rebellion. By 20 May they had reached York and entered the city, apparently without opposition as the rebellion faded away to nothing.

Basically the rebellion was a loyal protest against overly high taxation. It was respectable, law abiding, and basically nonviolent. Grievances concerning Henry VII's assaults on clerical privileges, especially SANCTUARY, added to local discontent, as did factional rivalries within the city of York. The rebellion remained small and was confined to eastern Yorkshire. Henry VII's investigators bothered to indict only forty-four people for rebellion, of whom five were condemned to death. At the same time, the king refused to back down on his program of taxation. Therefore, the chief result of the rebellion was the elimination of Henry Percy, the earl of Northumberland, who potentially could have become a dangerous, overmighty subject. Tudor authority in the north was strengthened with his replacement by the loyal THOMAS HOWARD, earl of Surrey (later 2nd duke of Norfolk), as the king's lieutenant.

Bibliography: M. A. Hicks, "The Yorkshire Rebellion of 1489 Reconsidered," *Northern History* 22 (1986): 39-62.

Ronald Fritze

Chronology

1457	28 January	Birth of Henry VII.
1461	4 March	Accession of Edward IV.
1476		William Caxton returns to England and brings the knowledge of printing with moveable type.
1483	9 April	Death of Edward IV and accession of Edward V.
	25 June	Deposition of Edward V.
	26 June	Accession of Richard III.
1485	22 August	Battle of Bosworth Field and accession of Henry VII.
	September	Outbreak of sweating sickness.
1486	18 January	Henry VII marries Elizabeth, daughter of Edward IV.
	March	Yorkist Risings.
1486	19 September	Birth of Prince Arthur.
1487	May-June	Rebellion of Lambert Simnel.
	16 June	Battle of Stoke.

1488	11 June	Battle of Sauchieburn, death of James III, and accession of James IV.
1489	10 February	Treaty of Redon.
	27 March	Treaty of Medina del Campo
	April-May	Yorkshire Rebellion.
	29 November	Birth of Princess Margaret.
1491	28 June	Birth of Henry VIII.
1492	October–November	English invasion of France and Treaty of Etaples.
1494	December	Poynings' Laws enacted by Irish Parliament.
1495-1497		Rebellion of Perkin Warbeck.
1496	24 February	Intercursus Magnus.
	? March	Birth of Princess Mary.
1497	May-June	Cornish Rebellion.
	17 June	Battle of Blackheath.
	24 June	John Cabot lands at Labrador in North America.
	20 September	Treaty of Ayton.
1498		Mysterious second voyage of John Cabot.
1501	14 November	Marriage of Prince Arthur and Catherine of Aragon in person. It had been done by proxy in May 1499.
1502	2 April	Death of Prince Arthur.
1503	7 August	Marriage of James IV and Margaret Tudor.
1506	30 April	Intercursus Malus.

1509	21 April	Death of Henry VII.
	22 April	Accession of Henry VIII.
	11 June	Marriage of Henry VIII and Catherine of Aragon.
1511-1514		First Anglo-French War of Henry VIII.
1513	9 September	Battle of Flodden, death of James IV, and accession of James V.
1514	December	Disturbances over Richard Hunne case.
1515	December	Thomas Wolsey becomes lord chancellor and cardinal.
1516	18 February	Birth of Mary I.
1517-1518		Great outbreak of sweating sickness.
1518	June	Wolsey appointed papal legate *a latere*.
	October	Treaty of London.
1519	?	Birth of Henry Fitzroy.
1520		Discussions of Martin Luther's ideas held at White Horse Inn, Cambridge.
	June	Meeting of Field of Cloth of Gold.
1521	May	Trial and execution of the duke of Buckingham.
	May	Burning of Luther's books in London before Wolsey.
	October	Henry VIII presents *Assertio Septem Sacramentorum*, an attack on Luther, to Pope Leo X.
		Pope Leo grants Henry VIII the title *fidei defensor*.
1522-1525		Second Anglo-French War of Henry VIII.

1525		Appearance of William Tyndale's translation of the New Testament into English.
	April-May	Amicable Grant Rebellion.
1527	May	Henry VIII publicly asserts his dissatisfaction over his marriage to Catherine of Aragon by having Wolsey cite him for illicit cohabitation.
1528		Outbreak of sweating sickness.
1529	18 October	Wolsey vacates the lord chancellorship and falls from power.
1529-1536		Reformation Parliament.
1530-1540		William Hawkins's voyages to Brazil.
1531	February	Pardon of the clergy.
1532		First Act in Restraint of Annates.
	March	Revival of Common's Supplication Against the Ordinaries.
	May	Submission of the Clergy.
1533	25 January	Henry VIII marries Anne Boleyn.
	February	Thomas Cranmer appointed archbishop of Canterbury.
	March	Act in Restraint of Appeals.
	7 September	Birth of Elizabeth I.
1534-1537		Kildare Rebellion in Ireland.
1534	January-February	Second Act in Restraint of Annates.
	"	Dispensations Act.
	"	Act for the Submission of the Clergy.

	January– February	First Act of Succession.
	November– December	Act of Supremacy.
1534	"	Act Concerning First Fruits and Tenths.
1535	January	Thomas Cromwell appointed vicegerent and vicar-general in spirituals.
		Compilation of the *Valor Ecclesiasticus*.
	May	Execution of the Carthusians.
	22 June	Execution of Cardinal John Fisher.
	6 July	Execution of Sir Thomas More.
1536	February– April	Act for the Dissolution of the Lesser Monasteries.
	19 May	Execution of Anne Boleyn.
	30 May	Henry VIII marries Jane Seymour.
	July	Ten Articles.
	22 July	Death of Henry Fitzroy.
	August	First Royal Injunctions.
	1 October	Outbreak of Pilgrimage of Grace in Lincolnshire.
	6 December	Robert Aske's followers in Pilgrimage of Grace disperse on promise of pardon.
1537	January– February	Fresh outbreaks of the Pilgrimage of Grace.
	July	Execution of Robert Aske.
	September	Publication of the *Bishops' Book*.
	12 October	Birth of Edward VI.

1537	24 October	Death of Jane Seymour.
1538	September	Second Royal Injunctions.
1538	September	Beginning of the persecution of the Pole family and the supposed Exeter Conspiracy.
1539		Great Bible.
	April-June	Act for Dissolution of the Greater Monasteries
	"	Statute of Proclamations
	May	Act of Six Articles.
1540	6 January	Henry VIII marries Anne of Cleves.
	10 June	Fall of Thomas Cromwell.
	9 July	Annulment of marriage to Anne of Cleves.
	28 July	Henry VIII marries Catherine Howard, and Thomas Cromwell is executed.
1541	June	Henry VIII assumes title of king of Ireland.
1542	13 February	Execution of Catherine Howard.
	24 November	Battle of Solway Moss.
	8 December	Birth of Mary, Queen of Scots.
	14 December	Death of James V.
		Beginning of the debasement of the coinage.
1543	May	Publication of the *King's Book*.
	12 July	Henry VIII marries Catherine Parr.

1543	July	Treaty of Greenwich.
1544-1546		Third Anglo-French War of Henry VIII.
1544	January-March	Third Act of Succession.
	14 September	Capture of Boulogne from the French.
1545	July-August	French naval expedition against the southern coast of England repulsed.
1546	29 May	Murder of Cardinal Beaton in Scotland.
	July	Trial and burning of Anne Askew.
1547	28 January	Death of Henry VIII and accession of Edward VI.
		Publication of Thomas Cranmer's *Book of Homilies*.
	11 September	Battle of Pinkie.
	November-December	Act of the Dissolution of the Chantries.
1549-1550		Anglo-French War.
1549	21 January	Parliament approves Book of Common Prayer.
		First Act of Uniformity.
	June-August	Western or Prayer Book Rebellion.
	July-August	Kett's Rebellion in Norfolk.
	17 August	Defeat of Western Rebels at Sampford Courtenay.
	27 August	Defeat of Kett's Rebels at Dussindale.
	10 October	Duke of Somerset deprived of the office of lord protector.
1551		Outbreak of sweating sickness.

1552	22 January	Execution of duke of Somerset.
	April	Second Act of Uniformity requires use of the revised Book of Common Prayer.
1553	June	Issuing of the Forty-two Articles.
	6 July	Death of Edward VI and accession of Lady Jane Grey.
	19 July	Deposition of Lady Jane Grey and accession of Mary I.
	22 August	Execution of the duke of Northumberland.
	Autumn	First Marian Statute repealing Protestant legislation.
1554	January-February	Wyatt's Rebellion.
	November	Second Marian Statute repealing Protestant legislation.
1555	4 February	Execution of John Rogers, the first martyr of the Marian Reaction.
	25 July	Marriage of Mary I and Philip II of Spain.
	16 October	Burning of Hugh Latimer and Nicholas Ridley.
	12 November	Death of Stephen Gardiner, lord chancellor and bishop of Winchester.
1556-1558		Series of epidemics ravage England.
1556	21 March	Burning of Thomas Cranmer.
1557-1559		Anglo-French War.
1557		John Knox returns to Scotland from Geneva.
	10 August	Battle of San Quentin.

	3 December	First Covenant in Scotland and formation of the Lords of the Congregation.
1558	6 January	French capture Calais.
	13 July	Battle of Gravelines.
	17 November	Death of Mary I and accession of Elizabeth I.
	18 November	Death of Reginald Pole, cardinal and archbishop of Canterbury.
1559	April	Passage of the Acts of Supremacy and Uniformity.
1560-1562		First rebellion of Shane O'Neill in Ireland.
1560		Publication of the Geneva Bible.
	27 February	Treaty of Berwick.
	6 July	Treaty of Edinburgh.
	August	Scottish Parliament adopts Calvinism.
	8 September	Death of Amy Robsart, wife of Robert Dudley.
	December	Beginning of the recoinage, which was completed in October 1561.
1561	19 August	Mary, Queen of Scots returns to Scotland.
1562		Publication of John Jewel's *Apology of the Church of England*.
		John Hawkins's first slaving expedition to Guinea and the New World.
	October	Elizabeth almost dies from smallpox.
1563		Publication of John Foxe's *Acts and Monuments*.

1563		Convocation approves the Thirty-Nine Articles.
		Outbreak of plague.
1564		John Hawkins's second voyage to Guinea and the New World.
	23 April	Birth of William Shakespeare.
1565-1566		Vestiarian Controversy.
1565	29 July	Marriage of Mary, Queen of Scots and Henry Stewart, Lord Darnley.
1566-1567		Second rebellion of Shane O'Neill in Ireland.
1566	March	Matthew Parker's "Advertisements."
	19 June	Birth of James VI and I amd murder of David Rizzio.
1567	10 February	Murder of Henry Stewart, Lord Darnley.
	15 June	Battle of Carberry Hill.
	July	Separatist congregation discovered in London.
	24 July	Abdication of Mary, Queen of Scots and accession of James VI as king of Scotland.
	October	John Hawkins's third voyage to Guinea and the New World.
1568		Publication of the Bishops' Bible.
	13 May	Battle of Langside.
	19 May	Mary, Queen of Scots flees to Carlisle.
	September	John Hawkins fights the Spanish at San Juan d'Ulloa.

1568	December	Elizabeth seizes the Duke of Alva's treasure ships.
		William Allen founds seminary for Roman Catholic exiles at Douai.
1569-1573		Fitzmaurice Revolt in Ireland.
1569	Spring	Norfolk Conspiracy.
	October-November	Rebellion of the Northern Earls.
1570	February	Issuing of *Regnans in Excelsis*, excommunicating Elizabeth.
		Marriage negotiations between Elizabeth and Anjou.
1571		Subscription Act gives statutory basis for the Thirty-nine Articles.
	September	Ridolfi Plot.
1572-1573		Admonition Controversy.
1572	April	Treaty of Blois.
	May	Francis Drake's voyage to the New World.
1574		Arrival of the first seminary priests in England.
1576	December	Archbishop Grindal is ordered to suppress Prophesyings but refuses and offers his resignation.
1577-1580		Francis Drake's circumnavigation of the world.
1577		James Burbage opens The Theatre.
	June	Archbishop Grindal is suspended from his duties.
	29 November	Execution of the first seminary priest, Cuthbert Mayne.

1578	12 March	Morton resigns as regent, and James VI assumes control of the Scottish government.
1579-1583		Desmond Revolt in Ireland.
1579		Foundation of the English college at Rome.
	August	Alencon comes to England to court Elizabeth personally. Their courtship lasts until February 1582.
1580	Summer	Arrival of the first Jesuits in England: Edmund Campion, Robert Parsons, and Ralph Emerson.
1581	1 December	Execution of Edmund Campion.
1582		Beginning of the puritan "classical" movement.
		Publication of the Roman Catholic Gregory Martin's translation of the Bible, the Rheims New Testament.
	22 August	Ruthven Raid.
1583	23 September	John Whitgift confirmed as archbishop of Canterbury.
	October	Throckmorton Plot discovered.
1584-1591		Roanoke voyages and colony.
1585-1604		Anglo-Spanish War.
1585-1586		Francis Drake's expedition to the West Indies, resulting in the burning of Cartagena.
1585	August	Treaty of Nonsuch.
	December	Leicester's expedition to the Netherlands.
1586	August	Babington Plot revealed.

1586	17 October	Death of Sir Philip Sidney as a result of wounds received at the battle of Zutphen.
1587	February	Anthony Cope's Bill and Book.
	18 February	Execution of Mary, Queen of Scots.
	April	Drake's raid on Cadiz.
1588	May-July	Campaign of the Spanish Armada.
	29 July	Battle of Gravelines and defeat of the Spanish Armada.
	October	Marprelate Tracts first appear.
1589	April-June	Portugal Expedition.
	Summer	Marprelate group smashed by authorities.
1590		Edmund Spenser publishes the first three books of *The Faerie Queen*.
1591	3 September	Death of Sir Richard Grenville and loss of the *Revenge* fighting the Spanish during the Azores Expedition.
1592	September	William Shakespeare working as an actor and playwright in London.
1593		Publication of Richard Hooker's *On the Laws of Ecclesiastical Polity*.
		Appearance of the plague.
		Executions of the Separatists Henry Barrow, John Greenwood, and John Penry.
	30 May	Death of Christopher Marlowe in a tavern brawl.
1594-1603		Tyrone Rebellion in Ireland.
1594	February-June	Lopez Plot.

1594-1595		Wisbech Stirs.
1594-1597		Adverse weather, poor harvests, and continued warfare cause subsistence crisis in parts of England.
1596	June-July	Cadiz expedition of the earl of Essex.
	October	Second Spanish Armada dispersed by storms.
1597	August	Islands Voyage.
	October	Third Spanish Armada dispersed by storms.
1598		Archpriest Controversy.
	4 August	Death of William Cecil, Lord Burghley and lord treasurer.
	14 August	Battle of Yellow Ford in Ireland.
1599		Building of the Globe Theatre.
	April-September	Essex campaigns in Ireland.
1600	5 August	Gowrie Conspiracy.
1601	8 February	Essex's Rebellion.
	24 December	Mountjoy defeats Tyrone outside of Kinsale, Ireland.
1602	2 January	Spanish forces at Kinsale surrender to Mountjoy.
1603	24 March	Death of Elizabeth I and accession of James I.

Bibliography

This bibliography is intended simply to provide a list of important and recent books dealing with topics of general interest to beginning students of the Tudor era. Most of these books will contain footnotes and bibliographies that will guide the reader to other more specialized books and articles.

BIBLIOGRAPHIES

"Great Britain, Commonwealth, Ireland, and Canada." In *Recently Published Articles*. Washington, D.C.: American Historical Association, 1976-1990.

Levine, Mortimer, comp. *Tudor England 1485-1603*. Cambridge: Cambridge University Press, 1968.

Read, Conyers. *Bibliography of British History: Tudor Period 1485-1603*, 2nd ed. Oxford: Oxford University Press, 1959. Reprint 1978.

Royal Historical Society Annual Bibliography of British and Irish History. Brighton, England: Harvester Press, 1976- .

Writings on British History. London: Institute of Historical Research, 1937- .

COLLECTIONS OF PRIMARY SOURCES

Byrne, Muriel St., Clare, ed. *The Lisle Letters*. 6 vols. Chicago: University of Chicago Press, 1981.

Dickens, A. G., and Dorothy Carr, eds. *The Reformation in England, to the Accession of Elizabeth*. New York: St. Martins, 1968.

Elton, G. R., ed. *The Tudor Constitution: Documents and Commentary*, 2nd ed. Cambridge: Cambridge University Press, 1982.

Foxe, John. *Acts and Monuments of John Foxe*. 8 vols. London: 1837-41. Reprint 1965.

Gee, H. and W. J. Hardy, eds. *Documents Illustrative of English Church History*. London: Macmillan, 1910.

Tanner, J. R. *Tudor Constitutional Documents a.d. 1485-1603 with an Historical Commentary*. Cambridge: Cambridge University Press, 1922.

Tawney, R. H., and E. Power, eds. *Tudor Economic Documents*. 3 vols. London: Longman, 1924.

Williams, C. H., ed. *English Historical Documents, 1485-1558*. New York: Oxford University Press, 1967.

GENERAL SURVEYS

Ashton, Robert. *Reformation and Revolution, 1558-1660*. London: Paladin, 1984.

Bindoff, S. T. *Tudor England*. Harmondsworth, England: Penguin, 1950.

Black, J. B. *The Reign of Elizabeth, 1558-1603*. 2nd ed. Oxford: Oxford University Press, 1959.

Davies, C. S. L. *Peace, Print and Protestantism, 1450-1558*. London: Paladin, 1977.

Elton, G. R. *England Under the Tudors*, 2nd ed. London: Methuen, 1974. Originally published 1954.

——————. *Reform and Reformation: England 1509-1558*. London: Arnold, 1977.

Graves, M. A. R., and R. H. Silcock. *Revolution, Reaction and the Triumph of Conservatism: English History 1558-1700*. Auckland, New Zealand: Longman Paul, 1984.

Guy, John. *Tudor England*. Oxford: Oxford University Press, 1988.

Lander, J. R. *Government and Community: England, 1450-1509*. London: Arnold, 1980.

Loades, D. M. *Politics and the Nation 1450-1660: Obedience, Resistance and Public Order*. London: Collins, 1974.

Lockyer, Roger. *Tudor and Stuart England 1471-1714*, 2nd ed. Harlow, England: Longman, 1985. Originally published 1964.

Mackie, J. D. *The Earlier Tudors, 1485-1558*. Oxford: Oxford University Press, 1952.

Ridley, Jasper. *The Tudor Age*. London: Constable, 1988.

Smith, Alan G. R. *The Emergence of a Nation State: The Commonwealth of England, 1529-1660*. Harlow, England: Longman, 1984.

Solt, Leo. *Church and State in Early Modern England, 1509-1640*. Oxford: Oxford University Press, 1990.

Williams, Penry. *The Tudor Regime*. Oxford: Oxford University Press, 1979.

Williamson, James A. *The Tudor Age*. London: Longman, 1979. Originally published 1957.

REIGN OF HENRY VII AND BEFORE

Alexander, Michael Van Cleave. *The First of the Tudors: A Study of Henry VII and His Reign*. London: Croom Helm, 1980.

Chrimes, S. B. *Henry VII*. Berkeley: University of California Press, 1972.

Lander, J. R. *Crown and Nobility 1450-1509*. London: Arnold, 1976.

Ross, Charles. *Edward IV*. Berkeley: University of California Press, 1974.

——————. *Richard III*. Berkeley: University of California Press, 1981.

REIGN OF HENRY VIII

Elton, G. R. *Policy and Police: The Enforcement of the Reformation in the Age of Thomas Cromwell*. Cambridge: Cambridge University Press, 1972.

——————. *Reform and Renewal: Thomas Cromwell and the Common Weal*. Cambridge: Cambridge University Press, 1973.

Fox, Alistair. *Thomas More: History and Providence*. Oxford: Blackwell, 1982.

Fox, Alistair, and John Guy. *Reassessing the Henrician Age*. Oxford: Blackwell, 1986.

Guy, John. *The Public Career of Sir Thomas More*. New Haven: Yale University Press, 1980.

Gwynn, Peter. *The King's Cardinal: The Rise and Fall of Thomas Wolsey*. London: Barrie and Jenkins, 1990.

Ives, E. W. *Anne Boleyn*. Oxford: Blackwell, 1986.

Lehmberg, S. E. *The Reformation Parliament 1529-1536*. Cambridge: Cambridge University Press, 1970.

——————. *The Later Parliaments of Henry VIII 1536-47*. Cambridge: Cambridge University Press, 1977.

Mattingly, Garrett. *Catherine of Aragon*. New York: Little Brown, 1941.

Pollard, A. F. *Henry VIII*. London: Goupil, 1902.

——————. *Wolsey*. London: Longman, 1929.

Redworth, Glyn. *In Defence of the Church Catholic: The Life of Stephen Gardiner*. Oxford: Blackwell, 1990.

Ridley, Jasper. *Statesman and Saint: Cardinal Wolsey, Sir Thomas More and the Politics of Henry VIII*. New York: Viking, 1983.

Scarisbrick, J. J. *Henry VIII*. Berkeley: University of California Press, 1968.

Warnicke, Retha. *The Rise and Fall of Anne Boleyn: Family Politics at the Court of Henry VIII*. Cambridge: Cambridge University Press, 1989.

REIGN OF EDWARD VI

Beer, Barrett L. *Northumberland: The Political Career of John Dudley, Earl of Warwick and Duke of Northumberland*. Kent, Ohio: Kent State University Press, 1973.

Bush, M. L. *The Government Policy of Protector Somerset*. London: Arnold, 1975.

Hoak, Dale. *The Reign of Edward VI*. London: Longman, 1991.

Jordan, W. K. *Edward VI: The Threshold of Power, the Dominance of the Duke of Northumberland*. Cambridge, Mass.: Harvard University Press, 1970.

——————. *Edward VI: The Young King, the Protectorship of the Duke of Somerset*. Cambridge, Mass.: Harvard University Press, 1968.

Loach, Jennifer and Robert Tittler, eds. *The Mid-Tudor Polity c1540-1560*. London: Macmillan, 1980.

REIGN OF MARY

Loades, D. M. *The Oxford Martyrs*. New York: Stein and Day, 1970.

Loades, D. M. *The Reign of Mary Tudor*. New York: St. Martins, 1979.

——————. *Mary Tudor: A Life*. Oxford: Blackwell, 1989.

Prescott, H. F. M. *Mary Tudor*. London: Eyre and Spottiswoode, 1952.

Tittler, Robert. *The Reign of Mary I*. London: Longman, 1983.

REIGN OF ELIZABETH

Erickson, Carolly. *The First Elizabeth*. New York: Summit Books, 1983.

Haigh, Christopher. *Elizabeth I*. London: Longman, 1988.

Haigh, Christopher, ed. *The Reign of Elizabeth I*. London: Macmillan, 1984.

MacCaffrey, Wallace T. *The Shaping of the Elizabethan Regime: Elizabethan Politics 1558-72*. Princeton: Princeton University Press, 1968.

——————. *Queen Elizabeth and the Making of Policy, 1572-1588*. Princeton: Princeton University Press, 1981.

Neale, J. E. *Queen Elizabeth: A Biography*. London: Cape, 1934.

Read, Conyers. *Mr. Secretary Cecil and Queen Elizabeth*. London: Cape, 1955.

——————. *Lord Burghley and Queen Elizabeth*. London: Cape, 1960.

CONSTITUTIONAL AND LEGAL HISTORY

Baker, J. H. *The Reports of Sir John Spelman*. 2 vols. London: Selden Society, 1977-1978. Vol. 2 is a historical introduction to the legal history of the early Tudor era.

Brooks, C. W. *Pettyfoggers and Vipers of the Commonwealth: The "Lower Branch" of the Legal Profession in Early Modern England*. Cambridge: Cambridge University Press, 1986.

Cockburn, J. S. *A History of English Assizes 1558-1714*. Cambridge: Cambridge University Press, 1972.

Coleman, Christopher, and David Starkey. *Revolution Reassessed: Revisions in the History of Tudor Government and Administration*. Oxford: Oxford University Press, 1986.

Elton, G. R. *The Tudor Revolution in Government: Administrative Changes in the Reign of Henry VIII*. Cambridge: Cambridge University Press, 1953.

Elton, G. R. *The Parliament of England 1559-1581*. Cambridge: Cambridge University Press, 1986.

Graves, Michael A. R. *The Tudor Parliaments: Crown, Lords and Commons, 1485-1603*. London: Longman, 1985.

Guy, John. *The Court of Star Chamber and Its Records to the Reign of Elizabeth I*. London: Her Majesty's Stationery Office, 1985.

Heinze, Rudolph W. *The Proclamations of the Tudor Kings*. Cambridge: Cambridge University Press, 1976.

Hoak, Dale. *The King's Council in the Reign of Edward VI*. Cambridge: Cambridge University Press, 1976.

Youngs, Frederic A., Jr. *The Proclamations of the Tudor Queens*. Cambridge: Cambridge University Press, 1976.

RELIGIOUS HISTORY

Collinson, Patrick. *The Elizabethan Puritan Movement*. Berkeley: University of California Press, 1967.

——————. *The Religion of Protestants: The Church in English Society 1559-1625*. Oxford: Oxford University Press, 1982.

Cross, Claire. *The Royal Supremacy in the Elizabethan Church*. London: Allen and Unwin, 1969.

——————. *Church and People, 1450-1660: The Triumph of the Laity in the English Church*. London: Collins, 1976.

Dickens, A. G. *The English Reformation*, 2nd ed. London: Batsford, 1989.

Haigh, Christopher, ed. *The English Reformation Revised*. Cambridge: Cambridge University Press, 1987.

Harper-Bill, C. *The Pre-Reformation Church in England, 1400-1530*. London: Longman, 1989.

Hill, Christopher. *Society and Puritanism in Pre-Revolutionary England*, 2nd ed. New York: Schocken, 1967.

Houlbrooke, Ralph. *Church Courts and the People During the English Reformation 1520-70*. Oxford: Oxford University Press, 1979.

Hughes, Philip. *The Reformation in England*. 3 vols. London: Hollis and Carter, 1950-1954.

Jones, Norman. *Faith by Statute: Parliament and the Settlement of Religion 1559*. London: Royal Historical Society, 1982.

King, John N. *English Reformation Literature: The Tudor Origins of the Protestant Tradition*. Princeton: Princeton University Press, 1982.

Lake, Peter. *Moderate Puritans and the Elizabethan Church*. Cambridge: Cambridge University Press, 1982.

Lake, Peter, and Maria Dowling, eds. *Protestantism and the National Church in Sixteenth-Century England*. London: Croom Helm, 1987.

MacCulloch, D. *The Later Reformation in England, 1547-1603*. New York: St. Martin's, 1990.

O'Day, Rosemary. *The Debate on the English Reformation*. London: Metheun, 1986.

Scarisbrick, J. J. *The Reformation and the English People*. Oxford: Blackwell, 1984.

Sheils, W. J., *The English Reformation 1530-1570*. London: Longman, 1989.

Thomas, Keith. *Religion and the Decline of Magic*. New York: Scribners, 1971.

Whiting, Robert. *The Blind Devotion of the People: Popular Religion and the English Reformation*. Cambridge: Cambridge University Press, 1989.

Youings, Joyce. *The Dissolution of the Monasteries*. London: Allen and Unwin, 1971.

SOCIAL AND ECONOMIC SURVEYS

Appleby, Andrew B. *Famine in Tudor and Stuart England*. Stanford, Calif.: Stanford University Press, 1978.

Clay, C. G. A. *Economic Expansion and Social Change: England 1500-1700*. 2 vols. Cambridge: Cambridge University Press, 1984.

Coleman, D. C. *The Economy of England 1450-1700*. Oxford: Oxford University Press, 1977.

Cressy, David. *Literacy and the Social Order: Reading and Writing in Tudor and Stuart England*. Cambridge: Cambridge University Press, 1980.

Hoskins, W. G. *The Age of Plunder: The England of Henry VIII 1500-1547*. London: Longman, 1976.

Houlbrooke, Ralph. *The English Family 1450-1700*. London: Longman, 1984.

Palliser, D. M. *The Age of Elizabeth: England Under the Later Tudors 1547-1603*. London: Longman, 1983.

Sharpe, James. *Crime in Early Modern England, 1550-1750*. London: Longman, 1984.

Slack, Paul. *The Impact of Plague in Tudor and Stuart England*. London: Routledge, 1985.

Thirsk, Joan, ed. *The Agrarian History of England and Wales*. Vol. 4: *1500-1640*. Cambridge: Cambridge University Press, 1967.

Wrigley, E. A., and R. S. Schofield. *The Population History of England 1541-1871*. Cambridge: Cambridge University Press, 1981.

Youings, Joyce. *Sixteenth-Century England*. Harmondsworth, England: Penguin, 1984.

DIPLOMATIC HISTORY

Crowson, P. S. *Tudor Foreign Policy*. London: Black, 1973.

Doran, Susan. *England and Europe 1485-1603*. London: Longman, 1986.

Mattingly, Garrett. *Renaissance Diplomacy*. London: Cape, 1955.

Wernham, R. B. *After the Armada: Elizabethan England and the Struggle for Western Europe 1588-1595*. Oxford: Oxford University Press, 1984.

——————. *Before the Armada: The Emergence of the English Nation, 1485-1588*. London: Cape, 1966.

——————. *The Making of Elizabethan Foreign Policy*. Berkeley: University of California Press, 1980.

MILITARY AND NAVAL HISTORY AND EXPLORATION

Andrews, K. R. *Elizabethan Privateering*. Cambridge: Cambridge University Press, 1964.

——————. *Trade, Plunder and Settlement: Maritime Enterprise and the Genesis of the British Empire, 1480-1630*. Cambridge: Cambridge University Press, 1984.

Boynton, L. *The Elizabethan Militia, 1558-1638*. London: Routledge and Kegan Paul, 1967.

Cruickshank, C. G. *Elizabeth's Army*, 2nd ed. Oxford: Oxford University Press, 1966.

Fletcher, Anthony. *Tudor Rebellions*, 3rd ed. London: Longman, 1983.

Mattingly, Garrett. *The Armada*. Boston: Houghton Mifflin, 1959.

INTELLECTUAL HISTORY AND HISTORY OF SCIENCE

Bennett, H. S. *English Books and Readers, 1475-1557*. Cambridge: Cambridge University Press, 1952.

——————. *English Books and Readers, 1558 to 1603*. Cambridge: Cambridge University Press, 1965.

Levy, F. J. *Tudor Historical Thought*. San Marino, Calif.: Huntington Library, 1967.

McConica, James. *English Humanists and Reformation Politics under Henry VIII and Edward VI*. Oxford: Oxford University Press, 1965.

McConica, James, ed. *The Collegiate University*, Vol. 3 of *The History of the University of Oxford*. Oxford: Oxford University Press, 1986.

McLean, Antonia. *Humanism and the Rise of Science in Tudor England*. New York: Watson, 1972.

Morris, Christopher. *Political Thought in England: Tyndale to Hooker*. Oxford: Oxford University Press, 1953.

O'Day, Rosemary. *Education and Society, 1500-1800: The Social Foundations of Education in Early Modern Britain*. London: Longman, 1982.

IRELAND

Bagwell, R. *Ireland Under the Tudors*. 3 vols. London: Longmans, 1885-1890. Reprint 1963.

Bradshaw, Brendan. *The Irish Constitutional Revolution of the Sixteenth Century*. Cambridge: Cambridge University Press, 1979.

Canny, Nicholas. *The Elizabethan Conquest of Ireland: A Pattern Established 1565-76*. Hassocks: Harvester Press, 1976.

Ellis, Steven G. *Tudor Ireland: Crown, Community and the Conflict of Cultures, 1470-1603*. London: Longman, 1985.

Moody, T. W., F. X. Martin, and F. J. Byrne, eds. *A New History of Ireland*. Vol. 3: *Early Modern Ireland, 1534-1691*. Oxford: Oxford University Press, 1976.

Moody, T. W., F. X. Martin, and F. J. Byrne, eds. *A New History of Ireland*. Vol. 2: *Medieval Ireland 1169-1534*. Oxford: Oxford University Press, 1987.

SCOTLAND

Donaldson, Gordon. *The Scottish Reformation*. Cambridge: Cambridge University Press, 1960.

——————. *Scotland: James V to James VII*. Edinburgh: Oliver and Boyd, 1965.

Fraser, Antonia. *Mary Queen of Scots*. New York: Delacorte Press, 1969.

Lee, Maurice, Jr. *Great Britain's Solomon: James VI and I in His Three Kingdoms*. Urbana: University of Illinois Press, 1990.

Reid, W. Stanford. *Trumpeter of God: A Biography of John Knox*. New York: Scribner, 1974.

Wormald, Jenny. *Court, Kirk, and Community: Scotland 1470-1625*. Toronto: University of Toronto Press, 1981.

——————. *Mary Queen of Scots: A Study in Failure*. London: Philip, 1988.

WALES

Williams, Glanmor. *Recovery, Reorientation and Reformation: Wales c. 1415-1642*. Oxford: Oxford University Press, 1987.

Index